D1104879

THE WESTMINSTER DICTIONARY OF

Theologians

THE WESTMINSTER DICTIONARY OF

Theologians

General Editor
Justo L. González

Associate Editors
Carlos F. Cardoza-Orlandi
Ismael García
Zaida Maldonado Pérez
Luis G. Pedraja
Luis Rivera Rodríguez
José David Rodríguez

Translator
Suzanne E. Hoeferkamp Segovia

Westminster John Knox Press
LOUISVILLE • LONDON

Translated by Suzanne E. Hoeferkamp Segovia from the Spanish *Diccionario de Teólogos y Teólogas* (Terrassa, Sp.: CLIE, 2004).

Book design by Sharon Adams
Cover design by Mark Abrams

First edition
Published by Westminster John Knox Press
Louisville, Kentucky

This book is printed on acid-free paper that meets the American National Standards Institute Z39.48 standard.

PRINTED IN THE UNITED STATES OF AMERICA

06 07 08 09 10 11 12 13 14 15—10 9 8 7 6 5 4 3 2 1

Library of Congress Cataloging-in-Publication Data is on file at the Library of Congress, Washington, D.C.

ISBN-13: 978-0-664-22989-4
ISBN-10: 0-664-22989-1

Preface

This dictionary was originally written in Spanish and published in Spain, as a project of the Hispanic Association for Theological Education (AETH). This is an organization of approximately a thousand members who are committed to Hispanic theological education. The dictionary itself was written and edited with no remuneration by members of AETH, as a contribution both to Hispanic theological education and to the coffers of AETH. For this reason, it is a product of love and commitment. But it is also such a product because the authors and editors of this volume are deeply committed to the subject of their study, and they hope that the use of the dictionary will move others toward similar commitments.

As is always the case in projects such as this, there will be disagreements as to who should have been—or should not have been—included. Our guidelines have been relatively simple, but not always easy to apply. On the one hand, we have sought to make this dictionary as ample as possible. Thus, the persons included here are not only those who are part of our direct theological ancestry, but also people belonging to other theological traditions within Christianity, so that here the reader will find articles about Protestants, Roman Catholics, Orthodox, Copts, Ethiopians, and so on. Following the same goal of amplitude, we have paid special attention to theological work taking place outside the traditional theological centers of Europe and North America. Thus, in the pages that follow the reader will find a wide representation of theologians from Africa, Asia, and particularly Latin America. On the other hand, given the mission of AETH, we have paid particular attention to Latino and Latina theologians working within the United States, as well as to other minorities in the same context.

One of the more difficult decisions was what to do about a number of philosophers who, while not being Christians, have had such an impact on theology that a knowledge of their thought is necessary in order to understand the work of many theologians. Such are the cases, for instance, of Plato, Aristotle, and Marx. They have been included, clearly not because they were theologians, but because they have been the background of much theological work.

The number of abbreviations has been kept to a minimum, and those employed are sufficiently common or self-evident that a list of abbreviations was not deemed necessary.

There are many to whom thanks are due as this volume goes to press. The dictionary itself is a work of thanks to the generations of theologians who have gone before us and who even today pursue the tasks of theology. I am also grateful to the editors and authors, whose time and efforts have been so graciously given. The translator, Dr. Suzanne Hoeferkamp Segovia, is a theologian in her own right, so that in the very process of translation she has been able to correct, improve, and clarify many a point. Her work was made possible by a grant from the Griffith Foundation, to which all of us are exceedingly grateful. My wife, Dr. Catherine Gunsalus González, has proofread and suggested significant corrections when I had read the manuscript so many times I could no longer concentrate on it. To all of them, thanks! And thanks also to the God who has given them to us!

Justo L. González
Decatur, Georgia
March 2006

List of Contributors

AEM	Dr. Aquiles Ernesto Martínez is Associate Professor of Religion at Reinhardt College, Waleska, Georgia
ALG	Dr. Alberto L. García is Professor of Theology at Wisconsin Concordia University, Mequion.
ALN	Agustina Luvis Núñez is Assistant Professor of Theology at the Evangelical Seminary of Puerto Rico, San Juan.
AMID	Dr. Ada María Isasi-Díaz is Professor of Christian Ethics and Theology at Drew University, Madison, New Jersey.
AP	Dr. Alvin Padilla is Academic Dean and Associate Professor of New Testament at Gordon-Conwell Theological Seminary, Boston, Massachusetts.
AZ	Dr. Ariel Zambrano, deceased, was Professor of Old Testament at the United Evangelical Seminary of Mexico, Mexico City.
CCO	Dr. Carlos F. Cardoza-Orlandi is Associate Professor of World Christianity at Columbia Theological Seminary, Decatur, Georgia.
CEA	Carmelo E. Álvarez is Adjunct Professor of Church History and Theology at Christian Theological Seminary, Indianapolis, Indiana.
CGG	Dr. Catherine Gunsalus González is Professor Emerita of Church History at Columbia Theological Seminary, Decatur, Georgia.
CJP	Dr. Carmen Julia Pagán is Associate Professor of Theological Studies at the Interamerican University of Puerto Rico, San Juan.
CMB	Dr. Claudio M. Burgaleta, SJ, is an independent scholar in the New York Province of the Society of Jesus.
CS	Carmelo Santos Rolón is a PhD candidate in systematic theology at the Lutheran School of Theology in Chicago.
DCF	Dr. David Cortés-Fuentes is Associate Professor of New Testament and Director of Academic Services at San Francisco Theological Seminary in Southern California, Pasadena.
DTG	Dr. David Traverzo Galarza is a lecturer at Mount Sinai College in Newburgh, New York.
EA	Dr. Efraín Agosto is Professor of New Testament and Director of the Hispanic Ministries Program at Hartford Seminary, Hartford, Connecticut.
ECF	Dr. Elizabeth Conde-Frazier is Assistant Professor of Religious Education at Claremont School of Theology, Claremont, California.
EDA	Dr. Edwin David Aponte is Associate Professor of Christianity and Culture and Director of Advanced Studies at Perkins School of Theology, Dallas, Texas.

EDB	Dr. Esther Díaz-Bolet is Associate Professor of Administration at the School of Educational Ministries, Southwestern Baptist Theological Seminary, Fort Worth, Texas.
EF	Dr. Eduardo C. Fernández, SJ, is Associate Professor of Pastoral Theology and Ministry at the Jesuit School of Theology and the Graduate Theological Union, Berkeley, California.
EH	Dr. Edwin Hernández is Foundations Research Director, the DeVos Family Foundations.
ELR	Dr. Ediberto López Rodríguez is Professor of New Testament at the Evangelical Seminary of Puerto Rico, San Juan.
EPA	Dr. Eliseo Pérez Álvarez is Associate Professor of Theology at the Lutheran Seminary Program in the Southwest, Austin, Texas.
EV	Dr. Eldin Villafañe is Ricardo Tañón Distinguished Professor of Hispanic Christianity, Ethics, and Urban Ministry at Gordon-Conwell Theological Seminary, Boston, Massachusetts.
EZ	Dr. Edward Zaragoza is the pastor of Eliot Presbyterian Church, Lowell, Massachusetts.
FMA	Dr. Felipe Martínez Arroyo is Associate Professor of Religion and Philosophy at the Interamerican University of Puerto Rico, San Juan.
GC	Dr. Giacomo Cassese is Associate Professor of Church History and Director of Hispanic Programs at the South Florida Center for Theological Studies, Miami.
GCC	Dr. Gonzalo Castillo-Cárdenas is Emeritus Professor of Church and Society and Third World Studies at Pittsburgh Theological Seminary, Pittsburgh, Pennsylvania.
GRK	Dr. George R. Knight is Professor of Church History at Seventh-day Adventist Seminary, Berrien Springs, Michigan.
HMT	Dr. Hugo Magallanes Tejera is Assistant Provost and Associate Professor of Church in Society at Asbury Theological Seminary, Florida Campus, Orlando.
IG	Dr. Ismael García is Professor of Christian Ethics at Austin Presbyterian Theological Seminary, Austin, Texas.
JDR	Dr. José David Rodríguez is Augustana Heritage Professor of World Christianity and Mission and Director of ThM and PhD programs of study at the Lutheran School of Theology at Chicago, Illinois
JDRR	Dr. José David Rodríguez Rivera is Adjunct Professor of Systematic Theology and Ethics at the Evangelical Seminary of Puerto Rico, San Juan.
JFM	Dr. Juan Francisco Martínez is Assistant Dean for the Hispanic Church Ministries Department and Associate Professor of Hispanic Studies and Pastoral Leadership at Fuller Theological Seminary, Pasadena, California.
JLG	Dr. Justo Luis González is General Editor of the Dictionary of Theologians.
JNR	Dr. José Norat Rodríguez is Area Director for Hispanic America and the Caribbean of the American Baptist Churches.
JR	Dr. Jesús Rodríguez is Director of the Doctoral Program in Theology at the Interamerican University of Puerto Rico, San Juan.

JRI   Dr. José Ramón Irizarry is Associate Professor of Cultural Studies in
           Religion and Education at McCormick Theological Seminary, Chicago,
           Illinois.

KD   Dr. Kenneth G. Davis, OFM, Conv., is Associate Professor of Pastoral
           Studies at Saint Meinrad School of Theology, St. Meinrad, Indiana.

LC-O   Leopoldo Cervantez-Ortiz is Director of the Basileia Research and
           Support Center, Mexico City.

LGP   Dr. Luis G. Pedraja is Executive Assistant Director, Middle States
           Commission on Higher Education.

LMcA   Dr. Lester McGrath Andino is a Professor of Humanities at the
           Mayagüez Campus of the University of Puerto Rico.

LRP   Dr. Luis Rivera Pagán is Henry Winters Luce Professor of Ecumenics at
           Princeton Theological Seminary, Princeton, New Jersey.

LRR   Dr. Luis Rivera Rodríguez is Associate Professor of Theology and
           Director of the Center for the Study of Latino/a Theology and Ministry
           at McCormick Theological Seminary, Chicago, Illinois.

MAD   Dr. Miguel Ángel De La Torre is Associate Professor of Social Ethics
           and Director of the Peace and Justice Institute at Iliff School of
           Theology, Denver, Colorado.

MAG   Dr. Michelle A. González is Assistant Professor of Religious Studies at
           the University of Miami, Miami, Florida.

MJM   Dr. Manuel Jesús Mejido Costoya teaches social theory and sociology at
           the Universidad Academia de Humanismo Cristiano and the Universidad
           de Arte y Ciencias Sociales, Santiago, Chile.

NLD   Dr. Nora O. Lozano Díaz is Assistant Professor of Theology at the
           Baptist University of the Americas, San Antonio, Texas.

NRG   Nelson Rivera García is Assistant Professor of Systematic Theology and
           Hispanic Ministry at the Lutheran Theological Seminary at Philadelphia,
           Pennsylvania.

ODV   Dr. Osvaldo D. Vena is Associate Professor of New Testament
           Interpretation at Garrett-Evangelical Theological Seminary, Evanston,
           Illinois.

OLM   Dr. Osvaldo L. Mottesi is Professor Emeritus of Religion and Society at
           Northern Baptist Seminary, Lombard, Illinois.

OOE   Dr. Orlando O. Espín is Professor of Systematic Theology and Director
           of the Center for the Study of Latino/a Catholicism at the University of
           San Diego, California.

PAJ   Dr. Pablo A. Jiménez is senior editor for Chalice Press, an imprint of the
           Christian Board of Publication, Indianapolis, Indiana.

PB   Dr. Paul Barton is Associate Professor of Hispanic Studies at the
           Episcopal Theological Seminary of the Southwest, Austin, Texas.

PBA   Dr. Plutarco Bonilla A. is a retired Professor of Philosophy at the
           University of Costa Rica, former Rector of the Seminario Bíblico
           Latinoamericano, and translations consultant for the United Bible
           Societies.

PP   Dr. Pablo Polischuck is Professor of Pastoral Counseling and Psycho-
           logy at Gordon-Conwell Theological Seminary, Boston, Massachusetts.

RA   Dr. Rubén Armendáriz is Associate Executive for Church Development, Mission Presbytery, San Antonio, Texas.

RAR   Dr. Roberto Amparo Rivera is Director of Pastoral Care for the Church of God in Puerto Rico.

RPT   Dr. Rubén Pérez Torres is Associate Professor of Religion at the Interamerican University of Puerto Rico, San Juan.

SHR   Dr. Sharon H. Ringe is Professor of New Testament at Wesley Theological Seminary, Washington, DC.

TCS   Dr. Teresa Chávez Sauceda is Associate for Racial Justice and Advocacy, National Ministries, the Presbyterian Church (U.S.A.).

ZMP   Dr. Zaida Maldonado Pérez is Associate Professor of Theological Studies at Asbury Theological Seminary, Florida Campus, Orlando.

Abaud (early 12th century). An abbot who wrote *Treatise on the Breaking of the Body of Christ* during the eucharistic controversies surrounding the doctrines of ⇒Berengar. He holds that although the bread is the body of Christ, when the bread is broken each one of its parts contains the totality of that body.

_____

                                         JLG

Abbot, George (1562–1633). Theologian and professor at Oxford; ardent defender of Puritanism, but also of the episcopal system of government. As a Puritan, he had several conflicts with William Laud while the latter was archbishop of Canterbury. In 1611 he himself came to occupy that seat, from which he defended the Calvinism of the Puritans. It was partly due to his intervention that the Church of England had representation at the Synod of ⇒Dort.

_____

                                         JLG

Abbott, Edwin A. (1838–1926). Theologian and Anglican scholar who devoted himself to philological studies of the New Testament and to the writing of religious novels. His three main works are *Philochrist, Onesimus,* and *Silvanus.*

_____

                                         JLG

Abelard, Peter (1079–1142). One of the main promoters of the intellectual renaissance of the twelfth century, and a forerunner of scholasticism. His life is particularly interesting since he himself commented on it in his *History of Calamities,* and also because his relations with Héloïse have been the subject of numerous works of fiction.

There is no doubt that A. had extraordinary intellectual gifts, but he does not seem to have been a person of much tact, particularly when it came to his relationship with his teachers. He studied with the most famous teachers of his time and won the enmity of all of them: ⇒Roscelin, ⇒William of Champeaux, and ⇒Anselm of Laon.

After distancing himself from Anselm in Laon, A. went to Paris, where he taught philosophy and theology. It was there where he had Héloïse, the niece of a canon of the cathedral, first as a disciple and then as a lover.

They named the child Astrolabe, in celebration of an instrument they considered one of the greatest human inventions. A. and Héloïse were married, but they had kept it a secret because it would have been very difficult for A. to keep his teaching position if he were known to be married. Héloïse's relatives believed that A. had kept the marriage a secret because he was planning to ask the pope for an annulment. In revenge for what they considered to be a dishonor, they assaulted A. and castrated him. Héloïse then became a nun, and A. joined the monastery of Saint Denis on the outskirts of Paris.

In Saint Denis he won the enmity of the other monks when he declared that the founder of the famous monastery could not have been ⇒Dionysius the Areopagite, as they believed. In 1121 a synod that gathered in Soissons condemned his opinions about the doctrine of the Trinity and forced him to burn his work on the subject.

He then retired to an isolated place where he hoped to find tranquility. Some disciples followed him there, and with them he founded a school that he called "the Paraclete." Héloïse followed him also and founded a convent near the Paraclete. But his enemies pursued him, especially the spirited ⇒Bernard of Clairvaux, who could not tolerate the way in which A. combined dialectics with theology, applying reason to questions of faith. As a result of the actions of Bernard and others, in 1141 A. had to appear before a synod gathered in Sens that condemned his doctrines without giving him the opportunity to defend himself. A. appealed to Pope Innocent II, but the following year he received news that the pope had died. Disappointed and having lost hope, he retired to the famous monastery of Cluny, where he was well received by ⇒Peter the Venerable, and he died shortly thereafter, having become reconciled with Bernard.

The works of A. are many, although there is doubt about the paternity of some that are attributed to him. His principal philosophical work is *Dialectics*, and his treatise *Know Thyself*, commonly known as *Ethics*, plowed new ground in that discipline. In the field of biblical exegesis, he wrote *Exposition of the Hexaemeron* and *Commentary on Romans*. His treatise *On the Divine Unity and Trinity* is not preserved, because it was burned at the council of Soissons in 1121. The best sources for his theology are *Introduction to Theology* and *Christian Theology*. His most famous work is *Sic et non* (Yes and No), which made a notable contribution to the scholastic method.

The point at which his interests in logic, metaphysics, and theology converge is the much-debated question of the universals. A. defines his position on this matter in opposition not only to the realism of William of Champeaux but also to the nominalism of Roscelin. Between both extremes, A. affirms that universals are not "things," as realism would say, nor are they merely "names," as nominalism would say, but rather they are concepts which, although they are in things, are extracted from them through a mental process. This position, called conceptualism, would exert great influence on subsequent generations.

The most notable contribution of A. in the field of systematic theology is the method that can be glimpsed in *Sic et non*. As the title suggests, A. poses questions (a total of 158) and then offers a list of "authorities"—biblical texts, quotations from the fathers of the church, and so on—that appear to respond to them in one way, and others that appear to respond in the opposite way. In the foreword A. explains that his purpose was not to question the value of the authorities quoted, but simply to point out some of the issues that theologians needed to explain. A. seems to have been convinced that, properly interpreted, the authorities quoted did not contradict one another. Given the spirit of the times and the fact that A. had won for himself a good number of enemies, it is not surprising that the work was received as an attempt to undermine the authority of the Bible and of the Fathers. In spite of this, *Sic et non* had a strong impact on scholastic theology, whose method consisted of posing a question, quoting authorities that appeared to lean toward contradictory answers, and then offering a "solution" and some "answers" that would solve the apparent contradictions. In this sense, the scholastics simply went a step beyond A., who been content with posing difficulties without attempting to solve them.

In his *Ethics*, A. said much that has become part of the moral capital of Western civilization.

In particular, he distinguished between the action itself and its intention. Whoever shoots an arrow aimed at a deer but kills a human being is not morally guilty of homicide. But this provided an opportunity for his enemies, who persuaded the council of 1141 to condemn those who held that "whoever crucified Christ without knowing what they were doing did not sin," or that "what is done out of ignorance is free of guilt."

In that same work, A. also declared that individuals cannot be guilty of what they have not done. In the field of theology, this implied that what is transmitted of Adam's sin to subsequent generations is not guilt, but only punishment. This in turn seemed to imply that God punishes entire generations for something for which they are not at fault. For this reason the same council likewise condemned the proposition "that we did not contract the guilt of Adam, but only the punishment."

The doctrine of A. that is possibly best known in modern times is his theory of atonement. A little earlier, Anselm had rejected the traditional theory that Christ came to the world to free people from the yoke of the devil and of sin, and in its place had proposed a theory according to which Christ came to pay the debt that sinners had incurred with God. A. rejected both theories, affirming that by his life, teachings, and death on the cross, Christ gives us such an example of love that it calls us to obedience and reconciliation. Such a theory was not well received for two main reasons: First, because it contradicted the doctrine that was commonly received. For that reason the council of 1141 condemned those who would hold "that Christ did not become incarnate in order to free us from the yoke of the Devil"—which, strictly speaking, would have implied also a rejection of Anselm's views. Second, this doctrine was not well received because it appeared to come too close to Pelagianism (⇒Pelagius), implying that in order to obey and follow God it suffices to decide to do it. For that reason, the same council condemned those who would say "that free will by itself is sufficient to do some good."

In spite of being repeatedly condemned, A. had a strong impact on the development of theology, even beyond the influence of his *Sic et non* in shaping the scholastic method. Several authors, most of them anonymous, continued expounding aspects of his doctrine, although with greater moderation. One of them wrote *Summary of Christian Theology*, which was later attributed to A. himself. The influence of A. is seen also in the anonymous *Sentences* of

Saint Florian and even in the work of Pope Alexander III, who, before reaching that office, under the name of Roland ⇒Bandinelli, wrote his own *Sentences*. Finally, A. and his followers influenced the thought of ⇒Peter Lombard and his *Four Books of Sentences*, which for centuries was the most widely used textbook on theology.

JLG

Abelly, Louis (1604–91). French theologian educated at the Sorbonne and associated with Vincent de Paul. In 1662 he was named bishop of Rodez. His most important work was *Life of the Venerable Servant of God, Vincent de Paul (Vie du vénérable serviteur de Dieu, Vincent de Paul)*, the first biography of St. Vincent. His *Medulla theologica* is a manual of probabilistic doctrine. His book *Tradition of the Church regarding the Devotion of Christians to the Holy Virgin (Tradition de l'église touchant la dévotion des Chrétiens envers la Sainte Vierge)* became a popular source for later Mariology.

JDR

Abercius, Epitaph of (2nd century). The epitaph of A., bishop of Hierapolis, was discovered in 1838 by archaeologist W. Ramsay. In a mystical and symbolic way, the inscription summarizes the life and deeds of A., who is believed to have composed it at the age of seventy-two. The epitaph is one of the most ancient monuments that mention the Eucharist.

ZMP

Aberlé, Mortiz von (1819–75). German Catholic theologian, professor of New Testament at the University of Tübingen until his death. Many of his opinions were rejected by the majority of his contemporaries. For instance, he held that the Gospel of Matthew was written to refute a slanderous manuscript published by the Sanhedrin to discredit Christianity and that the writings of Luke were prepared for the appearance of Paul before the Roman courts. Beginning in 1851 he was one of the main writers of *Theologische Quartalschrift*, a journal of the Catholic faculty of Tübingen. The theses proposed in his articles are summarized in a posthumous work, *Introduction to the New Testament (Einleitung in das Neue Testament)*.

JDR

Abesamis, Carlos H. (1934–). Jesuit priest, professor of sacred Scripture at Loyola School of Theology and at the Center for the Study of Religion and Culture in Manila. He has made contributions in comparative religion, intercultural studies, theology of religion, and liberation theology, all from an Asian perspective.

CCO

Abgar, Epistle of Jesus to. A very brief, spurious document that claims to be a letter sent by Jesus to King Abgar V of Edessa, who died in the year 50. In it he promises that, after his ascension, he will send the king one of his disciples. It was highly venerated among Syrian Christians who considered it authentic.

JLG

Abraham Ecchellensis (17th century). Prolific Catholic author whose name is derived from the village of his birthplace, Ecchel, on the slopes of Lebanon. He spent the greater part of his literary career in Rome and Paris, where he publicized the texts and traditions of Eastern Christianity, devoting himself especially to translating and editing works written in Syriac and Arabic.

JLG

Abraham, Kuruvilla Cherukara (1936–). A native of India, professor of theology and ethics at the United Theological School in Bangalore, India, and former president of the Ecumenical Association of Third World Theologians. He has made contributions in the theology of liberation from an Asian perspective, the relationship between theology and culture, and popular religiosity and spirituality.

CCO

Acacius of Berea (ca. 322–432). Bishop of Berea who actively participated in the controversies surrounding ⇒Apollinaris of Laodicea, whom he opposed. He attended the Council of ⇒Constantinople (381) and supported its decisions. Then he distanced himself from Pope ⇒Damasus, and in Constantinople was one of the opponents of ⇒John Chrysostom. When the controversy surrounding ⇒Nestorius broke out, he tried to be reconciled with ⇒Cyril of Alexandria, but without success. Because of his advanced age (109 years), he did not attend the Council of ⇒Ephesus in 431.

———

JLG

Acacius of Caesarea (?–366).

Defender of Arianism, specifically in its Homoean form. Because his Arianism was moderate, he was condemned not only by the extreme Arians but also by the orthodox. His importance for the Homoean party was such that for some time those who followed that interpretation were called Acacians.

———

JLG

Acacius of Constantinople (5th century).

Patriarch of Constantinople (471–89), known for giving his name to the schism of Acacius (482–519) between the churches of Constantinople and Rome. His chief theological work consisted of collaborating with Emperor Zeno in the composition of the Proclamation of Union or ⇒Henoticon (482). A. had gained a reputation for orthodoxy thanks to his tenacious opposition to the ⇒Encyclion of Emperor Basiliscus, who tried to gain the sympathy of the Monophysites by declaring the decisions of the Council of ⇒Chalcedon to be null and void. In addition, he presided over the synod that judged and condemned ⇒Peter the Fuller as a Monophysite.

The document of A. and Zeno was one of many attempts to heal the division between Monophysites and Chalcedonians. A. seems to have realized that much of that division was based on semantics, and that there were, besides a few true Monophysites, many others whom the historians would later call verbal Monophysites. While this verbal Monophysitism agreed with the orthodox on the need to affirm not only the divinity but also the humanity of Jesus, it was not willing to accept the formula "in two natures" that the Council of Chalcedon had promulgated. Nevertheless, the Henoticon does not state this clearly, but instead tries to return to the situation that existed before the Council of Chalcedon, reaffirming the doctrines of the councils of ⇒Nicaea (325) and of ⇒Constantinople (381).

Furthermore, probably in order to win the support of the Monophysites, he reaffirmed the *Twelve Anathemas* of ⇒Cyril of Alexandria against the Nestorians.

Instead of producing unity, the Henoticon led to greater divisions. In the East, some rejected it and others accepted it. In the West, Pope Felix rejected it for several reasons: First, because it seemed to take away authority from the Council of Chalcedon and the *Dogmatic Epistle* of ⇒Leo the Great. Second, because it lent itself to an openly Monophysite interpretation. And, finally, because it was an imperial edict, as if the emperor had the authority to judge in matters of doctrine.

The result of all of this was the schism of Acacius, which continued after his death, and was not healed until the accession of Justin to the imperial throne (518).

———

JLG

Acosta, José de, SJ (1540–1600).

Theologian, ethnologist, and Spanish Jesuit missionary to Peru, born in Medina del Campo, in a Portuguese family probably converted from Judaism. He wrote the first book published in South America (1585), the trilingual catechism in Aimara, Castilian, and Quechua, *On Christian Doctrine*, at the direction of the Third Provincial Council of Lima (1582). His masterpiece was probably *Natural and Moral History of the Indies* (1590), in which he offers the best description of the time of the cultural and natural novelties of the New World, and for which contemporary anthropologists consider him one of the fathers of Amerindian ethnology. With his first American work, *De procuranda indorum salute*, a missiological manual written in 1576 but not published until 1589, this literary trilogy constitutes a major contribution to Latin American theology. It is characterized by an eclectic theological method that combines the Thomist scholasticism of the Dominican School of Salamanca, the literary elegance and reformist concerns of humanistic theology, and Ignatian spirituality. The theological and ethical judgments of A. tend to be realistic and balanced, representing an intermediate position between the prophetic character of Bartolomé de ⇒Las Casas and the abuses of the conquest. He was also the first Jesuit superior who accepted and articulated the pastoral course of action for the first settlement or mission among the indigenous American peoples in Juli, near Lake Titicaca. This would be the model for the Jesuit settlements of Paraguay. After fourteen years in Peru, in 1587 he returned to Castile, where his most important activities had to do with the internal government of the Company of Jesus. He served as an agent of the failed plan of Philip II to exert greater control over the Company in

Spain, with the expulsion of the centralizing superior general Claudio Aquaviva.

———

CMB

Acta apostolicae sedis. Official journal of the Holy See. Its publication began in September 1908. Canon law considers it authorized and official. Every decree and decision of the Roman Rota published is officially announced and becomes effective three months after the date of its publication in the *Acta*. Nominally published on a monthly basis, it actually appears as often as necessary in order to keep the faithful informed of the official decisions made by the Catholic Church.

———

JDR

Acta sanctorum. Elaborate project, begun by a group of Jesuit scholars in the seventeenth century, to compile and narrate the lives of the saints in the order in which their feasts are celebrated. Interrupted by the suppression of the Jesuits in 1773, the project was not completed until the twentieth century, more than three hundred years after its inception.

———

JLG

Acton, Baron John E. E. D. (1834–1902). Catholic historian; a friend and collaborator of J. J. I. ⇒Döllinger and of J. H. ⇒Newman. Like them, he was a moderate Catholic. He tenaciously opposed Ultramontanism, and in 1869 went to Rome to try to prevent the First Vatican Council (⇒Vatican I) from promulgating the infallibility of the pope. When he lost that battle, he submitted to the authority of the council, but from then on focused his work on historical studies.

———

JLG

Acts of the Martyrs. Texts that narrate the trials, sufferings, and deaths of the Christian martyrs. In the strict sense, this category should include only those documents that are truly judicial "acts," that is, government minutes or records drafted by officials of the tribunals. The majority of scholars consider two documents of this nature to be authentic: *The Acts of the Scillitan Saints* and the *Proconsular Acts* of the martyrdom of ⇒Cyprian. The first refers to events in the year 180, and the second to the year 258.

In a broader and more common sense, the name "acts of the martyrs" is given to an entire collection of texts that record the trial, torture, and death of the Christian martyrs. Some of these are very ancient and show indications of being based on events that were witnessed or at least corroborated by those who wrote them. Such is the case, for example, of the *Martyrdom of* ⇒Polycarp and the *Martyrdom of St. Perpetua and St. Felicity*. The latter seems to have autobiographical elements, and in its present form could well be the work of ⇒Tertullian. In addition, ⇒Eusebius of Caesarea preserved references and narratives of martyrdoms that he apparently took from ancient archives.

The glorification of martyrdom brought about a series of fictitious "acts," the majority of which were written long after the events they claim to narrate. To distinguish between such products of the imagination and other documents that are more trustworthy is a difficult task, and consequently scholars do not always agree in their judgments on these matters.

———

JLG

Adam, Karl (1876–1966). Catholic theologian, part of a generation that worked toward the renewal of Roman Catholicism, and that turned out to be a forerunner of the Second Vatican Council (⇒Vatican II). The greater part of his career as a professor was spent in Tübingen, where he taught from 1919 to 1949. Among his main works is *Una sancta* (1951), in which he deals with the problems and the hope for rapprochement between Catholics and Protestants. His christological works were also very popular: *Christ Our Brother* (1926), *Jesus Christ* (1933), and *The Christ of Faith* (1954).

———

JLG

Adam of Marsh ⇒Marsh, Adam

Adam of St. Victor (?–ca. 1185). Liturgical poet who expressed in verse the piety and theology of the school of St. Victor (⇒Hugh of St. Victor; ⇒Richard of St. Victor). A dictionary of difficult terms in the Bible is also attributed to him.

———

JLG

Adamantius (4th century?). Antignostic author of whom nothing more than the name is known. He probably lived at the beginning of the fourth century in Syria or in Asia Minor. Although some confused him with ⇒Origen, this identification is not correct. His *Dialogue of the Proper Faith in God* is presented as a series of debates, first with the followers of ⇒Marcion and then with those of ⇒Bardesanes and ⇒Valentinus.

———

JLG

Adams, Hannah (1755–1832). The first North American woman theologian who was able to support herself financially through the books she wrote. Her scholarship in the field of comparative religion was highly regarded.

———

EPA

Adelard of Bath (ca. 1125). English philosopher about whose life very little is known, but who seems to have traveled throughout western Europe as well as North Africa and Asia Minor. He thus compiled an enormous quantity of scholarly material, which he used in his effort to reconcile the doctrines of ⇒Plato and those of ⇒Aristotle concerning the universals.

———

JLG

Adelmanus (?–ca. 1053). A disciple of ⇒Fulbert of Chartres who wrote a letter against the eucharistic doctrine of ⇒Berengar. In it he holds that the Lord, having promised that he would give us his flesh to eat, kept that promise in the institution of the Eucharist.

———

JLG

Adson of Luxeuil (?–992). Also known as Adso, Asson, or Azon. Brought up in the monastery of Luxeuil, he became the abbot of the monastery of Montierender. There he wrote on the lives of several saints and probably a history of the bishops of Tours. In those supposedly historical works, pious legends and fables abound. He also wrote *Treatise of the Antichrist*, which has been attributed to several other authors (among them, ⇒Augustine of Hippo and ⇒Alcuin).

———

JLG

Aeneas of Gaza (450–518). Alexandrian philosopher. One of the few Christian intellectuals of his time who opposed Neoplatonism. He wrote especially against metempsychosis or the theory of the transmigration of souls, which his teacher, the Neoplatonic Hierocles, proposed. He dedicated his *Dialogue on the Immortality of the Soul and the Resurrection* to this topic. It refuted the idea that such transmigration and the successive incarnations are a reward or punishment for deeds done in another life, arguing that reward and punishment do not make any sense if the one who receives them does not know their cause.

———

JLG

Aeneas of Paris (?–870). Chancellor of Charles the Bald and bishop of Paris who, apparently at the request of Nicholas I, wrote a treatise, *Against the Greeks,* on the occasion of the schism of ⇒Photius. In it he defends Western practices and positions and criticizes the Eastern ones, providing numerous quotations from ancient writers.

———

JLG

Aetius (?–ca. 350). Principal exponent of the most extreme form of Arianism. His followers, known as Anomoeans, held that the Father and the Son are different in everything, since only the Father is God. A native of Antioch, he traveled to Alexandria, where he studied the logic of ⇒Aristotle and thus became an able polemicist. He was made bishop by the Arians, although he does not appear to have had a particular see.

———

JLG

Afraates (?–ca. 350). Persian Christian, also known as the Wise Persian. Converted from Judaism to Christianity, he adopted the name of Jacob and proved himself a constant adversary of Arianism. Modern criticism substantiates that he was the author of twenty-two homilies whose Syriac text was found in the middle of the nineteenth century. As he himself tells us, he wrote them in 344, 345, and 347, during the persecution of Sapor II. They deal with various matters of ethics and controversy and provide valuable testimony on the faith and discipline of the Syriac church of fourth century. Although A. does not comment directly on the Scriptures, in all of his books he has a great many references to them. In certain interpretations he shows the influence of rabbinic doctrine.

———

JDR

Agobard of Lyon (ca. 780–840).
Archbishop of that city who participated in the political struggles of his time and therefore was removed from office. A highly scholarly man for his time, A. attacked many popular superstitions, including magic and witchcraft, as well as the excessive veneration of images. His main theological work, which is still extant, is a refutation of the adoptionism of ⇒Felix of Urgel.

———

JLG

Agop, John ⇒Holov, John

Agricola, Johann (ca. 1494–1566).
German theologian, first a student and then a colleague of ⇒Luther. When A. declared himself an antinomian, Luther disowned him. A. later recanted, and his apology was apparently accepted by most Lutherans, but not by Luther himself. He was also involved in the preparation and promotion of the Augsburg Interim of 1548, a document and a policy that the stricter Lutherans rejected.

———

JLG

Agricola, Rudolph (1433–85). Dutch philosopher, philologist, poet, musician, and painter. His true name was Rolef Huysmann. He was one of the restorers of the arts and sciences in Europe. He studied in Louvain, from 1473 traveled throughout France and Italy, and in 1480 returned to his country, saturated with the teachings of the Renaissance. A. held a teaching post in philosophy at the University of Heidelberg, of which he was a trustee. Due more to his personal actions than to his writings, he is one of the founders of German humanism. He taught the philosophy of ⇒Aristotle and was an irreconcilable enemy of the barbaric Latin of certain schools. He was the first modern author to seek practical means for teaching the Word to people who could not hear or speak. His works have been highly regarded, not only because of the classic elegance of his thoughts, but also because of the ease and precision of his style. Two volumes were published together in Cologne (1539) under the title *Elucubrationes aliquot lectu dignissimae.* Outstanding among them is *In laudem philosophiae* and the treatise *De inventione dialectica.* The latter, in which he tried to demonstrate the true function of logic as a fundamental element of rhetoric, became one of his most influential works. In addition, he wrote

letters, speeches, poems and several translations from the Greek. During the last years of his life he devoted himself to the study of theology and the Hebrew language. His discourse *De nativitate Christi* shows a spirit of profound piety.

———

JDR

Ailly, Pierre d' (1350–1420). Professor of the Sorbonne, and then archbishop of Cambrai (1397). Regarding the question of the universals, his position was a nominalism similar to that of ⇒Ockham and other philosophers at the end of the Middle Ages. Partly as a result of that nominalism, he refused to think of the church as a hierarchy headed by the pope. To him the church was instead a communion of the faithful, represented by the bishops. Thus some have said that for A. the church was an aristocracy rather than a monarchy. In any case, this means that a council of bishops has more authority than the pope. In his treatise *On the Reform of the Church*, he proposed precisely that thesis, which at that time was very well received, particularly since the papacy was divided in the midst of the Great Schism of the West, and in any case it seemed hopeless to wait for an ecclesiastical reform coming from it. He was one of the chief promoters of conciliarism and an important actor in the councils of ⇒Pisa and ⇒Constance, and he presided over several sessions of the latter.

———

JLG

Ajayic Crowther, Samuel (1807–91).
A native of the land of the Yoruba in western Nigeria, A. was one of the first African theologians and missionaries to their own land, working in Niger. In 1864, under the leadership of Henry ⇒Venn, A. was named the first bishop of the nations in the west of Africa beyond the limits of British political control. His theology of mission, contextual in nature and based on the use of the vernacular in the transmission of the gospel, is found in his works *Journal of an Expedition Up the Niger in 1841* (1843) and *The Gospel on the Banks of the Niger* (1859).

———

CCO

Alain of Lille (ca. 1114–ca. 1203).
Professor and then rector of the University of Paris. Later he retired to a monastic life among the Cistercians. Known as the Great by his contemporaries, he wrote a work, *On the Articles*

of the Catholic Faith, that many regard as superior to the *Sentences* of ⇒Peter Lombard, although it did not have the same influence. In some sections this work borrows from the geometric method, presenting its arguments in terms of axioms, theorems, and so on.

———

JLG

Albertus Magnus (1206–80). Also
known as Albert the Great. Teacher in the Dominican order, a native of Swabia, whose academic career transpired mainly in Paris and then in Cologne. In spite of the many interruptions in his studies due to ecclesiastical responsibilities, he was an original thinker and prolific author of voluminous works. A. was the most important teacher of ⇒Thomas Aquinas, who continued his work and carried it to its culmination.

A. lived at a time when the philosophy of ⇒Aristotle, recently reintroduced into European universities, was the cause of great controversy. The majority of the theologians of that period thought that Aristotle and his philosophy were radically incompatible with Christianity. To a great extent this was because the West knew Aristotle chiefly through his commentator ⇒Averroës. Therefore, it was thought that Aristotelian philosophy necessarily led to conclusions that are contrary to the Christian faith, such as the eternity of matter and the "unity of the active intellect" (that is, that ultimately all souls are but one, and in the end they lose themselves in that unity). In response to the challenge of Aristotelianism, many theologians and ecclesiastical leaders insisted that philosophy ought to be subordinate to theology, and that it had to arrive at the same conclusions as theology. In addition, there were a number of ecclesiastical prohibitions against the study of Aristotle (or at least against the most recently translated works of Aristotle, since his logic was generally known and accepted).

Over against almost all of his contemporaries, A. sought to show that the philosophy of Aristotle was not incompatible with the Christian faith. With that purpose, he established a clear distinction between philosophy and theology. Philosophy, like every other science except theology, is derived from autonomous principles that the mind can know apart from revelation. Theology, on the other hand, is based on revealed principles that the mind cannot know or discover by itself. What philosophy demonstrates on the basis of those autonomous principles is true; but philosophy should take care not to exceed the limits of it own data and its method. This happens, for example, when philosophers seek through reason to prove that matter is eternal. It also happens when other philosophers seek to prove creation out of nothing.

Though philosophy can in fact offer arguments that show the possibility and perhaps even the probability that God has created matter out of nothing, such arguments never become absolute proof. Thus, the question of whether matter is eternal or was created out of nothing cannot be settled by philosophy but only by theology, which sets out from the revealed principle of creation.

Concerning the supposed unity of the soul, A. points out that in all concrete and particular reality the *quod est* (the *what is*, the essence) must be distinguished from the *quo est* (the fact *that it is*, its concrete existence). Although the essence of all the souls is the same, it is God who gives each one its particular and concrete existence.

Another controverted point due to the reintroduction of Aristotle was the theory of knowledge. The theory that was traditional among Christian theologians was derived from ⇒Augustine and is known as the theory of illumination: it is God, through the eternal Word, who illumines the understanding, thus giving one knowledge. Aristotelianism, on the other hand, insisted on the importance of the senses in the process of gaining knowledge. A. resolves the tension by indicating that in the human being there is a "passive intellect" and an "active intellect." Through divine illumination, the latter manages to extract the true knowledge of the essence of things from the data that the senses provide, and then impresses it on the passive intellect.

The literary production of A. was immense, and the greater part of it still survives. In the field of theology, he wrote exegetical works as well as commentaries on the *Sentences* of ⇒Peter Lombard and on the writings of ⇒Dionysius the Areopagite. His most mature work in this field is his *Summa theologiae*. In the field of philosophy, he proposed to comment on all of the writings of Aristotle, which led him to write about logic, metaphysics, ethics, and politics. As a philosopher, he also wrote a number of works against the Averroists.

However, perhaps his chief contribution lies in his many writings about natural sciences (astronomy, zoology, botany). Thanks to the reintroduction of Aristotle, A. believed that the senses were an important source of knowledge.

So, in contrast with previous philosophers and theologians, who thought that true knowledge is obtained apart from the senses, A. was convinced that observation offers materials for true knowledge. For that reason, save few exceptions, A. was the first theologian of the Middle Ages who truly took into account the data of the senses and devoted himself to the observation of nature as a means to arrive at knowledge. Thanks to him and to his disciple Thomas Aquinas, western Europe began to pay attention to the physical world. Therefore it could be said that here is the origin of the sciences as we know them, and even of modern technology.

A bull of Pius XI, in 1931, added A. to the list of ⇒doctors of the church.

————

JLG

Albigensians. A neo-Manichean sect in the medieval period that originated in northern Italy and southern France. Its Manicheism was manifested mostly in dualistic teachings and an ascetic life. Among its fundamental doctrines is a duality of divinities. From eternity the prince of light rules over all that is invisible and the prince of this world rules over all that is visible. Lucifer is the son of the prince of this world.

Lucifer's chief task was to seduce some of the angels of the prince of light to enter the world of darkness. The work of redemption is to restore the liberty of "the lost sheep of the house of Israel." The divine light has manifested itself through the Psalms, the prophets, and Christ. Christ is the completely perfect celestial being and is the leader of all the good angels. His work of redemption consisted in proclaiming the truth in an ethereal body and in performing miracles, then returning to the invisible celestial world after his death.

In all of this the A. exhibit a docetic Christology. Believers attain their salvation in the baptism of Jesus through the Spirit, which they receive through the laying on of hands by their teachers. Their wandering souls can return to their celestial home only when they are incorporated in the true church of the believers. Since many of those souls perished before and after the work of Christ without knowing this true church, the A. believed in the transmigration of souls. This doctrine is necessary for the wandering souls to join that "true church" or community of A. in one of their transmigrations or reincarnations.

————

ALG

Albright, William Foxwell (1891–1971). North American archaeologist who specialized in Near Eastern studies. A son of missionaries, he was born in Chile. He studied at John Hopkins University, where he would then teach for nearly thirty years. His archaeological studies were an effort to prove the historical validity of the Old Testament in spite of the doubts caused by historical-critical studies of the Bible.

————

LGP

Alcuin of York (735?–804). English scholar and educator in the court of Charlemagne, and a leading figure in the intellectual renaissance of the time. As abbot of the monastery of St. Martin of Tours, he turned it into the center of scholarship for the entire French kingdom.

A. was Charlemagne's minister of public instruction and his chief intellectual. As such he was in charge of the Palatine School of Aachen and for eight years directed a movement of cultural renewal. What stands out in his extensive work is the introduction of Celtic styles into continental art, the renewal of liturgy, and the promotion of literature. In his leadership of the Carolingian renaissance, he made use of the best of the knowledge of the ancients and of the cultural heritage of the period. As theologian he was the chief adviser to Charlemagne on ecclesiastical matters. He published a revised and official edition of the Bible, promoted the instruction of the clergy, and defended orthodoxy.

————

CJP

Alexander, Archibald (1772–1851). Outstanding Presbyterian pastor and professor. He was born in Rockbridge County, Virginia, and studied at Liberty Hall Academy (now Washington and Lee University). After his ordination at the age of nineteen, he worked as pastor in various churches in Virginia. In 1796 he assumed the presidency of Hampden-Sydney College, where his leadership brought rapid growth. In 1807 he was assigned as pastor of Pine Street Church in Philadelphia, one of the most important congregations of that period, a position he occupied for five years. In 1812 he was named professor of pedagogy and polemical theology at the seminary that had been recently founded in Princeton, thus becoming its first faculty member. He served in that capacity until his death on October 22, 1851.

—

Alexander, Joseph Addison (1809–60).

Third son of Archibald ⇒Alexander. Having recently graduated from Princeton University, in 1826 he devoted himself to the establishment of Edgehill Seminary. In 1830 he was named adjunct professor of ancient languages at Princeton Seminary. He resigned this position in 1833 in order to visit German universities (Halle and Berlin). Upon his return the next year, he was named professor of Oriental literature at Princeton Seminary. In 1852 he was named director of the Department of Church History at the same institution. He died in Princeton in 1860.

—

Alexander III ⇒Bandinelli, Roland

Alexander of Afrodisias (?–211).

Aristotelian philosopher who, although not a Christian, influenced Christian theology because he was one of the chief ancient commentators of the work of ⇒Aristotle.

—

Alexander of Alexandria (?–328).

Bishop of that city, and the first to attack the doctrines of ⇒Arius. Against Arius, A. declared that the Father is eternally Father, by virtue of the Son's presence, which is also eternal. When the controversy led to the Council of ⇒Nicaea, A. attended it, in spite of his advanced age, taking with him the young deacon ⇒Athanasius. The council confirmed his position against that of Arius.

—

Alexander of Hales (1180–1245).

First Franciscan teacher at the University of Paris. (A. was a teacher at the university before becoming a Franciscan in 1236.) Known in his time as the Irrefutable Doctor, A. wrote many works, the majority of which have been lost. The chief one among those that survive is his *Summa theologiae*, which follows the outline of the *Sentences* of ⇒Peter Lombard: (1) God; (2) the creatures; (3) Christ and the virtues; (4) the sacraments and eschatology. Since A. died before finishing this work, his disciples completed it (which makes the task of determining the exact content of his theology much more difficult).

Although he was aware of the new currents of thought, A. remained firm in the Augustinian line of interpretation and allowed himself to be very little influenced by the growing Aristotelianism of that time. Augustinian in his epistemology, A. held that knowledge comes through illumination from God, which became the characteristic doctrine of many of the first Franciscans.

But, above all, A. expresses his Franciscan spirit by insisting that theology, more than knowledge, is wisdom, and that its aim is not to satisfy curiosity, but to perfect the soul and its virtues.

—

Allen, Alexander V. G. (1841–1908).

Episcopal clergyman and professor of church history in Massachusetts. He is known chiefly by his work *Continuity of Christian Thought* (1884), in which he interprets that thought differently than his contemporaries did, adopting a Hellenistic point of view that begins with ⇒Clement of Alexandria. He is also known by his works *Life and Letters of Phillips Brooks* (1900) and *Life of Jonathan Edwards* (1894).

—

Allen, Roland (1868–1947).

British Anglican pastor who studied at the University of Oxford and was ordained to the ministry in 1892. He was a missionary in northern China sponsored by the Society for the Propagation of the Gospel, a missionary agency that was supported by the evangelical wing of the Church of England. In 1904 he became the priest of a small parish, from which he resigned when he was required to baptize infants whose families had no commitment to the church. During the 1920s he collaborated with different groups and missionary agencies seeking to revitalize ecumenical missionary commitment. He died in Kenya, Africa, where he had worked as a missionary since 1931.

A. was a tireless writer. He wrote letters and articles informing congregations and missionary agencies on the progress of the mission. He is mainly remembered for two important books. The first, *Missionary Methods: St. Paul's or Ours* (1912), is a biblical and theological proposal for the church, inviting it to imitate the missionary methods of Paul. It emphasizes the missionary role of the church in proclamation, and not in the effort to establish churches that would be a copy of those in the West. The second book, *The Spontaneous Expansion of the Church and the Causes which Hinder It* (1927), proposes focusing on the work of the Holy Spirit in the mission of the church and questions the professional character of the ministry, recommending a return to a charismatic ministry.

A. also proposed better training for the missionary corps, cooperation between governments and missionary agencies in the expansion of Christianity, and an emphasis on education as a missionary task. His theological works represent a revolution in the missiological thought of his time.

—
CCO

Allis, Oswald Thompson (1880–1973).
Professor of Semitic philology at Princeton Seminary (1910–29) and of Old Testament and exegesis at Westminster Theological Seminary (1930–36). Editor of *Princeton Theological Review* and of other theological journals. He was moderator of the Philadelphia Presbytery of the Presbyterian Church and served on the Committee of Biblical Versions of the American Bible Society (1915–61). Among his chief works is *The Five Books of Moses* (1943).

—
ALG

Althaus, Paul August Wilhelm Hermann (1888–1966).
German Lutheran theologian who sought to make the theological legacy of ⇒Luther more relevant. He wrote prolifically on exegetical and systematic theology. Among his works are *Die letzten Dinge* (The Last Things); *Grundriss der Dogmatik* (Outline of Dogmatics); *Grundriss der Ethik* (Outline of Ethics); *Die Theologie Martin Luthers* (The Theology of Martin Luther); *Die Ethik Martin Luthers* (The Ethics of Martin Luther); and *Der Brief an die Römer übersetzt und erklärt* (The Letter to the Romans Translated and Expounded).

—
JDR

Altizer, Thomas J. J. (1927–)
Leading exponent of the theology of the death of God, which was in vogue in the United States and England during the 1960s. The assertion "God is dead" expresses theological as well as social

and cultural convictions. It was a more radical way of pointing out, as ⇒Bonhoeffer, ⇒Cox, and ⇒Tillich did, that in secularism the God of the theistic religions is no longer an important factor in the determination of human life. For A. this declaration implies that human beings are not governed by transcendent powers and are totally responsible for their fulfillment as individuals as well as for the well-being of their social and political communities.

—
IG

Altmann, Walter (1941–).
Brazilian Lutheran theologian. Professor of systematic theology at the School of Theology in São Leopoldo, Brazil. Author of a great number of articles on themes concerning Latin American theology, ecumenism, and ecclesiology. Besides exercising his leadership in the contemporary ecumenical dialogue, he has made great contributions to the most recent studies on Luther from a Latin American perspective. Among his publications are *Confrontation and Liberation* (1987), *Lutherans in Brazil* (1990), and *Luther and Liberation* (1992).

—
JDR

Álvarez, Carmelo (1947–).
Puerto Rican pastor, historian, and ecumenist. A leader in the ecumenical movement in Latin America, he has contributed to research on the impact of Protestantism and Pentecostalism on the continent.

—
CCO

Alves, Rubem (1933–).
Born in Brazil and reared in the conservative Presbyterian tradition, A. is one of the chief renewers of Latin American theology. The stages of his thought are distinguished, first, by a search for the activity of God in history and, second, by an investigation of the ludic and erotic possibilities of life. With his master's thesis (*A Theological Interpretation of the Meaning of the Revolution in Brazil*, 1963; Portuguese, 2004) which he defended at Union Seminary, New York, he took up the theme of revolution, which his mentor Richard ⇒Shaull was treating in those years, precisely at the time when the movement ⇒Iglesia y Sociedad en América Latina (ISAL) was surfacing.

After a government coup in 1964, A. was forced to return to the United States because he was persecuted by the military and by his own church. In Princeton he wrote the thesis

Towards a Theology of Liberation (1968; *Da esperança*, 1987). This title was changed to *Theology of Human Hope*. There he addresses the theologies of ⇒Barth, ⇒Bultmann, and ⇒Moltmann, criticizing them because they are not rooted in concrete human circumstances and because they do not adequately express the liberating discourse. His fundamental ethical principle, which he takes from Paul ⇒Lehmann, is "how human life can remain human in the world." He thus engages two kinds of discourse that lead to human liberation: messianic humanism and humanistic messianism. Both point to a project of liberation that includes not only the material but also the spiritual. The last part of the book explores the possibilities of a new language for faith and theology vindicating joy and play. Here he follows ⇒Bonhoeffer's concept of polyphony. With this work, A. in many ways anticipates Gustavo ⇒Gutiérrez and Hugo ⇒Assmann. They agreed that "theology and development" was not the correct formulation, since conditions in Latin America depended rather on the dynamic of oppression-liberation.

The imaginative emphasis of A.'s theology began to show itself in *Tomorrow's Child* (1972; *Gestação do futuro*, 1986), the fruit of a course on ethics that he gave at Union Seminary. This book was much misunderstood, since in it he analyzes the dominant technological system on the basis of his own cultural premises. One of his metaphors compares the present world with the huge dinosaurs whose voracity prevented them from surviving, as opposed to lizards, which survive until the present time. Back in Brazil, he gave up his membership in the church in 1974 and began his career as university professor. In that year he published *Confessions: On Theology and Life*, a self-critical confession about his ecclesiastical and theological experience. Later he became deeply involved in psychoanalysis.

In the 1970s he produced a series of critical works on Protestantism and religion, and in *Dogmatismo e tolerância* (1982; Dogmatism and Tolerance), he attempted to recover the values of the Reformed tradition. In *Variações sobre a vida e a morte* (1981; Variations on Life and Death), *A teologia como jogo* (1982; Theology as Play) and *Créio na resurreição do corpo* (1982; I Believe in the Resurrection of the Body) he exploits his ludic, erotic, and poetic style. Since then he has begun to write what he calls "chronicles," essays in which he gives free rein to his many ideas, including theological and pedagogical theories. He has also written children's stories in a vein that is very close to psychoana-

lytical research. *Pai Nosso* (1987; Our Father) and *The Poet, the Warrior, the Prophet* (1990) give witness to his literary and poetic maturity. He has also gathered in other volumes his reflections on education, which are followed with much interest by scholars because of his audacious pedagogical proposals. *Lições de feitiçaria* (1998, 2003; *Lessons on Sorcery*) and *Transparências da eternidade* (2002; Transparencies of Eternity) bring together some theological and antidogmatic texts.

———

LC-O

Amalric of Bena (12th century). Also

known as Amaury, and as "of Chartres." A student and then a professor at the University of Paris. His doctrines are similar to those of John Scotus ⇒Erigena. God is the only real being; therefore the essence of all things is the essence of God. In addition, the distinction between the sexes is the result of sin; therefore in the original creation that distinction did not exist, nor will it exist after the resurrection. (If sin had not interfered, human beings would have reproduced in some other way, as the angels do.)

Some time after the death of A., the sect or movement of the Amalricians, whose connection with the teacher of Paris is not entirely clear, arose. They were condemned in 1210, and thereafter repeatedly, for different reasons, but above all for two doctrinal points. First, they held that since God is present in everything, the eucharistic consecration does not make God more present in the bread and wine, nor present in a different way, but simply announces that presence, which in any case is universal. Second, they adopted a Trinitarian scheme according to which the Father became incarnate in Abraham and acted alone in the world until the Son became incarnate in Jesus and put an end to the old Law. Now the Holy Spirit, who becomes incarnate in human souls, puts an end to the law of Christ.

It is hardly likely that A. himself taught such doctrines, which the Amalricians and others later attributed to him.

———

JLG

Amaury of Bena (or of Chartres) ⇒Amalric of Bena

Ambrose (ca. 333–97). Bishop of Milan,

famous for his oratory, his contribution to liturgy, and his firm resistance to Arianism (⇒Arius). A native of the city of Trier and the son of a Christian high civil servant, he learned about the Christian faith at the same time as he was being trained for a career in the civil administration of the empire. He advanced rapidly in that career until he became governor of Liguria and Aemilia, residing in Milan. Upon the death of Bishop Auxentius, who had Arian convictions, A. feared that the election of his successor would cause a riot. In order to safeguard order, A. attended the election. Suddenly and unexpectedly, the people began to cry out that they wanted him as bishop. After seriously resisting, and finally deferring to the imperial mandate, A. accepted that office. Since he was not yet baptized, in the space of one week he went from being a catechumen to a bishop. A.'s first two steps signaled the direction of his episcopate. He began by distributing his possessions among the poor. Next, he invited the priest Simplicianus to Milan to teach A. Scripture and theology. These two interests, the poor and theology, characterized the rest of A.'s career.

In that career, two culminating moments were confrontations with the imperial authorities. One of them, with Theodosius, had to do with matters of morality. Theodosius had ordered a terrible slaughter, and A. refused to restore him to the communion of the church until he would give signs of repentance and issue orders that would prevent the incident from being repeated. The other confrontation, with the empress Justina, had mainly theological motives, for Justina promoted Arianism, and she demanded that A. surrender one of his churches for Arian worship. A. refused, and he and his followers occupied the church for a long time, singing hymns while the imperial authorities besieged the place. In the end, Justina had to abandon her project.

The other high point in the episcopal career of A. was the conversion and baptism of ⇒Augustine, who returned to the Christian faith thanks to the preaching of A. But A. himself does not seem to have perceived the exceptional gifts of Augustine.

A.'s chief literary work are his sermons, many of which are extant. The most notable deal with the six days of creation, the vineyard of Naboth, and the Psalms. Among the most outstanding of his works of moral exhortation are the essays *On the Virgins*, which deals with the chastity of both women and men, and *On the Duties of the Clergy*, which treats of the ethics and practice of ministerial functions and how to reconcile both. Against the Arians he wrote three main works, *On the Faith*, *On the Holy Spirit*, and *On the Mystery of the Incar-*

nation of the Lord. While these works reflect the rhetorical and logical ability of A., they also show a strong dependence on other authors, and above all on ⇒Basil of Caesarea. The same can be said of his essay *On the Mysteries*, in which he discusses the sacraments of initiation based on the work of ⇒Cyril of Jerusalem. Against the Novatians (⇒Novatian), he wrote the essay *On Penitence*.

In his doctrine of God and of the Trinity, A. follows the Greek writers closely, especially Basil of Caesarea, ⇒Gregory of Nazianzus, and ⇒Gregory of Nyssa, as well as ⇒Hilary of Poitiers, who lived in the West but wrote in Greek. Thus one of the main theological contributions of A. lay in translating Greek theology into Latin. This came to be of vital importance shortly after his death, when the invasion of the Germanic peoples who had been converted to Arianism compelled the Latin-speaking church to defend its doctrine against the Arians. In a way, A. prepared the church for that challenge, which he himself barely perceived.

In his biblical interpretation he is also guided by the same authors as well as by ⇒Origen, whom he also follows on several points of his eschatology.

Concerning the Eucharist, A. affirms that the nature of the bread gives place to the nature of the body of Christ, but he insists on the need to distinguish between the rite itself and the grace that acts in the believer.

The Ambrosian chant is usually attributed to him, as well as the liturgy of the same name. However, it is not entirely clear how much of these are the work of A. himself.

———

JLG

Ames, Edward Scribner (1870–1958).
Educator and clergyman who served chiefly as professor in the Faculty of Philosophy of the University of Chicago. There, along with other luminaries such as John ⇒Dewey and George Herbert ⇒Mead, he collaborated in the development of the pragmatic philosophy of the university. He was a pioneer in studies in the psychology of religion and a leader in the movement of liberal religion. For forty years he served simultaneously as minister of the University Church of the Disciples of Christ and as founder and dean of the House of Theological Studies in the university. His chief works are *The Psychology of Religious Experience* (1910) and *Religion* (1929).

———

ALG

Ames, William (1576–1633). Also known as Amesius. English Puritan clergyman and professor of theology at Cambridge and at Franeker, Frisia. He participated in the Synod of ⇒Dort (1618–19), where he affirmed Calvinist orthodox theology against ⇒Arminius. He was one of the first theologians to systematize Calvinist theology in the philosophical context of the French Huguenot Pierre de la Ramée (Petrus ⇒Ramus). A. also was one of the leading figures in the Puritan federalist theology of the seventeenth century. He lived mainly in Holland and died in Rotterdam as he prepared to emigrate to the colonies of New England. His work was hailed in the new colonies, where he was dubbed the father of American theology. His theological work *Medulla theologicae* (1623) became the principal text used in theological education at Harvard and Yale until the middle of the eighteenth century. His essay *De conscientia et ejus jure vel casibus* (1631) laid down the standards of moral conduct for the Puritans of the same period. But his greatest contribution is *Technometria* (1631), in which he systematizes the Puritan philosophy of Ramus. His systematic delineation of the nature and use of art in general, and of each one of the liberal arts, seeks the integration of theology with other disciplines. With his new outlook, he was able to offer an alternative to the traditional Aristotelian metaphysics.

———

ALG

Amollus of Lyon (9th century). Author of a letter against ⇒Gottschalk's views on predestination. Also against Gottschalk, he wrote a collection of propositions distilled from the works of ⇒Augustine. He also wrote a treatise against the Jews, lamenting their presence in Lyon. This writing is indicative of the anti-Semitism of many medieval theologians.

———

JLG

Amphilochius of Iconium (ca. 340–ca. 395). Contemporary, friend, and collaborator of the ⇒Cappadocians, and probably a relative of ⇒Gregory of Nazianzus. Although he wished to devote himself to the ascetic life, he was made bishop of Iconium by ⇒Basil of Caesarea. His principal theological work consisted in the defense of the divinity and consubstantiality (with the Father and the Son) of the Holy Spirit, in opposition to the teaching of the so-called Pneumatomachians or "enemies of the Spirit." He was at the Council of ⇒Constantinople in the year 381, where such doctrines were condemned. He also wrote against the Apotactite and Gemelite sects, which were extremely ascetic groups with apparently gnostic tendencies.

———

JLG

Amsdorf, Nikolaus von (1483–1565). German Protestant theologian. He studied at the University of Wittenberg, where he was a professor of theology and a friend of ⇒Luther, who encouraged him to study the works of ⇒Augustine. He accompanied Luther on the trips to Leipzig and Worms, and collaborated with him in the translation of the Bible. After Luther's death, he was expelled from Wittenberg (1547) and together with other faithful Lutherans (⇒Flacius) tenaciously combated the Interim and participated in the adiaphoristic, synergistic, and eucharistic controversies, as well as in lively debates on free will and original sin. He was always on the side of the most extreme Lutherans, among whom he stood out because of his fanatical intransigence. He was a bitter enemy of ⇒Melanchthon, fought against any effort to agree or compromise, and was intransigent over against every attempt to "modify" the doctrine of justification. The principle he established—that good works are detrimental to the salvation of the soul when they are done in order to obtain worldly goods and honors—was much debated. His teachings attracted many followers, who eventually formed the Amsdorfian sect. He was one of the founders of the University of Jena and was responsible for the Jena edition of Luther's works.

———

JDR

Amyraut, Moïse (1596–1664). Distinguished French Calvinist theologian who opposed the prevailing interpretation of ⇒Calvin. Although that opposition revolved around the doctrines of predestination and limited atonement, it really went further, since A., like Calvin, shared in the intellectual breadth and the aesthetic and literary tastes of the humanists, while ⇒Dort and orthodox Calvinism had turned Calvin into a rigid character with categorically incisive teachings.

The orthodox Calvinism of the period was defined in terms of the canons of the Synod of Dort, particularly as it relates to the doctrine of predestination and limited atonement. A.

insisted that Dort had misrepresented the doctrine of Calvin, for whom predestination was never something that could be proven on the basis of divine omniscience; rather, it was a way of expressing the experience of salvation through the grace of God. In addition, A. compiled numerous texts which proved that Calvin had never supported a limited atonement in the style of Dort.

In a synod of the Reformed Church of France that met in Alençon in 1637, there was an attempt to condemn him as a heretic, but A. had enough support to prevent this. With the passage of time that church became more Calvinist in the orthodox sense, and it soon became common to speak of the "heresy of Amyraut."

JLG

Anastasius Sinaita (d. 700). A monk on Mount Sinai. He was called a "new Moses" and revered as a saint in the Byzantine church. He stood out as an orthodox apologist against Monophysitism. A. was an author of many works on apologetic, monastic, and exegetical themes, usually following an allegorical interpretation. His main works are *Hodegos*, *Eratopokriseis*, and *Anagogicae contemplationes in hexaemeron ad theophilum.*

LRR

Anchieta, José de (1534–97). Jesuit, a relative of Ignatius of ⇒Loyola. Known as the "apostle of Brazil." Author of several catechisms, dialogues, and religious dramas in the Tupi language.

JLG

Andersen, Wilhem (1911–80). German Lutheran missiologist. His work consisted of developing theological relations between missions as church practice and as missionary organizations, and ecclesiology. He wrote *Towards a Theology of Mission: A Study of the Encounter between the Missionary Enterprise and the Church and Its Theology*, a critical reflection on the development of missiology and ecclesiology in the World Missionary Conferences up to the conference of Willingen in 1952. He was director of a school of missionary training in Germany and contributed significantly to the integration of missiology into theological curricula.

CCO

Anderson, Gerald (1930–). North American Methodist missiologist whose academic works center on the history of missiological thought and the biography of important figures in missiology and in the missionary field. Some of his most recent works are *Mission Legacies* (1995) and *A Biographical Dictionary of Christian Mission* (1998).

A. was director of the Overseas Ministries Study Center, which was located first in New Jersey and then in New Haven, Connecticut. This center sponsors programs and workshops for students and missionary personnel from the United States and other parts of the world. He was also one of the editors of the missiological journal *International Bulletin of Missionary Research*, one of the most important resources for the discipline in the United States. In retirement, he continues publishing missiological studies and supports the development of a new generation of missiologists in North America.

CCO

Anderson, Rufus (1796–1880). Born in Yarmouth, Maine, A. studied at Bowdoin College and at Andover Seminary. He was executive secretary of the American Board of Commissioners for Foreign Missions from 1832 until his retirement in 1866. He was also ordained as an evangelist and, though he volunteered to go to India, his work centered on the administration of the board and on theological reflection on the mission of the church.

Together with Henry ⇒Venn, A. developed a theology of mission that would secure the indigenization of congregations in missionary territories. He proposed three goals to bring this about: the congregations should govern themselves, support themselves, and propagate themselves. Progressively these congregations would participate in the expansion of the faith, becoming missionary congregations.

In 1855 he visited India, where he put some of his missiological principles into practice. His visit stimulated the dispersion of the missionaries who, up until that time, had lived together in their own communities. It also stimulated the organization of local congregations in villages, without the direct supervision of missionaries, and the ordination of nationals to the ministry. By 1856 he had designed and written the *Outline of Missionary Policy* of the American Board, in which he included his theories about the establishment of congregations. Other publications were *Foreign Missions:*

Their Relations and Claims (1869) and several works on the history of missions.

———

CCO

Andrea, Jacob (1528–90).

German Lutheran theologian. Born in the city of Waiblingen in Württemberg, he studied at the University of Tübingen. He was ordained at the age of eighteen in Stuttgart and in that same year married Anne Entringer. He was the only Lutheran clergyman who remained at his post during the occupation of Stuttgart by the Spaniards during the Schmalkald War. He received his doctorate in sacred theology in 1553. In 1561 Duke Christopher appointed him as professor of theology, provost, and president of the University of Tübingen, positions he held until his death.

Together with other Lutheran leaders he worked arduously for the adoption of the Formula of ⇒Concord (1577), of which he was one of six signatory theologians, and for which he wrote the Epitome (Summary). According to his friends and detractors, A. was a vain person with little tact, frequently imprudent in his choice of words, but at the same time possessed of a deep piety, conscious of his own faults, diligent and industrious, a powerful preacher, tenacious, and a devoutly honest proponent of Lutheran unity. His more than 200 books and pamphlets are mostly polemical or of a practical nature. These works exhibit a great loyalty to Lutheranism and deliberately avoid any novelty.

———

JDR

Andres, Juan (15th century).

Spanish theologian. He was born a Muslim in Jativa and converted to Christianity. He wrote a book on apologetics titled *Refutation of the Mohammedan Sect. A Treatise on Practical Arithmetic*, printed in 1515, is also attributed to him.

———

JDR

Angela of Foligno ⇒Foligno, Angela of

Anicetus (?–ca. 166).

Bishop of Rome from approximately 155 to 166. He debated with ⇒Polycarp on the difficult matter of the date on which the resurrection of the Lord should be celebrated. Although they were not able to agree on this matter, they insisted on maintaining communion with each other.

———

JLG

Anorius (14th century).

Ethiopian monk who stood out as the central figure in the reformist movement centered in the Dabra-Lebanon monastery. This monastery, which housed hundreds of monks, became the intellectual center of the Ethiopian church. The movement emerging from it included sharp criticism against the policies of King Amda-Sion (who reigned from 1312 to 1342) and called for theological and cultural reform. Together with other companions, A. held that the Hebrew Sabbath had been abolished. The king took this as a reason or excuse to attack A. and his monastery, counting on the support of rival monks who defended the Ethiopian tradition of observing both Saturday and Sunday. The result was the condemnation and flagellation of A. and the closing of his monastery.

———

JLG

Anselm of Canterbury (1033–1109).

Philosopher and theologian who is considered to be the father of the scholastic theology that ruled in the schools and universities during the High Middle Ages. He was born in Aosta, Italy. His father was a landowner, which in that period indicated that his family had attained a certain level of wealth and power. In 1059, after a dispute with his father, he left his home to travel throughout Europe. Three years later, at the age of twenty-nine, he entered the monastery of Bec in Normandy, attracted by the fame of its abbot, ⇒Lanfranc. There he had the opportunity to study theology with Lanfranc, who used a dialectical method that A. appropriated.

In 1063 Lanfranc was transferred to another monastery, and A. took his place as abbot. During his stay in Bec, A. wrote several of his most famous works, among them *Monologion, Proslogion,* and *Epistle on the Incarnation of the Word.* During a visit to England in 1093, he was named archbishop of Canterbury by William the Conqueror. A., who did not desire that post, protested against the action of the king, which he considered inappropriate. Due to his differences with the king over the right of monarchs to invest clergy, A. abandoned his see in 1097 and went into voluntary exile. During that time of exile he wrote *Cur Deus homo?*

(Why Did God Become Human?), one of his most famous works.

Although he felt miserable during his stays in England, A. returned to Canterbury in 1100. His difficulties with the king continued, and A. was compelled to leave his see once again after only three years. In 1106, having resolved his differences with the king, A. returned to Canterbury, where he served as archbishop until his death in 1109.

A. began a theological era that would continue for several centuries and whose culmination would be the scholasticism of the thirteenth century. In his time, theology was mainly a product of the monasteries. But with the rise of cities thanks to the rapid growth of trade, theology came to be centered in cathedral schools, and eventually in the universities that arose around them. It was there that scholastic theology reached its high point.

Scholastic theology is characterized by the use of reason to achieve an understanding of the Christian faith. Although other theologians had applied philosophy and human reasoning to their understanding of the faith, A. carried this practice to a new level. Before him it was common to use Scripture and the works of the church fathers as authorities for the validation of theological arguments. With A. this practice changed. In *Proslogion*, A. expresses his famous motto that would characterize the scholastic era: "Faith seeking understanding." Although faith and divine revelation are still above human reason, the possibility of using understanding in order to deepen faith emerges with vigor in the works of A. This gave rise to an age in which theologians endeavored to solve problems through the systematic use of reason.

This new application of the human intellect to the Christian faith is evident in the works of A. Until then, the existence of God, divine revelation, and Christian doctrines had been accepted by faith and through the authority of divine revelation. Although logic, philosophy, and rhetoric were used to explain the content of the faith or to combat heresies, they were not applied to theology in order to prove, ratify, or understand the reason for which Christian doctrines were true. For A. and the other theologians who followed in his footsteps, God was the supreme example of reasoning and intellect, and therefore the Christian faith should also demonstrate a high rational level.

A. uses a systematic method for understanding Christian doctrines. Employing a dialectical method of questions and answers, he looks for the solution to problems in Christian doctrines which could be wrongly interpreted or used by heretics in order to deny them. This method is evident in the development of his arguments, which are made up of a series of questions followed by answers that progressively arrive at the final conclusion of the argument.

Among the various arguments developed by A., the two that stand out are his ontological proof of the existence of God and his explanation of why God became human in the incarnation (*Cur Deus homo*). In these arguments it is also evident that he presupposes certain aspects of the philosophy of Plato, which was still dominant in the eleventh century. In Platonism all that exists in nature has an ideal prototype, of which it is an imperfect copy. These universal ideas are in the divine mind and are more real than the material world. Therefore, logic and reason are sufficient to demonstrate the validity of an argument.

This influence of Platonism is evident in *Proslogion*, in which A. applies his methodology and logic to prove the existence of God. Much later the proof of A. would acquire the name "ontological," a term derived from two Greek words that mean "the reason or logic of being."

A. was the first Christian theologian who attempted to prove the existence of God by using reason alone and arguing that God necessarily has to exist according to logic and human reasoning. To demonstrate this, he begins by defining God as the supreme being, who is above all beings, so that it is impossible to conceive anything greater. Using his dialectical method, A. asks himself: What is greater and more perfect, something that exists or something that does not exist? Naturally, something that exists. Then A. asks himself: What is greater and more perfect, something that necessarily exists outside the intellect or something that exists only in the intellect? Something that exists necessarily without depending on the intellect is more perfect. A. then concludes that the idea of God which we have requires that God exist. Naturally, A. believes in the objective truth of concepts and ideas, and thus shows the influence of Platonism on his thought.

The ontological proof of the existence of God was immediately disputed by ⇒Gaunilo, a monk who was a contemporary of A. According to Gaunilo, it is possible to imagine the most perfect island, but that does not indicate that it really exists. Likewise Gaunilo denies that the atheist can conceive of a supreme being. A. responded to these criticisms by indicating that an island is distinguished from God in that it is never what could be conceived of as the greatest and most perfect. A.'s argument does not indicate that the most perfect of every genre necessarily has to exist, but only that existence is part of supreme perfection. Likewise A. responds that it is possible to conceive of the idea of God, and as proof he refers to those who, like Gaunilo, have faith in God. But in truth A. does not solve the objection of Gaunilo to the effect that the atheist does not believe it to be possible to join existence with the idea of God.

In the eighteenth century, the philosopher Immanuel ⇒Kant also attacked A.'s proof, arguing that the existence of any being is not an attribute that can be postulated on the basis of its conceptual essence. The thought that something has to exist does not indicate that it actually exists. Existence is a property peculiar to being that cannot be derived from definition. Although many theologians and philosophers have for centuries disputed the proof of A., it continues to emerge as an important theme, most recently in the work of the philosopher Charles ⇒Hartshorne.

A.'s second important contribution was in the field of Christology. In order to understand the argument, it is necessary first to understand the Platonic concept of universals: all beings of the same kind, including human beings, participate in a common quality or essence. For this reason, the action of a single human being affects all humanity. With these presuppositions, A. tries to understand why it was necessary for God to become a human being in order to save us.

He begins by stating that, because of Adam's sin, all of humanity is under the power of sin and in debt to God. A. compares this to the debts of honor that frequently occurred in his time. Offenses against honor could be satisfied only in a duel unto death. Blood had to be shed to satisfy the debt. For this reason, some have named the argument the "theory of satisfaction." According to A., humanity's offense against God was so great that no human being could pay the great debt. Only a being that was both divine and human could satisfy it. It was necessary that a God-human shed his blood in order to pay the debt, and for this reason God became human. Likewise, because the action of a single human being affects all of humanity, and because Christ is human and infinite at the same time, Christ's death can satisfy the debt caused by sin.

Although A. began a new theological era, in his own time he was prominent chiefly because of his correspondence, prayers, and meditations. Nevertheless, the work of A. continues to influence theology and philosophy even today.

———

LGP

Anselm of Laon (?–1117). Teacher of ⇒Abelard and of ⇒William of Champeaux. His *Sentences* is probably the first systematic theology of its time, although it was soon eclipsed by a work with the same title by ⇒Peter Lombard. He is considered a precursor of the school of St. Victor (William of Champeaux, ⇒Hugh of St. Victor, ⇒Richard of St. Victor).

———

JLG

Antony of Padua (1195–1231). Franciscan mystical theologian. His main work, aside from his very famous sermons, is *Moral Concordances of the Holy Books*, comprising five books, four of which follow the order of the moral and mystical life. The first book treats of sin and its effects; the second, of conversion; the third, of the struggles of the spirit against temptations; the fourth, of the process of perfection. The fifth book deals with the different conditions in which humans live and how the spiritual life relates to each one of them. His theology, which was strongly influenced by a recent translation of the works of ⇒Dionysius the Aereopagite, is characterized by the allegorical and mystical interpretation of biblical texts. He was canonized by Gregory IX scarcely one year after his death.

———

JLG

Apelles (2nd century). A follower of ⇒Marcion. After he became independent of Marcion, he established his own school in Alexandria. He was more extreme than Marcion in his rejection of the Old Testament, saying that it was not even the revelation of a lower god, but a collection of fables and lies. Only a few quotations from him are preserved in a work of ⇒Ambrose, *On Paradise*. ⇒Tertullian wrote against Apelles in his treatise *On the Flesh of Christ* and more specifically in a lost work, *Against Apelles*.

———

JLG

Apollinaris of Hierapolis (2nd century). One of the Christian apologists of the

second century. All his writings are lost. We know about him chiefly through ⇒Eusebius of Caesarea, who praises him and affirms that A. wrote a *Discourse* presented to the emperor Marcus Aurelius, two books *On Truth*, five books *Against the Greeks*, two books *Against the Jews*, and another *Against the Heresy of the Phrygians* (that is, Montanism).

———

JLG

Apollinaris of Laodicea (ca. 310–ca. 390).

Bishop of the city of Laodicea in Syria (which should not be confused with the city of the same name in Asia Minor, whose church was the addressee of one of the seven letters in Revelation). He was a defender of the decisions of the Council of ⇒Nicaea against ⇒Arius and his followers, as well as a friend of ⇒Athanasius and teacher of ⇒Jerome. In the end, he himself was condemned by the Council of ⇒Constantinople in 381.

A. was a prolific author, but the greater part of his exegetical and polemical works are lost. Several of his doctrinal works do exist. This is strange, since normally the doctrinal works of those who were condemned as heretics are lost. In this case, some of his disciples, precisely in order to preserve his writings, published them under respected names like those of ⇒Gregory of Neocaesarea (the Wonderworker), Athanasius, and others. In addition, a good share of his book *Demonstration of the Incarnation of God* is preserved in passages in which ⇒Gregory of Nyssa quotes it in order then to refute it.

Although he was a native of Syria, A. was an exponent of the type of theology frequently associated with the city of Alexandria. When the members of that theological tradition broached the christological question, the crucial matter for them was the divinity of the Savior, rather than his humanity. They certainly believed in his humanity. But if, in order to explain the way in which a human being could at the same time be divine, it became necessary to deprive him of some of that humanity, they were ready to do so. The characteristic manner in which these theologians then dealt with the union of divinity and humanity in Jesus is what historians have called the Christology of the *logos-sarx* (or the Word-flesh). According to that Christology, the eternal Word of God assumed human *flesh*, but not necessarily a complete humanity.

This teaching, which many before him had held without having given it much thought, was the reason why A. was declared a heretic. In contrast to his predecessors in the same theological tradition, A. proposed to explain clearly how it was that the incarnation of the Word took place. He did this principally in order to refute some arguments of the Arians. But the final result was that once the teaching of A. and of the *logos-sarx* was clearly explained, other Christians decided that it was necessary to reject it.

A. starts from the anthropology that was common in his time, according to which there are three components in the human being: the body, the "animal soul" (which is what gives life to bodies, both human and animal), and the "rational soul" (the center of the consciousness, what we today call "mind"). Consequently, A. says, in Jesus the eternal Word takes the place of the human rational soul, so that Jesus had a human body but his rational soul or mind was purely divine.

This explanation, which at first sight could appear quite satisfactory, poses serious difficulties. The most serious is that, when all is said and done, the Jesus of A. is not truly human, but is a human body with a divine mind and consciousness. If the Word assumed human nature in order to save it, how can the Word save the human mind without assuming it? As ⇒Gregory of Nazianzus said, if only the human body had fallen, such a Christ would be sufficient to save humanity. But since the whole human being has fallen and is therefore a slave of sin, the divine Word assumed the entire human nature in order to save it entirely.

———

JLG

Apostolic Fathers.

A name which, beginning in the seventeenth century, was given to a group of writings whose authors had supposedly known the apostles. Although this may be true in some cases, for the most part it is not. All of them, except the *Letter to Diognetus*, are writings that arose within the church and are addressed to other believers.

The oldest of them is possibly the *Didache* or *Teaching of the Twelve Apostles*. Its date is uncertain, some scholars dating it as early as the year 70 and others a century later. Apparently it was written in Syria or in some other semiarid region, and its main concern is the order of the church and its worship. It includes one of the most ancient references outside the New Testament to the eucharistic celebration. It is the first text to suggest the possibility of practicing baptism by pouring water on the head, when the scarcity of water demands it. In general, it reflects the conflicts and difficulties that soon led the church to establish procedures for selecting and authorizing its leaders.

The Apostolic Fathers include another work of the first century: the *Epistle to the Corinthians* by ⇒Clement of Rome. (The so-called *Second Epistle of Clement* is in reality a homily of later date.) From the beginning of the second century come the seven authentic letters of ⇒Ignatius of Antioch, and shortly afterward the letter of ⇒Polycarp to the Philippians. Later in the second century, ⇒Papias of Hierapolis collected a number of "sayings of the Lord," of which only quotations in later authors survive. Around the middle of the same century, in Rome, ⇒Hermas, brother of the bishop of that city, published a number of visions and "prophesies"—that is, messages from the Lord to the church—known as *The Shepherd*.

The so-called *Epistle of* ⇒*Barnabas*, which in reality is a homily on the relationship between Christianity and the Hebrew Scriptures, has a very uncertain date. It appears to have been composed in Alexandria, possibly during the second half of the second century.

Finally, the Apostolic Fathers include the *Letter to* ⇒*Diognetus,* which in reality is an apology or defense of the faith. Some scholars believe that it is the lost apology of ⇒Quadratus, in which case it would be from the middle of the second century. But others think that this document has a much later date, perhaps even in the fourth century.

———

JLG

Appasamy, Aiyadurai (1891–1976).
Bishop of the Church of South India. His theological works highlight the responsibility of the Church of India in the struggle for independence. He also wrote studies on Christian and Hindu mysticism.

———

CCO

Aquinas, Thomas ⇒Thomas Aquinas

Aquino, María Pilar (1956–).
Feminist Latina theologian, currently professor at the University of San Diego. Born into a poor family, A. was reared in the frontier region on the border of Mexico and the United States and was educated chiefly in Mexico and Spain. She was the first Roman Catholic woman to earn a doctorate at the Pontifical University of Salamanca. As a former president of the Academy

of Catholic Hispanic Theologians of the U.S. (ACHTUS), she has contributed in a significant way to the development of feminist theologies, both Latin American and U.S. Latina, through criticism aimed at theologians of both regions because of their frequent lack of interest in the epistemologies and perspectives of women. In the United States as well as in Latin America and Europe, she has participated in a profound and prolonged dialogue with critical and theoretical feminist thought. In this way she has made important contributions to theological epistemology and methodology and has come to be a distinguished lecturer in Europe as well as in Latin America and the United States. In addition to articles and chapters in other books, she has published *Our Cry for Life* (1993); *La teología, la iglesia y la mujer en América Latina* (1994; Theology, Church and Women in Latin America); *Entre la indignación y la esperanza* (Between Indignation and Hope), with Ana Maria ⇒Tepedino (1998); and *Teología feminista latinoamericana* (Latin American Feminist Theology) with Elsa ⇒Tamez (1998). She is a member of the editorial committees of the *Journal of the American Academy of Religion, Concilium,* and the *Journal of Hispanic/Latino Theology,* and is associate director of the Center for the Study of Latino/a Catholicism at the University of San Diego. In May 2000, the Faculty of Theology of the University of Helsinki granted her an honorary doctorate in theology.

———

OOE

Aranguren, José Luis (1909–).
Spanish Catholic moral philosopher. His work contributes to the understanding of the relationship between religion and ethics in Catholicism and Protestantism. He deals also with the central place of the constant "frame of mind" (mood) vis-à-vis life in intellectual, moral, and religious experience. A. has also contributed to the European dialogue between Christians and Marxists. His main works are: *Ética* (Ethics), *El marxismo como moral* (Marxism as Morality), and *Catolicismo y protestantismo como formas de existencia* (Catholicism and Protestantism as Forms of Existence).

———

LRR

Araquel of Tauriz (17th century).
A prominent figure in the intellectual awakening of the Church of Armenia in the seventeenth century and author of *Book of Histories,* in

which he narrates the glories and vicissitudes of Christianity in Armenia.

—

Araya, Victorio (1945–). Costa Rican theologian and professor at the Latin American Biblical University in Costa Rica, A. is a Protestant liberation theologian. His book *Dios de los pobres* (God of the Poor) reflects the ecumenical spirit of the preferential option for the poor.

—

Arias, Mortimer (1924–). Uruguayan Methodist professor of mission and evangelization in Latin America and the United States. He was a bishop in Bolivia. He has written on liberation theology, evangelization and mission, and biblical hermeneutics. Two books highlight his contribution and the integration of these topics: *El clamor de mi pueblo* (The Cry of My People) and *Announcing the Reign of God: Evangelization and the Subversive Memory of Jesus.*

—

Aristides (2nd century). Author of the most ancient Christian apology that is still extant. This work had been lost, but at the end of the nineteenth century a Syriac version was discovered in the monastery of Saint Catherine on Mount Sinai. Upon reading this text, other scholars determined that the Greek text was preserved as part of the medieval work *Life of Barlaam and Joasaph.* Apparently the author of that legend, on reaching a certain point in his narrative, simply adapted the *Apology* of A. Besides these Syriac and Greek texts, fragments in Armenian have been found. On that basis, it has been possible to reconstruct the lost work of A.

The text begins with an introduction on the nature of God, the prime mover of the world, who has created everything because of God's love for humanity. God is so exalted that God has no name; therefore it is possible to speak of God only by denying God limitations: God has no beginning nor end, nor parts, and so on.

A. then goes on to defend the Christian faith by dividing humanity into four categories: barbarians, Greeks, Jews, and Christians (in the Greek version there are three: pagans, Jews, and Christians). The barbarians and the Greeks have made for themselves gods who are not gods,

who cannot even care for themselves, and who even practice vice and immorality. According to A., the Jews have also fallen into idolatry because they worship not the God of the heavens, but the angels and their own laws. Thus only Christians have found and followed the truth. For this reason, not only their teachings but also their customs are superior, as can be seen in the love that they show among themselves.

—

Aristo of Pella (2nd century). Author of the treatise *Disputation between Jason and Papiscus concerning Christ*, whose existence was known through ⇒Eusebius of Caesarea, and which recently has been recovered, at least partly, among texts attributed to other authors. In that dialogue, Jason, a Jew who has accepted Jesus as the Messiah, convinces the Alexandrian Jew Papiscus, who in the end requests baptism.

—

Aristotle (ca. 384–322 BCE). Greek philosopher of Thracian origin who studied in Athens under ⇒Plato. He was the teacher of Alexander the Great and then returned to Athens, where he founded his own school, known as the Peripatos. He wrote on logic, physics, metaphysics, ethics, and practically all the fields of human knowledge of his time. During the first centuries of the history of Christianity, the philosophy of A. had little influence on Christian theology, except insofar as the diverse eclectic systems of late Hellenism, particularly Stoicism and Neoplatonism, assimilated some elements of his teachings. Among the theologians, it was particularly those of the school of Antioch (⇒Ibas of Edessa, ⇒Theodore of Mopsuestia, ⇒Theodoret) who made greater use of A. When the Council of ⇒Ephesus condemned Nestorianism (⇒Nestorius) and the less moderate positions of the Antiochenes, many of these found refuge in the Persian Empire, particularly around the famous theological school of Nisibis. They brought with them the works of A., which were translated into Syriac and Persian. Meanwhile, the Platonic tradition prevailed over the theology of the rest of the church. Thus, although the majority of Western philosophers and theologians had always been acquainted with the logic and with some elements of the ethics of A., his metaphysics and his texts on the natural sciences were practically forgotten until they were reintroduced to the West, mainly through Spain and Sicily (Domingo ⇒González), where they had arrived with the Muslims who had become acquainted with them in Persia.

The reintroduction of A. into western Europe caused a great theological and philosophical disturbance in the thirteenth century. Those who accepted him unconditionally, even at the expense of Christian orthodoxy, received the name of Latin Averroists, in honor of the great Arabic commentator of A., ⇒Averroës (⇒Siger of Brabant). There were many condemnations of supposedly Aristotelian theses (Council of ⇒Paris; Stephen ⇒Tempier), several of which were Averroist rather than Aristotelian. In such cases, what worried the theologians most were three consequences of this type of Aristotelianism.

The first such consequence was the eternity of the world. Commenting on A., Averroës had declared that the eternal existence of a "first unmoved mover" requires the eternity of the world which such a mover moves. This contrasted with the traditional Christian doctrine, according to which only God is eternal and the world is the creation of God in time.

The second consequence was the "unity of the active intellect," which ultimately implied that there is a single universal soul, of which individual souls are only parts that in the end return to the universal soul. This created difficulties with regard to the fate of the soul after death.

The third consequence, which stemmed from Averroës rather than from A., had to do with the independence of reason vis-à-vis the doctrines of the faith. Averroës had been obliged to face the pressures of Muslim orthodoxy and for this reason had declared it was possible to hold one thing on the basis of faith and something else on the basis of reason. The Latin Averroists adopted similar positions, while their enemies saw in this a subversion of the faith, which thus appeared to be irrational.

Although these themes were the chief causes of disagreement in the thirteenth century, what in the end would have greatest impact was his theory of knowledge. A., in contrast to Plato, attributed a central and necessary place to the senses in the cognitive process. During the first centuries of the Middle Ages, hegemony of Platonic philosophy, joined with the mystical and ascetic tendencies of Christianity, had led to such excesses that whoever truly was interested in knowledge paid no attention to the data of the senses and concentrated on mystical contempla-

tion and intellectual exercise. After the reintroduction of A., there was a new interest in sense data and therefore in the observation of the world and its phenomena. The work of ⇒Thomas Aquinas and of ⇒Albertus Magnus consisted in good measure in reconciling Aristotelian philosophy, and particularly Aristotelian epistemology, with Christian orthodoxy. Thus an unpredictable result of the reintroduction of A. into the West was the observation of the created world. This eventually led to the development of scientific methods and to the technology that today characterizes Western civilization.

———

JLG

Arius (ca. 250–336). Theologian whose characteristic doctrine, known as Arianism, incited the Trinitarian debates of the fourth century and was condemned by the councils of ⇒Nicaea (325) and ⇒Constantinople (381).

It is said that A. was a native of Libya, and that he had studied under ⇒Lucian of Antioch. His general theological position followed the outlines of ⇒Origen, and with respect to the relation between the Father and the Son he was part of the so-called left wing of Origenism, which tended to safeguard the immutability and transcendence of the Father by emphasizing the difference and even distance between the Father and the Son—a position that receives the generic name of subordinationism. (Although this was not debated in his time, it also appears that A. denied that Jesus had a human soul, and therefore he could have been a forerunner of the doctrines of ⇒Apollinaris of Laodicea in the second half of that same century.)

A. was a pastor of renowned holiness in the city of Alexandria, where he served as a presbyter in the church of Baucalis, when a serious theological difference appeared between him and Bishop ⇒Alexander of Alexandria. What was ultimately debated was the absolute and real divinity of the Son, which in this case was posed in terms of his coeternity with the Father. In other words, when he was asked if both the Father and the Son are eternal, Alexander responded affirmatively, while A. said that only the Father is eternal. This was like saying that the Son is a creature, a product of the will of the Father, and therefore is not divine in the strict sense of the word.

The debate was long and bitter. A synod that Alexander summoned in Alexandria rejected the doctrines of A. and removed him from office. For his part, A. received the support of his congregation in Alexandria, which went out into the streets exclaiming that "there was [a time] when he was not" (in other words, there was a time when the Son did not exist). In addition, A. appealed to his fellow students, whom he called "Fellow Lucianists," meaning that the attack was not directed against himself, but against the whole school and the teachings of Lucian, who by then was dead.

Among those who angrily objected to the actions of Alexander and came out in defense of Arius was Bishop ⇒Eusebius of Nicomedia, who in addition to being recognized as an able theologian was a relative of Emperor Constantine. Thus, what had started as a local dispute threatened to divide the church.

Constantine, who had cherished the hope that the church, with its unity, would be "the cement of the empire," commissioned Bishop ⇒Hosius of Cordova to go to Alexandria and try to heal the schism that was emerging. When Hosius reported that the differences were too profound to be settled through such conversations, Constantine convened a great assembly of bishops, which met in Nicaea in the year 325. There, after a series of debates, maneuvers, and negotiations, a creed was promulgated that almost everyone present signed. This creed, with some variations that were later introduced, is still the most commonly used creed in all Christian churches. The Nicene Creed includes several phrases that are emphatic negations of Arianism: "begotten by the Father before all worlds, God from God, light from light, true God from true God, begotten not made, of one being with the Father." In addition, at the end of the creed was added a list of anathemas, which are not recited today: "Those who say, therefore, that there was [a time] when the Son of God did not exist, and that before being begotten he did not exist, and that he was made of things which are not, or that he was formed from another substance [hypostasis] or essence [ousia], or that he is a creature, or that he is mutable or variable, these the church catholic anathematizes."

But this did not put an end to Arianism. Even though A. himself was deposed and sent into exile, after a few years, thanks to the intervention of Eusebius of Nicomedia, he was able to return to Alexandria. There the new bishop, ⇒Athanasius, the great opposer of Arianism and defender of the doctrines of Nicaea, received the imperial order to admit A. to communion, but he refused to do so. A. died shortly afterward, although the date is unknown.

In the meantime, Eusebius of Nicomedia and others continued to defend the doctrines of

A. and the "Fellow Lucianists." Because of his efforts, several of the chief defenders of the Nicene doctrine were deposed, among them ⇒Marcellus of Ancyra and ⇒Eustathius of Antioch. At the death of Constantine, and after a brief period in which the government was divided among his sons, the entire empire was once again under one of them, Constantius, who was a resolute defender of the Arian cause. Hosius, by this time an old man, was forced to renounce the Nicene faith. So was the equally elderly bishop of Rome, ⇒Liberius, after strong imperial pressure. As ⇒Jerome said, "the world awoke from a deep sleep and discovered that it had become Arian." A new generation of Arians came forward, among whom ⇒Eunomius, ⇒Aetius, ⇒Ursacius, and ⇒Valens were best known. In the year 335 the Arian leaders promulgated a document, known by posterity as "the blasphemy of Sirmium," which practically made Arianism the official faith of the church.

But little by little, the Nicene party reorganized and clarified its positions. Athanasius, who had suffered exile and persecution repeatedly, was able to respond to the fears of some who thought that the Nicene doctrine rejected every distinction between the Father and the Son. These were some of the Homoiousians, so called because they were not willing to affirm, together with Nicaea, that the Son was "of the same substance" (homoousios) as the Father, although they were willing to declare that he was of a similar substance (homoiousios).

In the next generation, the chief defenders of the Nicene faith were the Cappadocians, ⇒Basil of Caesarea, ⇒Gregory of Nazianzus, and ⇒Gregory of Nyssa. These three established and explained the difference between "hypostasis" and ousia. The result was that almost all the theologians were willing to declare that the Father and the Son have one ousia or essence but different hypostases. This doctrine was reaffirmed at the Council of Constantinople in the year 381 (Second Ecumenical Council), and from then on Arianism progressively disappeared.

But in the meantime, when Arianism was at its peak, several of the Germanic peoples (the so-called barbarians) had been converted to Arian Christianity. When shortly afterward those peoples (Lombards, Goths, Vandals, and others) invaded the Latin West, they brought with them their Arian convictions, and consequently Arianism revived in the West, where it had never been a true threat. But with the passage of time, these Germanic conquerors came to accept the Nicene faith of the conquered and abandoned their Arianism. In this process the culminating point, which practically marks the end of Arianism, was the conversion of the Visigothic king of Spain, Recared, who in the year 587 embraced the Trinitarian faith.

Although with this event Arianism disappeared, it has appeared again, with modifications, in other movements, chiefly in that of the Jehovah's Witnesses.

———

JLG

Arminius, Jacob (1560–1609). Dutch theologian and pastor whose arguments against the Calvinist doctrine of predestination were the beginning of the Arminian movement. A. was born in Oudewater, Holland, and studied in the universities of Leiden and Geneva. In the latter he devoted himself to the study of Calvinism under the direction of Theodore ⇒Beza, ⇒Calvin's successor. Upon completing his studies he returned to Holland, where he served as pastor of a church in Amsterdam.

During his pastorate in Amsterdam, A. began to develop his theology of predestination under the influence of Dirck Koornhert, a Dutch theologian who had objected to certain characteristics of Calvinism. Originally A. had opposed the ideas of Koornhert. But when he studied Koornhert's arguments he concluded that Koornhert was right in his objections and that his arguments agreed with biblical teachings and Christian theology.

In 1603 A. accepted a position as professor in the University of Leiden. There his differences with the strict teachings of Calvinism soon gave rise to conflicts with one of the other professors, Franciscus ⇒Gomarus. A. died six years later, but his teachings continued to be disseminated in spite of the opposition of Gomarus, who tried to expel those followers of A. who held academic posts. In 1610, forty-six pastors who opposed Gomarus signed a document titled "Protest" (or "Remonstrance") that rejected the positions of strict Calvinism. Although the movement that would bear his name came to be understood as a form of anti-Calvinism, A. never ceased to be a Calvinist, nor did he deny the existence of predestination. But his understanding of predestination was different from that of Calvinism.

In strict Calvinism, the doctrine of double predestination was the logical conclusion of the doctrine of justification by faith. If faith is acquired only by divine grace and not through human action, it follows that those who are saved must have been elected by God for salvation. In the same way, unbelievers must have been condemned by God to perdition. For this reason, Calvin understood that predestination is the divine decree which determines the destiny of humanity. But when does God carry out this decree? Calvinists adopted either one of two opinions. One position, called supralapsarian, stated that the decree concerning predestination is prior to the decree concerning the fall. The other position, called infralapsarian, maintained the opposite.

A. denied both positions. According to A., the biblical doctrine of predestination is based on the foreknowledge of God, who from the beginning knows who will believe and be saved and who will not believe and will be condemned. Taking a christocentric position, A. maintained that the divine decree does not establish who will be saved; rather, it establishes through whom humanity will be saved. According to A., it is incorrect to say that Christ died for only part of humankind.

In order to avoid denying justification by faith, A. proposed what he called the "prevenient grace" of God, an idea he took from ⇒Augustine. This grace, given to all humanity, enables the free will to decide in favor of God, although God already knows the result of our decision. Without this grace, the sinful state of all human beings would not allow anyone to attain salvation. A. concludes that free will, restored by this grace, also permits a saved person to deny faith and to fall from grace. He thus denies the certainty given to believers by predestination.

Condemned by the Synod of ⇒Dort, the positions of A. were henceforth excluded from orthodox Calvinism. Nevertheless, some of A.'s teachings later influenced John ⇒Wesley and some evangelical Protestant movements.

———

LGP

Armitage, Thomas (1819–96). Founder of the American Bible Union (1850) and author of *A History of the Baptists* (1890). He became a Baptist in 1848 because of his disagreement with the Methodist system of government and became pastor of Fifth Avenue Baptist Church in New York (1849–89).

———

EZ

Arnauld, Antoine (1612–94). French theologian, philosopher, and author whose prestige was such that he was known as "the great Arnauld." His very numerous family included his sister Jacqueline Marie Angélique ⇒Arnauld, with whom he was in agreement on many theological points. In 1641 he withdrew to Port-Royal, where for some years his sister Angélique had promoted the teachings of ⇒Jansen, as they were interpreted and defended by ⇒Saint-Cyran. When he published in 1643 a treatise *On Frequent Communion*, in which he revealed a Jansenist position, he was strongly attacked by the Jesuits. ⇒Pascal, as well as a number of Dominicans, defended him. In spite of this, the Sorbonne, where he had studied, condemned him officially. He was obliged to retire from public life until 1669, when Louis XIV intervened on his behalf and restored to him all the honors of which he had been stripped. When the Jansenist controversy flared up again, A. went into exile in Holland, where he continued writing in defense of Jansenism and against Calvinism, which the Catholics frequently confused with the teachings of Jansen.

———

JLG

Arnauld, Jacqueline Marie Angélique (1591–1661).
Sister of Antoine ⇒Arnauld, the third of twenty children, and better known as Mother Angelica. She became abbess of Port-Royal. Her imperious reforming will was thwarted when her community in Port-Royal replaced her as abbess in 1630. Even so, her influence in the community continued through the introduction of Jean Du Vergier de Hauranne, abbot of ⇒Saint-Cyran, as spiritual director of the convent in 1633. Mother Angelica had known the abbot as a friend of the family for ten years, but had little sympathy for his writings. Nonetheless, beginning in 1633, she took his side, introduced him to her community, and made him the confessor of the nuns. This relationship indicated her inclination toward Jansenism. Collections of her letters, conversations, lectures, and memoirs still survive.

———

JDR

Arndt, Johann (1555–1621).
German Protestant theologian. His popularity is due to his familiar and suggestive style, which contrasts with the rough and cold mode of expression of most theologians of the period. His works show great skill in incorporating the best of the diverse medieval sources, of ⇒Luther, and of the later figures of the Reformation. He combined theological orthodoxy with a profound interest in the practical development of the Christian virtues. In the field of theology, he highlighted the mystical union of the believer with Christ, which was characteristic of the Lutheran dogmatic tradition. He is mainly known for his *Vier Bücher vom wahren Christentum* (Four Books on True Christianity).

———

JDR

Arnobius of Sicca (?–ca. 327).
Pagan philosopher who had attacked Christianity, but who was unexpectedly converted. When he requested baptism from the bishop of Sicca (in North Africa), the bishop was not entirely convinced of the sincerity of his conversion and asked him to make public profession of his Christian faith. Toward this end A. wrote the only work of his that still survives, *Against the Nations* (i.e., against the Gentiles), in seven books. In them he attacks ancient Greco-Roman beliefs, but says little about the content of the Christian faith, of which he apparently knew little. His work is particularly interesting because A. refers to a multitude of customs, beliefs, and myths about which we would know very little without his testimony. But as far as theology or doctrine is concerned, A. has little to say. Possibly the most interesting section of his work in this sense is the passage in the second book where he quotes Plato in support of the immortality of the soul and then tries to show that the Christian doctrine of life after death differs from that of Plato.

———

JLG

Arnold, Matthew (1822–88).
Literary critic, poet, and social political critic, one of the chief intellectuals of Victorian England. His principal works include commentaries on education and on religion. He lived in a period of turbulent changes, when all social and moral norms were being questioned. As he expressed it, he was a wanderer between "two worlds, one dead, and the other powerless to be born." In his poetry and literary work, he expresses his religious doubts and questions the possibility that human beings can be happy and live together in harmony.

———

IG

Arrastía, Cecilio (1922–95).
An evangelist and professor of homiletics who was the most eloquent Protestant preacher of Latin

America during the twentieth century. Born in Cuba, he received his theological education in that country and in the United States. Disillusioned with the Cuban revolution, which he had supported, he went into exile and lived in New York. His preaching was characterized by the freshness of his biblical exegesis, the theological depth of his sermons, his creative use of language, and the contextualization of his message in Latin America. He wrote many articles (some gathered in the journal *Pastoralia*, no longer published) and other books related to preaching.

—

PAJ

Artemon (late 2nd century). Also called Artemas. Obscure figure, proponent of adoptionism in the style of Theodotus and ⇒Paul of Samosata. Excommunicated by the bishop of Rome, ⇒Victor. According to the historian ⇒Theodoret, ⇒Hippolytus wrote a work against him titled *Little Labyrinth*.

—

JLG

Asbury, Francis (1745–1816). Early leader in the Methodist movement, born near Birmingham, England. A local preacher at age eighteen and an itinerant evangelist at twenty-one, in the Methodist conference of 1771 he offered to go as a missionary to the British colonies in North America. His effectiveness was so great that John ⇒Wesley named him and Thomas Coke superintendents of the Methodist Societies in North America. A. and Coke organized the Methodist Episcopal Church at the "Christmas Conference" meeting in Baltimore in 1784, and they were elected as the first two bishops of that church. Traveling half a million miles on horseback throughout the United States, A. promoted Methodism to such an extent that he turned it into the largest Protestant denomination of the United States at the beginning of the nineteenth century.

—

PB

Assmann, Hugo (1933–). A Brazilian Catholic and one of the most important exponents of Latin American liberation theology. A. has developed an intense and sophisticated dialogue between revolutionary Marxism and Christian theology. Among his themes is the claim of orthopraxis on orthodoxy, the first being a praxis of liberation in favor of the poor. His most important book is *Teología desde la praxis de la liberación* (1975; Theology Starting from the Praxis of Liberation).

—

CCO

Asterius the Sophist (?–ca. 341). One of the first Arian theologians (⇒Arius). He is known as the Sophist because that was his occupation before his conversion. Although several of his writings on the Psalms have been discovered, his main theological work, *Syntagmation*, has disappeared and only a few fragments of it survive, as quoted by ⇒Athanasius and by ⇒Marcellus of Ancyra in order to refute them. He appears to have been one of the most moderate Arian authors.

—

JLG

Athanasius (ca. 295–373). Bishop of Alexandria who was most noted for his defense of the Nicene faith against those who followed the teaching of ⇒Arius. Even before the Council of ⇒Nicaea, A. had shown great interest in the doctrine of the incarnation. Then, when the controversy between Bishop ⇒Alexander of Alexandria and the presbyter Arius arose concerning the divinity of the Word, A., who at that time was a young deacon, sided decisively with his bishop. Together they attended the Council of Nicaea in the year 325, although it is not clear how active A.'s participation was in the deliberations of that assembly. They returned to Alexandria, and when Alexander died in 328, A. was elected to succeed him.

Although he retained that bishopric until his death, A. did not always live in his see. Shortly after his election to the episcopate, having been accused of not being totally faithful to the emperor, he departed for the first of several exiles. Later, when Emperor Constantius was determined to promote the Arian faith, A. was exiled in Rome, where he made contacts that later proved valuable. He spent a third exile of three years hidden among the monks of the desert in Egypt. To these three major exiles were added several other occasions when he felt obliged to leave the city.

In the midst of such vicissitudes, A. was a prolific writer. His chief exegetical texts deal with the Psalms. His *Life of St. Anthony* had a decisive impact on later monasticism. Some of his letters are actually extensive theological essays; others are encyclicals sent to the nearby bishops in defense of his teaching and his action; the majority deal with the date and celebration of Easter. From the theological point of view, the most interesting are his four letters *To Serapion*, in which he proclaims and defends the divinity of the Holy Spirit. (There were those who were ready to accept the divinity of the Son, but not of the Holy Spirit; ⇒Macedonius of Constantinople.) The majority of his doctrinal essays are refutations of Arianism or reports of controversies and synods in which the same matter was discussed. He also wrote an apologetic work against paganism, *Discourse against the Greeks*.

The theology of A. is practical and religious rather than speculative. In Alexandria, where a little more than a hundred years earlier ⇒Origen had flourished, the speculative theology of that great teacher dominated the theological field. Thus it could be said that both Arius as well as his opponent, Alexander of Alexandria, were Origenists. But the case of A. is different. Although a good portion of his theological vocabulary, above all, that which refers to the doctrine of the Trinity, derives from the Origenist tradition, what most interested A. was not philosophical speculation but the relationship between theological teaching and the religious life of the church and of the faithful.

From this point of view, two theological poles were of special interest to A.: Christian monotheism and the doctrine of salvation through the incarnation of God in Jesus Christ. Monotheism was fundamental in the conflict between Christianity and the ancient religions. Those religions worshiped a multitude of gods, each with a field or fields of specialization. The conflicts, jealousy, and even fickleness of those gods explained and determined the course of history and of human life. It was not that way for Christianity, and certainly not for A., who insisted on the oneness of God. The Christian worldview does not require us to appease this or that god with every step we take, according to the sphere of action we are in, and it certainly does not require us to worry about supposed conflicts between the gods. Christianity holds that there is only one God and that, although at the present time there are conflicts between that God and the powers of evil, in the end and unfailingly that God will be victorious and God's purposes will be fulfilled. The result is a life of hope and joy based on faith in that sole and sovereign God.

This is the reason why A. opposed so tenaciously the teaching of certain Arians who made of the Word a kind of inferior God. This appeared to him to open the breach for a new form of polytheism and therefore to threaten the very essence of the Christian faith.

However, this one God is not distant. On the contrary, "for us and for our salvation" (as the Nicene Creed states) God became human. By taking on human flesh, God has injected divine reality into human life; or, stated in another way, God has assumed humanity and therefore has conferred God's own immortality on it. As an example, A. compares God with a great king who visits a city. From the moment of that visit, the city will never be the same. The same thing has happened to the human race with the advent of the God-human. Since God has become one of us, we will never be the same again. Salvation consists in this.

Also for this reason, A. was tenaciously opposed to Arianism, which seemed to say that the one who became incarnate in Jesus Christ was not "true God from true God." If whoever became incarnate was not God, then that incarnation is of little value. Stated differently, the work of salvation is as great as that of creation, and therefore the Savior cannot be less than the Creator.

While he opposed Arianism for these reasons, with the passage of the years A. discovered that a good part of the opposition to the Nicene doctrine came from those who feared that all distinction between the Father and the Son would be erased. The Nicene Creed included a series of anathemas condemning whoever would declare that the Father and the Son are not of the same *ousia* or hypostasis. Many feared that this would end up in Sabellianism (⇒Sabellius). A. came to realize that there were some who insisted on a difference of hypostasis as a way of safeguarding the distinction between the Father and the Son, and therefore he granted that those who affirmed this were not heretics, as long as they likewise affirmed the complete divinity of the Son and the existence of one God. It would be the responsibility of the next generation of theologians, above all the Cappadocian Fathers (⇒Basil of Caesarea, ⇒Gregory of Nazianzus, ⇒Gregory of Nyssa), to clarify the difference between *ousia* and hypostasis and thus arrive at what came to be the traditional Trinitarian formula: "one *ousia* and three hypostases."

———

JLG

Athenagoras (?–ca. 160). Philosopher and Christian apologist who flourished in Athens in the mid-second century. What little is known of A. is found in his only two surviving writings, *Apology* (or *Legatio* in Latin) and *Treatise on the Resurrection of the Dead*, and in ⇒Methodius of Olympus, who mentions him in one of his writings.

It is believed that the *Apology* was written and presented to Emperor Marcus Aurelius (161–80) and to his son Commodus in the year 176 or 177 on the occasion of their visit to Athens. It is a defense of Christian teaching against accusations of atheism, cannibalism, and incestuous practices, for which Christians unjustly suffered persecution and death. A.'s goal was to obtain a decree that ordered the judges of the Roman Empire (normally the governors of the provinces) to base their decisions on the pious and highly moral conduct of the Christians and not on such false accusations.

In his argument against the accusation of atheism, A. has recourse to the philosophers and poets of antiquity whose utterances about God were similar to those of Christians. A. censured the inconsistency of the Romans, reminding them that such philosophers were not branded as atheists. This and other accusations are the result of the evil that always opposes virtue. Christians, like Socrates before them, are its victims.

In his *Apology,* A. also expounds the Christian doctrine of the Trinity. This exposition makes A. one of the first to use philosophy to explain the Trinity and makes his treatise one of the oldest evidences for that doctrine. His teachings about the Father, the Son, and the Holy Spirit are deeply influenced by Platonism and the philosophical eclecticism of the times. For A., God is Mind and consequently can be perceived only through the mind and reason. The Son of God is the Logos or *Sophia* of the Father, and the two are one in power but distinct in rank. In this, A. resembles ⇒Justin Martyr. Although the Logos is conceived by the Father, it is also preexistent with the Father, since as Mind the Logos always existed in God. The Logos is the idea and the energizing power of the material world. (A. appears to avoid the doctrine of the incarnation, or at least he does not speak about it.) For A., the Holy Spirit is an emanation from God, just as the ray emanates from the sun, and is also the source of unity between the Father and the Son.

In his *Treatise on the Resurrection of the Dead*, whose authorship is still debated, A. argues on the basis of the philosophical point that the just God desires and has both the knowledge and the power to bring about the resurrection of the dead, which is predestined by God for humanity.

A.'s writings are lucid, elegant, and, in the particulars of thought and effectiveness, supe-

rior to the majority of the apologetic essays of his time. Of great importance is the ample information that they provide on pagan worship, sculpture, and religious art.

ZMP

Atto of Verceil (?–961).

Bishop of that city and chancellor of King Lothar II of France. He is particularly known for his works on morality and canon law, and for his *Commentaries on Saint Paul,* which show much scholarship, although little originality. A. was one of the many medieval teachers who maintained that the presence of Christ in the Eucharist is spiritual rather than physical.

JLG

Augsburg Confession (1530).

The chief document that defines the character and basic content of the Lutheran faith. This confession was presented before Emperor Charles V of the Holy Roman Empire on June 25, 1530, by its public reading during the Diet of Augsburg. From the beginning there were two versions of the confession, one in German and another in Latin, with small differences between the two.

The confessors wished to demonstrate their adherence to the faith of the Catholic Church as well as their appreciation for the civil government as the guarantor of worship and preaching. The language of the confession is very careful in simultaneously maintaining faithfulness to the Scriptures, orthodoxy in doctrinal terms, and deference to the civil authorities. For this reason, in its time it had both a theological and a political function. Although it was written by theologians (its chief author was ⇒Melanchthon), the confession was signed by princes and other authorities of evangelical territories.

The confession is composed of twenty-eight articles and is divided into two main parts: the doctrinal articles (1–21), which present a summary of what was preached and taught in the evangelical congregations, and the articles in controversy (22–28). Originally the reformers thought that there would not be a major discussion about the first articles, but rather about the last ones. But it did not turn out that way. At that time many already recognized the need for changes and reforms in the practices of the Roman Catholic Church. The Roman theologians understood that the confession introduced new doctrinal emphases, such as: the centrality of justification by faith as the very definition of the gospel and as the central dogma; the reformulation of the unity of the church as centered exclusively in preaching and the sacraments, which were now reduced to baptism and Holy Communion (with confession and absolution still occupying an important place); and the emphatic distinction between the ecclesiastical and the secular governments.

The immediate antecedents of the confession are to be found in the "Instruction for Visitors" (1528), written by Melanchthon and based chiefly on the model that Melanchthon had prepared in his previous "Articles of Visitation" (1527). The "Instruction" served as a guide for those who were commissioned to go to the parishes (churches and schools) of Electoral Saxony to initiate the programmatic reforms (educational, liturgical, and administrative) that had been formulated for those territories. There were other antecedent documents, such as the Schwabach Articles, the Torgau Articles, and the "Confession concerning the Holy Supper of Christ" of ⇒Luther. These documents sought to clarify the chief teachings of the reformers vis-à-vis Roman criticisms and demands.

The genius of the confession is its theology of the Word of God, a theology at the service of the preaching of the gospel and therefore at the service of the Christian ministry. It is characterized more by conciliation than by denunciation. Luther himself admitted that he would not have been able to "step as softly" as Melanchthon had done in the confession. In order to defend their position, the confessors appealed in general to Scripture and to the teachings of the fathers of the church.

———

NRG

Augustine of Hippo (354–430).

One of the most prolific Christian authors of antiquity, and the one who had the greatest impact on Western theology throughout the Middle Ages and even until the present. His life and his spiritual pilgrimage are better known than those of other Christians from antiquity, partly because A. himself tells about them in his *Confessions*.

A. was born in the north of Africa, in the city of Tagaste, of a pagan father who served in the Roman administration and a Christian mother, Monica. Monica, a very devout person, prayed constantly for the conversion of her husband and son. Her influence on A. was enormous—at least, so it appears from what A. allows to be seen in his *Confessions*.

From Tagaste, A. continued his studies in the neighboring city of Madaura and then, at the age of seventeen, in Carthage, the principal city of the region. There he devoted himself to the study of rhetoric, which in those times was the way to advance in public administration. It was also there that he took a concubine, with whom he lived for many years and who gave him his only son; but he never married her because of Monica's opposition. Finally, it was in Carthage that A. spent some time in the study of Cicero, which led him to the conviction that if rhetoric was important to formulate arguments well, much more important than rhetoric was the truth that it ought to express. From then on, A. searched for that truth.

That search led him first to Manicheism (⇒Mani). This was a dualistic doctrine according to which there are two principles or substances that mix on earth and in earthly life: the principle of good and the principle of evil. The principle of good has been revealed in prophets such as Zoroaster, Jesus, and Mani himself. Perfection then consisted in separating oneself from every expression of the principle of evil by means of an asceticism that in extreme cases leads to death by starvation.

Although A. never went beyond being a "hearer" among the Manicheans (that is, a sympathizer and even a believer, but without undergoing the asceticism of the "perfect ones"), he did come to think that Manicheism offered a rational interpretation of the world and of life, especially concerning the origin of evil. Whenever he had some doubt, or when something did not seem to him to agree with Manichean doctrines, he was told that there was a wise Manichean, a certain ⇒Faustus of Milevis, who could resolve all of his doubts. But when the highly acclaimed Faustus arrived, he was not able to clear up the doubts of A., who became disillusioned with Manicheism, even though for the time being he did not completely distance himself from the Manicheans.

His career then led him across the Mediterranean, to Rome. There he devoted himself to the study of a number of Platonic authors, who showed him that the problem of the origin of evil was not insurmountable. Besides, they made him see that reality did not consist solely of matter, but that there were intellectual or spiritual realities.

From Rome A. moved to Milan, where he went to listen to the preaching of the famous bishop of that city, ⇒Ambrose. His purpose was not so much to listen to what Ambrose said, but rather to study how he said it. This interested him as a professor of rhetoric. But as he himself tells us, "when I opened my heart to receive what he eloquently said, at the same time the truth that he said entered it, even though gradually." Little by little, Ambrose convinced him that his former objections to the Christian faith were not valid.

Yet this was not enough to make a Christian out of Augustine. His mother, Monica, had taught him a strict form of Christianity, and the Platonic authors that he had studied convinced him that the "philosophical life," that is, life according to the truth, is a life of renunciation and contemplation. A. was not ready for such a thing. As he himself tells us, at that time he prayed, "Give me chastity, but not yet."

It was then that the famous episode in the garden of Milan took place. A. had already been anguished for some time by that truth which he had discovered with the intellect, but to which he could not dedicate himself with the heart. One of the Platonic authors whom Augustine most respected, ⇒Marius Victorinus, had been converted and had declared his Christian faith publicly. A friend then told him about the conversion of two government officials who had just abandoned their careers in order to devote themselves to the ascetic life. A. fled to the garden and cried out: "When, when, tomorrow! tomorrow!? Why not today?" On the other side of the iron gate he heard a voice like that of a child at play repeating, "Take and read, take and read." Interpreting that as a message from on high, he took a codex of Paul's Letter to the Romans that he had left on a bench and read some words from Romans 13:13–14 that moved him deeply. He went and told Monica, who was with him in Milan, that he had decided to become a Christian, and he left with her and some friends to Cassiciacum, a remote place on the outskirts of Milan.

After a time of study and meditation, A., his son Adeodatus, and a good friend were baptized in Milan by Ambrose. They then began the return trip to Tagaste, but Monica became ill and died in the Roman port of Ostia. This delayed their return to Tagaste by nearly a year, which A. spent writing his first Christian books, directed mainly against the Manicheans.

Upon returning to Tagaste, A. sold a good portion of what he had inherited from his parents, gave the money to the poor, and devoted himself to study, prayer, and meditation. Such was the life that he wished to live for the rest of his days. But when A. visited the nearby city of Hippo, with the purpose of recruiting a friend for his community of meditation, the bishop of that city compelled him to accept ordination as priest and then as bishop. Consequently, A. spent the rest of his life as bishop of Hippo. He died there in the year 430, when the Vandals were approaching the gates of the city.

The theological work of A. revolved mainly around the controversies in which he found himself involved as bishop and defender of his flock and of his faith. Because of this, most of his first works were directed against the Manicheans, whose doctrines he had previously followed and defended, and which he now felt compelled to refute. It was in those works against the Manicheans that A. developed two of his characteristic doctrines: his interpretation of the origin of evil and his doctrine of free will.

Borrowing from his Platonic readings, A. declared that evil is not a reality of independent origin. After all, all of reality comes from God, the Creator. All creatures draw more or less near to God. Those that come the nearest are better than others; but this does not mean that the others are evil. Evil then is not a substance, but consists rather in becoming distant from the Creator. Therefore, the soul, for example, created for the contemplation of God, falls into what is evil when instead it turns to the contemplation of creatures.

In order to explain how such a thing can happen, A. appeals to the doctrine of free will. Humans and angels have freedom to determine their own actions. That freedom, like everything that God has made, is good. But humans used it for evil, for self-separation from God, and therein lies the root of sin and evil. In this matter A. also opposed the Manicheans, who held that the actions of the soul are determined by the mixture of the principles of good and evil which it contains, since what is good cannot but do good, and what is evil cannot but do evil.

The second great controversy of A. had to do with the Donatists (⇒Donatus). This was a movement that emerged when persecutions ended. It held that those who had yielded before the threat of persecution were unworthy, and therefore their ministerial actions were not valid. And the same was true of whoever would remain in communion with such unworthy persons. Therefore only the Donatists were faithful, and only their baptisms, communion services, and ordinations were valid.

A. responded to this by insisting that validity of a sacrament does not come from the one who officiates, but from God, and that therefore the sacrament administered by an unworthy person, even though it may be irregular, is in fact valid—in technical terms, the sacrament acts *ex opere operato*.

The third great controversy revolved around ⇒Pelagius and his doctrines. Pelagius was a monk who maintained that humans, even in their state of sin, can decide to do good and accept the grace of God. What is more, at birth children have no sin; rather, the only sin is that which each person commits personally—thus there is no such thing as original sin. Over against this teaching A. held that, even though there is free will, sin deprives humans of the freedom to do good. In other words, before sin humans could do good or not do it; but now, after sin, they no longer have the ability to do good on their own. This does not mean that we have no freedom, but that, in the state of sin, all of the options before us are sinful. We have therefore the freedom to choose among all of them, but not to not sin. It is then that grace intervenes, giving us the capacity to do good—and above all, to accept grace itself, something that we could not do without divine grace. Before conversion, grace "operates" in us so that we accept it; and once we have accepted it, it "cooperates" with us to do what is good.

That grace is " irresistible," since if we could resist it, sinners that we are, we would do so. No one can therefore boast of having accepted grace, nor believe oneself better than the one who did not accept it. If we can say that we have been saved, all the merit and glory are due to the grace of God, and not to ourselves.

This in turn leads to the doctrine of predestination. Since all humankind has sinned, it is all "a mass of perdition," and nobody has any right to demand anything other than condemnation. Only those whom God has predestined to receive this irresistible grace will accept it and be saved. The rest will be condemned. On this point, although the entire Middle Ages called itself Augustinian, the truth is that almost all of the medieval theologians distanced themselves from the teachings of A.

However, although many Protestants regard A. as the great defender of the doctrine of salvation by grace, it must be acknowledged that A. held that salvation requires the merits of good works—even though those good works can be performed only through the operation and cooperation of divine grace.

A.'s last great controversy took place after the Visigothic capture of Rome in the year 410. There were pagans then who argued Rome had fallen because it had abandoned the gods that made it great, and therefore they blamed Christians for that fall.

Over against such opinions A. wrote *The City of God*, a voluminous work that reviews the whole history of humanity as it was known then, attempting to show that the reason why Rome had fallen was not that it had abandoned the old gods. To achieve that goal, A. says that in history there are two great cities (perhaps today we would say two great orders or systems). The first is the earthly city, built on the basis of love for creatures, or rather on the concupiscent desire to possess them. The other is the city of God, founded on the love of God. All the political orders that have existed in history are expressions of the earthly city, and therefore are destined to disappear. Only the city of God, represented in the world by the church, remains forever.

Finally, the way in which A. interprets knowledge is important, since his epistemology dominated the first centuries of the Middle Ages, and determined a good portion of the course of theology, philosophy, and sciences. Like ⇒Plato before him, A. believed that the senses cannot be the source of true knowledge. True knowledge does not refer to the things that pass and that the senses perceive, but to the eternal truths, to the reality of things, which the senses could never penetrate. How then is knowledge attained? Plato had suggested the preexistence of souls. According to him, our souls existed previously in a world of ideas, and from there have fallen to this world of material realities and transitory things. So what we call "knowledge" is nothing but a reminiscence or vague memory of what we knew there. A. cannot accept Plato's solution, for that would lead him to affirm the preexistence of souls, which would deny the teachings of Christianity. Others held that the soul is capable of knowing the divine realities because it is part of the essence of God, and therefore its knowledge is innate. The soul knows the eternal truths because they are engraved on its own nature as God's emanation. But such a doctrine is also not acceptable to A., for it is not any more compatible with Christian teachings than is the hypothesis of the preexistence of souls.

In response to all this, A. developed his theory of knowledge as "illumination." According to him, the eternal Word of God illumines the human mind, placing in it all true knowledge. If we know that two plus two is four, this is not because we saw it in a previous world, nor because such knowledge is innate in our minds, and much less because we have seen it, for nobody has ever seen "two" without its reference to two transitory objects, which are unworthy of the true knowledge (two apples, two mountains, and so on). That knowledge is due rather to the fact that the eternal Word of God has placed it in our mind—has illumined it.

Clearly, this is very similar to what ⇒Justin, ⇒Clement of Alexandria, and others had previously said about the Word or Logos who illumines everyone who comes into this world (John 1:9). What A. has done is simply to develop that theory more thoroughly. Yet what previously was an apologetic argument in Justin, or an argument to justify the use of philosophy in Clement, with A. became the way in which nearly the entire Western Middle Ages understood knowledge. Early medieval thinkers, building on the authority of A., were convinced that knowledge cannot come through research nor through the observation of material realities. This was one of the reasons why the Middle Ages, until the rediscovery of ⇒Aristotle, were hardly or not at all concerned with the physical and natural sciences.

The influence of A. was enormous, not only on the theory of knowledge, but also on the whole field of theology and philosophy. It was chiefly through A. that the Middle Ages learned about Christian antiquity. Even though A. was an innovator in his time, and for a few years after his death there were those who attacked his doctrines (⇒John Cassian, ⇒Vincent of Lérins, ⇒Faustus of Riez, ⇒Prosper of Aquitaine, ⇒Gennadius of Marseilles), in the end the early Middle Ages came to believe that A. was the most faithful exponent of ancient Christianity. Today we know that the Neoplatonic interpretation of Christianity that A. proposed was an innovation—perhaps a valuable innovation for his time—but was certainly not the only way in which Christians had thought about such matters.

At any rate, A.'s influence and prestige were such that his name appears repeatedly, not only in the Middle Ages, but also at the time of the Protestant Reformation, when reformers such as ⇒Luther and ⇒Calvin appealed to his authority, and said that their teachings were those of the revered bishop of Hippo. Their Catholic rivals made the same claim for their positions. Later on, in the controversies on Jansenism, once more the debate revolved around the teachings of A.

Thus, although his influence on the Eastern church (the Greek-speaking church) was not comparable to his influence on the Western church (Latin-speaking), it is fair to say that, except for Paul, no other Christian writer has been more read and discussed than A.

———
JLG

Aulén, Gustaf Emmanuel Hildebrand (1879–1977).

Theologian, educator, lecturer, writer, and leader of the ecumenical movement. Born in Ljungby, Kalmar, Sweden. Studied at the University of Uppsala, where he began his teaching career (1907–13). He moved to the University of Lund as professor of dogmatics (1913–33). In 1933 he was elected bishop of the diocese of Strägnas, a position he occupied for twenty years.

Together with other Swedish Lutheran theologians (Anders ⇒Nygren, Ragnar Bring), he was a leader in what has been called the Lundensian school of theology. This school tried to establish a strictly scientific method for systematic theology through the study of specific themes (*motivforschung*), highlighting the theology of Luther as a legitimate renewal of the thought of the New Testament. This theology played an important role in contemporary ecumenical debates.

Some of the distinctive elements of the theology of A. are his interest in the historical-critical study of the Bible, the history of dogma divided into periods, and the modern study of the theology of Luther carried out by Karl ⇒Holl and his students.

In 1917 he published *Dogmenhistoria* (History of Dogma) as a textbook for students of theology. The work presents the development of Christian doctrine from its beginnings until the early twentieth century. Ten years later he published *Den kristna gudsbilden* (The Christian Idea of God). In this book he establishes a parallel between the theologies of the first centuries of Christianity and of the Reformation of the sixteenth century, offering a critique of medieval scholasticism and Lutheran orthodoxy. For A. there is more affinity between Luther and the theology of the first centuries of Christianity than between Luther and the Lutheranism that followed the Reformation. He treated this subject again in one of his most famous works, *Den kristna forsoningstanken* (The Christian Idea of Atonement), an abbreviated version of which was published in English under the title *Christus Victor* (1931). Here he points out the similarity between ⇒Irenaeus and Luther in the formulation of the doctrine of atonement. Both theologians reject or give secondary importance to the idea of atonement as a sacrifice offered to God. The emphasis falls on the work God carries out in Christ by struggling against the forces of sin and evil that enslave humanity. A. calls this perspective the *classical* theory and contrasts it with the *Latin* theory, characteristic of medieval scholasticism (⇒Anselm of Canterbury) and of orthodox Lutheranism, which sees the atonement as a human sacrifice to God, effected chiefly by the human nature of Christ.

One of his most widely read books in English is his systematic theology, *The Christian Faith.*

————
JDR

Aurifaber, Johann (1519–75). German Lutheran pastor, compiler and editor of the works of ⇒Luther. Studied at the University of Wittenberg (1537–40), and from 1545 was a personal servant of Luther until the death of the reformer in 1546. He was noted for the support he gave to ⇒Flacius in several of the controversies among Lutheran theologians. He signed opinions against the Interim of Augsburg (1548) and the position of ⇒Osiander on justification (1552); challenged the Adiaphorists and Majorists (1556, ⇒Major); and edited (with Flacius) the refutation produced in Weimar (1558). A.'s major contribution was his effort to gather, edit, and publish the works of Luther (the Jena edition, completed under his direction). His editions helped determine the norm for characterizing the personality of Luther until the nineteenth century, when scholars began to question his methodology. Subsequently, however, a number of scholars (mostly of the psychological school of ⇒Jung) have shown great appreciation for the veracity of the work produced by A.

————
JDR

Averroës (1126–98). Born Ibn Rushd in Cordoba, Spain, to a prestigious Muslim family, Averroës (as he is known in the West) was an important religious philosopher, Muslim jurist, and interpreter of the philosophy of ⇒Aristotle and ⇒Plato. He integrated in his thought Islamic traditions and Greek philosophy. Trained in jurisprudence and medicine, he served as the chief medical doctor of several caliphs, in addition to becoming *qāḍī* or the principal judge in Seville and then in Cordoba. He devoted many years of his productive life to writing commentaries on the principal works

of the Aristotelian corpus known in his time, such as the texts on logic, physics, metaphysics, ethics, rhetoric, and the natural sciences. From the Platonic corpus he commented mostly on works about politics.

A.'s commentaries became very influential among Jewish and Christian philosophers and theologians. His work is of great importance in understanding, for example, ⇒Thomas Aquinas. In his writings, the most important of which is the *Decisive Treatise on the Agreement between Religious Law and Philosophy*, A. defended the use of philosophy to establish and prove the truth and significance of religious beliefs. Through his work he wished to strengthen the use of demonstrative methods for interpreting civil and religious law and the writings of the Koran, although some accused him of undermining the Muslim religion.

In the thirteenth century his doctrines, as interpreted by the philosophers of the University of Paris, were the source for what has been called Latin Averroism (⇒Siger of Brabant).

————
NRG

Azariah, Vedanayakam Samuel (1874–1945). Son of a pastor, born in Vellalanvilai, Tinnevelly, South India. He was the first Indian bishop of the Anglican Church in India. He represented the "young churches" at the missionary conferences of Edinburgh, 1910, and Tambaram, 1938. He was one of the architects of the structure for the union of the Church of South India, the first great project of interdenominational unity in the third world.

————
CCO

Azor, John (1533–1603). Spanish Jesuit. He taught theology in Compostela, then in Plasencia, and finally in Rome, where he attracted general attention by his lectures, mostly on the subject of moral theology. Like most Catholic theologians of his time, in his teaching he followed ⇒Thomas Aquinas.

He was rector of several colleges and published a work, *Moral Institutions*, that was very much admired in the seventeenth and eighteenth centuries. This work has been reprinted many times and has been translated into almost all the European languages. He also wrote *Commentaries on the Song of Songs*, as well as other works on morality that did not attain the success of the *Institutions*.

————
JDR

Babai the Great (ca. 551–628).

Prolific Nestorian theologian from Mesopotamia. According to ⇒Ebedjesus bar Berikha, he wrote, among some eighty books, a commentary on the entire Bible. He also wrote hymns and several lives of saints and martyrs to serve as inspiration for the monastic life. His chief theological work is the *Book of the Union*, which treats of the two natures of Christ and the manner in which they unite.

Faithful to his Nestorian tradition, B. emphasizes the integrity of each of the two natures in Jesus Christ, and particularly the human nature. Thus he can refer, for instance, to the "man of our Lord Jesus Christ." While he affirms that in Jesus Christ there is a perfect union of divinity with humanity, he rejects the "hypostatic union" which by that time had become a characteristic mark of Chalcedonian orthodoxy (Council of ⇒Chalcedon). For B., a hypostatic union is that which takes place, for example, between the body and the soul, the result of which is a new nature, the human being. Yet B. is clear that, although it is not called "hypostatic," but rather "voluntary," the union of the two natures in Christ is "unique and adorable."

The phrase "voluntary union" had brought the Nestorians strong criticism, and for this reason B. insisted on clarifying that this does not mean that the human will of Jesus, through his submission to the divine will, deserved union with the Word. It rather means that the union is voluntary because inhabiting a human being is an act of condescension on the part of the Word. Nevertheless, Jesus Christ does have a human will as well as a divine will, although in perfect agreement.

—

JLG

Bacon, Francis (1561–1626).

Empiricist philosopher and English politician. He studied at the University of Cambridge. Like his father, he occupied important positions in government. Accused of taking bribes, he was incarcerated for a short time.

B. postulated that the human mind tends to make uncritical generalizations. Only a disciplined mind can succeed in advancing knowledge, and this is translated into power. A critical mind is one free of four "idols" or biases: (1) trusting in our perceptions; (2) judging on the basis of experience, tastes, and preferences; (3) using words in an informal and ambiguous way that leads to confusion; (4) accepting the traditional or dogmatic ways of thinking.

True knowledge is obtained only by the inductive method, through which we determine the causes and effects of phenomena. This implies (1) observing all the circumstances in which a phenomenon occurs, (2) considering all the cases in which the phenomenon does not occur, (3) noting all the cases in which the phenomenon occurs in some measure, (4) and then relating these three in order to discover the true causes of the phenomenon. This gives us knowledge about the causes of phenomena and adds to our power over nature and history.

His passion for scientific knowledge did not lead B., as it did other scientists of his period, to repudiate religion. His mother came from a Puritan tradition and had a certain influence on his education. B. did not belong to a church or have an active religious life. He thought that church was necessary to attend to the spiritual needs of the community and to give legitimacy and stability to the state. He denounced as arrogant those who pretended to understand the totality of the nature and purposes of God. He respected religious space as well as scientific space. These two human concerns belong to different spheres and ought to respect their mutual autonomy.

—

IG

Bacon, Leonard Wolsey (1830–1907).

Pastor of the Central Church (Congregationalist) in New Haven for many years and author of the classic work *Genesis of the New England Churches* (1874). He was also a strong defender of religious and racial tolerance.

—

EZ

Bacon, Roger (1215–94).

Franciscan philosopher and theologian, and a professor at Oxford. He was famous, among other things, for his corrections of the text of the Vulgate. This, his critique of some of the most famous teachers of the period, and, above all, his interest in the works of Aristotle cost him numerous enemies and condemnations. But in the end he was recognized as one of the best thinkers of his time. In his *Opus majus* he discusses the obstacles to true knowledge and singles out among them the excessive weight that is given to some authorities, and even more to common opinion, in addition to insisting on one's own opinions. In the face of this, B. proposes that preference should be given to reason above custom or common opinion and that, while ancient writers are respected, it should be remembered that they are fallible and that in fact they were mistaken on more than one occasion. He also insists on the knowledge of languages, especially Greek, Hebrew, and Arabic, in which several of the seminal writings of human knowledge are found.

Concerning the relationship between theology and philosophy, which was so much debated during his time, B. maintained that the two disciplines are interdependent and that they are mutually enriching, since the philosophers of antiquity could not have reached their high level of knowledge had it not been revealed to them by God. Certainly theology knows objects and truths which philosophy can neither know nor prove; nonetheless, philosophy can contribute to theology a good part of its methodology and its arguments. B. himself gives an example of this in the fourth part of his *Opus majus*, which is apologetic. There he shows that, although philosophy cannot reach the knowledge of revealed truths, it can help make them credible, giving preference to reason over human weakness.

—

JLG

Báez Camargo, Gonzalo (1899–1983).

A Mexican Protestant scholar in biblical studies and one of the most important thinkers of Latin American Protestantism in the twentieth century. He excelled as a writer, justifying the presence and role of the Protestant faith in the development of Latin American society. Many of his works, published under the pseudonym of Pedro Gringoire, are a call to Protestants to develop an authentically Latin American faith. His participation in the first missionary congresses in Latin America (Panama, 1916; Montevideo, 1925; and Havana, 1929) marks a milestone in the development of the ecumenical movement in the continent, as his work *Toward a Religious Renovation in Hispanic America* shows.

—

CCO

Baillie, Donald Mac (1887–1954).

Professor of systematic theology at the University of Saint Andrews in Scotland, his nation of origin. Together with his brother John ⇒Baillie, during the first half of the twentieth century he was part of a movement called "the theology of reconstruction," which was a neo-orthodox answer to what he considered to be the liberal gospel of the first half of the twentieth century in Europe. Especially in his great

work on the incarnation, *God Was In Christ: An Essay on Incarnation and Atonement*, B. proposed to reestablish the balance in Christology, vis-à-vis scholars such as ⇒Bultmann, who said that nothing can be known with certainty about the "Jesus of history," but that the "Christ of faith" was the core of biblical theology. B. argued that there cannot be a "Christ of faith" unless that Christ has been manifested in a completely human form in history. After his death, his brother John published some of his sermons about this and other themes, such as the Trinity. J. Baillie also published some appendixes to *God Was In Christ* that his brother had written before his death in 1954.

—

EA

Baillie, John (1886–1960).

Professor of theology in Toronto and in Edinburgh, Scotland, his nation of origin. Together with his brother Donald ⇒Baillie, B. represented a moderately conservative reaction to the most liberal elements among the neo-orthodox. His numerous works include *Our Knowledge of God* (1939), in which he enters into debate with ⇒Barth and ⇒Brunner on the theme of natural theology. He also evaluated what appeared to him to be the crisis of the study of religion in various works, among them *The Interpretation of Religion: An Introductory Study of Theological Principles* (1928). In a more popular work, *Invitation to Pilgrimage* (1942), B. demonstrated his intense interest in defending the evangelical Christian faith in the midst of doubt resulting from the crisis of the world war.

—

EA

Baius, Michael (1513–89).

Belgian theologian born in Melun who served as professor of theology and biblical hermeneutics in the College of the Pope in Louvain, the College of Standonk, and the College of Adrian. B. and others proposed new ideas and methods, based mainly on the study of ⇒Augustine. On this basis, he emphasized the primacy of grace, whose power is irresistible, and this led him to affirm the doctrine of predestination. At the instigation of the Franciscans, the Sorbonne condemned eighteen of his propositions, and this gave rise to a bitter controversy.

In 1563 B. was one of two theologians sent to the Council of Trent to represent the king of Spain. The council was on the verge of condemning B. and his companion, and only the prestige of the king of Spain set them free.

In 1564 he published his *Opuscula omnia*, of which Pius V condemned some seventy-five propositions, although without naming B. The latter defended himself, but he was compelled to submit, although he did not sign the retraction. In 1570 he published *Explicatio articulorum*, in which he defended the theses that had been condemned. A new condemnatory bull was subscribed to and accepted by the entire faculty in which he taught. In his last years he professed his controversial ideas with great zeal, but it is said he retracted them before dying.

B. was a precursor of Jansenism (⇒Jansen) and endeavored to reduce the study of theology to the Scriptures and to the ancient fathers of the church, especially Augustine. He was reproached for imitating the Protestants and for resorting to the same authorities as they did, to which B. and his partisans replied that they did so in order to fight the heretics more effectively, attacking them on their own ground. His doctrinal system was called Bayanism, which professes to be nothing but the teaching of Augustine on human freedom in each of its different states: before the fall, in the state of fallen nature, and in the state of the redeemed.

—

JDR

Ballou, Hosea (1771–1852).

North American theologian born in New England. Originally he was of Calvinist persuasion, but later he came to affirm the salvation of all humankind. He was very influential in the Universalist Church. Among his many writings, the most important are *Treatise on Atonement: In Which the Finite Nature of Sin Is Argued, Its Cause and Consequences as Such, the Necessity and Nature of Atonement, and Its Glorious Consequences in the Final Reconciliation of All Men to Holiness and Happiness*, in which he reexamines important aspects of Calvinism, and *The Ancient History of Universalism: From the Time of the Apostles, to Its Condemnation in the Fifth General Council, A.D. 553*, in which he challenges and revises the doctrine of eternal punishment. In addition, his theology developed toward a unitarian, not a Trinitarian, conception of God.

—

NRG

Balmes, Jaime Lucio (1810–48).

Spanish priest and theologian. Born in Catalonia (Vich), where he also died. B. studied in the seminary of Vich and in Cevera, was ordained as a priest in 1833, and for a time worked as a teacher in his native city. Political conditions forced him into exile, and he eventually settled in Madrid, where founded and published the journal *El pensamiento de la nación* (The Thought of the Nation), which gave publicity to the thoughts of the conservative Catholic party. In 1847 he published a pamphlet in favor of the political reforms of Pope ⇒Pius IX, resulting in conflict with the conservative party. B. then wrote several works in which he explains his position and his staunch opposition to Protestantism. These include *Protestantism Compared with Catholicism in Their Relationship with European Civilization* (1842–44), *Fundamental Philosophy* (1846), and *Course on Elemental Philosophy* (1837).

In these and other writings, B. criticized English empiricism (⇒Locke), Kantianism (⇒Kant), and the philosophy of ⇒Hegel. He defended Catholicism and had a positive influence on Cardinal Mercier and the school of Louvain. Due to serious health problems, he returned to his native city, where he died.

—

HMT

Balthasar, Hans Urs von (1905–88).

Theologian and Swiss Jesuit priest. He was an interdisciplinary thinker who explored the dialogical nature of all knowledge. Among the key themes of his theological research are the relationships between nature and grace and between immanence and transcendence. He studied the relationship among the transcendental categories of beauty, truth, and virtue, thus exploring important themes for classical Western philosophy. Central to his hermeneutics are the mystery of the Trinity and that of the incarnation in the drama of creation. He was influenced by his compatriot Karl ⇒Barth and by ⇒Maximus the Confessor in his effort to discover in the life and historical particularity of Jesus of Nazareth the universal meaning of salvation. For B. all experience and human culture fall under the interpretive experience of the concrete history of Jesus.

His interpretation is not dogmatic but phenomenological. He was always willing to observe, listen to, and understand the figures, sounds, and relations that are expressed in culture, literature, and musical compositions. He was therefore a great scholar and lover of literature, art, and music as texts of the Creator. He drank with pleasure from the sources of patristics, from the theological works of Henri de ⇒Lubac and others, as well as from the literature of Goethe, from the poetry of Schiller,

Rilke, and Homer, and from the symphonies of Mozart. Although he sometimes found himself marginalized in his order, as a Jesuit priest he lived out his call and following of Christ influenced by the *Spiritual Exercises* of ⇒Loyola, especially by Nos. 53 and 91–100. His most important works in the field of theology are his trilogy: *The Glory of the Lord*, *Theodrama*, and *Theologic*.

—

ALG

Bandinelli, Roland (ca. 1105–81).

Better known as Pope Alexander III (elected in 1159). B. defended the spiritual (and moral) authority of the papacy over kings and emperors, although he admitted the secular authority of the latter. He studied theology and law in Bologne, and came to see the Holy Roman Empire as a "benefit"—meaning a possession—of the papacy. He bemoaned yet survived the division of the papacy in Rome and two exiles in France. Long before becoming pope, B. supported the reforms of the church initiated by ⇒Gregory VII. As pope, he showed a strong interest in education and in the development of the universities.

—

NRG

Báñez, Domingo (1528–1604).

Dominican professor of theology in Ávila, in Alcalá, and finally in Salamanca. In Ávila he was a teacher and for six years the confessor of ⇒Teresa, whose reforming work he defended throughout his life. There is no doubt that it was B. who helped the saint to navigate the difficult waters of the suspicions of the Inquisition and who instructed her in theology in such a way that Teresa could avoid being condemned as a heretic. Also, in the process of the canonization of Teresa, B. was one of the principal witnesses. But it was in Salamanca that he became famous as a theologian when he participated in several of the most important controversies of his time, in particular those having to do with grace and predestination.

B. feared the Pelagian tendencies (⇒Pelagius) of some of the Spanish theologians, who in their opposition to Protestantism appeared to concede too much to free will. According to B., salvation is by grace, and God grants efficacious grace leading to salvation only to the elect, but does not give it to the reprobate. Soon the controversy became a conflict between the Dominicans, who supported the theses of B., and the Jesuits who, led by ⇒Lessius, upheld the opposite theses. With the publication of the work of Luis de ⇒Molina on free will, which was attacked by B. and other Dominicans, the controversy reached Rome. Numerous theological conferences were held there (in the *congregationes de auxiliis*), which in the end resolved nothing. The decision of Rome was that none of the parties in conflict was heretical and that each one could support and teach its position as long as it did not declare the other to be heretical. In the end this controversy was eclipsed by a similar one revolving around ⇒Jansen and Jansenism.

Although in the matter of grace and predestination B. was closer to ⇒Calvin than to many Catholics, this does not mean that he was in any way inclined toward Protestantism. On the contrary, he insisted on the authority of the Catholic Church and its tradition, eventually declaring that the core of the Scriptures is not in the written text but in the heart of the church.

Another important point in the teaching of B. was his insistence on the priority of existence over essence. This led him to difficulties with the Inquisition, because it appeared to imply that in the Eucharist the existence of the bread remains, although in essence the bread has become the body of Christ. Many Catholics objected that position came too close to the teaching of ⇒Luther.

—

JLG

Bar Berikha, Ebedjesus
⇒Ebedjesus bar Berikha

Bar Hebraeus, Gregory (1226–86).

One of the most prolific writers of the Jacobite or Monophysite Syrian church, he became bishop of Aleppo and then patriarch of that church. His literary work includes not only works on theology, the Bible, and ecclesiastical law, but also writings on medicine, astronomy, grammar, and history. His great encyclopedia, *The Best of Knowledge or The Cream of Science*, remains for the most part unpublished, and the same is true of his *Candelabrum of the Sanctuaries*, which is his chief theological work. Also of great interest is his universal history, which consists of two parts, the *Syriac Chronicle* and the *Ecclesiastical Chronicle*.

As far as theology is concerned, the work of B.H. is important because it shows that many supposed Monophysites were such only in the formulas they used ("one nature and one person"), but actually believed that Jesus Christ is divine and human at the same time and that his divinity does not diminish or destroy his humanity. B.H. himself says that the differences between his church, the orthodoxy of Chalcedon, and even the views of the Nestorians is mainly a matter of words.

—

JLG

Bar Koni, Theodore ⇒Theodore bar Koni

Bar Nun, Isho ⇒Isho bar Nun

Bar Senaja, Elijah ⇒Elijah bar Senaja

Barbieri, Sancte U. (1902–92). Protestant leader of Italian origin, who nevertheless wrote in Spanish and Portuguese and lived mainly in Argentina. He was a bishop of the Methodist church and the first Latin American president of the ⇒World Council of Churches. Among his publications is a book on *The Teachings of Jesus* and several volumes of religious poems. He belonged to a generation that helped Latin American Protestantism recover its cultural roots, above all concerning those having to do with literature.

—

CCO

Barclay, Robert (1648–90). Scottish theologian, educated in Paris, and an apologist for the Society of Friends (the Quakers). B. was the only systematic theologian among the early Quakers. His principal works are *Catechism and Confession of Faith* (1673) and *Apology for the True Christian Religion* (1678). The latter is his masterpiece, in which he presents in a systematic way the mystical spirituality of the Quakers, a spirituality giving structure and coherence to his theology.

—

AP

Barclay, William (1907–78). Scottish New Testament scholar, educated at the University of Glasgow, where he later served as professor. While serving his pastorate among factory and pier workers, he learned to communicate biblical and theological truths to ordinary folk and not to underestimate the intelligence of the common people. These experiences provided the pedagogical basis of his very famous commentaries, the *Daily Study Bible*, published between 1954 and 1978 and translated into several languages, including Spanish.

—

AP

Bardesanes (154–222). Writer in the Syriac language, although of Persian origin, who refuted the teachings of ⇒Valentinus and ⇒Marcion, but retained some gnostic tendencies. B.'s parents were pagan priests and therefore astrologers. B. was converted to Christianity in Edessa in the year 179. Later he occupied an important place in the court of King Abgar IX, who was converted to Christianity at the beginning of the third century.

Possibly due to his upbringing, he attempted to reconcile astrology with Christianity. He then proposed the theory that, although the human spirit is free to make decisions, what concerns the body—health and illness, fortune and misfortune, life and death—is determined by the stars.

What earned B. the title of heretic, besides this theory, was his teaching on creation. According to him, God initially created the elements, among which were light and darkness. The latter attempted to penetrate the light, and the resulting confusion led God to create the present world through the Word. Thus this material world, although a creation of God, is not good.

Although it is not certain that B. himself said so, at least his later disciples declared that, since matter is the result of evil, Jesus did not have a body like ours, and for this reason they rejected the resurrection of the body. For this, they were called gnostics, and later Manicheans.

His followers, known as the sect of the Bardesanites, continued living in the Arab world at least until the twelfth century.

—

JLG

Barlaam (?–ca. 1348). Calabrian monk of great learning, and one of the chief forerunners of the humanism of the Renaissance. He abandoned the Latin church in order to transfer to the Greek church, which he served for the greater part of his life; but at the end he returned to obedience to the pope and became a bishop in Italy.

His chief theological works were refutations of the Hesychastic mysticism defended by Gregory ⇒Palamas. The Hesychasts claimed that their methods of contemplation led them to a vision of the same divine light that the blessed see in heaven. B. attacked them not only with theological arguments, but also by mocking their methods of contemplation and their supposed ignorance.

While he belonged to the Eastern church he also wrote numerous treatises against the Latins. Later, on returning to the Latin church, he wrote against the Greeks.

——

JLG

Barmen, Declaration of (1934). Representatives of the Reformed, Lutheran, and United churches convened the First Confessional Synod of the German Evangelical Church on May 29 to 31, 1934, in Wuppertal-Barmen. The Declaration was born there as a confession of the faith of the church. This confession was adopted in a period of crisis because of the rise to power of the Third Reich and of the movement of "German Christianity." In it the Confessing Church gives its testimony of faith against the neopaganism and totalitarianism of the German Christian movement. It rejects the syncretism of the "German Christians," which joined the Christian faith with the ideology of Hitler's National Socialism or fascism. The fascist creed proclaimed "race, nationality, and nation as forms of order in life given by God." This fascist religiosity was the source of persecution of Jews, pacifists, and anyone who opposed the Third Reich as the messenger of the kingdom of God.

The six articles of B. are not chiefly a summary of the content of the faith; rather, they are a theological exposition as the answer of the church in a situation of crisis. The theological hand of Karl ⇒Barth can be perceived in the Declaration's emphasis on the sovereign God and on the centrality of Christ. The influence of the ⇒Augsburg Confession (1530) can also be noted in its emphasis on the Word and the sacraments as the fundamental basis for the formation and mission of the ecumenical church. The Declaration is recognized as one of the historic confessions of the Reformed Church in Germany. The majority of the Lutheran and United churches (Reformed and Lutheran) in Germany have included several themes of B. in their constitutions. The Presbyterian Church (U.S.A.) includes the Declaration in its *Book of Confessions*.

——

ALG

Barnabas, Epistle of (2nd century). The erroneously titled *Epistle of Barnabas* is one of the oldest and most enigmatic writings of Christianity. Its anonymous author combines an apocalyptic fervor with the allegorical hermeneutics of ⇒Philo of Alexandria. The first to speak of Barnabas as its author is ⇒Clement of Alexandria, who, like his disciple ⇒Origen, quotes B. as an authoritative source. Despite the ancient evidence, no scholars believe that its author is the Barnabas of the New Testament. To determine the date of its composition is difficult, if not impossible. The lack of obvious references to writings of the New Testament suggests a date before the year 100. The reference to the reconstruction of the temple in Jerusalem suggests a date after the rebellion of Bar Kokhba (132–35).

The epistle can be divided into two parts. The first (chaps. 1–17) is basically a very exaggerated allegorical interpretation of the Old Testament that denies its literal and traditional interpretation. According to this writing, the purpose of those texts was spiritual (that is, allegorical), but an evil angel deceived the Jews so that they would understand them literally. The author apparently feels that his readers are threatened by Judaizers who still view Judaism with nostalgia. Without a rigorous order, it jumps from speculation to exhortation, from the theoretical to the practical, emphasizing above all the relationship of Christianity with the Old Testament and stressing the superiority of Christianity over Judaism.

The second part (chaps. 18–20) is a comparison of the two ways, following the ⇒*Didache* step by step, although here the ways are called paths "of light" and "of darkness," presided over by angels of God and angels of Satan. This exposition in B. lacks the unity and clarity of the *Didache*.

——

AP

Baronius, Cesare (1538–1607). Controversial figure whose chief work was the elaboration of historical arguments in defense of Roman Catholicism vis-à-vis Protestantism. He intervened with Pope Clement VIII in order to effect a reconciliation between the papacy and Henry IV of France. Clement named him librarian of the Vatican, which gave him access to the documents necessary for writing his great work, *Ecclesiastical Annals*. This is a detailed history of the church with the purpose of refuting the ⇒*Centuries of Magdeburg*, a history of the church published between 1559 and 1574 in defense of Protestant teachings. B. was able to complete the first twelve volumes of this great undertaking, in which he took the history of the church up to the year 1198. After his death, others continued it. This work, containing detailed documentation that until then was not accessible to the historians, earned B. the title of "father of church history."

——
JLG

Barot, Madeleine (1909–). Protestant of French origin; outstanding leader in the Student Christian Movement, as well as in ecumenism and in feminism. Her deep interest in developing Christian ministry within the ecumenical spirit of the time and the historical reality of the moment led her to the organization of Comité inter-mouvement auprés des évacués (Intermovement Committee for Refugees). She stood out in helping Jewish refugees to escape from the Nazis during the German occupation of France.

After World War II, B. involved CIMADE in two projects of great importance in western Europe: (1) the reconstruction of France and the relocation of thousands of displaced people, and (2) reconciliation with Germany. B. reached the conclusion that it was necessary to maintain a certain distance from the church in order to be able to take greater risks and try more radical initiatives. While engaged in this work, she contributed to the development of a theology of mission that is centered not on the church but rather on the ecumenical spirit of the body of Christ and the response of Christian communities to the needs of the world. Indirectly she also contributed to the development of the theology of secularization. B. also was an active leader in the ⇒World Council of Churches, in tasks related to the life and renewal of the church in the world.

——
CCO

Barsumas. Name of two individuals who lived at the same time, one a Nestorian and the other a Monophysite.

1. The Nestorian B. (?–ca. 495) was one of the main founders of the school of Nisibis, the intellectual focus from which Nestorianism spread throughout the Persian Empire. He conspired against the Nestorian patriarch of Seleucia-Ctesifon, who was put to death by imperial order, apparently as the result of maneuvers or at least of accusations by B.

2. The Monophysite B. (?–458) was accused of being one of the architects of the "*latrocinium* of Ephesus" (the council that in 449 deposed all who supported the doctrine of the "two natures" in Christ), and above all of being the instigator of the death of ⇒Flavian of Constantinople, who was so badly assaulted in that council that he died within a few days. When the Council of ⇒Chalcedon undid what was done in Ephesus, B. rejected its decisions and was therefore anathematized. For the same reason, several Monophysite churches count him among their saints.

——
JLG

Barth, Karl (1886–1968). Pastor and theologian of the Reformed church of Switzerland and one of the most important theologians of the twentieth century, the founder of dialectical or neo-orthodox theology. Born in Basel, Switzerland, he was reared in a family with a high degree of education. His two grandfathers were pastors. His father, Fritz, was a pastor and teacher in a Protestant school and became professor of church history and New Testament at the University of Bern. Two of his brothers also followed the career of academic theology and philosophy.

Although B. received his theological education at the universities of Bern, Tübingen, and Marburg, and studied under several eminent theologians of the time, among them ⇒Harnack, he never completed a doctorate in theology. His theology emerged from the challenge presented by the demands of his ministry and preaching. In 1909, at the age of twenty-three, he finished his theological studies and was ordained to the ministry. That year he began to serve as assistant pastor of the Reformed church in Geneva, where he worked until 1911. He then served as pastor in the small city of Safenwil, also in Switzerland, until 1921.

During his years as pastor in Safenwil, B. devoted himself to matters of social justice as part of the Christian Socialist Movement in Switzerland, helping the poor workers who made up the greater part of his congregation. In 1913 he married Nelly Hoffman.

It was during his time as pastor in Safenwil that B. began to develop his own theology. Educated in the liberal theology that prevailed in the universities of his time, B. was disillusioned with it when ninety-three German academics signed a document supporting the German kaiser and his policy during the First World War. Confronting the challenges of sermon preparation and biblical study, he prepared his first commentary on the Epistle to the Romans, published in 1919. Although that first edition had limited circulation, it was sufficient to attract the attention of the academic circles of his day.

In 1921, due to the impact of the commentary on Romans, B. was offered a post as professor of Reformed theology at the University of Göttingen. That year he also finished revising the first edition of his commentary, and this resulted in a second edition, published in 1922. B.'s drastic critique of liberal theology in that second edition had a greater impact on the theological world than the first edition. As a result of that publication, B. discovered other theologians who also were dissatisfied with the state of liberal theology. He, Eduard ⇒Thurneysen, and Friedrich ⇒Gogarten joined in founding the journal *Zwischen den Zeiten* (Between the Times) in 1922. In 1925 B. accepted a post at the University of Münster,, where he remained until 1930. During his time in Münster, he continued writing and publishing several biblical commentaries, in addition to lecturing on the history of systematic theology. It was there that he published *The Doctrine of the Word of God: Prolegomena to Christian Dogmatics* (1927), his first attempt to develop a dogmatic theology.

In 1930 B. accepted a post at the University of Bonn as professor of systematic theology. The decade of the 1930s was turbulent in Germany, with the rapid rise to power of Adolf Hitler and the National Socialist (Nazi) Party. Always firm in his political and social convictions, B. attacked the abuses of the Nazi Party. In 1933 he and his friend Thurneysen launched the journal *Theologische Existenz Heute* in order to combat the complicity of the official German church with Nazism. As a result, B. emerged as one of the principal personalities of the Confessing Church that opposed Hitler. On May 31, 1934, the Confessing Church, gathered in Barmen, issued the famous Declaration of ⇒Barmen, drafted chiefly by B., which affirms faith exclusively in Christ and condemns the support granted to Nazism by the official church in Germany.

Because of his strong opposition to the National Socialist government, B. was expelled from Germany and from his position in the University of Bonn in 1935. In that year, at the age of forty-nine, he accepted a post at the University of Basel, in Switzerland. From there he continued his opposition to the Nazi Party through correspondence and writings. Although B. thought some day he would return permanently to Germany, he was never able to do so, except for some short trips and for one year

(1946–47) as visiting professor in his old university post in Bonn.

During his time at the University of Basel, B. was able to complete his chief work, *Die Kirchliche Dogmatik*, the most complete Protestant theological work produced in the twentieth century. It consists of four volumes in thirteen books, written during a period of more than thirty years (beginning in 1932 and finishing with the publication of the last volume in 1967). One year after the last volume of the *Church Dogmatics* was published, B. died in Basel, on December 10, 1968.

B. was a prolific writer. Among his chief works are his commentary on the Epistle to the Romans, his study *Fides quaerens intellectum* on the theological methodology of Anselm, and his principal theological work, the *Dogmatics*.

The theology of B. developed initially in opposition to the Protestant liberal theology that had emerged from ⇒Schleiermacher and other theologians of the nineteenth century. In response to the criticism that was generated by rationalism and empiricism, the theology of the nineteenth century centered on the human capacity to know God by means of reason alone. According to the theologians of the time, the immanence of God in the world and the continuity between God and the human being made it possible to construct an entire theological system without the need for biblical revelation. This had created an optimistic expectation concerning human nature and the possibility of establishing the kingdom of God on earth through human efforts.

B.'s dissatisfaction with this liberal Protestant theology first manifested itself in the commentary on Romans. There he points out that the historical-critical method used for biblical interpretation is insufficient for an adequate understanding of the Bible. The commentary takes a position opposed to the methodology of Protestant liberal theology, which took human religiosity as its starting point. In its place B. affirms the Reformed tradition of ⇒Calvin, denying the ability of humanity to reach any knowledge of God apart from divine revelation. This opposition to the anthropocentric and cultural theology of liberalism is still more evident in the second edition of the commentary.

B.'s criticism of liberalism is focused mainly on two points. First, according to B., liberal theology had abandoned the concept of divine transcendence. Because of that abandonment, God had been placed on the level of the human being, obliterating the difference between God and creation. This made Christianity vulnerable to the criticism of persons like ⇒Feuerbach, who claimed that God was only a projection of human ideals.

Over against this tendency, B. refers to God as "totally Other." The transcendence of God is supreme. There is an "infinite qualitative difference" between God and the human being. Only through God's self-revelation can something about God be known, and only through divine grace can one enter into communion with God. The human being can reach God only through divine action and initiative.

The second criticism of B. was that liberalism had forgotten the limitations of human knowledge caused by sin. Sin does not allow us to come to know God through human reason, philosophy, or anthropocentric theology. Likewise, sin does not permit us to be saved without the intervention of the grace of God. Human effort can never result in salvation.

One of the most notable changes in the second edition of the commentary on Romans is the dialectical method, which led to one of the names given to this new theological era that was begun by B. This method, derived from Danish philosopher Søren ⇒Kierkegaard, emphasizes the enormous difference that exists between the human being and God. Like Kierkegaard, B. stressed the moment of decision, the existential crisis, and the paradox of the divine-human encounter, always maintaining a dialectical tension between what pertains to the human being and what pertains to God.

In contrast to the continuity and divine immanence of liberal theology, the dialectical theology of B. maintains the tension caused by the difference that exists between human concepts and God. For B., the abyss that separates the human being from God can be crossed only through the divine revelation that is manifested principally in the incarnation in Jesus Christ. Only by means of this divine initiative in the incarnation can the human being know something about God.

This theme of divine initiative is fundamental for the theology of B. In Christ, God elects the human being for salvation and restores communion with humanity. All that humans can grasp in relation to God comes from God and not from humans.

B. argues that the human ability to express any theological concept is limited. Every theological affirmation that refers to God has to be conditioned through a negation. This premise maintains the tension and the difference that exists between human concepts and the reality of God.

B. also rejects the possibility of using metaphysics or philosophy as the point of departure to develop a theology. Although he recognizes that philosophy and metaphysics have their place in the development of theology, he gives priority to the Word of God, proposing that the starting point for all theological reflection should be the tripartite Word of God: the proclaimed Word, the written Word (the Bible), and the revealed Word (Christ).

During his time in Bonn, B.'s theology began to diverge from that of other dialectical theologians. This change is evident in his books *No! An Answer to Emil Brunner* and *Fides quaerens intellectum*. Starting from the premise of ⇒Augustine that reason should begin with revelation, and analyzing ⇒Anselm's proof of the existence of God, B. reached the conclusion that theology can be developed only through divine revelation and within the circle of faith which is the church. This separated him from other dialectical theologians who used philosophy, existentialism (⇒Bultmann), and natural revelation (⇒Brunner) as means of theological reflection.

In the *Dogmatics* B. developed his theology in full, beginning with the doctrine of the Word of God in his prolegomena and finishing with the ethics of the doctrine of reconciliation under the title of "Baptism as the Foundation of the Christian Life." In the intermediate volumes, B. develops a fundamentally christocentric theology based on the revelation of the triune God in the incarnation of Jesus Christ.

Even though in his final writings B. mollifies his emphasis on the radical contrast between the human being and God, he always maintained the emphasis on divine transcendence. The dialectical method, which is fundamental in his first works, is no longer so evident in the *Dogmatics*, where B. admits to the possibility of using analogical language to speak of God. But it is always the grace of God that "justifies" our words so that they can refer to the divine reality.

For B. the biblical God is alive, active, and free, manifesting Godself to humanity through God's revelation and historical deeds. For this reason, theology should not start with static concepts derived from philosophy, nor with anthropological premises. B.'s theological language uses dynamic expressions, relations, events, and works initiated always by God. Like his earlier works, *Dogmatics* emphasizes divine revelation as the beginning of theology. This revelation occurs fundamentally in the life, death, and resurrection of Jesus Christ, who is the definitive word of God to humanity.

Only through the historical and objective revelation of God in Christ does humanity obtain salvation, knowledge of God and of itself. Through Christ we know God as a triune and personal God, who reveals God's love toward humanity.

The being of God is relational and manifests itself as Trinitarian in three relational modes that do not deny the unity of God, but rather demonstrate God's communal being.

In Christ God elects humanity for salvation. Christ presents to us the objective form of salvation, while the Holy Spirit gives us the subjective possibility of salvation, giving us the power to respond with faith. Once again, B. maintains the sovereignty and initiative of divine grace. In Christ God elects all of humankind for salvation.

It is impossible to determine B.'s full influence on the theology of the twentieth century. The *Dogmatics* is one of the most important theological works of the century, and it will have to be seriously studied for a long time. By placing theology back in the ecclesial sphere, B. recovered many of the patristic and classical doctrines that had been abandoned by liberalism. At the same time, he offered an alternative to liberalism without denying the critical advances of the modern era.

——

LGP

Basel, Council of (1431–49). Council convened by Martin V as part of the conciliar movement, and following the decree of the Council of ⇒Constance, *Frequens*. Shortly after the council was convened, Eugenius IV declared it dissolved. But the council, under the direction of Nicholas of ⇒Cusa, refused to accept the papal decree and sought the support of the secular princes, and in the end Eugenius was forced to annul his decree. In the meantime the council took reforming measures that limited the power and finances of the pope and the curia.

These tensions led to a definitive rupture in 1437, when Eugenius IV transferred the council to Ferrara in Italy, arguing that union was being sought with the Eastern churches, for whose representatives Ferrara proved more accessible. Cusa and other leaders accepted the papal decree. However, others did not, but continued meeting in Basel, and thus the council was divided.

While the group that remained in Basel declared Eugenius IV deposed and named Felix V in his place, that in Ferrara (later transferred to Florence) reached an agreement of union with the Eastern churches. This gave it great prestige and lessened the prestige of the remnant at Basel. In the end Felix V resigned. The council, before dissolving, accepted Nicholas, successor of Eugenius IV, as the legitimate pope.

These episodes marked the end of the conciliar movement, since the councils were originally convened to heal the schism in the papacy, and now that schism had ended, but the council itself was divided.

——

PB

Basil of Ancyra (?–ca. 370). Bishop of that city, today Ankara in Turkey, and chief exponent of the Homoiousian party in the controversies that took place after the Council of ⇒Nicaea. This party refused to accept the equality of substance between the Father and the Son that Nicaea had declared, as well as the extreme opposite of the true Arians or Anomoeans, who maintained that the Son was "different" from the Father. While the Nicenes maintained the formula *homoousion to Patri* (of the same substance as the Father), B. and his own preferred *homoiousion to Patri* (of similar substance to the Father). B. said that the Son is "spirit of spirit, life of life, light of light, God of God, true Son of the true Father, wisdom born from the wise God; in one word, as Son, absolutely similar to the Father in all things." Although B. and his followers were branded as Semi-Arian, in the end, thanks to the clarifications of ⇒Athanasius, ⇒Basil of Caesarea, and others, B. and the majority of the Homoiousians became reconciled with the Nicene party. This led to the triumph of the Nicene cause at the Council of ⇒Constantinople in 381.

——

JLG

Basil of Caesarea (330–79). Also known as Basil the Great. One of the chief theologians of the second generation after the Council of ⇒Nicaea, who continued the work of ⇒Athanasius in favor of the Trinitarian doctrine, and was also a reformer of the liturgy, a social activist, and one of the principal founders of Eastern monasticism.

B. was born in a family of deep Christian conviction. His paternal grandmother had been a disciple of ⇒Gregory of Neocaesarea. His maternal grandfather had died as a martyr. His oldest sister, ⇒Macrina, was recognized as a teacher of the spiritual life. Two of his brothers were bishops: ⇒Gregory of Nyssa and ⇒Peter of Sebaste. He wished to devote himself to rhetoric, following the steps of his father, who was professor of that subject at Neocaesarea in Pontus. With that purpose in mind, he studied in Caesarea of Cappadocia, in Constantinople, and finally in Athens. It was in Athens that he met, ⇒Gregory of Nazianzus, who would become one of his main friends and collaborators. He returned to his native land in search of glory in the field of rhetoric, but his sister Macrina called him to a new life of asceticism. After being baptized, he traveled throughout Egypt, Palestine, Syria, and even Mesopotamia to learn about monastic life in those regions. On returning, he wrote with Gregory of Nazianzus two monastic *Rules* that became the foundation of Eastern monasticism, sometimes called Basilian monasticism (although the text of the second of these rules, which is the most influential, contains many elements that were added long after the death of B.). He was ordained as a priest in 364 and six years later became bishop of Caesarea, the main city of the region.

As bishop, B. endeavored to put the Christian life into practice and to invite his parishioners to do the same. For this reason, he strongly attacked those who accumulated riches while others died of hunger, accusing them of homicide and declaring that whoever had shoes that were not used while others went barefoot was no better than a thief. In addition, on the outskirts of Caesarea he founded a "city" or community which he called the "Kingdom"—*Basileia*—where shelter, work, food, and hope were given to abandoned and hungry people.

The Liturgy of Saint B., attributed to him, is still used in Eastern churches on the Sundays of Lent and other special days. Scholars have long discussed the authorship of that liturgy. It appears most likely that in essence it preceded B., who revised and expanded it, and that after his death several other revisions were made. Thus, although this liturgy shows what the worship of B.'s time was like, and could in good measure bear his seal, it is not strictly his work.

B. was a prolific writer, and a number of his works are preserved. Among them are moral and educational essays, sermons and letters. In the field of theology, his most interesting works are his exegetical writings and those he wrote against Arianism (⇒Arius).

In his exegetical writings, B. rejects allegorical interpretation, which had become common in the circles influenced by ⇒Origen. His nine homilies on the Hexaemeron—the six days of creation—are devoted to refuting the cosmologies of the pagans and Manicheans and to praising God for the goodness of the world and of the human creature.

The chief defender of Arianism in the time of B. was ⇒Eunomius, and therefore the main work of B. against Arianism is his treatise *Against Eunomius*. He also attacked the Pneumatomachians (⇒Macedonius of Constantinople) in his treatise *On the Holy Spirit*.

Since Eunomius represented the most extreme wing of Arianism, which maintained a radical difference between the Father and the Son, basing itself on philosophical arguments, B. refutes him with similar arguments. Thus, for example, Eunomius said that being unbegotten is part of God's own nature, and therefore the Son, who is begotten, cannot be God, but rather a creature. B. responds by declaring that the nature of God is something positive, and therefore to say that being unbegotten is part of the nature of God is a contradiction. What is negative, such as being invisible or immortal, can be a characteristic of God, but it is not part of his essence. What is being debated, then, is whether God can be begotten, to which B. responds with an emphatic affirmation. God has no beginning in time. But being begotten does not indicate an origin in time but a relationship of substance. The substance of the Son is the same as the Father's. This is what the generation of the Son indicates, and therefore, far from being a negation of his divinity, it is rather an affirmation.

In his treatise *On the Holy Spirit*, B. refutes the Pneumatomachians (on occasion called Semi-Arians, although this results in confusion in the use of that term). The Pneumatomachians declared themselves willing to accept the divinity of the Son but not that of the Holy Spirit. B. writes his treatise around the text of the doxology. While the most common text said, "Glory to the Father, through the Son and in the Holy Spirit," B. preferred to say, "with the Son, together with the Holy Spirit." What was at stake in this difference was the affirmation of the divinity of the Son and of the Holy Spirit, since in the first case it could be said that the glory belongs only to the Father, while in the second it belongs to the three; hence the most common form of the doxology today states: "Glory be to the Father, to the Son, and to the Holy Spirit; as it was [that is, as the glory was] in the beginning, [it] is now and shall be forever." In any case, although it begins around the question of the text of the doxology, B.'s argument centers on the divinity of the Holy Spirit. Through a series of arguments, B. tries to show that the divine glory belongs to the Holy Spirit as well as to the Father and the Son. This treatise was the foundation for a similar one by ⇒Ambrose (who in good measure limited himself to translating what B. had written). Thus a good part of the pneumatology, Eastern as well as Western, bears the seal of B. The result was that when the Council of ⇒Constantinople (381) met, the decisions that were made were genuinely Trinitarian, since not only the divinity of the Son was affirmed, but also that of the Holy Spirit.

On the other hand, perhaps B.'s chief contribution to the Trinitarian doctrine is not found in these treatises but in his epistles. In correspondence with several other theologians, but particularly with Gregory of Nyssa and Gregory of Nazianzus, B. and his colleagues established and clarified the distinction between *ousia* and *hypostasis*. Both words could be translated as "substance" or "essence," and it was in this way that the Council of Nicaea had used them, condemning whoever would say that in God there are three *ousias* or hypostases—which would lead to tritheism. The distinction that B. establishes, and which the two Gregories later developed, sees the *ousia* as the essence of a thing, its "what it is," and the hypostasis as its existence, the fact "that it is." Thus the divinity, the "what it is" of God, God's *ousia*, is one; but God exists in three hypostases (three that exist as such, but subsist in the same *ousia*).

This began to relieve the tensions, not only in the East, but also between the Greek-speaking East and the Latin-speaking West. Little by little, thanks to this distinction established by B., the agreement was reached to translate *ousia* as "essence" or "substance," and *hypostasis* as "person." With this agreement between East and West, the way was prepared for the general acceptance of Trinitarian doctrine.

JLG

Basilides (ca. 200) Founder of a gnostic movement known as the Basilidians. It is believed that he was a disciple of ⇒Menander in Antioch and that he taught in Alexandria during the time of Emperors Adrian and Antoninus Pius (120–45). Various works on which we have very limited information are attributed to B. According to ⇒Irenaeus, B. believed that Jesus had not died on the cross, for Simon of Cyrene had taken his place. Likewise he taught that only by means of certain esoteric knowledge (*gnosis*) could the human being save its

soul and free itself from the corruptible world. For B. everything that was done with the body here on earth was indifferent from the moral point of view.

AEM

Bastian, Jean Pierre (1947–). Historian and sociologist of religion whose work focuses on the social and political role of Protestantism in Latin America, highlighting the ambiguity of minority groups in the continent. Subsequently he has carried out studies on the growth of Pentecostalism in Latin America. He is the author of several books, including *History of Protestantism in Latin America* and *Protestants, Liberals, and Freemasons: Societies of Ideas and Modernity in Latin America, Nineteenth Century.*

CCO

Baur, Ferdinand Christian (1792–1860). German theologian and historian. Born in Württemberg, he studied at the University of Tübingen, where he continued as professor on completing his studies. Considered the originator of historical theology, B. was the first to apply a historical and systematic method to the study of Christian theology.

B. began his theological work at a time when the advances in science, naturalism, rationalism, and critical studies had put theology and the Christian faith on the defensive. The influence of ⇒Kant and ⇒Hegel on philosophy and of ⇒Schleiermacher on theology had initiated an era in which theology sought to rationalize the Christian faith for those intellectuals who doubted the validity of revelation and of all supernatural teaching. His student and colleague D. F. ⇒Strauss had published the controversial book *The Life of Jesus* (1835), in which he investigated the relation of the ideal image of Christ with the reality of the historical figure.

B. was influenced in his method by the philosophy and historical perspective of Hegel, and he therefore applied the Hegelian dialectical structure of thesis, antithesis, and synthesis to the history of Christianity.

B. differed from Hegel in his Christology, because he wished to solve what he considered the christological problems of Hegel, and also because of his more radical emphasis on history. For B., Christology is the chief starting point in the development of a historical and critical Christian theology. Insisting that Christianity had a historical base that a historian could get to know, B. devoted himself to studying the New Testament and the primitive church.

In his historical studies of the New Testament, B. looked for a reconciliation between theology and the scientific method, which had become popular in his century. He concluded that there was a historical basis for the faith of the church without the need to appeal to myths, miracles, and revelation. He also used the dialectics of Hegel to examine the development of the teachings in the Gospels and the tension between the Judaic tendencies of Peter and the Hellenistic tendencies of Paul. The result was what came to be called the Tübingen school of New Testament studies.

———

LGP

Bavinck, Herman (1854–1921). Dutch pastor who worked mainly as professor of dogmatic theology at the University of Leiden and the Seminary of Campen in Holland. With Abraham ⇒Kuyper, he led the neo-Calvinist movement of the Reformed Church of Holland. His principal work is *Gereformeerde Dogmatiek*, in four volumes. His theology upholds the principles of the ⇒Heidelberg Catechism and the canons of the Synod of ⇒Dort. Nonetheless he was open to ecumenism and willing to use all the available resources to reform the dogmatism of the Reformed scholasticism of the seventeenth century. His theology, although based on the revelation of God in Jesus Christ and subject to the Scriptures, contrasts with that of Kuyper in that it uses a realist philosophy rather than idealism. While he affirmed the revelation of God in creation and in the divine image in the human being, he insisted on the priority of the Scriptures in the theological task. He showed genuine appreciation for the neo-Thomist renaissance in Roman Catholicism.

———

ALG

Baxter, Richard (1615–91). A powerful Puritan preacher and prolific writer who ministered to the rebels of Kidderminster for twenty years. He also served for two years as military chaplain in Cromwell's army. At the time of the restoration of the monarchy, he was expelled from the church with other moderate dissidents. He proposed tolerance toward dissidents in the church. He is best known for *The Saints' Everlasting Rest* (1650), *The Reformed Pastor* (1656), and *Call to the Unconverted* (1658).

———

EZ

Beatus of Liebana (?–798). Benedictine abbot in Asturias and one of the chief opponents of the adoptionism of ⇒Elipandus of Toledo. Against him he wrote a long *Epistle to Elipandus* in two books. He is also known for *Commentary on the Apocalypse* (Revelation), which in reality is a collection of notes and glosses by previous authors and which therefore is one of the best sources for the history of the interpretation of Revelation in the first centuries of the Middle Ages.

———

JLG

Beaver, R. Pierce (1906–87). North American missiologist. He was born in Ohio and studied at Oberlin College and Cornell University. He served in China as a missionary from 1938, and in 1942 became a professor at the United Seminary in Central China. After returning to the United States, he became director of the Missionary Research Library at Union Theological Seminary in New York, where the journal *Occasional Bulletin from the MRL* began to be published. This journal, which promoted missiological studies, later became the *International Bulletin of Missionary Research*, published by the Overseas Ministries Study Center (OMSC). In 1955 he was named professor of mission in the School of Theology of the University of Chicago. He became director of the OMSC in 1976, after his retirement from the University of Chicago. Under his leadership and at a time when the critical study of mission was disappearing from theological seminaries, the OMSC developed a variety of programs to strengthen the critical study of missiology.

B. published prolifically. Among his most important works are *Ecumenical Beginnings in Protestant World Mission: A History of Comity* (1962) and *All Loves Excelling: American Protestant Women in World Mission* (1968, rev. 1980). He was a founding member of the Association of Professors of Mission in North America in 1956. From that base he supported studies on mission.

———

JLG

Bede, the Venerable (ca. 673–735). Considered the "Father of English History" and, with some presumption, the "teacher of the Middle Ages."

In this Benedictine monk we have a luminous aspect in the contribution of monasticism: the preservation and transmission of human knowledge. B. is linked to the interest which the England of his time manifested in Latin Christian classical culture and to the resulting Carolingian renaissance carried out by ⇒Alcuin (735–804), who joined the court of Charlemagne after having been educated in the monastery of York under the supervision of a disciple of B.

B. was born in the Anglo-Saxon kingdom of Northumbria, in what today is Durham (in the northeast of England). As far as is known, he never went beyond the limits of Northumbria. When he was seven years old, his parents handed him over to the cloister. He was educated under the supervision of the abbot Benedict Biscop and later under the care of the latter's associate, Ceolfrede. He spent his life in the abbeys of Wearmouth and Jarrow, both of which made up one single monastery. The abbeys were built on the shore of the Tyne and Wear rivers, close to Scotland. Contrary to what was customary, he became a deacon at nineteen. At the age of thirty he received priestly orders.

B. is the author of approximately forty works, in which he deals with a variety of disciplines: astronomy, chronology, mathematics, the natural sciences, poetry, music, grammar, history, and theology. His life's ideal was to spend all his time reading, teaching, and writing. As a faithful observant of his monastic vows and participant in biblical meditation and liturgical chant, his Marian piety inspired him to compose the hymn *In natali Sanctae Maria* (On the Birthday of Saint Mary).

His *Ecclesiastical History of the English Nation* (55 BCE–731 CE) is the obligatory source for the study of the origins and the initial activity of the British church. It is a masterful history of the great personalities of the religious and political world, although it also includes some reference to the common people. B.'s research is important because he wrote from the perspective of the total history of the English people. He recovered written and oral traditions and, through his friends, had access to archives in Rome.

His biblical commentaries reveal his familiarity with patristic authors. B. was the first to place ⇒Gregory the Great on the level of ⇒Jerome, ⇒Ambrose, and ⇒Augustine as a great teacher or doctor of the church (⇒Doctors).

He died on Ascension Eve and, in accordance with his will, was buried with his face turned toward his church. Shortly after his death he was named "the Venerable." In the eleventh century his remains were taken to Durham cathedral and placed in a silver and gold coffin. In 1899 Pope Leo XIII proclaimed him a doctor of the church. His feast is May 25, formerly 27, the probable date of his death.

——

EPA

Bediako, Kwame (1944–). Ordained minister of the Presbyterian Church of Ghana and one of the most distinguished African theologians in Protestant circles. He has doctorates from the universities of Bordeaux and Aberdeen. Outstanding among his works is *Theology and Identity: The Impact of Culture upon Christian Thought in the Second Century and in Modern Africa.* He is founder and director of the Akrofi-Kristaller Memorial Center for Mission and Theology and founder of the African Theological Fraternity.

——

CCO

Beecher, Henry Ward (1813–87). Pastor and Presbyterian theologian who influenced social causes. He was born in Connecticut in a prominent family; his father was the noted pastor and preacher Lyman ⇒Beecher, and his sister was Harriet Beecher Stowe, author of the book *Uncle Tom's Cabin.* After graduating from the University of Amherst, he enrolled in Lane Theological Seminary. He then served as pastor of Presbyterian churches in Indiana and New York. In 1847, after a famous trial, he was absolved of accusations of adultery. He wrote several books, of which the best known were *Seven Lectures to Young Men* (1844) and *Norwood* (1887). In his work *Evolution and Religion* (1885), he attempted to resolve the tensions between Christian doctrines and evolutionary theories. He was also editor of the journals *The Independent* and *The Christian Union.*

With the passage of time, B. left behind his original ultraorthodox Calvinism and began to be more concerned with social concerns. Although he was opposed to slavery, he did not associate with the abolitionists, who seemed extremist to him. He supported the North in the Civil War but then advocated for a policy of reconciliation. Like his father, he worked in favor of temperance and women's suffrage.

——

PB

Beecher, Lyman (1775–1863). Highly successful Presbyterian pastor in New York,

Connecticut, and Masachusetts. Born in New Haven, Connecticut, he studied at Yale University in the same city, where he came under the influence of his mentor Timothy ⇒Dwight and felt the impact of the Second Great Awakening. He was founder of the American Bible Society and the first president of Lane Seminary in Cincinnati (1832). As a famous preacher he gave his support to several reforming movements: the abolition of slavery, women's suffrage, laws against duels, and temperance. He was strongly anti-Catholic and antiunitarian, and argued in favor of the evangelization of the lands of the North American West as a way of protecting the region against the advance of the European Catholic powers.

—

PB

Béguines. A semimonastic movement of women without formal vows that had its origin in the twelfth century, as a response to the scandalous urban poverty in the Low Countries. The B. had a male counterpart in the Béghards. Some historians derive their origin from the priest Lambert the Stammerer, who invested his fortune in works of charity.

Although they enjoyed the freedom to own private property and to marry, they organized themselves in groups whose goods were held in common. They were particularly numerous in the great cities of what today is Holland, Switzerland, Belgium, and Germany. These groups were characterized by mystical practices, devotion to the ideal of the apostolic life, and, above all, their contribution to the formation of the religious opinion of the lower classes in medieval Europe.

Aside from the strong mystical influence, it is difficult to determine the sources that contributed to the theology of these groups. Frequently they are linked with many of the heterodox groups that existed in the interior of Europe, although in 1216 Pope Honorius III recognized them verbally, but without an official rule or affiliation with a monastic order. The rumors about their ties with heresy led them to be a favorite target of the inquisitors. When in 1311 the Council of Vienna determined that the theology of the B. was similar to that of the "spiritual Franciscans," they were declared heretics. But in spite of the attempt to suppress them, they continued to exist for several centuries.

—

GC

Bellamy, Joseph (1719–90). New England Congregationalist and participant in the Great Awakening with Jonathan ⇒Edwards. In the end he departed from the strict Calvinism of Edwards by rejecting the theory of limited atonement and the interpretation of the work of Christ in juridical terms or of "satisfaction" (⇒Anselm of Canterbury).

—

JLG

Bellarmine, Roberto Francesco Romolo (1542–1621). Italian Jesuit, born on the outskirts of Florence, of a noble but relatively poor family. He was eighteen years old when he joined the Company of Jesus. After studying philosophy and teaching literature, he studied theology, first in Padua and then in Louvain. After his ordination in 1570, he began to teach theology and devoted himself to preaching. Known for his tenacious opposition to Protestantism, in 1576 he was named professor of controversy at the Roman College, where his main task was to train the Germans and the English who were preparing to return to their countries as priests. Since in those countries Protestantism was dominant, a very important part of the preparation of these priests was to arm them with arguments against Protestant teachings and in defense of Catholicism.

B. continued to give courses on apologetics against Protestantism for twelve years. The result of those years was his main work, *Controversies about the Christian Faith against the Heretics of These Times,* known simply as *Controversies.* This great work, which some have called "a summa of controversy," develops the Catholic arguments against Protestantism in a systematic way and was for a long time the guide for anti-Protestant polemics. His arguments are based on reason, Scripture, and the history of the church—above all, the writings of the fathers of the church. Certainly many of the arguments that were commonly used against Protestantism, at least until well into the twentieth century, found their classical formulation in B. An example among many is the argument according to which it was the tradition of the church that produced the canon of the Scriptures, recognizing some books as inspired and others as not. Therefore the church and its tradition are to determine the way in which Scriptures are to be interpreted, and Protestants are mistaken when they claim that the Bible can be employed to refute or contradict the church and its tradition.

In addition to this great work of controversy, B. wrote on moral theology or ethics, in which he maintained the moral positions of the Roman Catholic Church.

In 1588 B. abandoned his teaching post in order to undertake administrative functions in the Company of Jesus. Eleven years later, in 1599, he was made cardinal. He became actively involved in the internal politics of the church in Rome, where he enjoyed great influence, except during a brief period in which he clashed with the pope and was ordered to return to the see of Capua, where he was titular archbishop.

Because Roman Catholicism became more and more conservative in doctrinal matters until the Second Vatican Council (⇒Vatican II), the fame and popularity of B. continued to increase until the second half of the twentieth century. In 1930 he was canonized, and one year later he was added to the select list of ⇒doctors of the church.

———

JLG

Benedict XVI ⇒Ratzinger, Joseph

Benedict of Nursia (480–547).

One of the main promoters of Western monasticism. Born in central Italy, he studied in Rome, from which he fled to the countryside because of the religious confrontations of the period, establishing himself as a hermit in Subiaco. After a period of meditation, discipline, reflection, and vigils, he decided to found a monastic community. In 529 he moved to a secluded place and founded the monastery of Monte Cassino, center of his monastic and missionary work until his death. His twin sister, Scholastica, founded a similar order for women.

In spite of political and religious turbulence in Italy, B. concentrated on organizing the monastic life and as a result gave Christianity one of the most important and best-organized religious orders. With Roman practicality and on the basis of the experience of other monks, such as ⇒John Cassian and ⇒Basil of Caesarea, B. elaborated his *Rule*, which became the cornerstone of monastic discipline and medieval spirituality.

Among the distinctive elements of the *Rule* were the hours of prayer. In a regimen in which work and prayer were balanced, this system provided a liturgical order for personal and community worship. Very soon this system for the life of daily prayer attained great popularity, being known until this day as the liturgical hours: Matins, Lauds, Prime, Terce, Sext, Nones, Vespers, and Compline. The Psalms and other portions of the Scriptures were organized in a kind of weekly and annual lectionary.

The *Rule* promoted a moderate regimen of ascetic practice. By means of an adequate balance between agricultural work, community tasks, and the life of prayer and study, a community-oriented style of life was achieved.

The chief emphases were permanence or stability (precluding monks from wandering from one monastery to another), absolute obedience, a simple life, and constant work. Everything was summed up in the principle *ora et labora* (pray and work), with an alternate regime of work in the field and times of prayer. This lifestyle, with an abbot presiding over a community of work, study, and meditation, became the key to the missionary success of the Benedictine orders. The Benedictine ideal was a community of material and spiritual goods based on simplicity of life, evangelizing fervor, commitment to service, and the educational task.

One of the permanent contributions of the Benedictine monasteries was the copying and preservation of manuscripts. Of particular importance was the gathering of the religious and cultural legacy of patristic and medieval literature, which gave continuity and consistency to Christianity in successive generations.

The Benedictine monastic movement expanded throughout Europe through its monastic schools, particularly for children, being thus a fundamental vehicle in the intellectual formation of the entire continent. The Benedictine *Rule* extended to the British Isles, the kingdom of the Franks, Spain, and other European territories. The influence of the *Rule* of B., the propagation of the faith, and its educational work are permanent contributions of a monastic movement that today is scattered throughout the world. It is noteworthy that the cultural and educational influence of Benedictine monasticism has been able to take root in the countries of the third world with a visible presence that extends to political and public life. Benedictine monasticism's simple and practical theology, affirming the dignity of work, constant effort, and physical and spiritual discipline, continues to exert an important influence on Christian spirituality in the twenty-first century.

———

CEA

Bennett, John C. (1899–1995).

North American ethical theologian who rejected the situational ethics of Joseph ⇒Fletcher, although he shared with him and other adherents of that ethic the conviction that principles are always provisional and that ambiguous and complex situations demand pragmatic ethical responses that take into account the particular circumstances in which decisions are to be made.

This disciple of Reinhold ⇒Niebuhr, whose chair at Union Theological Seminary he inherited, developed the idea of intermediate principles. These principles are less formal than universal principles and less specific than a program or particular plan of action. The intermediate principles are not mandatory for all times or in all circumstances, but rather provide a provisional but specific direction for the type of conduct that should define Christian practice in particular circumstances. B. developed these principles in the areas of politics, economics, and international relations.

—
IG

Bentham, Jeremy (1748–1832). Educated in Queens College, Oxford, B. was one of the founders of English ethical utilitarianism. He postulated that individuals act and decide what to do in the light of what they calculate will give greater pleasure and less pain. One of our primordial moral duties is to produce the greater good (pleasure) for the greater number of people. B. believed that in most cases it is easy to harmonize the individual good and the common good.

An important difference between B. and other hedonistic utilitarians is that he thinks that the principle of maximizing pleasure is neither individualistic nor egotistic, but has a social character. Like other utilitarians, he proposed and constantly supported legal and social reforms that advance the common good, even at the expense of the pleasure of the individual. The goal of moral action is the common good and not individual pleasure. His reforming spirit motivated him to support any social and political action that would produce the greatest happiness in and for society in its totality.

—
IG

Beozzo, Oscar (1941–). Sociologist of religion, Roman Catholic, and native of Brazil. He contributed to the dialogue on the relationship between Marxist thought and Christian faith in Latin America. In addition, he has written on the topic of ecumenism and the history of the church in that continent.

——
CCO

Berdyayev, Nikolay (1874–1948). Russian existentialist philosopher noted for his opposition to modern secularism and materialism. He studied natural sciences and law, but his passion was philosophy. Several spiritual crises led him to question the privileges of the aristocracy into which he had been born. In 1894 he approached Marxism, but his spirit of independence did not permit him to submit to the discipline required by the party or to accept its doctrines. His commitment to the struggle of workers cost him two years of incarceration and three of exile. There he wrote *Subjectivism and Individualism in Social Philosophy*, in which he expresses his critique of Marxism.

It is ironic that his contact with Marxists led him to Christianity and to the Russian Orthodox Church. The essay *The Great Inquisitor* by ⇒Dostoyevsky converted him to Christianity. He had conflicts with the official church, but in spite of his critical attitude he respected the authority of the sacraments, which he understood were the essence of life.

When the Russian Marxists took power, he denounced the Bolsheviks and predicted that they would cause the destruction of all moral values. He expressed his criticism of the revolution in *The Philosophy of Inequality*.

In 1922 the Soviet state exiled him for life. He died in Paris, sitting at his desk, writing. His literary production makes him one of the most prestigious Christian thinkers of his time.

B. defined himself as a philosopher of religion and not as a theologian. Following ⇒Kant, he makes a distinction between the world of objects, ruled by natural laws, and the world of the spirit, founded on freedom. The human being distinguishes itself by being a member of both worlds, but the spiritual is fundamental. It is in the spiritual sphere that life gains meaning. The determination of the meaning of life is a subjective, not an objective, task. In its denial of God and the spiritual sphere, materialist philosophy violates human dignity and personality. This violation of human dignity distorts creation and the purposes of God and is the root of sin, evil, and injustice.

Human personality is the supreme value within creation. But personality is not a given. We become persons to the extent that our spiritual reality conquers our natural reality. This purpose has been revealed to us in the life of Jesus Christ, the God-human. Jesus reveals to us that humans can become transformed from mere natural beings into divine-human beings. This deification or *theosis* is the unity of the spiritual and the material, in which the spiritual dominates. The meaning and goal of history is this transformation of the human being.

Only an authentic Christianity gives us the hope of being able to create a good and just society. This is the kingdom of God, concretely realized in the hearts of those who submit their lives to God. The kingdom will be fulfilled in its totality at the end of time. For now, we have to fight for a better world. Social justice is not attained by changing social structures, but rather through spiritual changes. Both capitalism and communism are destined to fail because of their emphasis on the economic life and their lack of vision in the spiritual dimension that mobilizes the human will.

The status of a complete personality is equivalent to salvation. Salvation depends on the grace of God and on our will to accept it. The mission of the church consists in bringing humans to God, whose grace and love give us the opportunity to re-create our being.

For B., human reason cannot exhaust and systematize the experience of God. Although God is revealed in history and nature, it is only the revelation in Christ that fully shows us the divine nature and will. We know God in the subjective sphere. God, who is not object, can only be known in a subjective, intuitive, mystical, or experiential way.

—
IG

Berengar of Tours (ca. 1000–ca. 1088).

Central character in a great eucharistic controversy that frequently receives his name. B. was a disciple of ⇒Fulbert of Chartres, although the latter eventually repudiated him. After the death of Fulbert, B. established himself in the monastery of St. Martin of Tours, where he became famous for his learning, and where many went to study with him.

B. claimed he based his eucharistic teaching on the writings of John Scotus ⇒Erigena, and soon attracted the opposition of ⇒Lanfranc, who held to the teachings, at that time traditional, of ⇒Paschasius Radbertus. Condemned repeatedly by councils and other authorities, B. retracted more than once and then returned to his earlier teachings, or at least to something very similar.

The exact nature of the eucharistic teaching of B. is still being discussed. He certainly refused to affirm that the eucharistic bread becomes the body of Christ—what was later called transubstantiation. According to B., the heavenly body of Jesus is incorruptible and indivisible, and therefore cannot be present physically and materially in the eucharistic bread, which exists at the same time on a multitude of altars that are distant from one another. This probably does not mean that Jesus Christ is not present in Communion, but simply that his presence is spiritual rather than material or physical.

—
JLG

Bergson, Henri (1859–1941).

Vitalist philosopher who affirms that nature is always in the process of overcoming everything that wants to immobilize it, and that it reveals a process of continuous development full of spontaneity, novelty, and creativity. Our intuition, not our reason, permits us to capture the vital character of nature. The intellect perceives the world from an external and practical perspective. Intuition and instinct, on the other hand, take on an internal perspective that shares the vital impulse of the world.

For B., God is incessant life, creative action, and freedom. Morality and religion manifest themselves in one of two opposite ways: in a static or in a dynamic way. Static morality is closed and therefore unauthentic. It is determined by traditions, habits, and customs regulated by our social roles and social pressure. Dynamic morality is one of aspirations in which the moral agent spontaneously seeks to fulfill the ideal. This morality remains open and dynamic in that it goes beyond what social functions and roles and moral conventions require. It is a heroic morality, the morality of the saints. These are creative agents that are nurtured by the vital impulse of life. Intimate contact with the principle of life is what permits them to obtain creative energy and to go beyond what is required. In the history of morality, every creative impulse is petrified into rules and social expectations and needs to find the source of life that breaks through the ruling moral structures and opens up to new possibilities of attaining the good.

Closed morality belongs to a particular society, while open morality is concerned with all of humanity. Only religion can close the gap between what belongs to a particular group and what belongs to all of humanity.

There are also two types of religion: closed religion and dynamic religion. Closed religion is that of the dominant groups, replete with myths and rituals, but whose function is to domesticate every vital impulse of other groups seeking to change the social order. Open and dynamic religion breaks through or relativizes myths and rituals, centering on the vital impulse of creation's absolute energy, that is, the impulse of life and love which is God. This religiosity is not rational and academic but intuitive and mutually binding and culminates in the union of the soul with God.

—

IG

Berkhof, Louis (1873–1957). U.S. theologian of the Reformed or Calvinist tradition. He was born in Holland but emigrated to the United States in 1888 at the age of fifteen. He studied theology at Calvin Seminary, where he then taught for thirty years, coming to serve as president of the seminary. His Calvinist theology influenced many generations of pastors of the Reformed Christian Church. His main book, *Systematic Theology* (1941), originally titled, more appropriately, *Reformed Dogmatics*, served as the chief textbook for the pastors of his denomination.

—

LGP

Berkouwer, Gerrit Cornelis (1903–96). Neo-Calvinist theologian whose theology revolves around the correlation between faith and revelation. He was born in Amsterdam in a home of the Reformed confession. In 1940 he was hired as a professor at his alma mater, the Free University of Amsterdam, and five years later he obtained the chair of dogmatics that Abraham ⇒Kuyper had occupied.

B. was a prolific author. Chief among his works are *Studies in Dogmatics* (1952–83), which in the English translation fills fourteen volumes; *Karl Barth* (⇒Barth's comment on this book was that "it has a pretty cover"); and *The Triumph of Grace in the Theology of Karl Barth* (1954), in which he developed his critical dialogue with his interlocutor in Basel. It is clear that B. never accepted the Barthian distinction between Scripture and the Word of God.

He was an official observer during the Second Vatican Council (⇒Vatican II). Nevertheless, after the celebration of such a great event, his position on authority was not modified, and he continued to criticize Rome for giving too much weight to tradition, to the slighting of Scripture.

—

EPA

Bernard of Chartres (ca. 1070–1130). Leader of the renowned school of Chartres and one of the principal representatives of western Platonism in the twelfth century. Among his works are *On the Interpretation of Porphyry* and a comparative study of ⇒Plato and ⇒Aristotle. In his zeal to demonstrate the existence of universals beyond the objects that designate them ("realism"), he established a clear distinction between "the world of ideas" and the "world of matter." Reality included three immutable elements: God, ideas, and matter. God is eternal. Ideas are coeternal with God, but only in a derivative sense. Matter is the form in which such ideas exist in the world and serve as "engendered form" or "copy" of God.

—

AEM

Bernard of Clairvaux (1090–1153). Monastic reformer and theologian born in Fontaines, near Dijon, France, of a noble family. In spite of his youth, B. persuaded his five brothers and his sister to live in isolation and under a strict regimen in their father's house. In 1113, B., his brothers, and other sympathizers (a total of thirty) moved to Citeaux, where they were admitted to the Cistercian monastery. In 1114, because of his dedication and piety, B. was selected to initiate and found a new monastic house in Clairvaux. He soon became the abbot of the monastery and the central character of the recently created order.

The fame and talent of B. extended to other places and churches, so much so that in 1128 he won the recognition of the Order of the Knights Templar during the Synod of Troy. His power and influence were evident when he took part in the controversy surrounding the election of Innocent II. B. defended the cause of Innocent II, who was finally confirmed as pope. In gratitude for this support, Innocent II granted special privileges both to B. and to the Order of the Cistercians.

B. incessantly attacked ⇒Abelard for his teaching on the Trinity and for his use of dialectics, and eventually had Abelard condemned at the Council of Sens (1141). In addition, his work and actions were essential in the condemnation of the doctrines of Arnold of Brescia and ⇒Henry of Lausanne.

He likewise took part in another important controversy, this one concerning the immaculate conception of the Virgin Mary. The controversy began when several churches in France began a festival to celebrate the immaculate conception of Mary. The Church of Lyon was the first to begin this celebration, which soon extended to other churches and nearby places. B. was one of the first to respond to this celebration, severely criticizing it. He argued against the immaculate conception of Mary, alleging that such an honor belongs only to Christ. Some churches adopted the tradition begun by the church of Lyon, while others adopted the position of B. This controversy continued for centuries, until ⇒Pius IX in 1854 promulgated the dogma of the immaculate conception of Mary.

B. was also the organizer and preacher of the Second Crusade, during the years 1146–47, which ended in a painful defeat in Damascus. This defeat was the source of great discouragement for him.

B. of Clairvaux was a sincere man and a devoted defender of the church as an institution, so much so that Martin ⇒Luther said of him, "If there is someone among the monks who has been pious and God-fearing, his name has to be Saint B. of Clairvaux, whom I greatly esteem, more than any other monk in the world." It is also important to note that his *Meditations* are read and admired even among Protestants.

When B. died on August 23, 1153, the Cistercian order had grown to a total of 160 monasteries. For his work as a theologian and defender of the faith, he was canonized in 1174 by Alexander III, and proclaimed a ⇒doctor of the church in 1830. The Roman Catholic Church celebrates his work and his memory on August 20.

—

HMT

Bernard of Constance (?–ca. 1088).

Writer and professor born in Saxony. His numerous letters to students reveal his theological thought, especially those sent to Bernold of St. Blas. B. was learned in the classical and canonical literature, an attribute that he used to defend the cause of ⇒Gregory VII in his many conflicts with the empire. With that objective in mind, he wrote the *Report of Saxony* in 1085. He also wrote the *Liber canonum* and *On Schismatic Donations*, and compiled the complete collection of the letters of Gregory VII. His convictions led him to retire to monastic life, where he spent his last years under the name of Bernard of Saxony.

—

GC

Bernard Silvester (?–ca. 1167).

Philosopher, poet, and humanist. Also known as Bernard of Tours, presumably the city of his birth. B. sought to correlate biblical thought with Greek mythology in order to obtain, through the use of Greek ideas, a more rational comprehension of biblical cosmology. In his works, that search for philosophical integration manifests itself, above all, in his cosmography *De mundi universitate*, in which he deals extensively with the theme of creation. He also wrote commentaries on the *Aeneid* of Virgil and a work called *Experimentarius*. B. opened the doors to a new methodology for the study of biblical literature that would have its golden age in the Renaissance.

—

GC

Bertold of Rumania (1210–72).

Monk and great preacher also known as Bertold of Ratisbon. Born in Regensburg, Germany, he traveled and preached throughout most of Europe and became particularly famous in Slovakia, Hungary, and Rumania. Even though he was never outlawed by the Catholic hierarchy as a heretic, some heterodox groups sympathized with his ideas because of his ardent preaching against indulgences and his iconoclastic theology.

—

GC

Bessarion, John (1403–72).

Scholar and Roman Catholic theologian born in Greece and educated in Constantinople. He was archbishop of Nicaea and was a key participant in the Council of ⇒Ferrara-Florence (1431), the purpose of which was to unite the Western church with that of the East. Of Greek background, but converted to Roman Catholicism and successively occupying several bishoprics in the Near East, B. fought for the unity of the church. This made him unpopular in Constantinople, and for this he spent his last years in Italy. He wrote a treatise *Against the Slanderers of Plato*, in which he defended the teachings of Plato over against the Aristotelians. In addition, he devoted a great part of his life to the collection of manuscripts in Greek, which today form part of the library of the Cathedral of St. Mark in Venice.

—

CCO

Betto (1944–).

Brazilian Dominican author, known by his religious title, Fray Betto, although his name is Alberto Libanio Christo. Leader of the opposition against the military regimes that ruled in Brazil from 1969 to 1985, and subsequently organizer of base communities and popular education programs. Author of more than thirteen books, he is chiefly known for his lectures and the book *Fidel and Religion*, which provided a novel perspective on the relationship between Cuban Marxism, the Christian religion, and liberation theology, from the middle of the 1970s through the next decade.

———
CCO

Bevans, Stephen (1944–). Missiologist and missionary of the Order of the Divine Word. Author of several books and editor of projects in the field of missiology. His book *Models of Contextual Theology* has contributed significantly to the discussion on the relationship between the gospel and culture, and the different ways in which some theologians treat that relationship.

———
CCO

Beyerhaus, Peter (1929–). German evangelical missiologist who was an ardent participant in the controversies on mission and evangelization in the ⇒World Council of Churches during the 1970s and 1980s. He is author of *Missions—Which Way?* and *Shaken Foundations* and coauthor of the *Frankfurt Declaration on the Fundamental Crisis in Christian Mission*.

———
CCO

Beza, Theodore (1519–1605). Humanist, poet, theologian, biblical scholar, and successor of ⇒Calvin in his functions as reformer of Geneva. He was born in Vezelay, Burgundy, of a family that belonged to the minor nobility of France. He left his native town in 1534 to study law in Orléans and Bourges, under the sponsorship of his uncle Nicholas, who functioned as counselor of the Parliament in Paris. B.'s family wanted him to take religious vows, but he secretly married Claudine Denosse in Paris, where he practiced law beginning in 1539. His education under the great humanist Melchor Wolmar, from whom he learned Latin and Greek, helped him to become acquainted with poetics and the reformist ideas. His studies with Wolmar continued until his father, Pierre B., asked him to return to Orléans to complete his law studies—which did not prevent him from pursuing classical literature.

In 1548 in Paris, B. published a book of poems, *Poemata juvenilia*, the fruit of his humanist passion. That year he became gravely ill and, finding himself at the edge of death, he again asked himself the most basic existential questions, in the end becoming a Protestant. He fled to Geneva, where he publicly married Claudine. His departure for Paris in pursuit of the Reformers was the reason for the symbolic burning of his body in Mambert in 1550. He presented himself to Pierre ⇒Viret, the great Reformed biblical scholar in Lausanne, who employed him as professor of Greek and then as professor of theology at the local academy, of which he was later rector.

B. was called by Calvin in 1557 to be rector of the new Academy of Geneva, a position he held until the death of Calvin in 1564. He performed pastoral duties (1559–1605) and presided over the council of pastors from 1564 until 1580. B. participated in several colloquies, among them those of Poissy (1561) and St. Germain (1562). He presided over the Synod of La Rochelle (1571) and was present at the colloquy of Nantes (1572). Although he failed in his attempt to reconcile Catholics and Protestants in Poissy, he did achieve, jointly with ⇒Bullinger, the reconciliation of those who followed Calvin with ⇒Zwingli's followers, in the Second Helvetic Confession (1566), which became the authorized confession for the Reformed churches of France and Switzerland.

B. was very influential in sixteenth-century Geneva. His relationship with Henry IV of France gave him authority beyond Geneva's borders. He also functioned as counselor of Gaspar II de Coligny and of the Huguenot movement in France. He traveled to Lutheran Germany and Sweden to secure support for the Huguenots in the religious war in France.

His writings are many. He finished the translation of the Psalms into French that was begun by Clement Marot, which was later published. He wrote a short apology in favor of Calvin in the case of the execution of the anti-Trinitarian theologian Michael ⇒Servetus under the title *Regarding the Heretics Who Ought to Be Punished by the Magistrate* (1554). In 1556 he published an edition of the New Testament in Greek, to which he added the Vulgate and his own French translation. In 1572, in reaction to the massacre of St. Bartholomew's Day, he published a short but important text on the history of political literature, *De iure magistrate*, which advocates the right to regicide for religious reasons. In 1580 he published the second edition of his Greek New Testament, which, together with his work on textual criticism, would influence the English version of 1611, known as the King James Version. He also published a manual for the study of Greek and French.

B. spent a great part of his last years refining Calvinist doctrine on themes such as the Eucharist and double predestination, and struggling against heresy. Among those he influenced were William Perkins, Lambert Daneau, and the very controversial ⇒Arminius. His works, which were translated into several languages, made him influential in the entire area in which the Reformation took root.

———

GC

Biel, Gabriel (1420–95).

German philosopher and theologian. He was born in Speyer and was educated in Heidelberg and Erfurt. B. is regarded as an important German scholastic theologian and one of the outstanding nominalists of the late Middle Ages. B. knew how to integrate the nominalism of ⇒Ockham with the theology of ⇒Thomas Aquinas, ⇒Bonaventure, and Duns ⇒Scotus.

B. was a cofounder of the University of Tübingen, where he taught theology from 1484 and later became rector. Outside of the academy, B. became known as an excellent preacher, and in his last years he joined the Brothers of the Common Life. His writings exerted great influence on the theology of Martin ⇒Luther. Among his best-known works are *The Epitome*, in which he developed his nominalist ideas following those of Ockham; *Conference and Exposition of the Canon of the Mass*, in which he gave form to his sacramental theology; and finally his *Sermons*.

———

GC

Biko, Stephan Bantu (1946–77).

Born in Kingwilliamstown, South Africa. Studied at the Catholic missionary school in Mariannhill before entering the University of Natal to study medicine. Because of his opposition to apartheid, he was expelled from his country in 1973. After returning, he was arrested and killed at the hands of the authorities, without having been taken to trial. His writings, the majority of which were brief and secretly published, were an inspiration for the theological and liberationist labors of ⇒Boesak, ⇒Tutu, and others.

———

CCO

Bisschop, Simon (1583–1643).

Also known by the names Bischop, Biscop, and Episcopius. One of the chief promoters of the thought of ⇒Arminius. He was professor at the University of Leiden, from which he was later expelled. Together with other religious leaders, he was excommunicated in 1619 by the Synod of ⇒Dort. In 1621, at the petition of the Arminian leadership of Holland, he drew up a confession of faith in twenty-five chapters, which was circulated widely and was subscribed to by the most eminent leaders of Holland and France. His works also include studies of liturgy.

———

JDR

Blanco White, José María (1775–1841).

Priest and journalist converted to Anglicanism. Born in Spain, B.W. graduated from the University of Seville and was ordained into the ministry, but his liberal ideas compelled him to leave Catholicism. In 1810 he arrived in England, where he worked as a journalist and was supported by the English government, which was interested in promoting the revolt against Spain in its American colonies. He was converted to Anglicanism, and from London, through his journal, *The Spaniard*, he promoted republican agendas, forcefully attacking the complicity of Catholicism and the monarchy in their colonial policies. The Catholic Church censured his writings, believing them to be seditious, fanatical, and markedly anticlerical.

———

GC

Blandrata, George (1515–90).

Italian physician who for some time lived in Geneva, and who there clashed with ⇒Calvin because he opposed Trinitarian doctrine. One of his disciples declared that to worship a triune God was equivalent to worshiping "three demons." In 1558 Calvin convened a consultation on the Trinity that produced a confession of Trinitarian faith. Refusing to sign it, B. took refuge in Poland, where for some time he enjoyed the welcome of the country's Protestants. When in 1562 he openly declared that the Trinity was "the foundation of all heresies," Polish Protestantism was divided between orthodox Calvinists and B.'s followers. In the end the orthodox prevailed, and B. was compelled to leave for Transylvania, where he was murdered by a nephew.

———

JLG

Blaurock, Georg (1492–1529). Leader of the Anabaptist movement in Zurich during the sixteenth century. He was one of the first Anabaptists to reject his own baptism as an infant and to require adult baptism. He was an eloquent preacher with a great popular following. Persecuted for his religious opinions, he was incarcerated, cruelly tortured, and on September 6, 1529, sentenced to die at the stake in the city of Clausen. Among the reasons given for his condemnation were sedition, his conflict with the clergy and the Catholic Church, and his repudiation of the Mass, of confession, and of the veneration of the Virgin Mary.

In the history of the Anabaptist movement, he is remembered for his efforts in support of the freedom of religion and the equality of every citizen before the law. He is also remembered as the author of several hymns.

—
JDR

Blondel, Maurice (1861–1949). Roman Catholic lay philosopher who is associated with modernism. Like ⇒Bergson, he viewed reality in dynamic terms, but he rejected the vitalism and naturalism of Bergson. The center of his philosophy is not life but action. Human nature consists of being a practical agent. Action is the key to understanding ourselves, the world, and God.

It is our actions which lead us to philosophical thought, for they raise the question of their meaning. The only thing that we can never avoid is acting. Life is given in the dialectic between thinking, which is a form of acting, and the concrete carrying out of our actions. That gap contains the most profound dissatisfactions of our lives, while it also gives us the incentive to continue acting in search of our fulfillment. Here B. sees a process of humanization that begins with those actions which seek one's own well-being and benefit, continues with actions that seek the well-being of others, and culminates in actions that include the well-being of all of humanity. The human being, in its search for God, is moved by the demands of the action itself from what is natural to what is supernatural. The positive affirmation of God is not a theoretical postulate but a practical attitude vis-à-vis the challenges of life. The natural and the supernatural exist in continuity and discontinuity. We should discern the nature and purpose of God in our actions. Only as active agents do we find God. Action is the genuine form of thinking about God.

—
IG

Blumhardt, Johann Christoph (1805–80). Evangelist and Lutheran pastor in Germany. Studied in Tübingen. Served as pastor at the Institute of Missions in Basel (1830–38) and in Göttingen (1838–52). In that very rationalist era, he had experiences of healing by faith and maintained a profound spirituality, with the result that he had great influence on the spiritual pilgrimage of others. In 1852 he established himself in Bad Boll, which became a center of faith healing.

—
AP

Boehme, Jacob (1575–1624). German mystic, born in Silesia, a shoemaker by profession and possessed of a natural intelligence, although without formal academic education. B. combined a profound mystical passion with study and reflection. His restless spirit and inquisitive mind took the form of penetrating writings in which he tried to express and share his experiences, telling about his visions and his drawing near to God.

During his own life, these works were considered confused and disturbing documents, in style as well as in content. They created uneasiness among theologians and common believers of his time, mostly because B., imbued with the spirit of those times, tried to be a free person, challenging the traditional dogmas, the fixed liturgies, and the devotional routines of his own Lutheran tradition.

His radical spirit led him to an extreme spiritualism, calling attention to a fundamental fact: Christian life ought to combine personal enthusiasm with community life, in a shared and lived faith. This is the *theologia cordis*—theology of the heart—that attempts to unite heart and mind in an authentic piety.

His ideas about God, the world, and human nature, and his own visions, induced him to write as a kind of amanuensis of God. He preferred to write as a great visionary rather than to preach, feeling like a standard-bearer of a new revelation.

His *Brilliant Dawn*, as well as his teachings and later writings, did not win many followers at first, but in later decades his influence and effect expanded and increased, influencing that modern spirituality which seeks to be a polemical and challenging movement of renovation for the Christian churches. To some extent B. was a forerunner of movements such as the Quakers and Pentecostals, although with different emphases and content.

During the twentieth century the study of the works of B. became popular, and today many movements of spirituality point to his heritage and influence. The concern to translate the Christian faith into a real appropriation or experience of faith continues to be valid, although it is always in need of reflection and study, which are essential ingredients for an integral and solid Christian life. We owe to B.'s pen and inspiration a heritage which, beyond its excesses and deviations, calls attention to a piety that is felt and not feigned.

———

CEA

Boesak, Allan (1945–).

Minister of the Dutch Reformed Church in South Africa, the country where he was born and where he experienced the multiple humiliations and degradations that the regime of apartheid imposed on its black citizens. His father died when he was six years old, and his mother worked as a seamstress to support the family. It was she who educated him in the Christian faith. The B. family has a history of struggle and resistance. He expresses pride in the fact that the first B. led a slave rebellion in South Africa.

He studied at the University of Western Cape and in the theological school of Belville. He then studied in the United States at Union Theological Seminary and at Colgate Rochester Seminary in New York. At Union he studied the thought of Martin Luther ⇒King Jr., who strengthened his pride in being black and his commitment to the nonviolent method of social change. In 1976 he became a doctor of theology at the Theological Academy of Kampen in Holland. While in Holland, he wrote a series of essays comparing the thought of King and Malcolm X. In 1982 he was elected president of the World Alliance of Reformed Churches.

From his point of view, the Reformed tradition distinguishes itself by its commitment to the poor. The dominant Reformed theology of the Afrikaners is a distortion of this tradition. For B., the struggle against apartheid is a struggle against a diabolic and pseudoreligious ideology born within the Reformed tradition itself. Beginning with the massacres of Soweto, B. became one of the chief voices of theological protest against apartheid.

In spite of his radical criticism of the white regime, B. always conceived of the possibility of reconciliation between the black and white populations. His political theology is distinguished by his notion of reconciliation, which is not possible between oppressor and oppressed, but certainly is between human beings who, in spite of their past, recognize and respect one another as human beings. B. understands that racial oppression is not the only problem that humiliates blacks in South Africa. The capitalist development that promotes economic and social inequality also has to change.

His most important books are *Farewell to Innocence* (1977), *Black and Reformed* (1984), and *If This Is Treason, I Am Guilty* (1987).

———

IG

Boethius (ca. 475–ca. 524).

Christian scholar who lived in Rome under the Ostrogothic regime. Of noble origin, he had the opportunity to study in the best centers of the time, including Athens. For some time the Gothic king Theodoric was his friend and admirer, granting him honors and duties. But the growing tension between the Ostrogoths and the Byzantines at last gave rise to suspicions of treason or at least of disloyalty against B. Since B. professed the orthodox faith promulgated at Nicaea, just as the emperors of Byzantium did, while Theodoric was Arian, these suspicions were blended with theological differences. In the end B. was incarcerated, tortured, and killed by order of Theodoric.

Among the works of B. are five *Theological Opuscles*, whose purpose is to expound Christian doctrines in philosophical terms. The first three treat of diverse aspects of the Trinitarian doctrine, which was precisely the point of conflict with the Arians. The fourth deals with a great variety of themes. The fifth centers its attention on the christological dogma and seeks to refute both the Nestorians and the Monophysites. He also wrote several philosophical essays, as well as translations and commentaries on classical philosophy, and two scientific essays: one on music and the other on arithmetic.

But his most famous work is *The Consolation of Philosophy*, written in prison. It is a literary jewel, the most read work of all those written in Ostrogothic Italy. In it the author, in the midst of his incarceration and torture, seeks consolation in ancient philosophy, above all in Neoplatonism and Stoicism. What is surprising is that in this entire essay, written in such difficult circumstances, the name of Jesus is not even mentioned. This has led many scholars to think that B. was not a Christian. Certainly the book itself could have been written by any cultivated and refined pagan. Thus apparently B., although of Christian profession, and although capable of writing about topics like the Trinity, found the meaning of life and consolation in his misfortunes not so much in his Christian faith as in pagan philosophy.

———

JLG

Boff, Clodovis (1944–). Catholic liberation theologian born in Brazil. A priest of the Order of the Servants of Mary, university professor of theology, and adviser to the Conference of the Religious of Brazil. His priesthood, teaching, and theology have been shaped by his experience and work among the poor. He has contributed to the development of the methodology of liberation theology, and to the theology and practice of the ecclesial base communities (*comunidades eclesiales de base*). Among his chief works are *Theology and Praxis: Theology of the Political and Its Mediations, Option for the Poor*, and *Liberty and Liberation*.

———

LRR

Boff, Leonardo (1938–). Brazilian Catholic liberation theologian. Ordained as a Franciscan priest in 1964, he completed his doctorate in theology in Germany under the guidance of K. ⇒Rahner and has had an outstanding career as professor of systematic theology, editor of theological journals, theological adviser of bishops and religious orders in Latin America, consultant and theologian of base communities, activist in human rights, and international lecturer. His theological work is prolific and is characterized by the reinterpretation of the Christian faith from a liberationist perspective, especially the doctrines of the Trinity, Jesus Christ, grace, salvation, the church and its mission, the sacraments, Mariology, Saint Francis, eschatology, evangelization, and themes of spirituality and ecology. His fame in Latin America began with his book *Jesus Christ the Liberator* (1971). His worldwide recognition increased with the gag order imposed by the Vatican in 1985 because of his book *Church: Charisma and Power*. He resigned from the priesthood in 1993 under the threat of another silencing by the Vatican. Eventually he married, and obtained the professorship of philosophy, ethics, and ecology at the University of the State of Rio de Janeiro.

Beginning in the 1990s, B. has been rearticulating his theology from an ecological-liberationist paradigm. He attempts to connect in theory and practice listening to the outcry of the exploited and poor and listening to the outcry of the other great poor entity, the earth, an assaulted planet that suffers from oppressive productive practices. The condition of exploitation and oppression of the poor and of the earth is due to modern anthropocentric culture and also to the capitalist and industrialist economy. It is necessary to construct a praxis, a theology, an ethic, a spirituality, and a new planetary culture that will lead to a civil and cosmic democracy, to a new alliance between human beings and the earth.

Ecological integrity, social and economic justice, and democratic governments and cultures committed to peace are inseparable values and goals in the latest works of B. Among these are *Ecology, Globalization, Spirituality; New Era: The Planetary Civilization; Ecology: The Cry of the Earth, The Cry of the Poor*; and *The Eagle and the Hen: A Metaphor of the Human Condition*.

———

LRR

Boisen, Anton (1876–1965). Considered to be the founder of clinical pastoral education (CPE), used by hospital chaplains. B. was the person of greatest influence in the development of pastoral theology and psychology of religion in the United States. His most important contributions in the field of chaplaincy and pastoral theology are (1) to take theological education out of the seminaries and transfer it to the hospital, thus making experience with psychiatric patients the primary laboratory for doing pastoral theology; (2) to understand the person as a "living human text," who requires a pastoral hermeneutic similar to the one used when examining any text; and (3) to criticize the theory of Sigmund ⇒Freud for its lack of depth, and the method of Carl ⇒Rogers for the distancing that made it difficult for students to cultivate their pastoral identity and their ability to think theologically about the experience of suffering and the mental health of their patients. His students Seward ⇒Hiltner, Carroll ⇒Wise, and Charles ⇒Gerkin refined his thought. Among the most important works of B. are *Exploration of the Inner World* (1936) and his autobiography, *Out of the Depths* (1960).

—

JR

Bolsec, Hieronimus Hermes (ca. 1522–84). Physician and lay theologian born in Paris, who possibly died in Lyon. He belonged to the Order of the Carmelites until he was expelled from Paris in 1545 because of the content of his sermons. He took refuge in Ferrara and then in Switzerland. He was also expelled from there because he publicly rejected ⇒Calvin's double predestination. B. could not visualize predestination from a perspective of eternity, that is, as a result of a logical speculation of cause and effect without any relation to history. Since sin is a historical human fact and not an eternal decree, God relates to the sinner in a historical way through God's grace, which is manifested in a universal way in Jesus Christ. For B., faith does not depend on an election before creation, but rather the election takes place in the act of faith that appropriates the grace of God in Christ.

———

ALG

Bonaventure (1221–74). Main theologian of the first Franciscan generation, also known as the Seraphic Doctor. He studied at the University of Paris under ⇒Alexander of Hales, the first Franciscan professor of that university—since Alexander was already a professor when he decided to become Franciscan. The university closed its doors to both Dominicans and Franciscans, and B. fought together with ⇒Thomas Aquinas in defense of the mendicant orders. It was in that context that he wrote his "debated questions" *On the Poverty of Christ.* In 1257, together with Thomas, he was finally recognized as a "doctor" of the university, with the right to teach in it.

In that same year he was elected general minister of the order, at a time when it experienced severe difficulties due to the struggles between the strict Franciscans, who insisted on absolute poverty, and the more moderate ones. What was debated was whether the primitive *Rule* of ⇒Francis of Assisi and his *Testament* were binding for the Franciscans, or whether they should adhere to the more moderate practices authorized by the pope. B. took the second of these paths and strongly opposed the more extreme Franciscans, whose leader he incarcerated. His work in this sense was of such significance that it has been said that he was the "second founder" of the order.

In June of 1273 he was made a cardinal. The following year, by order of Gregory X, he traveled to Lyon, where a council that sought unity with the Greek church was meeting. B. witnessed the success—although ephemeral—of that council eight days before he died. In 1588 Pope Sixtus V declared him to be a ⇒doctor of the church.

As was the custom at the University of Paris, B. wrote several biblical commentaries as well as a commentary to the *Sentences* of ⇒Peter Lombard and several series of "debated matters"—*Quaestiones disputatae*—on topics such as the knowledge of Christ and evangelical poverty. (These latter were directed against ⇒William of Saint Amour, who rejected the Franciscan ideal of poverty and accused as heretics those who said that this ideal was found in the Gospels.) He also wrote a brief systematic theology under the title *Breviloquium,* a series of lectures on the six days of creation, a brief essay on *How the Arts Are Reduced to Theology,* and a multitude of sermons and briefer tracts. His two most widely read works are *Itinerary of the Mind towards God* and *Meditations on the Life of Christ.* (Although at times the *Meditations* have been attributed to other authors, for the most part they appear to be genuine.) The *Itinerary* was written as a guide for the soul that seeks to contemplate God. In it all of reality is ordered as a hierarchy or ladder, in such a way that upon contemplating each rung, and then transcending it, the soul comes closer to the pure contemplation of God. This is a mysticism in which the influence of ⇒Dionysius the Areopagite and of the entire mystical tradition of Neoplatonic inspiration can be seen. The *Meditations,* in contrast, center on the life of Jesus, and particularly on his sufferings. In them the influence of ⇒Bernard of Clairvaux can be seen.

B. lived in a period when the philosophy of Aristotle, for the most part unknown in western Europe until that time, made its entrance into the University of Paris and gave rise to strong controversies. Although B. accepted some points of Aristotelianism, his philosophy always continued to have a Platonic flavor, in contrast to Thomas Aquinas, who attempted to produce a new synthesis between Aristotelian philosophy and Christian theology. For this reason he insisted, as ⇒Anselm had done before, that the existence of God is eminently rational, so rational that it does not need to be proved, since the nonexistence of God is an absurd contradiction. Following the Platonic tradition, B. thought that the ideas in the mind of God are the "models" of which the present realities are a copy, shadow, or trace. For this reason the "itinerary" toward the contemplation of God leads us from the contemplation of shadows or traces in creatures to the contemplation of models or ideas in the mind of God.

Such knowledge—any true knowledge—is not attained without illumination from the Word of God, the light that illumines every human being. For this reason, B. argues that all the "arts," that is, all knowledge, have their foundation and culmination in theology, in the knowledge of God. In all of this B. is a faithful exponent of the Augustinian tradition and its lack of trust in the senses as the source of knowledge.

———

JLG

Bonhoeffer, Dietrich (1906–45).

German theologian killed by the Nazis. He imbibed the thought of some of the most distinguished European theologians: ⇒Troeltsch, ⇒Harnack, and ⇒Barth. He also became a friend of Reinhold ⇒Niebuhr when he visited Union Theological Seminary in New York. His theological education was shaped in conjunction with his pastoral practice and his commitment to the international Christian community. When the official German church declared itself in favor of German Nazism, he struggled so that the international church would recognize the Confessing Church as the only legitimate one in Germany. In 1944 the Nazis discovered his participation in a conspiracy to assassinate Hitler. He was detained in the high-security prison of Flossenberg, and in April of 1945, only a few days before the Allied forces liberated the prison, he was hanged.

The dramatic element in the life and death of B. explains the influence of his book *The Cost of Discipleship*. But what makes it truly important is the originality of his biblical and theological interpretation. This work criticizes the notion of "cheap grace," which distorts the doctrine of salvation through faith. The alternative is "costly grace," which is an intrinsic part of all genuine discipleship. Discipleship is costly because it can cost us our life, and it is grace because it gives us the only true life.

B. redefines the traditional Protestant interpretation of the relationship between faith and works. The tradition says that only those who have faith are obedient, and that only works performed in faith are truly good. Nevertheless, B. insists that only those who obey have faith, and that only the faith that is expressed in works is true. Discipleship is defined in terms of the combination of faith and obedience. The ethics of the Sermon on the Mount describes the life of the disciple, which implies the death of one style of life and the beginning of another. Baptism is the symbol of this new life and makes us members of that alternative community which is the church. It is in the church that we become disciples. B. establishes a very intimate relation between the church and the presence of Christ. "The Church is the presence of Christ in the same way that Christ is the presence of God." It is in the church that the deeds of God take concretion, continuity, and historical unity, and where the human being develops its character as moral and religious agent.

His last book, *Ethics*, which he could not complete, gives witness to how a Christian confronts and responds to the moral bankruptcy of the Western world. *Ethics* concerns itself with the formation of the human being. For Christians this means imitating and following Christ. Being like Christ implies acquiring the freedom that allows us to be faithful to our human condition. While we humans vainly make an effort to be more than human, God, by becoming human, affirms our humanity.

Ethical life is a combination of simplicity and wisdom. To follow and to be like the Crucified One means submitting to the will of God and liberating ourselves from the criteria of success as the world defines it. Simplicity is to live in the light of the will of God. Wisdom means having a profound and intimate knowledge of the world. Both are possible because in Christ God has become incarnate and is reconciled with the world. Our experience of God takes place in history, in the world. The ethics of Christ is an ethics of service and reconciliation. It is an ethics that goes beyond the formulation of laws, duties, and prohibitions. It is a positive ethics of liberty. Besides being positive, it is a concrete and situational ethics (⇒Fletcher). B. insists that the will of God does not adjust to rules and principles.

Although the ethics of B. is contextual, it is not intuitive. All our faculties, reason, feelings, discernment, observations, and experiences are placed at the service of discerning the will of God.

The commandments of God become concrete through the "divine mandates": marriage, work, culture, the state, and the church. The divine mandates, in contrast with the "orders of creation," are not conservative, nor do they justify a particular social order. Every social order is relative and provisional. Our duty is to transform our world when there is the possibility of increasing justice. Finally, B. uses the categories "ultimate" and "penultimate" to distinguish the divine from every human approximation. The purpose of these two terms is to avoid dualism or thinking in two spheres: the Christian and the non-Christian; the order of grace and the natural order. Everything that is has its beginning and unity in God. The ultimate reality of the grace of God does not in any way annul the penultimate values that we have to fulfill in our historical and social life. On the contrary, the ultimate values give validity to our moral struggles, while they at the same time reveal their historical and passing character. Our historical responsibility calls us to determine what is relatively better and to distinguish it from what is relatively worse. Not to make this distinction means that, with or without our intention, we hand over the historical, social, and political sphere to the forces of chaos.

Only Christians can affirm the secular world in its secularity. In Christ it has been revealed to Christians that the supernatural is incarnate in the natural, the divine in the profane, revelation in reason. The Christian recognizes that God accepts, affirms, and redeems the world in all its secularity and naturalness. Christians are called to be worldly. The secular world is an adult and mature world that includes the reality of God at every level. God exists in the center of life, and not at the margin. God is found in the fullness of life, and not only at the hour of death; in health, and not only in illness; in creativity, and not only in sin.

The church is an essential part of the Christian life, as B. demonstrates in his book *Life Together.* That church has to serve human beings in their world. It is called to promote human reconciliation and not to waste energy on its own preservation. Therefore we need to find a new language that, without being traditionally religious, is capable of communicating the biblical vision of a secular world. God makes Godself concretely present in the demands of others. Transcendence and religiosity, therefore, always have more of an ethical than an epistemological character. In all of this B. laid out a standard or norm for the secular theology of later decades.

—

IG

Boniface VIII (pope from 1294 to 1303).

Pope whose bull *Unam Sanctam* is a milestone in the pontifical declarations on the power of the papacy. According to B., there are two "swords" or powers, the temporal and the spiritual. The first belongs to the kings and lay lords, and the second to the church and in the final instance to the pope. The spiritual power is above the temporal power, so that if the latter goes astray, the former has the authority to correct it. But if the spiritual power errs, only God can correct it. In spite of such declarations, B. suffered humiliation at the hands of the agents of the king of France. Thus, while the papacy claimed greater power, in reality it was losing it.

—

JLG

Bonino, José Míguez ⇒Míguez Bonino, José

Booth, Catherine Mumford (1829–90).

Fervent Christian, feminist, preacher, and defender of temperance, B. shared with her husband, William ⇒Booth, a passionate commitment to social reform, especially with regard to women. Together they founded the Salvation Army when, in 1864–65, they created in London the Christian Mission of the East End, which included revival services in the open air.

—

EZ

Booth, William (1829–1912).

Local Methodist preacher, ambulant pastor, and open-air evangelist, B. founded the Salvation Army with his wife, Catherine Mumford ⇒Booth. From Methodism he acquired an emphasis on Christian perfection. Inspired by Catherine, he invited women to participate fully in the ministry.

—

EZ

Bornkamm, Günther (1905–90).

German New Testament scholar who taught in Königsberg, but was dismissed by the Nazis in 1936 because of his participation in the Confessing Church. Later he was professor at the University of Göttingen and then in Heidelberg. He was a student of ⇒Bultmann, although he differed from him regarding the possibility of knowing about the historical Jesus. He did pioneering work in redaction criticism (the study of the distinctive contributions of the authors of the Gospels), with particular reference to Matthew. His book *Jesus of Nazareth* (1956) was one of the outstanding contributions in the "new search for the historical Jesus." This work was followed by *Paul,* on the thought of the apostle. Both works popularized the results of critical studies of the Bible that were produced in Germany.

—

JDR

Borromeo, Charles (1538–84).

Cardinal-Archbishop of Milan. Nephew of Pius IV, for whom he directed the papal secretariat with political skill during the third period of the Council of ⇒Trent. An outstanding administrative promoter, B. was recognized as a model bishop of the Catholic Tridentine reform. He contributed to the legislation and implementation of the decisions of Trent in Rome and Milan. He emphasized the centrality and authority of the bishop as reformer, model, and preacher, and underlined the difference between clergy and laity. He implemented the new reformist emphases: episcopal visits, diocesan synods, provincial councils, the creation of seminaries, and the reform of religious houses. He championed ecclesiastical discipline, the spirituality of clergy and laity, and the autonomy of the diocese over against temporal authorities. He was canonized in 1610.

LRR

Bosch, David (1929–92). South African missiologist and a member of the Dutch Reformed Church. Bosch was a biblical theologian of the New Testament by formation and a missiologist by vocation. His most important work is *Transforming Mission* (1989), in which he shows that in reality a single theology of mission does not exist, but rather many, each one with the seal of the contexts and tendencies of its place and time. Each one of them is specifically related to a different theological paradigm.

CCO

Bossuet, Jacques Bénigne (1627–1704). Catholic bishop of Meaux, in France, possibly one of the greatest religious orators of all time. As a theologian, he distinguished himself by his writings against the Protestants and by his opposition to the mystical quietism of Madame de ⇒Guyon and François ⇒Fénelon, whose condemnation he obtained in 1699. Against the Protestants, he wrote an *Exposition of the Catholic Doctrine on the Debated Topics* (1671) and *History of the Divergences of the Protestant Churches* (two volumes, 1688).

His opposition to Protestantism led him to urge the king to revoke the Edict of Nantes (1685) and therefore to expel the Huguenots from France. On the other hand, he maintained an ample correspondence with the German Protestant ⇒Leibniz, in the hope of arriving at a reunification between Catholics and Protestants.

JLG

Boston, Thomas (1676–1732). Prolific theologian and Scottish pastor, expert in biblical languages, and principal figure in what was commonly called the Marrow controversy. B. and his adherents argued that, based on the doctrine of grace, it was not necessary to abandon sin before coming to Christ. To support their position, they republished the book *The Marrow of Modern Divinity*, published years before as a summary of Reformed theology.

The General Assembly of the Church of Scotland rejected their position, accusing them of antinomianism, while they accused the assembly of "neonomianism"—that is, of turning the gospel into a new law.

JLG

Bourdieu, Pierre (1930–2002). French sociologist, also an anthropologist and critic of globalization. He is known especially for his *Distinctions: A Social Critique of the Judgment of Taste* (1984). His sociological contribution is in the use of the term—taken from the moral psychology of the Middle Ages—"habitus," which refers to the system of dispositions and functions that create the principles of action and organization within a culture. The work of B. has helped theology not only to discover its contextual character but also to recognize the particularities of culture and class within groups in the same context. This requires the creation of a system of symbols for the theological task.

CCO

Bousset, Johann Franz Wilhelm (1865–1920). German theologian, expert in the New Testament and patristic literature, who together with Hermann ⇒Gunkel has been cataloged as one of the creators of the school of comparative religions or history of religions. B. is recognized for his investigations into and contribution to the contextual understanding of late Judaism and primitive Christianity (especially in regard to their literary and intellectual relationship with the Hellenistic religions of the period); for his investigations on theological themes that are central to the study of primitive Christianity (for example, the concepts of Christ and antichrist, Gnosticism); and for his contribution to methodological matters that are linked with the textual criticism of the New Testament. Among his best-known works are *Evangelienzitate Justins des Märtyrers*, (1891; Gospel Quotations of Justin Martyr), *Textkritische Studien* (1894; Text-Critical Studies), *Die Religion des Judentums im späthellenistischen Zeitalter* (1903, 1926, 1966; The Religion of Judaism in the Late Hellenistic Age), *Hauptprobleme der Gnosis* (1907, 1973; Chief Problems of Gnosticism), *Kyrios Christos* (1913), and *Apothegmata: Studien zur Geschichte des ältesten Mönchtums* (posthumous publication, 1923; Studies on the History of Ancient Monasticism).

AEM

Bowne, Borden Parker (1847–1910).
A lay theologian, philosopher and educator,
author of fifteen books, and founder of personalist idealism. His appointment in 1876 as professor of philosophy at Boston University
marks the beginning of the modern period of
Methodist theology in the United States.

————

EPA

Boyce, James Petigru (1827–88).
Theologian and Baptist educator who, in 1859,
was one of the founders of the Southern Baptist Seminary. As an adherent of Reformed theology, he envisioned a seminary for the training
of scholars, but open to anyone called to the
ministry, regardless of their previous educational experience.

————

AP

Boyd, Frank Matthews (1883–1984).
Educator, writer, pioneer in the birth of the
Assemblies of God. He was prepared as a missionary in Nyack, New York. He held that there
is a correspondence between the dispensations
according to ⇒Scofield and Pentecostal experience.

————

EPA

Braaten, Carl E. (1929–). North American Lutheran theologian. He taught systematic
theology at Luther Theological Seminary, St.
Paul, Minnesota (1958–61); Chicago Theological Seminary, Maywood (1961–62); and the
Lutheran School of Theology at Chicago
(1962–91).

Among his works are *History and
Hermeneutics* (1966), *The Future of God*
(1969), *Christ and Counter Christ* (1972), *The
Whole Counsel of God* (1974), *Eschatology
and Ethics* (1974), *Principles of Lutheran Theology* (1983), and *The Apostolic Imperative*
(1985). The textbook he coedited with Robert
⇒Jenson, *Christian Dogmatics* (1984), is generally used in seminaries and universities to
familiarize students with the history of the fundamental doctrines of the Christian faith.

————

JDR

**Bradwardine, Thomas (ca. 1290–
1349).** English theologian and philosopher,
known above all for his opposition to Pelagianism (⇒Pelagius), and considered a precursor of ⇒Wycliffe and ⇒Luther. He spent
the greater part of his career at Oxford,
where he was given the title of Profound Doctor. While abroad in Avignon, he was made
archbishop of Canterbury, but he died only a
week after returning to England to occupy
this see. He wrote several treatises on mathematics and a commentary on the *Metaphysics
of Aristotle.*

His chief theological work is *Against Pelagius.* In this work, B. first deals with God and
God's sovereign freedom, then with human
freedom, and finally with the relationship
between them. According to B., everything that
occurs is the will of God, since nothing can
occur against that will. Human will is free in
the sense that it is not predetermined by the
stars or by a mechanical necessity, but not in
the sense of being able to act against God's will.
Sin consists in acting against the general will
of God by opposing the divine plans, but it only
takes place because this particular action is, in
effect, the will of God. What this implies is that
B. maintains a theological determinism, in contrast with the determinism of the astrologists or
that of mechanistic rationalism. His critics have
accused him of making God responsible for sin
and of denying the reality of sin.

————

JLG

Braga, Erasmo (1877–1939). Brazilian Protestant leader. He stood out as an interpreter and interlocutor of Latin America for the
world missionary movement. B. was a member
of the Committee of Cooperation for Latin
America and wrote the book *Panamericanism:
Religious Aspect*, which is an interpretation of
the Missionary Convention of Panama in 1916,
in addition to several articles in the journal *La
nueva democracia.*

————

CCO

Brent, Charles Henry (1862–1929).
One of the founders of the Faith and Order
movement at the beginning of the twentieth
century. Of Canadian origin, B. worked as an
Anglican priest until his appointment in 1901
as bishop of the Philippines. As bishop and missionary, he struggled arduously against the
opium traffic in Asia.

Bishop B.'s vision of the unity of the church
informed and formed what is now the ⇒World
Council of Churches and its Commission on
Faith and Order.

————

CCO

Brenz, Johann (1499–1570). Defender of the Reformation in the south of Germany. Collaborated with ⇒Luther, ⇒Melanchthon, ⇒Jonas, and others in the formulation of the Schwabach Articles, which later formed part of the Marburg Articles, and then served as the foundation for the first twenty-one articles of the ⇒Augsburg Confession. A moderate Lutheran, in Württemberg he opposed the position of ⇒Calvin regarding the Lord's Supper. After the defeat of the peasants, he did much in favor of those who were defeated. After the death of Luther, he was also a reconciler between the more moderate Lutherans (called Philippists because they followed Philipp Melanchthon) and the more radical Gnesio-Lutherans led by ⇒Flacius. This led him to contribute effectively to the Formula of ⇒Concord, although it was produced after his death.

———

ALG

Briggs, Charles Augustus (1841–1913). Professor of Hebrew at Union Theological Seminary in New York (1874–91) and editor of the *Presbyterian Review* (1880–90). B. was later named professor of biblical theology (1891–1904) and then of theological encyclopedia and symbolics (1904–13). At his inauguration in 1891, he commented on the authority of the Bible, rejecting the notion of inerrancy. The result was his heresy trial before the Presbytery of New York. Although the presbytery absolved him, the General Assembly of the Presbyterian Church suspended him from his clerical functions in 1893. He continued teaching at Union and took orders in the Episcopal Protestant Church in 1899. He was one of the editors of the International Critical Commentary series (1880–90) as well as a coauthor of an important Hebrew dictionary.

———

TCS

Brightman, Edgar S. (1884–1953). U.S. philosopher who devoted himself to the philosophy of personalism developed at Boston University. His chief interests were religion, personal values, and the necessity of faith for the rational function. His philosophy also gave importance to activity, creativity, and the potential of the person, which everyone has the obligation to develop. His interests and his correspondence with philosophers in Latin America helped to establish his fame in that region and to call the attention of the United States to Latin American philosophy. B. also established the first program of Latin American studies in the United States.

———

LGP

Brindisi (or Brindis), Lawrence of (1559–1619). Theologian, biblical scholar, and preacher born in the Italian city of Brindisi. First educated by the Conventual Franciscans in his native town, he entered the Order of the Capuchin Franciscans in 1575. He studied philosophy and theology at the University of Padua, where he demonstrated extraordinary ability in European and Semitic languages. A great preacher, he left a collection of sermons in eight volumes. His intelligence, academic training, gift of preaching, and fame for holiness made him known in almost all the European continent and enabled him to serve in positions of leadership among the Capuchins as well as in the church throughout Catholic Europe. Although he was respected as a theologian, his fame is due more to his gift of preaching.

———

OOE

Brown, Robert McAfee (1920–2001). U.S. theologian born in Carthage, Illinois. He studied at Union Theological Seminary in New York and at Columbia and Oxford universities. He taught in several universities and seminaries, among them Macalaster College, Union Theological Seminary, Stanford University, and the Pacific School of Religion in California. He became known as one of the principal interpreters of the liberation theologies and their challenge to North America. His works deal mainly with matters of justice, human rights, and liberation.

———

LGP

Brown, William Adams (1865–1943). Pastor and Presbyterian theologian. He studied at Yale, at Union Theological Seminary in New York (where he also taught), and in Berlin under A. ⇒Harnack. He worked on the subjects of missions, theological pluralism, the dialogue between theology and science, and, most of all, on ecumenism. His most widely read work was *Christian Theology in Outline* (1906). In 1913 some in his denomination questioned his writings, but their accusations of heresy came to naught.

———

EPA

Browne, Robert (ca. 1550–1633).
Puritan Congregationalist leader and one of the original proponents of the free or separatist churches, a movement that demanded separation from the Anglican Church and total freedom from government control. Those who agreed with him and refused to accept the norms and doctrines of the Church of England were called nonconformists. His followers were also known as Brownists. Educated at the Corpus Christi College of Cambridge, he was ordained a priest by the Church of England. Together with Robert Harrison, he gathered a separatist congregation in Norwich in 1580. Owing to these and other actions, he was incarcerated thirty-two times and exiled in 1582. Eventually he returned to England and submitted to the state religion.

LMcA

Browning, Don S. (1934–). Pastoral psychologist and supervisor of clinical pastoral education in the United States. He tries to recover the moral context of pastoral care and emphasizes the function of ethics in pastoral care and pastoral theology. In *The Moral Context of Pastoral Care* (1976), he offers a model of pastoral counseling in which he outlines his theology, which is directed toward a pastoral morality and an ethics that is based on five levels of analysis. His other chief works are *Practical Theology* (1983), *Religious Ethics and Pastoral Care* (1983), *Religious Thought and the Modern Psychologies* (1987), and *A Fundamental Practical Theology* (1991).

—

JR

Bruce, F. F. (1910–90). Scottish biblical scholar. Born in Elgin, son of a preacher of the church of the Plymouth Brethren. In his denomination, Frederick Fyvie Bruce promoted gender justice in ecclesiastical ministries. He also was a mentor of many through his copious correspondence. His theological education took place in Aberdeen, Cambridge, and Vienna. He taught in Edinburgh, Leeds, Sheffield, and Manchester.

B. wrote fifty books and some two thousand articles. He commented on most of the New Testament. He edited the New International Commentary on the New Testament series and the journals *Evangelical Quarterly* and *Palestine Exploration Quarterly*. He was distinguished by a vast scholarship joined to an orthodox and relatively traditional reading of the biblical text.

—

EPA

Bruner, Frederick Dale (1932–). New Testament scholar, Presbyterian missionary, and writer. He studied at Princeton and Hamburg. He became widely known as a specialist in Pentecostal doctrine and history, as is seen in his book *The Holy Spirit: Shy Member of the Trinity* (1984).

—

EPA

Brunner, Emil (1889–1965). Pastor and Protestant theologian who served as professor of dogmatic theology in Zurich. In his early years, B. was a liberal theologian, emphasizing the social and ethical dimensions of the gospel and our rational ability to discern the truths of the faith. After the First World War, as was the case with many theologians of his time, he became critical of liberal theology. He rejected the postulate of ⇒Schleiermacher that Christian doctrine can be derived from personal or communal experience.

B. insists on the necessity of biblical revelation to define the distinctive character of Christianity. He understands that, from the rational point of view, Christianity is contradictory and paradoxical. Not that faith is intrinsically contradictory, but rather that our reason cannot capture the totality of divine revelation. These postulates led him to support the theological dialectic proposed by ⇒Barth.

In spite of his affinity with Barth, B. kept his distance from that theologian. In contrast to Barth, he affirmed the value of critical philosophy, which recognizes its limits and its inability to understand the divine sphere. In addition, he affirmed that the human being has the ability to respond to the call of God. From his point of view, Barth's total dependence on the grace of God denies human initiative and responsibility.

The contrasts of the theology of B. with theological liberalism, on the one hand, and with the theology of Barth, on the other, become more evident in his social and ethical philosophy. In contrast to Barth, B. defends natural theology, since all human beings have limited, though valuable, knowledge of God. Like ⇒Luther, he postulates the existence and importance of the "orders of creation." Such orders are institutions or social practices (e.g., the family and the state) of human origin.

Although these institutions and practices are not derived from biblical revelation, revelation accepts them as part of the purposes of God. They provide standards of conduct that help to regulate our relationships. Their contribution, nevertheless, is not, as liberal theologians allege, to promote personal well-being and the common good; rather, their contribution is negative: they are standards that aid in limiting the consequences of sin.

Like ⇒Buber, B. used the categories "Thou" and "I" and the centrality of dialogue as a model to express and understand the relationship between the believer and God. The task of the Christian theologian is to establish a constructive dialogue with the secular world and with representatives of other religions. Human life develops fully in a communal context as long as the community does not deny the individuality of each of its members. On the other hand, sin is expressed primordially through our resistance to living in dependence on God and in our demanding more autonomy than is fitting for a creature. Our inclination is for our will to be self-sufficient and independent of the will of God. Only biblical revelation presents us with the person of the Christ, who represents true freedom and human fulfillment.

—
IG

Bruno, Eusebius (11th century).
Apparently a disciple and friend of ⇒Berengar, initially condemned by the same synods that condemned Berengar. But finally he rejected the views of Berengar, accepted the eucharistic doctrines of the majority of his contemporaries, and devoted himself to the administration of his diocese of Angers.

—
JLG

Bruno, Giordano (1548–1600). Theologian and philosopher burned as an archheretic, whom history vindicated as a martyr of theological and scientific freedom. A native of Nola, in 1562 he entered the Order of the Dominicans in Naples, where he changed his name from Philippo to Giordano. His chief interest was Copernican astronomy. In 1572 he was ordained a priest. In 1576, under suspicion of heresy, he fled, beginning a peripatetic life. Excommunicated by Genevan Calvinists and by German Lutherans, expelled by the Anglicans of Oxford, he was finally delivered over to the Inquisition of Venice in 1592. Extradited to Rome, he was incarcerated for eight years

and executed on February 17, 1600, in the "Field of Flowers."

His teachings on the infinite number of planets, suns, and constellations, on the possibility of extraterrestial life, and on the world soul gained for him the epithets of mystical-naturalist, monist, emanentist, and pantheist. Today we have to reexamine such judgments in the light of astrophysics, ecotheology, and the concept of the world as a living organism.

His last words still resound: "Perhaps you should tremble more when you pronounce the sentence than I when I receive it."

—
EPA

Buber, Martin (1878–1965). Jewish existentialist thinker who was educated in Vienna, Zurich, Berlin, and Leipzig. He served as editor of various Jewish newspapers and as professor of Jewish ethics and philosophy at the University of Frankfurt am Main. From a very early age he was a member of the Zionist movement, and he grew more militant when Germany became Nazi. Later, in Palestine, he worked as professor of the sociology of religion in the Hebrew University of Israel and promoted Arab-Israeli unity.

His chief work is *I and Thou* (1923), whose central idea has made a lasting impact in the fields of theology, ethics, philosophy, education, sociology, and psychiatry. The fundamental idea of his work is that a radical difference exists between our relationship with the world of things ("I and it") and our relationship with the personal world ("I and Thou"). The interpersonal world questions me and demands my recognition and response. The "I and it" relation consists in observing and manipulating objects and processes. The "I and Thou" relation defines our most essential relationships in terms of dialogue and mutuality. These are the relations that ultimately define personality.

When we relate to people as if they were objects, they become distorted, and we, as well as our relationship with God, become distorted. B. defines this relationship in terms of a continuous dialogue in which God as well as we preserve our own identity and integrity. Religion is a continuous dialogue based on faith.

—
IG

Bucer, Martin (1491–1551). Leader of the Protestant reformation in Strassburg. Born in Selestat, Alsace, in a modest home. At the age of fifteen, he entered the Order of the

Dominicans. At the Heidelberg Disputation (1518), he heard ⇒Luther and became a Martinian. Three years later, he was granted a dispensation from his vows.

B. not only married three years before Luther, but also focused on finding wives for the reformers. In 1522 he was excommunicated because of his own marriage. With his wife Elizabeth, he had thirteen children, but in 1541, the year of the great plague, only five survived, and that calamity took Elizabeth with it. Subsequently he married Wibrandis, who was a widow of the reformers ⇒Oecolampadius and ⇒Capito.

In 1523 he arrived in Strassburg, a city through which the imperial highway passed, which made it very vulnerable. There he joined the reforming current of Matthäus ⇒Zell, Wolfgang Capito, and Gaspar Hedio. His religious tolerance made Strassburg a citadel of refuge. From 1538 to 1541, ⇒Calvin took sanctuary in it. There, with the help of B., Calvin developed topics such as predestination, the glory of God, Christian certainty, the unity of the church, liturgy, and a method for commenting on the Bible. Unfortunately, B. did not turn out to be liberal enough to give asylum to Anabaptists.

B. always mediated between the Lutheran and the Reformed. In the Marburg Colloquy (1529), he specified that discrepancies on the Eucharist were more verbal than in depth, as Luther believed. B., the peacemaker, knew how to differentiate between what is basic and what is only *adiaphora*—that which is not essential to the faith.

His decisive participation in the Tetrapolitan Confession (1530) contributed to the cohesion that Protestants showed at the Diet of ⇒Augsburg. Likewise in 1531 he made Strassburg a member of the League of Smalkald, in order to resist the imminent attack of Charles V.

As an opponent of the Augsburg Interim (1548), he was exiled, but he was welcomed in England by Thomas ⇒Cranmer. There he became Regis Professor of Divinity at the University of Cambridge. He also participated in the revised edition of 1552 of the Book of Common Prayer, which made the pendulum swing toward the Protestant faith.

B. shared in the collective error of Luther and ⇒Melanchthon of blessing the bigamy of Prince Philip of Hesse.

———

EPA

Budé, Guillaume (1467–1540).
French humanist interested in a reform of the church in

the style proposed by ⇒Erasmus. Although he never declared himself a Protestant, his enemies considered him to be one, since he always maintained cordial relations with the Reformers. Through his work in Paris, he influenced the young ⇒Calvin, who launched into humanist studies under the inspiration of B. and others like him. Years after the death of B., Calvin wrote to his relatives, who had become Protestants, offering them refuge in Geneva. His most important theological work is *From Hellenism to Christianity* (1534).

———

JLG

Bugenhagen, Johann (1485–1558).
German Lutheran theologian who was a member of the intimate circle of Reformers in Wittenberg. He received his higher education at the University of Greifswald, where he became familiar with humanism (1502–4). He was inspired by ⇒Erasmus to devote himself to biblical studies. He studied theology at the University of Wittenberg (1521) and very soon was named lecturer of that university in the area of Psalms. He became a follower of ⇒Luther in 1520 after reading his work *The Babylonian Captivity of the Church.* He was one of the first Reformers to marry (1522). He received his title of doctor of theology in 1533 and was promoted to the rank of professor in 1535. He was pastor of the church of St. Mary in Wittenberg (1523–58) and Luther's confessor. B. helped Luther in the revision of the Bible and remained at his side during several controversies. He was also one of the first professors at the University of Wittenberg to oppose ⇒Zwingli, against whom he wrote a treatise in 1525. King Christian III called him to Denmark to introduce the Reformation in his country. In addition to his work in the reform of the church, he introduced Protestant theology in the University of Copenhagen and crowned the king and queen of Denmark. In spite of declining three bishoprics and many other positions, he was named general superintendent of the Church of Saxony. He was also the preacher at the funeral rites of Luther. After the capture of the University of Wittenberg by the empire, he was treated well by Charles V. This motivated B. not to oppose the Augsburg Interim. But in 1550 he again promoted strict Lutheranism with his *Commentary on Jonah*, in which he protested against the errors of Roman Catholicism. Shortly before his retirement, he warned all the pastors against the temptation of compromising their theological position.

His greatest contributions to the Reformation were his tireless zeal and his skills as an organizer of the church. He was likewise a great organizer of schools, for which he has been called the father of the *Volksschule*.

—

JDR

Bulgaris, Eugenius (1716–1806).

Greek theologian, famous preacher, and director of the Academy of Mount Athos until political circumstances compelled him to establish himself in Constantinople, where he was professor of philosophy and mathematics. Later he left that city and went to Germany, and then to Russia, where he enjoyed the favor of Catherine the Great. He wrote against Catholics and Protestants and in defense of Eastern Orthodoxy. At the same time, he distinguished himself through his openness to modernity and his criticism of a good deal of religious tradition, in the style of Voltaire, whom he admired and translated into Greek.

—

JLG

Bullinger, Johann Heinrich (1504–75).

Swiss reformer educated at the school of the Brothers of the Common Life and at the University of Cologne, where he became familiar with the works of ⇒Erasmus, ⇒Melanchthon, and ⇒Luther. Upon his return to Switzerland in 1523, he joined the Reformation of ⇒Zwingli and took part in the controversy of 1528, which won Zurich over to the Reformation. In contrast to Zwingli, B. had a reconciling attitude toward his opponents. Even during his pamphlet struggles with Luther and others on the meaning of the Lord's Supper, B. avoided personal polemics and treated those who differed from him with charity. After the battle of Kappel, in which Zwingli died, B. had to flee, but later he returned to Zurich, where in December of 1531 he became Zwingli's successor. He showed a particular interest in England and provided theological support to the English monarchs.

B. wrote *The Decades* (fifty sermons on Christian doctrine) and *Diarium*, as well as *The History of the Reformation*. He helped to shape the First Helvetic Confession. Together with ⇒Calvin, he completed the *Consensus Tigurinus* (1549). This was a careful study of the Lord's Supper that gave unity to the Reformed tradition. He also wrote the Second Helvetic Confession (1566). This compendium of the teachings of Reformed theology was adopted as the official position of the church in Switzerland, Hungary, Bohemia, and elsewhere.

—

JDR

Bultmann, Rudolf Karl (1884–1976).

German scholar educated in Marburg, Tübingen, and Berlin, and later professor of New Testament in Marburg (1921–51). One of the most influential Protestant theologians of the twentieth century, he worked intensely on the New Testament, making use of historical criticism. He tried to understand Christianity in its own context and as a possibility of faith for people in the twentieth century. Among his works of greater influence are *Die Geschichte der synoptischen Tradition* (The History of the Synoptic Tradition, 1921), *Jesus* (1926), *Das Evangelium des Johannes* (The Gospel of John, 1941), *Theologie des Neuen Testaments* (Theology of the New Testament, 1948–53), and many others.

Following the line of interpretation traced by ⇒Bousset and ⇒Reitzenstein, B. detected a strong influence of ⇒Gnosticism in the sociocultural background of the Gospel of John. At the same time, he was one of the first to use the method of form criticism (developed by Hermann ⇒Gunkel, Karl L. ⇒Schmidt, and Martin ⇒Dibelius) in his interpretation of the Synoptic Gospels. Based on the presuppositions of this method, B. thought that the content or informative material of the Gospels could be reduced to "small units of tradition," which emerged and circulated in an oral form before being finally fixed in writing. This approach eventually led him to doubt the authenticity of these units of tradition and, in particular, of several aspects relative to the historicity of the person of Jesus.

With the help of this exegetical tool, B. concludes that the mission of Jesus is, in essence, a "call to decision." B., in fact, interpreted the mission of Jesus as an effort to call his disciples to accept his message and obey his demands. Jesus saw himself as the person in whom God made Godself present and in whom God offered salvation. That is, there was an "implicit Christology" in his self-understanding. This understanding subsequently caused the disciples to work out a Christology so developed that now it is almost impossible to know who was the real historical Jesus. According to B., the language of faith in the Gospels and the discrepancies among them make this task very difficult. Aside from some basic historical data, such as his existence and his death on the cross, for B. there is very little that we can know about Jesus.

In spite of his skepticism, B. maintained a profound interest in making the New Testament more relevant to modern people. But in order to achieve such a goal, B. had to find a "conceptual frame" that would allow the human being to interpret the message of the NT, not only from a historical-critical perspective, but also in a comprehensible language which is more in accord with modern times. In the existentialism of Martin ⇒Heidegger, B. found a solution to this need, a solution which culminated in a hermeneutical process that he called "demythologization." According to B., the ability to make decisions is what makes the human being unique. But this ability to make decisions can only happen in a context of options that make such decisions possible. For this reason, the human being cannot concentrate on the past but rather on the future. But there is an obstacle that does not allow the human to be fully aware of this quality which belongs to the human: unfortunately, humans still live in their traditions, legalisms, or dead systems of the past that do not permit them to open themselves to the future. The vision of the world, the beliefs and practices of the New Testament contribute to this state of alienation, since the New Testament is "prescientific" or "primitive" and, therefore, alien to the experience and worldview of the contemporary human being. For this reason, human beings need to be liberated from this mythical understanding of reality so that their faith can be pertinent. Therefore, "salvation" for B. means opening to the future in a radical way, placing faith in the kerygma of the gospel and bringing the message of the New Testament up to date by emptying it of all that is irrelevant. B. dedicated practically all his life to reading the New Testament through this theoretical frame. His effort to demythologize the New Testament left a deep mark in the field of theology and biblical studies.

AEM

Bunyan, John (1628–88). English Puritan pastor and author of the allegory *The Pilgrim's Progress* (1678, 1684). He was born in the town of Elstow, near Bedford, where he was a pastor for many years. His father and mother were poor, and they raised him in such a strict way that B. developed great remorse for his youthful sins, such as cursing, dancing, and playing with the bells of the local church. That

intense feeling of sin and total dependence on the grace of God is reflected in most of his works, including his spiritual autobiography, *Grace Abounding to the Chief of Sinners* (1666). B. wrote sixty books and treatises, but we do not have copies of them all. He only studied the first years of elementary school, but he learned to read and write by reading the Bible and works such as the *Book of Martyrs* by ⇒Foxe. He participated in the civil war of England (1644–46) and then suffered many years of imprisonment (1660–72) for preaching "separatism." Although basically loyal to the Anglican theology of Puritanism and of Calvinism, B. did not agree with the close relationship of the church with the state. For this reason, he was pastor of an independent congregation in Bedford from 1672 until his death in 1688. Also, as a result of the popularity of his writings, he preached in many places in England. In his last work, *Antichrist and Her Ruin* (1692, published posthumously), he showed his anti-Catholicism and his theological perspective, according to which in this world we live in spiritual warfare, and the salvation of the soul is of supreme importance.

EA

Burgess, Stanley Milton (1937–). Born in India, son of missionaries of the Assemblies of God. He is best known for his work as writer and editor of *The New Dictionary of Pentecostal and Charismatic Movements*.

EPA

Bushnell, Horace (1802–76). Pastor in the Congregational Church, and preacher of great oratorical power. One of the most important figures of the discipline of religious education, he was the first to develop a "theology of childhood," in his classic *Christian Nurture*. His starting point is a concern for two postulates of faith that prevailed in the New England theology during his years of ministry. The first understood the baptism of infants as a regenerative act and, therefore, a fact that is detached from the subsequent life of the child. The second, supported by a revivalist mentality, viewed the baptized child as potentially religious as long as it did not have an adult experience of conversion. In response to these postulates, B. proposed a "perpetual baptism" in which grace is not confined to the sacramental moment but is instead an integral part of the process of Christian growth. Baptism transcends its immediate function and takes on significance in the future as an anticipation of the care which in matters of faith the child will receive in the home, church, and school. B.'s maxim that "the child is to grow as a Christian, and never know himself as being otherwise" became famous. The Christian character is formed in an organic social experience through a process that begins with birth. Long before developmental psychology appeared, B. had already emphasized the importance of the first years of life as formative for religious experience.

—

JRI

Butler, Joseph (1692–1752).

Theologian who occupied high positions in the Church of England, and who in 1747 refused to accept the archbishopric of Canterbury. His theological work centered on the refutation of Deism, as is evident in his most famous work, *The Analogy of Religion, Natural and Revealed, to the Constitution and the Course of Nature.* In this work, he argues that the order and beauty of nature are proof of the existence of the God of religion, who is not only Creator, but also has a purpose for creation.

—

JLG

Buttrick, David G. (1927–).

Outstanding preacher and teacher of homiletics in the United States. He followed the footsteps of his father, George ⇒Buttrick, and devoted himself to teaching the art of preaching at the theological seminaries of Pittsburgh and of St. Meinrad (Indiana), and at the School of Theology of Vanderbilt University, where he is professor emeritus. B. has written and edited fourteen books, among which *Homiletic: Moves and Structures* stands out as his most important work. There he explains his method of "phenomenological preaching." He uses principles of structural analysis to determine the episodes (or "movements") of a biblical text. According to this complicated method, the sermon should follow the logic of the argument of the biblical text.

—

PAJ

Buttrick, George Arthur (1892–1980).

Pastor, preacher, theologian, and teacher. B. was one of the twentieth century's most influential experts in homiletics in the United States. He served twenty-seven years as pastor of Madison Avenue Presbyterian Church in New York City. His sermons from that pulpit made him famous in the entire country. From there, he went on to teach in theological seminaries: Union, Harvard, Garrett, and Louisville. B. wrote fifteen books and twice offered the prestigious Lyman Beecher Lecture on Preaching at Yale University. As a teacher of preaching, he paid great attention to the structure of the outline of the sermon. As a preacher, he excelled by being a biblical preacher who invited his audience to enter into a deeper relationship with God.

—

PAJ

Cabasilas, Nicholas (ca. 1322–71).

One of the most remarkable Byzantine theologians of the fourteenth century. He was an ardent defender of ⇒Palamas and his teachings, although his own position was much more moderate than those of the Palamites of his time. He also tenaciously opposed the union between the Roman and the Byzantine churches.

The titles of his two main books, *Life in Jesus* and *Interpretation of the Liturgy*, indicate his theological and mystical interests. C. was interested in promoting a christocentric mysticism based on meditation on Jesus and intimate union with him. According to C., our union with Jesus is even more intimate than our union with ourselves. In that union, human beings acquire and recognize their own true dignity, which is higher than the sun and the stars. True happiness is found in that union.

Worship has an extremely important place in the process of reaching that union. Hence C.'s interest in liturgy. Union with Jesus is reached through liturgy and especially through the mysteries of baptism, chrismation, and Communion. On the other hand, neither the temple nor the altar, nor worship itself, are as holy as the human being, who is made in the image of God.

It is important to note that C.'s mysticism did not regard that union as a goal exclusively for monks or anchorites. Instead he insisted that this union is possible for every human being. Since the law of the Spirit is love, the presence of other people is the ideal means to exercise oneself in it. Therefore there is no need to abandon daily life or the surrounding society.

—

JLG

Cabasilas, Nilo (14th century).

Bishop of Thessalonica, frequently confused with his nephew Nicholas ⇒Cabasilas. He opposed the union with Rome that was then being planned for political reasons. This opposition served as inspiration and guidance for his nephew Nicholas, one of the most important Byzantine theologians of the time.

—

JLG

Cadbury, Henry Joel (1883–1974).
North American Quaker, professor of New Testament and theology at Harvard. He wrote chiefly on Luke-Acts and on ⇒Fox.

—

JLG

Caesarius of Arles (ca. 470–543).
Bishop of that city from 503 and defender of the positions of ⇒Augustine regarding grace, free will, and salvation. He wrote treatises *On the Trinity* and *On Grace*. Before being bishop he was a monk in Lerins, where ⇒Faustus of Riez taught the diluted Augustinianism that is known as Semi-Pelagianism. As bishop, he opposed such doctrines and was the chief theologian in the Synod of ⇒Orange (529), which accepted several Augustinian theses, although not the most extreme, such as the predestination of the condemned. He is also known for his distinction between "capital" and "minor" sins. Among the first are sacrilege, homicide, adultery, and several others, even intoxication and rage when they are habitual. These sins require repentance, confession (usually public), and penitence. The minor sins are those which no believer escapes; the best remedy against them is good works.

—

JLG

Cajetan, Thomas de Vio (1468–1535).
Dominican, general of the order, professor of theology, cardinal and apostolic nuncio in Germany, defender of Catholicism against Protestantism, participant in the discussions regarding the divorce of Henry VIII of England, but known above all in the field of theology for his commentaries on the *Summa theologica* of ⇒Thomas Aquinas. It was his lot to live at a time of transition from the Middle Ages to modernity, and to promote the reform of the church even while he opposed the doctrinal reforms proposed by the Protestants. For this reason he faced strong resistance, not only among Protestants, but also within Roman Catholicism.

During the first years of his intellectual career as professor in Padua, his chief opponents were the Averroists of that city (⇒Averroës; ⇒Siger of Brabant), as well as the followers of Duns ⇒Scotus who opposed the Thomism of C. The main Averroist in Padua at that time was Pietro Pomponazzi, against whom C. wrote a commentary on ⇒Aristotle's *De anima*. But C. himself does not appear to have been convinced that the immortality of the individual soul could be proved by philosophical means, and because of this some of his own Dominican colleagues accused him of coming too close to Averroism.

C. wrote several treatises against Protestantism, but above all a series of exegetical works in which he refuted some of the Protestant interpretations. Because in those works C. used the best scientific and exegetical methods of his time, there were those who considered him an unbeliever. But centuries later many biblical scholars have seen in him a precursor of modern biblical studies.

The commentaries on the *Summa theologica* are the most famous and influential work of C., so much so that when Leo XIII ordered the publication of the works of Thomas, he also ordered the publication of C.'s commentaries along with the *Summa*. This work took C. years to complete; the first commentary was published in 1507 and the last in 1522.

On the other hand, these commentaries of C. were not always well received, for some thought that in certain points he distorted the teachings of Thomas. Thus, Pope Pius V ordered some passages to be removed. This included, for example, some paragraphs in which C. said that children who die without being baptized can be saved through the faith of their parents.

Later there were controversies among the followers of C. (mostly Dominicans) and those of Francisco ⇒Suárez (mostly Jesuits) concerning the Thomist doctrine of analogy. C. maintained that the analogy between God and creatures was an "analogy of proportionality," while Suárez also proposed an "analogy of attribution," based on the relation between the Creator and creatures.

—

JLG

Calixtus, Georg (1586–1656).
German Lutheran theologian. In 1611 he published his first work (on the fifteen most important doctrinal differences between various theological traditions), thereby disclosing his moderate Melanchthonian Lutheranism. In 1614 Duke Frederick Ulrich of Brunswick-Wolfenbuettel

granted him a professorship at Helmsted, where he remained for the rest of his life.

The criticism of some of his contemporaries and subsequent generations does not change the fact that C. was one of the most independent and original thinkers among the Lutheran theologians of his time. His theological system has to be reconstructed from a number of his works: *Epitome theologiae* (1619; Summary of Theology), *Apparatus theologicus* (1628), his fragmentary *Epitome theologiae moralis* (1634; Summary of Moral Theology), and a great variety of monographic studies on individual topics. His concern for Christian unity occupied him during the last twenty-five years of his life. It provoked the syncretistic controversy, which reached a climax in the colloquy of Thorn (1645) and provided a foundation for subsequent but failed efforts toward union. C. died in Helmsted.

His contemporaries did not always realize that "orthodox" Lutheranism had moved beyond Luther and developed a number of principles that are embodied in the thought that characterizes the sixteenth century. These principles are quite different from those elaborated by C. and his associates. The laudable concern of C.'s group for the external unity of the empirical church and its appeal to antiquity and universal tradition embody in an authentic way intellectual discernment that is properly Lutheran. Nonetheless, his tendency to reduce the minimum requirements of faith to the baptismal creed and his occasional extreme confidence in the *consensus quinquesaecularis* (the supposed agreement among the Christian teachers of the first five centuries, a term that was developed by others and which C. never used) should be deplored as a case in which concern for polemics and irenic interests interfered with an adequate evaluation of the historical facts.

The general adoption of the analytic method that is theologically oriented toward dogmatics in order to make of theology a practical science is broadly identified as one of C.'s contributions. He is also recognized for the establishment of ethics as one of the subdisciplines of theology. After its notable development following the colloquy of Regensburg (1601), his epistemology takes loyal account of Lutheran biblical principles. His eucharistic teaching rejects what he considers to be Roman Catholic as well as Reformed aberrations. Among his many works, he is best remembered not only for his commentaries and other titles that have already been mentioned, but also for his books

on the authority of the Bible, the doctrine of the Trinity, the Lord's Supper, the Council of Trent, the marriage of pastors, and the primacy of the pope.

———

JDR

Calixtus I (?–ca. 223). Bishop of Rome from approximately 217 until his death. He was condemned to work in the mines of Sardinia— some say because of his faith, but his adversary ⇒Hippolytus claimed that it was because of his shady financial maneuvers. Pardoned through the intervention of the emperor's favorite mistress, he returned to Rome, where he was assistant to Bishop Zephyrinus, whom he succeeded.

His controversy with Hippolytus revolved around moral as well as doctrinal concerns. Regarding moral matters, Hippolytus accused him of being too lax when he forgave and readmitted to the communion of the church those who had fallen into fornication. (When he discusses this, Hippolytus makes assertions about the personal character of C. that many historians question.)

Concerning doctrinal matters, the controversy revolved around Trinitarian doctrine, and specifically around the teachings of ⇒Sabellius. Also in this case it is difficult to know exactly what C. taught, since the main testimony that we have about such teachings is that of his opponent Hippolytus. According to Hippolytus, although at first C. rejected the teachings of Sabellius, in the end he accepted them, affirming that "the Spirit who became incarnate in the Virgin is not different from the Father, but one and the same. Because what can be seen, the man, he [C.] calls Son; while the Spirit that was in the Son he calls Father."

C. died a natural death in 222 or 223, but the controversy continued under his successors Urban and Pontianus.

———

JLG

Calov, Abraham (1612–86). German Lutheran theologian born in Mohrungen (Eastern Prussia). He studied in Königsberg, the university in which he was later a professor of theology (1637). Subsequently he was appointed rector of the Institute of Danzig (1643), professor of theology in Wittenberg, and general superintendent (1650). A champion and classical representative of the militant Lutheran orthodox theology of the sixteenth century, he fought ardently against the "syncretism" of

Georg ⇒Calixtus, and also against the Calvinists, the Socinians, and the Arminians.

Among his works are *Consensus repetitus fidei vere Luteranae* (1655; Repeated Consensus of the True Lutheran Faith), in which he attacked sixty-five "syncretistic" propositions while he made a new Lutheran confession of faith, a work that did not merit or secure general approval because of its excessive subtlety and dialectics; *Syncretistic History* (1682); *Illustrated Bible* (1672), a refutation of the commentaries of ⇒Grotius; and *System of Theological Common Themes* (1677), which can be considered the masterpiece of Lutheran scholasticism.

—

JDR

Calvin, John (1509–64).

The foremost Protestant theologian of the second generation. In a certain way, he was a systematizer of the thought of ⇒Luther, but he differed from the great reformer in several points. The Reformed tradition arises from these differences. Among the chief theologians of this tradition in the early years are ⇒Zwingli, ⇒Bucer, ⇒Knox, and C. This tradition, although Protestant, is distinguished from the Lutheran tradition.

C. was born in France, in Noyon, which at that time was an episcopal city whose bishop and lord was the protector of C.'s family. As a result of that relation, when he was only twelve years old, the young C. received the first of the ecclesiastical "benefits" (that is, positions whose income he received without being present), by means of which he was able to study and support himself financially. C. retained these benefits until, in 1534, the reforming impulse led him to renounce them.

In the meantime, C. studied in some of the best schools of Paris, with the goal of following an ecclesiastical career. Some time afterward he decided to study law, which he began to do in Orléans and continued in Bourges. Although by that time he seems to have read several Protestant works, for the time being what attracted him was humanism, so that he dreamed of emulating the works of ⇒Erasmus.

In this humanist spirit, he published his first important work, a commentary on *De clementia* by Seneca. Although generally well received, this work did not make the impact that C. had hoped for.

Shortly afterward, around the years 1533–34, C. became a Protestant. This occurred through what he himself calls "a sudden conversion," although he does not give further explanations or details. For the time being he continued living in France, where the moderate reformation proposed by ⇒Lefèvre d'Étaples enjoyed a certain favor. His first theological work, published around that date, carries the title *De psychopannychia* (On the Sleep of the Soul). It is a refutation of the teaching of some Anabaptists, according to which the souls of the dead sleep until the day of the final resurrection.

In October 1534, C. fled from France because of the "episode of the placards." Someone (perhaps some of C.'s friends) posted "Lutheran" lampoons throughout Paris, which the authorities interpreted as an assault against them. C. as well as others of his friends felt compelled to flee.

C. headed for Basel, where he devoted himself to a project he had cherished for some time: the preparation of a catechism for French-speaking Protestants. With that aim, he applied himself to the assiduous study of theology and to reading the works of ⇒Augustine, Luther, ⇒Melanchthon, Bucer, and others. The book that emerged from these efforts, published in Basel in 1536, was titled *Institutes of the Christian Religion*. It was a small pocketbook (that is, for a pocket of those times, which was rather capacious) which comprised six chapters and a total of 516 pages.

After that publication, C. traveled through Italy and France, and was heading for Strassburg when the military conflicts of the time compelled him to take a route that would lead through Geneva. There the reformer ⇒Farel urged him to remain in the city and take charge of the reforming work. Although at first C. resisted, in the end he felt compelled by God to accept Farel's challenge. But after a few years in Geneva, the tensions between C. and Farel, on the one hand, and the civil authorities, on the other, forced both reformers to abandon that city. Farel went to Neuchâtel and C. to Strassburg, where he established a fruitful dialogue with Bucer and where he also married, in 1540. During those years he came to know personally Melanchthon, in whom he found a kindred spirit. Meanwhile, in Geneva the absence of the reforming leaders was felt more than ever, and they were invited to return. In September 1541, C. returned to Geneva, where he would spend the rest of his life.

C.'s efforts in Geneva moved in two directions. On the one hand, he did all he could to lead the city to become adjusted to what he considered to be the best Christian practices in matters such as worship, morality, and the organization of ecclesiastical life. In these efforts he was always in tension with the civil authorities, and he never was able to establish all his reforms. Therefore it is not correct to think that the Geneva of C. was a theocracy, as some affirm.

On the other hand, C. continued his theological work, writing commentaries on almost all the books of the Bible, several treatises on theology and on the government of the church, and, above all, a series of new editions of the *Institutes*, each more extensive than the earlier ones.

These two interests, the work of reforming and that of theology, came together in the question of how to deal with heretics, especially in two famous cases. The first was that of Sebastian ⇒Castello, who dared to affirm that the Song of Songs was an erotic poem, rather than a spiritual canticle between the soul and God, as almost everybody then held. He also insisted on affirming that Jesus literally descended into hell. C. opposed Castello on both points and persuaded the authorities to expel him from the city. The other case, much more famous, was that of Michael ⇒Servetus. Servetus was a Spanish physician who had been condemned in his absence by the Spanish Inquisition for denying the doctrine of the Trinity. When Servetus was passing through Geneva, he was recognized and captured by the authorities. C. accused him of heresy, and, after consultations with other Protestant cities, Servetus was burned as a heretic (which has remained a stain on the career of the Genevan reformer).

C.'s theology can be known chiefly from his *Institutes of the Christian Religion*. Indeed, in the successive editions of that work, the evolution of C.'s thought can be seen, and the pastoral and theological concerns that were shaping his theology become apparent.

The last edition of the *Institutes* (Latin ed. in 1559, and French in 1560) is divided into four great parts or books, with a total of eighty chapters. The first book deals with the knowledge of God as creator and governor of the world, and consequently it also deals with the human being and its condition; the second, with the knowledge of God as revealed in Jesus Christ, with its antecedents in the Old Testament; the third, with the work of the Holy Spirit and with grace and its effects; and the last, with the "external means" that God has provided to lead us to accept Jesus Christ and to hold fast to him.

In the *Institutes,* C. begins by declaring that practically all that we can know can be grouped under two headings: the knowledge of God and the knowledge of oneself. If we really knew ourselves, we would know that our sin is such that we have to turn to the knowledge of God. But, precisely because our sin hides our reality from us, true wisdom begins in the knowledge of God.

Such knowledge does not simply consist in knowing that God exists, but also in knowing how to glorify God. Although every human being has a certain awareness of the existence of God, and although traces of God can be seen in nature, this is enough only to condemn us, to leave us without excuse. We cannot know God directly, not only because of our sin, but also because of the infinite distance between the Creator and the creature.

It is for this reason that God reveals Godself. Revelation itself requires a certain accommodation. God makes Godself known in ways that are adjusted to our limited capacity. For this reason, in the Bible God is spoken of in anthropomorphic terms. If it were not this way, we could not understand God.

God is known to us in the Scriptures as the only God, sovereign and triune. This God is radically distinguished from the idols, since these are made by us, while the true God is the creator of all that exists, including the angels and the demons. In any case, the most important point about the doctrine of creation is not the details about God's creative activity, but the fact that all of this has been done for us and for our good.

The human being is the crown of creation and is made of body and soul. The soul, although immortal, is created, and is not, as Servetus would say, part of the divine substance. But the human being has sinned, and because of this fall the image of God that was in it remained, not totally destroyed, but horribly deformed. Ever since the fall we live under the sign and the slavery of sin. It is for this reason that, although an important part of wisdom is knowledge of oneself, and although the philosophers of old defended this, the fact is that such knowledge is beyond our reach. This is the doctrine of human "depravity," which includes the intellect as well as the will, and which much later would become one of the marks of orthodox Calvinism. Such depravity does not mean that the will and the intellect have been destroyed or that they have lost all of their love for the good and the truth; but it does mean that, above all when it comes to "heavenly things," we can only see and hear them through the eyes and ears which the Spirit grants us.

God made Godself known long ago through the Law. When speaking of the Law, C., in contrast to Luther, does not understand it as the counterpart of the gospel, but rather as the revelation of God to Israel in the Old Testament. Between the Law and the gospel there is not such a contrast or counterpoint as there is in Luther, but instead there is a continuity. At the same time, this implies that C. gives more weight than Luther to the role of the Law in Christian life. The purpose of the Law is to show us our sin and corruption and also to curb human evil; but the Law also has a "third use," which consists in showing believers the will of God. This "third use of the Law" came to be one of the characteristics of the Reformed tradition.

C.'s Christology is essentially orthodox. The work of Christ consists in the triple office (*triplex munus*) of priest, prophet, and king, although C., like the majority of the theologians of his time, understands that work in terms that are very much like those of ⇒Anselm of Canterbury: the sacrifice of Christ as payment for our sins. Regarding the hypostatic union, C. is inclined toward the Antiochene Christology, which emphasizes the full humanity of God incarnate and, in order to safeguard that humanity, underscores the distinction between it and the divinity. The union must be such that it does not destroy any of the characteristics of humanity, nor any of its intrinsic limitations, with the sole exception of sin. Besides, when Christ was in the womb of the virgin, his divinity still filled the universe and was not limited to the virginal womb. This is the doctrine of the *extra calvinisticum*, which would be another of the characteristics of the Reformed tradition. On the other hand, C.'s christological position would be reflected in his teaching regarding the presence of Jesus Christ in the Lord's Supper.

Justification is by faith, but faith is not the mere acceptance of propositions that reason cannot demonstrate. Such "faith" would be nothing but another work. Against ⇒Osiander, C. rejects the proposition that the essence of Jesus Christ is in the believer, and that we are "justified in essence." In other words, according to Osiander, justification consists in the presence of the divinity of Jesus in us. C. cannot accept such a thing, which not only makes the cross unnecessary, but also confuses the creature with the Creator.

As far as the Christian life is concerned, although the sinner continues to be a sinner, justification is also a regenerating action that permits the believer, with the aid of the Holy Spirit and the direction of the Law of God, to enter into a process of sanctification which is to continue throughout life. Such sanctification is to be not only individual, but also collective; and because of this, the Reformed tradition has been characterized by its efforts to produce societies that are more conformed to the will of God, even to the extent that on various occasions it has made room for rebellion against the existing order.

In the context of his discussion of the Christian life, in the third book of the *Institutes*, C. discusses the doctrine of predestination. According to C., through an eternal decree God has determined the final destiny of each human being. Such predestination does not depend on God's foreknowledge, according to which God knows who will believe and who will not. It is an absolute and sovereign decree of God. What is more, the eternal decree of God has determined not only who will be saved, but also who will be condemned. The justice of God manifests itself in that condemnation, for all deserve it; and in the election of some, God's love is manifested. The believer must affirm such predestination, because otherwise believers would be claiming for themselves the merit of their faith. Predestination is also the basis of the confidence which the elect have that they will persevere in the grace of God. This is the teaching of the "perseverance of the saints," which would become another of the marks of orthodox Calvinism.

C. makes a distinction between the visible and the invisible church. The latter, which consists of all the elect throughout the ages, is the true body of Christ, of which only the predestined can be members. But this does not mean that the visible church is not important. On the contrary, it is important, because only by means of it do we know the invisible church. Therefore, while we are in this life, we are to be faithful members of the visible church, which is a sign of the invisible. Every visible church in which "the pure Word of God is preached and heard and in which the sacraments are administered according to the divine institution" is true and is a sign of the invisible church. What is more, even in those churches, such as the Roman Catholic, in which C. believes he sees a profound corruption of Christian teaching, there is a certain "vestige of church," as long as the Word is preached and the sacraments are administered.

C. paid more attention than other Reformers to the organization and government of the church, which he believed ought to follow the patterns of the ancient church. Thus, C. proposed a system of government that would allow each local church to elect its own pastor, yet always with the approval of the rest of the pastoral body. This is the origin of the presbyterian system of government, which, with certain variants, is characteristic of the majority of the Reformed churches.

Although there were sacraments in the Old Testament, such as circumcision, purifications, and sacrifices, C. recognizes baptism and the Eucharist as the two sacraments of the new covenant. For him, a sacrament is an external sign through which God imprints God's promises on us in order to sustain us in the faith. C. holds, against the majority of the Anabaptists and against Zwingli, that the sacraments have their own efficacy, but that efficacy is not such that the sacraments produce justification or confer grace.

It was in his teaching on the Eucharist that C. distanced himself not only from the position of the Anabaptists, who saw in it a mere symbol, but also from the Lutherans, for whom the body of Christ was physically present in the sacrament. Luther could affirm such a presence by maintaining that the resurrected body of the Lord possesses the gift of "ubiquity," that is, of being present in many places at one time. C., whose Christology did not allow such a confusion between the divinity and the humanity, insisted that the body of the risen Christ continues to be human, and that therefore the presence of Christ in the sacrament, although real, is not physical, but spiritual. What is more, in a certain sense what happens in the sacrament is not that Christ comes down to the altar, but that the communicants ascend to heaven in a kind of anticipation of the heavenly banquet. Since this happens "in virtue [by the power] of the Holy Spirit," this position receives the name of virtualism.

Although Luther had spoken favorably of C.'s theology, some Lutherans of the second generation, among whom ⇒Westphal stood out, underscored the contrast between the Swiss reformer and the one from Wittenberg. This gave rise to a long series of controversies which little by little distanced the followers of Luther from those of C., thus originating two traditions, the Lutheran and the Reformed. In the meantime, Calvinism had expanded throughout Switzerland, Scotland, and Holland, as well as in certain regions of Germany and Hungary, among the Protestants of France, and among many in the Church of England.

In the seventeenth century, a series of disputes among Calvinists led to a more strict definition of Calvinist orthodoxy (⇒Arminius; ⇒Dort; ⇒Westminster), which was now characterized by its emphasis on the total depravity of humankind, irresistible grace, predestination, the expiatory sacrifice of Jesus Christ being limited to the elect, and the perseverance of the saints. Although all of these points find support in the writings of C., this later orthodox Calvinism became very distant from the spirit of C. himself, for whom theology was never a series of dogmatic propositions, but rather an expression of the experience of the grace of God and of the work of the Holy Spirit.

——
JLG

Cámara, Hélder (1909–99). Brazilian Catholic archbishop, defender of the poor, promoter of a Christian pacifist and socialist militancy in favor of social change, human rights activist, and in his writings a contributor to the spirituality of the theology of liberation. He was an organizer of the National Council of Bishops of Brazil, of the Latin American Episcopal Council (⇒CELAM), of the Bishops of the Third World, and of the Conference of ⇒Medellín, and promoter of the grassroots education movement. He was a candidate for the Nobel Peace Prize on three occasions.

——
LRR

Camerarius, Bartholomew (?–1564). Italian Catholic jurist who lived mainly in Naples. His chief theological work is *On Predestination, Free Will and Grace*, in which he refutes the teachings of ⇒Calvin. He also wrote on marriage, fasting, and purgatory.

——
JLG

Cameron, John (1579–1625). Calvinist theologian of Scottish origin who worked mainly in France. There he clashed with the strictest Calvinists when he rejected the theory of limited atonement, which in the end was affirmed by the Synod of ⇒Dort. Because of his scholarship and his humanist spirit, he influenced ⇒Amyraut and his school.

——
JLG

Cameron, Richard (?–1680). Leader of Scottish Calvinism and of the movement that, on the basis of a series of solemn oaths and in defense of Presbyterianism, refused to accept the authority of the king of England.

After the resolution of the conflict in 1690, some of the earlier followers of C. refused to accept the agreement. These more unyielding Presbyterians, known as Reformed Presbyterians, were also called Cameronians.

———

JLG

Campbell, Alexander (1788–1866).

Principal founder of the Christian Church, the first native Protestant denomination in the United States, of which the present-day Christian Church (Disciples of Christ) and the Churches of Christ are heirs.

The Campbellites worked specifically among marginalized groups, broke away from the larger church, and questioned confessional documents as means to maintain the monopoly of knowledge. Their social conscience led them to repudiate slavery and war. They also practiced the Eucharist weekly, a custom which had been lost in a large part of North American Protestantism; promoted the universal priesthood; and discarded speculative theology. One of their emphases was to achieve Christian unity through a return to the simple practices and beliefs of the New Testament.

C. was born in Antrim, Ireland, and studied theology at the University of Glasgow, Scotland. In 1809, with all his family, he arrived in Pennsylvania, where he would meet with his father, the Presbyterian pastor John Thomas ⇒Campbell. That same year he was ordained pastor by his father in the Brush Run Church, and soon he assumed the leadership of the Washington Christian Association. His theology, written at a popular level, was disseminated through the *Millenial Harbinger* newspaper (1830–70) and through his book *The Christian System* (1835).

In 1823 he visited Barton Stone (1772–1844), a Presbyterian pastor who would break away from his church because of his disagreement with the doctrines of unconditional election and total depravity. Between 1830 and 1833 they created a new church with some ten thousand members led by Stone and some twelve thousand directed by C. In the process of founding a new denomination, Stone preferred the name of "Christians," and C. that of "Disciples." Thus from the former Christian Church the present-day Christian Church (Disciples of Christ) emerged.

———

EPA

Campbell, John McLeod (1800–72).

Scottish Calvinist whom other Calvinists regarded as a heretic. He was born in Kilninver, near Glasgow, son of a Presbyterian pastor. He studied in Glasgow and Edinburgh. In 1826 he contradicted orthodox Calvinism by rejecting the doctrine of limited atonement (⇒Dort). C. maintained that Christ's death on the cross is for every human being. In 1831 the General Assembly excommunicated him. Subsequently C. carried out an independent ministry in Glasgow. His book *The Nature of Atonement and Its Relation to the Remission of Sins and Eternal Life* (1856) has been considered one of the best Scottish theological works of that century. Four years before he died, the University of Glasgow granted him an honorary degree.

———

EPA

Campbell, John Thomas (1763–1854).

Together with his son Alexander ⇒Campbell and with Barton Stone, C. inspired the establishment of the Christian Church. He had an ecumenical spirit and a social conscience. In 1798 he was ordained a Presbyterian pastor in Ireland and devoted himself to denouncing intolerant Protestant secret societies that went as far as to take up arms against the Roman Catholic Church.

In 1807 he emigrated to a region in Pennsylvania that was populated by many very rigid branches of Scottish and Irish Presbyterians. His ecumenical spirit led him to practice open communion with the entire Calvinist family. He was disciplined for this practice. Then he abandoned his denomination and created the Washington Christian Association, whose *Declaration and Address* (1809) maintained that the church is "essentially, intentionally, and constitutionally one." This set of ideas created for them more conflicts with the established denominations, and for this reason they founded the Brush Run Church. In the end all of this resulted in the creation of the Christian Church.

———

EPA

Canisius, Peter (1521–97).

Theologian of the Catholic Reformation of the sixteenth century and persistent opponent of Protestantism. He studied in Cologne, where in 1543 he had the distinction of being the first German to join the Jesuits. Ordained a priest three years later, shortly thereafter he was sent to the Council of ⇒Trent, which was then meeting in Bologna. There he worked with Diego

⇒Laínez and others in drafting several of the council's doctrinal decrees. After a brief visit to Rome, he returned to Germany in 1549. Although his work was centered at first in the University of Ingolstadt, he traveled throughout Germany, Austria, Bohemia, and Poland, defending Catholicism and attacking Protestant teachings. His work focused on education, preaching, and literary work. In 1581 he went to Switzerland, where he remained for most of the rest of his life. In 1864 he was beatified by Pius IX.

Among his works are three catechisms, of which two were published: *Summa doctrinae Christianae* (Summary of Christian Doctrine) and *Parvus catechismus Catholicorum* (Small Catholic Catechism). His chief work, which in reality is a new edition of the former two, is *Commentariorum de verbi Dei corruptelis* (Commentaries on the Corruptions of the Word of God), in which he tries to refute the ⇒*Centuries of Magdeburg*, not on the basis of historical studies, as ⇒Baronius would do, but on the basis of texts of the New Testament. Thus, C. relates each of the chief controverted points to some character close to Jesus. For example, John the Baptist provides him the opportunity for debating penitence, the Virgin Mary for celibacy, Peter for ecclesiology.

————

JLG

Cano, Melchor (1509–60).

Spanish Dominican. He studied in Salamanca under Francisco de ⇒Vitoria, whom he succeeded in 1546. In 1553, apparently pressured by Charles V, he abandoned the professorship in order to be consecrated Bishop of the Canary Islands, a post that he soon resigned in order to return to the peninsula, where he participated in various controversies and repeatedly clashed with the archbishop of Toledo and primate of Spain, Bartholomew Carranza.

His chief work is *De locis theologicis* (On Theological Places), which deals with the method and the sources of theology. These sources are ten: Scripture, oral tradition, the universal church, the councils, the Roman church, the fathers of the church, the scholastic theologians, reason, philosophers, and history. The next volume deals with the use of each of these sources in polemical theology. According to C.'s plan, the following volume of the work, which remained unfinished, was to deal with how to use each source in biblical interpretation.

————

JLG

Capito, Wolfgang Fabricius (1478–1541).

German Benedictine monk who was attracted to the reforming movement of the church by the preaching of ⇒Zwingli and by his reading of the personal letters of ⇒Luther. He received his degree in medicine from the University of Freiburg. He then became interested in law and afterward studied theology. He was preacher in the cathedral of Basel (1515) and in Mainz (1519). In 1523 he moved to Strassburg, where he actively participated in the affairs of the Reformed church until his death. He helped with the writing of the Tetrapolitan Confession (1530) and the Wittenberg Concord (1536), by which an agreement with the Lutheran party was achieved.

————

JDR

Cappadocians.

A group of important theologians who flourished in the region of Cappadocia, in Asia Minor, in the second half of the fourth century. Traditionally they are referred to as "the three great Cappadocians," and that number includes ⇒Basil of Caesarea, his brother ⇒Gregory of Nyssa, and ⇒Gregory of Nazianzus, the friend of both. But to these must be added ⇒Macrina, the sister of Basil and of Gregory of Nyssa, who was spiritual director to both during difficult times in their lives, and whom Gregory calls the Teacher.

The two families to which the C. belonged were deeply Christian. Peter, another brother of Macrina, Basil, and Gregory of Nyssa, became bishop of Sebaste. Another brother, Naucratius, was a monk known for his wisdom and holiness. The parents of this family had suffered during the recent persecution of Diocletian. The father, Basil the Elder, had been obliged to flee as a child with his parents and his brother Gregory and had remained hidden for seven years. The maternal grandfather had perished as a martyr. As far as Gregory of Nazianzus is concerned, his father, Gregory the Elder, had also been bishop of the same city.

Cappadocia is an arid and forbidding region in the center of Asia Minor, where the soil is thin and the rain unpredictable. For this reason, in the writings of the C. there are frequent references to famine and to the obligation of Christians to take care of the hungry and the abandoned.

The C. lived when the decisions of the Council of ⇒Nicaea were still being debated. Being somewhat younger than ⇒Athanasius, it was primarily their responsibility to defend and clarify Trinitarian doctrine until its final promulgation in the Council of ⇒Constantinople in 381. The point of discussion in this generation was how both the unity and the distinction between the several persons of the Trinity should be articulated. While in Nicaea the primary concern was the relation between the Father and the Son, by the time of the C. the person of the Holy Spirit was also being debated because of the challenge of the ⇒Pneumatomachians. The C. were convinced of the need to affirm the divinity and coeternity not only of the Son but also of the Holy Spirit.

Among the four great C., Macrina was the only one who was able to realize the dream of all: to lead a peaceful life of devotion and meditation. It was she who called her brothers to a life of greater devotion, and this is why Gregory calls her the Teacher.

Basil, also known as the Great, was beginning a promising career as professor of rhetoric when the death of Naucratius and the exhortations of Macrina led him to the monastic life. In order to understand that life better, he traveled through Egypt and Palestine, visiting the great centers and teachers of monasticism. Upon his return to Cappadocia, he led a monastic life for several years, until the needs of the church and of the poor compelled him to become more directly involved in the administration of the support of the poor. In the end, even against his will, he was elected bishop of Caesarea. In that position, he clashed repeatedly with the imperial authorities and even with Emperor Valens, who supported Arianism.

Although he could not lead a monastic life for long, Basil wrote several treatises on that life. Other writers later wrote works on the same subject that were attributed to Basil, and others interpolated extensive additions into the authentic writings of Basil. Consequently Basil is generally recognized as the organizer of Eastern monasticism, although a good portion of what is attributed to him is not really his work.

In the field of theology, Basil's main contribution can be seen in his treatises *On the Holy Spirit* and *Against* ⇒Eunomius. In this latter treatise, as well as in several of his *Epistles*, Basil establishes a difference between *ousia* and *hypostasis.* These terms, which at Nicaea had been used as synonyms, are different. While the first refers to the essence, the second refers to the particularity, the individuality, the subsistence. Thus, in God there is only one *ousia,* but three hypostases. In the statement "I believe in God the Father," "God" refers to the *ousia,* to the common divinity, while "Father" refers to the hypostasis, to what makes the

Father subsist as such and is not the same as the Son or the Holy Spirit. This distinction, defended by Basil with firmness but with subtle diplomacy, and also accepted and defended by the other C., finally prevailed in the Council of Constantinople.

While Basil distinguished himself as an organizer and diplomat, Gregory of Nazianzus was the poet and orator among the C. Like Basil, he repeatedly attempted to retire to monastic life, but the struggles of the moment prevented him from doing so. Having been made a priest and bishop against his will, he repeatedly fled to the monastic life. In 380, while on a visit to the cathedral of Saint Sophia in Constantinople with Emperor Theodosius, he was elected bishop and therefore patriarch of Constantinople. As such, he presided over the first sessions of the Council of Constantinople. But when the council was still in session, he resigned from his office in order to devote himself once more to the life of contemplation. In this effort, his success was such that the date of his death is unknown.

In the field of theology, the most important work of Gregory of Nazianzus is his series of *Theological Discourses*, in which he treats the character and method of theology, as well as the Trinitarian issue. Concerning theology, he underscores its character as wisdom and discipline rather than as objective knowledge.

Gregory of Nyssa, the younger brother of Basil and Macrina, was a theologian of mystical experience. To a much greater degree than his companions, he made use of Greek philosophy and above all of the Platonic tradition to interpret reality. He was an assiduous scholar and imitator of ⇒Origen, whose exegetical method he followed, in contrast to Basil, who always insisted on the literal sense of the text. Like ⇒Augustine, and as part of the same tradition, which had a Neoplatonic outlook, Gregory affirmed that evil, far from being a reality, is simply the absence of the good. Moreover, all of corporeal creation is real only in a secondary sense, for all of reality is spiritual, and what is corporeal is nothing but a constellation of categories that ultimately are incorporeal, categories such as form, weight, quantity, and so on.

Like Basil and Gregory of Nazianzus, Gregory of Nyssa wrote on the Trinity, a theme to which he dedicated three of his chief works: *Against* ⇒*Eunomius, On the Holy Trinity,* and *There Are Not Three Gods.*

Although the Trinitarian teaching of the C. is perfectly orthodox, it tends to underscore the distinction between the three persons more than their unity. This contrasts with the tendency of Augustine, who was inclined in the opposite direction.

— JLG

Capps, Donald (1939–). American pastoral psychologist particularly interested in the pastoral use of the Bible, the practice of moral direction, the function of religious rites in pastoral care, and the integration of psychology and theology. His most important works are *Pastoral Care: A Thematic Approach* (1979), *Life Cycle Theory and Pastoral Care* (1983), *Pastoral Care and Hermeneutics* (1984), and *Deadly Sins and Saving Virtues* (1987).

— JR

Cardenal, Ernesto (1925–). Priest, poet, and Nicaraguan minister of culture in the Sandinista government. He studied literature at the universities of Managua, Autonomous of Mexico, and Columbia in the United States. He had a religious conversion and became a monk under the tutelage of Thomas ⇒Merton. In 1964 he founded the famous Christian base community in Solentiname which was destroyed by the army of dictator Somoza. In his exile C. excelled as a spokesperson for the Sandinista Front of National Liberation, and after the triumph of the revolution, back in Nicaragua, as minister of culture. His poetic contribution, his Christian revolutionary identity, and his spirituality and liberationist theology are evident in his works: *The Psalms* (*Los Salmos*), *The Gospel in Solentiname* (*El Evangelio en Solentiname*), and *Flights of Victory* (*Vuelos de victoria*).

— LRR

Carey, William (1761–1834). One of the most prominent missionaries and missiologists of his time, he worked in India and is known as the father of modern missions. He was born in Paulerspury, Northants, England, where he served as a Baptist pastor until the foundation of the Particular Baptist Society for Propagating the Gospel among the Heathen in 1792.

C. wrote the important book *An Inquiry into the Obligations of Christians to Use Means for the Conversion of the Heathen* in 1792. Three methods and tasks for missionary work derived from this book appeared revolutionary at that time: the meticulous study of the languages, customs, and religion of the people to be addressed; the proclamation of the gospel in the towns and villages; and the translation and publication of the Scriptures in the greatest possible number of languages. For this reason, his work is considered to be an important forerunner of the theory of the contextualization of the gospel among the peoples who are the recipients of missionary work.

C., who devoted his entire life to learning Sanskrit, Bengali, and Marati, translated the Bible or parts of it into thirty-seven languages of India. His works of translation and his mastery of languages place him among the founders of prose in Bengali. He also founded the mission of Serampore College, which developed programs for the instruction of leaders and pastors.

C. was at the forefront in the struggle against the practice of *sati,* the act of burning a widow on her husband's funeral pyre. He also proposed a missionary conference to achieve greater cooperation in the missionary field. Such a conference did not take place until one hundred years later in Edinburgh. C.'s missionary work established the foundations for the multiple missionary tasks of the nineteenth century.

More critical work is required in the analysis of the work of C. Nevertheless, he is remembered for his vigor, dedication, and creativity in the missionary field.

— CCO

Carlstadt, Andreas Rudolph Bodenstein (1480?–1541). Also Karlstadt. Radical German reformer. He was a colleague of ⇒Luther in Wittenberg until his positions turned out to be too radical for Luther. He studied at the universities of Erfurt and Cologne. He was originally a follower of the teachings of ⇒Thomas Aquinas, but after a spiritual crisis he joined the Reformers.

In 1521, during Luther's absence from Wittenberg, he tried to lead the reforming efforts in the direction of a revolution, advocating the abolition of private confession, as well as of the elevation of the host, priestly vestments, clerical celibacy (he married in 1522), and the use of paintings and images. There were riots against the Mass, with much destruction of art and the property of the church. Upon Luther's return in March of 1522, C. had to leave the city in disgrace. He lived in obscurity and poverty for the greater part of the rest of his life. For a while he was a staunch critic of Luther, and then, in 1530, he established himself in Switzerland, where he worked until his death with the reformation directed by ⇒Zwingli.

Carnell, Edward J. (1919–83). Conservative Protestant theologian who, while defending traditional theology, tried to distance himself from some of its most extreme positions. He completed two doctorates, one in Harvard with a specialization in the thought of Reinhold ⇒Niebuhr, and another in Boston centered on ⇒Kierkegaard. After teaching in Gordon College near Boston for three years, he transferred to Fuller Theological Seminary in Pasadena, California. There he served as professor and for four years as president. His chief work is *The Case for Orthodoxy* (1960), in which he criticizes fundamentalism, at the same time defending orthodoxy.

Cartwright, Thomas (1535–1603). Principal Puritan theologian in the sixteenth century. He was professor of the University of Cambridge, although his presence there and in England was repeatedly interrupted by his conflicts with the authorities. He was removed from office when Mary Tudor became queen of England. Under the new regime of Elizabeth, who succeeded Mary, his position was not much better, for when he sought to cleanse the Church of England of all that was not the "pure Christianity" of the New Testament, this Puritan position brought him new difficulties. As a result, he abandoned England and went to live in Ireland. In 1569 he was restored to his professorship, but once again he was removed from office the following year. He then spent some time in Geneva, where his contacts with ⇒Beza reinforced his Puritan and Presbyterian positions. Back in England, he attacked the episcopal system of government of the Church of England, and his Presbyterianism found an echo in many persons who saw the bishops as officials of the state rather than as leaders of the community of believers. He was arrested for his ideas in 1590 and absolved in 1592. Upon the death of Elizabeth, he addressed to King James a Millennial Petition, which received that name because it claimed to express the opinions of a thousand ministers. Although it did not say anything against the episcopacy, it asked the new king to free the Puritans from a

number of ceremonies that they considered false, such as confirmation, the use of rings in marriage, and certain ecclesiastical vestments. It also asked the king to promulgate laws against the profanation of the Lord's Day, another subject of great interest to Puritans.

Case, Shirley Jackson (1872–1947). Liberal Baptist theologian who spent the greater part of his academic career at the University of Chicago. His field of specialization was the New Testament, to which he applied the historical-critical methods that were then at their peak. Among his chief works are *Social Origins of Christianity* (1923) and *Jesus: A New Biography* (1927).

Cassian ⇒John Cassian

Cassiodorus (477?–573?). His complete name was Magnus Aurelius Cassiodorus Senator. An important and respected official in the court of the Ostrogothic king Theodoric and his successors, C. was notable for his mediating efforts between the Arian conquerors (⇒Arius) and the ancient traditions of the conquered, who followed the Nicene faith (Council of ⇒Nicaea, 325). When he was sixty years old, he retired to a monastery he founded on land he had inherited in Vivarium. Toward the end of his life, he resigned from the office of abbot of this monastery and lived as a simple monk until his death.

A scholar who combined physical work with study, C. wrote two historical works: *Chronicle from Adam until the Year 519* and *On the Origins and Deeds of the Goths*. He also was the promoter and compiler of the *Tripartite History*, in which he continued the famous *Ecclesiastical History* of ⇒Eusebius of Caesarea by appending the contributions of ⇒Socrates the historian, ⇒Sozomenos, and ⇒Theodoret. An assiduous student of ⇒Augustine and of some later Augustinian theologians such as ⇒Claudianus Mamertus, C. attempted to unite secular and classical learning with religious knowledge, above all in his great work *Institutions of the Divine and Secular Letters*, known as *Institutions*.

The influence of C. on the Middle Ages was enormous, because the *Tripartite History* as well as the *Institutions* became the fundamental texts through which the Middle Ages received and interpreted much of the learning of antiquity.

JLG

Castellio, Sebastian (1515–63).

Protestant theologian and French Hellenist, famous translator of the Bible. In Strassburg he met ⇒Calvin (1540), who offered him the rectorship of the college he had established in Geneva. Soon deep differences flared up between them, since the uncompromising attitude of Calvin and his followers could not accept the broad tolerance of C.'s spirit. In addition, he denied the dogmas of the descent into hell and predestination and proposed the removal from the Bible of the Song of Songs, which he judged to be obscene. Having severed relations with Calvin, he resigned as rector of the College of Geneva. Because he feared the persecution of his adversaries, he found refuge in Lausanne and then in Basel (1544), where he was welcomed, but did not find support of any kind. To support himself and his family, he was compelled to perform difficult and ill-paid manual labor, which undermined his health. Finally he secured a professorship of Greek, which he occupied until his death.

The execution of Michael ⇒Servetus, ordered by Calvin and ⇒Beza, and which C. greatly condemned, inspired him to write the book *De haereticis an sint persequendi* (1554; Whether Heretics Are to Be Persecuted), a defense of religious tolerance. This teaching, which he always maintained, provoked the indignation of the Calvinists to the point that after his death they exhumed his remains and scattered his ashes (a desecration for which some of his disciples made amends by erecting a monument to his memory in the cathedral).

JDR

Castro, Emilio (1927–).

Uruguayan Methodist who has been a leader in the world ecumenical movement. He was coordinator of UNELAM (Provisional Commission for Latin American Evangelical Unity), subsequently director of the Commission for Mission and Evangelism, and then general secretary of the ⇒World Council of Churches. C. has a doctorate from the University of Lausanne and is an author of articles and books on mission and the unity of the church, including *Freedom in Mission* (1985) and *A Passion for Unity* (1992).

CCO

Catharinus, Ambrosius (1487–1553).

Dominican who excelled through his polemics against Protestantism and his contributions to the Council of ⇒Trent, but who was also strongly criticized by the Dominicans themselves for the boldness of some of his teachings. His birth name was Lancelot Polito, but he adopted the religious name of Ambrose C., by which he is known. Part of the opposition of some of the Dominicans was because C. combined the Thomism of the Dominicans (⇒Thomas Aquinas) with some positions of Duns ⇒Scotus that his critics saw as typically Franciscan. The most disputed point of his theology is his opinion regarding predestination. According to C., there are a small number of elect, predestined by God and whom, without destroying free will, God impels by irresistible grace. Among such are found the apostles, the Virgin Mary, and a few more. The majority are elect in a secondary sense, for God gives them the grace that is necessary to choose salvation, but this salvation depends on the use that they make of that grace. Because of such opinions, C. has been considered a predecessor of Luis de ⇒Molina and his theory of a "middle knowledge" (*scientia media*).

JLG

Catherine of Genoa (1447–1510).

Italian mystic of aristocratic origin whose father was the viceroy of Naples. In the midst of an unhappy marriage of convenience, she had a mystical experience of conversion, in which her husband followed her shortly afterward. Both then devoted themselves to a simple life, living in a hospital where they cared for the sick and poor. After the death of her husband, C. began to share her experiences and thoughts with her disciples. These disciples have preserved for us some of her thought, for no work written by C. has survived. Perhaps the most interesting feature of her theology is what she says about purgatory. For her, purgatory has nothing to do with punishment; it is the purifying fire into which the soul casts itself for the love of God, seeking the purification that is necessary to be closer to God. C. was canonized in 1737.

JLG

Catherine of Siena (1347–80).

She was designated a ⇒doctor of the church in 1970 in recognition of the importance of her writings and her exemplary life. She died when she was only thirty-three years old. Daughter of a prosperous wool merchant, she was the twenty-fourth of twenty-five children. She resisted her father's wish for an advantageous marriage, stating that she was called to be married to Christ. After imposing on her a painful punishment, her father came to recognize that C. was called by God when he saw a dove hovering over her head while she prayed. Without entering a religious order, C. took the habit of a Dominican tertiary.

For three years she suffered doubts and demonic visions. When she finally overcame those doubts and Christ appeared to her, C. reproached him: "And where were You while all of this was happening?" The divine answer, "I was in your heart," led her to trust in herself. This first phase culminated in the "mystical betrothal" with Christ, who put a ring on her finger that only she could see.

In a second phase, C. went out of her way to be kind to others. In this way she obeyed the order of Jesus, "What you cannot do for me, you should do for your neighbor." For several years she cared for the ill, gave alms to the poor, helped prisoners and victims of the plague, and mediated between the feudal families of Siena. In spite of her young age, she attracted female and male disciples who affectionately called her Mother.

In 1374 she began the last stage of her life, during which she wrote the *Dialogues*, in which she describes her mystical conversations with Christ. During those last years of her life, C. devoted herself to politics in the secular world and in the universal church, writing hundreds of letters to the pope, to kings, and to other leaders, advising them how to carry out their functions. Apparently influenced by a vision of Christ crowned with the papal tiara, she mediated the conflict between Florence and the papacy in Avignon. She traveled there to interview Gregory XI and convinced him to return to Rome, but Gregory died shortly thereafter and was succeeded by Urban VI, whose reign was so disastrous that the cardinals elected a second pope. When Urban refused to abdicate, a war between the two popes began, in which C. remained faithful to the unworthy Urban for having been legitimately consecrated as pope. Praying to obtain the grace to be able to expiate the sins of the church, C. had a final vision: the church was a great ship that she carried on her shoulders. After several weeks of intense pain and paralysis, C. died on April 30, 1380. Her visions and mystical experiences did not separate her from the world, but led her to become deeply involved in it, always guided by the belief that she had to "redeem" with her life the time that God had given her.

AMID

CELAM. In 1955, as a result of the first general conference of Latin American bishops, celebrated in Rio de Janeiro, the Latin American Episcopal Council (CELAM) was created. As an organ for consultation, the aim of CELAM is "to study the problems of the Church in Latin America, coordinating its activities and preparing conferences for its episcopate."

Between 1955 and 1968, the year of the Second Episcopal Conference held in ⇒Medellín, Colombia, CELAM concentrated on two areas: the life of the church (catechesis, mission, education) and social and economic research.

CELAM took upon itself the task of developing an "Integrated Pastoral Action," the intention of which is to integrate pastoral work with the social reality of the continent. These studies led the Latin American episcopate to a new awareness of the reality of extreme poverty and exploitation that the people of Latin America suffer, along with the stagnation of the church in its evangelizing efforts.

On the other hand, these investigations also led the Latin American episcopate to become acquainted with the movements of biblical and liturgical renovation in Europe, with the new theological tendencies, and with the church's various forms of social action promoting justice in the world. Even more, the Second Vatican Council (⇒Vatican II) created a fertile space so that the Latin American episcopate could share and discuss the concerns of the region on a global and ecumenical level. In addition, the Second Vatican Council gave a prominent place to regional conferences of bishops, articulating a new model of relationship between the Vatican and the Latin American episcopate and promoting the regional and communal task of the church in the region.

With this impulse, with exposure to new theological tendencies, and with a solid foundation in theological and social research in the region itself, CELAM prepared its Second Episcopal Conference in Medellín. Aware that beyond adapting the documents of Vatican II, it was necessary to create a theology and an ecclesiastical documentation rooted in the life and reality of the continent, Medellin proposed to study the condition of the church within the complex social and economic transformation of the continent. The method, which is evident in the documents of Medellín, is the well-known hermeneutical model of "seeing," "judging," and "acting."

Although a uniform line of thought does not exist in the documents of Medellín, there are some important themes, such as: (1) the church is understood as an integral part of the Latin American people; (2) Latin America should be conceived of as a geographical unity, even though there is great diversity among the nations and cultures; (3) the condition of underdevelopment in the continent requires concrete action on the part of the church; and (4) the church must read the signs of the times and discover the plan of God for Latin American humanity. All of this theological reflection served as leaven so that the Latin American theology of liberation could be born.

In 1979 CELAM celebrated its third conference in ⇒Puebla, Mexico. This conference concentrated its efforts on ecclesiology, debating in particular the ecclesial base communities (*Comunidades eclesiales de base*, CEBs). One of the questions that occupied CELAM is the relationship of the CEBs with traditional ecclesiology, that is, the life of the church as a sacramental and missional community.

In Puebla, the documents also reflected an absence of agreement concerning the task, function, and mission of the church, and therefore many are of the opinion that Puebla was a movement backward in comparison with Medellín. On the other hand, although in an ambiguous way as compared with Medellín, Puebla continued to affirm the religious and social role of the church in a continent marked by poverty, oppression, and political persecution. To a large extent, Puebla reflected the ambiguity that is born of the violent conflicts and ideological controversies of the continent. Puebla also did not discard the development and influence of the theology of liberation, but neither did it issue a declaration that would signal approval of that theology which was indigenous and consonant with the concerns of the episcopacy a decade earlier.

In 1992 the fourth conference of the Latin American episcopate was held in Santo Domingo, Dominican Republic. Under the theme of the encounter between two cultures, the "discovery" of America, CELAM changed the tone of its political, social, and economic agenda for another that is more ecclesiastical and founded on the life and mission of the church. Pope John Paul II and CELAM debated the theme of the "new evangelization," remem-

bering and recognizing that the history of the evangelization of Latin America is full of errors, with a certain level of success, and in need of renewal. In Santo Domingo, CELAM (1) continued to affirm the popular character of the church and the importance of solidarity in the struggles of the Latin American peoples; (2) named the new agents of evangelization, acknowledging the action of marginalized groups such as blacks, Amerindians, women, and children, and the need for the gospel in their lives; (3) recognized the challenge of environmental damage and the need for an ecclesiastical effort that protects creation; (4) affirmed the quest and the theological task of the Latin American church to become inculturated on its own soil; and (5) affirmed the missionary character of the church in its efforts toward justice and solidarity with excluded peoples.

For many, Santo Domingo was in close continuity with Medellín and Puebla, providing more clarity and definition for the life of the church. On the other hand, some liberation theologians, and especially Leonardo ⇒Boff, saw in Santo Domingo the beginning of a process whereby the social and economic commitment to overcome underdevelopment is replaced by cultural and anthropological analysis.

Between 1992 and 2002, CELAM focused its work on the theme of the church in the third millennium and its pastoral challenges. In recognition of the transformations in the culture, the economy, politics, the family, the means of communication, and the religious phenomenon, among others, CELAM endeavors to redefine the encounter with Jesus Christ in life in community, solidarity, and inculturation. With these changes in mind, CELAM has identified six ecclesiastical expressions: (1) the church in permanent conversion, (2) the church in communion, (3) the church in solidarity, (4) the inculturated church, (5) the missionary church, and (6) the church closer to the gospel. In its pastoral efforts, CELAM continues to emphasize that the gospel should appeal to the people, over against a coercive type of evangelization; that pastoral work is based on action and gestures of solidarity which have a sacramental character; and that pastoral work ought always to be in defense of those who are excluded. It is evident that Santo Domingo did not take up again the theme of liberation theology, although foundations and elements of that theology can be identified in the theological reflection of CELAM in the last decade of the twentieth century.

CCO

Celestine (?–432). Pope, successor of ⇒Zosimus, who, like his predecessor, clashed with the bishops of the province of Africa over matters of jurisdiction, and who also participated in the debate surrounding ⇒Nestorius, whose doctrines were declared heretical by a Roman synod convened by C. In addition, his legates supported the position of ⇒Cyril of Alexandria against Nestorius in the Council of ⇒Ephesus (431). Apparently at the request of ⇒Prosper of Aquitaine, C. wrote a letter in which he praised the theology of ⇒Augustine. Someone interpolated in that letter, possibly in the sixth century, a series of "chapters" or headings against Semi-Pelagianism. Since posterity believed that those chapters were part of C.'s original letter, for some time they were taken as a trustworthy interpretation almost contemporary with the teachings of Augustine. But in reality, its teachings are closer to the moderate and modified Augustinianism of the Synod of ⇒Orange.

—

JLG

Centuries of Magdeburg. A history of the Christian church prepared in Magdeburg in defense of the Lutheran positions and under the direction of Matthias ⇒Flacius. The thesis of this work, published in Basel between 1559 and 1574, is that Lutheranism is simply the restoration of the most authentic Christian tradition, from which Roman Catholicism has strayed in its doctrines as well as in its practice and worship. It was given the name of *Centuries* because each volume was dedicated to one century of the history of the church. The death of Flacius interrupted the project, which did not get past the thirteenth century.

Although the work was interrupted by the death of its chief promoter, its impact was notable, and the Roman church saw the need to respond. After several partial refutations of minor importance, the great reply to the *Centuries* began to be published in 1588. This is the *Ecclesiastical Annals* of ⇒Baronius.

—

JLG

Cerdo (2nd century). A native of Syria, C. lived in Rome around the year 140. He was one of the first proponents of Christian ⇒Gnosticism, according to ⇒Irenaeus. It was he who taught ⇒Marcion that the God of the Old Testament and the God of the New Testament are different, the first evil and the latter good. The God of the New Testament could not be known

outside of Jesus Christ—and certainly not in the Old Testament. He also maintained that what is physical is bad, and therefore Jesus Christ could not have come in the flesh, but only in spirit. This Docetism is a common element in the teachings of C. and Marcion and of Gnosticism in general.

—

EA

Cerinthus (ca. 100). Leader of a Judeo-Christian sect with gnostic tendencies. He believed that the world had been created by "an inferior divinity" (demiurge) or by the angels. He also taught that Jesus had received "Christ" during his baptism. This was the manifestation of the power of God, which revealed the Father and enabled him to preach and do miracles. Nevertheless, this divine gift abandoned Jesus before his death and resurrection. C. accepted circumcision and the observance of the Sabbath but rejected all the writings of the New Testament except Matthew. According to ⇒Irenaeus, "the false teachings" of C. led John to write his Gospel. Several ancient writers attributed the creation of the gnostic heresy to C. or to ⇒Simon Magus.

—

AEM

Cerularius, Michael (?–1059). Patriarch of Constantinople from 1043 to 1058, and therefore at the time of the rupture with Rome in 1054. C. was not well versed in theology, but he was a person of firm convictions who had actively and bravely participated in several conflicts in Byzantium. When he became patriarch, he did not seem to have been aware of the claims that Rome had been making for some time of possessing the primacy among all the patriarchates (Rome, Constantinople, Jerusalem, Alexandria, and Antioch). But he did have a deep conviction of his authority in spiritual matters, even above the emperor. Later, when Cardinal ⇒Humbert of Silva Candida, the papal legate, wanted to have the Roman primacy recognized in Constantinople, C. refused, even though for political reasons the emperor favored the efforts of Humbert. In the conflict that ensued between the patriarch and the crown, for some time the former was able to resist thanks to the support of the faithful; but in the end he was deposed and died two months later in exile.

Although in the West historians frequently refer to the "schism of Cerularius" or to the moment when Humbert placed the letter of excommunication on the altar of the church of

Saint Sophia as the definitive break between East and West, the truth is that his contemporaries did not give much importance to the matter. C.'s biographers—among them Michael ⇒Psellus—hardly mention the event, while they give great importance to other actions of C., particularly to his unusual courage in facing the authorities.

The few works of C. that survive include a sermon on the festival of the restoration of images and several synodical epistles.

―――

JLG

Chafer, Lewis Sperry (1871–1952).

Known chiefly as the founder and first president of Dallas Theological Seminary (or Evangelical Theological College) in 1924, a school recognized as the principal academic center of dispensationalist theology. He was considered the successor of his friend C. I. ⇒Scofield, who trained him theologically.

His theological interest was to present the Scriptures in a systematic way, especially emphasizing (1) the grace of God in Christ as the center of salvation and of Christianity, (2) the importance of understanding and interpreting the Bible by following the dispensationalist scheme, and (3) the spiritual development of the believer. He created his educational vision on the basis of these principles, which led to the foundation of the seminary in Dallas.

―――

ALG

Chakkari, Vengal (1880–1958).

Born in Madras, C. was an originator of contextual theology. Together with ⇒Chenchiah, he stimulated and took the first steps to contextualize Christian missionary theology in India. His two most important works are *Jesus the Avatar* (1927) and *The Cross and Indian Thought* (1932).

―――

CCO

Chakko, Sarah (1905–54).

Born in Trichur, Kerala, South India, she was one of the forerunners who, at the beginning of the development of the ecumenical movement, emphasized the place and participation of women. For many years she served as president of the Commission on Life and Work of Women in the Church, in the ⇒World Council of Churches.

―――

CCO

Chalcedon, Council of (451).

Fourth ecumenical council, the chief task of which consisted of defining the doctrine of the two natures in the one person (or hypostasis) of Jesus Christ. The debate that characterized this council arose from the contrast between two christological tendencies. The Antiochene tendency insisted on safeguarding the humanity of the Savior, while the Alexandrian underscored his divinity. The first feared that if the unity between the humanity and the divinity in Jesus were too greatly emphasized, what is human would be absorbed or eclipsed by what is divine; therefore this Christology tended to be "disjunctive," that is, to insist on the distinction, difference, and even separation between the humanity of Jesus and his divinity. The second tendency, the Alexandrian, feared that Jesus would be divided into two persons, one divine and another human; therefore its Christology was "unitive." Among the exponents of the Antiochene tendency before Chalcedon (although there were serious differences among them) were ⇒Paul of Samosata, ⇒Eustathius of Antioch, ⇒Diodore of Tarsus, ⇒Theodore of Mopsuestia, and ⇒Nestorius. Among the Alexandrians (although they also had serious differences among them because of their diverse circumstances and times) were ⇒Apollinaris, ⇒Cyril of Alexandria, ⇒Dioscorus, and ⇒Eutyches.

In the Council of ⇒Ephesus (431), the extreme Antiochene position of Nestorius had been condemned. N. underscored the distinction between the divinity and the humanity in Christ to such a point that he seemed to be speaking of two different persons. From then on, the Alexandrian party began gaining strength, to the extent that it began seeking to condemn even the most moderate Antiochenes. Dioscorus, who was at that time patriarch of Alexandria, eventually got the weak emperor Theodosius II to summon a council with that purpose. Pope ⇒Leo the Great wrote a *Tome* in which he essentially reaffirmed the ancient formula of ⇒Tertullian, that in Christ there are "two natures" or substances and "one person." When this council gathered in Ephesus in 449, Dioscorus, who presided over it, did not allow the representatives of Leo to read his epistle to the assembly, nor did he allow any defense of the Antiochene position. Without further deliberation, all the Antiochenes were condemned and the bishops who did not affirm Alexandrian Christology were deposed.

In Rome, Leo called the council that had just met "the robbers synod" or *latrocinium*—a name by which it is now generally known—and he requested the convocation of a new council. Several of the Antiochene bishops who had been deposed did likewise (⇒Flavian of Constantinople, ⇒Ibas of Edessa, and Domno of Antioch, among many others). Dioscorus had imperial support, and the Alexandrian party seemed to have won the game when Theodosius II died in an equestrian accident and his sister Pulcheria succeeded him. Pulcheria and her consort, Marcian, convened a new council, which assembled in Chalcedon in 451.

At the Basilica of Saint Euphemia, in Chalcedon, 520 bishops met, besides a dozen and a half imperial officials, in the greatest of all the councils up to that day. The first thing that the council did was to examine the acts of the *latrocinium*, verifying the way in which Dioscorus had led it. Dioscorus was declared a heretic, deposed, and sent into exile, but all the other participants in the "robbery" were pardoned. Then the council devoted itself to finding an intermediate position between the Alexandrians and the most extreme Antiochenes. To show that the whole affair was not simply an attack on all that was Alexandrian, the council read and approved the *Synodical Epistles* of Cyril of Alexandria, in which he explained, among other things, why Nestorius had been condemned. In addition, the council listened to and approved the *Tome* of Leo.

Instead of offering a new creed, the Council of Chalcedon proclaimed a Definition of Faith, which was not meant to be spoken as a creed, and therefore does not use liturgical language, but is rather an explanation of the faith of the church with respect to Jesus Christ. According to that definition, Jesus Christ is

> perfect in divinity and perfect in humanity; true God and true man, of rational soul and body [against Apollinaris]; consubstantial with the Father according to the divinity [against Arius], and also consubstantial with us according to the humanity [against Eutyches] . . . of the Virgin Mary, the Mother of God [against Nestorius] . . . in two natures [against Eutyches and Dioscorus], without confusion, without mutation, without division, without separation, and without the disappearance of the difference in the natures because of the union, but conserving the properties of each nature, and uniting them in one person or hypostasis [with all this the council adopts an intermediate position between the Alexandrians and the Antiochenes], not divided or split into two persons

[against Nestorius], but one and the same only-begotten Son.

Although there were other christological controversies after that date, it can be said that the Council of Chalcedon established what would be christological orthodoxy from then on. Some did not accept it because it seemed too inclined toward the Alexandrian position. These persons gathered beyond the borders of the Roman Empire, in Persia, where they formed what is now called the Nestorian church, which still exists today. Others did not accept it for the opposite reason, because it seemed to them too Antiochene. These churches are called Monophysite, because they supposedly affirm that in Christ there is only "one nature": the Coptic Church, the church of Ethiopia, the church of Armenia, the Jacobite church of Syria, and others.

—

JLG

Chandler, Samuel (1693–1766).
Presbyterian pastor, author of two volumes on *The Life of David*. He provoked debates by comparing David with the deceased King George II of England.

—

JLG

Channing, William Ellery (1780–1842).
Urban pastor, eloquent preacher, and liberal theologian, C. is known as the founder of Unitarianism. He broke with the theological orthodoxy of the New England of his day, which was centered on Calvinism and its teachings on depravity, election, and irresistible grace (⇒Calvin, ⇒Dort). Upon breaking with Calvinism, C. redefined human nature as well as grace and helped to change the intellectual climate in the United States of the nineteenth century.

In 1803 he was ordained and called to the Federal Street Church in Boston, where he served until his death. In his famous Baltimore sermon (1819), he explained the basis of the Unitarian movement. C. maintained that Unitarianism was a biblical faith and that the Bible is the only source of truth. According to him, reason supports and aids revelation, especially when the historical and critical method is used for the interpretation of the Holy Scriptures. On this basis, C. opposed not only the doctrine of the Trinity but, even more and with greater tenacity, the Calvinist vision of a depraved humanity and an angry God. Against Calvinism, C. affirmed the human experience of being able to develop morally and spiritually. This led him to redefine both human and divine nature, which, according to him, finally are the same. C. located the divine attributes in the individual human soul, which in his opinion could be developed infinitely in the likeness of God. Because of his vision of humanity, C. promoted education and moral persuasion as the best ways to change society.

—

EZ

Chao, Tzu Ch'en (1888–1979).

A Chinese theologian, native of the province of Kuching. He devoted his work to the conceptualization of the Christian faith in Chinese culture and society, particularly in relation to elitist groups. His works, *Christian Philosophy* and *Life of Jesus*, make no reference to the supernatural, focusing rather on the ethical, which is typical of Confucian thought. He was also a distinguished ecumenical leader on the world Protestant scene.

—

CCO

Chauncy, Charles.

Name of two theologians from one family. The great-grandfather (1592–1672), a native of England, was the second president of Harvard University. His extreme Puritanism caused conflicts with the authorities until he finally recanted. Later he changed his mind about that retraction, published a treatise defending his previous Puritan positions, and left for New England. His best-known work is a treatise, written in the style of a catechism, with questions and answers, *Doctrine of the Sacrament, with the Right Use Thereof* (1642).

The great-grandson (1705–87) studied at Harvard and distinguished himself through his defense of Presbyterianism, particularly in his *Complete View of the Episcopacy*. He was known above all because toward the end of his life he adopted a universalist position, affirming that all will be included in the final restoration. He wrote several works on this theme between 1782 and his death in 1787. Possibly the most important is *Divine Glory Brought to View in the Final Salvation of All Men* (1783).

—

JLG

Chemnitz, Martin (1522–86).

Lutheran theologian born in the city of Treuenbrietzen. He died in Brunswick. Due to the poverty of his family and in order to earn his living, he repeatedly had to interrupt his study of mathematics and astronomy, which began in Frankfort on the Oder (1543) and continued in Wittenberg (1545). As a consequence of the Smalkald War, he was granted the post of rector of the cathedral school of Königsburg. In the university of that city, he received the master's degree. During his stay in Salfeld, where he sought refuge to avoid being a victim of the plague that terrorized the city of Königsburg, he began his theological studies. Upon his return to Königsburg (1550), he was appointed librarian to Duke Albert of Prussia. He applied himself with great enthusiasm to the study of theology, and in 1553 he left for Wittenberg, where he was one of the most faithful companions of ⇒Melanchthon, whose *Loci communes* he expounded in public. The influence of the latter led him to understand better the distinction between the law and the gospel. He joined the faculty of philosophy of the university and was ordained to the ministry in St. Mary's Church in November of 1554. In 1558 he received his doctorate in sacred theology from the University of Rostock. Together with his colleague Joachim Moerling, he participated in the reorganization of the Lutheran Church in Prussia, and in 1567 he was called to be superintendent of the Lutheran Church in Brunswick.

In spite of his constant devotion to his mentor Melanchthon, C. developed a conservative position which combined a biblical posture with a candid traditionalism, thus avoiding the extremes of the uncompromising position that was characteristic of the Gnesio-Lutherans who followed ⇒Flacius, as well as that of the no-less-extravagant disciples of Melanchthon called Philippists. As a resource against the schismatic sectarianism that divided the Lutheran movement after 1546, the pragmatic administrative instinct of C. led him to insist on symbols of authority, thus proposing his teaching of the *ubivolipraesentia* of the humanity of Christ (Christ's humanity can be present wherever he wills) in the hypostatic union which is affirmed in the Formula of ⇒Concord, of which he was coauthor (1577).

By nature C. was a reflective theologian, although eclectic, and a man of profound scholarship. He was also a linguist, but above all he was a great representative and leader of the church. His main goal was to present the teachings of the gospel in a practical, simple, and concise way. His insistence on the creation of a particular ecclesiastical policy, such as the use of a black garment without adornment by women in the celebration of the Lord's Supper, established certain patterns in the liturgical customs of the church.

His masterpiece is *Loci theologici* (1591; Theological Topics). In addition, he wrote *Vera et sana doctrina de praesentia corporis et sanguinis Christi in Coena Domini* (1560; True and Sound Doctrine concerning the Presence of the Body and Blood of Christ in the Lord's Supper), and *Repetitio sanae doctrinae, etc.* (1561; Repetition of Sound Doctrine). In collaboration with J. ⇒Andrea, he wrote *Corpus doctrinae Julium* (1569; Julian Body of Doctrine), which was the ecclesiastical code of the duchy of Brunswick-Witenbuttel. For Prussia he published, with Moerlin, *Corpus doctrinae Pruthenicum* (1566; Prussian Body of Doctrine), and against the Jesuits he wrote *Theologiae Jesuitarum praecipua capita* (1562; Main Chapters of the Theology of the Jesuits) and *Examen Concilii Tridentini* (1565–73; Analysis of the Council of Trent).

His chief work, which exhibits extraordinary scholarship with biblical foundations, patristic references, and ample knowledge of the history of Roman Catholic dogma, is an analysis of the decisions of the Council of ⇒Trent. This work enlarged his reputation beyond the borders of Germany, gaining for him the respect of the Jesuit movement as a formidable opponent and scholar. This made him a valuable resource person who was in great demand during the doctrinal disputes of his time.

———

JDR

Chenchiah, Pandipeddi (1886–1959).
A native of Madras, C. was one of the most prominent lay theologians in India and in the ecumenical movement. He and his brother-in-law ⇒Chakkarai founded the organization Christo Samaj, which promoted the Indian character of the Christian church. In addition, he participated in the group Rethinking Christianity, the purpose of which was to promote a secular mission of the church, and which generated support for Indian identity.

———

CCO

Ch'eng Ching Yi (1881–1939). Also
Cheng Jingyi. Born and raised in Beijing, C. was one of the outstanding leaders of Protestantism in China at the beginning of the twentieth century. Between 1910 and 1930 he focused on creating an authentically Chinese church, independent of the missionary movement. At the World Missionary Conference of Edinburgh in 1910, he declared himself in favor of the indigenization of the faith in its context and promoted the elimination of denominationalism in the work of the "younger" churches in the non-Western world.

———

CCO

Chenu, Marie-Dominique (1895–1990). A French Dominican, C. was a leader
of the movement in Catholic theology of the twentieth century known as *ressourcement.* He pursued a return to the historical sources of the Christian tradition in order to revitalize and shape contemporary theology. Underneath that impulse was the desire to free Roman Catholic theology from the antimodern and anti-Protestant position that had emerged in connection with the Councils of ⇒Trent and ⇒Vatican I. C.'s theology centered on a historical understanding of the theology of ⇒Thomas Aquinas in particular, and of medieval theology in general. His studies on the history of theology resulted in controversies. In 1942, his book *Une école de théologie: Le Saulchoir* (A School of Theology: *Le Saulchoir*) was removed from circulation because of its "modernist" inclinations. C., like other theologians of the *ressourcement* such as Henri de ⇒Lubac and Yves ⇒Congar, was accused of reducing the final truth of Catholic dogma to relativism, because of his emphasis on historical investigation. Today that emphasis, as well as the essential place of the incarnation in C.'s theology, are seen as forerunners of the Second Vatican Council (⇒Vatican II).

———

MAG

Cherbury, Lord Herbert (1583–1648).
British theologian and philosopher, he was one of the forerunners of British Deism, which in turn would influence some of the North American revolutionary leaders, such as Benjamin Franklin. Deism, based on empiricism and rationalism, pursued a natural and universal religion that would be grounded only on reason. C. applied himself to seeking the fundamental basis of human religiosity aside from historical events and divine revelation. He determined that universal religion, to which all the true religions could be reduced, had five essential teachings: the existence of God, the duty to worship God, the need for repentance, rewards, and punishments. The emphasis of

Deism would fall on the importance of the universal law, morality, and duty.

———

LGP

Chrysologus, Peter ⇒**Peter Chrysologus**

Chrysostom, John ⇒**John Chrysostom**

Chung, Hyun-Kyung (1956–). Korean feminist and associate professor of ecumenical theology at Union Theological Seminary in New York. Among her works is *Struggle to Be Sun Again: Introducing Asian Women Theology* (1990), in which she proposes a syncretistic and feminist theology in the context of Asian women, intersecting shamanist practices and the Christian faith and therefore incorporating the primal religious aspect into the call of liberation. Besides her written works, she is known for her polemical and controversial lectures relating to the Christian faith and the feminist Asian worldview of poor women.

———

CCO

Church and Society in Latin America ⇒**Iglesia y Sociedad en América Latina**

Chytraeus, David (1531–1600). German Lutheran theologian, professor at the University of Rostock, and one of the coauthors of the Formula of ⇒Concord (1577). Influenced mainly by the thought of ⇒Melanchthon, he worked constantly in favor of intra-Lutheran and ecumenical unity. He published works on theology and history, and commentaries on nineteen books of the Bible.

———

NRG

Clarembaud of Aras (12th century). Disciple of both ⇒Thierry of Chartres and ⇒Hugh of St. Victor. As a follower of the school of Chartres (⇒Bernard of Chartres, ⇒William of Conches), on the question of the universals he supported realism. As a follower of the school of St. Victor, he was also concerned about orthodoxy and therefore refuted the Trinitarian doctrine of ⇒Gilbert de La Porrée, making use of his realism to reject what appeared to him to be the tritheism of Gilbert.

———

JLG

Clark, Gordon Haddon (1902–86). Evangelical philosopher who defended theism against the attacks of modernism, arguing that biblical theism is intellectually sustainable. While he rejected modernism, he also rejected neo-orthodoxy. He wrote important works on the history of Western thought and of Christianity, and on contemporary thought. In his writings, he insisted that logical reason is proof of the truth, and he therefore clashed with the fideist position of Cornelius ⇒Van Til, who affirmed the incomprehensibility of God. Because of this conflict, he withdrew from the Orthodox Presbyterian Church and joined the Reformed Presbyterian Church. Among his works are *What Presbyterians Believe* (1956), *Three Types of Religious Philosophy* (1973), and *The Biblical Doctrine of Man* (1984).

———

AP

Clarke, William Newton (1841–1912). Baptist theologian, professor principally at Toronto Baptist College and at Colgate University. He sought to reconcile biblical doctrines and the Christian tradition with modern thought. His chief work is *The Use of the Scriptures in Theology* (1905).

———

JLG

Claudianus Mamertus (?–ca. 474). Follower and defender of ⇒Augustine, above all in what relates to the spirituality of the soul. Many theologians, among them ⇒Tertullian, ⇒Jerome, and ⇒Cassian, had attributed to the soul a material substance. Augustine's teaching to the contrary had aroused the criticism of ⇒Faustus of Riez. Against him, C.M. wrote his work in three books, *On the Nature of the Soul*, in which he defends the spirituality of the soul on the basis of philosophy and the authority of revelation, and then refutes the arguments of Faustus. He has been criticized, nevertheless, for thinking that angels have a material body.

———

JLG

Clement of Alexandria (ca. 150–ca. 215). Theologian born in Athens, converted from paganism to Christianity. After traveling in search of wisdom, in Alexandria he came upon ⇒Pantaenus, who from then on was his teacher, and whom he succeeded around the year 200. But the persecution of Septimus Severus two years later compelled him to flee. After this, we know that he was in Cappadocia and in Antioch, but the rest of his life is unknown.

His most important works are *Who Is the Rich Man Who Is Saved?* and a trilogy under the titles *Exhortation to the Greeks, Pedagogue,* and *Stromateis* (*Miscellanies* or Tapestries, Snippets).

Who Is the Rich Man Who Is Saved? is a homily, directed mainly to a relatively influential audience, and it is a sign that the church was beginning to make its way among the more affluent classes of Alexandrian society. What concerned C. is the saying of Jesus that it is easier for a camel to go through the eye of a needle than for a rich man to enter the kingdom of heaven. While this homily utters strong and sometimes even sardonic words about the customs and the extravagances of the rich, C. concludes that, although it is more difficult for the rich to enter heaven, they can do it as long as they remember that they should not hoard riches for themselves, but share them with the needy.

The *Exhortation to the Greeks* refers to the first of the three functions of the Word to which C. will refer in his trilogy: the Word as exhorter, then as guide, and finally as teacher. Thus, the *Exhortation* is a call, in the name of the Word, to abandon pagan beliefs and practices and to adopt Christianity. It is an apology or defense of the faith, and is therefore a continuation of the work of earlier apologists, particularly ⇒Justin.

Pedagogue receives its name from the slaves who took children to the schools, and who sometimes were also their teachers. Here the Word is presented as teacher, and the believer is invited to follow the Christian life and above all to be freed from the dominion of the passions. On this point, the influence of Neoplatonism on C. is evident.

The third work does not appear to be complete, but is instead a compilation of notes and ideas. When he planned his trilogy, C. thought that the third would be the *Teacher* or *Didaskalos*. But what we have instead is this strange collection, seemingly disjointed. Thus its title, *Stromateis* (*Miscellanies*), which could be translated as "tapestries" or "snippets," and which indicates a series of threads that appear and disappear following their own design, or a series of snippets sewn together without a fixed or clear pattern. Unfortunately, in this work that is so minimally systematic or ordered, C. expounds the best of his theology.

Following the tradition of Justin and of ⇒Athenagoras, C. shows a deep admiration for the best of classical culture, and especially for Greek philosophy. Like Justin, C. starts from the doctrine of the Logos or Word, and affirms that the Greeks learned the truth through their philosophers, just as the Jews learned it through Moses, and that in both cases it was God who was making Godself known through the Word. The Law and philosophy are thus two parallel covenants that God established to lead humanity to Jesus Christ.

On the other hand, both philosophy and theology have their foundation in faith. Certainly philosophy seeks rational proofs; but philosophy itself concedes that its own "primary principles," that is, its basic axioms, cannot be proven. Thus, the very foundation of philosophy requires an act of faith. On the other hand, something similar happens with theology, which requires the use of reason in spite of being founded on faith. Therefore, C. says, "faith should be known and knowledge should be believed, through something like a divine reciprocity."

Within this frame of reference, theology has ample justification to refute and reject heresies, for although the heretics claim to have faith, they do not have the proper knowledge of the Scriptures, and therefore come to a false faith.

On the other hand, those Scriptures that the heretics cannot understand should be interpreted allegorically. On this point C. shows himself to be a faithful member of an Alexandrian tradition that will find its culmination in the work of his disciple ⇒Origen. According to C., just as the realities of this world point to the eternal truths (as ⇒Plato would say), so do the Scriptures point spiritually toward those realities. Therefore, the Scriptures have two senses, a literal one and a spiritual one. The "literal" sense is not always literalist, since in the case of a parable the "literal" sense does not consist in understanding the parable as a historical account, but in the sense of the parable, which is figurative.

In any case, the highest meaning of Scripture is the spiritual sense. The Christian who truly understands—whom C. calls the "true gnostic"—will always seek that sense, although without abandoning the literal meaning, which is for all the faithful. In this distinction, we see one of the characteristics of the theology of C., as well as of a good part of the Alexandrian school: its elitism. There is a simple truth for all believers, but above it there is a truth reserved for those who truly understand, the "true gnostics"—a phrase with which C. also rejects the so-called gnostics. Thus, for example, the Eucharist has a literal meaning for the common people among the faithful, but a deeper spiritual meaning is added for those who truly understand what the Eucharist symbolizes.

As a good Neoplatonist, C. understands that the greatest thing one can acknowledge about God is God's lack of all limitation. God is so exalted that God cannot be defined, and the best way to refer to God is through negative attributes such as "infinite" and "impassive."

This eternal God is also triune. C. appears to make of the Word of God an intermediary or bridge between the immutable One and the changing world. In this sense, he may be seen as a forerunner of ⇒Arius, although C. never denies nor explicitly limits the divinity of the Word.

Concerning the incarnation, C. rejects the Docetism of the gnostics, but his Neoplatonic inclination leads him to explanations with docetic tendencies. Thus, for example, in a passage full of internal contradictions, C. affirms that Jesus ate not because he really needed to, but in order to refute the opinions of the Docetists who might think that his body was not real.

———

JLG

Clement of Rome (?–101?). According to the episcopal lists of ⇒Eusebius of Caesarea and ⇒Irenaeus of Lyon, C. was the third bishop of Rome. Apparently this C. was very well known, but, as happens with most of the initial names on these lists, we know little about his life and deeds. ⇒Origen mistakenly identified this C. with the collaborator of Paul who is mentioned in Philippians 4:3. Then history and tradition affirmed that C. was bishop of Rome during the reign of Domitian (ca. 96). Because of the vast literature that was associated with him, it is evident that C. was held in high esteem. Of these writings only one, the *First Epistle of Clement*, is definitely authentic. In reality it is an anonymous document, for in its solemn heading the document presents itself as written by the "pilgrim Church of God in Rome to the pilgrim Church of God in Corinth." But since the days of ⇒Hegesippus (ca. 150), the author has been identified as C., the third bishop of Rome. The date of the composition of this letter is an object of debate. Some scholars, basing their arguments on the references to the temple in Jerusalem and the traditions about Paul and Peter, are of the opinion that it was written before C. became bishop, that is, during the decades of the 70s or 80s. Others, taking as the starting point the ecclesiastical

dissensions that occasioned the letter, think that they do not reflect the conditions of the first century, and suggest a date in the middle of the second century. The academic consensus is that the calamities and tribulations that, according to the letter, prevented an immediate response to the conflicts in Corinth allude to the persecution under Domitian, and thus that the letter was written during some pause of that persecution or immediately after it (ca. 95/96). Since recent studies have refuted the truthfulness of the tradition of Domitian as a second Nero, and because of the ecclesiastical structure that is reflected in the epistle, my opinion is that it was written near 150.

In spite of the doubts regarding its author and the date of composition, the document is of great importance for the study of the development of Christian doctrine, for here we find data on the development of the canon of the New Testament, liturgical and ecclesiastical practices of the primitive church, and much more. The literary character of the document is parenetic (ethical exhortation). This exhortation is not based on Hellenistic rhetoric, as many think, but on Jewish tradition and that of early Christianity. The literary structure of the letter is difficult to determine with certainty because of the length and serpentine character of the content, which obscures the logic of the argument. After announcing the occasion and purpose of the letter (1:1–34), the author launches into a long exposition of the Christian life (4:1–36), which apparently has nothing to do with the conflict that occasioned its composition. The response to the conflicts in Corinth is finally offered in chapters 37–44, alluding to apostolic succession as the basis of the ecclesiastical hierarchy. C. suggests that the apostolic tradition initiated by Peter and Paul demands that contemporary believers accept and respect those who have subsequently been installed as bishops. Consequently, those who cause division should be expelled for the good of the community—a practice that has appeared over and over again in church history. As he finishes the main theme, the author concludes by instructing his readers on love and obedience. He offers a solemn liturgical prayer and appeals to the intimate relation between Rome and Corinth as a basis for his instruction.

———

AP

Clement of Smolensk (12th century). Russian theologian, metropolitan bishop of Kiev from 1147. Although he enjoyed

great fame as a scholar and theologian, of his writings there remains only a letter directed to a presbyter who did not like his allegorical exegesis. C. responds by indicating that the purely literal reading does not always make sense. Thus he says, for example, "What does it matter to me that Jacob walks around limping?" Then, with a series of quotations, he tries to prove that allegorical exegesis was always the one preferred by the ancients.

———
JLG

Climacus, John (ca. 570–649).

Ascetic and mystic Christian who withdrew from the world to lead a contemplative life. C. arrived at the monastery of Mount Sinai at the age of sixteen, and after his conversion to the monastic life he dedicated the rest of his days to silent meditation, prayer, and the mortification of the body. In his work *The Ladder of Paradise* or *The Ladder of the Divine Ascent*, C. reflects about the many vices and virtues linked with the monastic life. He presents thirty steps that can lead the Christian to "spiritual perfection," a number that corresponds to the age of Christ when he was baptized by John the Baptist in the Jordan River.

———
AEM

Clinebell, Howard (1922–).

American specialist in the psychology of religion. He has worked as a pastor, counselor, and supervisor of clinical pastoral education, and has published in all of these areas. His books have been very influential on pastoral psychology. His theory on "integral health and development" should be understood as a reaction to the influence of Rogerian theory (Carl ⇒Rogers) on American pastoral care. In response, C. developed a less individualistic theory of pastoral care, with greater focus on interpersonal dynamics. His best-known book is probably *Growth Counseling: Hope-Centered Methods of Actualizing Human Wholeness* (1979).

———
JR

Cobb, John B. (1925–).

U.S. theologian and founder of the Center for Process Studies. He was born in Japan, the son of missionaries, and lived there until 1939. His experience there awakened his interest in the dialogue between Christianity and Buddhism. He studied at the University of Chicago, where he received a master's degree and then a doctorate in 1952,

under the supervision of Charles ⇒Hartshorne. Although his chief interest is the process theology developed by A. N. ⇒Whitehead and Hartshorne, he has also become interested in ecology, lay theology, and more recently in liberation theologies. In his chief works he uses process theology to interpret the main Christian doctrines, especially the doctrines of God, of humanity, and of Christ.

———
LGP

Cocceius, Johannes (1603–69).

Also known as Koch, Cox, Coccejus. German Protestant theologian, professor of Hebrew in Bremen (1630), then in Franeker (1636), and finally professor of dogmatic theology in Leiden (1636). Starting from the principle that the Bible, and only the Bible, is the Word of God, he ardently applied himself to the study of the Scriptures. The fruit of those efforts was his work *Summa doctrinae de foedere et testamento Dei* (Summa of the Doctrine of the Covenant and Testament of God), in which he developed his theology of the covenant. C. distinguished two covenants of God with humanity. The first he called the covenant of works (also the covenant of nature). This was in force before the sin of Adam and was a covenant by which God demanded good works from the human being, and for his part made the commitment to give salvation to the human being. This covenant was annulled by the sin of Adam and Eve. Once this covenant was abrogated, God in his mercy condescended to make a second covenant of grace with humankind. This second covenant had three successive phrases: before the law, under the law, and after the law. In the patriarchal stage, before the Mosaic law, the covenant was limited to a chosen family; in times of the law, the chosen family came to be a beloved nation, the people of Israel; after the fulfillment of the law by Christ, the covenant expanded, and all human beings were called to the kingdom of God.

This theological perspective won such popularity among Protestant theologians of the time that a movement called the Cocceians arose. The biblical basis assumed by C. for the development of his theological proposal also stimulated the study of the Bible in its original languages.

———
JDR

Cochlaeus, Johannes (1479–1552).

Humanist, priest, theologian, and opponent of Luther. He was born in Wendelstein, near

Nüremberg, and died in Breslau. He came from peasant origins, and studied humanities first in Nüremberg and then more intensively in Cologne (1504–7). He published books and made contributions in the area of education. He studied law in Bologna (1515–17) and received an academic degree in scholastic theology at the university of Ferrara in 1517, although he preferred the humanist method. He was ordained as a priest during his stay in Rome (1517–19). In 1510 he was rector of the school of St. Lawrence in Nüremberg and in 1520 dean of the Church of Our Lady in Frankfurt am Main, performing several chapter duties in the cathedrals of Mainz, Meissen, and Breslau. While in Frankfurt (1520), he entered the controversies of the Reformation, supporting the need for a reformation of the church and trying to debate theologically with ⇒Luther. When Luther rejected his initiatives, C. began the publication of the first of his numerous polemical treatises, to which Luther replied only once. As secretary of George of Saxony (1529–39), he took part in the Diet of ⇒Augsburg and prepared the refutation of the Lutheran confession.

Of his many polemical writings, noted for their scholarship and keenness, but generally also characterized by insult and offense, the most notable is *Commentaria de actis et scriptis Martini Lutheri, 1517–46* (1549; Commentaries on the Deeds and Writings of Martin Luther). He also published *Historia Hussitarum libri XII* (1549; History of the Hussites in Twelve Books).

JDR

Coe, George Albert (1862–1951).

Psychologist of religion and professor of religious education in North America for more than forty years. He published eleven books and hundreds of articles. *The Spiritual Life: Studies in the Science of Religion* (1900), *What Does Religion Do to Our Consciences?* (1943), and *What is Christian Education?* (1929) are among his most important contributions. C. founded the Religious Education Association in 1903 and remained as its honorary president until his death in 1951. His theory regarding Christian education integrates two fundamental theological presuppositions: the existence of God and the infinite value of the human being. He sought to establish the reciprocal relationship that exists between the disciplines of theology and psychology.

EDB

Colet, John (1466–1519).

English humanist, reformer in the style of ⇒Erasmus. He was born in London and educated at Oxford University. After Oxford, he traveled to Paris and Italy, where he continued his studies for seven years. During that time he came to know Erasmus. After his return to Oxford, he gave a series of lectures in 1497 on the Epistles of Paul, which were very well received. Through these lectures and in his writings and classes, C. shared the concern of the humanist Renaissance for reforming the clergy and the institutions of the church and for improving education. He attacked clerical abuses and, although he did not advocate a doctrinal reform, he was never exempt from suspicions of heresy. He founded St. Paul's School in London and was named dean of that institution in 1505. He occupied that position until his death in 1519.

HMT

Comblin, Joseph (1923–).

Belgian Catholic theologian and missiologist, proponent of liberation theology. He has lived and taught in Latin America since 1958. He is the author of more than fifty books in Spanish, Portuguese, French, and English. Among his works are *Theology of Revolution, Os sinais dos tempos e a evangelização* (The Signs of the Time and Evangelization), *Théologie de la ville* (Theology of the City), and *The Meaning of Mission*.

CCO

Comenius, Johannes Amos (1592–1670).

Pastor and educator, C. was born in Moravia. Because of the persecution of the Protestants and the Thirty Years' War in central Europe, he lived most of his adult life in exile in Poland and Holland. He was a member of the Bohemian Protestant movement known as Union of the Brethren (*Unitas Fratrum*). He was ordained to the ministry of that church in 1616 after studying in the schools of the same church and in the Reformed universities of Herborn and Heidelberg. C.'s elementary educational experience was so strict, especially for an orphan child such as himself, that in his professional life he strove to institute pedagogical reforms. He wanted to eliminate the use of force in the education of children and promote the use of the senses and the development of character by stages. All of these were pioneering ideas in teaching. In addition, C. was a pioneer of ecumenism. His experience of war and religious persecution moved him to seek peace and Christian unity through educational reform. He was the last bishop of the *Unitas Fratrum*, but his grandchild was the first bishop of the Renewed Moravian Church. C. wrote more than 150 books, but many manuscripts, including a great Czech and Latin dictionary, were lost in a fire in 1621. Works such as *Didactica magna* (1657), in which C. presented his pedagogy, and *The One Thing Necessary* (1668), in which he presented his hope for a united Christianity, have been studied more closely in the last hundred years, especially in Moravia, Bohemia, and Germany.

—

EA

Concord, Formula of (1577).

Early in the history of Lutheranism, an intense discussion about the correct interpretation of the ⇒Augsburg Confession (1530) took place. After the death of Martin ⇒Luther (1546), the controversy among his many followers, all interpreters of his thought on the chief themes of the Protestant Reformation, flared up again.

Chief among the issues were the following: the teachings and practices that are not essential for salvation (the so-called *adiaphora*); the use and extension of the doctrine of justification by faith; the place of the law and the commandments in the Christian life; the importance or, on the contrary, the possible harm of good works for faith and salvation; the relationship between divine providence and human will; and the correct understanding of the "real presence" of Christ in Holy Communion.

As a consequence of the attempts to achieve an agreement or concord among the different factions within Lutheranism by means of dialogues and meetings, in addition to the publication of theological treatises or doctrinal agreements, a Formula of Concord (or of Concordia) was finally produced, which mainly consists of a "solid declaration"—which is really the second part of the document—and a summary of its content ("epitome"). In no small measure it can be said that this formula emerged from the exchange of ideas between Luther and Philipp ⇒Melanchthon, and between the disciples of each one. The followers of the first were called Gnesio-Lutherans (authentic Lutherans) and the others Philippists. The Formula of Concord was drafted chiefly by Martin ⇒Chemnitz, David ⇒Chytraeus, and Jacob ⇒Andrea. It is a summary of the themes and doctrinal concerns that define

Lutheranism, in spite of internal differences, over against the other Reformed movements. In its twelve articles, it emphasizes the absolute authority of the Holy Scriptures as well as the role of the Lutheran confessions. The majority of Lutherans adhered to it and, consequently, the way was opened for the appearance of the *Book of Concord* (1580) in its totality.

—

NRG

Cone, James H. (1947–).

Professor of systematic theology at Union Theological Seminary in New York, whom many consider the father of African American liberation theology. His book *Black Theology and Black Power* incorporates elements of the theologies of ⇒Barth, ⇒Tillich, and ⇒Moltmann, and shows how a radical and liberating exegesis of biblical texts justifies black power. In *A Black Theology of Liberation,* he elaborates and explains that blackness points to something more profound and meaningful than the color of the skin. Blackness in the United States is a symbol of the essence of oppression which affects all, not only African Americans. Black experience leads to a particular way of doing theology which seeks to be in solidarity with other struggles of liberation and their particular theological expressions. Solidarity among various oppressed groups is necessary and possible because all forms of oppression offend God.

—

IG

Congar, Yves (1904–95).

French Catholic theologian of the Dominican order, known for his strong ecumenical vocation and his contributions to historical theology. He began his studies with the Carmelites, while being influenced by Neo-Thomist currents. His interest in the church fathers led him to dedicate several writings to doctrinal and liturgical themes. He was also familiar with Orthodox and Lutheran theologies. His ecumenical work was resisted by Roman Catholic authorities, leading to a brief exile in Jerusalem. Eventually he was named theological *peritus* ("expert") for ⇒Vatican II (1962–65).

The unity of the church was one of his favorite themes, to which he devoted several books, including *Disunited Christians, Christians in Dialogue,* and *Diversity and Communion.* Through books like *True and False Reform in the Church,* among others, he insisted on the necessity of reform in the church. Among those who influenced him are

Protestant theologians such as ⇒Luther, because of his emphasis on the primacy of grace and the Scriptures, in addition to ⇒Calvin and ⇒Barth, for their emphasis on the sovereignty of God and God's revealed Word. C. moved from a foundational theology in his initial stages to the theme of ecclesiology, and in his mature production he emphasized the doctrine of the Spirit.

——
NRG

Conner, Walter Thomas (1877–1952).

Southern Baptist theologian who insisted that divine revelation precedes the act of writing it, and should therefore not be confused with the Scriptures, which are subsequent. Even while he defended the doctrine of predestination, he insisted on love above all things. In addition, he maintained that the Trinity, more than a description of God, is an analogy.

——
MAD

Constance, Council of (1414–18).

Considered the Sixteenth Ecumenical Council by the Roman church. The chief reason for which it was convoked by Emperor Sigismund was the Great Schism of the West, which had deteriorated to such an extent that instead of two popes there were three. But this council was also the culmination of the conciliar movement, which held that the church was in need of reform, that such reform would not come from the papacy, and that, in any case, an ecumenical council had more authority than a pope.

Since the previous Council of ⇒Pisa had not been able to overcome the schism, but quite the contrary, the emperor now made sure that representatives of all nations would participate and, as far as possible, representatives of the different factions in conflict.

In one of the first sessions of the council, the conciliar leaders made very clear their position on the superiority of the council over any pope. The conciliar decree *Sacrosancta* explicitly declares this, affirming that the authority of the council comes directly from Christ, and that all, including the pope, owe it obedience.

With that authority, the council declared two of the three popes (or pretenders) deposed: John XXIII (the pope named by the Council of Pisa, who should not be confused with the pope of the same name and number in the twentieth century) and Benedict XIII (the pope of Avignon). The pope of Rome, Gregory XII (considered legitimate today by the Roman church),

resigned. After long debates about the way to implement the reforming movement, Martin V was elected pope. Although for some time Benedict refused to accept the council's decrees, the schism was healed.

In order to continue the impetus of renewal, the council issued the decree *Frequens*, according to which the council should meet again five years later, then seven years later, and from then on every ten years. This did not happen.

One of the most notable and lamentable actions of the council was the condemnation of John ⇒Huss. In spite of having gone to the council under a safe-conduct guaranteed by Sigismund, Huss was taken before the assembly, where he was not allowed to defend himself, but was only invited to recant. Condemned to the stake, he manifested exemplary courage, and his death remained an indelible stain in the annals of that council, which otherwise would have shone for its achievements and its reforming spirit.

——
JLG

Constantine Economos
⇒Oikeconomos, Constantine

Constantinople, Council of (381).

Second Ecumenical Council (⇒Councils), in which the teaching of the Council of ⇒Nicaea and the condemnation of ⇒Arius and his followers were reaffirmed. In addition, the C. of C. rejected the doctrines of the ⇒Pneumatomachians and of ⇒Apollinaris of Laodicea.

Although at first it seemed that the Council of Nicaea had put an end to the Arian question, many were dissatisfied with the decisions of that council. Such dissatisfaction existed not only among the convinced Arians, but also among a good number of bishops and theologians who feared that by declaring that the Son is consubstantial (*homoousios*) with the Father, the Council of Nicaea had fallen into Sabellianism (⇒Sabellius), which did not leave room for distinctions among the three persons of the Trinity. Also, when the empire was united once again under Constantius, who was Arian, the Arian cause progressed rapidly. As ⇒Jerome said, "The world awoke from a deep sleep and discovered that it had become Arian."

This situation required an arduous labor of diplomacy and of theological clarification, initially by ⇒Athanasius and in the next generation by the ⇒Cappadocians. When Constantius died and his pagan cousin Julian succeeded him, the new political situation permitted a more open theological discussion, without fear of imperial intervention. When, shortly afterward, Theodosius ascended to the throne, everything was ready for the convocation of a new council that would reaffirm what was done in Nicaea.

In the meantime, other questionable teachings had emerged. One of them was that of the ⇒Pneumatomachians, who appeared willing to affirm the full divinity of the Son, but not of the Holy Spirit. In response to them, the C. of C. discussed the question of the Holy Spirit (which does not appear to have been a prominent theme in Nicaea) and determined that the Holy Spirit is also God, together with the Father and the Son. It is for this reason that, while the old Creed of Nicaea simply confesses faith in the Holy Spirit, the creed which we now call Nicene, but which in reality is a product of the C. of C., says much more in this regard: ". . . in the Holy Spirit, the Lord and giver of life, who proceeds from the Father [the Western church has added "and the Son," *filioque*]; who with the Father and the Son is together worshiped and glorified; who spoke through the prophets."

The other theological position that the C. of C. rejected was the Christology of Apollinaris, who held that the humanity of Jesus Christ does not include a rational human soul, since the place of such a soul is occupied by the eternal Word of God. The Cappadocians had opposed this, arguing that Jesus assumed human nature in order to save it, and that if he did not assume a complete humanity, then salvation is not complete either.

———
JLG

Constantinople II, Council of (553).

Council convoked by Emperor Justinian, who attempted to consolidate his empire by promoting a series of conversations among the parties in conflict regarding the doctrinal decisions of the Council of ⇒Chalcedon.

In reality, this was simply the continuation of the old christological controversies between the Antiochene and the Alexandrian tendencies. Opposition to the decisions of Chalcedon persisted. Theologians such as ⇒Severus of Antioch, whom some historians call verbal Monophysites because they were not true Monophysites but simply opponents of the formula of Chalcedon, criticized what had been done in that council. The political circumstances were difficult, since those who felt oppressed by the Byzantine yoke frequently

attacked the decisions of Chalcedon as a way of fortifying their opposition to the empire. Consequently, Emperor Basiliscus published in 476 a decree (⇒Encyclion) in which he declared the decisions of Chalcedon null and void. In 482 Emperor Zeno promulgated a ⇒Henoticon or edict of union in which he adopted a type of verbal Monophysitism in the style of Severus, and which, without condemning what was done in Chalcedon, tended to deprive it of its authority. Since the patriarch ⇒Acacius of Constantinople was behind the imperial edict, and since the pope protested against this attempt by the civil authority to pass judgment in matters of doctrine, this resulted in the "schism of Acacius" between the East and the West. Finally, in the year 519, during the reign of Justin, the Henoticon was withdrawn and the schism healed.

With all of these events as background, Justinian convened a number of conferences between the parties in dispute. As part of that process, the emperor tried to win the sympathy of the verbal Monophysites by condemning the "Three Chapters." With this name, the opponents of Chalcedon referred to three Antiochene theologians and their work: ⇒Theodore of Mopsuestia, ⇒Ibas of Edessa, and ⇒Theodoret of Cyrus. Shortly afterward Justinian forced Pope Vigilius to follow his lead and condemn the Three Chapters. But in spite of all this, the dispute continued. Then Justinian convened the Second Council of Constantinople, which today is generally recognized as the Fifth Ecumenical Council, and which condemned the Three Chapters.

———
JLG

Constantinople III, Council of (680–81).

Also known as the Sixth Ecumenical Council and as the Council *in Trullo* (for the salon of the imperial palace, called *trullus*, in which it took place). What was debated in it was a continuation of the old christological controversies that revolved around the earlier councils of ⇒Constantinople (381 and 553), ⇒Ephesus (431), and ⇒Chalcedon (451). The decisions of Chalcedon were not well regarded by these Monophysites of Armenia, Syria, and Egypt, and this theological difference threatened to impair the unity of the Byzantine Empire. For this reason, the emperors were interested in overcoming the disagreements between Chalcedonians and Monophysites. It appeared that this was also the purpose of the patriarch of Constantinople,

⇒Sergius, who proposed that in Christ, although there are two natures in one person, the two natures have a single will: the divine will. Since in Greek "will" is *thelema*, this position received the name of Monothelitism. The patriarch ⇒Sophronius of Jerusalem strongly objected to this teaching. But Pope ⇒Honorius allowed himself to be convinced by the arguments of Sergius and accepted Monothelitism. The emperor then promulgated an edict that made Monothelitism the official doctrine of the church. With this measure, he attracted the goodwill of many moderate Monophysites, but also the criticism of several bishops who insisted that the emperor did not have authority in theological matters. Among such critics the new pope, Martin, stood out. He rejected Monothelitism and for that reason was exiled to Crimea, where he died in 655.

Finally, in 680, a new emperor convened a council to settle the issue. By that date the ancient sees of Alexandria and Jerusalem, as well as other regions where Monophysitism was strong, had fallen into the hands of the Arabs, and therefore the Byzantine Empire was not greatly interested in gaining the sympathy of the Monophysite or Monothelite Christians. Consequently, the council condemned Monothelitism with relative ease and reiterated the rejection of Monophysitism that had taken place in Chalcedon.

An interesting consequence of all this is that Pope Honorius, who was now dead, turned out to be a heretic. Centuries later, when the promulgation of papal infallibility was being considered, one of the obstacles that the First Vatican (⇒Vatican I) Council had to face was the case of the heresy of Honorius.

———

JLG

Constantinople IV, Council of (869–70).

The fourth council gathered in that city, considered the Eighth Ecumenical Council by the Roman church, but not by the Eastern Orthodox churches. It met because of the so-called schism of ⇒Photius. Photius, a scholar of recognized fame, had succeeded Patriarch Ignatius, who was deposed for political reasons. Pope Nicholas (858–67) refused to accept what was done and excommunicated Photius in 863. Photius responded in kind four years later, excommunicating the pope. The schism lasted until a new emperor deposed Photius and restored Ignatius. It was then that the council met and anathematized Photius, who refused to accept the authority of the council.

In addition, the assembly confirmed the decisions of the Second Council of ⇒Nicaea (787) with respect to the veneration of images and declared that there are five patriarchs, in this order of precedence: Rome, Constantinople, Alexandria, Antioch, and Jerusalem.

Shortly after the sessions of the council, the political situation changed again. Photius was restored, and a new council that met in Constantinople in 879–80 undid what was done ten years earlier. For the Eastern churches, this is the Eighth Ecumenical Council. With it the schism came back to life. But the chaos in the West was such that the pope does not appear to have done a great deal to resolve the schism, and gradually the dispute was forgotten, as if it had not existed.

———

JLG

Cook, William (1946–99).
Born in Argentina of evangelical missionary parents, he was instrumental in the conversations between Latin American evangelical and liberation theologies. His work *The Expectation of the Poor* is a milestone in the discussion about ecclesiology and mission. His last works reflect his interest in the contextualization of the gospel in Latin America. He was also a member and leader of Fraternidad Teológica Latinoamericana.

———

CCO

Coquille, Guy (1525–1603).
French Catholic who together with Pierre ⇒Pithou and Edmond ⇒Richer defended the "Gallican liberties" vis-à-vis the pretensions of the papacy. As the aristocrat that he was, he based his arguments on an aristocratic vision of the church, in which the bishops had the authority, and the pope was not superior to them except in honor. His two chief works are *Treatise on the Liberties of the Church of France* and *Discourse on the Liberties of the Church of France*.

———

MAD

Cornelius (?–253).
Bishop of Rome from 251. He clashed with ⇒Novatian regarding the restoration of those who had fallen in times of persecution. In contrast to the rigorism of Novatian, C. was inclined to grant such restoration, perhaps sometimes by the simple action of those who had confessed the faith in times of persecution (the "confessors"). In this he differed from ⇒Cyprian, who was willing to

restore the fallen, but only after a formal process. This led to a lengthy and sometimes bitter correspondence.

—

JLG

Costas, Orlando (1942–87).

Theologian and missiologist born of Puerto Rican parents and reared in Bridgeport, Connecticut. The life and ministry of C. are outstanding because of his theological productivity and his practice as pastor, evangelist, missiologist, professor, lecturer, preacher, and writer.

C. pursued his university studies in Puerto Rico (1966) and completed two master's degrees in theology and divinity (1967, 1969). He received his doctorate in theology from the Free University of Amsterdam (1976). A good part of his ministry took place in Costa Rica, where he served as a professor in the Latin American Biblical Seminary. He wrote more than a hundred contributions to books and journals, in addition to seventeen books. He was recognized internationally for his theological contributions. When he died, he was dean of Andover Newton Theological School, near Boston, Massachusetts.

His unique contribution is that of a contextual theologian with an integrative vision of the church of Christ. The proclamation of the gospel and the incarnation of the justice of God are fundamental to the thought and work of C. Christ is proclaimed holistically, starting from the world of the poor and the oppressed as a crucial part of the mission of God. Such a methodology and praxis can be described as a radical Latino evangelicalism coming from the periphery or the world of the abandoned. The model of such ministry is Jesus Christ, who ministered starting from the world of Galilee and going toward the marginalized of society. All in all, this is a holistic, prophetic, and contextual gospel that proclaims life and hope in the midst of death and oppression.

Among his works are *The Church and Its Evangelizing Mission* (1971), *The Church and Its Mission: A Shattering Critique from the Third World* (1976), *Christ outside the Gate* (1982), *Contextual Evangelization: Theological and Pastoral Foundations* (1986), and *Liberating News* (posthumous, 1989).

—

DTG

Cotton, John (1584–1652).

Puritan who contributed to the development of "congregationalism," a word he invented to describe a nonconformist polity. A native of England, from the time of his youth and academic formation he was inclined to Puritanism. The Puritans, a generation of Reformers inside the Church of England, had been influenced by the Continental Reformers ⇒Calvin, ⇒Beza, ⇒Bucer, and ⇒Zwingli, and therefore they were Calvinists. In 1630 C. was invited to preach the farewell sermon to a group of colonizers who were leaving for America. With this sermon he legitimized the migration to New England in North America and pointed to a model for colonial doctrine and theology. Three years later, in 1633, to escape persecution because of his Puritanism, C. resigned his post in the church of St. Botolph and, with his wife and daughter, left for New England. It was in Massachusetts that C. made his major contribution to independence, both in the ecclesiastical and in the civil sphere, through his publication of *The Keys* in 1644. C. explains that the keys of the kingdom are the ordinances of Christ, which are preaching, the sacraments, and discipline, and that these keys do not include civil or legislative powers. Civil authority is limited to the responsibility of assuring that a pure religion exists, but it cannot force the people to enter into communion with a certain congregation. On this foundation C., although not completely convinced, proposes the separation of the civil state and the church.

—

RA

Councils.

This article will deal with the ecumenical councils in general and trace their history in broad strokes, leaving the details of the principal councils for the corresponding articles on each one.

Since the most ancient times, it was a custom among Christian leaders to meet in order to make decisions together or to resolve some debated issue. This can be seen in the episode described in Acts 15:6–29, which some call the Apostolic Council or Council of Jerusalem. But in the time before Constantine, such meetings were always limited, sometimes by the danger of persecution and always by the scarcity of resources and the difficulties in communication. Thus we have, for example, a series of regional councils in North Africa presided over by ⇒Cyprian in the third century.

When Constantine began to give his support to the church, such circumstances changed. Constantine himself gathered in Arles bishops who represented the entire West, in order to deal with the challenge of Donatism (⇒Donatus).

1. But it was some years later, in 325, that the First "Ecumenical" Council (that is, universal, for the term *oikoumene* refers to the entire inhabited earth, and it was only in recent times that it acquired its present meaning of "interconfessional" or "interdenominational") met in ⇒Nicaea. Constantine convened this meeting to deal with some practical and liturgical matters, such as the date on which the resurrection of the Lord should be celebrated. But the summons had above all the purpose of resolving the conflict that arose in connection with the teachings of ⇒Arius, who made of the Son an entity who was inferior to the Father, and a creature. After a series of complicated debates, the council adopted a creed that appears to be an adaptation of the one which ⇒Eusebius of Caesarea presented, with a number of additions whose purpose was to reject Arianism. Thus the Nicene Creed affirms that Jesus Christ is "begotten as the Only Son of the Father, that is, of the substance of the Father, God from God; light from light; true God from true God; begotten, not made; consubstantial with the Father."

Of all these declarations, the one which became the touchstone of Nicene orthodoxy was "consubstantial [*homoousios*] with the Father," a phrase which made some fear that every distinction between the Father and the Son had been denied and that therefore the council had fallen into the error of ⇒Sabellius.

After the closure of the council, the debate continued. The extreme Arians, known as Anomoeans (from the Greek *anomoios*, unequal or different), affirmed that the Son was "different" from the Father. The Homoeans (from the Greek *homoios*, similar) said that the Father and the Son are "similar," but without explaining how. For this reason they have been called political Arians, since their position allowed them to adapt themselves to what the emperor who reigned at that time maintained. The Homoiousians (from the Greek *homoiousos*, of similar substance) maintained the divinity of the Son but feared the Sabellian connotations of the *homoousios*. (Note the *i* that distinguishes the *homoiousios* of this group from the *homoousios* of Nicaea.)

During this time there were a whole series of councils, several of which gave themselves the title of "ecumenical," but which today are not recognized as such. At the same time, ⇒Athanasius, the ⇒Cappadocians, and others made an effort to explain the doctrine of Nicaea

in a way that appeased the fears of those who, like the Homoiousians, were afraid of falling into Sabellianism, which denied the real distinction between the Father, the Son, and the Holy Spirit. After a number of theological clarifications, it was possible to establish the distinction between *ousia* (essence, substance) and *hypostasis* (subsistence). These theologians declared that in God there is one single *ousia* in three hypostases (or, in terms of the Latin of the West, one substance and three persons).

2. This position was endorsed by the council that eventually was recognized as the Second Ecumenical Council, which gathered in ⇒Constantinople in 381. There not only the condemnation of Arianism was reaffirmed, but also the issue was broadened with the affirmation of the full divinity of the Holy Spirit over against the teachings of the ⇒Pneumatomachians. The council also rejected the christological position of ⇒Apollinaris of Laodicea, who held that in Jesus Christ there is a human body and soul, but that the "rational soul" was not human, for it was the very Word of God.

The creed recited in churches today as the Nicene Creed is in reality the Niceno-Constantinopolitan Creed, since it is an adaptation of the one promulgated in Nicaea. (In addition, as the result of a much later process, in the West the *filioque* is included, which the East rejects because it is not a part of the original creed. Thus in the West it is said that the Holy Spirit proceeds from the Father *and the Son*.)

3. The Third Ecumenical Council took place in ⇒Ephesus in 431, and the main topic of debate was the Christology of the patriarch of Constantinople, ⇒Nestorius. What was at stake was the contrast between two ancient Christologies, the one known today as Antiochene and the other as Alexandrian. The Antiochene tradition insisted on the need to affirm the full humanity of Jesus Christ, which was always in danger of being eclipsed by his divinity. Consequently, in Antioch there was the tendency toward a Christology which historians call "disjunctive," that is, which defends and upholds the full humanity of the Savior, safeguarding it against a union with the divinity that is too close. In contrast, Alexandrian Christology was "unitive," for what was most important for it was the true and complete union between the divinity and the humanity in Jesus Christ, even when the latter would lose some of its reality. This was affirmed in the principle of the *communicatio idiomatum*, or the participation of the properties, which maintained that the unity of the Savior is such that everything that is said

about his humanity also has to be said about his divinity. For this reason, if the Antiochenes risked losing the unity of the Savior, the Alexandrians risked losing his true humanity. Apollinaris, whom the Council of Constantinople had condemned, was a faithful exponent of the Alexandrian Christology of his time.

What finally made the controversy break out was a number of sermons preached in Constantinople by Nestorius's chaplain and then endorsed by the patriarch, in which it was said that Mary should not receive the title of *Theotokos* (mother or bearer of God), but rather of *Christotokos* (mother or bearer of Christ). This appeared normal to the Antiochenes, for whom it was necessary to distinguish between God and Christ. But it shocked the Alexandrians, who opposed such a contrast between the humanity and the divinity of the Savior.

When the assigned date of the council arrived, the head of the Alexandrian party, ⇒Cyril of Alexandria, began the sessions without waiting for the defenders of Nestorius, especially for John of Antioch, and this council declared Nestorius a heretic. John and his followers then formed a separate council. The result was a number of mutual condemnations that did not end until the imperial authorities forced a supposed reconciliation between both sides. But in the end it was the council of Cyril that managed to be recognized as the Third Ecumenical Council, and henceforth received the official name of Council of Ephesus.

But the issue was not resolved with this measure. For some time, imperial pressure forced the Alexandrians as well as the Antiochenes to adopt more conciliatory positions. However, peace could not last, and the *Twelve Anathemas* of Cyril against Antiochene Christology stirred up a new controversy that finally led to the Council of Chalcedon.

4. The process that led from the third to the Fourth Ecumenical Council, which met in ⇒Chalcedon in 451, was complicated, and in a certain way was a continuation of the disputes that led to the Council of Ephesus. In this case the crisis focused on the monk ⇒Eutyches. Although it is clear that Eutyches was an exponent of the Alexandrian Christology in its most extreme form, the exact content of his teaching is not very clear. He certainly affirmed that in Christ there is "one nature and one person," and some ancient authors add that he said that the body of Christ was made of a celestial substance and that Jesus, although "of the same substance" (*homoousios*) as the Father, is not of the same substance as the rest of humanity.

In any case, the successor of Cyril in Alexandria, ⇒Dioscorus, took advantage of the occasion to achieve what he hoped would be the definitive triumph of his party. With imperial support, he convened a council that met in Ephesus in 449 and which today only the churches called Monophysite (that is, which teach the "one nature") consider as ecumenical. The bishop of Rome, ⇒Leo the Great, had written a *Tome* in which he criticized and rejected the position of Eutyches. But Dioscorus, who presided over the assembly, did not allow it to be read. When ⇒Flavian, the patriarch of Constantinople, attempted to expound his Antiochene position, he was treated with such violence that he died a few days later. In Rome, Leo gave that council the name by which it is known in history: "the robbery (*latrocinium*) of Ephesus."

Shortly thereafter, when Emperor Theodosius II had died in a riding accident, Empress Pulcheria and her husband Marcian convened a new council, which this time met in Chalcedon. This council adopted a moderate position, although perhaps it leaned toward the Antiochene position. On the basis of the *Tome* of Leo, the council adopted a formula very similar to what had been proposed centuries earlier by ⇒Tertullian, and thus arrived at the affirmation that in Jesus Christ there are "two natures in one person." The Definition of Faith which the council adopted (quoted extensively in the article ⇒Chalcedon) became the classical expression of orthodox Christology for the entire church, except for those churches that were dubbed Monophysite (among them the Coptic Church of Egypt, the Church of Ethiopia, that of Armenia, and the Jacobite Church of Syria), and the Nestorians.

These first four councils are recognized by the majority of the churches, including the Eastern Orthodox, the Roman, and the oldest churches among the Protestants.

5. The Fifth Ecumenical Council, also known as the Second Council of ⇒Constantinople, met in that city in 553. The principal topic debated was the orthodoxy of the so-called Three Chapters, the phrase denoting the persons as well as the works of three great Antiochene teachers: ⇒Theodore of Mopsuestia, ⇒Theodoret of Cyrus, and ⇒Ibas of Edessa. The council, at the insistence of Justinian, condemned the Three Chapters.

6. The Sixth Ecumenical Council, which met in ⇒Constantinople in 680–81, resulted from another attempt at reconciliation between the Antiochene and the Alexandrian tendencies.

There the Monothelite teaching of ⇒Sergius of Constantinople was condemned. He had proposed an intermediate position between both parties when he said that while in Christ there are two natures, there is only one will (thus arose the name *Monothelitism*, from two Greek words that mean "one" and "will").

7. The Seventh Ecumenical Council, or Second Council of ⇒Nicaea, met in the year 787, and while it restored the veneration of images, it regulated their use and established a distinction between the legitimate veneration due such images (*doulia*) and the adoration (*latria*) that belongs only to God.

8. The Eighth Ecumenical Council, Fourth Council of ⇒Constantinople (869–70), put an end to the schism of ⇒Photius.

9. From then on, what are called the "ecumenical councils" are really Western councils, in which there was seldom a true representation of the Eastern churches. While normally the previous councils had been convened by the emperors, from this point on they would be convened by the popes. Therefore, although the Roman church considers them ecumenical, the other churches do not accept them as such.

The Ninth Ecumenical Council, according to the Roman method of counting, is the First ⇒Lateran Council (1123), which confirmed the Concordat of Worms between the papacy and the empire.

10. The Second Lateran Council (1139) was convened by Innocent II in order to remove from office those who had supported his rival Anacletus II. In addition, measures were taken to continue the reforms begun by ⇒Gregory VII, and against several dissident groups whose teachings are not entirely known.

11. The Third Lateran Council (1179) continued the reforming process, above all establishing the rule that from then on the election of a pope would require two-thirds of the vote.

12. The Fourth Lateran Council (1215) was convened by the most powerful pope of all time, Innocent III. In three short sessions, in the course of less than three weeks, the council adopted a whole series of measures prepared beforehand by the pope and his curia. Various reforming measures were thus adopted. The most notable was the mandate that every believer should confess and receive Communion at least once a year. The council also condemned the ⇒Albigensians, established rules for the Inquisition, and condemned ⇒Joachim of Fiore and his followers. In the field of theology, the most notable action of this council was the promulgation of the doctrine of transubstantiation, as a rejection of the opinions of ⇒Berengar.

13. The First Council of Lyon (1245) deposed the emperor Frederick II.

14. The Second Council of ⇒Lyon (1274), which met at a time when the Byzantine Empire was seriously threatened, saw the submission of the patriarch of Constantinople and of several of his followers to papal authority. But that "union" did not last long, for the faithful of the Eastern church never accepted it, and Pope Martin IV, at the same time that he was accepting the submission of Byzantium, was making plans with the king of Naples for the conquest of Constantinople. In addition, the council established new rules for the election of popes, and those rules, with slight alterations, still exist today.

15. The Council of Vienna (1311–12) suppressed the Order of the Templars and adopted several reforming measures.

16. The Council of ⇒Constance (1414–18) saw the triumph of the conciliarist ideas (⇒Marsilius of Padua, ⇒Dietrich of Niem, Jean ⇒Gerson, Pierre d'⇒Ailly). These ideas, which had gained special force because of the corruption of the papacy and the Great Western Schism, when for a long time there were two popes, proposed a reform of the church through the convening of a series of councils. According to the conciliarists, the church is the congregation of the faithful, and therefore a universal council that represents all the faithful has more authority than the pope.

It was on this basis that, when the two pretender popes could not agree, a group of cardinals of both parties, weary with the situation, convened a council that would meet in Pisa in 1409. This council declared the two rival popes deposed and in their place named another, who took the title of John XXIII. Since the other two pretenders did not accept the decisions of the council, the result was that there were now three rival popes. (The Roman Catholic Church does not accept this council or the pope which it named, and for this reason in the twentieth century there could be another pope with the name of John XXIII).

The rivalry between the pretenders led Emperor Sigismund of Germany to convene a new council, that of Constance, which the Roman church accepts as ecumenical, but whose members considered it to be the continuation of the Council of Pisa.

When John XXIII saw that the council would not submit to his pretensions, he fled, but was made prisoner and deposed by the council.

The council then sought the resignation of the other popes. The one from Avignon refused, but the council declared him deposed, and he had lost so much of his prestige that he soon became isolated and had no support. The one from Rome, Gregory XII, abdicated, and in his place the cardinals who were present, together with representatives from the council, elected Martin V. With these measures the Great Schism of the West was practically healed, and apparently the conciliar movement triumphed.

In spite of its reforming impulse, it was this Council of Constance which condemned John ⇒Huss. In addition, in its decree *Sacrosanct*, the council declared that its authority was superior to that of the pope and, by means of the decree *Frequens*, dictated the periodic meeting of the councils for the purpose of protecting and promoting the welfare of the church.

17. But soon the popes began to recover their ancient power. The next council, which was to meet in 1423, was poorly attended, and the pope dissolved it. By 1430, when the next assembly was to take place, the tensions between the papacy and the conciliarists were serious, but even so Martin V convened a meeting that began in Basel in 1431. When Eugenius IV, Martin's successor, attempted to dissolve the assembly, it refused to disperse and fell into the hands of the most extreme conciliarists. Nicholas of ⇒Cusa, one of them, declared that the council did not have to obey the pope. Eugenius IV finally capitulated, and the council showed signs of wanting to continue indefinitely and to impose its authority on the pope.

What saved the pope was a call for help that came from Constantinople, which was strongly besieged by the Turks. In exchange for military aid, Byzantium declared itself willing to submit to papal authority and thus heal the schism between East and West. With the pretext of making the trip easier for the Greeks, the pope ordered the council to move to Ferrara and then to Florence. The most moderate members obeyed, because they favored the proposed unity with the Greeks, while the others decided to continue their sessions in Basel. The result was that the conciliar movement, which had reached its high point as a means to overcome the papal schism, was now divided into two councils. This practically put an end to the movement, although it always had its defenders.

Although the council achieved union with the Greeks, this union turned out to be disastrous, for once more the faithful of Constantinople refused to accept what their leaders had done for political motives, and in the end the rupture became official again, and mutual suspicions were worse than before.

18. The Fifth Lateran Council (1512–17) condemned those who still continued in the Council of Basel, and thus put an end to the schism and the conciliar movement.

19. The Council of ⇒Trent (1545–63) was convened mainly to reply to the Protestant challenge, both condemning the Protestant teachings and reforming the morality and the life of the church. In contrast to other councils, this one dealt with practically the whole body of Christian doctrine, for on all those points serious differences existed between Protestants and Catholics. This is one of the most important councils, for it gave shape to all of modern Roman Catholicism to such an extent that frequently Catholicism between Trent and the Second Vatican Council is called Tridentine Catholicism, from the Latin name for Trent.

20. The First Vatican Council (⇒Vatican I) (1869–70) met when papal authority was being strongly attacked, not only by modern intellectual currents, but also by the new Italian nation, which demanded the old papal states for itself. The chief action of this council was to proclaim the infallibility of the pope. Although this proclamation caused strong reactions in theological circles, the political powers paid little attention to it—a sign of the lack of importance that was given to the papacy. A few months after being proclaimed infallible, the pope was losing all the papal states, including Rome, and his temporal power was limited to the tiny Vatican City.

21. The Second ⇒Vatican Council (1962–65) was convened by Pope John XXIII with the purpose of "bringing the church up to date" (*aggiornamento*). In contrast to the first ecumenical councils and to the Council of Trent, its purpose was not to refute some enemy or heretic, but to examine the whole life of the church and adjust it for mission in the present time. Thus it can be said that with Vatican II, a new era in Roman Catholicism began.

———

JLG

Cox, Harvey Gallagher (1929–).
North American Baptist theologian of international fame. He worked as a university chaplain and then as professor of theology at Andover Newton and Harvard. He was an activist in the civil rights and peace movements. Through his books, he has contributed to the theological

dialogue on various topics: the secular city, political and liberation theology, interreligious dialogue, and Pentecostalism.

LRR

Cragg, Albert Kenneth (1913–2000).
British Anglican, and one of the most prominent interpreters of Islam to the Western world. He is a prolific writer in the field of Islam and the Christian-Muslim dialogue, with a doctorate from Oxford and experience in the Middle East. He edited the journal *The Muslim World* while he was professor at Hartford Seminary. Among his books are *The Call of the Minaret*, which proposes a theology of mission in the Muslim context, stressing a ministry of mutual enrichment, service, and social action, and the interpretation of the gospel within the scriptural frame of the Koran.

Among his most recent works that have influenced the Christian-Muslim dialogue and encounter are *The Christ and the Faiths: Theology in Cross Reference* and *Jesus and the Muslim: An Exploration*. The work of this interreligious theologian reflects a deep interest in finding a point of convergence between the Christian and the Islamic faiths.

CCO

Cranmer, Thomas (1489–1556).
Archbishop of Canterbury at the time of the break between Henry VIII and Rome. His ideas became progressively Protestant, and during the reign of Edward VI he did much to promote the Reformation in England. He is considered one of the chief authors of the Book of Common Prayer. His position concerning the relationship between the state and the church was similar to that of ⇒Erastus, which created great difficulties when Mary Tudor succeeded Edward VI. Under pressure, he recanted his Protestant position. Later he publicly repented of his recantation and died at the stake.

JLG

Croatto, José Severino (1932–2004).
Professor of Old Testament and Semitic languages at the ISEDET (Evangelical Higher Institute of Theological Studies) in Buenos Aires. He is best known for his work *Biblical Hermeneutics* (1984). Together with many Latin American theologians of the late twentieth century, he made clear the role of ideology

in the interpretation of the Scriptures and developed a hermeneutic that gives preference to the poor in the Latin American context.

CCO

Cudworth, Ralph (1617–88).
One of the chief thinkers of the group known as the Cambridge Platonists. He was born in Aller, Somerset, in England. In 1639 he was named professor of Emmanuel College in Cambridge. In 1642 he published *Discourse concerning the True Notion of the Lord's Supper* and a treatise with the title *The Union of Christ and the Church*. Three years later, he was named director of Clare College and Regius Professor of Hebrew. In 1654 he became director of Christ College, where he died. He also wrote *The True Intellectual System of the Universe*, *Treatise concerning Eternal and Immutable Morality,* and others which remain unfinished or unpublished.

AZ

Cullmann, Oscar (1902–99).
New Testament scholar, specialist in biblical theology. He was born in Strasburg, France, and received his doctorate in theology at the university of that city (1930). For the greater part of his career, he was professor of New Testament, history, and theology at the University of Basel in Switzerland and at the Sorbonne in Paris. In two of his most recognized works, *Christ and Time* (1946) and *Salvation in History* (1964), C. challenged ⇒Bultmann and the proponents of existentialism and of the "demythologization" of the New Testament. He argued that history is very relevant in the study of the New Testament, where it is not only a matter of the crisis of individual decision—which Bultmann and his followers maintained. God in Christ intervenes in human history. Therefore Christ is the "center" of time. The New Testament represents the key stage of the "history of salvation." In addition, C. rejected the theory that Jesus did not proclaim an eschatological vision. In Christ the end begins, although the culmination of history is in the future. This is the New Testament perspective of time and history, according to C. In addition to his theological work, C. dedicated much time to ecumenism, serving as official observer at the Second Vatican Council (⇒Vatican II) and founding the Ecumenical Institute of Jerusalem. He was also concerned about various topics in the New Testament related to the ministry of the church, in works such as

Baptism in the New Testament (1950) and
Prayer in the New Testament (1994).

———
EA

Curaeus, Joachim (1532–73). Faith-
ful disciple of Philipp ⇒Melanchthon. He was
born in 1532 and studied philosophy and
theology in Wittenberg in 1550–54. He later
studied medicine in Padua and Bologna in
1557–59. He established himself in Glogan,
where he worked as a doctor until his death in
1573. He defended the position that some
called Semi-Calvinist in relation to the sacrament of Communion, especially in the book
*Integral Exegesis of the Controversial Holy
Supper*, which appeared as an anonymous work
in 1574 and was reprinted in 1853.

———
HMT

Cusa, Nicholas of (1401–64). Mathe-
matician, experimental scientist, expert in the
arts, mystic, and Neoplatonic philosopher.
Considered one of the outstanding and many-
sided personalities of the Renaissance. He was
ordained to the priesthood in Brixen in 1440 by
Pope Nicholas V and was named bishop of that
city in 1450.

In order to purify and unite the church, C.
became involved in the conciliar movement. In
the Council of ⇒Basel in 1432, he defended the
theses that the pope was a member of the church,
that only the church was infallible, and that the
general councils were above the authority of the
pope and could depose him—even though he
later changed his mind. In 1433 he demonstrated
the falsehood of the "Donation of Constantine."

C. argued that the human being could not
know God and the universe in its totality. Nevertheless, through mystical experience or the
"higher state of intelligence," the human being
could know God, although such knowledge
could not be expressed in words. According to
C., that person is wise who recognizes his or her
own ignorance (*docta ignorantia*). In a sense,
C. got ahead of Copernicus when he insisted on
the movement of the universe and posited that
the earth is not its center. In his study of the
growth of plants, he affirmed that the plants are
nurtured by the air. The creation of several maps
of Europe is also attributed to C., as well as having given impulse to the Renaissance in Germany through his notable library.

———
AEM

Cyprian (ca. 210–58). Bishop of
Carthage from 249 until his death as a martyr
in 258. Born of a well-to-do family, he received
an excellent education, and for a while was a
lawyer. As a result of his conversion in 245, he
sold a good portion of his properties in order to
do works of mercy among the poor. He was
made a priest in 247, and two years later was
bishop of his native city. Since Carthage was
the main city of the province of Africa, C. soon
was a leader of the hundred or so bishops in the
province, who sometimes called him "pope
[that is, papa] Cyprian." When persecution
broke out under Emperor Decius, C. went into
hiding. The reason that he gave was the wish to
avoid martyrdom in order to continue leading
his flock, mostly by means of a copious correspondence. He thus saw the need to defend
himself not only against those who criticized
him in Carthage and its surroundings, but also
against those who from afar echoed the same
accusations. Among them was the Church of
Rome, which repeatedly wrote to him asking
him to account for his actions. In addition, his
situation was growing more difficult, since
from the very moment of his election there was
a small group that opposed it, and after a long
debate C. excommunicated its leaders. These
then took refuge in Rome, where they joined
the schismatic movement of ⇒Novatian and
continued attacking C.

After the persecution had passed, in the summer of 251, C. returned to Carthage, where he
convened the bishops of the region for a synod.
A little more than half of the bishops of the
province attended. The main question that was
debated was how to proceed with the "fallen,"
that is, with those who, in times of persecution,
had abandoned the faith. Some were inclined to
forgive them with no conditions. Others said
that the "confessors"—persons who had suffered for the faith but had survived the persecution—were the ones with moral authority to
restore the fallen. They maintained that C.,
even though a bishop, did not have such authority, because instead of showing himself willing
to suffer for the faith he had gone into hiding.

C. dealt with this matter in the treatise *De
lapsis* (On the Fallen). There he maintained that
the only persons who could be restored to the
communion of the church on the sole basis of
their repentance were those who, when Decius
ordered that all should have a document certi-
fying that they had worshiped the gods,
obtained such documents by diverse means, but
had not in fact worshiped the gods. For the rest,

the only hope was a period of penitence that would last a lifetime, unless a new persecution should give them the opportunity of witnessing to their faith by means of martyrdom. This was in essence what the synod decided, although not without the displeasure of many confessors who claimed to have an authority which the synod had now usurped.

Shortly afterward the plague broke out in Carthage. Many pagans accused the Christians of having caused the plague, which had been sent by the gods as a punishment because their previous followers had abandoned them upon becoming Christian. C. responded to this in a treatise *To Demetrian*, in which he said that the reason for the recent calamities was that the world was aging and that such calamities were similar to the illnesses of old age. At the same time, C. wrote works directed to the faithful to invite them to give an adequate response to the challenge of the plague, *On the Loss of Life* and *On Works and Charity*. The first exhorts believers to face death with faith. The second encourages them to practice love toward sick and afflicted persons.

In the year 257 persecution broke out again, this time under Valerian. C. refused to flee. After a brief exile, he was taken before the authorities and died as a martyr the following day.

C.'s writings comprise treatises and letters. Several of his works are revisions of writings by ⇒Tertullian, whom C. called the Teacher, such as the treatises *Idols are Not Gods*, *On Prayer*, *On the Good of Patience,* and *On the Habit of the Virgins*. The most important of his writings is his treatise on the unity of the church, *De unitate ecclesiae*.

In this writing, C. affirms that the unity of the church lies in its bishops and in their mutual communion. The bishops are successors of the apostles, and therefore their authority is the same as that which Jesus gave the apostles. This is true to such an extent that where there is no bishop, there is no church—that is, believers who for whatever reason distance themselves from the bishop distance themselves from the church, and, therefore, from Jesus Christ. On the other hand, the unity of the episcopate is not hierarchical, in the sense that the bishops are one because all owe obedience to one among them, to a "bishop of bishops." On the contrary, the episcopate is one because it is united with Jesus Christ to such an extent that the totality of the episcopate is represented in each bishop. As C. says, "The episcopate is one, of which each one has a part through the totality." This vision of the episcopate caused friction between C. and Rome, whose bishop C. accused precisely of pretending to be a "bishop of bishops."

Another of the elements that soured the relations of C. with Rome was the question of the baptism of heretics. When a baptized person within a group of heretics joined the church, should that person be baptized again or not? The custom in some churches was to accept the baptism of the heretics as valid, as long as it was with water and in the name of the Father, the Son, and the Holy Spirit. This is what was done in Rome as well as in the churches of Palestine and Egypt. But in Antioch and the province of Africa, the custom was not to accept such baptism, and therefore to rebaptize the converts. When someone in Carthage pointed out this diversity of practices, C. came out in defense of the African custom of rebaptizing heretics. The next provincial synod, presided over by C., confirmed this position, and C. communicated it to the church of Rome in a letter written in the name of the synod. This led to a long controversy with Stephen, the bishop of Rome, who insisted that the church of Carthage should follow the customs of Rome, while C. and the other bishops of the province refused to do so. C. wrote to other bishops of other regions who agreed with him and insisted on their vision of the episcopate, which is one, and does not allow any single bishop to exercise hegemony over the others. Stephen threatened to break the bonds of communion between Rome and Carthage. C. and his friends remained firm in their position, and a schism might have taken place if it had not been for the death of Stephen in 257. His successor, Sixtus II, did not insist on the matter. Tempers calmed down, although no formal agreement was reached. In spite of everything, half a century later the Roman custom had become generalized in Carthage, apparently without great controversy or opposition.

———

JLG

Cyril of Alexandria (?–444).

Patriarch of Alexandria from 412, when he succeeded his uncle Theophilus. A theologian of great ability, although he was also very rigid and dogmatic. In his works there are strong attacks against the Jews and the philosophers. In 415, when an angry crowd attacked and killed the Neoplatonic philosopher Hypatia, some attributed this deed to C. Although it has not been proved that C. planned the attack, there is no doubt that his preaching against the pagan philosophers inspired it.

But the great theological controversy of C. had to do with the teachings of ⇒Nestorius, who had defended his chaplain Anastasius. Nestorius himself followed his chaplain's lead by preaching against the title *Theotokos* (mother of God or, more literally, bearer of God), which was applied to the Virgin Mary. What was at stake was not so much what was said about Mary as what was said about Jesus. Following a typically Antiochene position, Nestorius sought to safeguard the humanity of the Savior, which always ran the risk of being eclipsed by his divinity. Therefore he clearly distinguished between them, and said that the one who was born of Mary was Jesus, or Christ, but not God, and that the proper title of Mary was therefore *Christotokos* (bearer of Christ).

Over against Nestorius, C. adopted a typically Alexandrian position. The school of Alexandria had for a long time been inclined to emphasize the union of the humanity with the divinity in Jesus Christ, even when this would appear to result in the diminishment of the true and total humanity of the Savior. That union manifests itself, among other things, in what theologians call the *communicatio idiomatum*, that is, the communication or transfer of the properties or predicates. It is in virtue of the *communicatio idiomatum* that we can say that in Jesus God walked in Galilee. And, as C. affirmed, it is for the same reason we can say that God suffered and died on the cross. Although this might be difficult to accept, the contrary affirmation would make the incarnation senseless, for then we would need to distinguish at every step what Jesus does as God and what he does as a human. And if this distinction is taken to its final conclusion, the result is that the one who suffered and died on the cross was a human being, and it is difficult to see what saving power that suffering and that death can have. For this reason C. insists on calling the Virgin *Theotokos*. In virtue of the *communicatio idiomatum*, it must be said that the one who was born of Mary was not only human, but also God. Therefore the one who was born of Mary was God. And consequently it is feasible to say that Mary is the mother or bearer of God, not in the sense that God's origin was in her, but in the sense that the one who was in her womb was very God.

The controversy was long and complicated. In his *Easter Epistle* of 429, C. defended the title *Theotokos*. Then he convinced ⇒Celestine, who presided over a Roman synod that condemned the teachings of Nestorius, while another synod in Alexandria, presided over by C. himself, did the same. This last synod sent Nestorius a condemnatory epistle that included twelve anathemas directed not only against Nestorius, but also against a good portion of the traditional positions of the school of Antioch.

All of this brought about the convocation of the Council of ⇒Ephesus, which met in 431, and which C. opened before the delegation of Antioch arrived. The result was a divided council and a series of vicissitudes which in the end led to a Formula of Union (433) between Cyril and the more moderate Antiochenes. C. more or less repudiated his twelve anathemas, Nestorius was permanently deposed, and for a brief time the controversy calmed down. (Concerning its continuation, ⇒Nestorius, ⇒Dioscorus, Council of ⇒Chalcedon.)

C.'s Christology is refined and subtle, and therefore has frequently been erroneously interpreted. According to C., the union between the humanity and the divinity in Jesus Christ is "hypostatic." This phrase, "hypostatic union," soon came to be the common way of referring to the union that takes place in the incarnation. What this means for C. is that in the incarnation the human nature is united with the hypostasis of the Second Person of the Trinity (concerning the difference between hypostasis and *ousia*, ⇒Basil of Caesarea, ⇒Cappadocians). Thus, in Christ there is no human hypostasis or subsistence, but the humanity subsists in the subsistence or hypostasis of the Word. For this reason C. refers to the "anhypostasis" (the lack of hypostasis) of the humanity of Jesus.

This has led some interpreters to think that according to C., in Jesus Christ the Word was united not to a particular human being, but to a generic "humanity." Although there are some texts in the works of C. that lend themselves to such an interpretation, C. does not pretend to deny the human individuality of the Savior. What C. does deny is that this humanity has its own subsistence, separate from that of the Word. Jesus' humanity subsists in his divinity. This in turn is the foundation of the *communicatio idiomatum*, for the properties are predicated of the hypostasis, and in Jesus there is only one hypostasis, both for the divinity and for the humanity. This was the basis on which the theologians who worked in conjunction with the Council of Chalcedon developed what in the end came to be the orthodox christological expression.

On the other hand, several phrases and passages in the works of C. supported the position that is known as Monophysitism, that is, the doctrine of "one nature" in the Savior. Frequently C. uses the term *physis,* nature, as a synonym for "hypostasis," subsistence or, in its orthodox use in Christology as well as in the Trinitarian doctrine, "person." What is more, the Monophysites based themselves on a phrase that C. believed came from ⇒Athanasius, but which appears rather to have come from ⇒Apollinaris of Laodicea or one of his followers: "one nature incarnate of God the Word." Consequently, while the orthodox theologians (that is, those who agree with the decisions of Chalcedon) see the champion of their Christology in C., the Monophysitists see in him the champion of theirs.

—

JLG

Cyril of Jerusalem (ca. 313–86).
Bishop of that city in the fourth century whose opposition to the Arianism of ⇒Acacius of Caesarea cost him persecution and exile. Nonetheless, C. preferred the term *homoiousios* to the one that had been adopted in ⇒Nicaea, *homoousios,* and therefore can be considered part of the Homoiousian party which the Cappadocians convinced of the orthodoxy of Nicaea. His chief work is his *Catechetical Lectures,* in which he comments on a creed which apparently is that of Jerusalem and which appears to have influenced the formulation of the Nicene Creed adopted in the Council of ⇒Constantinople (381), where C. was present. Much more important than his position regarding the Trinity is his discussion and description of the Eucharist, which is our main source for the details of the eucharistic celebration as it was practiced in the East in the fourth century. According to C., in the Eucharist we become participants of the body and blood of Jesus Christ (*synsomoi* and *synaimoi*) and therefore bearers of him (*Christoforoi*).

—

JLG

Cyril of Turov (12th century).
Russian theologian and mystic of whose life little is known. In his Christology he highlights the role of Jesus Christ as conqueror of the powers of hell and death. He interpreted the Bible allegorically and consequently accused the Jews of foolishness and blindness for not seeing the promised messiah in Jesus. Apparently he knew the Old Testament better than the New,

for occasionally he is mistaken when he quotes the latter.

—

JLG

D'Ailly, Pierre ⇒Ailly, Pierre d'

Dagg, John Leadley (1794–1884).
Educator, writer, and slaveholder. He presided over and taught at the University of Mercer, in Georgia. He was the first systematizer of Baptist theology in the United States. He promoted the American and Foreign Biblical Society.

—

EPA

Daly, Mary (1928–).
One of the best-known and most radical feminist theologians. From 1967 until 1999 she taught at Boston College, a Jesuit institution, where she had many conflicts due to her theological positions. During that time her writing was becoming ever more radical, in a process that began with the book *The Church and the Second Sex* (1968) and continued with *Beyond God the Father* (1973), *Gyn/Ecology* (1978), *Pure Lust* (1984), and several others. Although she had been reared and educated within Roman Catholicism, in the end she declared herself "a graduate" from the church and therefore no longer a Christian, but a philosopher of radical feminism. A characteristic of her writings is the reinterpretation of words on the basis of their roots. In that process, D. radicalized old terms and created new ones. Many Christian feminists, without leaving the church, have appreciated and used D.'s criticism as a starting point of support for their own less-radical feminism. Thus, although D. no longer considers herself a part of the church, her work continues to influence the theological endeavor in Catholic as well as in Protestant circles.

—

CGG

Damasus (ca. 304–84).
Bishop of Rome and author of a number of epistles in which, among other things, he insists on his own authority (although some documents that bear his name, and in which the relations between Rome, Antioch, and Alexandria are discussed, appear not to have been written by him, but were composed one hundred years later). He intervened in the schism of Antioch, taking the side that was opposed to ⇒Meletius of Antioch. Also, at the urging of ⇒Basil of

Caesarea, he condemned the Christology of ⇒Apollinaris.

———

JLG

Daniélou, Jean (1905–74). Jesuit theologian, expert in patristics, who became bishop and cardinal. He entered the novitiate in 1927 and was ordained to the priesthood in 1938. He lived in Paris from 1941 and carried out the rest of his career there as teacher, scholar, and chaplain. He served as professor of the history of primitive Christianity in the Faculty of Theology of the Catholic Institute. As a scholar, he excelled as a church historian. His chief publications were on the theology of ⇒Gregory of Nyssa, patristic exegesis, and primitive Judeo-Christian theology. He was also university chaplain at the Sorbonne and the Superior Normal School. He was consecrated bishop on April 21, 1969, and named a cardinal by Pope Paul VI seven days afterward. Together with Henri de ⇒Lubac, D. considered himself one of the proponents of the movement known as *nouvelle théologie* (lit., new theology) in France. Outstanding among his works are *Scandal of the Truth* (1962), *History of Salvation and Liturgy* (1965), and *The Infancy Gospels* (1969).

———

PAJ

Dante Alighieri (1265–1321). The poet shared with Boccaccio and Petrarch, the great men of letters of the fourteenth century, the honor of shaping the Italian tongue. He is recognized as one of the greatest poets of the Middle Ages and of all times.

D. was born in Florence, an opulent city-state and a cradle of the fine arts with a very developed banking system and far-flung foreign trade. Florence, together with Venice, Milan, and Genoa, acquired its riches thanks to the high rates of interest that it charged for financing the Crusades and through the absolute control that it established over the commercial routes to India in the twelfth and thirteenth centuries. D.'s father was probably a landowner and moneylender, with his eyes turned toward the nobility. His great-grandfather, Cacciaguida, died in Jerusalem during the Second Crusade.

He studied in cathedral schools and in the universities of Bologna, Padua, and probably Paris. When he was young he enlisted in the army and fought in the battle of Campeldino against the Aretins. In 1290, he entered a mar-

riage of convenience with Gemma Donati, with whom he had at least four children.

From 1295 on, he participated in the political and military matters of his native city, occupying different public posts. He was a member of the Guelph party that favored the pope, in opposition to the Ghibellines, partisans of the emperor. In 1301 a sector of the Guelph party that opposed D. won control of the city and expelled him, condemning him to the stake should he return to Florence. D. died in his exile in Ravenna.

The Divine Comedy, his masterpiece, was written between 1307 and 1321. It is an epic poem that portrays the theology of the time. In this allegory, D. visits the church in purgatory. (The adjective "Divine" in the title is a late addition to the Venetian edition of 1555. The word "Comedy" has to do with its happy ending.) Virgil, the symbol of philosophical knowledge, guides D. through hell and purgatory. In the second part, the Florentine Beatrice Portinari (1266–90), D.'s platonic love, guides him with her theological knowledge toward the contemplation of the supreme good in paradise. Through a mystical rapture, D. discovers the meaning of life and of the cosmos.

Beatrice also appears in his poetic history, *Vita nuova* (New Life). Some of his other works are *The Monarchy, The Banquet, On the Eloquence of the Vernacular, The Dispute about Water and Earth, The Two Eclogues, The Thirteen Epistles*, besides other letters and poems.

———

EPA

Darby, John Nelson (1800–82). Key character in the establishment of the denomination called the Plymouth Brethren, who are still known in Europe as Darbyites. He came from an aristocratic Anglo-Irish family. He studied law and then theology at Trinity College in Dublin. In 1825 he was ordained in the Anglican Church, from which he broke away a few years later. In Dublin he began to frequent nonconformist groups who called themselves "believers," "Christians," "brothers," or "saints." There he made contact with Anthony Groves, Francis William Newman, and J. G. Bellet. In 1829 he wrote the first text of the movement, *On the Nature and the Unity of the Church of Christ*. Finally his followers took their name from the second and largest center founded by D., in Plymouth, England.

The leadership of D. was reflected in his doctrinal contributions: dispensationalism, which influenced Cyrus I. ⇒Scofield and his annotated Bible; the assurance of salvation; the presence of God in the congregation of the devout; and the universal priesthood of believers.

In 1848 the movement suffered a division between an exclusivist group and another that was more open to having contacts with the "nonbrothers." D. led the first group, adopting positions that were increasingly legalistic.

The Plymouth Brethren emphasized returning to the simple Christianity of the New Testament (Matt. 18:20); sharing the bread of Communion weekly; doing without an ordained clergy (Matt. 23:8–13); moving away from fixed liturgies; and focusing on the imminent return of Jesus Christ.

With the aid of others among the Brethren, D. translated the Bible into English, French, and German. His writings are contained in thirty-two volumes published in London (1867–83). He was a commentator, poet, and hymnologist (he edited the official songbook of the denomination). He also wrote devotional literature and sermons. His unmarried status made possible his peripatetic work in the West Indies, the United States (where he broke with D. L. ⇒Moody), Australia, New Zealand, and Europe.

———

EPA

Darwin, Charles Robert (1809–82).
English scientist—and supporter of Christian missions—who proposed the theory of evolution by natural selection. In *The Origin of Species* (1859) and *The Descent of Man* (1871), he postulated that in the natural world there is a constant competitive struggle between members of the species whose physiological traits allow some to adapt themselves to changing environments and survive and reproduce while others perish. This natural selection explains the evolution of species and also the emergence of new ones, including humanity. The reaction in modern theology toward D. has been acceptance, adaptation, or rejection. His vision challenged traditional concepts of the authority of the Bible, the action of God in the world, the privileged status of humanity, and natural theology.

———

LRR

David de Dinant (13th century).
Theologian declared a heretic by the provincial council of Sens in 1210. His works were burned by the order of that council, which accused him

of upholding teachings similar to those of ⇒Amalric of Bena. Although it is difficult to know his thought, since all of his written work was destroyed, from the testimony of ⇒Albertus Magnus and ⇒Thomas Aquinas it is inferred that D. maintained that, since individuals are included in their class, the supreme class, God, includes everything. Upon this foundation D. seems to have declared that God is the matter of everything that exists. His adversaries have called this teaching materialist pantheism.

———

JLG

Dayton, Donald Wilber (1942–).
Author, educator, and scholar who has specialized in the Holiness movement of the nineteenth century and its contributions to Pentecostal thought. His book *Theological Roots of Pentecostalism* (1987) identifies in the Holiness movement four christological themes that characterize Pentecostal thought and ethos: Christ as Savior, as the one who baptizes in the Holy Spirit, as Healer, and as King who comes.

———

EV

De Dietrich, Suzanne ⇒Dietrich, Suzanne de

De Guyon, Madame ⇒Guyon, Madame de

De La Ramée, Pierre ⇒Ramus, Petrus

De Lubac, Henri ⇒Lubac, Henri de

De Maistre, Joseph-Marie ⇒Maistre, Joseph-Marie de

De Nobili, Roberto ⇒Nobili, Roberto de

Deiros, Pablo (1945–).
Argentinian Baptist historian and evangelical theologian, member of Fraternidad Teológica Latinoamericana. He was the first Latin American to write a history of Christianity in Latin America, under the title *A Vision of Christianity in Latin America*. His theological contribution in evangelical circles stimulated a more critical reflection on the relationship between the Christian faith and politics in Latin America during the 1980s.

———

CCO

Deloria, Vine Victor (1933–2005).

One of the most prominent figures in the defense of the history, rights, and philosophy of the indigenous nations of North America. He was born in South Dakota and received his master's degree in theology at the Lutheran School of Theology in Maywood, Illinois (1963). In 1970 he received his doctorate in jurisprudence at the University of Colorado.

D. was executive director of the National Congress of Indigenous North Americans and a member of the National Office for the Rights of Indigenous Persons. He was also professor of history, law, religious studies, and political science at the University of Colorado in Boulder.

D. published a great number of books, including *Spirit and Reason*; *God is Red*; *Red Earth, White Lies*; *Custer Died for Your Sins: An Indian Manifesto*; and *Behind the Trail of Broken Treaties: An Indian Declaration of Independence*.

In the field of theology, D. held that the merciless exploitation of nature by Western civilization is related to the words of Genesis in which God gives the human being sovereignty over creation. He also valued religion that, like the indigenous religions of North America, gives special attention to place rather than to time.

———

JDR

Demetrius of Cycicus (10th century).

Greek bishop of that city who wrote a treatise against the Christology of the Jacobite and Armenian churches.

———

JLG

Demetrius of Lampe (12th century).

Obscure personality, of Phrygian origin, around whom a controversy in Constantinople broke out concerning the meaning of Jesus' words, "My Father is greater than I." Accused of returning to doctrines that had already been condemned as Arian (⇒Arius), he was declared a heretic by a synod that met in 1166.

———

JLG

Denck, Hans (1495–1527).

One of the first Anabaptist theologians. Educated as a humanist, he was later a disciple of ⇒Oecolampadius. Convinced at last by Anabaptist preaching, in 1526 he was baptized by Balthasar ⇒Hübmaier and devoted himself to defending the Anabaptist teachings, infusing in them strong mystical and individualistic elements.

For him the internal Word of God is superior to the Scriptures, and all the Christian ceremonies, including baptism, are only a sign and reminder of what takes place within the soul.

———

JLG

Derrida, Jacques (1930–2004).

French philosopher born in Algeria, and later professor at the Sorbonne, Yale, Johns Hopkins, and other universities. He is considered the founder of deconstructionism, denying that the author is the only source of meaning in a text. On the contrary, the same text acquires different meanings according to who reads it and from where it is read (*polysemia*). This has opened new horizons in biblical hermeneutics and, to a lesser degree in the present, in historical and theological studies.

———

JLG

Descartes, René (1596–1650).

Known as the father of modern philosophy, this French philosopher, scientist, and mathematician invented analytic geometry and was the first of the philosophers of modernity to describe the physical world in terms of matter and movement. His two best-known works are *Discourse on Method* and *The Principles of Philosophy*.

D.'s philosophy is dualistic. The world is formed by two basic substances: matter and spirit. Matter is the essence of the physical world, of which our bodies are a part. Spirit is the essence of the conscious life and of our rationality. The spirit is unified and interacts with the body but can exist without it.

In his *Discourse on Method*, D. begins from his famous methodological doubt. Nothing should be accepted as true except that which is free of all doubt. When I think, however much I doubt, I can still have the absolute certainty that it is I who think, and therefore I have the certainty that I exist. Thus the famous phrase: *cogito ergo sum* (I think, therefore I am). This certainty serves him as a foundation to prove the existence of God, the immortality of the soul, and the existence of the physical world.

In a similar way, it can be proved that God exists, since the idea of a perfect God cannot be created by an imperfect being. As far as the existence of the soul is concerned, he alleges that the capacity to think is what gives us certainty of our own existence as a thinking being; and as a thinking being, each one can conceive of his or her own existence even apart from the body. The existence of God is what allows D. to be sure that the physical world exists, and that it is possible to know its physical properties. The benevolent character of God assures us that when we think carefully, our clear perceptions, including those of the physical world, are true.

— IG

Deusdedit (11th century). A cardinal who, at the end of the eleventh century (1087 and 1097), published two works in defense of the autonomy of spiritual power: *Collection of Canons* and *Against the Invaders and Simoniacs*. While he defended priestly and papal autonomy, he also affirmed that the secular power has its own functions, and that one power should not invade the responsibilities of the other.

— JLG

Devanandan, Paul David (1901–62). Professor of philosophy and the history of religions in Bangalore, India. D. developed a Christian theology of dialogue with other religions, particularly Hinduism. This theological posture and evangelizing conception helped the Church of South India to move away from a position of antagonism and isolation and to participate more fully in the culture of India.

— CCO

Dewey, John (1859–1952). North American philosopher and educator who was influenced by the pragmatism of W. ⇒James. He advocated a reconstruction of philosophy that would take experience as a starting point of resolution. D. characterized his philosophy and his ethical theory as "naturalism," arguing that both facts and values can be discovered and ratified by experience.

In the method of philosophical inquiry that D. proposed, a problem is posed, information is researched, options are examined, and conclusions are evaluated. D. understood that the democratic system was the best laboratory, since this type of research requires freedom to make intelligent decisions as well as each individual's will to act. It is common in the Deweyan tradition to speak of democracy as religion because, as he said in his book *A Common Faith*, religion is nothing else than an active relation between the actual and the ideal.

With these ideas, D. established an experimental school at the University of Chicago, seeking to help students in their formation as citizens of democracy. With this purpose in mind, students were to learn to regulate themselves; education was centered on one's own efforts to develop and to gain technical and intellectual competence. "Progressive education," as this pedagogical effort has been called, has influenced religious education, as the works of G. A. ⇒Coe demonstrate.

— JRI

Dias, Zwinglio (1941–). Brazilian Presbyterian. One of the Protestant theologians and historians who have provided a critical analysis of the development of Protestantism and the history of the ecumenical movement in Latin America, particularly in Brazil.

— CCO

Dibelius, Martin Franz (1883–1947). German New Testament scholar, Lutheran theologian, and promoter of the ecumenical movement, who is known as one of the founders of the form-critical method. D. became interested in the problems linked with literary criticism and the oral tradition behind the written message of the Gospels. According to him, the Gospels, rather than being the creation of independent authors, were the fruit of the work of compilers and editors of the oral tradition. In this sense, the church was the principal medium of transmission of the sayings of Jesus. D. also studied the origin of the ethical instructions of the New Testament from the eschatological point of view. Among his best-known works are *Die Geisterwelt im Glauben des Paulus* (1909; The Spirit World in the Faith of Paul); *Die urchristliche Überlieferung von Johannes dem Taufer* (1911; The Early Christian Tradition about John the Baptist); *Geschichte der christlichen Literatur* (1926; History of Christian Literature); *Evangelium und Welt* (1929; Gospel and World); *Paulus* (1951; Paul); and several exegetical commentaries on the Pauline Epistles.

— AEM

Dickinson, Jonathan (1688–1747). Prominent Presbyterian minister, author, and theologian in the North American colonial period. He is recognized chiefly through four elements in his career: He influenced the formation of the original constitution of the new colonial Presbyterian Church when he recommended that ecclesiastical powers should be granted to the presbyters and not to the central synod. He offered a moderate position of accepting in the Presbyterian church those who did not subscribe to the ⇒Westminster Confession. He accepted as valid George ⇒Whitefield's movement of renewal, as long as discipline and order were maintained and antinomianism was not promoted. Together with other prominent leaders he founded the College of New Jersey (known today as Princeton University) and served as its first president. Part of his purpose was to make room in theological education for those who participated in Whitefield's renewal movement.

———
ALG

Didache ⇒Apostolic Fathers

Didymus the Blind (ca. 312–98).
Blind from the time he was four or five, he devoted himself to study and prayer, so much so that his contemporaries regarded him as an example of scholarship. ⇒Athanasius made him the head of the catechetical school of Alexandria, where he restored the study of ⇒Origen, although giving an orthodox interpretation to some of the most daring assertions of his famous predecessor. He wrote, among others, treatises *Against Arius and Sabellius*, *Against the Manicheans*, *On the Trinity*, and *On the Holy Spirit*. Some attribute to him the third and fourth books of *Against Eunomius* of ⇒Basil of Caesarea. A faithful follower of Origen, like him he upheld theories such as the eternity of creation and the preexistence of souls. For this reason, half a century after his death the Council of ⇒Constantinople of 553 (Fifth Ecumenical) declared him a heretic.

———
JLG

Dietrich of Niem (ca. 1340–1418).
Member of the Roman curia, but at the same time one of the chief proponents of conciliarist theory, which he developed in his treatise *On the Schism* and in a *Dialogue* that he wrote shortly afterward agreeing with the proposals of ⇒Ockham and ⇒Marsilius of Padua.

———
JLG

Dietrich, Suzanne de (1891–1981).
French engineer, D. stood out as a leader of the Christian and ecumenical student movements and became a member of the Executive Committee of the World Student Christian Federa-

tion. A lay member of the Reformed Church of France and instructor at the Ecumenical Institute of Bossey of the ⇒World Council of Churches, D. was one of the first women to leave an indelible mark in the ecumenical movement and in ecumenical theology. A good part of her theological viewpoint reflects the influence of Karl ⇒Barth.

———
CCO

Dilthey, Wilhelm (1833–1911).
German philosopher whose chief contribution was the development of a distinctive methodology for the humanities.

He attempted to establish the humanities as interpretive sciences in their own right. He sought the philosophical foundation of what he called "the sciences of man, society, and the state," which he later called *Geisteswissenschaften* (sciences of the spirit), a term that in time gained general recognition.

The ideal of the humanities at that time was to copy the methodology of the natural sciences. D. objected to the diffusive influence of the latter and thus developed a philosophy of life that perceived the human being in its contingency and historical mutability. Fundamental to this notion was the interaction between personal experience, its fulfillment in creative expression, and the reflective understanding of this experience. According to him, the essence of the human being cannot be captured by the scientific method, but only through knowledge of all of history. The comprehensive conception of history from the cultural point of view, established by D., has been of great consequence in modern scholarship, particularly in the study of literature.

Very little is known about his personal life. He was a peaceful scholar, calm, reserved, and enigmatic, and totally dedicated to his work. Even his most intimate circle of disciples and collaborators acknowledged knowing very little about his deepest sentiments.

———
RAR

Diodore of Tarsus (ca. 350–ca. 392).
Respected teacher, chief founder of the Antiochene tradition of biblical interpretation, and bishop of Tarsus from 378. Earlier he had founded in Antioch a monastery where ⇒John Chrysostom and ⇒Theodore of Mopsuestia were his disciples. His main work on hermeneutical theory, *Distinction between Theory and Allegory*, has been lost. D. rejected Alexandrian allegory and preferred an exegetical method in

which the literal sense of the Bible led to moral and spiritual teachings. On this basis he produced commentaries on several books of the Bible, which do not survive. He also wrote a good number of works on theological topics, which also have been lost. In them he was concerned above all with christological matters, although he also refuted the Manicheans (⇒Mani), the ⇒Pneumatomachians, and others.

As a good Antiochene, D. proposed a "disjunctive" Christology, that is, one that seeks to preserve the true humanity of Jesus Christ, underscoring the difference and even the distance between that humanity and the divinity of the Lord. Thus he says, for example, that "the Son of God" inhabited the "Son of David," very much "as in a temple." On the basis of such assertions, later generations saw in him the origins of the teachings of ⇒Nestorius. It is probably for this reason that only fragments of his writings quoted by other authors are preserved (although some scholars attribute to him a *Commentary on the Psalms* of unknown origin).

—

JLG

Diognetus, To (2nd? century).

One of the writings that is commonly found among the ⇒Apostolic Fathers (together with ⇒Clement of Rome, the *Didache*, ⇒Ignatius of Antioch, ⇒Polycarp of Smyrna, ⇒Papias, the so-called *Epistle of* ⇒*Barnabas,* and the *Shepherd* of ⇒Hermas). This document was discovered and published for the first time in the sixteenth century, but the question of its exact date has been broadly debated. Some locate it as late as the thirteenth century. Others believe that it is the lost apology of ⇒Quadratus, and that it therefore is earlier than ⇒Justin and the other apologists. The study of the language and the style appears to indicate that it indeed is a document of the second century, but this is not sufficient to attribute it to Quadratus.

The so-called discourse is directed to a certain Diognetus, whom the author gives the title of "most excellent" (the same title that the author of Luke-Acts gives to Theophilus), but who otherwise is unknown to us. We have here an elegant and moderate writing, the intention of which is not to attack the customs and beliefs of the pagans, as in the writings of ⇒Hermias and ⇒Tatian, but to show the goodness of the Christian faith. In this way it is very similar to the writings of ⇒Athenagoras.

The most famous passage of this writing is found in chapter 5, where the author points out the way in which Christians are both similar to and different from the rest of humanity. They are a part of humanity in that they live in the same lands and in the same flesh, and they subject themselves to the same laws. But they distinguish themselves from the rest because, although they inhabit the same earth and conduct themselves as the citizens of any nation in which they happen to be, everywhere they are treated as strangers, and for them every country is a strange land. Consequently, chapter 6 says, "Christians are to the world what the soul is to the body."

—

JLG

Dionysius of Alexandria (ca. 195–264).

Disciple of the Origenist ⇒Heraclas, whom he succeeded, first as director of the school of Alexandria (ca. 232) and then as bishop of the same city (ca. 248). Among his many controversies, the most important was his struggle against the teachings of ⇒Sabellius, who appeared to him to erase every distinction among the persons of the Trinity. In the course of that controversy, he emphasized the difference between the Father and the Son to such an extent that some accused him of subordinationism (that is, of making the Son an inferior being, and not strictly divine). The result of this was a correspondence with ⇒Dionysius of Rome in which the Alexandrian explained his position, the Roman warned him of some of its dangers, and D. accepted the recommendations and comments. Subsequently the Arian controversy (⇒Arius) awakened interest in that correspondence, since D. appeared to have been a precursor of Arianism. It was for this reason that ⇒Athanasius commented on the correspondence between the Dionysiuses.

—

JLG

Dionysius of Rome (?–268).

Bishop of that city, whose interesting correspondence with ⇒Dionysius of Alexandria is preserved. In his efforts to refute Sabellianism (⇒Sabellius), the latter seemed to have come too close to subordinationism. D. of Rome warned him of this danger, pointing out that, just as light always has brilliance, the Father always has the Son next to him; that is, the Son is coeternal with the Father. In addition, D. warned the Alexandrian that he should avoid using the term "creature" when referring to the Son: the Son is not a creature of the Father.

—

JLG

Dionysius the Areopagite (ca. 500).
Pseudonym by which an unknown author published a series of mystical works, to whom modern authors usually refer as Pseudo-Dionysius. Since the authentic D. the A. was a disciple of Paul (see Acts 17:34), during the Middle Ages these writings were given an authority almost equal to that of the Scriptures, and therefore their influence on theology as well as on medieval religiosity and worldview was great. Also, since Gregory of Tours affirmed that the founder of the church in what today is Paris was "Dionysius," toward the ninth century the belief began to appear that, besides having written all these works, D. of A. was the apostle of the Gauls. Already in the twelfth century ⇒Abelard expressed doubts about that identification of Dionysius of Paris with D. the A. Today scholars agree that the author of those works was neither a disciple of Paul nor founder of the Parisian church.

The works of the fictitious D. the A., in addition to some letters, are four: *On the Divine Names, Mystical Theology, The Celestial Hierarchy*, and *The Ecclesiastical Hierarchy*. In all of those works, D. the A. shows his philosophical position. His conception of reality was essentially Neoplatonic, as was his understanding of the relationship between physical and spiritual reality. To a great extent it was through the influence and prestige of D. the A. (as well as of ⇒Augustine) that Neoplatonism imposed itself on the first centuries of the Middle Ages, to the extent that it was believed that it was part of Christian revelation and therefore that different philosophical systems (such as Aristotelianism, which was reintroduced in western Europe in the twelfth and thirteenth centuries) were not compatible with the Christian faith.

In the first of the works mentioned above, the author affirmed that the only way to know God is through the Scriptures, in which God is given different names, and that such investigation can be done only in a spirit of prayer, since God reveals Godself only to those who come near God in faith and devotion. Among the names he studies are "goodness," "beauty," "love," "being," "power," "justice."

Mystical Theology is much briefer. It speaks of a knowledge of God that reaches the believer in the silence of prayer. This knowledge is mysterious and "superluminous." In search of such knowledge, the believer should begin by denying any limitation to God, since God can be spoken of only in a negative sense, expressing what God is not. At the end of this process, the soul is purely passive and in contemplation experiences a profound unity with the Eternal.

The Ecclesiastical Hierarchy and *The Celestial Hierarchy* deal with the process of "deification" or sanctification. This process has three stages: purification (*catharsis*), illumination, and perfection. In order to lead us to such an experience, God provides a whole hierarchy of beings, like a divine ladder, that lead us toward mystical union. This hierarchy has two levels: an earthly or ecclesiastical hierarchy, and another which is angelic or celestial.

The Celestial Hierarchy made a profound impact on medieval angelology. According to D. the A., the celestial hierarchy, in imitation of the Trinity, is composed of three hierarchies, each one of which is tripartite. The result is that the first hierarchy includes the seraphim, cherubim, and thrones; the second, the dominions, authorities, and powers; and the third, the principalities, archangels, and angels. The first level surrounds the celestial throne; the second concerns itself with the whole of creation; the third takes special care of the human creature, so that there are particular angels that concern themselves with nations and individuals.

The ecclesiastical hierarchy is similar. Its purpose is also to purify, illumine, and perfect believers. As with the celestial, this hierarchy is also subdivided into three: the sacraments or rites provided for purification, illumination, and perfection of the faithful; the ministers devoted to the consecration and distribution of those sacraments; and the recipients of their benefits. Each one of these three is likewise divided into three. The three rites are baptism, the Eucharist, and confirmation. The ministers are the bishops, priests, and deacons. And the recipients are, first, the catechumens (those who have not yet received baptism) and the penitents (those who because of their sins are temporarily excluded from the Eucharist). For these what is demanded is purification, which the catechumens obtain in baptism and the penitents receive through penance. The next level of this subhierarchy is made up of the baptized faithful and the communicants, who are progressively illumined with the aim of perfection. And the third level are the "perfect ones," that is, those who embrace the monastic life.

It has been suggested that D. the A. was a Monophysite (⇒Eutyches, ⇒Severus of Antioch, Council of ⇒Chalcedon), or at least a theologian of Monothelite tendencies (⇒Sergius of Constantinople, Council of ⇒Constantinople III, 680–81). It is difficult to determine if such assertions are true, but at least it is clear that his theology is a great deal closer to the Alexandrian tendencies than to those of the Antiochenes, and therefore his Christology is unitive and tends to lessen the importance of the humanity of Christ.

———

JLG

Dioscorus (5th century). Successor of ⇒Cyril as bishop of Alexandria in 444, deposed in 451 by the Council of ⇒Chalcedon. As a defender of the traditional Alexandrian Christology, he declared himself a defender of ⇒Eutyches and as such presided over what ⇒Leo the Great called "the *latrocinium* [robber council] of Ephesus" (449). The churches of the Monophysite tradition venerate him as a saint and a defender of that tradition.

———

JLG

Doctors of the Church. The principal teachers of the church, officially recognized as such by the Roman authorities, usually by papal proclamation. The first official proclamation in this sense was made by ⇒Boniface VIII in 1295, declaring that the four great D.'s were ⇒Ambrose, ⇒Jerome, ⇒Augustine, and ⇒Gregory I the Great. Three hundred years later (1567) Pius V added ⇒Thomas Aquinas to the list. The following year the same pope declared that the four great D.'s of the Greek church were ⇒Basil of Caesarea, ⇒Gregory of Nazanzius, ⇒John Chrysostom, and ⇒Athanasius. Shortly afterward, in 1588, Sixtus V added ⇒Bonaventure to the list, in an apparent effort to recognize the contribution of the Franciscans to theology and thus to balance the previous proclamation of Thomas Aquinas as a D. After that date, it was not until 1720 that a new name was added, that of ⇒Anselm of Canterbury. From then on, the list has continued growing. In 1754, when he declared ⇒Leo the Great a D., Benedict XIV also declared that in order to obtain such a title three conditions are required; the eminence and distinction of the teaching of the person; personal holiness; and the official declaration, either by the pope or by an ecumenical council.

In 1970 Paul VI named the first two women to obtain this honor, ⇒Teresa of Ávila and ⇒Catherine of Siena. At the present time the list includes thirty-two names.

Within this list are eight to whom a special place is granted, being called the "great D.'s of the C." Four of them represent the Western church (Ambrose, Jerome, Augustine, and Gre-

gory the Great), and four the Eastern (Basil of Caesarea, Gregory of Nazianzus, John Chrysostom, and Athanasius).

The current list, with the year in which each one was honored, and the pope who took this action:

Ambrose, 1295, Boniface VIII
Jerome, 1295, Boniface VIII
Augustine, 1295, Boniface VIII
Gregory the Great, 1295, Boniface VIII
Thomas Aquinas, 1567, Pius V
Basil of Caesarea, 1568, Pius V
Gregory of Nazianzus, 1568, PiusV
John Chrysostom, 1568, Pius V
Athanasius, 1568, Pius V
Bonaventure, 1588, Sixtus V
Anselm, 1720, Clement XI
Isidore of Seville, 1722, Innocent XIII
Peter Chrysologus, 1728, Benedict XIII
Leo the Great, 1754, Benedict XIV
Peter Damian, 1828, Leon XII
Bernard of Clairvaux, 1830, Pius VIII
Hilary of Poitiers, 1851, Pius IX
Alphonsus Liguori, 1871, Pius IX
Francis de Sales, 1876, Pius IX
Cyril of Jerusalem, 1882, Leo XIII
Cyril of Alexandria, 1882, Leo XIII
John of Damascus, 1890, Leo XIII
Bede, 1899, Leon XIII
Ephraem Syrus, 1920, Benedict XV
Peter Canisius, 1925, Pius XI
John of the Cross, 1926, Pius XI
Robert Bellarmine, 1931, Pius XI
Albertus Magnus, 1931, Pius XI
Antony of Padua, 1946, Pius XII
Lawrence of Brindisi, 1959, John XXIII
Teresa of Ávila, 1970, Paul VI
Catherine of Siena, 1970, Paul VI

About each one of these, see the corresponding article.

———

JLG

Dodd, Charles Harold (1884–1973). New Testament scholar and renowned English theologian, a graduate of Oxford, an ordained minister of the Congregational Church, and lecturer and professor at Oxford, Manchester, and Cambridge. Among his best-known writings are *The Parables of the Kingdom* (1935), *The Apostolic Preaching and Its Development* (1936), *According to the Scriptures* (1952), *The Interpretation of the Fourth Gospel* (1953), and *Historical Traditions behind the Fourth Gospel* (1963). His contributions to the study of the New Testament are of incalculable value. D.

discovered a "nucleus" or "essence" common to all the apostolic writings that is constitutive of the gospel itself, and which he calls the "kerygma" (preaching). The historical foundation of the religious tradition behind the Gospel of John stood out in relief. He showed the unity that exists in the way the authors of the New Testament interpret the Old Testament and present Jesus as the key to such a process. And he proposed the concept of "realized eschatology." According to D., all the promises of the Old Testament and the words of Jesus about the coming of the kingdom of God saw their fulfillment (that is, were realized) in the incarnation of Christ and in the implications that this great event has for humanity.

———
AEM

Döllinger, Johann Joseph Ignaz von (1788–1890).

Roman Catholic theologian and historian whose key principle, which he called organic growth, was an attempt to accept some of the changes that had taken place in the church throughout the centuries, but at the same time to limit such changes in the Roman Catholic Church of his time. Beginning in 1826 he was professor of church history at the University of Munich.

At the beginning of his career, D. used his recognized scholarship to defend contemporary Catholicism. His works on the Reformation (1846–48) and Luther (1851) are a strong criticism of the Protestants for having caused a break in the church.

But later he began to rebel against what he considered to be the new obscurantist positions that the Roman hierarchy was assuming. Without ecclesiastical sanction, he organized a conference of Catholic theologians and historians (1863) where he defended the use of critical tools, independent of Roman authority, in the investigation of history. As part of his historical studies, he affirmed that the theory of papal infallibility was an innovation that ran contrary to the tradition of the church. When the First Vatican Council (⇒Vatican I) promulgated such infallibility, D. refused to accept it, and this resulted in his excommunication (1871). The Old Catholic Church, which arose as a movement of protest against the direction that the Roman Church was taking, offered him the position of bishop, but D. declined. He continued to attend the Catholic mass until his death, although the sacraments were denied to him.

———
AP

Dominic of Guzmán (1170–1221).

Founder of the Order of Preachers or Dominicans. Born in Caleruega, Spain, of an aristocratic family. As a member of the Augustinian Order, he accompanied Bishop Diego on a missionary trip to the south of France to preach to the ⇒Albigensians. When he saw the violence and the inability of the Crusades to convert the Albigensians, D. recognized that the best method of evangelization is persuasion.

Inspired by the work of the apostles in the book of Acts and persuaded to create an order of itinerant, mendicant preachers, not bound by the duties that characterized the monastic movement, D. obtained the approval to create his order in 1215 under the papacy of Innocent III. D. instilled in his order a commitment to study for missionary work, thus acquiring for it an important place in the universities and great cities.

D.'s legacy is found in the conviction that missionaries should have the best possible theological preparation for communicating the gospel to other cultures and religions. The Order of Preachers or Dominicans is known as one of the most scholarly and missionary in the medieval, modern, and contemporary worlds.

———
CCO

Donatus (4th century).

Apparently the name of two different persons, but both bishops in North Africa, one in Casa Nigra in Numidia, and the other in Carthage. The ancient writers ⇒Optatus and—in some texts—⇒Augustine do not distinguish between these two, simply affirming that Donatism receives that name from its leader D., but then attributing to this person episodes in the lives of both bishops. Augustine himself later made clear that there were two persons of the same name. Following Augustine on this point, and also relying on other indications, historians doubt that the one who was bishop of Casa Nigra was later bishop of Carthage, and they therefore tend to distinguish between two persons of the same name.

Apparently D. of Casa Nigra was somewhat earlier, and was included among the first promoters of the movement that finally received the name of Donatism. This movement arose as a result of the persecution of Diocletian, and it maintained that the ministry of those who had lapsed in times of persecution was not valid. In addition, D. of Casa Nigra accused the bishop of Carthage, Mensurius, of having surrendered the sacred books in times of persecution. Upon the death of Mensurius, D. of Casa Nigra and others proposed as a candidate a member of their party, but the one who was elected was the deacon Cecilianus. Dissatisfied with such an election, D. of Casa Nigra convened a synod in Numidia which declared that the election and consecration of Cecilianus were invalid, since bishops had participated in it who were *traditores* (that is, bishops who supposedly had surrendered the sacred books to be destroyed). In his place they named Majorinus, from which action arose a schism in North Africa.

Emperor Constantine asked the bishop of Rome, Miltiades, to intervene in the matter. A synod that gathered in Rome in the year 313 declared itself in favor of Cecilianus and against D., Majorinus, and the bishops of Numidia who had rejected Cecilianus. Since these people of Numidia refused to accept the decision of the synod that had met in Rome, a new council was convoked, this time in Arles in 314, but with the same result.

The other D. was named bishop of Carthage by the group that had followed Majorinus, and it was he who gave the movement the name of Donatism. Now when the imperial authorities wanted to intervene again, the Donatists declared that they did not have to obey those authorities (although it was they who had appealed to the emperor against Cecilianus). The schism grew to the point where there were almost 400 Donatist bishops in North Africa. In the meantime, the most extreme anti-Roman groups, made up for the most part of Numidian believers, launched into armed rebellion and were called "circumcellions." Although some Donatist bishops opposed the circumcellions, the majority saw in this movement an ally against the official church and the empire that supported it. Thus the schism continued for several centuries.

The main theological matter that was debated as a result of this controversy was the validity of sacraments administered by an unworthy minister. The Donatists said that some of the bishops of the other church had been *traditores*, and therefore the ordinations performed by them were invalid. The result was that, according to the Donatists, the sacraments administered by the official church were not valid either, since the priests who celebrated them were not true priests. This in turn revived the old question, which was much discussed in North Africa, of the rebaptism of heretics (⇒Cyprian). For this reason the Donatist movement and the refutation of its teachings by authors such as Augustine were one of the factors leading to the development of sacramental theology, and particularly to the insistence on the view that the validity of the sacrament does not depend on the virtue or character of the one who administers it.

On the other hand, the schism also had other social and ethnic roots. In North Africa, the ancient population of Punic and Numidian origin resented the presence and authority of the Romans and Greeks, who had arrived at a relatively recent date. Since the latter were part of the official church, the most dispossessed and marginalized groups tended to support Donatism and frequently also the circumcellions.

—

JLG

Donne, John (1572–1631). English poet, considered the most illustrious representative of metaphysical poetry and later the best exponent of English religious oratory in the seventeenth century. Born of a Catholic family, he was educated in the faith of his ancestors. During the 1590s, he studied theology intensively in order to investigate the contradictory claims of Catholicism and Protestantism. Finally he embraced the official Anglicanism of the state, in which he excelled as an orator. His sermons, some of which were preached in situations of great prestige and influence, are the theological key to understand the depths of his poetry. Very little of his poetry was published during his life. He was rediscovered in the twentieth century, when he exerted notable influence on British and North American poetry, especially in the poetic styles of T. S. Eliot and W. B. Yeats, two of the dominant forces in modern English poetry. Among his collections of poems, *Divine Poems* and *Holy Sonnets* deserve special attention because of their religious dimensions.

—

RAR

Dort (or Dordrecht), Synod of (1618–19). Assembly of the Reformed Church of the Netherlands, convoked by the government of that country to put an end to the controversy surrounding the teachings of ⇒Arminius. The five theological principles enunciated by that synod have come to be the distinctive mark of Calvinist orthodoxy. (Concerning orthodox Calvinism, ⇒Westminster and François ⇒Turretin.)

The origin of the controversy went back to the positions of the theologian Dirk Koornhert. Although a Calvinist with respect to all of the issues that until then had been distinctive of the Reformed tradition, as opposed to the Lutheran, Koornhert had doubts regarding the doctrine of predestination. After studying them in order to refute them, Arminius became the chief defender of the opinions of Koornhert over against the strict Calvinist ⇒Gomarus. The latter maintained the supralapsarian opinion, that is, the opinion that the decree of predestination, which elects some and condemns others, precedes the decree of the fall. At first Arminius was inclined toward infralapsarianism, according to which God decreed the fall first and then the election of some and the condemnation of others. But in the end, partly due to his studies of Koornhert, he decided that the doctrine of predestination itself, at least the way the Calvinists of his time taught it, was wrong. According to Arminius, this doctrine should be rejected because it did not place Jesus Christ at the very center of salvation and it made God responsible for the condemnation of the reprobate. The great absolute decree of God is the one which makes Jesus Christ mediator between God and humanity. Following this is the decree according to which God would forgive and save whoever would repent and believe, and the decree which provides the means for that repentance and that faith. The decree that saves some and condemns others is based on the divine foreknowledge, according to which God knows who will repent and believe, and who will not.

In order to explain how it is possible for a sinner to repent, if he or she is bound to sin, Arminius spoke of the "preventive [or prevenient] grace" of God, which is given to all of us as human beings and which allows us to take the step of repentance and faith.

Arminius died in 1609, but his followers continued to uphold his teachings. His successor in the professorship was ⇒Bisschop, who was clearly an Arminian, and who together with ⇒Uyttenbogaert is probably one of the authors of a document, the *Remonstrance*, in which a good number of Arminian pastors and theologians manifested their opposition to the Calvinism of Gomarus—and from then on were called Remonstrants. While it affirms predestination, the *Remonstrance* leaves open the question whether God predestines on the basis of God's foreknowledge of the future actions of human beings, or if the divine decree of election and reprobation precedes this foreknowledge. What is important for the Remonstrants is to affirm that Christ died for all, and that no theology should pretend that he died only for

the elect. Other points of fundamental divergence were the doctrine of irresistible grace and the total depravity of the human race. For the Gomarists these two points are parallel, since human depravity, which makes us incapable of repenting and believing, requires the grace of God for our salvation. And since depravity is total, grace must be irresistible, for otherwise we would resist it.

Political and social considerations were added to all of these theological questions. In the maritime provinces of Holland, the growing middle class supported the Remonstrants, whose position appeared to fit better with free commerce with other nations, including staunchly Catholic Spain. The peasantry of the interior, and the fishermen of the coast, supported the most extreme positions of Gomarus, which were joined with a strong nationalism opposing Spanish domination and influence, and proclaiming the heterodoxy of almost all other nations. Joining them were the exiles who had been compelled to take refuge in the Netherlands because of their Calvinist convictions. All of this became complicated by the struggle of Maurice of Nassau to obtain power. When this was achieved in 1618 with the support of the Gomarists, everything was ready for the convocation of a synod that would put an end to the resistance of the Remonstrants.

That synod, meeting in Dort, included representatives not only from the Dutch provinces, but also from Scotland, England, Switzerland, and the Palatinate, and it promulgated five points which from then on were the mark of orthodox Calvinism. Until then the term "Calvinist" was used mainly in contrast to "Lutheran," and the distinction was established mainly in terms of the Eucharist, the use of the Law, the importance of sanctification, and other such matters. From the time of Dort, "Calvinist" was understood above all as the opposite of "Arminian," and what distinguishes such Calvinism are precisely the five points of Dort: the total depravity of the human race; unconditional and double predestination, some to salvation and others to condemnation; the doctrine according to which the atoning work of Christ is only for the elect; irresistible grace; and the "perseverance of the saints"—that is, that the elect cannot fall from grace and be condemned.

———

JLG

Dositheus of Jerusalem (1641–1707).

Patriarch of that city and strong defender of the positions of the Greek church against the

Western, Catholic as well as Protestant. In his attacks against the West, he made use of great scholarship, although his work is mainly a compilation of sources, not only in Greek and Latin, but also in Arabic and Russian.

———

JLG

Dostoyevsky, Fyodor (1821–81). An interesting phenomenon of the nineteenth century in Russia was the role that certain notable novelists played in strengthening the Orthodox faith. Outstanding among them was Nikolai Gogol, who insisted that the Orthodox Church has universal significance and the capacity to resolve the problems of humanity. Even more prominent than Gogol was D., one of the major literary figures of all times and one of the most complex personalities in the Russian spiritual life of the time.

The work of D. was a vital stimulus for Russian literature. This coincided with the evolution of literary taste that grew out of the literary scope and range of the nobility, whose greatest representative was Leo ⇒Tolstoy. Such a scope included the bourgeois class, made up of intellectual officials, clergy, and other related elements. *Crime and Punishment* (1865–66) was the first of D.'s great novels that made him famous abroad, and even today it endures as the best known. In *The Brothers Karamazov*, he narrates the parable of the Grand Inquisitor to express his understanding of Christ and his mistrust of the Catholic Church.

Imprisoned for his socialist ideas, he was condemned to death. Moments before his execution, the sentence was commuted to four years of forced labor in Siberia. Afterward he took refuge in literature, convinced that it ought to reveal to the world the problems that human beings carry without daring to recognize or resolve them by themselves.

———

RAR

Du Plessis, David Johannes ⇒Plessis, David Johannes du

DuBose, William Porcher (1836–1918). U.S. Episcopal pastor and theologian. He was born in Winnsboro, South Carolina, and fought in the Civil War with the Confederate army. He was a chaplain and a professor of ethics, moral philosophy, and Aristotle at the University of the South in Sewanee, Tennessee. He cultivated dialogue with modernist Anglicans.

———

EPA

Duns Scotus, John ⇒Scotus, John Duns

Durandus of Troarn (ca. 1012–89). Benedictine monk employed by William the Conqueror in his efforts to organize monastic life in his dominions. He wrote a treatise *On the Body and the Blood of Christ*, in which he refutes the opinions of ⇒Berengar.

———

JLG

Dussell, Enrique (1934–). One of the chief promoters of the Latin American theology and ethics of liberation. His writings, as well as his ability to organize conferences and meetings, have accelerated the diffusion of this theology. He has worked above all in the history of the Latin American church, as chief promoter of CEHILA (Commission for the Study of the History of the Latin American Church). His work *History of the Latin American Church: From Colonialism to Liberation (1492–1979)* was the first attempt to write the history of the Latin American church in one volume. His *Latin American Ethical Philosophy* (5 vols.) is an attempt to establish the philosophical foundations for the ethics of liberation. In both works he expounds his conviction that philosophy and history are among the weapons that the poor need in their liberating struggle.

—

IG

Dwight, Timothy (1752–1817). North American Congregationalist minister, theologian, poet, hymn writer, and educator. A prominent figure in the Second Great Awakening and influential in the development of Protestantism in the United States. D. was born in Northampton, Massachusetts, and was a grandson of Jonathan ⇒Edwards. He began his studies at Yale University when he was thirteen and graduated in 1769. He was named tutor at Yale, where he was the founder of the Connecticut Wits, a group of North American literary critics. He served as a military chaplain during the American Revolution. After the war he studied with his uncle Jonathan ⇒Edwards Jr., who was a member of the group called the New Divinity. Beginning in 1783 he was a pastor in Greenfield, Connecticut. During his pastorate of twelve years, he established a private school and became well known through his sermons. In 1785 he published his long epic poem *The Conquest of Canaan*, an allegory about the United States based on the book of Joshua.

D. became president of Yale in 1795 (after Ezra Stiles) and served in that post until his death in 1817. He endeavored to revise the curriculum of the university, emphasizing the study of classics and literature. It seemed to him that many of the students had been negatively influenced by the French Enlightenment and that their conduct was impious. Therefore he regularly preached his vision of Christianity. This preaching coincided with a spirit of revival outside of Yale. The result was a series of revivals among the students of Yale, beginning in 1802.

Revivalism was also making headway in other universities (e.g., Dartmouth, Williams, and Amherst) as part of the Second Great Awakening. The movement touched several of D.'s students who later became prominent leaders of the church. Among them were Moses ⇒Stuart, Lyman ⇒Beecher, and Nathaniel W. ⇒Taylor. Many of the graduates of Yale in that generation played a role in the church and in society in general. The talks of D. *On Christianity* were published in 1818 and were a resource for a whole generation of theological students.

In his theology, D. used the Bible and what the Scots called "common reason." He dialogued with the faction that supported the "new theology" of New England, upheld by Samuel ⇒Hopkins and Joseph ⇒Bellamy, disciples of Jonathan Edwards. There is a difference of opinion among historians as to whether D. himself should be considered part of that school. In any case, there is no doubt that D. was the source of the theology of New Haven that his student Taylor later developed.

D. was not a strict disciple of Edwards, but rather advocated a modified Calvinism. He affirmed the depravity of humanity and its need for salvation, but at the same time he granted a role to human participation in salvation through preaching, the reading of the Bible, prayer, the sacraments, education, and active piety in daily Christian life. He believed that true faith was reasonable and consistent with religion lived in experience.

———

EDA

Ebedjesus bar Berikha (?–1318).

Metropolitan bishop of Nisibis, poet, and one of the last Nestorian theologians who wrote in Syriac. His chief theological work is the *Book of the Pearl, or the Truth of the Christian Faith.* Of this work in five books, the most important is the third, which deals with the incarnation and which therefore expounds the official Nestorian doctrine at that time. When he refers to the humanity of Jesus, E. uses several of the typical images of Nestorianism. Thus God inhabited Jesus as "in a temple" or "in a home." The most interesting image, and the one that gives the whole book its title, is the one that explains the presence of the divinity in the man Jesus as that of the sun in a pearl which reflects it, so that the "illuminated nature becomes like the nature which illuminates it."

———

JLG

Ebeling, Gerhard (1912–2001).

Lutheran theologian who was born in Berlin. He was a professor of church history (1946–64) and then of systematic theology (1954–65) at the University of Tübingen. From 1968 to 1979 he was professor of theology at the University of Zurich. Considered to have been one of the most distinguished ⇒Luther scholars, he presided over the commission for the publication of the works of Martin Luther. He was influenced by his teachers R. ⇒Bultmann and E. ⇒Brunner. His theology emphasized the experience of faith and the place of prayer at the root of theological work. Among his publications are *The Study of Theology* (1977) and *The Nature of Faith* (1963). His complete works in German began to be published in 1995 and total twelve volumes.

———

JDR

Eck, Johann Maier (1486–1543).

Also known as Johann Eck of Ingolstadt. One of the most important Catholic polemicists during the rise of the Protestant movement in Europe in the sixteenth century, and the chief adversary of ⇒Luther. He was born in the Swabian town Egg an der Günz, from which he later took his name (Eck). Michael Maier, his father, was a magistrate in that town. He received his academic preparation at the universities of Heidelberg (1498), Tübingen (1499), Cologne (1501), and Freiburg (1502). In 1508 he was ordained at the age of twenty-two, with a special dispensation. He became a doctor of theology in 1510, distinguishing himself by his oratorical skills. At the invitation of the Duke of Bavaria, he taught theology in the University of Ingolstadt for thirty-two years. His prestige made that university the center of the reaction against the Protestant movement.

His first writing against Luther was his refutation of the Ninety-Five Theses, which he called *Obelisks* (1518). This writing was like a declaration of war. In May of 1518 ⇒Carlstadt published some theses against this work of E. The latter challenged him to a debate, which took place in Leipzig from June 27 to July 16, 1518, under the auspices of Duke George of Saxony. In order to involve Luther in the debate, E. wrote twelve theses that subtly attacked the doctrinal position of the reformer, especially his practical rejection of the primacy of Rome. As a consequence of the debate, Luther was accused of heresy and E. was considered the champion of the Roman Catholic cause. After the debate, E. wrote a treatise on the primacy of the pope, which he took to Rome. The pope named him nuncio to publish in Germany the bull of excommunication against Luther, *Exsurge Domine*, which was partially written by E.

Without leaving his professorship, E. made numerous trips for the cause he defended. He visited Rome (1521–23), traversed Germany promulgating the condemnation of Luther, went to debate with the Swiss reformers in the city of Baden, traveled to Holland and England, and, as a Roman Catholic theologian, took part in the diets of ⇒Augsburg (1530) and of Ratisbon (1541). In Augsburg he became convinced of the futility of public debates on theological theses. He died with the reputation of a man full of zeal and wisdom. The Protestants responded to his criticism of the reforming movement in a document titled *Propositiones in Eccium de vino, venere et balneo* (Propositions against Eck on Wine, Love and the Bath).

Many of his works were edited in four volumes in Ingolstadt (1530–35). His chief theological writing was *Chrysopassus*. In it he treats the topics of predestination, grace, and free will. This work served as preparation for his controversy with Luther. One of his most prominent works, which between 1525 and 1576 went through forty-six editions, was *Enchiridion locorum communium adversus Lutherum et alios hostes ecclesiae* (Manual of Common Themes against Luther and Other Enemies of the Church). Many of his scholastic writings remained unpublished. At the insistence of the Duke of Saxony, E. made a translation of the Bible that was hardly successful.

———
JDR

Eckhardt, Johann (1664–1730).

He studied in Leipzig and was an assistant to ⇒Leibniz in 1694. This gained for him a post as professor at Helmstedt in 1706. He then became the librarian of the royal family of Hanover.

For unknown reasons he fled from Hanover and became a Catholic in Cologne in 1724. Under the influence of French historians, he developed a rigorous scientific and critical method in such works as his *Corpus historicum Medii Aevi* (1723; Historical Corpus of the Middle Ages) and *Commentarii de rebus Franciae Orientalis et Episcopatus Wirceburgensis* (1729; Commentaries on the Affairs of East France and the Episcopate of Würzburg).

———
JDRR

Eckhart, Johannes (ca. 1260–ca. 1327).

Also known as Meister Eckhardt, Eckart, Eckardt, Eccard, Eckehart. Dominican exponent of German mysticism and a contributor to the formation of the German language. He probably studied with ⇒Albertus Magnus. He was a professor in Paris, Strasbourg, and Cologne. He served as Dominican provincial of Saxony and vicar general of Bohemia. He influenced the thought of ⇒Suso, ⇒Tauler, and ⇒Cusa.

Of all his theological work, only fragments from his *Opus tripartitum* (Tripartite Work) remain. The first part deals with one thousand propositions, the second debates several themes that are questioned, and the third is a selection of sermons and interpretations of the Bible. His methodology and style are scholastic. His scholastic and mystical theology shows that E. did not believe in the opposition in principle between mysticism and scholasticism. E. expressed in his theology the need that every soul has for reaching complete union with God. He taught that although that union could be sought in the traditional faith of the church, human beings had to go further and look for it in their own understanding. By looking for that understanding outside the tradition of the church, he distanced himself from ⇒Bernard of Clairvaux and ⇒Hugh of St. Victor. His Trinitarian theology sees the manifestation of God in all its fullness in all the creatures. Therefore his theology in a certain way comes close to and in another way distinguishes itself from pantheism.

In 1326 he was accused of heresy in Cologne. He appealed to the pope, but died before being exonerated. In 1329 John XXII condemned twenty-eight of his propositions, but nonetheless considered E. a son of the church, declaring that he had retracted his supposedly heretical teachings.

———
ALG

Ecolampadius ⇒Oecolampadius, John

Eddy, Mary Baker (1821–1910). Founder of Christian Science and of the Metaphysical School of Massachusetts, where she taught until the school was closed in 1889. Throughout her life she suffered from an infirmity of the spinal column. In the midst of one of the worst episodes of her illness, in 1866, she declared that she had found a cure for her condition in the story of the paralytic in Matthew 9:1–8.

Her ideas evolved. She first published them in *Science and Health* (1875), and after revising them she published them again under the title *Science and Health with Key to the Sacred Scriptures.*

Her disciples considered this work to have been divinely inspired. Together with the Bible it provides the theological foundation for the Christian Science movement. According to this movement, God is the Mind of the universe, the All-in-All, the Divine Principle of all that really is, since everything else is appearance. Jesus is the Teacher, and in his sacrifice he reveals to us the love of God. By his crucifixion and resurrection, Christ inspires in us such a faith that we can understand eternal life, the fullness of the soul and the Spirit, and the nothingness of the material. This "fullness of the Spirit" and the "nothingness of the material" is the fundamental teaching of E. For her all reality is found in God, and creation is not a material reality, but an eternal harmony. All that God creates is good. Therefore the only reality that sin, illness, or death possess is that of unreal things which appear to be real only to humans who fail in their faith. God shows us their falsity. These evils are not real because they do not belong to the reality of God.

———

ALG

Edwards, Jonathan (1703–58). One of the most important North American theologians, pastors, philosophers, and educators during the English colonial period, and without a doubt one of the most significant figures in the Great Awakening of the eighteenth century. His writings are still influential in theology, philosophy, and literature. He tried to identify the characteristics of true Christian discipleship. He also developed an intellectual understanding of the revivals.

Born in Connecticut, E. was the son and grandson of Congregationalist ministers and was raised in the New England Calvinist tradition. He began his studies at Yale University at the age of thirteen and remained there for two additional years of theological studies. In 1722 he became pastor of a Presbyterian church in New England, then was tutor at Yale for two years, and in 1726 joined his grandfather Solomon ⇒Stoddard in the pastorate in Northampton, Massachusetts. In 1727 E. married Sarah Perrepont, with whom he would have eleven children. After the death of his grandfather in 1729, E. became the sole pastor in Northampton, remaining there until 1750.

E. believed in the need for a personal and genuine experience of conversion. The impression that the life of the youth and of the community in general did not reflect such an experience worried him. Therefore, beginning in 1734 he preached a series of sermons on justification by faith which began a regional revival that E. describes in his treatise *A Faithful Narrative of the Surprising Work of God* (1737). This essay was widely read in the English colonies and in Great Britain. E. tells about what happened in Northampton, and thus inspired other people to work in favor of revivals in their own surroundings and helped to prepare the way for the ministry of the Anglican evangelist George ⇒Whitefield in North America.

In his sermons and writings, E. emphasized his belief that true religion depends totally on the grace and sovereignty of God. Salvation implies a radical conversion and the experience of divine forgiveness. E. thereby reaffirmed the Reformation teaching on justification by faith. True religious experience includes personal knowledge of the grace of God and results in a change in personal life.

E. is probably remembered above all for his revivalist sermon "Sinners in the Hands of an Angry God." His other writings include *The Distinguishing Marks of a Work of the Spirit of God* (1741) and *Some Thoughts concerning the Present Revival of Religion in New England* (1742), in which he defended the authenticity and validity of the revivals. In *A Treatise concerning Religious Affections* (1746), he argued for the practice of a true faith.

E.'s emphasis on the visible expressions of authentic Christianity gave rise to a dispute, and the congregation of Northampton dismissed him. He then went to a church in Stockbridge, Massachusetts, which was considered an isolated place and a marginal area of the colony. He continued there with his work, serving both the Indians of the Housatonic tribe and his own congregation. Among his many other important works are *A Careful and Strict Enquiry into the Modern Prevailing Notions of . . . Freedom of the Will* (1754) and *The Great Christian Doctrine of Original Sin Defended* (1758).

In January of 1758, E. became the third president of the College of New Jersey (Princeton). He died of smallpox two months later and was buried in Princeton.

—

EDA

Edwards, Jonathan, Jr. (1745–1801).
Congregationalist minister, theologian, and president of Union College. He was the ninth son of Jonathan ⇒Edwards. He graduated from the College of New Jersey (Princeton) in 1765 and then studied theology for an additional year. In 1766 he returned to Princeton as a tutor. In 1769 he was ordained and became pastor of a congregation in New Haven, Connecticut. He was named president of Union College in Schenectady, New York, in 1799, and occupied that post until his death. He was also a private teacher of his nephew Timothy ⇒Dwight. Theologically E. was part of the New Divinity group of New England and constructed a juridical interpretation of the atonement based on the work of his father. He was a strong adversary of slavery and also played an important part in the Plan of Union of 1801, which was a cooperative effort between the Congregationalists and the Presbyterians on the western frontier, the area where the United States was then expanding.

—

EDA

Eliade, Mircea (1907–86).
Hungarian historian of religions who spent the greater part of his academic career at the University of Chicago. He is known for his contribution to the study of comparative religions. He wrote numerous articles and essays, and among his books in the field of the history of religions are *Patterns in Comparative Religion* (1958), *Cosmos and History* (1959), and *The Sacred and the Profane* (1959). He also contributed in a significant way to methodological studies in religion. Works such as *Myths, Dreams, and Mysteries* (1960), *Images and Symbols* (1961), and *The Quest* (1969) represent new frontiers in the discipline, rediscovering the significance of myths in the history of peoples and questioning the historicism that characterized the philosophy of history in the twentieth century.

E. also edited the book *From Primitives to Zen* (1967), an anthology of myths from various religious traditions, compiled for students in the field of religion. He was cofounder of the academic journal *History of Religions* and editor of the *Encyclopedia of Religion* (1986). His methodological creativity and his contribution to the discipline of comparative religions significantly influenced the way in which Christian theology evaluates the religious phenomenon and its role in human life.

—

CCO

Elijah bar Seneja (10th–11th century).
Metropolitan bishop of Nisibis from 975 until approximately 1050. He wrote in Arabic and Syriac and published an Arabic-Syriac dictionary. His works are numerous, but those that stand out are his polemical writings against Jews, Muslims, and Chalcedonian Christians (that is, the "orthodox"; Council of ⇒Chalcedon).

Among these controversial works, the best known is a summary of conversations that he had with the vizier, approximately in the year 1025, about the truth of the Christian faith. In this book he explains and defends the doctrine of the Trinity, the incarnation, and other doctrines. Some of the arguments he uses are based on the Koran. Others are based on reason, miracles, and the life of Christians.

—

JLG

Elipandus of Toledo (ca. 715–ca. 800).
Together with ⇒Felix of Urgel, he was the chief exponent of Spanish adoptionism. The doctrine of the Trinity was very much debated in Spain during the time when the greater part of the peninsula was in Muslim hands. A certain ⇒Migetius, of whom little is known, appears to have come too close to Sabellian Modalism (⇒Sabellius), and in reaction E. declared that the Son is not only different from the Father, which was perfectly orthodox, but also that in Jesus Christ a distinction must be made between the eternal Son of God and the human son. Although it does not appear that E. had expressed himself in such terms, the opinion was attributed to him that, while the second person of the Trinity is the Son of God by nature, the humanity that he assumes, that is, the man Jesus, is the son only by adoption. For this reason his teaching was given the name of adoptionism, although it is most likely that E.'s position was nothing but a new expression of

the ancient concern of the Antiochenes (Council of ⇒Ephesus, Council of ⇒Chalcedon, ⇒Diodore of Tarsus, ⇒Theodore of Mopsuestia) that the humanity of Jesus is not to be eclipsed by his divinity. In addition, the term "adoption" was used in the Mozarabic liturgy, which at that time was in use in Spain. Therefore E. believed he had support in the liturgy, and through it support in the ancients who had composed it. His chief opponent was ⇒Beatus of Liebana. Condemned repeatedly, E. remained firm in his theological convictions—partly because he lived in Moorish territories, and therefore the anathemas and condemnations of the pope and others did not reach him directly.

—

JLG

Elizondo, Virgilio P. (1935–).

Priest, educator, and theologian known as the great pioneer of Hispanic theology in the United States. He was rector of the Catholic Cathedral of San Fernando in San Antonio, Texas, from 1983 to 1995. After studying in the East Asian Pastoral Institute of Manila, he obtained the doctorate in theology from the Institute Catholique de Paris. He was the founder and first president (1972–87) of the Mexican American Cultural Center (MACC) in San Antonio. His numerous articles and several books have influenced Hispanic theological production, which continues to develop some of his key themes. Among these is the relationship between Christianity and culture, *mestizaje,* and the Virgin of Guadalupe.

One of his best-known works is *Galilean Journey: The Mexican-American Promise* (1983). There E. establishes a relationship between two identities that would not seem to have much in common: what was understood by "Galilean" in Jesus' time, and what today is understood by "mestizo." The book deals with the similarities between these identities. To E., the term "mestizo" designates a state of marginalization. Both the Galileans and the mestizos are marginalized peoples. E. emphasizes the importance of such peoples in the history of salvation.

In the theological method of E., human experience is fundamental, since all theological work reflects a particular context. A hermeneutic of the gospel ought to consider both the sociopolitical climate of Jesus' time and the present social context. Thus the importance of the binomial Galilean-mestizo.

Another of his works is *The Future Is Mestizo: Life Where Cultures Meet* (1988), an autobiographical book. In *Guadalupe: Mother of the New Creation* (1997), E. brings out the evangelical element of the Guadalupan devotion, basing it on the *Nican Mopohua* (the oldest extant document narrating the apparitions of the Virgin of Guadalupe).

—

EF

Ellacuría, Ignacio (1930–89).

Spanish Jesuit and liberation theologian who lived in El Salvador from 1949. Rector of the Central-American University of San Salvador. He was murdered in 1989 with other Jesuits and their servants by members of the Salvadoran army. Among his chief works are *Political Theology* (1973), *Freedom Made Flesh: The Mission of Christ and His Church* (1976), *Conversion of the Church to the Kingdom of God* (1984), and *Philosophy of the Historical Reality* (1984).

—

LRR

Ellul, Jacques (1912–94).

This French lawyer, activist, and Protestant theologian discovered the writings of ⇒Marx early in his academic career. This led him to use Marxist categories for social analysis. During his youth, E. became involved in French politics, mainly with anarchist and socialist groups. He taught law at the University of Strasbourg from 1937 until 1940, when the Vichy government removed him from his post. He was also active in the French Resistance. From 1944 until his retirement, E. taught law, history, and sociology in the University of Bordeaux. His many writings fall mainly into two categories: Marxist sociological writings and Reformed theological works. One of his chief theological ideas was that the relationship between God and the world is contentious, for the world is in a constant struggle against the will of God.

—

PAJ

Ellyson, Edgar P. (1869–1954).

Minister, theologian, and one of the founders of the Church of the Nazarene. Initially he served as a Quaker minister and director of the Biblical School of the Friends (Quakers) in Marshalltown, Iowa. During his presidency of a college in Texas, he became a great sympathizer of the Holiness movement and attended its historic conference in Pilot Point, Texas, where the Church of the Nazarene (1908) was born. He was elected as one of the chief superintendents of the new denomination, and for several years he devoted himself to its development. Later he served as president of Pasadena College and of Olivet Nazareth College. During this period he left his mark on the educational development of the new denomination. He also stood out as a theologian when he published his *Theological Compend* (1908), the first systematic theology produced by the Holiness movement in the United States.

———
ALG

Elxai, Elquesai, or Elcesai (3rd century?).

Obscure character who claimed to have a book that had been revealed in the time of Trajan (second century) by two angels, each with a height of more than seventy-five miles, and who were called "Son of God" and "Holy Spirit" (the first masculine and the second feminine). At the beginning his followers were particularly numerous among the Judeo-Christians of Asia Minor. They insisted on circumcision, and if they committed serious sins, they were rebaptized. From the fourth century on, their number declined, but they existed for centuries in Arabia, where apparently the prophet Mohammed met some of them.

———
ALG

Emerson, Ralph Waldo (1803–82).

U.S. philosopher, writer, and poet, a native of Boston. Ordained in the Unitarian Church, he left the ministry after three years, turning to writing, lecturing, and traveling. His transcendental philosophy rejected the miracles of Christ in favor of the divine immanence that is present in all of nature and in every person. His emphasis on the divine spirit as moral guide, his antilegalism, his theory about the human ability to obtain salvation through moral intuition, and a mysticism combined with a good dose of rationalism were the main characteristics of his philosophy.

———
LGP

Emmons, Nathaniel (1745–1840).

New England Congregationalist whose thoughts are frequently confused with those of Samuel ⇒Hopkins. The distinctive elements of his theology are as follows:

1. Holiness and sin are based on free and voluntary action.
2. The human will is free, and subsists as part of the action of God.

3. Even the smallest transgression deserves eternal punishment.
4. The difference between what is just and what is unjust is found in the very nature of things.
5. Sinners are forgiven and justified through the atonement of Christ by the work of the grace of God.
6. Although the depravity of the human race is total, God still requires holiness from sinners.
7. Preachers should exhort sinners to love God, repent of their sin, and immediately believe in Christ.
8. Human beings are active agents, not passive, in their regeneration.

———
MAD

Encinas, Francisco de (1520–52).

Spanish scholar with a broad academic formation in the prestigious universities of Alcalá de Henares, Paris, Louvain, and Wittenberg. Having been influenced by the growing Protestant literature, he joined the Reformation. In Wittenberg he lodged in the home of the Lutheran leader and thinker Philipp ⇒Melanchthon, who encouraged him to translate the New Testament into Spanish. When he moved to Louvain in order to be able to print his work, he encountered opposition from theologians of the university who considered biblical translations into vernacular languages to be the seed of heretical ideas. He left for Antwerp, where a printer agreed to edit and print what would become the first Spanish edition of the NT. This edition was requisitioned by the ecclesiastical authorities, and E. was imprisoned in Brussels, accused of Lutheranism. After a little more than a year of imprisonment, he escaped and returned to Melanchthon's home. Later he left for England, where he would teach Greek at Cambridge University.

———
JRI

Encratites (2nd century).

Movement of extreme ascetic tendencies, which prohibited sex and in some cases limited drink to water and food to vegetables. Several of the ancient Christian writers refer to this movement, especially ⇒Tatian, ⇒Clement of Alexandria, ⇒Irenaeus, and ⇒Epiphanius. Apparently the first E. based their asceticism on a dualism according to which God the Father of Jesus Christ is not the author of the material world. Soon the title of Encratite was given to anyone who practiced extreme asceticism.

———

JLG

Encyclion. Imperial edict promulgated by Emperor Basiliscus in the year 475 or 476. In it he rejected the decisions of ⇒Chalcedon and convoked a new council. What was at stake was the opposition of many believers, above all in Egypt and Syria, to the Chalcedonian formula, and the interest of the emperor (who had usurped the throne) in gaining their support. The fall of Basiliscus shortly afterward put an end to such projects.

———

JLG

Enzinas ⇒Encinas, Francisco de

Eon of L'Etoile ⇒Eudes of Stella

Ephesus, Council of (431). Generally recognized as the Third Ecumenical Council. Aside from the first skirmishes having to do with Apollinaris and his teachings, this council marks the beginning of the long battle between the Antiochene Christology and its Alexandrian counterpart, that is, between a Christology concerned with safeguarding the humanity of Jesus Christ, even at the expense of his union with the divinity, and another which emphasized the reality of the union of both natures, even at the cost of the full humanity of the Savior.

⇒Nestorius, whom the Council of Ephesus condemned, was a faithful exponent of Antiochene Christology. Therefore he declared that in Jesus Christ there are "two natures and two persons" and he distinguished between the divinity and the humanity, rejecting the *communicatio idiomatum* (that is, the principle according to which, in virtue of the union of the two natures, the attributes of one can be predicated of the other, and vice versa). Thus Nestorius declared, for example, that he who was born of the Virgin Mary was Christ, but not God. Debate broke out around that issue when Nestorius, defending sermons on the nativity of the Lord preached by one of his chaplains, declared that Mary had not given birth to God, but only to Christ. Therefore what became the touchstone of this controversy was the question whether Mary is *Theotokos* (bearer of God) or *Christotokos* (bearer of Christ). On this point, it is important to make clear that the topic of debate was not so much a mariological question as a christological one, and therefore Protestants who believe they see in Nestorius a forerunner of their objections to Marian devotion are mistaken.

The council followed questionable procedures when ⇒Cyril of Alexandria made himself master of the process and began the sessions before the arrival of John of Antioch and his companions who were coming to defend Nestorius. When the latter arrived in Ephesus and learned what Cyril and his followers were doing, they formed their own rival council. The two assemblies proclaimed reciprocal condemnations, each one declaring that the other was not valid. Shortly afterward the delegates from Rome arrived, and with their support and that of Emperor Theodosius II the decisions of the council of Cyril prevailed in the end, although not without a series of vicissitudes which for some time included the imprisonment of both Cyril and John.

Even after that victory, Cyril continued attacking the Antiochenes, issuing against them *Twelve Anathemas*, and thus continuing a dispute that finally led to the Council of ⇒Chalcedon.

———

JLG

Ephraem Syrus (?–373). Native of Nisibis, on the border between Syria and Persia, and son of pagan parents. When E. was converted, his father, a priest of one of the gods of the place, threw him out of the house, and E. took refuge with Bishop Jacobus of Nisibis. Then he followed an ascetic life, the details of which are not known, although it is said that eventually he directed the theological and catechetical school that Jacobus had founded in the city. When the Persians invaded the region, he moved to Edessa, where he continued his ascetic life and his teaching. Among his numerous works his hymns stand out, many of which have the intention of communicating theological truths. Thus, for example, he wrote a series of fifty-six hymns against ⇒Bardesanes, ⇒Marcion, and ⇒Mani. He wrote abundantly and vividly about the terrors of hell and purgatory, as well as about paradise, which the redeemed will not enter until after the final resurrection, since nothing imperfect is admitted there, and the soul without the body is not perfect. Since E. lived before the great christological controversies of the fifth century, both the Monophysites and those who accept the decisions of ⇒Chalcedon claim him.

———

JLG

Epictetus (50?–138?). A native of Asia Minor, this Greek philosopher became affiliated with the Stoic movement, which developed shortly before the establishment of Christianity and had great influence on the new faith. In his youth he was enslaved. When he recovered his liberty, he taught in Rome until the emperor Domitian expelled him in the year 89. He went to Greece and continued teaching.

E. recommended discipline in the face of adversity. Behind all events, good as well as bad, there is a divine providence that governs everything. What at first appears to us to be a calamity is in reality part of a divine plan that orders everything for the good. The wise Stoic can confront every calamity in a spirit of serenity and perfect calm.

In addition, he taught that all human beings, in spite of differences in race, nationality, birth, and social position, are equal, since all participate in the divine reason. This equality is the fundamental moral reality.

Much of this was assimilated into Christian ethics and spirituality.

—

IG

Epiphanius (ca. 315–403). Ascetic and wise man, a native of Judea, whom ⇒Jerome honors with the title of Pentaglot. He is known above all as a heresiologist. In that role, he attacked Origenism in particular (⇒Origen), which seemed to him the most frightful of the heresies of his time. Convinced that ⇒John Chrysostom was an Origenist, he went to Constantinople and participated in the efforts to depose him. When he finally discovered that he had been deceived by the enemies of Chrysostom, he left for Cyprus, where he was bishop at that time, but died before arriving. His chief work was *Panarion* or *Pharmacopea against All the Heresies*. He counts among such heresies not only those that appeared in the church, but also the previous errors of the pagan philosophers and of various Jewish groups. Although in his works there is much doubtful data, they are nonetheless one of the best sources that we have for the study of the ancient teachings and positions condemned by the rest of the church.

——

JLG

Erasmus of Rotterdam, Desiderius (1466?–1536). Outstanding transitional figure between the Middle Ages and the modern era, classical scholar *par excellence*, rec-

ognized and acclaimed by his contemporaries. He was a writer on popular subjects, a humanist, critic, and satirist of the abuses and the ignorance of his time. For some time he wore the habit of a monk. He was editor of the Greek New Testament and of several of the works of Christian antiquity.

In his edition of the New Testament, he endeavored to improve on the Vulgate through faithfulness to the Greek text, greater clarity of expression, the removal of solecisms (violations of grammatical rules or the approved idiomatic use of the language), and the improvement of style. His method of biblical interpretation combines a philological focus on the Scriptures (focusing on textual, literary, and historical criticism) with a spiritual one (allegorical and tropological).

With some Protestant inclinations in spirit, but not identified with the Protestant cause, E. is indissolubly linked with the first days of the Reformation. He welcomed the initial protests of ⇒Luther against the abuses in the church but did not approve of the corrections of the Reformers which he considered abusive and intemperate. E. kept an extensive correspondence with Luther. ⇒Zwingli visited him and had avidly read his works. Another Swiss Protestant reformer, ⇒Oecolampadius, had been his associate. Between E. and ⇒Melanchthon there was mutual admiration.

An illegitimate son of a priest and of the daughter of a physician, he was born Geert Geertsz (Gerhard son of Gerhard). Later he adopted the Greco-Latin name Desiderius E. (from *Desidarius,* desired, and *Erasmus,* lovable or loved). He was raised in the midst of the commercial activity of Holland, and in many respects his opinions reflected the common values of the bourgeois class. In 1506 he obtained the doctorate in theology in Turin. On more than one occasion he rejected the opportunity to become a cardinal under the pretext of his health and his studies.

In 1521, after an itinerant life, he established himself in Basel, from where he carried on an extensive correspondence with the kings and pontiffs of Europe. His fame was growing, and in the end he became the center of an international circle of humanists who hoped to reform the church, not by violent means, but by giving back to the church its simple and primitive faith. Luther and other Reformers cried out for a transformation in the doctrinal positions of the church, which to them had distanced itself from the teachings of the Scriptures. For E., on the other hand, doctrines were not the chief interest of the Christian life. He admitted that some doctrines, such as the incarnation, were fundamental, but he insisted that the upright life was much more important than orthodox doctrine. What the church urgently needed was a reformation of customs, the practice of decency, and moderation. The members of religious orders who devoted themselves to subtle doctrinal distinctions, simultaneously living scandalous lives, were a frequent object of E.'s scathing attacks.

He began to break with Luther openly on the teachings of the latter on predestination and total depravity, with which he was not in agreement. Instead, he favored the freedom of the will and the moral responsibility of humans. Concerned for what he considered violence on the part of the reformer, he composed the *Diatribe on Free Will*, to which Luther replied with *The Bondage of the Will*.

In his controversy with E., Luther alleged that the great humanist knew very little about the grace of God. Human beings have nothing to do to attain their salvation; instead, this is an exclusive matter of the grace of God. E. defended the synergistic point of view, that is, that human beings have the ability to grasp and hold the gift of salvation that is proclaimed. The human will, impelled by God, by its very nature cooperates in the moment in which the Spirit effects conversion and salvation.

The alienation of these two great men, to a great extent owing to their temperaments, was, in the estimation of many interpreters of the history of the Reformation, a tragedy of great consequences. Both were reformers and scholars of stature. But their dedication to the faith followed different paths. Luther defended a decisive, immediate, and total reformation of the church both in doctrine and in practice. E., who was devoted to the slower path of teaching and illumination, affirmed his neutrality because of his love of peaceful learning and because he was more disposed toward unity and peace.

In his youth E. had studied scholasticism, but he soon felt a great repugnance toward it. In his famous satire *In Praise of Folly*, written in 1508, he attempted to bury medieval scholastic science in ridicule. Using as a resource the figure of madness (folly), which had already been used by the satirist Sebastian Brant (1458–1521) in *The Ship of Fools*, E. fashioned a vast parody of the contemporary world. Madness in person presents itself before a great assembly of all nations, classes, and ages, and announces its wish to praise itself,

since no one pays any attention to it. Although the scope of the work is limited to the polemic of humanism against the Roman church, the splendor of the language, the spirit of the discourse, the wit of the satire, and its cultural background gave *In Praise of Folly* an immense success that has extended to modern times.

——

RAR

Erastus, Thomas (1524–83).

His name at birth was Lieber, Liebier, or Lüber. He was a Swiss-German theologian and professor of medicine at the University of Heidelberg. As a disciple of ⇒Zwingli, he opposed strict Calvinism and Lutheranism. He attended the theological conferences of Heidelberg (1560) and Maulbronn (1564) among Reformed and Lutheran theologians. In Germany he helped with the introduction of the ⇒Heidelberg Catechism (1562) as a confessional base of the Reformed faith in order to distinguish it from the Lutheran. When the radical Calvinists wanted to introduce the rule of "Holy Discipline" in the Palatinate, E. wrote his *Explicatio gravissimae quaestionis* (1568; Explanation of a Very Serious Matter), published for the first time in London in 1589. There he held that in a civil state in which the same religion is professed, the authorities have the obligation and the right to exercise all jurisdiction in civil as well as in ecclesiastical matters. The government can judge all moral conduct, arbitrate disputes, and work with the pastors to reprimand those who live immoral lives. Actions that appear to be merely ecclesiastical, such as excommunication, have to be approved by the civil government. In spite of all this, the church was not a servant of the state, and the state could not pass judgment in matters such as who can receive the sacraments and who cannot. His book was translated into English in 1659, giving birth in England to the movement called Erastianism, which was more radical than E. himself in terms of the power that was granted to civil authorities. Erastianism influenced R. ⇒Hooker, who defended the supremacy of the civil powers in his *Ecclesiastical Polity* (1594), and it is also reflected in the vision that Hobbes had of the secularization of the modern state.

——

ALG

Erdman, William Jacob (1834–1903).

Presbyterian pastor and biblical scholar born on April 28, 1834, in Allentown, Pennsylvania. He received his bachelor's degree from Hamilton

College (1856) and his theological education at Union Theological Seminary in New York (1859). He was ordained as pastor in the Presbyterian Church in 1860. He was secretary of the Niagara Bible Conference throughout its duration (1883–97).

As a pastor he was very much respected for his jovial personality, devotion to the work of the church, humility, humor, and great scholarship. He is best known for his educational work as leader of the Niagara Conference, through which he awakened a love for the Word of God and the consecration to Christian service of a great number of ecumenical leaders. His interest in the Bible was focused on New Testament studies related to the work of the Holy Spirit and the second coming of Christ. Among his works are *The Holy Spirit and Christian Experience*; *Notes on the Revelation*; and *The Parousia of Christ a Period of Time, or, When Will the Church Be Translated?*

———
JDRR

Erickson, Millard J. (1932–). Baptist pastor, prolific writer, and prominent theologian of the evangelical movement at the end of the twentieth century and the beginning of the twenty-first. He studied with the neo-orthodox theologian William Hordern and has also been influenced by the neo-evangelical theologians Carl F. H. ⇒Henry and Edward J. ⇒Carnell. He has been a professor at Wheaton College and at Bethel Seminary, and distinguished professor in Truett Seminary at Baylor University and at Western Seminary, Portland. Among his many writings are *Relativism in Contemporary Christian Ethics* (1974), in which he confronts the challenge of relativism, and *Christian Theology*, in three volumes (1983–85), where his theological position is more extensively developed. This position is characterized by a moderate Calvinist perspective. In his most recent works he dialogues with postmodernism in an apologetic manner. Among them are *Postmodernizing the Faith: Evangelical Responses to the Challenge of Postmodernism* (1998) and *Truth or Consequences: The Promise and Perils of Postmodernism* (2001). E. proposes a moderate postmodernism in which the hermeneutic of deconstruction is essential to disarm modern ideologies of power. At the same time he rejects the relativism of radical postmodernism as something absurd and harmful to the theological task.

———
ALG

Erigena, John Scotus (ca. 810–77). Philosopher and writer noted for his interpretation of Greek thought in the West. The place and date of his birth have not been clearly established. Several traditions exist that explain his origin. One of these traditions claims that E. was born and grew up in England and that he was a Saxon. Another says that he was born in Scotland and that he studied with the monastic order of Columba. The most accepted tradition among historians states that E. was born in Ireland and studied in Irish monasteries, which were then the only centers of higher religious instruction in Europe. This tradition seems to explain the quality of the education received by E. The origin of his name can be seen in an argument that gives support to this last tradition. The meaning of the name "Scotus" during the ninth century was literally "Irish." In addition, the Greek version of "Scotus" is "Erigena," with the same meaning.

E.'s presence in the royal court of France is well known. He appeared before King Pepin, son of Louis the Pious and grandson of Charlemagne. Although the reason for his presence is uncertain, historical data show that E. was received in the Frankish kingdom with enthusiasm, and that he was named director of the school of the royal palace. Years later, at the request of the king, E. translated the treatise *The Heavenly Hierarchy* into Latin. This treatise had been falsely attributed to ⇒Dionysius the Areopagite. In this work E. demonstrated not only his capacity as translator, but also his ability to explain the thought of the Greek philosophers. This ability gave him fame and prestige, which led King Pepin, persuaded by ⇒Hincmar, archbishop of Reims, to ask him to refute ⇒Gottschalk. E. accepted the challenge and brilliantly fulfilled this task—even though his arguments were such that Hincmar preferred to forgo his support.

Upon finishing this work, E. expanded the translation of *The Heavenly Hierarchy* and translated other works attributed to Dionysius. In addition, he wrote *De praedestinatione* and *De divisione naturae*, treatises in which he expounded his theology. These works attracted the interest of Pope Nicholas I, who called King Pepin to account for allowing the dissemination of theological writings without the approval of the church. The king did not respond to such a petition, and E. mysteriously disappeared. Some historians say that on the death of Pepin, E. went to England, where King Alfred put him in charge of his school in Oxford. Others, like Matthew of Westminster and Roger de

Hoveden, say that E. fled to the monastery of Meldum, where his teachings were not well received and his students murdered him in reaction to his demands and requirements. Another tradition claims that he died in France calmly and peacefully, after living in isolation.

E. was a prolific writer and translator. He translated all the works attributed to Dionysius. In addition, he wrote a treatise on Holy Communion, in which he denies the presence of Christ in the elements and argues that the ceremony is a reminder of the atoning sacrifice of Christ.

His most complete and controversial work is *De divisione naturae*. Here, E. uses elements of Greek and Neoplatonic philosophy to explain the nature of God and of creation. He affirms that all things come from God, all things subsist in God, and all things end in God. This relationship between God and creation is explained on the basis of four categories: (1) nature that is creative and not created, (2) nature that is created and creative, (3) nature that is created but not creative, (4) nature that is neither created nor creative.

It is important to note that the vocabulary used by E. reflects the limitations of his time. His conclusions, especially those that refer to the nature of God and the world, were soon questioned. They present God as an abstract idea and as a metaphysical entity, and not as a personal God. The creative nature of this God apparently makes no sense and has no purpose. His fourth point appears to make room for a sphere outside reality and outside the power of God. For these reasons E. is classified as a pantheist and is occasionally mentioned as a precursor of Spinoza. Some historians also consider him to be a forerunner of ⇒Leibniz.

E.'s writings were generally rejected by the church, since, in addition to the doctrinal problems already presented, E. denied transubstantiation and affirmed that the authority of the church should be subordinate to reason. Consequently E. and his treatise *De divisione naturae* were condemned by Pope Honorius III in 1225, almost 400 years after its publication.

In defense of E., some historians and theologians point out that his doctrinal deficiencies are owing in great part to his use of the dialectical method, which has its origin in Aristotle. When he used this method, E. integrated authority with reason and theology with philosophy, thus offering a prelude to the great debate between realists and nominalists. Also in his defense, several authors argue that when E. affirmed that all things come from God and all things return to God and end in God, he did not teach an absorption of the divine nature in itself or in other created things. Rather, E. referred to the power of God that accompanies everything in the process of creation.

————

HMT

Escobar, Samuel (1934–).

Peruvian Baptist missiologist who is well known in evangelical circles. He was one of the founders of Fraternidad Teológica Latinoamericana, a member of the ⇒Lausanne Movement, and author of many books in the field of missiology. Some of the themes that characterize his work are (1) Latin American evangelical theology and liberation theologies, (2) the history of missions in Latin America, (3) the recovery of the theological legacy of the first Latin American Protestants, and (4) the contribution of Latin American Pentecostalism to the theological and missional task.

————

CCO

Eudes also ⇒Odo

Eudes of Stella (12th century).

Obscure person who supposedly declared himself the Son of God and judge of the world, and who, in response to the abuses of the nobility and clergy, proposed the community of goods. Although he was accused of being a Manichean (⇒Mani) and an ⇒Albigensian, his preaching does not appear to have included the dualism characteristic of such groups. He was condemned to prison by the council of Reims (1148) and died there.

————

JLG

Eudoxius (4th century).

One of the main Arian leaders (⇒Arius; Council of ⇒Nicaea), although not of the extreme party, but of the party that adapted itself to the conditions of the moment, whom historians call political Arians. Apparently, like so many other Arians, he was a disciple of ⇒Lucian of Antioch. In the midst of the highs and lows of politics, he was bishop of Antioch, then was deposed and exiled, and finally made patriarch of Constantinople after the deposition of ⇒Macedonius. From that position he mainly opposed the party of the Homoiousians, who have been called Semi-Arians, but who in reality sought an intermediate position that would allow them to accept what was done in Nicaea without capitulating to what appeared to them the Sabellianism (⇒Sabellius) of the Nicene *homoousios*.

———

JLG

Eunomius (4th century). Disciple of ⇒Aetius and, together with him, one of the chief defenders of the extreme Arianism (⇒Arius) of the Anomoeans. According to him, only the Father has no origin, and is therefore divine in the strict sense. The Son or Word, begotten of the Father, did not exist before being begotten. Because he was the first of the creatures of God and the origin of all the rest of creation, he is Lord and God over all those other creatures; but even so, he is still a creature. The Holy Spirit, created by the Son, is also divine only in this limited and secondary sense. Since in his time the Homoiousian party had gained many followers, E. attacked the Homoiousians as well as the Homoousians (that is, the strictly Nicenes). He wrote an *Apology* which ⇒Basil of Caesarea refuted. Then he also wrote a reply to Basil. His other important work is his *Confession of Faith*, presented in 383 to Emperor Theodosius. But already by that date the Council of ⇒Constantinople (381) had endorsed what was done in ⇒Nicaea, and Arianism was in full decline.

———

JLG

Eusebius, Bruno ⇒Bruno, **Eusebius**

Eusebius of Caesarea (ca. 263–ca. 340). Prolific author of the fourth century known especially for his *Ecclesiastical History,* which has gained for him the title of father of church history. He was born in Caesarea, where he was a disciple of ⇒Pamphilus of Caesarea. His admiration for that teacher was such that years later E. would give himself the name Eusebius of Pamphilus, that is, the son or disciple of Pamphilus.

Persecution compelled E. to flee from his native city, first to Tyre and later to the Egyptian desert, but even there he was imprisoned. When the persecution ended in 313, he returned to Caesarea, where he seems to have been elected bishop almost immediately.

Using the library that ⇒Origen had left in Caesarea, and that Pamphilus had augmented, E. wrote several historical and theological works. In addition to his *Ecclesiastical History,* he composed a *Chronicle* of universal history,

the purpose of which was to reaffirm the old argument of some apologists that the Judeo-Christian tradition was older than any religion and than Greek philosophy. This apologetic purpose is also found in his *Praeparatio evangelica* and in *Demonstratio evangelica*. The first of these was dedicated mainly to the criticism of paganism, and the second to the refutation of the arguments of Jews against Christianity. He also wrote several biblical commentaries, theological works with which he intervened in the Arian controversy (⇒Arius), epistles, and so on.

As E. read and presented the history of the church, the purpose of God in that history always included a positive role for the Roman Empire. Before E., ⇒Justin and several other apologists, such as ⇒Clement of Alexandria and ⇒Origen, had affirmed that, just as God gave the Law to the Jews to lead them to Christ, God gave philosophy to the Gentiles to lead them to the same Lord. E. belonged to that theological tradition which affirmed the positive place of philosophy, above all the Platonic version, in Christian theology. But also, now that in the person and work of Constantine the empire had become Christian, E. affirmed that the plan of God also included that new order, so that the empire had also been created by God to lead humanity toward God's purposes.

It is from this perspective that E. read all the earlier history of the church, and it is also this perspective which he has bequeathed to the historians who followed him. Thus, for example, for E. the entire history of the persecutions was the work of mad emperors like Nero, or of bad advice from ambitious court officials, or the result of a misunderstanding on the part of the empire. If it had not been for such circumstances, there should not have been any conflict at all between the church and the civil government, as the new order begun by Constantine now showed. (In more recent times church historians have begun to question this reading of the persecutions and to ask themselves if there were not in the doctrines and practices of ancient Christianity subversive elements that E. underestimated.)

E.'s stance vis-à-vis the imperial authorities found its greatest expression in his *Life of Constantine* and his *Eulogy of Constantine* (which in reality is a compilation of a discourse pronounced in celebration of the thirteenth anniversary of Constantine's government and another treatise on the occasion of the dedication of the church of the Holy Sepulchre). In these works E. ignores all the negative elements of Constantine's government (for example, his having ordered the death of his own son) and underscores the virtues of the emperor. Although this is why E. has been branded as a flatterer who was willing to hide the truth for reasons of convenience, it must not be forgotten that E. had suffered because of his faith and therefore that the peace which Constantine had brought the church was for him an unexpected miracle. Thus, perhaps it would be more exact to say that rather than flattery, in E. there is boundless gratitude.

E. also participated in the controversies of his time, and above all in the Arian (⇒Arius) controversy. Apparently E. never became convinced of the danger of Arianism and instead always feared Sabellianism (⇒Sabellius). In the early stages of the controversy, he appeared to be concerned above all that the actions of ⇒Alexander of Alexandria against Arius might disturb the peace of the church, and therefore he wrote letters in defense of Arius. A synod in Caesarea, under his direction, declared that Arius was orthodox. In reply, shortly before the Council of ⇒Nicaea, another synod, now in Antioch, condemned Arius as well as E. himself.

When the council met in Nicaea, E. was part of a majority group of bishops who apparently were more concerned about Sabellianism than about Arianism. For them, the chief danger was not an excessive distinction between the Father and the Son, but the loss of such a distinction. E. would have preferred that the council simply reaffirm the divinity of the Son using biblical phrases and without entering into greater details. But the position of the Arians, who insisted that the Son was not divine in the same sense as the Father, made the council seek other ways of rejecting Arianism. When the emperor suggested the term *homoousios* (consubstantial) to express the relation between the two divine persons, E. and almost all the rest acceded. Furthermore, the creed that Nicaea adopted, and which E. and almost everyone present signed, appears to be an adaptation of the creed that was traditionally used in Caesarea, with the changes that were necessary to reject Arianism, and above all to include the term *homoousios*.

Nevertheless, once the council had closed, E. began to have doubts about what had been done there. His own letter to the faithful of Caesarea already shows his hesitation and how difficult it was for him to explain what had been done. Shortly afterward he began to criticize the decisions of Nicaea and supported the efforts of ⇒Eusebius of Nicomedia to undo what had

been done. In 330 he actively participated in the synod of Antioch which deposed ⇒Eustathius of Antioch. Five years later he also participated in another synod in Tyre which declared ⇒Athanasius a heretic. He also wrote against ⇒Marcellus of Ancyra, whose removal the Arians obtained shortly thereafter. All of these measures were taken by the Arians against the leaders of the Nicene party, and therefore it is correct to say that without becoming an Arian, E. certainly was anti-Nicene. Such was his position until his death, which occurred shortly after the death of Constantine, when the conflicts between the three sons of the great emperor would give new life to Arianism.

———

JLG

Eusebius of Dorilea (5th century).

First he was an opponent of ⇒Nestorius, and then of ⇒Eutyches and ⇒Dioscorus. It is said that he was a layman, an official of the court, when on hearing Nestorius declare that Mary should not receive the title of *Theotokos* he protested loudly in the center of the cathedral itself. After protesting verbally, E. unfolded a placard in which he accused Nestorius of following the heresy of ⇒Paul of Samosata and invited other bishops to condemn him. This was the spark that lit the Nestorian controversy and the long series of debates and fights that would continue at least until the Council of ⇒Chalcedon. E. was concerned about the position of Nestorius, mainly because it seemed to deny the full incarnation of God in Jesus Christ. Part of the result of that action and of the controversies that followed was the ordination of E., who then occupied the episcopal see of Dorilea in Phrygia.

Years later E. noticed that Eutyches, an influential monk in Constantinople, was inclining too much toward the opposite extreme of Nestorius, and it was E. who once more provoked controversy, presenting to Patriarch ⇒Flavian of Constantinople a formal accusation against Eutyches. When the council of the year 449 (the so-called robber council of Ephesus, ⇒Councils, ⇒Chalcedon) met in Ephesus under the presidency of ⇒Dioscorus, E. was not allowed to be present, even when Flavian insisted that the complaint against Eutyches had been initiated by E. Without listening to him, E. was declared a heretic and deposed.

Shortly afterward, after the death of Emperor Theodosius II and with the support of ⇒Leo the Great and of Empress Pulcheria, E. accused Dioscorus of heresy and of unjust procedures—the third of his formal accusations against others. The result was that in the Council of Chalcedon E. was vindicated, and Dioscorus was declared a heretic and removed from his Alexandrian see. In all of this, the conduct of E., although legally irreproachable, can well be qualified as extremely rigid and legalistic.

———

Eusebius of Emesa (?–ca. 360).
One of the main Pneumatomachians, that is, of those who were willing to affirm the divinity and coeternity of the Son, but not of the Holy Spirit. Famous for his knowledge, he wrote not only on the Holy Spirit, but also against the Novatians (⇒Novatian) and others. Almost all of his work has been lost.

———

Eusebius of Nicomedia (?–ca. 342).
Chief defender of ⇒Arius and his doctrines. When ⇒Alexander of Alexandria declared Arius a heretic, E. came out in defense of the latter, who like himself had been a disciple of ⇒Lucian of Antioch. His protests and the actions of a synod convened by him led Emperor Constantine to the conclusion that it was necessary to convene a general council. This met in Nicaea, and there E. was the chief exponent of the teachings of Arius and the rest of the "fellow Lucianists." When he refused to accept the decisions of the council, he was sent into exile by the emperor. Three years later he was allowed to return to Nicomedia, where E. was bishop and where the emperor had his summer residence. He was one of the main authors of the accusations and judgment against ⇒Eustathius of Antioch, and then became one of the main opponents of ⇒Athanasius. His chief triumph took place when the political currents of that moment made him bishop of Constantinople.

———

Eustace of Sebaste (ca. 300–ca. 380).
Monk and bishop who according to some is the true founder of Eastern monasticism (an honor traditionally attributed to ⇒Basil of Caesarea). He studied in Alexandria, apparently under ⇒Arius. For this reason ⇒Eustathius of Antioch later refused to admit him into the clergy of that city. He then followed a confused theological career, at times leaning toward Arianism and at times opposing it. Apparently his stance was that of a good

many of his colleagues: while he rejected extreme Arianism, which was an assault on the divinity of the Savior, he feared that the *homoousios* of ⇒Nicaea came too close to Sabellianism (⇒Sabellius). For this reason it is feasible to count him among the Homoiousians. Finally he joined the Pneumatomachians.

———

Eustathius of Antioch (4th century).
Bishop of that city beginning in 324. He collaborated with ⇒Alexander of Alexandria in the condemnation of ⇒Arius and had an active role in the Council of ⇒Nicaea. He clashed with ⇒Eusebius of Caesarea, whom he accused of Arian tendencies, and the latter in turn branded him a Sabellian (⇒Sabellius). When the Arians gained the upper hand politically, they declared him a heretic, immoral and tyrannical, and they deposed him. With respect to his theology, E. was a faithful expositor of the Antiochene tradition, above all in what pertains to Christology. For this reason some consider him a forerunner of ⇒Nestorius.

———

Eutyches (378–ca. 455).
Archimandrite of Constantinople who was the catalyst for the clash between ⇒Flavian of Constantinople and ⇒Dioscorus that eventually led to the Council of ⇒Chalcedon. Traditionally he is considered the founder of Monophysitism, which sometimes receives the name Eutychianism. Dioscorus came out in defense of E., who had been condemned by a synod in Constantinople, and the result was the so-called robber council (*latrocinium*) of Ephesus (⇒Councils). Two years later, in the Council of Chalcedon, his teachings were condemned.

What these teachings were is difficult to know, since E. does not appear to have been well versed in theology, but was instead the pawn that Dioscorus used to promote the Alexandrian cause against the Antiochene. He certainly affirmed that in Christ there was "only one nature." But it is not at all certain that this was a denial of the humanity of the Savior, and much less that he said, as some have accused him of affirming, that the body of Jesus Christ was made of a heavenly substance. Perhaps the one who most aptly judged him was ⇒Leo the Great, who said that E. wanted to be a teacher of what he had not learned.

———

Evagrius Ponticus (345–99). Mystic monk and theologian, a native of Ibora in Pontus. He was made a lector or reader by ⇒Basil of Caesarea and ordained deacon (379) by ⇒Gregory of Nazianzus. He became a monk in the year 363. After traveling to several monasteries in Palestine and in Egypt, he took up residency in the valley of Celia where, for fourteen years, he developed and taught his mystical theology. During that time E. became renowned for his knowledge and austere life. In 381 he accompanied Gregory to the Council of ⇒Constantinople, where his intellectual gifts and rhetorical skills had a dazzling effect.

The influence of E. on the founding and promotion of monastic mysticism prevailed among the Greeks (John ⇒Climacus, ⇒Maximus the Confessor, ⇒Dionysius the Aeropagite), among the Latins through ⇒John Cassian, and among the Syrians through the Nestorians and Monophysites, who regard him as their great doctor of mystical theology.

Because of his radical dedication to the teachings of ⇒Origen, E. was accused of heresy and condemned after his death, in the Second Council of ⇒Constantinople (553). His many writings, biblical commentaries, and letters come to us in the original Greek and in Syriac, Armenian, or Latin translations. His most important writings are *Praktikos* (a trilogy) and *Chapters on Prayer*.

ZMP

Ewart, Frank J. (1876–1947). Minister and evangelist born in Australia who became one of the first leaders of Pentecostalism in the United States. He upheld the unity of God, which he placed over against the doctrine of the Trinity. Based on Acts 2:38, he believed that the name of God was in reality "Jesus," and therefore Jesus himself was the Father, the Son, and the Holy Spirit, and should not be identified only with the Son. His last accomplishments include his autobiographical narrative of the emergence of the movement of non-Trinitarian Pentecostalism (Oneness Movement) in his book *The Phenomenon of Pentecost* (1947). He was admitted to the United Pentecostal Church shortly before his death.

ALG

Ewer, Ferdinand Cartwright (1826–83). Priest, distinguished preacher, and Anglo-Catholic theologian. He served as rector of Christ Church (Episcopal) in New York, where he stood out as the most prominent defender of Anglo-Catholicism. Among his most distinguished works is *Catholicism in Its Relationship to Protestantism and Romanism* (1878).

ALG

Fackre, Gabriel Joseph (1926–). Minister and professor of systematic theology, Christian ethics, and mission. He served as pastor in Duquesne-West Mifflin, and then as a professor in Lancaster Theological Seminary, and Andover Newton Theological School, from which he retired in 1996. Among his numerous works are *The Religion of the Right and Christian Faith* (1982), *The Doctrine of Revelation: A Narrative Interpretation* (1997), and *Restoring the Center: Essays Evangelical and Ecumenical* (1998).

ALG

Farel, Guillaume (1489–1565). French reformer and preacher who began the Reformation in French-speaking Switzerland when he persuaded the Great Council of Geneva to promulgate an edict in favor of the reforming party. ⇒Lefèvre d'Étaples, the pioneer of the Reformation in France, influenced him with his studies on the Epistles of Paul and his teaching on justification by faith. He was recognized by the reformers ⇒Calvin and ⇒Beza, chiefly for his eloquence as an extemporaneous preacher. His style could be sharp and thunderous, and because of that he sometimes found himself in difficulties. He recognized his weakness and persuaded Calvin to take the lead as theologian of the reforming movement in Geneva. His debate in Latin, delivered in Bern in 1524, is among his most recognized accomplishments. There he converted the recognized Greek and Hebrew scholar, the Franciscan ⇒Pellican, to the cause of the Reformation. Although his sermons have disappeared, some of his books in French are extant, among them one on dogmatics and another on liturgy.

ALG

Farrer, Austin Marsden (1904–68). English theologian with philosophical training who also distinguished himself by his exegetical contributions. The son of a Baptist pastor, he was ordained to the Anglican priesthood in Oxford, where he served as chaplain and fellow of several colleges. He was the director of Keble College from 1960 until his death.

F.'s research on the composition of the Synoptic Gospels established the foundations for the development of one of the most important hypotheses that has been presented as an alternative to the two-source theory that has dominated studies on this subject. F. had a conservative but very creative spirit. At a time when systematic theology had distanced itself from biblical analysis, he invited scholars to assume stances that were critical of the accepted theories about the sources and the development of the Gospels. He proposed that the authors of these documents, far from serving as mere compilers of earlier sources (as editors), performed a very creative theological task in their composition. His most influential work on biblical criticism was his article "On Dispensing with Q."

———

JDR

Faustus of Milevis (?–ca. 400).
Manichean teacher whom ⇒Augustine, in his Manichean period, had anxiously awaited with the hope that he would free him from his doubts concerning Manichean teachings. Disappointed by F., Augustine abandoned Manicheism and composed a work in thirty-three books, *Against Faustus the Manichean*. Since in this refutation Augustine quotes him in extensive detail, this work makes it possible for us to learn a great deal about the teachings of F. and the Manicheans.

———

JLG

Faustus of Riez (ca. 410–500?).
Bishop of Riez, also known as F. of Lerins because he had been abbot of that famous monastery. F. was one of the chief critics of the Augustinian doctrine of grace (⇒Augustine). He also opposed Arianism (⇒Arius), and for this reason the Gothic king Eurich exiled him for approximately seven years. He criticized Augustine in a treatise in two books, *On the Grace of God*, and in a shorter one, *Against the Opinion of Those Who Say That There Are Incorporeal Beings That Are Not God*—that is, against Augustine, who maintained that both the human soul and the angels are incorporeal beings. Concerning grace F. maintained, against ⇒Pelagius, that original sin has affected humanity in such a way that without grace humanity can neither do good nor obtain salvation. Such "preventive [or prevenient] grace" has been given to all human beings. But, against Augustine, F. declared that grace is not

irresistible, that the human being always has the free will to direct itself toward God, and that therefore the need for grace should not lead to the assertion of predestination. This is what some have called Semi-Pelagianism, to indicate that it is an intermediate position between Augustine and Pelagius.

———

JLG

Febronius (1701–90). His birth name
was Johann Nikolaus von Hontheim, but he is better known as Febronius. He was suffragan bishop of Trier in Prussia, educated in Jesuit schools and universities in Prussia. On the completion of his studies, he visited Rome with the intention of learning more about the Roman Catholic Church. Upon his return to Prussia, he occupied several official positions in the church and finally was named suffragan bishop in 1748. He served in that position until 1788, two years before his death. In the capacity of bishop and using his pseudonym, Febronius, he published in Latin his work *The State of the Church and the Legitimate Authority of the Roman Pontiff: Book Composed with the Purpose of Uniting in Religion Christian Dissidents*. In it he makes a clear distinction between spiritual and ecclesiastical power, explaining in detail the church of the New Testament, the nature of councils, the tendency of the nuncios to usurp power, and the episcopal monopoly of authority. The reaction of the Roman church was almost immediate. Pope Clement XIII condemned the work in 1784, even though F. had dedicated it to him. Pius VI ordered the persecution of F. and his family. In spite of that, and as a consequence of F.'s work, papal power was restricted in several countries. After retracting on various occasions, F. submitted to the authority of the church shortly before his death.

———

HMT

Fee, Gordon David (1934–). New Testament
scholar who taught at Regent College in Vancouver, Canada. His father was a Pentecostal pastor, and F. is an ordained minister of the Assemblies of God. He has excelled in the textual criticism and exegesis of the New Testament. He has written major commentaries on 1 Corinthians (1987) and Philippians (1995). As a Pentecostal and an evangelical, he has represented both these theologies with intellectual integrity and passion. His monumental book *God's Empowering Presence: The Holy Spirit in the Letters of Paul* (1994) analyzes every

passage on the Holy Spirit in the Pauline letters. He has also concerned himself with teaching a good exegetical methodology, and consequently wrote *New Testament Exegesis: A Handbook for Students and Pastors* (1983, 1993) and, at a more popular level, *How to Read the Bible for All Its Worth: A Guide to Understanding the Bible* (1985).

—

EA

Felix of Urgel (?–818). Bishop of that city in Spain, and defender of the adoptionism of ⇒Elipandus of Toledo. Even though it is called adoptionism, the most accurate interpretation of this position appears to be that F. proposed a Christology in which, in the style of the ancient school of Antioch, he sought to safeguard the complete humanity of Jesus Christ through a clear and perhaps exaggerated distinction between it and the divinity of the Savior. For this reason he rejected the christological principle of the *communicatio idiomatum* (the sharing of predicates between the divinity and the humanity of the Savior) and said that, insofar as he is God, the Savior is the Son by nature, while insofar as he is human, he is this "by adoption." This does not mean, as in true adoptionism, that God, in view of the faithfulness of Jesus, adopted him as son in some moment of his life. It is, rather, a way of affirming the humanity of Jesus in such a way that he can truly be the guide and head of the faithful (and perhaps in the case of F. it is also a way of replying to the criticism of his Muslim neighbors).

Having been summoned to a council in Regensburg in 792 under the leadership of Charlemagne, F. is said to have recanted, but it is also said that on his return to Spain he insisted on his teachings. Summoned again to a council in Aachen in 798, F. debated his teachings with the famous ⇒Alcuin for six days. Although in the end F. said he was in agreement with Alcuin, Charlemagne did not allow him to return to his see in Urgel but instead kept him as a prisoner until he died in Lyon (four years after the death of Charlemagne). According to the papers that he left, he was never convinced that his teachings were erroneous.

—

JLG

Fénelon, François de Salignac de La Mothe (1651–1715). Catholic mystic and archbishop of Cambrai, France. Of a family of the high French nobility that had been reduced to poverty, F. first studied in Cahors and then in Paris, where he was ordained as presbyter in 1675 and served as pastor. In 1678 he was elected rector of Nouvelles Catholiques, an organization dedicated to the education of young women who had converted from Protestantism. From that time he devoted himself to ministering to former Protestants who returned or were converted to Catholicism. Although strict in doctrinal orthodoxy, F. was recognized for his kind and tolerant dealings with others. In 1689 he was named teacher of the grandson of Louis XIV and as part of his duties wrote *Télémaque*, in which he teaches that every king is subject to the same moral laws as the citizens—a teaching that aroused the suspicion of Louis XIV. An unforeseen encounter with the mystic Madame de ⇒Guyon led him to mysticism, but without her exaggerations. In 1693 F. was elected a member of the French Academy, and in 1695 he was named archbishop of Cambrai. In order to keep his mystical style of prayer from being confused with that of Guyon, he was compelled to sign the Articles of Issy, in which many of the proposals of the French "quietists" who were directed by her were condemned. In 1697 F. published his *Explanation of the Maxims of the Saints on the Inner Life*, which provoked strong reactions against him (especially from ⇒Bousset) as well as accusations of heresy and the partial condemnation of Pope Innocent XII. Exiled from the court, he devoted the rest of his life to the pastoral care of his diocese and to the spiritual direction of numerous persons who sought to learn from his spiritual experience and wisdom. He opposed Jansenism (⇒Jansen) and exerted great religious influence in France after the death of Louis XIV, even among Protestants. He died in poverty after distributing his resources among the most needy.

—

OOE

Ferrara-Florence, Council of (1438–52). In his conflicts with the Council of ⇒Basel, Pope Eugenius IV had ordered that it be transferred to Ferrara. The refusal of some to obey caused a schism in the conciliar movement, so that for a time there were two councils, one in Basel and another in Ferrara. The latter, which was more obedient to the papal mandate, appeared to be in danger when the plague, as well as its finances, forced it to transfer to Florence. But it achieved an unexpected victory when the emperor of Byzantium, John VIII Paleologos, and the patriarch of Constantinople came to it in search of aid against the threat of the Turks. The result was that the C. of F. became a process of union between Roman Catholicism and the Eastern churches, in which finally representatives of the patriarchs of Antioch, Alexandria, and Jerusalem, and also the archbishop of Kiev, participated.

The council agreed to include the *filioque* in the creed and also stated the primacy of the pope, "according to the acts and canons of the ancient councils." Apparently, while the West understood these words in the sense that such acts and canons affirmed papal primacy, the East understood them in the sense that such primacy was only that which was found in those acts and canons. The Russians explained that what was agreed upon constituted a pardoning of the Latins on the part of the Greeks. In any case, the easterners, especially the Greeks, were anxious to achieve a union that apparently promised them support against the Turks.

With great pomp, on July 6, 1439, the documents were signed and the union of the Latin and Greek churches was celebrated. Shortly afterward similar agreements with the Armenians and the Monophysites of Egypt were signed.

All of this fell apart in the face of the opposition of the Eastern faithful—clergy and the laity—who declared that those who had signed these documents were apostates and heretics. When in 1453 the Turks captured Constantinople, practically without any opposition from the West, the fictitious union promulgated by the council was forgotten.

The council itself continued its sessions, each time with less momentum, until in 1452 Nicholas V transferred it to Rome, where it disappeared.

———

JLG

Ferré, Nels F. S. (1908–71).
Theologian, author, and educator who was a native of Sweden. His career, which covered more than thirty years, unfolded mainly in the United States. His scholarly works include studies on theological philosophy, theology in Sweden, and contributions to modern theology, especially on the relationship between the traditional doctrine of God and the new process theology. Among his many publications are *Faith and Reason* and *The Universal Word: A Theology for a Universal Faith.*

He believed that the chief function of theology is the transforming work of the world under an incarnate biblical vision of *agape.*

This work is directed to the radical transformation of society, of the human being, and of Christianity.

———

ALG

Feuerbach, Ludwig A. (1804–72).
German theologian and philosopher whose interpretation of God was significantly influenced by ⇒Hegel. But in contrast to Hegel, F. rejects every notion of the transcendence and existence of God. According to him, any assertion that is made about God is really a declaration about the human being. The divine is only a projection of those human potentialities and possibilities that have not yet been historically fulfilled. Our ideas of God are mere projections of human desires and ambitions.

———

IG

Ficino, Marsilio (1433–99).
Renaissance philosopher, editor of the works of Plato in Greek, best known for his Neoplatonic ideas on the close relationship between the beautiful and the good. In addition to his career as translator from Greek into Latin, he was also a Catholic priest. He wrote treatises on theology, in which he considered the One (God) as the origin and unity of all things, thus articulating his universalist religion. Mystical elements can also be perceived in his thought, including something of the Jewish Kabbalah.

———

NRG

Finney, Charles Grandison (1792–1875).
Famous preacher born in Warren, Connecticut, within the Presbyterian tradition. In 1821, while he was studying law in Adams, New York, he had a religious experience that transformed his life. He described this as his experience of justification by faith and his baptism in the Holy Spirit. In 1823 he was commissioned by the Presbyterian church to preach the gospel as a missionary through the Women's Missionary Society of Western New York. This gave rise to a project of preaching and revival initiated by F. The revival consisted in calling the assembled people to a total surrender to Christ and to strict purity and holiness. F. was of the opinion that the Lutheran dictum of *simul justus et peccator* (saint and sinner at the same time) was a distortion of the gospel, and he insisted on a lifestyle in which believers would make the righteousness of God real in their

lives. F. distanced himself from the Calvinist image of salvation as a sovereign act of God for the elect and argued that salvation is available to all persons, who therefore should actively seek it. He claimed that the justification of the sinner was effective after the sinner repented and began to live in holiness. If the justified Christian sinned again, such Christian needed to be justified again and therefore was in danger of condemnation before the judgment of God. For F. the righteousness of God was not something imputed to human beings, but the actual practice of righteousness in daily life and in society. Other innovations of F. were allowing women to participate in public prayer in the worship services of his movement, increasing the number of services in addition to those on Sunday, using everyday language as part of preaching, and emphasizing the conversion, revival, and sanctification of the converted. In addition, F. claimed that in conversion the person automatically became a member of the church. In 1827 the Presbyterian Assembly discussed, as a topic of controversy, the school of revivalism that F. represented, but no decision was made against him. F. extended his preaching from towns to cities, with an emphasis on the revival of the faith and the present sanctification of converts. In 1834 his congregation in New York rejected Presbyterian polity and theology and adopted a Congregational polity. In 1835 F. began to teach in Oberlin Theological Seminary, where he continued his ministry until 1872. Under his leadership, in 1846 Oberlin admitted the first woman, Antoinette Brown, as a candidate to the ministry. In 1851 F. was elected president of Oberlin. During that period in Oberlin he published his works on holiness and revival and also his debates with the Presbyterian tradition. Another element in the theology of F. was his strong abolitionism, which was part of his understanding of holiness.

—

ELR

Firmilian of Caesarea (?–ca. 268).

Bishop of that city and admirer of ⇒Origen, to whom he went to listen in Palestine and whom he later invited to take refuge in Cappadocia. He participated, with ⇒Cyprian, in the conflict with Rome on the baptism of heretics. According to F. and Cyprian, those who became members of the orthodox church after receiving baptism from a heretic had to be baptized again. The bishop of Rome, Stephen, opposed this practice. The dispute slackened after the death

of the chief opponents, and eventually the rest of the church followed the Roman practice.

—

JLG

Fishacre, Richard (?–1248). Domini-

can theologian of Augustinian convictions and author of a *Commentary on the Sentences of Peter Lombard*. According to him, theology is above all knowledge inspired by the Holy Spirit, and although it does have a cognitive dimension, its main value is affective and moral.

—

JLG

Flacius, Matthias (1520–75). Austrian

Lutheran theologian, also known as Vlacich (a Croatian name that was Latinized as Flacius) and Francovich. He was born in the small village of Albon and died in the city of Frankfurt. In 1536 he began his studies in the humanities in Venice. Upon finishing these studies in 1539, he went to Basel, from there to Tübingen, and finally to Wittenberg, to study with teachers such as ⇒Luther and ⇒Melanchthon. In Wittenberg he finished his master's degree and in 1544 occupied a professorship of Hebrew in the faculty of philosophy. When Melanchthon consented to the Interim of Leipzig, F. began a virulent campaign against him and his school, writing anonymous tracts. On Easter of 1549 he left Wittenberg and went to Magdeburg where, together with ⇒Amsdorf, he led the attack of the strict Lutherans against the Melanchthonian attitude toward *adiaphora,* things neither commanded nor forbidden. He was also one of the protagonists in the ongoing controversies against ⇒Osiander and ⇒Schwenckfeld. When the Majoristic Controversy developed, he also played a prominent part by becoming involved in polemics with Justus ⇒Menius.

Although in the beginning he was held in high esteem, practically becoming the oracle of the Lutherans, he went into a complete decline and suffered the contempt of many of his colleagues when he asserted that original sin was a natural condition of the human being. His treatise on original sin, incorporated in the 1567 edition of his *Clavis* (Key), generated much criticism from those who had been his allies. Tilemann ⇒Hesshusen and Johann ⇒Wigand, professors at the University of Jena, took the lead in this attack. Although initially he was one of his friends, Jacob ⇒Andrea also became one of his strongest opponents after the Colloquy of Strasbourg in 1571.

F. is above all remembered as editor of the ⇒*Centuries of Magdeburg*. This was a pioneer work of Protestant scholarship on the sources and interpretation of the history of the church in its ongoing struggle to eliminate error and establish truth. His biblical studies were concentrated on grammatical and historical details. His work *Clavis Scripturae Sacrae* (1567; Key to the Sacred Scripture), which went through several editions, holds a prominent place in the history of hermeneutics. F.'s interpretation of the doctrine of original sin forced German Lutheranism to examine more carefully, in the Formula of ⇒Concord, the articulation of the relationship between creation and sin, as well as the restricted legitimacy of free will, and to resist the threat of both Manicheism and Pelagianism. In studies on church history F. is considered to be the most distinguished Lutheran opponent of his colleagues at Wittenberg after the Schmalkald War. He also wrote *Catalogus testium veritatis* (1556; Catalog of Witnesses to the Truth); *Missa Latina antiqua* (The Ancient Latin Mass); and *Contra Papatum Romanum a diabolo inventum* (Against the Roman Papacy Invented by the Devil).

F. spent his last years in the Lutheran convent of Frankfurt, which was presided over by Katerina von Meerfeld, who became his protector. In 1574 he decided to take a very long trip through Mansfel and Silesia to meet with friends and support groups. He died on his return to Frankfurt.

During the nineteenth century several important studies rehabilitated the value of F.'s contribution to church history. These efforts began with the essay by ⇒Twesten in 1844 and were strengthened by the monumental biography of F. written by William ⇒Preger in 1859–61.

—

JDR

Flavian of Constantinople (5th century).

Patriarch of that city beginning in 446. It fell to him to participate actively in the first episodes of the Monophysite controversy. The controversy broke out when ⇒Eutyches was condemned by a synod led by F. himself. In that synod F. declared his faith in "Christ, who is of two natures after the incarnation, in one single hypostasis and person." The phrase "of two natures," which F. had taken from ⇒Cyril of Alexandria, would later become typical of Monophysitism, which was prepared to assert

that Jesus Christ was "of two natures," that is, one divine and the other human, but not "in two natures." The Monophysites thereby declared that, although in Christ divinity and humanity were joined, the latter disappeared in virtue of the union. It was precisely against such an interpretation that F. added the words "after the incarnation." In the "robber council (*latrocinium*) of Ephesus" in 449, ⇒Dioscorus and his followers treated F. with such violence that he is said to have died shortly afterward as a result.

—

JLG

Fletcher, Joseph (1905–91).

Author who popularized situational ethics in the United States. This ethic rejects the necessity of formulating and using ethical principles. Ethical decisions must be spontaneous and free, not tied to principles, traditions, laws, and rules that in their abstractness are incapable of responding to what is distinctive in each situation. For F., the intuition that is based on Christian *agape*, that love which calls us to love God above all things and our neighbor as ourselves, is a sufficient guide for ethical decisions. In the best of cases, moral principles serve as general advice, but they should never acquire imperative or categorical authority. Aside from love, intrinsically obligatory rules or moral principles do not exist. Any principle or rule that refuses to practice love concretely in a given situation lacks moral relevance. For F., love has a utilitarian character. To love is to maximize the good of others or to minimize their pain. In summary, love justifies any means to achieve it and to make it concrete.

—

IG

Flórez, Enrique (1702–73).

Spanish Augustinian monk chiefly recognized as a church historian. He studied in Alcalá, where Ambrose of Morales (d. 1591) had established a strong tradition of historical research. Together with other Spanish scholars he edited volumes 1 through 29 of *España sagrada* (Sacred Spain, 1747–75). This work, which organizes the ecclesiastical history of Spain around dioceses, remains an obligatory reference for the history of the church in Spain.

—

ALG

Florovsky, Georges Vasil'evich (1893–1979).

A priest of the Russian Orthodox Church, F. contributed to the ecumenical dialogue between the patristic and Orthodox traditions on the one hand and other Christian traditions on the other. F. proposed that every theological and ecumenical dialogue should begin with the patristic tradition, which determined the canon of the New Testament. He was a professor of history in institutions such as the University of Odessa in Prague, St. Sergius Institute of Orthodox Theology in Paris, and Union Theological Seminary in New York.

CCO

Florus of Lyon (?–ca. 860). Poet and theologian, deacon of Lyon, and distinguished personality of the Carolingian renaissance. He wrote on canon law and on liturgy, in addition to commentaries on the Pauline epistles. He is known chiefly for his participation in the controversy on predestination that emerged around the teachings of ⇒Gottschalk. F. adopted a moderate position, affirming a double predestination—that is, some to salvation and others to suffer the consequences of their sin—but insisting at the same time that it is the human will which determines who will receive condemnation and who will be rewarded. When John Scotus ⇒Erigena intervened in the debate, establishing his extreme position on a rationalism that appeared to lead to absolute determinism, F. and several other colleagues rejected his theses, and Erigena withdrew from the struggle.

JLG

Fogazzaro, Antonio (1842–1911). A novelist, poet, senator, and pioneer of lay participation in Roman Catholicism, born in Vicenza, Italy. He was accused of being a modernist, and his books *Il Santo* (1906) and *Leila* (1910) appeared in the Index or list of forbidden books of the Inquisition.

EPA

Foligno, Angela of (ca. 1248–1309). A mystic who, on becoming a widow, entered the Franciscan order, gave away her wealth, and dedicated herself to the care of the poor. Her visions were gathered by her confessor, Brother Arnold, in a classic work of Franciscan spirituality, *Visions and Instructions*. As a "teacher of theologians," she was beatified by Innocent XII.

EPA

Fonseca, Peter of (1528–99). Portuguese humanist, philosopher, and theologian. He was a member of the Company of Jesus and professor at the University of Coimbra. F. promoted the rebirth of Thomist thought in the sixteenth century by developing the *scientia media*, a principle that strives to harmonize God's knowledge of the future and the freedom of human actions in that future.

CEA

Forell, George Wolfgang (1919–). Ethicist and missiologist who was unable to complete his university studies in Germany because of Nazi persecution. He was born in Breslau of a long line of Lutheran pastors. His father, Frederick, was a pioneer in his repudiation of Hitler. This deed cost him a forced retirement at the age of forty-four and a life of itinerancy. His mother was sent to a concentration camp in France.

He entered the Lutheran Seminary in Philadelphia in 1939 and became pastor of two congregations two years later. In 1943 he continued his studies in Princeton under J. L. ⇒Hromadka and then in Union Theological Seminary of New York with Reinhold ⇒Niebuhr (PhD, 1949).

F. was a world-famous lecturer, a prolific author, and a student of ⇒Zinzendorf and of the tradition that attributes feminine dimensions to the Holy Spirit. His best-known work is *Faith Active in Love: An Investigation of the Principles underlying Luther's Social Ethics* (1954).

EPA

Forsyth, Peter Taylor (1848–1921). Scottish Congregationalist, theologian, preacher, and prolific author. He is known chiefly for his criticism of liberalism and his high ecclesiology, with a parallel vision of the ministry and the sacraments. For twenty-five years he served in churches of the working class in England and for two decades as director of Hackney College (New College) in London. A liberal at the beginning of his ministry, he rethought his theological position when he came up against the harsh realities of the lives of his parishioners and congregations. In 1894 he abandoned liberalism, with the exception of his emphasis on the critical study of the Scriptures. On the basis of his reading of Paul, he proclaimed a theology and a faith that are lived until the end and centered on Christ and his cross. Chief among his works is *The Person and Place of Jesus Christ* (1909).

—

EZ

Fosdick, Harry Emerson (1878–1969). Pastor of the famous Riverside Church in New York, 1930–46. He was educated at Colgate University and Union Theological Seminary in New York. He was professor of practical theology at Union from 1915 until 1946. He excelled as a preacher and author of practical books on the application of the Christian faith to the modern world. His most famous sermon, "Shall the Fundamentalists Win?" (1922), proposed a modern faith, rejecting the doctrines of biblical inerrancy, the virgin birth, and the bodily resurrection and second coming of Jesus. Instead of these doctrines, F. proposed a faith centered on the love of God and the possibility of receiving spiritual help in order to lead an ethical life. This sermon brought him strong opposition not only from the fundamentalists but also from his own Presbyterian church, which asked him to resign. He then became pastor of the Park Avenue Baptist Church in 1926, which took the name of Riverside Church in 1930, when it constructed a magnificent Gothic edifice with the financial support of John D. Rockefeller Jr., who wanted an international and ecumenical place where the ministry of F. could shine. Later, in his sermon "Beyond Modernism" (1935), F. also challenged the modernists for being too optimistic and for concerning themselves only with the intellectual side of life and not holding to absolute moral values. After his retirement in 1946, he remained active in matters of social justice and wrote his autobiography, *The Living of These Days* (1956).

—

EA

Foster, Frank Hugh (1851–1935). A pastor, author, and Congregationalist theologian born in Springfield, Massachusetts. He taught church history, philosophy, and systematic theology at the Pacific School of Religion in Berkeley, California.

—

EPA

Foster, George Burnham (1858–1918). A Baptist pastor, professor at McMaster University in Toronto, and distinguished professor of systematic theology and philosophy of religion at the University of Chicago. He was an interpreter of liberal Protestant theology and was strongly influenced by Adolf von ⇒Harnack. In his methodology, he mainly affirmed a theology anchored in human experience. In his chief work, *The Finality of the Christian Religion* (1906), he asserted that the purpose of religion is found in the moral values taught by Jesus of Nazareth.

—

ALG

Foulkes, Irene (1932–). North American missionary and New Testament scholar who worked in Central America for many years, mostly as a professor at the Biblical University in Costa Rica. Among her works are *Theology from the Standpoint of Women in Central America* (1989) and *Pastoral Problems in Corinth: Exegetical-Pastoral Commentary on First Corinthians* (1996).

—

CCO

Fowler, James (1940–). Professor of theology and human development. The concept of theories of development received an enormous stimulus owing to the work of Charles ⇒Darwin and occupied a prominent place in the pedagogical investigations of the twentieth century. Among the most influential researchers in human development are Jean Piaget (cognitive development), Erik Erikson (emotional development), William Perry (intellectual development), Lawrence Kohlberg (moral development), Robert Kegan (the evolution of the ego), and Carol Gilligan (feminine adaptation of moral and emotional development). F. is recognized for his application of the theories of Piaget, Erikson, and others to the formulation of a thesis that clarifies the development of faith and vocation in the light of the phenomenologies of faith by H. R. ⇒Niebuhr and Paul ⇒Tillich. He describes the development of faith from the simplistic and imaginative faith of an infant all the way to adult faith, which is more integrated and in which there is greater congruity between beliefs and behavior. F. insists that human beings are genetically formed to have fellowship with God and that the context for the development of the tendencies and the innate potential for that fellowship is the community. Therefore the effort to facilitate growth through the stages of faith is not important. The concern of the community should be to proclaim the truths of God and to enable those truths to become deeply rooted in our lives. The movement through the stages occurs when this is done effectively.

Among the works of F. that describe his thesis on the development of faith are *Stages of Faith* (1981), *Becoming Adult, Becoming Christian* (1984), and *Faith Development and Pastoral Care* (1987).

———

RAR

Fox, George (1624–91). Founder of the Society of Friends, or Quakers, born in England. As a youth he worked as an apprentice to a shoemaker, but at the age of nineteen, disillusioned with the state of religion, he devoted himself to preaching. His emphasis on the direction of the Spirit led him to reject many of the rites and sacraments of the church. This rejection gave rise to criticism from many religious leaders. In spite of suffering persecution and being beaten, stoned, and imprisoned on several occasions, F. became successful, especially in the northeast of England, under the protection of the local judge. After the death of the judge, F. married his widow and traveled extensively throughout Europe and North America.

The theology of F. was guided by personal experience and the "inner light." According to him, all human beings have a spark of that inner light and can attain salvation. His religious emphasis fell on the direction of the Spirit, pacifism, and the love within the community. All who were led by the Spirit, including women, were allowed to preach—something that was unheard of in that time.

———

LGP

Foxe, John (1516–87). A native of Lincolnshire, England. He was a historian, tutor of the nobility, and pastor. Persecuted during the reign of Mary Tudor, while in exile he wrote *Foxe's Book of Martyrs*. This church history and martyrology was required reading for many for two and a half centuries. It was published in English in 1563 and dedicated to the new Protestant queen Elizabeth. In his lifetime, F. saw four editions of his work.

———

EPA

Francis de Sales (1567–1622). Bishop, writer, and founder of a congregation of nuns. He is better known for his spirituality and sermons than for his theology. In fact, he was more of an apologist than a theologian, since many of his writings refute those of ⇒Calvin. In spite of this, he influenced theology indirectly.

His spirituality underscored the role of the layperson at a time when the religious professional was considered to be the only Christian who could really pray. His perspective helped to correct some of the extreme tendencies of the Catholic Reformation.

Also, although the Jesuits took the devotion of the Sacred Heart of Jesus to Latin America, F. was a tireless promoter of this devotion, which has become common even in non-Catholic places in which images of Christ with the open heart are venerated. This is one of the few examples of popular religion that is practiced outside the denomination in which it emerged.

———

KD

Francis of Assisi (ca. 1182–1226). Founder of the Franciscan order, poet, and missionary. He never wrote systematic theology. Nevertheless, he is very important for this theology for four reasons:

1. Theologians such as Duns ⇒Scotus, ⇒Bonaventure, and ⇒Antony of Padua took him as their spiritual patron.
2. He inspires contemporary theologians who are defenders of the natural environment with his example and his poem "Brother Son, Sister Moon."
3. He was the first missionary among the Muslims who wished to win them by means of the word and not by a crusade.
4. He was a great defender of the preferential option for the poor, and he therefore links liberation theology with that of the ancients.

Finally, since his followers evangelized in Latin America in the sixteenth century, his spirituality forms the foundation of much of what is considered the popular religion of the continent. And since popular religion is now recognized as a necessary *locus theologicus*, F. can be considered a forerunner of the theology that is based on it.

———

KD

Francis Xavier (1506–15). Jesuit missionary in Asia who was born in Navarre, Spain. He studied in the same institution where Ignatius of ⇒Loyola was a student. This circumstance led to his conversion in 1533. By 1541, already ordained to the priesthood and a member of the Company of Jesus, he left for Goa, India. During his missionary activity he worked in Japan and for a brief time on an island on the edge of China, where he died because of physical exhaustion and fragile health.

His missionary work was catechetical, one of religious education and training. In India he worked with children, youth, servants, and the low castes—*paravas* or *bharathas*. Among his catechetical works are *Christian Doctrine* (1542) and *Exposition of the Creed*, both translated into Tamil, Malay, and Japanese. These works not only have a pedagogical purpose, but they were written with the intention of being sung and adapted to the musical and educational styles of the context. He was canonized in 1622, and Pope Pius XI proclaimed him the patron of missions in 1947.

———
CCO

Franck, Sebastian (ca. 1499–ca. 1542).

Printer of books, translator, priest, and German theologian, who was influenced by the ideas of ⇒Zwingli and ⇒Luther, but mainly followed his own intellectual route. He became involved in several controversies. He was persecuted for his ideas and was even expelled from various cities. He wrote more than twenty books, including commentaries on other authors. His chief work was the *Chronicle*. He developed a spiritualist theology with a strong ethical emphasis, which he claimed to have received from God and which he expounded with an almost missionary zeal. However, he never tried to organize a sect.

F. was very critical of institutions, religious as well as civil, and he was opposed to orthodoxies, in defense of the freedom of the internal spiritual word, which he understood as a manifestation of the living word of God that dwells in humans. For F., something of divinity exists in the essence of the human being. Historical experience points out the works of God in the past as well as the possibilities of the future, while the Holy Spirit shows us the working of God in the present.

Some scholars think that F. lived ahead of his time, since his ideas would find greater acceptance years after his death.

———
NRG

Francke, August Hermann (1663–1727).

German Lutheran minister, professor, and proponent of pietism. He was born in Lübeck and studied philosophy and theology in the universities of Erfurt, Kiel, and Leipzig. He also studied Hebrew, with great success, in Hamburg. In 1685, together with Paul Anton, he established a special program for the study of the Bible and practical exegesis. This program aroused great interest among the students, but the faculty of theology raised objections and forced him to resign. In 1687–88 he continued his studies of exegesis in Lüenberg, where he had a spiritual experience that led him to consecrate his work and academic life to the glory of God. In 1689 he returned to Leipzig, where he gave exegetical talks on the Pauline epistles. These talks were very well received by the community and created great enthusiasm for the study of the Bible. But opposition groups condemned him for being a pietist, and in 1690 he was forbidden to give his speeches at the university. In the face of this opposition, he accepted a pastoral charge in Erfurt, where his sermons attracted a great number of people, among them many Roman Catholics. His presence did not go unnoticed, and the elector of Mentz, who had Erfurt under his jurisdiction, ordered him to abandon the city within twenty-four hours. This rejection led him to the recently founded University of Halle, where he was named professor of Oriental languages and later of theology. At the same time he accepted the pastorate of Glaucha, a suburb of Halle. He devoted himself to helping and teaching orphaned children and to performing other works of charity, assisted by colleagues and members of the church. At the same time, with his own salary and with the help of others, he set out to construct an orphanage. He was able to do so thanks to generous donations from friends and colleagues who admired him for his testimony, his dedication to serving others, and his faithfulness to the Bible. In addition to the orphanage, F. was instrumental in fund-raising for many other institutions. Among the most important of these are the Normal School for the preparation of teachers and the School of Theology, designed to prepare for the ministry students with scarce financial resources. These institutions had so much success that by 1714 there were 1,775 students and 108 teachers.

F. is recognized for his ministerial and academic labor, for his desire to return to the Bible, and for his interest in cultivating the Christian life, which should be a life of love and service to the neighbor. Given that in his theological positions he came very close to ⇒Spener, it can be said that the main work of F. consisted in giving practical and institutional form to the theological positions of Spener. He died in Halle.

———
HMT

Frankena, William K. (1908–94).

Moralist philosopher who sought to express the close relationship among ethics, education, religion, and psychology. In his attempt to determine the concept of "the good," F. established a clear difference between being good for some purpose in life ("instrumental value"), being good in some skill or ability ("technical value"), being good as part of the whole ("contributing value"), and being good in a total sense ("final value"). His principal work is *Analytical Ethics* (1963).

Fraternidad Teológica Latinoamericana (FTL).

At the First Latin American Evangelism Congress in Bogotá, Colombia, in 1969 (CLADE I), the FTL was organized to reflect, from an evangelical perspective, on the theologies of mission and evangelism in Latin America and the Caribbean. At the beginning, the FTL developed as a place for strategic missional reflection. But by the time the Second Evangelism Congress (CLADE II) met in Lima, Peru (1979), the FTL became a voice that was critical of liberation theologies in Latin America.

FTL does not completely discard the contributions of the liberation theologies but reflects on their implications for evangelical theologies and praxis. During the 1980s, the FTL had moments of tension in its struggle to integrate an evangelical vision of mission with liberation themes.

In later decades, particularly after the fall of the Soviet bloc, the FTL took a new theological and missional turn, focusing on issues such as: (1) gospel and cultures of Latin America; (2) the contextualization of the gospel; (3) social justice in relation to evangelism; (4) the new missional agents (women, children, youth); and (5) the encounter between religions.

———
CCO

Fredegisus of Tours (9th century).

Abbot of St. Martin of Tours, disciple of ⇒Alcuin in York, and later chancellor of Louis the Pious. When ⇒Agobard of Lyon declared that the Scriptures contained grammatical and rhetorical defects, F. accused him of blasphemy against the Holy Spirit, arguing that such apparent errors pointed to deep mysteries, since the Spirit had put the exact words on the lips and in the pens of the sacred authors.

———
JLG

Freire, Paulo (1921–97).

One of the most important educators (secular and religious) of the last century; a native of Recife, Brazil. His most influential book, *The Pedagogy of the Oppressed*, illustrates his marked interest in a pedagogy for persons who live in poverty and marginality. Terms such as "praxis," "conscientization," and the descriptions of forms and practices of education as "banking," "liberating," and "dialogical" are some of his contributions to educational understanding.

F. cultivated the theme of politics in education. He affirmed the nonneutrality of Christians vis-à-vis social concerns and the centrality of the religious dimension in the analysis of reality. In order to understand F. and to evaluate his contribution, it is necessary to study his analysis of the role that ideology plays in the educational process and the function of education in the transformation of society.

———
CJP

Freud, Sigmund (1856–1939).

The founder of psychoanalysis. He was born in Freiberg, Moravia, in a Jewish home. His father had been widowed and entered a second marriage with a younger woman. Sigmund was the first son of this union, the "spoiled child" of his mother. When he was five, the family moved to Vienna, Austria, where F. lived and worked most of his life. He was displaced by the Nazis to England, where he died in 1939.

F.'s life has been expounded in biographical notes by Ernest Jones in three volumes. Space does not permit the presentation of all of the works published by F., beginning with *Interpretation of Dreams* in 1900 and ending with *An Outline of Psycho-Analysis* in 1940 (posthumously). His translated works form a collection of twenty-four volumes.

Influenced by the currents of thought coming from Newton, ⇒Darwin, and Goethe, he studied medicine and devoted himself to scientific research. He studied with Charcot in France, where he was exposed to the phenomenon of hysteria and its treatment by hypnotism. After a residency in Berlin, where he studied neurology, F. returned to Vienna and practiced medicine as a neurologist, with the assistance of another mentor, Breuer. Today his specialty could be defined as the practice of neuropsychiatry.

He began his own process of self-analysis in 1897, through which he deduced his concepts of personality and psychotherapy. He postulated notions based on the dualism between the body (*soma*) and the mind (*psyche*), with emphasis on intrapsychic "depth." He divided the properties of the mind into three regions: conscious, preconscious, and subconscious. To these concepts he added the dynamic constructs of the id (primitive aspect of disordered desires, with an unrefined irrational tinge), the ego (rational executive aspect), and the superego (ideal, moral, or judging aspect).

F. held that the motivating force of conduct and dynamic interaction between the id, the ego, and the superego was provided by the sexual or libidinal energy derived from the id. The result of his ideas became a dynamic topographical model that was characterized by intrapsychic conflicts and the resulting anxiety. Repressed desires and the anxiety generated by the internal conflict were, in his theory, the factors responsible for mental illnesses. Neurotic disturbances and physical symptoms were the result of the transformations of the psychic to the somatic and conductive. As a defense mechanism against anxiety, repression occupied the fundamental place, with other added defenses, such as negation, rationalization, intellectualization, and sublimation, among others. Discernment, perspicacity, and elucidation of the subconscious reality became the avenue of liberation, utilizing psychoanalysis for this end.

F. described human development in psychosexual stages (oral, anal, genital), emphasizing the possibility of regression and fixation as factors that interfere in the formation of the normal personality. He paid attention to the oedipal complex (the conflict with the father to obtain the mother for oneself) in the genital stage, alluding to the possible later consequences due to its adequate or inadequate resolution.

F.'s ideas were the seedbed of theories of personality and therapy that others continued to elaborate, refine, attack, or replace. The influence that F. has had on society and history over and beyond psychology and psychiatry has affected the humanities and the social sciences in general, including theological interpretations.

—
PP

Froland of Senlis (11th century).

Bishop of that city beginning in 1043, and possibly until 1074. All that remains of his work is an *Epistle to* ⇒*Berengar*. In it he expresses affection and esteem toward Berengar, above all for his piety. But at the same time he does not appear to be interested in the eucharistic teaching of Berengar. Perhaps this is because he accepted the ideas of Berengar, or perhaps he really was not acquainted with them.

—
JLG

Fulbert of Chartres (ca. 960–1028).

First a physician and then bishop of Chartres. He was a very influential person who maintained contact with the kings of France, Denmark, and Hungary, in addition to several prominent persons of the nobility and the clergy. Besides being a physician, pastor, and statesman, he was a poet, and he also supervised the reconstruction of the Chartres cathedral after a fire in 1020. Regarding the controverted question of the universals, he was a realist, maintaining that beyond particular objects that the senses perceive, there are intellectual essences and spiritual realities. The first are known through reason and the second through faith. This realism, in addition to the eucharistic debates and other matters, caused him to clash with the most famous of his disciples, ⇒Berengar.

—
JLG

Fulgentius of Ruspe (468–533).

Monk and bishop of North Africa, born when the region was under the power of Byzantium. The invasion of the Vandals, who were mainly Arian (⇒Arius), forced him to abandon the region repeatedly, which led him to Sicily, Sardinia, and Rome. During those exiles he became acquainted with and participated in the controversies surrounding ⇒Augustine's teaching on grace. In defense of the Trinitarian doctrine, he wrote, among several other short works, the treatise *Against the Arians*. Against Nestorianism (⇒Nestorius), he approved and defended the formula proposed by other monks, "one of the three divine persons suffered in the flesh." But he distinguished himself above all as a defender of the Augustinian teaching on grace.

In his treatise *On the Truth of Predestination and Divine Grace,* F. proposed what can well be described as a modified Augustinianism. He agreed with Augustine regarding the corruption produced by sin, which pertains to both the body and the soul. He also agreed that sin is inherited on account of the concupiscence that necessarily accompanies the very process of conception. Like Augustine, he insisted on the priority of grace in salvation, rejecting the Semi-Pelagianism of ⇒Faustus of Riez. But he refused to follow Augustine in his more extreme positions on predestination, denying that God predestines to evil or to condemnation. What takes place in that case, rather than predestination, is divine foreknowledge: God destines to evil and perdition those who God knows will choose evil and perdition.

———

JLG

Fung, Raymond W. M. (1940–). A secretary of mission for the Christian Council of Hong Kong. He likewise served as secretary of the Commission on Mission and Evangelism of the ⇒World Council of Churches and of the Christian Institute of Hong Kong. His work and theological reflection make a significant contribution to the history and mission of the church in China.

———

CCO

Gadamer, Hans-Georg (1900–2002). Philosopher whose works have deeply influenced the theory of communication, clarifying the difficulties of the modern conception of understanding. He was professor at the universities of Breslau, Marburg (his native city), and Leipzig, where he became rector. His opposition to and criticism of the modern scientific ideal of interpretation that is absolutely objective and free of prejudices make him one of the principal figures that announce the end of the modern age. His works *Philosophical Hermeneutics* and *Truth and Method* are required reading for those who concern themselves with themes such as biblical hermeneutics. His *Complete Works* were published in German from 1986 to 1991.

———

JLG

Galilea, Segundo (1928–). Chilean Catholic priest and pastoral theologian. D. has devoted the greater part of his ministry in Latin America to the renewal of pastoral work. Through his many publications, and particularly in *Spirituality of Liberation*, G. proposes an integration between liberation theology, pastoral work as liberating praxis, and Christian spirituality. In the last few years he has focused his work on missiology in Latin America.

———

CCO

Garnerius of Rochefort (12th–13th century). Author to whom the work *Against the Amalricians* is attributed. This text is one of the main sources for our knowledge of the doctrines of ⇒Amalric of Bena.

———

JLG

Gaunilo of Marmoutiers (?–1083). Monk of that community, who attempted to respond to the proof of the existence of God that ⇒Anselm offered in his *Proslogion*. Taking Psalm 14 as a starting point, Anselm had tried to show why whoever says there is no God is a fool. His conclusion was that reason itself compels the thought that "the greatest which can be conceived" must exist, because otherwise it would not be so great as what does exist. In his book *In Defense of the Fool*, G. argued that the most perfect island which can be conceived does not for that reason have to exist. Anselm answered him, insisting on his argument and asserting that, although what G. says is true of imperfect beings (even a perfect island has imperfections, and is not the perfect being), in the case of the absolutely perfect being, its very essence does require its existence.

———

JLG

Gautier of Saint Victor (12th century). One of the last teachers of the school of Saint Victor. He wrote a treatise *Against the Four Labyrinths of France*, namely: ⇒Abelard, ⇒Peter Lombard, ⇒Peter of Poitiers, and ⇒Gilbert de La Porrée.

———

JLG

Gay, Ebenezer (1718–96). Distinguished pastor of the Congregationalist Church of Suffield, Connecticut. He was born in Dedham, Massachusetts. He studied at Harvard University, where he received the Hopkins prize and participated in the graduation ceremony of 1737. He began his career as a preacher in 1740. He received a call to the pastorate of the church in Suffield in 1741 and was ordained the following year.

The content of his sermons was direct. They showed deep piety, moral principles, and disdain for prejudice. His great tolerance for other perspectives led him to establish relations with several prominent political leaders of his time. When he was not on preaching trips to other churches, he would devote himself to visiting his family and supervising the work at his plantation, where he had slaves. He also served as mentor of students who were preparing to study at Yale University.

Many of his sermons are found in *The Work of a Gospel Minister* (1755), *The Sovereignty of God* (1767), and *Evangelical Preacher* (1763). His sermons and diaries are preserved as a rich source of the religious and social thought that was characteristic of the eighteenth century in what was then one of the main cities of New England.

——

JDRR

Geisler, Norman L. (1932–). Apologist, theologian, and ethicist who is known for his contributions, from an evangelical perspective, in the fields of philosophy of religion, contemporary humanism, systematic theology, and comparative religion, and, above all, for his defense of the authority and historicity of the Scriptures.

——

AEM

Gelasius (?–496). Bishop of Rome from 492 until his death. He wrote several brief theological treatises. Most of them refer to the schism of ⇒Acacius of Constantinople and to the Monophysite controversy. In another he attacks the teachings of ⇒Pelagius.

G. was famous above all for the *Gelasian Decree* and the *Gelasian Sacramentary*, both falsely attributed to him. The *Decree* probably dates from the sixth century and apparently was not a product of Rome, but of someone in another part of Italy or in Gaul who wanted to have the right to appeal to the pope above the authority of bishops or other local prelates. The *Sacramentary* is essentially a collection of eucharistic prayers as well as prayers for other occasions. Although it perhaps reflects something of the practice in the times of G., in its actual form it probably dates from the seventh or the eighth century.

——

JLG

Gennadius of Marseilles (?–ca. 494). Author who sought to bring the *De viris illustribus* of ⇒Jerome up to date by adding ninety-one chapters to it. Many of his works have been lost, and we know of their existence because an anonymous author added a last chapter to G.'s version of *De viris illustribus* in which something is said of his literary work.

G. participated in the controversies that immediately followed the death of ⇒Augustine. He opposed the Augustinian doctrine of grace, and therefore is counted among the Semi-Pelagians, although all that is known about his stance regarding this is that he supported the positions of ⇒Vincent of Lérins. He also opposed the Augustinian doctrine of the soul as incorporeal, saying that the only incorporeal being is God, who thus can be omnipresent. The soul, like every other creature, has a body, although more subtle than the physical body.

——

JLG

Gennadius of Novgorod (15th century). Russian bishop who, when he did not find a complete Russian translation of all the books of the Old Testament, had twelve of them translated from Latin. While he attempted to reform the church through studies, his own writings are an index of the ignorance of the times.

——

JLG

George of Arabia (of Akula) (7th–8th centuries). Bishop who defended the custom of mixing water with the wine of the Eucharist against the arguments of the Armenians, who insisted on using only wine. He also wrote on the six days of creation and defended the dichotomist position (the human being consists of body and soul) in anthropology, against the trichotomist position (body, soul, and spirit).

——

JLG

George Scholarius ⇒Scholarios, Georgios

Gerard of Abbeville (?–1271). Defender of the vows of poverty and a participant in the controversy that surrounded ⇒William of Saint Amour and the mendicant orders. His chief work is *Against the Adversaries of Christian Perfection*, published in 1268.

——

JLG

Gerardo de Borgo San Donino (13th century). "Spiritual" Franciscan, follower of the eschatological schemes of ⇒Joachim of Fiore. He attacked the Franciscan moderates as well as the secular clergy who, led by ⇒William of Saint Amour, rejected and criticized the vows of voluntary poverty. His chief work is *Introduction to the Eternal Gospel*. As leader of the "spiritual" party, he opposed the reforms or modifications that were taking place in the Franciscan order. For this reason ⇒Bonaventure, at that time general minister of the order, had him shut away in a monastery, where he remained until his death.

—

JLG

Gerbert of Aurillac (?–1003). Pope, under the title of Sylvester II, from 999 until his death. Previously he had studied in Cordova and Seville and was professor in Reims and bishop of Ravenna. His studies in Spain led him to admire and imitate the science of the Arabs, which at that time was much more advanced than that of western Europe. Consequently he practiced and promoted the study of mathematics, the natural sciences, and philosophy. His chief work, *On the Reasonable Use of Reason*, influenced the way in which the question of the universals was posed. His most distinguished disciple might have been ⇒Fulbert of Chartres.

—

JLG

Gerhard, Johann (1582–1637). German Lutheran theologian who was born in Quedlinburg. He studied medicine in Wittenberg, but then, in fulfillment of a vow, he devoted himself to theology. At the age of fifteen he suffered a terrible illness that produced in him a deep depression, during which he thought he was going to die. This experience permanently deepened his piety and increased his understanding of Christian tribulation. His spiritual counselor persuaded him to devote himself to the study of theology. In 1606 he was named superintendent of Heldburg, in 1615 general superintendent of Coburg, and in 1616 professor of theology at the University of Jena, where he acquired such authority that not only the duke of Weimar requested his counsel on matters of state, but foreign princes also consulted him. His opinion was highly valued in colloquies or conferences on religion.

G. became the most influential Lutheran theologian of the seventeenth century. Very early he participated in the movement to renew Aristotelian metaphysics, which influenced the German universities during that century. His work was also a decisive invitation to the Protestant theologians of his time to study the evangelical character of Christianity prior to the Protestant Reformation.

His chief work is *Loci communes theologici* (1610–22). He also wrote *Meditationes sacrae* (1627), his most popular work; *Harmonia evangelistarum* (1626); and *Confessio Catholica et evangelica* (1624).

—

JDR

Gerhart, Emmanuel (1817–1904). Pastor, theologian, and president of several institutions of higher education affiliated with the German Reformed Church in the United States. He was born in Freeburg, Pennsylvania. He was president of Heidelberg College in Ohio (1851–55), and of Franklin and Marshall College (1855–66) and the theological seminaries in Mercersburg and Lancaster (1868–1904), all in Pennsylvania.

His academic work had a strong effect on the development of the German Reformed Church. His most important work was published under the title *Institutes of the Christian Religion* (1894).

—

JDRR

Gerhoch of Reichersberg (12th century). Opponent of the *Sentences* of ⇒Peter Lombard, which he wanted to have condemned, without any success, by the Third Ecumenical ⇒Lateran Council (1179).

—

JLG

Gerkin, Charles Vincent (1922–2004). North American chaplain, pastor, and clinical pastoral theologian. He followed the clinical-pastoral orientation of Anton ⇒Boisen, his teacher. G. attempted to recover the centrality of the significance of religious experience as the focus of pastoral action. Toward that end, and based on his own experience of crisis, he developed a theology of providence based on a hermeneutic that is in tension with the Freudian psychodynamic theory and the Rogerian client-centered theory. His principal books are *Crisis Experience in Modern Life* (1979) and *The Living Human Document* (1984).

—

JR

Germanus of Constantinople (ca. 635–733). Patriarch of Constantinople beginning in 715. In 725, when Emperor Leo the Isaurian promulgated his first iconoclastic decree, G., who earlier had shown himself obedient to the wishes of another emperor to restore Monothelitism (⇒Sergius of Constantinople), now tenaciously opposed the imperial edict and wrote in favor of the use of images in the church. Of his many writings in defense of images, only three letters escaped the destruction that was ordered by the emperor, who deposed him in 729. Even after his death he was declared a heretic by the iconoclastic council of 753. But in 787 the Seventh Ecumenical Council (Second of ⇒Nicaea) restored his memory.

G. defended the use of images by establishing the distinction between true worship, or *latreia*, and the sign of respect and veneration that is known as *douleia*. While the first belongs only to God, so that whoever renders it to any creature falls into idolatry, the second is owed to the saints and their images as a sign of respect and veneration.

JLG

Germinius (4th century).

Bishop of Sirmium, in the region of Illyria. Together with ⇒Ursacius and ⇒Valens, they are known as the Illyric trio. They were Arians (⇒Arius), although of the Homoean party. They preferred not to speak of the *homoousios* nor of the *homoiousios*—of the same and of similar substance, respectively—but rather to say that the Son is "similar"—*homoios*—to the Father. Sometimes they are called political Arians because of the ambiguity of such a posture. The steps taken by this trio led to the "Blasphemy of Sirmium," when a synod that met in that city prohibited the use of the terms *homoousios* and *homoiousios*, declaring that "nobody can doubt that the Father is greater than the Son in honor, dignity, splendor, majesty, and in the name itself of Father . . . and that the Son is subordinate to the Father."

JLG

Gerson, Jean (1363–1429).

Chancellor of the University of Paris who was born in Champagne and died in Lyon. He became a teacher of theology at the University of Navarre. In 1395 he replaced Pierre d' ⇒Ailly as chancellor of the University of Paris, a title he retained until his death, even though as a result of the Council of ⇒Constance (1414–18) he could not return to Paris. Following the tradition of the humanists, he was one of the most distinguished authors in the French language. He was a renowned theologian, a spiritual writer, a tireless champion for the peace of the church, and a poet when the muses inspired him.

It was his fate to live in the midst of the Western Schism, and thus he labored in favor of the unity of the church. He opposed the use of violence and favored the resignation of all who laid claims to the papacy in order to come to an agreement in these conflicts. He upheld the thesis that the council was superior to the pope. This he based on his nominalist posture regarding universals, which implies that the essence of the church does not rest in its hierarchy but rather in its members. He expressed himself very frankly on the limits of papal power.

G. believed that theological studies should serve spiritual and pastoral interests. His personal life was always in harmony with his teachings.

JDRR

Gezo of Tortona (10th century).

Abbot who, inspired by the treatise of ⇒Paschasius Radbertus on the Eucharist, wrote a *Treatise on the Body and the Blood of the Lord*. It is a work without originality, limited to repeating what others said, and which accepts and marvels at any rumor about eucharistic miracles that circulated at the time.

JLG

Gilbert de La Porrée (12th century).

Philosopher and teacher at the school of Chartres, defender of "dialectics," that is, the use of reason in theology. His philosophical position was either very subtle or very obscure, since his contemporaries understood it in different ways, and the same is true today among scholars of medieval philosophy. There does not seem to be any doubt that he established a pronounced difference between the essence that is common to a class and the presence of that essence in the individuals of that class. This brought him difficulties because of the way in which he appeared to apply it to the Trinitarian doctrine in his *Commentary on the Book of Boethius on the Trinity*. There he distinguished between the essence and the attributes of God, or, in other words, between "God" and God's "divinity." While God is eternal, God's attributes are not.

Accused of denying either the absolute simplicity or the eternity of God, he was condemned by a synod that met in Reims in 1148 under the direction of ⇒Bernard of Clairvaux. Although four propositions that were attributed to G. (and which he appeared to be willing to abandon) were condemned there, it appears that he was rejected because his theories, which were extremely subtle and obscure, seemed to be an affront to the common faith. It was partly to refute G. that ⇒Richard of St. Victor wrote a treatise *On the Trinity* in which he proposes that the Trinity ought to be understood within the context of love, which requires communication and therefore a plurality of persons.

——

JLG

Giles of Lessines (13th century).

Dominican, perhaps a disciple of ⇒Thomas Aquinas. He wrote a treatise, *On Usury*, which is sometimes attributed to Thomas. He also composed a sort of chronological concordance, *De temporibus*.

——

JLG

Giles of Rome (1246?–1316).

Famous disciple of ⇒Thomas Aquinas and an Augustinian. Beginning in 1292 he was the superior of that order and later the archbishop of Bourges, in France. It is said that he commented on the entire canon of Scripture, although only some of his commentaries are currently known. He also wrote works on dialectics and rhetoric. His defense of Thomas's Aristotelian synthesis led the archbishop of Paris, Stephen ⇒Tempier, to censure him officially and to prevent him from receiving the doctorate from the University of Paris. He then left for Italy, and it was not until years later, after the death of Tempier and through the intervention of Honorius IV, that he finally received his doctorate. His fame was such that all Augustinian teachers were ordered to submit in everything to his teachings.

——

JLG

Giles of Viterbus (ca. 1465–1532).

Conciliarist Augustinian theologian, named cardinal by Leo X, who sent him as ambassador to the court of Charles V, with the order to proclaim a new crusade against the Turks. He preached at the opening of the Lateran Council of 1512 (⇒Councils), proclaiming the need to reform the church and the hope that God would do so through the council. E. was also a poet, both in Italian and in Latin.

——

JLG

Gilkey, Langdon (1919–2004).

North American theologian. He studied at Harvard, Columbia, and Union Theological Seminary in New York, where he had the opportunity to study with Paul ⇒Tillich and Reinhold ⇒Niebuhr. He taught at Vanderbilt University and at the Divinity School of the University of Chicago. His main interest was in using the method of correlation developed by Tillich in order to relate science and religion. He also sought a correlation between philosophy and mythology.

——

LGP

Gilson, Étienne (1884–1978).

French philosopher, historian, and prominent interpreter of medieval thought. He founded the Institute of Medieval Studies in Toronto in 1929. His interest in medieval thought began while he was a student at the Sorbonne, where he studied the medieval roots of the thought of René ⇒Descartes. Thus he saw that there is a link between modern and medieval thought. His favorite theologian was ⇒Thomas Aquinas, from whom G. learned about "Christian philosophy," that is, the harmony between reason and revelation, and how faith guides the philosophical quest for truth. The indispensable books of G. are *The Christian Philosophy of Saint Thomas Aquinas* (1919) and *The Philosophy of the Middle Ages* (1955).

——

EZ

Girard, René (1923–).

Philosopher, literary critic, and Christian apologist. Although he was born in France, he spent most of his academic career in the United States, at Stanford University. G. points out that human desire is mimetic; that is, it is founded and grows by imitating the desire of others. This mimetism gives new value to what is desired and therefore produces an envy that is more refined and generalized. The rivalry that is born of it grows very rapidly and finally leads to violence and the need to blame someone for the evil that society suffers. What is sought then is someone to blame, a scapegoat, and it is punished in the name of all. This is so universally human that it is found in the fundamental myths and in the literature of all civilizations. What makes Christianity unique and at the same time of universal value is that it recognizes the need for such an expiatory personage. For Christianity this is Jesus Christ, someone without guilt. This breaks the cycle of violence, and it is therefore the answer to the deepest human needs.

The impact of G. has been enormous and the debate on his philosophy constant. Thus there are groups of his followers who declare themselves Christians because of his work, while others say that his arguments are fallacious, and still others declare that the true result of his work is not to shore up, but to undermine, the authority of the gospel.

———

JLG

Gnostics. The term "gnostic" comes from the Greek *gnosis,* which literally means "knowledge." This knowledge or gnosis nevertheless is not an intellectual knowledge but a mythical one mediated through a revelation from a heavenly agent. It is knowledge that reveals the means to salvation. Gnosticism manifested itself in different currents within Hellenism, apocalyptic Judaism, and gnostic Christian groups. Gnosticism is related to the idea of a special knowledge as the key to salvation. This was held by a group of Christians at the end of the second century and early in the third. The movement survived as a sector of Christianity, even though it was banned and persecuted, until the fifth or sixth century. The Mandaeans from the Iran and Iraq of our times are theological descendants of Gnosticism.

The primary sources for reconstructing the history and ideas of Gnosticism were traditionally the church fathers who wrote against the gnostics. One of the chief of those sources is a treatise by ⇒Irenaeus titled *Against the Heresies.* ⇒Tertullian, ⇒Hippolytus, ⇒Clement of Alexandria, and ⇒Eusebius of Caesarea also bequeathed us information on theological conflicts with groups that were related to Gnosticism. In 1945 an entire library of gnostic documents was discovered in Nag Hammadi, Egypt. Together with the texts of the fathers of the church, they are the basic sources for a reconstruction of gnostic thought.

Gnosticism is an alternative theological system in which it is understood that salvation is achieved through a special revealed knowledge that helps the initiated to escape from the prison of the human body and from the earthly cosmos in order to become united to spiritual reality.

Gnosticism had a particular understanding of the human and cosmic dilemma. The experience of human suffering, death, sickness, war, oppression, and other calamities was the sociological context for the origin of Gnosticism.

The gnostics explained suffering and human and cosmic privation through their account of creation. They believed that the world had been created by an inferior and evil god or demiurge. Some held that this demiurge was the son of one of the spiritual powers that the Supreme God had created: Wisdom. Wisdom gave birth to a defective god who in turn created this evil world. Some Christian gnostics were of the opinion that the God of the Old Testament was that demiurge creator.

On the other hand, the human being who was created by the demiurge had in its being a divine spark trapped in the body and in the earthly prison. This divine spark was asleep and forgotten in the prison of the human body made by the demiurge and in the evil world. In order to save this divine spark, it was necessary to articulate a process that would allow its return to a heavenly region. This salvific knowledge could be revealed only by a messenger from the heavenly world. A spiritual messenger had to come to the world to awaken the dormant spirits within the human body. The task of this messenger consisted in giving secret knowledge that would open the way of human beings to the heavenly fullness.

Concerning the practical life of the gnostics, they developed an ethic of rejection of the world and of the human body and an entire system of symbols and rituals that emphasized this salvific knowledge. The rituals and details about the spirituality of the gnostics show that they gave great importance to the Spirit and to charismatic experiences.

Gnostic Christians had an understanding of women that was much more egalitarian than the orthodoxy that was becoming predominant and which may be seen in the Pastoral Letters. Some gnostic literature has a heavenly feminine figure in the divinity called the Mother, which is parallel to the orthodox figure of the Father.

Christian Gnosticism had a different idea of the human being, the cosmos, salvation, and the sacraments from that of orthodox Christianity. It was a Christianity that regarded creation with a great deal of pessimism and hoped for a salvation beyond the world, the body, society, and human life. Salvation consisted in a mythical knowledge that would liberate the human being from its body and from the evil world and would guide it in the cosmic journey to reunification with the divine fullness. The gnostic savior was not really a human being but a divine figure in human appearance who granted knowledge for the cosmic liberation of the human being. In this sense, Gnosticism was pessimistic insofar as the possibility of transforming the world, enjoying the human body, and seeing the divine goodness in the creation.

———

ELR

Godfrey of Fontaines (?–ca. 1306).
Teacher who refused to accept the condemnation of Thomism by the ecclesiastical authorities. Nonetheless he criticized ⇒Thomas Aquinas on several points. He insisted on the priority of reason over the will, which later brought him criticism from the Franciscans.

—

JLG

Godfrey of St. Victor (12th century).
One of the last teachers of that famous school. In contrast to his predecessors, he tended to emphasize the importance of piety above reason, and therefore to break the equilibrium that until then characterized the school of St. Victor.

—

JLG

Godfrey of Vendôme (12th century).
Defender of the power of the pope in view of the need to reform the church. The investiture of ecclesiastical authorities by the temporal power is a heresy, although it is true that in the case of prelacies that include properties, there is room for a certain form of lay investiture. In any case, such lay investiture will never be with the staff and the ring, which belong only to the spiritual authorities.

—

JLG

Gogarten, Friedrich (1887–1968).
German theologian who taught theology at the University of Jena from 1927 until 1933, when he began to teach at the University of Göttingen. He adopted the anti-idealism of Søren ⇒Kierkegaard. His academic work was in dialogue with Karl ⇒Barth and Rudolph ⇒Bultmann. Using the dialectical theology of Barth, he formulated an interpretation of culture and history from a Lutheran perspective. In this period he developed his anthropology of the dependence of the individual on God, which was one of the basic presuppositions of the authoritarianism of the German Christians who supported German fascism in the 1930s. In his books *Politische Ethik* (1932) and *Der Mensch zwischen Gott und Welt* (1952), he tackles the problem of the relationship between the state and religion. In his main book, *Entmythologisierung und die Kirche* (1953; trans. Demythologization and the Church, 1955), he examines and expands the demythologizing project of Bultmann in order to remove the mythical elements from the New Testament as part of the project of hermeneutical secularization.

—

ELR

Goizueta, Roberto (1954–).
Roman Catholic theologian born in Havana, Cuba, who has lived in the United States since childhood. He received his master's and doctor's degrees in theology from Marquette University, the first in 1982 and the second in 1984. He has been professor at the universities of Southern Loyola, Emory, Loyola in Chicago, and Boston College. A lay theologian, he is a founding member of the Academy of Hispanic Catholic Theologians (ACHTUS). His first book was *Liberation, Method, and Dialogue: Enrique ⇒Dussel and North American Theological Discourse* (1988). This book marks the standard for his following works, for in it he appears willing to unite and weave together different theological currents. Since then he has published several articles, three other books, two collections of essays by different authors, and above all the book *Caminemos con Jesús: Toward a Hispanic/Latino Theology of Accompaniment* (1995). Among the Hispanic theologians in the United States, G. appears to be the most interested in methodological matters. He confronts the dominant theological paradigms in order to criticize and correct them. In that way he explores the liberating context where theology from a Latino perspective is produced. This includes the role of aesthetics in theological method and the challenges that Hispanics pose to North Atlantic theology. He has also served as president of the Catholic Theological Society of America.

—

EF

Gollwitzer, Helmut (1908–93).
German Lutheran theologian, a graduate of the University of Basel (1937). During the Second World War, he actively participated in the movement of Christian resistance against the Nazi government. He was arrested several times and prevented from teaching in state universities. Toward the end of the war, he was forced to enlist in the Nazi army. In 1945 he was imprisoned by the Soviet army, and he spent years as a prisoner of war in the Soviet Union. In 1950 he became a professor of systematic theology at the University of Bonn. His experiences in the Confessing Church and in concentration camps convinced him of the need to preach the implications of the kingdom of

God for the current political and economic life. This explains why he became passionately involved in the political conflicts that followed the Second World War in Germany.

— PAJ

Gomarus, Franciscus (1563–1641). Calvinist theologian and professor at the University of Leiden. He took a supralapsarian position, believing that God had predestined some to salvation and others to perdition before allowing or decreeing the fall of humanity into sin. He stood out because of his strict interpretation of Calvinism in opposition to ⇒Arminius and the Arminian movement.

— LGP

González, Domingo (12th century). Also known as Gundissalinus or Gundisalvo. One of the first translators who, in Toledo and under the inspiration of Archbishop Raymond, translated the classical works of antiquity from Arabic into Latin. He also wrote several of his own works in which, while demonstrating the impact of ⇒Aristotle and of different Arab philosophers, he also showed the Neoplatonic influence that dominated all philosophy of that time. His writings are *On the Origin of the World*, *On the Immortality of the Soul*, and *On Unity*. They deal with several of the issues that in the following century would be debated in the University of Paris in the face of the sudden appearance of the translations of Toledo and their many sequels.

— JLG

González, Justo Luis (1937–). Born in Cuba and subsequently naturalized in the United States. Eminent and prolific church historian and theologian; ordained Methodist minister. He has been a professor and lecturer in seminaries and universities in the Americas. His contribution is chiefly in four contexts: the academy, the church, the theological education of Latinos/Hispanics in the United States, and ecumenical organizations at the national and international levels.

His multiple books and articles make contributions in the following areas: the history of the church, missions, and theology; systematic theology; biblical commentaries, preaching and Hispanic hermeneutics; and materials for the educational and liturgical use of the churches. Among his most disseminated works, which have been translated into several languages, are *History of Christian Thought* (3 vols.), *The Story of Christianity*, *Christian Thought Revisited: Three Types of Theology*, and *Mañana: Christian Theology from a Hispanic Perspective*.

G. has contributed significantly to the development of Hispanic/Latino theological education through his writings and organizational initiatives. He has been the organizer and/or director of the theological journal *Apuntes*; the Association for Hispanic Theological Education (AETH); a program of scholarships, Hispanic Theological Initiative (HTI); and the Hispanic Summer Program, sponsored by more than forty institutions of theological education at the graduate level in the United States.

The academic and organizational work and mentorship of G. has inspired and contributed to the formation of several generations of Hispanic women and men who exercise Protestant, Catholic, and Pentecostal theological and ministerial leadership. He is recognized by these and other publics as one of the fathers of Latino theology in its academic, pastoral, and ecumenical dimensions.

— LRR

Goodspeed, Edgar Johnson (1871–1962). One of the most prominent North American scholars of the first half of the twentieth century, he specialized in the study of the New Testament and served as professor at the University of Chicago for thirty-five years. He was a member of the editorial committee for the Revised Standard Version of the Bible in English (1952).

— AEM

Gordon, George Angier (1853–1929). Born in Oyne, Scotland. Emigrated to the United States at the age of eighteen. Congregationalist author, pastor, and theologian. He combated the orthodox Calvinist doctrines of arbitrary election, limited atonement, and the total depravity of the human race.

— EPA

Gore, Charles (1853–1932). Born in Wimbledon, England. Prolific author, social activist, and Anglican theologian. A graduate of Oxford University. Pastor of Westminster Cathedral; chaplain of the royal family; bishop of Worcester, Birmingham, and Oxford. He founded the Christian Social Union (1889), was a member of the Workers' Educational Association, and created the Order of the Community of the Resurrection (1893). He was editor of the series *Lux Mundi* (1889), whose purpose was to relate the traditional faith of the church to modern issues, both intellectual and moral. He embraced social justice, struggled with the economic implications of the Christian faith, and promoted the ecumenical movement, as is evident in his *Christ and Society* (1928). He also traveled to Calcutta to promote missions in India.

EPA

Gospels, Apocryphal.

Gospels, Apocryphal. Name that is applied to several literary versions of the words and deeds of Jesus outside the canon of the New Testament. The Gospels of Matthew, Mark, Luke, and John gather what their authors considered to be vital for the faith of the first Christians, but at the same time draw a general picture of the person of Jesus. This situation motivated various religious groups to create and develop traditions about Jesus, for the purpose of filling lacunae and completing or expanding apparently inconclusive accounts in the Gospels. Some could see in this an opportunity to insert, defend, and promote new religious concepts, using Jesus for their own ends.

The term "apocryphal" comes from the Greek *apokryphon*, which translated literally means "occult" or "hidden," and by extension is applied to what is spurious or of doubtful value. As the church was closing the canon of the New Testament, it linked the word "apocrypha" with the word "gospels" to point out those writings which, in spite of speaking about Jesus, were considered not inspired by God and lacking authority in matters of faith and praxis.

Some apocryphal Gospels contain elements that belong to the Gnosticism of the period after the New Testament (⇒gnostics) and express the popular piety of a great number of persons at the margin of the institutional church of that period (that is, the so-called heretics). Generally these documents are legendary and not at all reliable from a historiographic point of view. Many of them were written in the name of the apostles (that is, they are pseudepigrapha) in an age when the lines of division between orthodoxy and heterodoxy were not clearly defined, and therefore contradictory points of view were circulating in the churches.

From a literary perspective, the material that can be designated as apocryphal Gospels is not homogeneous; there is a relative variety of genres under this heading. Having made this qualification, one can say that the *Gospel of Thomas* heads the list because of its close affinity with the canonical Gospels, and also because of the insertion of other sayings of Jesus that could well be original. To this are added the Gospels of Peter, Philip, James, Bartholomew, Andrew, Thaddaeus, Barnabas, Matthias, Nicodemus, Judas Iscariot, Cerinthus, Basilides, Valentinus, Apelles, and Eve. We also have the Gospels of the Hebrews, of the Egyptians, of the Ebionites, the *Arabic Gospel of the Infancy of Jesus,* and the Arab story of Joseph the carpenter.

The apocryphal Gospels constitute a valuable source of information for the study of the history, literature, religion, and culture of Christianity. They give testimony to the powerful influence that Jesus had in a sector of antiquity and to the different interpretations that were placed on his words and deeds. Seen as a whole, the apocryphal Gospels allow us to have broader knowledge of the diversity of thought that prevailed in the churches, as well as about the internal struggles of these churches to define their religious identity.

AEM

Gottschalk of Orbais (9th century).

Gottschalk of Orbais (9th century). Also known as Gottescalc. Monk of aristocratic origin who devoted himself to studying ⇒Augustine, ⇒Prosper of Aquitaine, ⇒Fulgentius of Ruspe, and others. On the basis of those studies, he came to the conclusion that predestination is absolutely double, for while God predestines the angels and the elect for salvation, God also predestines the demons and the reprobate to eternal condemnation. On this point, there is no doubt that G. interpreted Augustine correctly and literally. Perhaps the main difference between G. and Augustine is that, while for the saint of Hippo the doctrine of predestination was presented in the context of a hymn of praise to God for the unmerited gift of election, in the monk of Orbais it took a bitter and even morbid turn, as when G. rejoiced because he was convinced that his adversary ⇒Hincmar was among the reprobate.

The one who first raised the standard against G. was his old abbot in Fulda, ⇒Rabanus Maurus, who published against him a treatise *On Foreknowledge, Predestination, and Free Will.* A series of actions followed this, with the result that G. was arrested by Hincmar, archbishop of Reims, who had him beaten until he threw his works into the fire. Afterward he was imprisoned in a monastery for the rest of his days.

The controversies that G. stirred up extended further, provoking writings by John Scotus ⇒Erigena, ⇒Prudentius of Troyes, ⇒Servatus Lupus, ⇒Ratramnus of Corbie, ⇒Florus of Lyon, and several others.

———
JLG

Grabau, Johannes Andreas A. (1804–79).
Pastor from Magdeburg, Germany, who immigrated to Buffalo, New York, and founded the Lutheran Synod of Buffalo. Like ⇒Loehe, he believed that the authority in the church is given to the episcopate, which has the sole right to ordain to the ministry. His episcopal vision continues to be shared by some members of the Lutheran clergy in the United States, especially in the Evangelical Lutheran Church in America, but also among other Lutherans. This was a major point of theological controversy with other Lutherans, especially C. F. W. ⇒Walther.

———
ALG

Graham, William "Billy" Franklin (1918–).
International evangelist from the United States and founder of the Billy Graham Evangelistic Association. G. has been instrumental in the origin and development of the ⇒Lausanne Movement and other evangelical movements that reiterate the centrality of evangelization. G., who is considered one of the best evangelists in the world, has written several books on themes of interest to the general religious public.

———
CCO

Grant, Jacquelyn (1948–).
African American Protestant theologian, leading figure in womanist theology (which should not be confused with feminist theology or with mujerista theology; Ada María ⇒Isasi-Díaz). Her theological work has been developed on the basis of the experience of African American women who suffer from a triple oppression: racism, classism, and sexism. She proposes that if Jesus identifies with the most insignificant people, then he is immersed in the experiences of African American women as a Jesus who takes the form of a black woman. She is the author of *White Women's Christ and Black Women's Jesus: Feminist Christology and Womanist Response*.

———
NLD

Gratian (12th century).
Born in Chiusi, Italy. Camaldulensian monk and father of the science of canon law. Historian and lawyer, professor in the University of Bologna, tutor of the future pope Alexander III. His *Concordantia discordantium canonum*, or Harmony of the Discordant Canons, is an all-embracing work including the ecclesiastical law of more than a millennium. In it he recorded papal declarations and conciliar decrees, and included a group of patristic texts, all of which are related to the different areas of the discipline of the church. Having been influenced by the method of ⇒Peter Lombard, G. analyzed the texts and advanced possible solutions to their apparent discrepancies.

His *Decretals*, as his work is known, were published shortly after the Second ⇒Lateran Council (1139) and consist of approximately 3,800 texts. G. made use of both Roman imperial law and ecclesiastical law. With the passing of the years other texts were added, culminating in the *Codex Iuris Canonici* (1917–18). In 1983 a new edition appeared as a result of changes emanating from ⇒Vatican II.

———
EPA

Graves, James Robinson (1820–93).
Baptist pastor, editor, journalist, and author. Self-taught, he became a schoolteacher and editor of *The Tennessee Baptist* (1848), whose circulation reached 13,000 copies. Champion of Landmarkism, which held that the Baptists constitute the only true church, which is the heir to an uninterrupted succession of true Christians from the New Testament to the present.

———
EPA

Grebel, Conrad (ca. 1498–1526).
Radical Swiss reformer, known as the father of Anabaptism, and originally a follower of ⇒Zwingli. Before the City Council of Zurich, he proposed changes in ecclesiastical practices, such as worship and Communion, that were much more radical than Zwingli's. Like other Reformers, he also insisted on the reform of abuses and excesses within the church of his time, but he did not believe that this was enough, for it was necessary to return to a church such as that described in the New Testament. Insisting that the Bible was the only trustworthy authority above popes and councils, he proposed a church directed by lay leaders, where the baptism of adult believers was practiced. He also envisioned a church free

from the tutelage and protection of the secular state.

———

Green, William Henry (1825–1900).
Born in Groveville, New Jersey. Theologian, author, and Presbyterian pastor. A graduate of Princeton Seminary, where he later was professor of Hebrew and Oriental literature.

———

Gregory I, "the Great" (ca. 540–604).
Bishop of Rome from 590 until his death. Before his ordination he was prefect of the city of Rome, since his family belonged to the nobility. Later he entered the monastic life and the service of the church, which took him to Constantinople as representative of the pope for seven years. Five years after his return, he was elected bishop, succeeding Pope Pelagius II. Prior to being pope, G. promoted Benedictine monasticism (⇒Benedict of Nursia), and he continued that policy with greater energy on becoming pope. He paid great attention to missions, particularly to the Saxons of England, to whom he sent a group of missionaries under the direction of Augustine of Canterbury. In his honor a certain type of medieval chant is called "Gregorian," although he did not invent it, but simply promoted it.

His main work was in administration. Almost nine hundred letters by G. survive, most of which have to do with administrative matters: the organization of the church in Gaul, the transportation of wheat from Sicily to Rome, the management of the funds of the church, and so on. It was chiefly because of all these activities, which made the church of Rome the center of European life, and thus contributed significantly to the Roman primacy, that posterity knows G. as "the Great."

The theological work of G. was less original, but nevertheless quite important. Besides the aforementioned letters and two series of homilies (on Matthew and on Ezekiel), his many works include an *Exposition of the Book of Job*, commonly known as *Moralia*, in thirty-five books; four books of *Dialogues*; a *Pastoral Rule*; and many liturgical pieces attributed to G., but of doubtful authenticity.

G. was a scholar and follower of ⇒Augustine, although he never fully accepted, and apparently never completely understood, Augustine's teaching on grace and predestination. Thus, for example, instead of predestination by the sovereign decision of God, G. asserts that God predestines the elect as an act of divine foreknowledge. He also differed from the great teacher of Hippo in that, while Augustine granted a great deal of importance to Neoplatonic philosophy, the interest of G. was chiefly practical and devotional. His works are full of stories of miracles, many of them hardly credible, and some even ridiculous, although they always had the purpose of edifying the faithful. The existence of a purgatory or of a place where the souls of the deceased are purified before entering glory, which Augustine suggests as a possibility, becomes a doctrinal affirmation in G. The Mass as sacrifice, which could be deduced from some texts of Augustine, also becomes a point of doctrine in G., who maintains that such sacrifice includes merits that can be transferred both to the living and to the dead. And he affirms that a certain monk, for whom masses had been said during thirty days, appeared in the presence of his brothers to tell them that thanks to those masses he had been liberated from purgatory.

The veneration of relics and images and their miraculous powers are a repeated theme in the miracles that G. relates. He also writes about angels and demons with such conviction that his readers reached the conclusion that such knowledge came from divine inspiration. (For this reason iconography came to picture him as writing with a dove whispering into his ear, in representation of the Holy Spirit.)

G. also began to systematize what in the end would be the penitential system of the Western church, which requires contrition, confession (although in the time of G. this rarely took place privately), and satisfaction. Upon this follows absolution, conferred by the priest by the same authority that Jesus gave the apostles to bind and loose on earth and in heaven.

For all of these reasons, the importance of G. for medieval theology was enormous, although not so much for its originality, but rather because his medieval readers interpreted Augustine through G., whom they took as the definitive authority in matters such as the categories and activities of angels and demons.

———

Gregory VII (ca. 1020–85).
His original name was Hildebrand. He was raised in a Cluniac monastery where his uncle was the abbot. There he absorbed many of the reformist ideas that came to mark his life. He arrived in Rome with Pope Leo IX in 1049, where he carried out several responsibilities within the curia. These

activities would provide opportunities for him to work for the reformation of the church until he became pope in 1073.

From the time he acceded to the papal throne he was characterized as a hard-line reformist. He attempted to purge the papacy of all political interference by the civil authorities. Such claims and actions were to degenerate into the so-called wars of investitures.

G. had available a body of jurists and theologians who were also reformers, who sought to shore up the supremacy of the church over civil investitures. One of his chief advisers was the Spanish cardinal ⇒Humbert of Silva Candida, who led G. to define the church no longer as the assembly of believers but rather as the totality of the clergy. According to this vision, all of Europe formed the *corpus christianum*, but not all belonged to the church. With such an excluding declaration, G. sought to marginalize the Christian kings who were thirsty for power and anxious to influence the affairs of the church.

G. gave highly significant juridical weight to canon law, by which he justified many of his theological positions. Under G. the official theology of Rome was to become ever more reflective of canon law in its argumentation.

In 1075 G. promulgated his famous *Dictatus Papae*, a papal document of twenty-seven declarations of polemical content, through which the Roman see made its new ecclesiology clear. Some of the affirmations were that only the Roman pontiff is legitimately universal, that it is lawful for him to depose emperors, that his ruling is not to be rejected by anybody, and that only he can reject the ruling of all.

These positions of G. led to direct confrontations with several European kings, especially with Emperor Henry IV of Germany, who, after reacting to the articles of the *Dictatus Papae,* was excommunicated by G. in 1076. These conflicts, which were provoked by the theological positions of G., continued with great virulence for three centuries, until the days of ⇒Boniface VIII.

As part of his attempt to reform the church, of his vision of a church constituted above all by the hierarchy, and of his wish to remove the clergy from the power of civil authorities, G. insisted on ecclesiastical celibacy. Married priests were forced to expel their wives and children, and in many places there were riots in which the people, aroused in their religious fervor and inspired by the papal declarations, attacked married priests and their families.

Because G. was the spark of this great movement of confrontation between the church and the state, and because of his insistence on ecclesiastical celibacy, this entire period is known as that of the Gregorian Reforms. The theology that G. inspired was later counterattacked mainly by theologians and philosophers who were at the service of the kings of Europe, such as ⇒Marsilius of Padua and William of ⇒Ockham, among others.

———

GC

Gregory Acindinus (14th century). A follower of ⇒Barlaam, whose opposition to the Hesychasm of ⇒Palamas he continued. In the end both he and Barlaam were rejected by the Eastern church, which considered Palamas a saint and his opponents heretics.

———

JLG

Gregory of Catinus (12th century). Defender of the authority of temporal power who in his work *Orthodox Defense of the Empire* claimed that the emperor was the head of both the state and the church. Only God can give or remove kingdoms and empires. Because of this, the king ought to invest the bishops with the ring and the staff.

———

JLG

Gregory of Datev (14th century). Defender of the doctrines of the Church of Armenia, and especially of its Monophysitism, against the Roman doctrines, which some Armenians were beginning to accept. In his *Book of Questions* he poses to his adversaries some difficulties in the theological positions they have adopted. Thus, for example, when the Chalcedonians affirm the two natures in Christ, they have to decide whether they should worship his humanity or his divinity. In the first case, they worship "like the Jews," that is, they worship God separately from the incarnation. In the second, they are idolaters.

———

JLG

Gregory of Elvira (?–392). Disciple and defender of ⇒Lucifer of Cagliari. Since the conflict between the Luciferians and the rest of the church was political rather than doctrinal, G. appears to have been orthodox in his doctrine. Such is the case with his chief work, *On the Orthodox Faith against the Arians.*

———

JLG

Gregory of Nazianzus (ca. 330–ca. 390).

Together with ⇒Basil of Caesarea, ⇒Gregory of Nyssa, and ⇒Macrina, one of the "great ⇒Cappadocians" who flourished in the second half of the fourth century and who contributed so much to the final triumph of the Nicene faith (Council of ⇒Nicaea). While the other three were siblings, G. was a friend of Basil since their youth and consequently also knew the other two. After his initial studies in Caesarea of Cappadocia (in what today is Turkey), he went on to study in Caesarea of Palestine, then in Alexandria, and finally in Athens, where his companions were Basil and the future emperor Julian (whom posterity knows as "the apostate").

G. had always wanted to devote himself to study and contemplation, but the pressures of the times and of the friends who solicited his help repeatedly interrupted his studies and his retreats. His own father, who was bishop of Nazianzus, and who sought help in his pastoral tasks when old age drew near, compelled him to be ordained. G. fled and tried to hide, but finally he agreed to his ordination and for some time helped his father in Nazianzus. Basil, who for political reasons needed more bishops who would be faithful to him, had him named bishop of a small village, but G. never took possession of that semifictitious see. Shortly after the death of his father, he attempted to remove himself again for study and contemplation, but the Nicenes in Constantinople sought a leader who could strengthen them in the face of the attacks by the Arians, and thus G. agreed to be made bishop of that city. When the Council of ⇒Constantinople (381) began, G. presided over it as patriarch of Constantinople. But after a few days, weary of the quarrels among the Christians, he resigned the post and returned to Nazianzus, where he directed the life of the church until he was able to get another bishop to succeed him. Then he retired for the last time for study and contemplation, and on this occasion his success was such that the circumstances and exact date of his death are unknown.

Although here he interests us above all as a theologian, it must be pointed out that G. was famous in his time as a poet and orator, to the extent that his contemporaries called him the Christian Demosthenes. Thus, among his most important works are his forty-five *Orations*. Five of them, known as the *Five Theological Orations*, are of special importance. In them, besides refuting the doctrines of the Arians, G. discusses the character and method of theology.

They are one of the oldest and most complete reflections on theological method that survive.

It fell to G.'s lot to live during the second stage of the controversy surrounding Arianism (⇒Arius, ⇒Eusebius of Nicomedia, ⇒Eunomius) and the Nicene doctrine. Since there were many whose chief fear was Sabellianism (⇒Sabellius), that is, the doctrine according to which the Father, Son, and Holy Spirit are only external manifestations or "modes" of God, G. felt the need to assert the distinction of the persons in the Trinity. This distinction could not only be *ad extra*, as if the difference lay in the various functions or activities of God. G. did not wish to assert that God was sometimes Creator and other times Redeemer, so that when carrying out one function God was Father and when God carried out another function God was Son. This was precisely the Sabellianism that the vast majority of his colleagues and contemporaries feared so much. But at the same time he had to avoid falling into a subordinationist position, as if the difference between the three persons lay in the degree of divinity of each one of them. This was the essence and the scandal of Arianism, which ultimately made of the Son a "god" or divine being inferior to the Father.

What G. affirmed in response to such challenges was that the distinctions between the three divine persons are not mere passing modalities nor aspects in which God presents Godself in different circumstances and moments. On the contrary, what distinguishes the three persons of the Trinity is their mutual relation. What makes the Father be Father is not having an origin, for God is the source of God's own being. By contrast, what characterizes the Son is being "begotten." And what characterizes and distinguishes the Spirit is the "proceeding" or, in traditional terms, the Spirit's "procession." G. elaborates on this last point much more than the previous generation, when there were no discussions on the divinity of the Spirit like the ones that arose during the second generation of the debate between the Arians and Nicenes.

The Christology of G. is also important for the history of Christian theology. G., as well as the other Cappadocians, opposed the teaching of ⇒Apollinaris of Laodicea, who claimed that what in Jesus Christ had been united with divinity did not include a human "rational soul," since the mind of Christ was purely divine. G. argued that this makes of Jesus Christ a partially human being, but not completely, since a body without a rational soul is not a human being. In addition, G. began to transfer to the christological debate the vocabulary that until then had been developing in the Trinitarian debate, particularly the term *hypostasis*, on whose clarification he, Basil, and Gregory of Nyssa worked.

———

JLG

Gregory of Neocaesarea (?–ca. 270).

A native of that city in the Pontus, where he was later bishop. His old biographers, one anonymous and the other ⇒Gregory of Nyssa, tell about him a multitude of miracles, and for this reason he is also known as the Thaumaturge or the Wonderworker.

Having been born a pagan, he was converted to Christianity through the teachings of ⇒Origen in Caesarea. After five years of studies with that great teacher, he left to return to Pontus. On the occasion of that farewell, he composed a *Discourse of Gratitude to Origen*. Having returned to Pontus, he was elected bishop of his native city, where he carried out a widespread work of evangelization. Among all his writings, the chief ones are *On the Impassibility and Passibility of God*, a *Paraphrase of Ecclesiastes*, and a creed or *Confession of Faith*. In them he shows himself to be a faithful disciple of Origen, with speculative interests similar to those of his master.

The *Confession of Faith*, which survives because Gregory of Nyssa quotes it in his biography of G., is a testimony to the development of the Trinitarian doctrine in the interval between Origen and ⇒Nicaea. While other Origenists, basing themselves on the transcendence of God, tended to emphasize the distance between the Father and the Son, G. was inclined in the opposite direction. While G. affirms the distinction between the Father and the Son, he makes sure that this distinction would not be such that it would diminish the divinity of the second person of the Trinity. Thus he declares, in words that already point to the Nicene Creed, that the second person is "the Only of the Only, God of God, Image and Likeness of the divinity, efficient Word . . . true Son of the true Father, Invisible of the Invisible, Incorruptible of the Incorruptible, Immortal of the Immortal and Eternal of the Eternal."

———

JLG

Gregory of Nyssa (ca. 335–94).

One of the "great ⇒Cappadocians," brother of ⇒Basil of Caesarea and of ⇒Macrina. His formal education was not as polished as that of Basil or of ⇒Gregory of Nazianzus, the friend of both, but he owed it chiefly to the teachings of Basil and of Macrina (both of whom he called the Teacher). But in spite of this he was the most profound theologian among the Cappadocians. Basil had him named bishop of Nyssa for political reasons, to have more bishops who would support him. Although G. tried to carry out his pastoral responsibilities in Nyssa, in reality those were not his gifts. Later he was bishop of the much more important see of Sebaste in Pontus. He participated in the Council of ⇒Constantinople of 381. He also repeatedly visited the Constantinopolitan court, where he was regarded as wise. He was the orator on the occasion of the funeral of the empress Pulcheria.

His most important theological works were occasioned by the Arian controversy (⇒Arius, Council of ⇒Nicaea), which at that time was at the boiling point. Among them is a series of treatises *Against ⇒Eunomius,* which unfortunately were so mixed and confused in the manuscript tradition that it is difficult to distinguish between them or to place them in chronological order. He also wrote *To Ablabius: There Are Not Three Gods.* In these writings he defends orthodox Trinitarian doctrine over against the Arians, and especially against the extreme Arianism of Eunomius and others called Anomoeans. Basing himself on a radical Platonic realism, G. argued that just as the "human being" (that is, the idea of the human being, which is more real than particular human beings) is one, although it exists concretely as Peter, Paul, and John, in the same way "God" is one, although existing concretely as Father, Son, and Holy Spirit. For this reason some interpreters think that G. practically falls into tritheism. Nevertheless, it must be remembered that according to the Platonic realism that is at the base of his theology, the universal idea is the ultimate reality, and its particular concretions are secondary. Thus G. is not saying that there are three gods, but that there are three whose ultimate reality is in being God. Much more important than this, with regard to the Trinitarian teaching of G., is the way in which he makes the individuality of each of the three persons rest on their relations with each other, and not on their *ad extra* relations with the world or with the history of salvation. The difference between the Father and the Son is that the first is the cause of the second, the source of his being, and not that one is Creator and the other is Redeemer, or that one is immutable and the other is not. Likewise, what characterizes the Holy Spirit is the Spirit's proceeding from the Father through the Son.

G. lived at the dawn of the christological debates that finally led to the councils of ⇒Ephesus and ⇒Chalcedon. The christological doctrine that seems to have concerned him most was that of ⇒Apollinaris of Laodicea, against whom he wrote several treatises in which he insists on the existence of a rational human soul in the person of the Savior. He also refuted the theory of some according to which the flesh of Jesus Christ proceeded directly from heaven and was thus different from ours.

Regarding the future life, G. wrote a dialogue, *On the Soul and the Resurrection*, in which he holds a conversation with his sister Macrina, who is already on her deathbed. In that dialogue Macrina is the teacher and G. is the interlocutor. Therefore it is very possible and even probable that G. was presenting not his own teachings there, but Macrina's.

G. also wrote several exegetical works. In them his exegetical method is similar to that of Origen, and therefore allegorical interpretations abound. But this is not the case with his two writings on creation, *On the Six Days of Creation* (or *On the Hexaemeron*) and *On the Creation of the Human Being*. These two works were written to complete what his brother Basil had written. Given the fact that Basil preferred the literal sense and feared exaggerated allegorical interpretations, G. abstained from allegorisms and followed an exegetical method that was chiefly literal. (The fact that in this case G. made such an attempt to be faithful to the theological position of his brother is an indication that he was probably doing the same in his dialogue with Macrina, and therefore that the dialogue with her expresses the theology of Macrina rather than that of G.)

On the other hand, G. also made a strong impact on the mystical theology of later centuries. According to G., the communion of the human being with God is possible because the human being has been created in the image of God. Just as the eye can see the light because the eye itself is luminous, so also the human being can know God because the human being itself bears the image of God. But this knowledge is not easily attained. In order to be able to ascend toward God, it is necessary first to purify oneself from sin. Such purification or catharsis brings with it a process of struggle against sin and the passions, until one reaches the point of *apatheia,* in which the passions lose their power. It is then that the rise toward

God begins, which makes the human being ever more similar to God in terms of love, justice, and holiness, and which leads to a close communion that is characterized by ecstasy. At this point one is already in heaven, although still living on earth.

The importance of these mystical teachings lies in the impact that they appear to have made on the pseudonymous ⇒Dionysius the Aereopagite, who repeats and summarizes them. Through Dionysius, the mystical teaching of G. made itself felt in the later centuries, including many people who never read his works, but who did read those of Dionysius.

———

JLG

Gregory of Rimini (?–1358).

Teacher and eventually general of the Augustinians, who were divided because G. followed the teachings of William of ⇒Ockham. His enemies, making a word play on his natal surname (Tortoricci), called him *tortor parvulorum* (torturer or executioner of infants), apparently because, on the basis of certain writings of ⇒Augustine, he asserted that unbaptized infants were condemned. Over against such opposition, the pope gave him the title of *Doctor Authenticus*, by which his followers knew him. Centuries later ⇒Luther, who also was Augustinian, thought that among the great medieval teachers only G. had avoided falling into Pelagianism (⇒Pelagius).

———

JLG

Gregory of Sinai (14th century).

Mystic whose methods and teachings precipitated the Hesychast controversy (⇒Palamas). According to G., the best method of reaching ecstasy consisted in being seated, with the chin on the chest, looking at one's navel and constantly repeating "Lord Jesus Christ, have mercy on me." The ecstasy that was reached led the believer to contemplate the same uncreated light that shone on Mount Tabor, that is, Godself. This provoked the opposition of ⇒Barlaam, who caused the controversy to break out.

———

JLG

Groote, Geert de (1340–84).

Dutch educator and priest who after his religious conversion lived in service to the poor and as a reformer and preacher against the corruption and luxury of the clergy in Holland. His major contribution was the formation of centers where impoverished scholars devoted themselves to copying manuscripts, thus founding the Brothers of the Common Life—later approved by Pope Gregory XI. This order was successful in reforming primary and secondary education, first in Holland and Germany and then throughout Europe, with its humanist vision. Among its famous students was the scholar ⇒Erasmus. There was also a women's part of the movement, much devoted to study and to the copying of manuscripts.

———

ALG

Grosseteste, Robert (?–1253). Franciscan professor and later chancellor of Oxford University. A relatively conservative theologian who nevertheless promoted the study of the new sciences and philosophies coming from the Arab world. His interest in mathematics, and above all in its logical method, left its mark in Oxford, where others followed his lead.

———

JLG

Grotius, Hugo (1583–1645). Dutch Calvinist frequently considered the founder of international law. He expressed his sympathy toward ⇒Arminius and rejected the Calvinist doctrine of predestination. As a result, he was imprisoned, but he escaped and fled to France. There he wrote his great work *De jure belli ac pacis* (1625; On the Law of War and Peace), dedicated to Louis XIII, which continues to be read in courses on international law.

G. lived in the historical moment of the birth of modern sovereign nations. The destructive effects of war, especially of the Thirty Years' War, motivated him to formulate principles by which states could govern their relations. Like ⇒Erasmus, G. was a humanist who aspired to eliminate war. Nevertheless his political realism made him understand that this was not feasible and led him to formulate criteria to limit and make war more humane. Like ⇒Aristotle, he had faith in human reason, which shows the need for nations to fulfill their promises, honor their treaties, and respect property.

His contribution to the development of the theory of the just war is still recognized as significant. In addition, G. promoted the principle of religious tolerance, especially among Christians.

———

IG

Grumbach, Argula (von Stauff) (1490–1554). Friend of ⇒Luther and author of several pamphlets in defense of the Reformation. She was considered a great scholar of the Scriptures.

———

ALG

Grundtvig, N. F. S. (1783–1872). Educator, politician, philologist, theologian, hymnologist, poet, historian, member of parliament, student of Nordic mythology, Danish Lutheran pastor, and bishop. Nicholas Frederick Severinus G. was the first cousin of the bishop of all Denmark, Jacob Mynster. In 1824 G. began his religious reformation and with it what others called Grundtvigianism, which struggled for religious freedom and against the rampant rationalism of his time. As an educator he established the Folk High School, which continues to this day.

G. championed the cause of the "happy Danes," or the middle-class peasants, while his countryman Søren ⇒Kierkegaard opted for the "sad Danes," that is, the poor peasants and poor city folk. According to Kierkegaard, the Grundtvigians, including his own brother, Bishop Peter Kierkegaard, sinned as defenders of the status quo because of their inclination to support those with money.

———

EPA

Guardini, Romano (1885–1968). Roman Catholic theologian born in Verona, Italy. He was ordained a priest in 1910. He participated in youth and literary movements. At a very young age he excelled as a writer and speaker. He was very much admired as a local parish priest, but he preferred to continue on the path of teaching and research.

G. pursued theological studies at the universities of Freiburg and Tübingen, obtaining the degree of doctor of theology from Tübingen. He was a prolific writer who published books on such varied themes as religious psychology, pedagogy, biblical exegesis, liturgy, philosophy, and history. The influence of his work has been felt in Catholic and ecumenical theological circles. Two fundamental works show the diversity and breadth of the themes that he tackled: *Prayer* and *The Dusk of the Modern Age.*

———

CEA

Guitmund of Aversa (11th century). Author of a treatise *On the Truth of the Body and Blood of Christ*, in which he attacks the theories of ⇒Berengar. According to G., the power of the God who made all things out of what did not exist can well make something new out of what already exists, that is, transform bread into the body of Christ and wine into his blood. This change is "substantial" or "in substance," with which terms G. came close to the vocabulary that would soon be used in the doctrine of transubstantiation. Also, the bread is the body of Christ to such an extent that it does not nourish whoever eats it physically, but only spiritually.

———

JLG

Gunkel, Johann Friedrich Hermann (1862–1932). German Protestant biblical scholar and founding member of the school of the history of religions or comparative religions who devoted his efforts to the study of the popular mythology that is reflected in the biblical narratives. In collaboration with Wilhelm ⇒Bousset, he was one of the first to analyze the Bible from the historical-religious point of view. He is widely known for his application of the method of form criticism to the Old Testament, especially to Genesis, the Psalms, and prophetic literature.

———

AEM

Gustafson, James (1927–). One of the most original ethical theologians of our time. He has served as professor of theological ethics at Yale, Chicago, and Emory universities. A student of H. R. ⇒Niebuhr, his thought represents an elaboration on that of his teacher.

His greatest work, *Ethics from a Theocentric Perspective*, embodies his unique style of constructing theological ethics. He maintains that ethics must include the resources offered by theology, the natural sciences, the social sciences, and philosophy.

For G., ethics should have a theocentric foundation. It is God, and not only Christ, on whom we should base our practical positions. The theocentric vision allows us to value nature and not only culture and history. Ethics is based on our understanding of the purposes of God for all creation, which implies our respect for nature, personality, and cultures.

Ethics is neither objective nor subjective. Instead, it is born of the interrelation between the affective and the rational. Reason gives order and form to the natural impulses and desires, which in turn give content and direction to reason in its quest for meaning and purpose. Our beliefs about God, our interpretation of moral reality, and our spiritual feeling determine our understanding of human moral experience.

There are four pillars for constructing theological ethics: (1) analysis of the social situation; (2) theological affirmations; (3) formulation of moral principles; and (4) an interpretation of the human being or Christian anthropology. For G. it is important to remember that in every ethical-theological task, it is the human being who decides how to interpret the reality on which we act.

Others among his best-known works are *Treasures in Earthen Vessels* and *Christ and the Moral Life*.

———

IG

Gutiérrez, Gustavo (1928–). Peruvian Catholic priest. One of the fathers of Latin American liberation theology. Author of the first great book of that movement, *Theology of Liberation: Perspectives* (1971). He studied medicine, psychology, philosophy, and theology in Peru, Chile, Rome, Belgium, and France, and obtained his doctorate in theology from the University of Lyon, France.

Born into a poor family of urban workers, he learned the sufferings of a prolonged illness during his adolescence and the social impact of being mestizo. Ever since his student days and the beginning of his priesthood, G. has identified with the cause of the poor. His theological reflection was born of a Christian commitment to the struggles of the people and the ecclesial base communities that were active in the process of liberation. For many years he has been pastor of a poor parish in Lima and founder and director of the pastoral center Bartolomé de las Casas.

As one of the theological advisers of the Latin American Episcopal Council (⇒CELAM), his contribution was decisive in the formulation of some documents in the Conference of ⇒Medellín, Colombia, in 1968, from which much of the theology of liberation was born.

His theological production has been crucial in the development of this theological movement. What especially stands out are his contributions to classical theological themes such as the doctrine of God, salvation, the church, theological method, and the spirituality of liberation, and also the interpretation of the work and significance of Bartolomé de ⇒Las Casas.

At the center of the theology of G. is the confession of the God who has revealed Godself in Israel and in Jesus Christ as the God of life, love, and justice, who has made a "preferential option for the poor," and who works for their liberation in human history, where the saving action of the kingdom of God manifests itself. This liberation includes three concurrent and interdependent levels: liberation from economic exploitation and from the political oppression of countries, groups, and persons; cultural liberation or the formation of a new humanity that is free and in solidarity; and liberation from personal and social sin. Theology is a second act; that is, it is born from the commitment of love and justice to the liberation of the poor and occurs within transformative pastoral action. Theology is the critical reflection on the historical praxis of the church in favor of the liberation of human beings, especially the poor, in the light of the Word and having as a goal the transformation of the world for the construction of a new society that is just and fraternal.

Although G. has been harassed by conservative sectors and investigated by Rome about his orthodoxy, he has not been disciplined by the Vatican. His literary production has had worldwide influence, and the importance of his theology has been recognized ecumenically and internationally.

———
LRR

Guy of Osnabruck (?–1101). Teacher in that city and later its bishop from 1093 until his death. He wrote a treatise *On the Controversy between Hildebrand and Emperor Henry*. G. lived at the time of the gravest controversies between the pope and the empire, and he maintained that, since the election of Hildebrand as pope (⇒Gregory VII) was not confirmed by the emperor, it was not valid.

———
JLG

Guyon, Madame de (1648–1717). Catholic mystic who, through her spiritual writings, has also had great influence among Protestants. She lived and proposed a spiritual life based on personal and private prayer, the denial of the ego, and the experience of God within the person. She was educated in a convent of Ursulines, and she married at the age of sixteen through an arrangement by her parents. When she became a widow in 1676 she donated all of her possessions to charity and devoted herself completely to religious life, first in private and then in a religious community in France. Many persons came to her in search of prayers and spiritual discernment. Her work

with the people, proposing private prayer, and her association with mysticism resulted in the opposition of many, who accused her of quietism, that is, of maintaining that before God the only thing necessary is to adopt an absolutely passive attitude. Because of this she was censured by the bishop of Meaux and imprisoned in the Bastille in 1695. Among her many writings, the most famous is the book *Brief and Easy Method of Prayer*.

———
TCS

Habermas, Jürgen (1929–). German philosopher who was deeply influenced by ⇒Hegel, ⇒Marx, and ⇒Kant. He is part of a group of philosophers who have questioned the modern theory of knowledge, communication, and interpretation (⇒Gadamer, ⇒Derrida). His works of greatest influence for theology and for biblical hermeneutics are *Theory of Communicative Action* (2 vols.) and *Postmetaphysical Thought*.

———
JLG

Hadrumet, Monks of (5th century). Two of these monks, in what today is Tunis, were sent to consult with ⇒Augustine in the year 426, since the entire monastery was concerned over the apparent denial of human freedom by Augustine. Seemingly what most worried them was, if grace is an irresistible gift of God, and God gives it to whom God pleases, how can God justly punish those to whom grace is not given? Augustine responded with a letter to the abbot and another one to the monastery in general. In addition, he wrote two treatises in response to the concerns of the brothers in H.: *On Grace and Free Will* and *On Punishment and Grace*. This concern of the monks was an indication of the difficulties that the Augustinian doctrine of grace would soon stumble on and an announcement of the objections of the Semi-Pelagians.

———
JLG

Hallencreutz, Carl F. (1934–). Swede, dean of the faculty of Uppsala University and lecturer of the Swedish Institute of Missionary Research, scholar in the field of the political and missionary history of Africa, and theologian in the missionary movement and in the ⇒World Council of Churches. One of the most prolific missiologists in Europe in the last three decades of the twentieth century, he focuses particularly on the interreligious dialogue and on the political history of South Africa.

———

CCO

Häring, Bernard (1912–98). Catholic theologian who specialized in moral theology. He became prominent with his development of a theology of protest without violence, holding that Christians should be activists who confront the abuses of human rights without falling into violence, except in absolutely extreme cases and after exhausting all other options. His argument urges activism for human liberation, based on the love and justice of God.

———

LGP

Harkness, Georgia Elma (1891–1974). Prominent Methodist theologian. She studied at Cornell University and obtained a master's degree and a doctorate in philosophy at Boston University. While she studied in those programs, she taught at Elmira College, and in 1923 she joined the faculty of philosophy of that institution. Later she taught at Mount Holyoke College, Garrett Theological Seminary, and Pacific School of Religion.

She published her first book, *Conflicts in Religious Thought*, in 1929. It manifests her commitment to the personalist thought of ⇒Brightman. Her commitment to the education of laypeople defines the purpose of the rest of her literary work, since it inspired her to write thirty-six books in several branches of theology. All of her books are accessible and relevant to the religious needs of the laity. Among her best-known works are *The Dark Night of the Soul* (1945), *Understanding the Christian Faith* (1947), *Prayer and the Common Life* (1948), *Toward Understanding the Bible* (1954), and *Christian Ethics* (1957).

Her commitment to the church was firm. She was a leader of the Conference on Faith and Life in Oxford and served as a delegate to the first meeting of the ⇒World Council of Churches in Amsterdam. H. is one of the most prominent figures in the history of the Methodist church. She fought for the ordination of competent women. (Nevertheless, when in 1956 the Methodist Church allowed the ordination of women, she did not request it for herself.) She opposed the use of nuclear weapons. Although she tolerated the system of segregation that oppressed African American citizens,

her encouragement for the progress of all races created conditions that would lead to more liberal and progressive positions against racism.

—

IG

Harnack, Adolf von (1851–1930). German theologian, church historian, and one of the leaders of liberal theology. He wrote more than 1,600 books and articles. Among his most outstanding writings are *The History of Dogma* (1886–89); *The Essence of Christianity* (1900), which was translated into fifteen languages and of which more than 70,000 copies were printed; and *Marcion* (1921). His great achievements in the area of patristics earned him the title of "prince of church historians" of his time.

The work of H. as theologian and church historian revolved around his great urge to define the essence of Christianity. According to H., the intrusion of the "Hellenist spirit" in the patristic era made room for the development of dogmas that, to this day, hide the truth and simplicity of the message of Jesus. The result was a dogmatic deviation erroneously centered on teachings *about* Jesus, and not on the teachings *of* Jesus. Thus there is a "gospel within the gospel" that becomes evident only through the meticulous work of discovering the Hellenizing layers that cover it up.

The essence of this pristine Christianity is found, according to H., in the teachings of Jesus about the kingdom of God and the coming of this kingdom, the Fatherhood of God, universal brotherhood, the infinite value of the soul, and the commandment of love. For him, each one of these themes contains and exhibits in itself the totality of the gospel.

———

ZMP

Harper, William Rainey (1856–1906). Baptist educator and Hebrew scholar who was the first president of the University of Chicago (1891). He thus became one of the pioneers of education in the United States and made great contributions to that famous university, especially by giving a new scientific focus to religious education.

———

RPT

Harris, George K. (1887–1962). Baptist missionary, a graduate of the Moody Bible Institute, who worked with the China Inland

Mission, particularly among Chinese Muslims. His best-known book is *How to Lead Muslims to Christ*.

— JLG

Harris, James Rendel (1852–1941). English scholar, originally a Congregationalist, but in the end a Quaker. He distinguished himself above all by his theories about the influence of the surrounding cultures on primitive Christianity, especially of the ⇒*Sibylline Oracles*. He was also the discoverer of the Greek text of the *Apology* of Aristides. His studies of esoteric traditions and his interpretation of the origins of Christianity caused him to be regarded both as a notable scholar and as an eccentric theologian.

— JLG

Harrison, Everett F. (1902–99). Presbyterian theologian who insisted that although the Bible itself does not proclaim its authority and infallibility, such a teaching is a necessary corollary of the inspiration of the Bible itself.

— MAD

Hartenstein, Karl F. (1894–1952). German missiologist, director of the Missionary Society of Basel, and promoter of the concept of *missio Dei* in missionary circles in the West. H. was a strong critic of the missiological proposal of ⇒Barth. He insisted that between the ascension and the coming of the Lord, mission is focused on the historical and saving significance of the gospel of God and not on the centrality of the church. Such a position, while critical of Barth, allowed him to follow a course parallel to Barth's by being a prophet over against the Nazi ideology and joining the Confessing Church—a prophetic voice in Germany at the beginning of the Second World War—and the ecumenical movement.

— CCO

Hartmann, Eduard von (1842–1906). Born in Berlin, this German philosopher injured his knee and became partially handicapped at a very early age. Perhaps this circumstance explains his pessimism, his conviction that the world moves toward nothing, and his conviction that happiness cannot be reached in this life or in a future one. For him true religion seeks to free God from the agony

that it causes God to see the misery that dominates creation. The vitality of Christianity is based on its pessimism over against the world. His *Philosophy of the Unconscious* (1884), in which he develops his theory of the unconscious, brought him recognition. Many call him the forerunner of European nihilism and of the theories of ⇒Freud.

— IG

Hartshorne, Charles (1897–2000). North American philosopher and theologian, one of the founders of process philosophy. He studied in the universities of Haverford, Harvard, and later Freiburg and Marburg in Germany. He worked with ⇒Whitehead at Harvard in developing a philosophy of process in which reality is organic, dynamic, and relational. But he differed from Whitehead in his strict use of logic for developing his philosophy. He was professor at the universities of Chicago, Emory, and Texas. He is noted for his understanding of the universe as the body of God and for his arguments in favor of panentheism, ⇒Anselm's ontological argument, and the redefinition of the divine attributes as the actualization of the greatest possible potential. For him, God is dynamic, relational, and temporal. His books include *Man's Vision of God and the Logic of Theism*, *The Divine Relativity: A Social Conception of God*, and *Omnipotence and Other Theological Mistakes*.

— LGP

Hauerwas, Stanley (1940–). North American Protestant theologian, notable for his work in narrative theology and ethics. After studying at Yale University, he taught at Notre Dame University, and then at Duke University. His theology and ethics have become prominent through their emphasis on the need to locate the development of moral character within the Christian community. Rejecting human autonomy, that is, our capacity for self-determination to decide our own course of action, as the chief factor in the development of our sense of what is moral, H. argues that human beings develop their moral sense within the social context of their community. Within the context of community, there is a dynamic in which human beings construct themselves in a process of personal and social transformation. Instead of moral principles that presuppose a universal law, the community creates a series of narratives and stories that serve as a moral guide for its members. Rhetoric also functions in the intercommunity interchange as well as in the intracommunity, establishing the predominant narrative that defines the theology and ethics of the community through its arguments and narrative force. His books include *A Community of Character*, *The Peaceable Kingdom*, *Suffering Presence*, and *Wilderness Wanderings: Probing Twentieth-Century Theology and Philosophy*.

————

LGP

Haymo of Halberstadt (9th century).

Defender of the ascetic life, especially in his work *On the Love of the Heavenly Country*. Also attributed to him is a very brief treatise in which he speaks of the presence of Christ in the Eucharist in terms similar to the doctrine of transubstantiation, whose development came later. According to this treatise, what occurs in the Eucharist is a "substantial" transformation of the bread and wine into the body and blood of Christ. However, there are doubts concerning the authorship of this treatise, just as there are about other writings attributed to H. This is because there are at least three other authors with the same name who could just as well have written it: Haymo of Auxerre (contemporary of H. of Halberstadt) and Haymo of Hirschau and Haymo of Telleia (both in the eleventh century). Since what is expressed in the treatise on the Eucharist is similar to what other authors wrote in the vicinity of the eleventh century, many scholars are inclined to attribute it to one of these last two.

————

JLG

Hefner, Philip (1932–). North American

Lutheran theologian. He received his doctoral training in theology at the University of Chicago. After a distinguished career as professor of systematic theology in several Lutheran seminaries in the United States, he became professor emeritus of the Lutheran School of Theology at Chicago. He also distinguished himself as an international leader in the dialogue between religion and science, paying special attention to contemporary culture and the natural sciences. Beginning in 1990 he was director of the Zygon Center for Religion and Science and editor-in-chief of the journal *Zygon: Journal of Religion and Science*.

Among his many works are *Faith and the Vitalities of History: A Theological Study Based on the Thought of Albrecht Ritschl* (1966), *The*

Promise of Teilhard (1970), *Belonging and Alienation* (1976), *The Human Factor* (1993), and *Technology and Human Becoming* (2003).

————

JDR

Hegel, Wilhelm Friedrich (1770–1831). The most prominent of the Ger-

man idealist philosophers. He was born in Stuttgart and studied in Tübingen, which for a long time continued the Hegelian tradition. In contrast with ⇒Schleiermacher and the Romantics, for whom religion is understood intuitively and through the senses, H. affirmed that religion and the Absolute are understood in a rational way. For him, feelings are the underdeveloped expression of our awareness, while thought and rational concepts are its highest expression.

As opposed to ⇒Kant, H. maintains that the mind has the capacity to capture reality in itself, and in contrast to Platonic idealism, that ideal reality is dynamic and not static. What is real is essentially historical and can be understood only through ways of thinking that emphasize the dimension of process, becoming, and development. The chief contribution of the thought of H. is the attempt to capture and describe the historical evolution of all that he studied.

Absolute reality and true knowledge, therefore, can be captured only by the dialectical method, which is an intrinsic part of the historical reality itself. Against Aristotelian logic, which values consistency, Hegelian dialectics values opposition, the conflict of ideas and opposite truths. Hegelian dialectics describes every phenomenon as a unity of opposite poles, thesis and antithesis, that are conjoined in a synthesis. Every higher truth or synthesis, however, continues to be limited and contradictory, and becomes a new thesis that seeks to transcend itself in an even higher truth. This process has no end, or its end will occur when the idea embodies the totality of the Absolute Spirit. This is the way in which the Absolute Spirit (God) and the limited spirit (reason, culture, and the history of ideas) grow and fulfill themselves.

For H., philosophy and theology have the same object of study: the Absolute. These two disciplines exist in harmony, which allowed him to affirm that even God has a historical-dialectical character. Thus he developed a philosophical interpretation of the doctrine of the Trinity. God develops in three phases: (1) God as eternal idea, the kingdom of God the Father; (2) God as incarnate, revealing God's finitude in the kingdom of the Son; and finally, (3) God returning to Godself in unity with the congregation of faith, the kingdom of the Spirit. This interpretation led H. to affirm that Christianity is the absolute religion. The incarnation reveals that the spiritual and the material are poles of the same reality, and that God is the reconciliation of the finite and the infinite.

Among those who followed his ideas, but who diverged from them, are ⇒Feuerbach and ⇒Marx. Some European political theologians and Latin American theologians of liberation have also been influenced by his methodology and his historicism.

—

IG

Hegesippus (ca. 105–ca. 180). Apparently a Hellenistic Jew who was converted to Christianity. H. visited several of the principal churches of his time, arriving in Rome around the year 155. His purpose was to know what was taught in those churches, in order to reject and refute the doctrines and theories of the ⇒gnostics. On returning to his homeland, he wrote five books of *Memoirs*. These have been lost, and what remains of them is chiefly what we know thanks to quotations that appear in ⇒Eusebius of Caesarea.

—

JLG

Heidegger, Martin (1889–1976). German existentialist philosopher. Originally of Catholic convictions, to the point of beginning studies aimed at entering the priesthood. In 1919 he declared himself free from what he called the "dogmatism" of Catholicism, and in the end he was a key figure in the development of the nontheistic form of existentialism. He was a professor at several German universities, among them those of Marburg, Tübingen, and Freiburg. In 1933 he was elected rector of the University of Freiburg, and at about the same date he joined the Nazi Party, in which he remained until the end of the Second World War. Between 1945 and 1949 the French military government of occupation did not permit him to teach, and for a long time he was suspected of Nazi sympathies. Slowly he was reintegrated in the academic activities of the new Germany, although he never again occupied the distinguished positions he had during the war. His literary production was enormous, but in the middle of it stood out his great work, *Being and Time* (1927). In this book he argued that the investigation of being (*Sein*) ought to be based on the investigation and above all the experience of human existence (*Dasein*), with all its ambiguities and anxieties.

Although he abandoned every attempt to do theology from the time of his youth, H. was important for the theology of the twentieth century because several Christian existentialist theologians used his thought to interpret the Christian faith. Chief among them was R. ⇒Bultmann, who proposed a "demythologization" of the New Testament, which to a great extent was a rereading in terms of the philosophy of H.

—

JLG

Heidelberg Catechism (1562). Protestant and Reformed confession of the Christian faith. It was written at the request of Frederick III, elector of the German province of the Palatinate. With the support of the faculty of Heidelberg University, Frederick III commissioned Zacharias ⇒Ursinus, a twenty-eight-year-old professor of theology in that university, and Caspar ⇒Olevianus, a twenty-six-year-old court preacher. The Heidelberg Catechism was written to instruct and guide young people, beginning pastors, and teachers. This catechism was accepted and approved by the Synod of Heidelberg and was published in German on January 19, 1563, with a preface written by Frederick III himself. The edition was so well accepted that two more German editions with a few revisions were published when the first edition was exhausted. During that first year, 1563, it was also translated into Latin. Years later it was divided into fifty-two sections, to be read and explained each Sunday and thus to cover the entire catechism in one year. It was translated into Dutch by Peter Dathenus in 1566, and immediately this translation was widely accepted and enjoyed great popularity in the Low Countries. A pastor in Amsterdam, Peter Gabriel, designed a worship service centered on the weekly themes of the catechism. This was adopted and imitated by many other pastors and congregations. Years later the different union synods in Germany made up of Lutherans and Reformed adopted the Heidelberg Catechism as one of three formulas of unity, so that all the pastors and congregations who were affiliated with these synods were required to confess and teach this catechism. The catechism was translated into English in 1572, and then into many other languages. It is considered one of the most important confessional documents of the Reformation. In essence it reflects a moderate Calvinist theology, and thus it is more compatible with Lutheran theology than other Reformed confessions.

———

HMT

Heim, Karl (1874–1958). Lutheran theologian born in Württemberg, Germany. He studied at the University of Tübingen, serving as pastor for several years before assuming a teaching position in the University of Münster. Although he was a contemporary of ⇒Barth and ⇒Bultmann, he differed from them, particularly in his interest in natural theology and in the relationship between science and theology.

———

LGP

Heiric of Auxerre (9th century). Theologian of the monastery of St. Germain of Auxerre. He wrote chiefly commentaries on ⇒Augustine in which the influence of John Scotus ⇒Erigena is apparent. However, in contrast with Erigena, he rejects extreme realism, declaring that the reality of things is not found in the universals, but in the particular substance of each entity. The influence of ⇒Boethius, whom H. had studied at great length, is seen in this position.

———

JLG

Hellenus of Tarsus (3rd century). Bishop of that city and principal opponent of ⇒Paul of Samosata. H. convened a synod in 264, but the assembly was not able to determine the exact character of the teachings of Paul. H. then turned to the Origenist theologian ⇒Malchion, who in another synod was able to convince the assembly that the teachings of Paul of Samosata were false.

———

JLG

Hemmenway, Moses (1735–1811). Congregationalist leader of the "old Calvinists," a name the moderate Calvinists gave themselves and which provoked the anger of the strict followers of Johnathan ⇒Edwards, such as Samuel ⇒Hopkins and Nathaniel ⇒Emmons. He repudiated the practice of excluding from Communion those who would not make a public confession of faith. He also opposed the Baptists, whose number was growing, by insisting on the baptism of infants.

———

MAD

Henoticon. Word used to explain the union between the divinity and the humanity in Jesus, and also the title of a decree issued by Emperor Zeno in 482 to promote unity between the Monophysites, who held that in the incarnate Christ there was only one nature and not two, and the Chalcedonian orthodox, who held that in Christ there are two natures, the human and the divine, and that these remain after the incarnation. This decree was written by ⇒Acacius of Constantinople and ⇒Peter Mongo of Alexandria. It reaffirmed the creed of ⇒Nicaea (325) and ⇒Constantinople (381); the *Twelve Anathemas* of ⇒Cyril of Alexandria were accepted; and ⇒Nestorius and ⇒Eutyches were condemned, but without reference to the number of natures in Christ. Thus an ambiguous position with respect to the Council of ⇒Chalcedon is maintained, and any mention of the *Dogmatic Epistle* by Leo is omitted. This decree was generally accepted in the East, but not in Rome, which caused the so-called schism of Acacius that marks the first official break between the East and the West.

———

HMT

Henry, Carl F. H. (1913–2003). One of the principal representatives of the conservative evangelical movement in the United States. In his conception, biblical revelation has absolute authority in matters of faith and of moral conduct. The Bible is literally the word of God. His work *The Uneasy Conscience of Modern Fundamentalism* (1947) presents the biblical bases that give legitimacy to the involvement of evangelical Christians in the social issues of their time.

In his theological ethics he combines elements from the Anabaptist tradition (his antihumanist and antisubjective inclination) and from the Reformed tradition (by seeking in the Scriptures a pattern of divine order). The morality that is presented in biblical revelation is special and particular. It is an ethic for the community of believers and not a universal religious ethic that is accessible to all human beings. The Bible reveals the will of God through specific commandments that are specifically given to the elect in clear language. For Christians, the commandments are embodied in the Sermon on the Mount. However, H. insists on maintaining unity and continuity between the New and the Old Testament.

———

IG

Henry, Matthew (1662–1714). English Presbyterian biblical scholar who wrote a commentary on the whole Bible, with devotional and spiritual emphasis. His interpretation has influenced conservative and Pentecostal churches in the United States and Latin America, especially between 1930 and 1980.

————

RPT

Henry of Ghent (?–1293). Professor in Paris beginning in 1277 whose main work is a treatise on God. This was intended to be the beginning of a *Summa theologica,* which he never completed. Like many of his contemporaries, while he felt attracted by some elements of Thomism (⇒Thomas Aquinas), he was in reality an eclectic philosopher and theologian, still deeply committed to traditional Augustinianism.

————

JLG

Henry of Lausanne (1090–1145). Benedictine monk and heterodox theologian. He was born in the north of Italy and was in the monastery of Cluny for a time. Later he was detained for denouncing the corruption of the Catholic clergy. After having been set free, he settled in the south of France, where he began to preach and established his own movement (the Henryists), which subsequently joined the followers of ⇒Peter of Bruys. According to some, he claimed to know the thoughts and sins of people simply by looking at their faces. On that basis he accused the clergy of immorality (while his enemies accused him of the same thing) and therefore invited people to withdraw from worship and the sacraments. When H. was declared a heretic because of his incisive criticism of the church and because he disowned papal authority, ⇒Bernard of Clairvaux was given the responsibility of refuting him. Eventually he was incarcerated and died in prison.

————

GC

Heraclas (2nd–3rd century). First a disciple and later a collaborator of ⇒Origen in the catechetical school of Alexandria. Origen had been forced to leave Alexandria because of conflicts with Bishop Demetrius. When Demetrius died, H. succeeded him. But H. upheld the decisions of his predecessor, and Origen continued in exile. Very little is known of the theology of H., who was a teacher of ⇒Sextus Julius Africanus.

————

JLG

Hermas (2nd century). Christian author who lived in Rome during the middle of the second century, and brother of the bishop of that city. His work, the *Shepherd,* is the longest among the ⇒Apostolic Fathers. Written in the apocalyptic genre, the work consists of a collection of five visions, twelve commandments, and ten parables or comparisons. The source of the visions is an elderly woman (who represents the church), and they are interpreted by an angel-shepherd who instructs Hermas on the nature of Christian life.

In the first vision, Hermas describes how he felt attracted by his employer, a Christian called Rhoda. Further on an elderly woman (the church) accused him of his sin. In the second vision, he receives a revelation in the form of a book whose message is that repentance is possible. The third vision (the most important) is known as the "Vision of the Tower," because in it Hermas sees a tower under construction with stones brought from the sea and other stones that had been scattered over the ground. The woman (the church) explains that the tower is herself and that the different stones represent different persons. The good stones are those who live in holiness. Those of the sea represent the martyrs. The stones that were rejected (but were left near the tower because later on they can be used for construction) are those who have sinned but wish to repent. Other stones that are thrown far away and are broken represent the hypocrites who do not turn away from evil and do not have hope of salvation. In the fourth vision, the church is threatened by a beast with four colors on its head. The beast represents the tribulation that is to come, and the four colors symbolize this generation (black), its destruction (red), the salvation of the elect (gold), and the coming of the future world (white). The fifth and last vision has the function of introducing the twelve commandments and the ten parables or comparisons. In this fifth vision, the Shepherd appears who will accompany Hermas and will teach him the commandments and the parables.

The twelve commandments are a number of warnings in which some vices are contrasted with Christian virtues, such as faith in God, simplicity, and innocence as opposed to murmuring; and truthfulness, chastity, repentance, patience, self-control, continence, and joy as opposed to evil desire. This section is similar to the material in the ⇒*Didache* 1–6 and some sections of the Letter of James. Obedience to these commandments assures eternal life.

The third part of the work consists of ten parables. In one of them Christian life is compared with persons who live in a strange land (two cities). The parable of the elm tree and the vine illustrates the relationship between the rich and the poor in the church. The remaining parables are moral exhortations for the Christian way of life. The ninth parable returns to the image of the third vision (the tower), although in a more elaborate way. The construction is stopped for some time to provide an opportunity for repentance. In this parable H. introduces the Christian virtues with names of virgins (dressed in white): Faith, Continence, Fortitude, Patience, Simplicity, Innocence, Chastity, Joy, Truth, Intelligence, Harmony, and Charity. These virtues are contrasted with vices (dressed in black): Indifference, Incontinence, Disobedience, Deceit, Sadness, Evil, Dissolution, Impatience, Lying, Foolishness, Murmuring, and Hate.

The book is an ethical exhortation to purity and offers the opportunity for forgiveness after postbaptismal repentance (*metanoia*), from a perspective of the imminent end of the world. With respect to sins committed after baptism, it grants repentance once, but not more. H. reflects a Christianity that emphasizes the fulfillment of moral precepts and integrity. It is a morality that is very similar to the one presented in the *Didache*, the *Epistle of* ⇒Barnabas, the Letter of James, and the Sermon on the Mount. The entire work has the character of commandment and practical morality.

Some early sectors of Western Christianity included the *Shepherd* in the canon of the New Testament.

———

DCF

Hermias (2nd century?).

Author of a brief *Mockery of the Pagan Philosophers*, in which the teachings of diverse philosophers are compared in a satirical and even mocking tone, apparently with the purpose of showing that there is such confusion among them that they should not be given credit. It is generally counted among the apologists of the second century, although there is no internal evidence to assign the work to that date. It is also not possible to determine its date through external

evidence, since it is not quoted among the authors of antiquity. In any case, H. belongs to the group of apologists who, together with ⇒Tatian and in contrast to ⇒Justin, believed that philosophy, rather than being an aid to faith or to theology, is an obstacle.

———

JLG

Hermogenes (2nd–3rd centuries).

A native of Syria, and a painter by profession, who lived between the second half of the second century and the first part of the third, and whom the church at large declared a heretic. He spent most of his life in Carthage, and what we know of him today has reached us through his accusers. ⇒Theophilus of Antioch, for example, wrote a treatise against H. (a lost work), whose wide circulation and influence allowed many to attack the ideas of H. Subsequently, ⇒Tertullian wrote *Against Hermogenes* (our main source of information) and another document, which has disappeared, in order to counteract the theories of H. on the origin of the soul, which reflect a strong influence of Greek philosophy. According to H., the matter from which God gave form and ordered the world is eternal and preexistent. Evil does not come from God, but from this uncreated matter. Likewise the soul comes from matter, and not from the breath of God in the human being.

———

AEM

Hesshusen, Tilemann (1527–88).

German Lutheran theologian, a professor in Jena, and then a bishop. In the debates between Philippists and strict Lutherans or Gnesio-Lutherans, H. sided with the latter, under the leadership of ⇒Flacius.

———

JLG

Hick, John (1922–).

Philosopher and theologian, a native of Great Britain who studied in Edinburgh, Oxford, and Cambridge. He taught at the University of Birmingham and at Claremont Graduate School.

He excelled in the comparative study of religions and in theodicy. In the book *Evil and the God of Love*, he provides an interpretation of the problem of evil in light of the love of God, in which he uses ⇒Irenaeus to develop his argument that suffering and evil help us to develop human character and to appreciate the good. He rejected christocentric theology in favor of a theocentric position. His arguments on the relationship between Christianity and other religions, and especially his insistence on pluralism and on the possibility of finding salvation outside of Christ, resulted in accusations of heresy. His chief works are *The Myth of Christ Incarnate*, *The Myth of Christian Uniqueness*, and *The Metaphor of God Incarnate*.

LGP

Hickok, Laurens P. (1798–1888).
Congregationalist of the tradition of Jonathan ⇒Edwards, known above all as a philosopher. Having been influenced by ⇒Kant, H., who was skillful in the use of dialectics, attempted to use modern philosophy to lead into theism. The name he gave to the resulting philosophy was constructive realism.

MAD

Hiebert, Paul G. (1932–).
Conservative evangelical Protestant born in India of missionary parents. H. is an anthropologist and has published studies in the field of popular religiosity, syncretism, and mission, including *Anthropological Insights for Missionaries* and *Understanding Folk Religion*.

CCO

Hilary of Arles (ca. 399–449).
Bishop of that city beginning in 429. He had conflicts with ⇒Leo the Great, who reprimanded him for his wish to extend his influence to the rest of Gaul. He did not agree with the Augustinian doctrine of grace, as can be seen in his correspondence with ⇒Augustine (*Ep.* 226) himself, and was therefore part of the resistance to Augustinianism that was so strong in the south of France already in the time of Augustine.

JLG

Hilary of Kiev (11th century).
First Russian bishop of that city, which at that time was the capital of Russia. H. was the chief theologian the Russian church produced in its first years. His theology was characterized by his allegorical interpretation of the Scriptures, by his strong prejudice against Jews, and by his vast vision of the history of salvation, which was to culminate in a new world and a general resurrection.

JLG

Hilary of Poitiers (ca. 315–67).
Bishop of that city, and champion of Nicene orthodoxy against Arianism (⇒Arius). It was he who, in 355, succeeded in arranging a synod that met in Paris to reject the teachings of the Arians ⇒Ursacius and ⇒Valens. Because of his insistence on the Nicene teaching, Emperor Constantius exiled him to Phrygia, where he devoted himself to the study of the theology of his Eastern or Greek colleagues. There he wrote his great work in twelve books, *On the Trinity*, as well as the treatise *On the Synods*, in which he explained the course of the controversy in the Eastern church to his colleagues in Gaul. At the same time he showed openness to those who, fearful of the implications of the *homoousios* (of the same substance), were nevertheless willing to accept the *homoiousios* (of a similar substance). When the conflict with the emperor flared up again, H. wrote a strong treatise, *Against Constantius*. When shortly afterward he had to confront the ambiguities of the Homoean party (one of the groups into which the opposition to Nicaea had divided), he wrote a treatise *Against Auxentius*, the Homoean bishop of Milan. Because of this impressive record in favor of the Nicene faith, he is sometimes called the Athanasius of the West.

Since his chief theological concern was Trinitarian doctrine, it is in this field that H. made the greatest contribution. However, that contribution does not lie in his originality, but in his willingness to interpret the position of the Homoiousians as another way of expressing the divine essence of the Son, and therefore to create alliances between Homoiousians (whom others with less charity stigmatized as Semi-Arians) and Homoousians (that is, the Nicenes). This led to a process of clarification, showing that the Nicene faith did not necessarily lead to Sabellianism (⇒Sabellius) or to the blurring of the distinctions between persons. Thus little by little a coalition was being created that years after the death of H., would be victorious in the Council of ⇒Constantinople (381).

In the field of Christology his teaching is not clear. On the one hand, he insisted on the reality of the humanity of Jesus Christ. But on the other hand, he said that by virtue of its union with the divine, humanity could not suffer (or at least could not suffer the passions and internal pains that are the common lot of humanity). Because of this, some interpreters have accused him of Docetism, or at least of Aphthartodocetism (the theory that the body of Jesus was incorruptible).

JLG

Hildegard of Bingen (1098–1179).

Theologian, mystic, and German abbess. Tenth child of a well-to-do family of Böckelheim. From the time she was small, she stood out for her clairvoyance, her spiritual gifts, and the development of her internal senses. When she was eight years old, she entered a Benedictine convent. She wrote on theology, science, natural history, and medicine, in addition to writing hymns, homilies, biographies, letters, and her *Scivias*, which includes twenty-six visions. She was canonized by the people and not directly by the official hierarchy.

———

EPA

Hiltner, Seward (1909–84).

North American Presbyterian pastoral theologian. It is commonly said that Anton ⇒Boisen founded the discipline of North American pastoral theology and that H. was its theoretical architect. He introduced the method of Carl ⇒Rogers to pastoral counseling; he developed a method that emphasizes the creative potential of the person who is seeking help rather than a method of moralistic exhortation; and, in his *Preface to Pastoral Theology* (1958), he stressed that the task of pastoral theology is to seek the integral health and the emotional and spiritual support of persons and the development of activities aimed at providing guidance to the church. His chief work is *Pastoral Counseling* (1949).

—

JR

Himes, Joshua Vaughan (1805–95).

Main follower of William ⇒Miller, who predicted that Christ would return in 1843. The Adventist movement emerged from the ideas of Miller and H. When 1843 had come and gone, H. determined a new date: 1854. Disillusioned for the second time, in 1878 he returned to the Episcopal church, where he directed several missionary projects until his death.

———

MAD

Hincmar of Reims (ca. 806–82).

Scholar who was trained in the monastery of Saint Denys, in Paris, and was later bishop of Reims. He was a faithful servant of Louis the Pious and later of Charles the Bald, which brought him into conflict with Lothair. He was a skillful administrator, and to a certain extent he was a reformer of the church of his time.

In the field of theology the name of H. became prominent in the context of the controversies that dominated the Carolingian era, and above all in the controversy concerning the doctrine of predestination and the teachings of ⇒Gottschalk of Orbais. This monk, who was an implacable defender of double predestination (that is, the predestination of the elect and the reprobate), was declared a heretic by a council. It became the responsibility of H., as his ecclesiastical superior, to exercise discipline over Gottschalk. The severe measures taken by H. against the unfortunate monk, and the acknowledgment by some that Gottschalk based his teachings on the writings of ⇒Augustine, compelled H. to defend his actions. But the treatise in which he did so appeared to reject the traditional Augustinian doctrine of grace. In response, ⇒Ratramnus of Corbie wrote a treatise in which he refuted H. without agreeing with the extreme positions of Gottschalk. Perhaps knowing that what was being debated was too complex and profound for his own theological abilities, H. asked John Scotus ⇒Erigena to write on the subject. The treatise that Erigena wrote was full of abstract speculations and did not satisfy anyone. ⇒Prudentius of Troyes wrote a strong treatise against H., who in the end attempted to respond by means of a long work, *On Predestination and Free Will*, which was nothing but a compilation of biblical and patristic texts and which only stated that predestination to condemnation would make God guilty of evil.

H. was also involved in a controversy surrounding the doctrine of the Trinity, in which the protagonists were the same ones who had debated predestination. In a well-known hymn that was sung frequently during the festivities of the martyrs, the phrase *trina deitas* (triune deity) appeared. To H. this was too much like saying that there are three gods, and therefore he changed the hymn so that it said "great deity." This change in such a well-known formula made some doubt the orthodoxy of H. concerning Trinitarian doctrine. Ratramnus and Gottschalk wrote treatises accusing H. of heterodoxy. H. defended himself, as in the case of the other controversy, with a large compilation of quotations, but without in fact making his own position clear.

In summary, while he was a skillful ecclesiastical leader, H. was not a discerning or original theologian. His two main incursions in the field of theology did not have great success.

———

JLG

Hinkelammert, Franz J. (1931–). German by birth and Latin American by adoption, H. is an economist and theologian. He is a member of the working team of the Ecumenical Department of Research (DEI) in San José, Costa Rica. His writings focus on the relationship between Christian theology, capitalism, and foreign debt. H. might be one of the most sophisticated exponents of Latin American liberation theology, as has become evident in his work *Ideological Weapons of Death*.

————

CCO

Hippolytus (ca. 170–ca. 235). Eminent scholar, theologian, martyr, and leader in the Roman church, and probably the first antipope. History reveals very little about his life. ⇒Eusebius of Caesarea offers a list of some of his writings and incidentally mentions that he was bishop of a see, the location of which is unknown to him. ⇒Jerome calls him "martyr" and gives a more extensive list of his writings, but does not say much more.

During the Middle Ages, H. and his martyrdom were sources of poetic and legendary inspiration. More recently a number of discoveries have erased some of the mystery concerning his person and theology. Among them is the discovery in Rome (1551) of his effigy, a statue, which has inscribed on it the tables for the celebration of Easter as calculated by H. and a list of his works. Another great finding is the discovery and publication (1851) of the manuscript *Philosophoumena*, or Refutation of All the Heresies, which is one of the writings mentioned in the list. Thus it has been proved that H. was a bishop in or near Rome at the beginning of the third century. We also know that H. actively participated in the defense of the doctrines of the church and of its penitential discipline, which he carried out with fierce rigor. His purifying zeal led him to oppose two bishops of Rome, Zephyrinus (202–17) and ⇒Calixtus I (217–22). H. vehemently accused both of disciplinary laxity and doctrinal negligence.

According to H., the testimony of Calixtus was stained by previous banking embezzlements. Calixtus's action as bishop, readmitting to Communion persons who were guilty of adultery and fornication, as well as his apparent inclination toward the Sabellian doctrine (⇒Sabellius), provoked a severe attack from H., who saw the position of Calixtus as a betrayal and harmful compromise of Christian ideals. His vexation and hostility toward Calixtus were so extreme that he and his followers separated from the church and formed their own Christian community, where, under his supervision, orthodox teaching and disciplinary rigidity ruled. This is why H. is designated as an antipope.

According to the Liberian Catalogue, in the year 235, during the persecution of Emperor Maximinus, H. and Pontianus, the bishop of Rome (230–35), were exiled to the mines in Sardinia. It is believed that both died there and that, in honor of their confession of faith, they were included among the martyrs of the church. It was also said that they had become reconciled.

H. was the most scholarly and prolific writer of the Roman church in the second and third centuries. His writings, all in Greek, reflect his learning. According to his own testimony, he witnessed in person the speeches of ⇒Irenaeus (in Lyon or Rome), from whom he freely borrowed. Aside from his commentaries on the Scriptures, his chief work is *Philosophoumena*, which offers us data on the teachings of that time, on philosophy (which he considered to be the source of all the heresies), and on the state of the Roman church at the beginning of the third century. In addition, his *Apostolic Tradition* gives us important and penetrating details on the liturgy and the administration of the sacraments in the Roman church of the second and third centuries. The statue of H. is found in the Vatican Library.

————

ZMP

Hochstraten, Jacob (1460–1527). Roman Catholic theologian who was born in Hoogstraeten, Belgium, and died in Cologne. He studied the classics and theology with the Dominicans in Louvain, and in 1485 was one of the first to receive the master in arts degree from that institution. He entered the Order of the Dominicans and was ordained to the priesthood in 1496. He enrolled in the University of Cologne to continue his studies in theology and received the doctorate in 1504. He was named professor of theology in the Dominican college of Cologne. His great achievements in the area of theology, along with his natural ability to teach, made him an exceptional educator.

He was involved in controversies through his writing in defense of the mendicant orders, which had been accused of abusing their privileges. Its title was *Defensorium fratrum mendicatium contra curatos illos qui privilegia fratrum injuste impugnant* (1507). What followed were some writings against the eminent Italian jurist Pietro Tomasi de Ravenna. His greatest controversy was with ⇒Reuchlin. In his capacity as inquisitor, H. summoned Reuchlin to the court of Mainz to respond to the charges of favoring Jews and anti-Christian literature, thus reflecting the unfavorable attitude of the universities toward Jewish literature. Reuchlin appealed to Rome, which gave him its support and condemned H. as guilty of insult and abuse, with the result that H. lost his post as inquisitor. In 1520 the pope condemned Reuchlin and reinstalled H.

—

JDR

Hocking, William Ernest (1873–1966).
A student and then professor of philosophy at Harvard. He wrote extensively on philosophy and religion. Two of his most important works are *The Meaning of God in Human Existence* (1912) and *Human Nature and Its Remaking* (1918).

H. was designated to lead the visit to Asia of the Commission of Appraisal of the Laymen's Foreign Missions Inquiry and to write the controversial *Laymen's Report: Rethinking Missions,* published in 1932 and discussed at the World Missionary Conference of Madras, India (1938). This report created a great disturbance in missionary circles, since it was interpreted as an attack on the traditional style of mission and a threat to the missionary motivations of the time. The report also provoked an interesting debate with Hendrik ⇒Kraemer and his work *The Christian Message in a Non-Christian World* (1938). In this debate H. proposed an alliance with other religions in order to attain greater unity and progress in the world, while Kraemer insisted on the particularity of the Christian faith over against other religions.

Ironically, H. later published other books in which he affirmed the particularity of Jesus Christ, the Trinity, and the supremacy of the Christian faith, although never denying his appreciation for other religions.

—

CCO

Hodge, Archibald Alexander (1823–86).
Presbyterian pastor, Reformed theologian, and influential teacher. The eldest son of Charles ⇒Hodge, he was born in Princeton, New Jersey. He studied in Princeton, where he was a faithful follower of his father and an exponent of his ideas. After three years of service in India, H. and his wife returned to the United States for health reasons. After serving as a pastor in Maryland, Virginia, and Pennsyl-

vania for thirteen years, he began his teaching career in 1864 at Western Seminary in Allegheny, Pennsylvania, while he continued serving as a pastor. In 1878 he moved to Princeton, where his father had taught, and was part of the teaching body of that institution for nine years. There he held a strictly Calvinist position in books such as *Outlines of Theology* (1860, 1879) and *Popular Readings on Theological Themes* (1887). He argued in favor of the use of Calvinist principles in public life as a way of ordering the social, economic, political, and educational life of the nation.

—

EZ

Hodge, Charles (1797–1878).
A polemicist and systematic theologian, and defender of the "Princeton orthodoxy," H. affirmed that the purpose of life is to glorify God, that salvation is the work of the Holy Spirit, and that the proper source of theology is the Scriptures. He was educated in Princeton, where he completed his theological studies in 1819. Archibald ⇒Alexander, his professor of theology, had a profound effect on his thoughts and beliefs. In 1820 he began to teach at Princeton, a task which he continued for the rest of his life. He began as professor of Oriental and biblical literature and became professor of theology in 1840. He exercised a strong influence on his students thanks to his rigorous scholarship and his intense personal piety. His *Systematic Theology* (3 vols., 1872–83) is a firm expression of the Calvinism of the ⇒Westminster Confession, with strong emphasis on the infallibility of the Bible. He was also famous for several essays he wrote for the *Biblical Repertory and Princeton Review*, which had a strong impact on the thought and life of the Presbyterian Church. In 1837 he disputed against the theology of the New School, which held that happiness was the goal of life, that human effort was part of the history of salvation, and that human experience should serve as a starting point for theology.

—

EZ

Hoekendijk, Johannes Christian (1912–75).
Dutch missiologist who was born in Indonesia of missionary parents. His experience during the Second World War led him to be a strong critic of the missionary ecclesiocentrism of the times. His most important contribution in missiology, considered by many as radical, was the continuous claim that

the church cannot be more than a function of the missionary work of God for the *shalom* of the world and cannot mean more than the categories of "people of God" and "nation of God." As a result of his missiology, H. took secularization and the interaction between the reign of God and secularism very seriously and developed a theology of mission in which the terms *kerygma, koinonia,* and *diakonia* have an important meaning. In 1965 he accepted the chair of world Christianity at Union Theological Seminary in New York, teaching there until his death. He was the husband of Letty ⇒Russell.

CCO

Hoffmann, Melchior (1495–1543).
One of the most notable Anabaptist leaders at the beginning of the movement. He was born in Schwäbisch-Hall and died in Strassburg, after having been imprisoned for ten years. He received a good basic education and learned the trade of selling furs. From very early in his life he enjoyed religious literature, especially the works of the mystics. He also acquired a deep understanding of the Bible. He was enthusiastic about works of Martin ⇒Luther and became one of his most zealous followers.

In 1523 his fur trade led him to Lithuania, where he felt the call to participate in the religious reformation movement. Due to the limited number of preachers, he assumed that task. He was persecuted, made prisoner, and expelled from the region. In the fall of 1524 he arrived in Dorpat, where he began to preach against the use of images. His opponents demanded from the city council that his doctrines be approved by recognized theological authorities. He went to Riga, where some Protestant preachers gave him their support, and then to Wittenberg to receive Luther's approval for his preaching. With the support of Luther, he returned to Dorpat during the summer of 1525. Nonetheless, the experience of H. during his reforming work in the Baltic countries, in Holland, Sweden, and Denmark, and his conflicts with other Lutheran leaders, led Luther to repudiate him. This rejection drove him to establish a closer relationship with Anabaptist groups, especially those of the city of Strassburg.

H. had extraordinary gifts. His zeal for the cause of Jesus Christ consumed him. He showed a strange eloquence, combining an enthusiastic morality with a genuine interest in the truth. This explains his great influence and success with the masses. The great number of writings that he was able to publish during his highly unstable life is astonishing. Aside from his uncontrollable imagination, his arbitrary interpretation of the Bible, and his fanatical vision of the end of all times, his works also contain a great number of important Christian teachings on the hope for the return of Christ, on holiness in the life of the believer, and on the freedom of the believer as evidence of the power of the Spirit.

JDR

Hogg, William Richey (1921–2005).
A Methodist native of Pennsylvania, H. was educated at Duke and Yale, where he worked under the mentorship of Kenneth Scott ⇒Latourette. For some time he also worked as a missionary in Asia. Then he was professor of world Christianity at Southern Methodist University. His most important publication is *Ecumenical Foundations: A History of the International Missionary Council,* in which he traces the historical and theological relationship between the International Missionary Council and the development of the conciliar ecumenical movement (⇒World Council of Churches).

CCO

Holl, Karl (1866–1926).
Church historian and German Protestant theologian. After completing his theological studies, he taught at the University of Tübingen in 1900 and moved to Berlin in 1906. There he worked with Adolf von ⇒Harnack. He edited several patristic texts, among them the *Sacra parallela* of ⇒John of Damascus. H.'s work with patristic texts is widely recognized for his exactitude and for his understanding of the philosophical foundations of these texts.

HMT

Hollaz, David (1648–1713).
German theologian, considered the last of the great systematic theologians of Lutheran orthodoxy. He studied in the universities of Erfurt and Wittenberg. He was pastor in several cities and also rector of a preparatory school. His chief work, *Examen theologicum* (Theological Reflection), has chapters that are divided into questions and answers. There he emphasizes the themes of inspiration, natural law, illuminating grace, and the church from a pastoral perspective. This

work was republished multiple times, even many years after his death.

—
NRG

Hollenweger, Walter Jacob (1927–).

Author, ecumenist, educator, and theologian who is the best-known expert on world Pentecostalism. He was born in Antwerp and was reared in the Pentecostal church, although later he was ordained to the ministry by the Reformed Church of Switzerland. His studies in the University of Zurich culminated in a doctoral thesis of ten volumes, *Handbuch der Pfingstbewegung* (1966). This was revised, summarized, and published as *The Pentecostals* (1972). From 1965 to 1971 H. served in the ⇒World Council of Churches. Then for more than eighteen years he served as professor of missions in the University of Birmingham, England. H. is a prolific author. Among his most recent works is *Pentecostalism: Origins and Developments Worldwide* (1997).

One of the principal theses of H. is that the first ten years of the Pentecostal movement are the heart and not the infancy of its spirituality, thus his emphasis on authentic Pentecostalism as an oral religion with its testimonies, stories, and songs, and a spirituality that is marked by charismatic manifestations, healings, and dances in the Spirit. H. has attributed the phenomenal growth of Pentecostalism in the third world to, among other factors, its oral and charismatic spirituality. H. highlights such spirituality as a valuable contribution from Pentecostalism to the universal church in these postmodern times.

—
EV

Holov, John (17th century). Armenian

theologian, central character in the rebirth of studies in the Armenian Church during the seventeenth century. He wrote systematic, exegetical, and apologetic works.

—
JLG

Honorius (?–638). Bishop of Rome from

625 to 638 who was involved in the Monothelite controversy (⇒Sergius of Constantinople). The emperor was interested in finding a formula that would help him win the goodwill of those who rejected the decisions of the Council of ⇒Chalcedon, especially in Egypt and Syria. The Monothelite formula that Sergius proposed seemed to him a good solution.

Apparently H. shared the same thought, since he declared himself a defender of Monothelitism. That teaching was rejected by the Council of ⇒Constantinople in 681 (generally recognized as the Sixth Ecumenical Council). That council condemned both the teachings of Sergius and those of H. The importance of all of this is that the case of H., a pope who had been declared a heretic, was one of the main difficulties that were discussed in connection with the promulgation of papal infallibility by the First Vatican Council (⇒Vatican I).

—
JLG

Honorius of Augsburg (13th century). One of the many theologians and

jurists who became involved in the conflict between the secular and spiritual authorities, or between the papacy and the empire. His chief work is *Summa gloriae*, in which he defends the superiority of the priestly order to that of the secular with a long series of examples, beginning with Abel, who is a figure of the priestly office, and Cain, who is a figure of the royal office. According to H. the superiority of the priestly order is such that from that order the temporal order emerges. This has been true ever since Samuel anointed the first kings of Israel. His conclusion is that emperors should be named by popes.

—
JLG

Hooker, Richard (1553–1600). English

theologian and apologist. He was born near Exeter and was educated in the primary school of Exeter and in Corpus Christi College, Oxford. During his studies in Corpus Christi, Bishop ⇒Jewel assigned him a secretariat in the college. In 1573 H. began his master of arts program, and by 1577 he was already teaching in the same institution. In 1579 he was named professor of Hebrew. That year he was dismissed along with three other faculty members, but he was hired again in less than a month. After his ordination to the ministry, he served as preacher in several churches until the archbishop of York named him to a post that led him to defend the teachings of the Church of England. In the discharge of that office and against the positions of Walter ⇒Travers on the discipline of the church, he published eight books under the title *Laws of Ecclesiastical Polity*. In his works he had recourse to Thomism to explain the relationship between revelation and reason. He also demonstrated that a church could be properly constituted without claiming divine justification for every detail nor falling into the Roman error of continuing with medieval practices. His writings were very well received and recognized with honors. He is considered one of the most important theologians of the Church of England.

HMT

Hooker, Thomas (1586–1647). English pastor in the Congregational Church, born in Marfield, Leicestershire. He was a student and professor in Emmanuel College, Cambridge. In 1626 he was named assistant pastor in Chelmsford, but in 1630 he received a reprimand from Archbishop Laud for insulting behavior and for his Puritanical tendencies, for which he was fined and called to court. He fled to Holland, where he remained for three years. He traveled to Boston in 1633, where he was ordained and named pastor of the First Church of Newtowne (now Cambridge). But several disputes and disagreements forced H. and a great part of his congregation to go to the Connecticut valley, where the church continued and founded Hartford College in 1636. H. served as pastor of this church until his death in 1647.

HMT

Hooper, John (ca. 1495–1555). Anglican bishop and martyr. He was born in Somerset and studied in Oxford, then became a monk. The dissolution of his monastic order under Henry VIII led him to London, where he studied the writings of ⇒Zwingli and ⇒Bullinger, after which he returned to Oxford to promote the ideas of those Reformers. For that reason he was exiled and forced to travel throughout Europe from 1547 to 1549. Toward the end of 1549, he returned to England as a chaplain under the protectorate of Somerset, when Edward VI was king. In 1550 he was named bishop of Worcester, a function that he carried out with honesty and vigor, and in continuous service to the poor. In 1555, when Mary Tudor was queen, he was condemned for proclaiming heresies. He refused to deny his beliefs, for which he was burned in a public ceremony on February 9, 1555. The life and writings of H. influenced the Puritans of England.

HMT

Hopkins, Samuel (1721–1803). North American Congregationalist who studied under

Jonathan ⇒Edwards. The basis of his theology is the writings of Edwards. Although he was a defender of uniform Calvinism, his position was known as Hopkinsianism and as New England theology or (in England) as American theology. According to H.:

1. All the moral attributes of God are summarized in a "disinterested benevolence."
2. All sin consists of selfishness.
3. Regenerative grace does not work in those who are not spiritually reborn.
4. The inability of sinners to believe in Christ is not natural, but moral.
5. Sinners should be willing to suffer whatever punishment the will of God imposes on them (in his own words, should be willing to "be condemned for the glory of God").
6. The atonement of Christ is for all of humanity, for the elect as well as for the reprobate.
7. God rejects the moral evil that exists in the universe in order to give what is good to all.
8. Before faith in Christ can occur, the sinner should begin with regeneration, an imperceptible action of the Holy Spirit that leads the individual to the knowledge of God.
9. Although humanity became sinful because of Adam, each one is responsible only for one's personal sins.
10. The sinner is not under any obligation to carry out an action unless he or she has the natural capacity for it.
11. Individuals have the natural power to choose good or evil.
12. Even though believers are justified by the righteousness of Christ, that righteousness is not transferred to them.

H. exposed himself to persecution because he was one of the first to denounce the slave trade. He called for the emancipation of the Africans even though his church was in Newport, the chief slave market in North America.

MAD

Hormisdas (pope from 514 to 523). It was his lot to occupy the Roman see during the Theopaschite controversy, also called "of the Scythian monks." These monks, whose Christology belonged to the unitive tradition characteristic of the Alexandrian school, searched for a way to counteract the apparent triumph of the disjunctive Antiochene Christology through the abrogation of the ⇒Henoticon. To that end, they defended the formula "one of the Trinity suffered," for which reason they were called Theopaschites, that is, defenders of the suffering of God. The Scythian monks and their followers began a campaign for that formula to be declared official doctrine of the church. In this matter they counted on the support of Emperor Justin and his high command, who exerted pressure on H. so that he would join them. But the pope refused. When finally H. became reconciled with Justin, this was not well regarded by the Ostrogothic king Theodoric, and it is possible that the imprisonment and death of ⇒Boethius may have been, at least in part, a result of that annoyance of Theodoric.

——

JLG

Horton, Walter Marshall (1895–1966).
Baptist, promoter of what he called "neoliberalism." In dialogue with the works of Karl ⇒Barth, H. rejected the Barthian polemic against religion and natural theology, while he recognized the importance of the emphasis of Barth on revelation and redemption. Later he attempted to articulate a Christian theology that would support ecumenism by providing Christian answers to universal questions.

——

MAD

Hosius of Cordoba (256–357).
Counselor of Constantine in theological matters. Sent by the emperor to attempt to settle the dispute in Alexandria between ⇒Alexander and ⇒Arius, he realized the importance of the differences between them and seems to have advised Constantine to convene the Council of ⇒Nicaea. Some historians propose that it was he who suggested to Constantine the inclusion of the term *homoousios* in the creed, but there are no historical bases for this assertion. When, during the regime of Constantius, Arianism was prevalent everywhere, H., by then an old man, accepted the Arian formula known as the "blasphemy of Sirmium."

——

JLG

Hospinian, Rudolf (1547–1626).
Preacher and Reformed theologian. He was born in Altorf, in the canton of Zurich, and also died in Zurich. Beginning in 1565 he studied in the universities of Marburg and Heidelberg. In 1568 he began teaching and preaching in Zurich. In 1576 he directed the *Schola Carolina*,

and he maintained that position for nineteen years without interrupting his pastoral duties. In 1588 he was designated archdeacon and in 1594 pastor of the cathedral of Our Lady. He carried out extensive studies in church history in order to show the "papists" the error of their appeal to the supposed harmony of their teachings and institutions with the early church, especially in regard to baptism, the Lord's Supper, church festivals, fasting, the monastic orders, papal government, and funerals.

Among his works are *On the Origin and Development of Ecclesiastical Rites and Ceremonies* (1585), *On the Jewish and Gentile Festivals, that is, on the Origin and Development of the Ceremonies and Rites of Christian Feast Days* (1593), and *History of the Sacraments* (1598–1603).

——

JDR

Hromadka, Josef (1889–1969).
Reformed Czech theologian. He was born in Moravia and was educated in Vienna, Basel, and Heidelberg. He served as professor of theology in Czechoslovakia and was very active in the ecumenical movement, having served on the Executive Committee of the ⇒World Council of Churches. He was one of the chief critics of the Christians who use Christianity to justify the present social and political order and the benefits derived from it. For H., Christianity should be a critical voice that is free from the bonds of the status quo. This freedom allows Christianity to be a force that unifies social movements which contribute to the well-being of humanity. A great part of his educational and pastoral mission was devoted to the interpretation of the Christian life and the mission of the church in communist countries.

——

IG

Huber, Samuel (1547–1624).
Swiss Protestant who criticized the orthodox Calvinism of his country, especially the teaching of predestination. Orthodox Calvinism gave the name of Huberianism to the teaching that denies the limited atonement promulgated by the Synod of ⇒Dort. He also criticized the practice of using common bread, and not the wafer, in Communion.

——

MAD

Hübmaier, Balthasar (ca. 1480–1528).
German Anabaptist leader, the best

theological expositor of Anabaptism in its beginnings. Ordained to the priesthood, he earned a doctorate in theology and was then named preacher in Regensburg. There he became a populist leader and then traveled to other cities, where he established relations with several radical reformers. He was associated with ⇒Zwingli, with whom he shared theological ideas such as the spiritual interpretation of the presence of Christ in Communion. H. taught the baptism of believers, that is, of adults or children with the ability to be taught. He distinguished between different types of baptism: by the Holy Spirit, by water, and by blood through suffering and martyrdom. He was burned at the stake.

———

NRG

Hugh of Chartres (11th century).

Bishop of that city and adversary of ⇒Berengar, to whom he wrote in 1048 an *Epistle to Berengar* insisting that the eucharistic bread is truly changed into the body of Christ, although it continues to taste like bread. If this were not true, said H., the Eucharist would have no power and would be good for nothing.

———

JLG

Hugh of Fleury (12th century).

Author of a treatise *On Royal Power and Priestly Dignity*, in which he takes an intermediate position between those who defended papal supremacy and those who sided with secular power (concretely in the case of H., they were the defenders of the supreme authority of Henry I of England). According to H., bishops are to be elected by the people and the clergy, according to ancient custom, and the rulers are to accept such an election, except in the case of a true impediment. Ultimately both the people and the king have the right to veto an election. On the other hand, secular courts do not have jurisdiction over bishops, who can excommunicate the king in extreme cases.

———

JLG

Hugh of St. Victor (ca. 1095–1141).

Teacher of the monastery of St. Victor in Paris and the most famous theologian of the school of St. Victor, founded earlier by ⇒William of Champeaux. His chief work is *On the Sacraments of the Christian Faith*, which does not deal only with the sacraments but with a whole gamut of theological topics, from creation to the final consummation. But all this material is presented in such a way that the sacraments are the center of the work, so that creation, redemption, and the other topics point toward them.

According to H., the purpose of theological studies is not to satisfy curiosity or to answer intellectual questions, but to lead to a better and higher life. It is precisely because of this that what interests him above all is creation and its final restoration and, as the link between both, the sacraments. From this perspective, all of history is a movement that points and leads toward the final consummation, and knowledge is valid only insofar as it leads in the same direction. This is true of all intellectual disciplines: they are good as long as they lead to the improvement of the soul and to equipping it for the presence of God. The contrary is also true: any kind of knowledge, even if it is true in itself, is false if it does not lead the soul to God.

The mysticism of H. is derived from the pseudonymous ⇒Dionysius the Areopagite, whose works enjoyed great prestige, since it was believed that he had been a disciple of Paul. He was also especially popular in France because it was believed that he had been the founder of the Christianity in the region. Pseudo-Dionysius has to do with a mysticism of Neoplatonic type, centered in a process of ascent through contemplation of the hierarchies of creation, until the soul arrives at the contemplation of God and ecstasy.

Concerning the sacraments themselves, H. gives that title to anything that manifests God and thus leads to the sanctification of the soul. For this reason, and since the whole world is ordered toward the contemplation of God, the list of things, rites, and formulas that H. calls sacraments is enormous. H. pays special attention to only seven of them, which are the same as those which the Roman church soon declared to be the official list of seven sacraments. Apparently it was from H. that ⇒Peter Lombard took that number, and it was through the enormous influence of the latter that the scholastics from then on fixed the number of the sacraments at seven.

The school of St. Victor was significant for the development of medieval theology. Before H. and his school, strong clashes had taken place between those who were devout and at times even mystical, such as ⇒Bernard of Clairvaux, and those who were interested in "dialectics," that is, in the use of reason in philosophical and theological matters, such as ⇒Abelard. Now H. and the school of St. Victor combined a strong mystical impulse with intellectual rigor. This union of what until then had been two poles that seemed irreconcilable continued and broadened in the *Sentences* of Peter Lombard and thus led to the great flourishing of theology in the following century, with figures such as ⇒Bonaventure and ⇒Thomas Aquinas.

—

JLG

Hugh of Strasbourg (?–1277). Disciple of ⇒Albertus Magnus who wrote a *Compendium of Theological Truth* that was widely read during the rest of the Middle Ages.

—

JLG

Humbert, Cardinal (11th century). Zealous reformer and author of a famous treatise, *Against the Simoniacs.* As a defender of the reformation that had finally taken possession of the papacy, H. was one of the three legates whom Leo IX sent to the court of Constantinople in moments of high tension between Rome and Constantinople. ⇒Leo of Ochrid had written a strong attack against several Western customs. Among them was the practice of using unleavened bread in Communion. For Leo of Ochrid, this was an undue concession to Jewish customs. The patriarch Michael ⇒Cerularius supported him and strengthened his position with a *Synodical Edict* in which he reaffirmed the differences between the Greek East and the Latin West. This led to a debate on the primacy of the Constantinopolitan see in the East. In the midst of it all, H., who was not a person of irenic temper, wrote a *Response to Leo of Ochrid.* The conflicts continued to worsen until finally H. and the two other legates placed on the high altar of the Cathedral of Saint Sophia, in the name of the pope, a sentence of excommunication against Cerularius and all his followers. Generally that date (July 26, 1054) is considered the beginning of the final schism between East and West.

H. also participated in the eucharistic controversy in the West, in which context he wrote *Against* ⇒*Berengar.*

—

JLG

Hume, David (1711–76). Philosopher, economist, ethicist, and historian, born in Scotland. H. was an empiricist philosopher who rejected metaphysics as being merely speculative and incapable of providing truths that can be scientifically verified. True knowledge is based on experience. Therefore much of what we take for granted is not necessarily true, such as the principle of cause and effect and the idea of substance, because our senses have never shown us such things. For the same reason, the ideas of God as the First Cause and the existence of the soul as a substance are false—as is the very notion of substance.

Although he was reared in a Calvinist family, H. abandoned his religious beliefs at an early age. His attitude was not antireligious, but simply indifferent toward religion. In general terms he understood that religion is an obstacle to moral activity and formation, since it motivates persons to act on the basis of self-interest and not on the basis of love for the good and for justice. He also was convinced that religious persons have a tendency toward fanaticism and intolerance, two qualities that in the political sphere lead to war. In any case, religion is reduced to a probable theoretical postulate, which has its origin in passion and the fear of death, in the experience and fear of disasters, and in the hope for a better world. H. concludes that all of our postulates on God, the origin of the world, and other supposed realities that go beyond our experience cannot be proved and really do not make sense.

—

IG

Huntington, William (1844–1930). Pastor, educator, and president of Boston University. He was born on July 30 in Hillsboro, Illinois. He grew up on a farm, for which he later expressed gratitude. He enlisted when the Civil War began and served until it ended. He studied at the University of Wisconsin and then in the School of Theology of Boston University, in preparation for candidacy to pastoral ministry in the Methodist Church. On completing his studies, he enrolled in the universities of Leipzig and Göttingen (Germany) to pursue advanced studies. He served as a pastor for eight years. In 1882, at the age of thirty-eight, he was appointed dean of the College of Liberal Arts of Boston University, where he served for twenty-two years. In 1904 he was elected president of that university, and he served with distinction in that post until 1911.

—

JDRR

Huss, John (1369–1415). Important Czech prereformer. He was born of peasant parents in the small town of Husinec, in southern Bohemia. In 1390 he began his studies in the

University of Prague, where he became a member of the faculty in 1398. Two years later he was ordained to the ministry and appointed as preacher in the Bethlehem Chapel in Prague. His criticism of some of the errors of the church of Rome caused him to be identified as the head of the reformist party within Czech Catholicism.

H. often exposed himself to the thought of some of the clergy who held reformist ideas, such as Miles of Kromerz, Matthew of Janov, and above all John ⇒Wycliffe. His friend ⇒Jerome of Prague in 1401 brought to Bohemia a great number of theological works of Wycliffe, together with those of other writers of reformist convictions. H. began by incorporating the least radical ideas of Wycliffe in his reform, and he translated into Czech the work of Wycliffe titled *Trialogue*, even though the University of Prague censured the thought of the English reformer.

The thought of Wycliffe became so popular in Bohemia that Popes Innocent VII and Gregory XII exhorted the archbishop of Prague, Zbynek Zajic, to keep close watch over the proliferation of those ideas. Two of the friends of H., Stanislav of Znojmo and Stephen Palec, were tried by the Inquisition on charges of promoting the ideas of Wycliffe. This atmosphere of intolerance, together with the uncertain political situation created by the Western Schism, limited the radius of influence of H., who decided to seek refuge in southern Bohemia in 1412.

During that first withdrawal, the reformer was able to put into writing some of his ideas, which now were somewhat more developed. Some of those works were written in Latin and others in Czech. The best-known are *Expositions of the Faith*, *On the Decalogue and the Lord's Prayer*, and *On the Church*. In these works he reveals his theological profile and his vision of what a faithful church ought to be.

Although H. was on many points an orthodox theologian, his examiners did not limit themselves to an isolated analysis of his teachings, but also included his practices. Some of the "extremes" that were censured in the practices of H. were the use of the vernacular in preaching, his Utraquist position (that is, declaring that lay persons should also receive the wine in the Eucharist, and not only the bread), his criticism of the sale of indulgences, and the permission given to lay persons to interpret the Scriptures.

With the promise of a safe-conduct, H. was invited to the Council of ⇒Constance to defend his theological positions. The debate was centered mainly on his practices and on his work *De ecclesia*. In the latter there were forty-two articles that incriminated H. as a follower of Wycliffe, and on that basis he was condemned and taken to the stake in June of 1415.

Martin ⇒Luther was excommunicated in 1521 for agreeing with some of the ideas of H. The Hussite movement in Bohemia continued to resist Catholic pressure and several armed attempts to suppress it, and it continues to this day.

GCC

Hut, Hans (16th century).
Pacifist and apocalyptic Anabaptist who looked for the end of the world in 1528. He was a disciple of Hans ⇒Denck and Thomas ⇒Münzer. His followers formed a commune in Austerlitz that in the end followed Jacob ⇒Hutter, thus beginning the Hutterite movement.

JLG

Hutchinson, Anne Marbury (1591–1643).
Daughter of an Anglican pastor in Alford, England. Influenced by the Puritan pastor John ⇒Cotton, H. and her husband, William, moved to Boston in 1634. There she organized a group of women for Bible study. This group eventually included a hundred women and men who were interested in deepening and promoting Puritan theology. This led to a crisis in the church of Boston, when a conflict arose concerning the place of works in salvation. H. believed that salvation comes through the grace of God to each individual through the testimony of the Spirit and is not necessarily proven through works. Because this position and its growing influence clashed with the authorities of the church, the governor of the colony, John Winthrop, took her to court. Although she brilliantly defended her theological position, when she finally admitted the possibility of receiving direct revelations from the Spirit she was declared a heretic and expelled from the colony. In 1638, together with her family, she moved to Rhode Island, where her husband died. H. died on Long Island, surrounded by ten of her eleven children.

EA

Hutter, Jacob (?–1536). Successor of Hans ⇒Hut as leader of the Anabaptist commune of Austerlitz, and founder of the Hutterite Brethren. Like Hut, H. was a pacifist. His work consisted mainly in organizing community life in such a way that the practice of the common possession of goods continued among his followers long after his death. He died at the stake in Innsbruck, after being cruelly tortured.

—

JLG

Hutter, Leonhard (1563–1616). German Lutheran theologian. He studied theology in Strassburg, Leipzig, and Heidelberg. He taught in Wittenberg during the post-Philippist era, which tended to interpret the thought of ⇒Melanchthon in a more conservative vein, thus adapting it to the positions of the radical Lutherans or Gnesio-Lutherans (⇒Flacius). H. assumed a polemical and apologetic posture of great rigidity and dogmatism. He defended Lutheran orthodoxy against what he perceived as attacks from Calvinists and Roman Catholics.

—

CEA

Huxley, Thomas Henry (1825–95). One of the most prominent marine biologists of the time, in addition to being a paleontologist, biblical critic, and reformer of education. He defended and promoted the theory of evolution of ⇒Darwin, but rejected Darwinism morally. From the viewpoint of nature, domination and conquest through whatever means possible is normal. But in the moral and social sphere, the theory of the survival of the fittest must be rejected as offensive and cruel. For H., our natural impulses are immoral and thus ought to be domesticated and subjected to moral patterns given by reason.

—

IG

Ibas of Edessa (?–457). Bishop of that city from 435 until his death. A leading representative of the school of Antioch, and thus of the "disjunctive" Christology that characterized that school. His best-known writing, although not the most important, is *Epistle to the Maris of Adrashir* (433; it is possible that "Maris" was the title given to the bishop of that city, but it is more probable that it was the proper name of this specific bishop). In it he expounded the objections of the Antiochenes to the "unitive" Christology of the Alexandrians, and especially that of ⇒Cyril of Alexandria. The "robbers' synod (*latrocinium*) of Ephesus" (449) declared him a heretic and removed him from office, but the Council of ⇒Chalcedon restored him, after being assured that I. distanced himself sufficiently from the excessively disjunctive Christology of ⇒Nestorius.

Even after the death of its author, the letter of I. continued to be the reason for the controversies that culminated in the debate surrounding the "Three Chapters" (these were, in addition to the letter of I., the writings of ⇒Theodore of Mopsuestia and ⇒Theodore of Cyrus). Pope ⇒Vigilius defended the Three Chapters, affirming, as far as the letter of I. is concerned, that it was read and accepted by the Council of Chalcedon, and thus to declare it heretical would be to declare by implication that the council was also heretical. In the end, the Second Council of ⇒Constantinople (553, Fifth Ecumenical Council) condemned the Three Chapters. Regarding I., this council used a subterfuge, pretending that the letter read in Chalcedon could not be the same one.

The school of Edessa, of which I. was the chief teacher, had been formally closed by Emperor Zeno in 489. Its teachers then moved to Nisibis, where they continued to teach the disjunctive Christology that had always characterized them, even to the extent that the rest of the church gave them the name of Nestorians.

—

JLG

Iglesia y Sociedad en América Latina (ISAL). Ecumenical organization of a prophetic character, with origins in 1962, and parallel to other organizations in Latin America such as CELADEC (Latin American Evangelical Commission on Christian Education) and ULAJE (Latin American Union of Evangelical Youth). It received support from the Office of Church and Society of the ⇒World Council of Churches.

ISAL created a theological and ecumenical agenda for the region during a time of struggle and political division in the continent. Julio de ⇒Santa Ana, José ⇒Míguez Bonino, Elsa ⇒Tamez, Enrique ⇒Dussell, Pablo ⇒Richard, Rubem ⇒Alves, and others contributed to the development of the theology of ISAL. This theology, according to historians and critics of the movement, is centered in the following premises: (1) the centrality of the kingdom of God as eschatological and historical utopia, (2) a deep concern for the social and transforming participation of Christians in the continent, (3) an ecumenical spirit among Protestants and Catholics that promotes awareness of the theological and revolutionary task in the region, and (4) the development of an ecclesiology that promotes a militant and missional church. It is important to note that, in addition to theological inquiry, ISAL embodies the integration of the social sciences with the theological task.

The theological material of ISAL is found in the journal that carries the same name: *Iglesia y Sociedad en América Latina* (Church and Society in Latin America).

———

CCO

Ignatius of Antioch (ca. 35–ca. 107).

Bishop of Antioch of Syria who was martyred in Rome during the reign of Trajan (98–117). According to ⇒Origen and ⇒Eusebius, he was the second bishop of Antioch after Evodius, ca. 69. But some consider St. Peter the first bishop, in which case I. would be the third.

We know about his life almost exclusively through his seven letters written on the way to martyrdom, when he was guarded by ten soldiers. In Smyrna, ⇒Polycarp, the bishop of that city, received him together with delegates from the neighboring churches of Ephesus, Magnesia, and Tralles. From there he wrote letters to those three congregations and to the church of Rome. From Troas, the next stop on the way to martyrdom, he wrote to the churches of Philadelphia and Smyrna, with a personal note to their bishop, Polycarp. From there he may have crossed by boat to Neapolis, and then by land to Philippi, where, according to Polycarp in his letter to the Philippians (chaps. 9 and 13), he was received by the believers. The rest of the trip to Rome is not documented. He probably crossed Macedonia and from there went to Italy by sea.

The letters of I. reveal a person intensely devoted to Christ and joyfully facing imminent martyrdom, which could open the way to God, to true life. In his letter to the Romans, he asks them not to intercede for him before the authorities and not to get in the way of his access to life: "Do not wish death for me. Do not give back to the world someone who wishes to belong to God; do not deceive him with material things. . . . Allow me to imitate the passion of my God" (6:1–2).

I. was convinced that his death would make him a true disciple of Jesus Christ. Martyrdom was the goal of his life, the purifying vehicle that would take him into the very presence of God. Some of the metaphors that he uses to describe this vocation are truly dramatic. In his letter to the Romans (4:1–2) he speaks of himself as the wheat of God, which when crushed by the teeth of the wild beasts will become pure bread for Christ.

This fervent wish for martyrdom should be understood in the context of the forgiveness of sins. It was believed that baptism erased all sin committed until that moment. Since baptism could not be repeated, there were two ways to erase the sins committed after this. One way was penitence. The other was martyrdom, which was considered a second baptism, by blood, that took away all the sins committed since the first baptism. Just as I. did, many Christians offered themselves voluntarily, for they were convinced that this was the passage to eternal life.

Aside from voluntary martyrdom as an expression of faith, these letters show us two additional aspects of the congregations of the second century: their ecclesiastical organization and the struggle against alternative versions of the faith. A look at the organization of the church shows that the local congregation was led by a bishop who was supported in his task by a council of presbyters and assisted by deacons. These three offices were clearly delineated, with special importance granted to the bishop as the center of the liturgical and social life of the congregation. In this sense a development is noticed in relation to the Pastoral Epistles, the *Didache* and *1 ⇒Clement,* in which the titles of bishop and presbyter and the offices that they represent are not yet well delineated. Obviously, I. belonged to a later stage in the history of the church.

An interesting aspect of the way in which I. conceived of this organization is that an apostolic succession is not traced between the bishop and those who preceded him. Instead, they are presented as earthly offices of heavenly archetypes. For example, in *Letter to the Magnesians* 6:1 the bishop occupies the place of God, the presbyters that of the apostles, and the deacons that of Jesus Christ—a Platonic scheme of reality that is characteristic of I. and that is not found in other writings of the time.

I. does not concern himself with describing in detail the struggle against heretical movements. Instead he prescribes a church order that is presented as the best remedy against the schismatics: "Flee from the schisms that are the source of evildoing. All should follow the bishop as Jesus Christ followed the Father"

(*Smyrn.* 8:1). Nevertheless, there are indications in his letters that these opponents manifested Judaizing and gnostic characteristics (*Magn.* 8 and 9; *Trall.* 10; *Smyrn.* 2).

Against these divergent interpretations, I. emphasizes the divinity of Christ, apparently against "Judaizers" who saw Jesus as the last of the prophets. He referred to Christ as "our God" and also as "the Christ God" (*Smyrn.* 3). On the other hand, he underlines the reality of the incarnation, passion, and resurrection of Jesus, apparently against gnostics who believed that matter was fundamentally evil and that the divinity could not reside in a material body. I. affirms that Jesus retained his human nature even after the resurrection, although in spirit he was united with the Father (*Smyrn.* 3).

The letters of I. seem to have been first collected by Polycarp, who probably obtained them from Burro, the amanuensis of I. (*Phld.* 11:2). They have come down to us in three forms: a long text interpolated in the fourth century with elements that favored an Arian point of view and with six additional letters that were falsely attributed to I.; a short text of Syrian origin that represents a summary of the genuine letters; and finally a middle text that contains the original text of the authentic letters.

───
ODV

Ignatius of Loyola ⇒Loyola, Ignatius of

Ildefonsus of Toledo (ca. 607–69).
Archbishop of that city from 657. Among his works are a treatise, *In Defense of the Perpetual Virginity of Mary*, and an appendix to the *Illustrious Men* by ⇒Jerome, whose purpose was to bring that work up to date, after the additions of ⇒Gennadius of Marseilles and of ⇒Isidore of Seville. But while Jerome and his successors had been interested above all in the work of their "illustrious men," I. was most interested in their morality and holiness.

───
JLG

Inman, Samuel Guy (1877–1965).
North American, member of the Disciples of Christ, and leader in the missionary movement in Latin America. He participated in the Christian Congresses of Latin America in Panama (1916), Montevideo (1925), and Havana (1929). He was executive secretary of the Committee on Cooperation for Latin America and

promoter of missionary work under the auspices of religious panamericanism. With Erasmo ⇒Braga, Alberto ⇒Rembao, and others, I. helped articulate a missionary justification for the presence of the Protestant missions in Latin America. His best-known works are *Problems in Panamericanism*, *Christian Cooperation in Latin America*, *Ventures in Inter-American Friendship*, and *América revolucionaria*.

───
CCO

Irarrazával, Diego (1942–).
One of the most respected theologians in the field of contextualization and popular religiosity in Latin America, particularly in relation to the indigenous peoples of the Andean region. A Jesuit priest, I. has written *Inculturación: Amanecer eclesial en América Latina* (Inculturation: Ecclesial Dawn in Latin America) and *La fiesta, símbolo de la libertad* (The Fiesta: Symbol of Freedom).

───
CCO

Irenaeus of Lyon (?–ca. 202).
One of the main theologians of the ancient church. In the twentieth century the rediscovery of his theology, often ignored until then, produced movements of theological renovation in Catholicism as well as in Protestantism. In the latter, the rediscovery of I. was one of the main impulses of the Lundensian school, represented in theologians such as A. ⇒Nygren, G. ⇒Aulén, and G. ⇒Wingren.

Not much is known about the life of I. He was a native of Asia Minor, and probably of Smyrna, where he was a disciple of the bishop of that city, ⇒Polycarp. Around the year 170 he settled in the city of Lyon, in Gaul, where there were a good number of immigrants from Asia Minor, and he joined the church in that city. There he was a presbyter in 177, when he went on an embassy of his church to that of Rome. On his return to Lyon, he was elected to succeed Bishop Pothinus, who had suffered martyrdom.

As bishop, I. shepherded his flock and evangelized his Celtic neighbors, but above all he was concerned about the heresies that appeared to be gaining ground. It was in response to them that he wrote his chief work, *Denunciation and Refutation of the Reputed Gnosis*, generally known by the abbreviated title *Adversus haereses*. This work comprises five books. Originally written in Greek, it survives mostly in a Latin translation and in a partial version in Armenian.

The first book of this vast work is a description of some of the teachings that, according to I., threatened the integrity of the Christian faith. Chief among them is Gnosticism ($\Rightarrow$gnostics), particularly in the version of $\Rightarrow$Valentinus. Although I. refers to several other heresies, he does not try to summarize them, declaring that "in order to prove that sea water is salty, it is not necessary to drink it all."

The second book attempts to demonstrate the internal contradictions and the rational difficulties of the gnostic systems. This seems to be especially important to him, because Gnosticism presents itself as an eminently rational teaching. By showing its internal contradictions, I. hopes to eliminate its chief attraction.

In the last three books, I. expounds his own theological position, as he attempts to refute Gnosticism on the basis of Scripture. Although some of his refutations are more convincing than others, what is most interesting about these books is not those arguments, but the vision of Christianity that they reveal.

The other important work of I. is his *Demonstration of the Apostolic Preaching*, also known as *Epideixis*. This is a much briefer work, of a catechetical or rather a didactic character, since its purpose is not the instruction of those who prepare themselves for baptism, but the acquisition of greater depth in those who have already received baptism, helping them to see new dimensions of their faith and strengthening them in it.

All of this implies that I. does not offer an orderly and detailed exposition of his thought. This may be one of the reasons why he has not been read or studied as much as other more systematic theologians. But not having given a systematic presentation of his entire thought does not imply that I. did not have a coherent vision of the Christian faith. What it does imply is that in order to discover that vision his texts must be scrutinized, organizing what is stated in them in a more systematic way.

On the other hand, I. does not appear to have been, nor to have desired to be, an original thinker. Instead, his purpose was to reaffirm what he had received from his forerunners in the faith—especially from Polycarp and, through him, from "John," although it is not clear from which of the various persons in the ancient church with that name.

It is precisely because of this traditionalist attitude that I. is especially interesting, for if he wrote approximately in the year 170, that implies that he was expressing what had already been for a long time the teaching and practice of the church.

The doctrine of creation was of fundamental importance for I. That was partly because his opponents maintained a radical dualism between the spiritual and the material, so that the first appeared good to them, and the second evil. Over against this position, I. insisted that all that exists has been created by God and is therefore good.

God has created the world through what I. called "the hands of God," which are the Son and the Holy Spirit. Apparently the purpose of I. in using this image of the hands is to indicate that God creates directly, and not through intermediaries. The supreme God of the gnostics was a distant being who would never be contaminated with this physical matter that the world and bodies are made of. The God of I. is introduced directly and personally in the world through those "hands."

The human being was created "in the image of God." Since Paul declared that Jesus Christ is the image of God, what I. understood is that Jesus Christ, God made flesh, was the model that God used in the creation of the human being. The eternal purposes of God included the close union between the divinity and the humanity that takes place in Jesus Christ. The incarnation is not only a remedy for human sin, but it is the culmination of what God had foreseen and desired for humanity, even apart from sin.

The original perfection of humanity does not mean, as it did for later theologians and for the greater part of the Western tradition, that Adam and Eve were superior, stronger, greater, or wiser beings than we. Original perfection consisted in a perfection that was adequate for that moment in the designs of God. It is a perfection similar to that of a newborn, of whom we say that it is "perfect," not because it is big, wise, and strong, but because it is as it should be in that moment of its life. I. even declared that God made Adam and Eve "like children," with the intention that they grow in wisdom and righteousness until they would reach their own union with God.

What happens when human beings sin is that they become slaves of Satan, who keeps them from developing as God had intended. Human development continues, but it is a development that could be called monstrous, for the good that God had intended in it is joined with the distortion that evil produces. In such a situation, the law is given by God in order to restrain sin and its consequences. The law and its fulfillment are not the final purpose of human life. Their purpose is eternal communion with God. What the law does is to help us direct our growth toward God, and above all to give us a hint of what God has promised us. Briefly stated, in addition to being a rule, the law is promise.

Jesus Christ, God made human, is the culmination of the creative and redemptive work of God. On this point, I. underscores the continuity between God's creative work and God's redemptive work—in contrast to some heretics, for whom the discontinuity between creation and redemption was such that some postulated that they were the work of different gods or principles. This incarnate Son who served as model for the creation of the human being now comes to dwell among us for our new creation, our restoration.

I. spoke of the redemptive work of Jesus Christ in terms of what he calls "recapitulation." For I., a recapitulation was not a summary or brief repetition, as it is for us. Instead, recapitulation is, as its etymology indicates (in Latin *caput* is "head"), a "reheading" of humanity.

Because of sin, our old head, Adam, remained subject to death and Satan. Now, in Jesus Christ, a new humanity begins, a new body of salvation whose head is Jesus Christ. This is the "recapitulation" or "reheading" to which I. refers, basing himself on several Pauline passages, and above all on Ephesians 1:10, where the Greek literally says that the eternal plan of God is to reunite all things in Christ as under a single head.

This recapitulation also implies a victory over Satan, by whom humanity was enslaved. When he came into this world, and when through death he arrived at the very lair of the devil, in order to triumph in his resurrection, Jesus Christ conquered the evil one, "having taken captivity captive" (Eph. 4:8). Thus the entire life of Jesus Christ, from the time of his incarnation, is part of his saving work and of his battle and victory over the devil.

For I. the eternal purpose of God was being united with humanity, and therefore the christological problems that were later posed did not present him with major difficulties. These problems would have to do with the way in which it is possible for divinity and humanity to be joined in Jesus Christ, when they appear to be two opposing realities. For I. such a contradiction does not exist, for the humanity that is complete and true and that arrives at its goal is precisely the one which lives in communion with God.

The new humanity whose head is Jesus Christ is the church, the body of Christ. The church is the body of Christ because it is the joining together of those who have been grafted into him, as members of a body. This grafting begins in baptism, and is nourished by worship and the Eucharist. In the Eucharist, as we unite with the immortal body and blood of Jesus Christ, we become participants of his immortality.

In the end, this new humanity will live in communion with God. In some passages, I. appears to indicate that this purpose of salvation is universal, in such a way that all will participate in that union. Other passages appear to indicate that even the fall is part of the plan of God, as the means by which God directs the historical process that in the end would lead to the incarnation and the final consummation. But those passages are brief and are not entirely clear.

In any case, it is difficult to exaggerate the importance of I. for contemporary theology. His dynamic vision of reality, his christocentric faith, his doctrine of a God who is transcendent but near, his emphasis on the place of the church in the process of salvation, and his pastoral attitude in the refutation of error are contributions that the twentieth century began to appreciate and rediscover, and that today still deserve greater study and consideration.

———

JLG

Isasi-Díaz, Ada María (1943–).

Roman Catholic theologian, a native of Cuba who at a very early age emigrated to the United States. In 1977 she obtained a master's degree in medieval history from the University of the State of New York. Later at Union Theological Seminary she received a master's degree in theology (1985), a master's degree in philosophy (1989), and a doctorate in theology with a specialization in social ethics (1990, when she was the first Latina to obtain this academic title). Since 1991 she has taught at Drew University. In the last two decades she has stood out as a writer on pastoral theology for base communities, as an academic of international fame, and as a feminist activist. Her experience in parish ministry, as parish coordinator of religious education, as organizer of the Conference on the Ordination of Women, as a lecturer and facilitator of feminist reflection groups, led her to write, with Yolanda Tarango, a book whose theological innovation would make it a classic: *Hispanic Women: Prophetic Voice in the Church* (1988). These two Latina theologians explore a theology from the perspective of Latina women and illustrate this process through examples given by the women of their reflection groups.

I.-D. is known as the pioneer of mujerista theology, a liberating praxis that adopts a critical position over against North American feminism, which does not take into account race and social class, and over against Hispanic theology, which does not take into account feminine perspective and experiences—hence the name "mujerista," which distinguishes it from the feminism of the dominant groups. Other important works of I.-D., in addition to some twenty articles, are *En la Lucha: In the Struggle* and *Mujerista Theology: A Theology for the Twenty-First Century*, which is a collection of her essays. She participates in the Academy of Catholic Hispanic Theologians in the United States (ACHTUS), which in 1994 granted her the Virgilio ⇒Elizondo prize for her academic excellence.

—

EF

Isho bar Nun (9th century). Nestorian patriarch from 823 to 828. He wrote homilies, treatises on canon law, and a *Theology* that has been lost.

——

JLG

Isidore of Pelusium (?–ca. 445). Abbot of a monastery in Egypt from whom a collection of more than two thousand letters is preserved. A defender of Alexandrian Christology and collaborator of ⇒Cyril of Alexandria, he nevertheless opposed the excesses of that school, on occasion defending the Antiochene point of view, and in the end resisting the fanaticism of ⇒Dioscorus. Although he was an Alexandrian in the rest of his theological positions, he criticized the allegorical exegesis that always characterized that school. Furthermore, he criticized the tendency to interpret the entire Old Testament as if it always referred to Jesus Christ, and he insisted on the historical character of a major part of the Hebrew Bible.

——

JLG

Isidore of Seville (ca. 560–636). Bishop of that city beginning ca. 600, when he succeeded his brother Leander. He was a prolific author who devoted himself to preserving, summarizing, and transmitting the knowledge of antiquity. Among his works are *On the Difference of Words*, a study of the shades of meaning of synonyms; *On the Universe*, which attempts to explain natural phenomena on the basis of the best science of antiquity and to off-

set the superstitions surrounding such phenomena; a continuation of the *Illustrious Men* by ⇒Jerome; and the *Etymologies*, his most famous and influential work.

The *Etymologies*, which occupied several years of the life of I., are much more than a series of etymological studies. They are a vast encyclopedia of all the knowledge that I. could acquire and transmit to posterity. To demonstrate the breadth of this work, it is enough to list the topics that are discussed in his twenty books: grammar; rhetoric and dialectics; mathematics (which includes music and astronomy); medicine; laws and the divisions of time; books and ecclesiastical offices; God, the angels, and the faithful; the church and the sects; languages, nations, kingdoms, militias, cities, and kinships; words; the human being and strange beings; animals; the world and its parts; buildings and fields; rocks and metals; agriculture; war and games; ships, buildings, and clothes; provisions and domestic and rustic utensils.

Although it is hardly original, this vast encyclopedia was a channel through which the knowledge of antiquity was preserved and transmitted to the Middle Ages. It was therefore as a collector and transmitter of knowledge and theories rather than as an original theologian that I. contributed to the theological task.

——

JLG

Jacob Baradaeus (ca. 500–78). Bishop, Syrian missionary, and Monophysite who was called the apostle of Asia. He is credited with being the genius who succeeded in preserving the Syrian Monophysite tradition (known as the Jacobite tradition) in spite of frequent persecution by the authorities of Constantinople.

He was born in Tella, to the east of Syria, and was educated as an ascetic monk in a monastery near Nisibis. Having been consecrated to the bishopric in Edessa in 542, he faced many persecutions, from which he emerged victorious because of his peculiar way of evading them: using old clothing to confuse his persecutors. His extraordinary missionary and theological activity gave new life to the Monophysite tradition in Syria and Persia.

——

JLG

Jacob of Edessa (640–708). Theologian of the Jacobite Church of Syria. Encyclopedic author and biblical commentator, defender of the christological doctrine of the "one nature" in Christ.

———

JLG

Jacobs, Henry Eyster (1844–1932).

Lutheran theologian and historian, born in Gettysburg, Pennsylvania, professor at the Lutheran Seminary of Philadelphia, and prolific writer. J. had a deep influence on the formation of American Lutheranism between the Civil War and the Great Depression.

———

NRG

Jacopone da Todi (?–1306).

Italian mystical poet. He wrote a collection of *Laudas*, although many that are attributed to him are not his. His masterpiece is *The Weeping of the Virgin*, which is a typical example of the Marian devotion of the late Middle Ages. With great lyrical passion, J. pictures the pain of Mary, which culminates in an anguished cry to John: "figlio novello . . . morto è lo tuo fratello" (new son, your brother has died). The hymn *Stabat Mater,* in which such feelings are expressed, is also attributed to him.

———

JLG

James, William (1842–1910).

A scholar who pursued studies in art, natural science, medicine, psychology, and philosophy. A great part of his academic career took place at Harvard University, where he obtained a degree in medicine. He was named professor of philosophy at a time when that discipline enjoyed great prestige, and is therefore one of the founders of North American philosophy.

His philosophical interests, which were mostly devoted to resolving dualisms, led him to study the relationships between psychology and religious experience. His two volumes on *Principles of Psychology* and his *Pragmatism* were accompanied by two important studies on religion: *The Will to Believe and Other Essays* and *The Varieties of Religious Experience*. The latter work presents a synthesis of his pluralistic and holistic thought. It is a study of religious life based on the experience of ordinary believers, spiritualists, and mystics, through which J. attempts to demonstrate that the uniqueness of religious testimony and the causes of its experience are enough to prove that the religious hypothesis is true. This argument, which makes causality the point of validation of the truth, is known as pragmatism, a concept that J. popularized and that would predominate in a great part of early-twentieth-century North American philosophy.

———

JRI

Jansen, Cornelius Otto (1585–1638).

Catholic theologian and bishop who was born in Holland and died in Belgium. Not to be confused with his uncle, Cornelius Jansen the Elder (1510–76). He pursued studies in philosophy and theology in Louvain (1602–9) and at the University of Paris (1609–11), where he obtained his doctorate in theology (1617). He was ordained in 1614. He worked as professor of theology and Scripture (1617–35) and as rector of the University of Louvain (1635–36). He was bishop of Ypres, Belgium (1636–38).

His university and ecclesiastical teaching career caused him to be involved in several controversies. Between 1624 and 1626 he traveled twice to the court of Spain to defend the right of the University of Louvain to grant degrees. His participation in 1635 in the resistance against the French invasion of Louvain was outstanding. He was a critic of Cardinal Richelieu. He also published polemics against Protestant ministers. Controversy followed him, even after his death, with the publication of his *Augustinus*.

Among his published works are *Pentateuchus seu commentarius in quinque libros Moysis* (1639), *Tetrateuchus seu commentarius in quatuor Evangelia* (1639), and *Analecta in Proverbia* (1644). These books reflect his university teaching on the Bible. *Augustinus* (3 vols., 1640), published posthumously, is the most famous of his works because it precipitated the controversy and the movement known as Jansenism.

Augustinus was a lifetime project. By 1619 J. was convinced of the need to correct commonly held ideas about the doctrine of grace in ⇒Augustine, and he resolved to write on the subject. He began this work in 1627 and finished its revision in 1638, a few days before dying of the plague. The work was published in 1640. The first volume summarizes the opinions of the Pelagians and Semi-Pelagians according to Augustine. The second volume discusses the relationship between theology and philosophy, declares the ecclesiastical authority of Augustine, discusses the condition of the angels and of humanity after the fall, and argues about the power of concupiscence over free will and on the impossibility of the state of pure nature. The third volume presents a strict version (some would call it severe) of the theme of grace in Augustine, emphasizing, among others, these subjects: the need of grace for every good work, the infallibility and irresistibility of grace over against free will, and the absolute gratuity of predestination. His exposition of Augustine was very similar to that of ⇒Calvin and entered into controversy with the Catholic teaching of ⇒Trent and, especially, with Jesuit theology.

Augustinus was written in a context of great theological controversy in the Catholic Church on the subject of divine grace and human freedom, not only against Protestantism (Council of ⇒Trent), but within Catholicism itself (Michael ⇒Baius, Luis de ⇒Molina), where it was the main issue in a controversy between Dominicans and Jesuits. Members of the Jesuit order opposed the publication of this book and brought about its condemnation. The defense of J. was led by J. A. Du Vergier, Abbot of ⇒Saint-Cyran, who had lived and worked with J. Both aspired to a reformation of the church centered on Augustinian teaching. Several important persons associated with the abbey of Port-Royal, which was under the spiritual tutelage of Saint-Cyran, also joined in that defense, especially A. ⇒Arnauld (1612–94), who published a defense of J. in 1644.

The condemnation by Rome appeared initially in the papal bull *In eminenti*, and again in *Cum occasione* (1653). This last document condemns five propositions that were associated with the position of J. in his *Augustinus*:

1. Some commandments of God are impossible for the righteous to obey with the present strength they have, however much they may desire and strive to do so, if they also lack the grace with which it is possible.
2. In the state of fallen nature, grace is irresistible.
3. In order to be worthy and unworthy in the state of fallen nature, the human being does not require the freedom of necessity, but rather the freedom of compulsion suffices.
4. The Semi-Pelagians admitted the need for inner prevenient grace for every action, even to begin in the faith, and they were heretics because they desired that grace to be such that the human will could decide to resist it or obey it.
5. It is Semi-Pelagian to say that Christ died or that he shed his blood for absolutely all.

The defense of the theological ideas of J. and the project for reformation led by Saint-Cyran

were the main foci of Jansenism in its early stages. But circumstances eventually led to the development of Jansenism as a religious and political movement of great magnitude. This movement deeply influenced France and the Low Countries during the seventeenth and eighteenth centuries and generated strong opposition in religious and political circles both in and outside of France.

——

LRR

Jenson, Robert W. (1930–).

Lutheran theologian who was born in the United States and was educated there as well as in Europe, and who has taught in universities and seminaries. A prolific writer, he has made contributions in systematic (Trinitarian and sacramental), confessional (Lutheran and Reformed), and ecumenical theology (evangelical, Catholic, and Orthodox). He recognizes ⇒Luther and ⇒Barth as his greatest influences.

——

NRG

Jerome (347–419).

One of the most distinguished Christian authors of antiquity, famous above all for his translation of the Bible into Latin, known as the Vulgate. A native of Panonia, as a young man he went to Rome to study. There he was baptized by Bishop ⇒Liberius. Then he traveled through the Levant, where for a time he led an extremely ascetic life, and where he also met theologians and pastors as distinguished as ⇒Gregory of Nazianzus and ⇒Gregory of Nyssa. On his return to Rome in 382, he served as secretary to Bishop ⇒Damasus, who assigned him the task of establishing a uniform text of the Latin Bible that was then in use, and which is now known as the Vetus Latina. While he devoted himself to this task, J. also instructed a group of distinguished women whom he taught Greek and Hebrew so that they could study the Bible with him. Chief among them were Paula and her daughter Eustochium, who later accompanied J. in Palestine. Being at heart an ascetic, J. did not care for life in Rome, with its sophisticated customs and excessive lavishness.

The last thirty-five years of J.'s life were spent mainly in Palestine, where, after some wanderings, he settled in Bethlehem and devoted himself to study and the ascetic life. Nearby, Paula and Eustochium founded a convent for women and continued studying under the direction of J. In Bethlehem J. finally devoted himself to his great translation of the

Bible from the original languages into Latin. But he could not do this without interruptions, such as the one that took place during the prolonged controversy on Origenism. J. had been an enthusiastic student of the works of ⇒Origen and had translated several of them. But little by little he became convinced that the opinions of Origen were not all orthodox. When controversy broke out around the teachings of Origen, J., who was no longer a convinced Origenist, became involved. His enemies pointed out his old sympathy for Origen. They criticized him for having learned Hebrew from Jewish rabbis, and they even accused him of illicit relations with Paula and her followers.

This was only one of the many controversies in which J. became involved. His ardent spirit, his vitriolic style, and frequently a profound rigidity in his opinions led him to strong clashes with a good many of his contemporaries. One of them was ⇒Augustine, who questioned some of the biblical translations of J. The latter responded with arrogant and even derogatory words. But in the end, united in their opposition to Pelagianism (⇒Pelagius), Augustine and J. became reconciled.

A good part of J.'s literary work consisted of translations. He translated the Psalms from Hebrew into excellent Latin poetry, and these texts were long used in Gregorian chant. The translation of the Bible far surpasses all his other works, and made the strongest impact, since until very recently the Vulgate was the official Bible of Roman Catholicism. He also translated several of the chief works of Origen, ⇒Eusebius of Caesarea, ⇒Didymus, and others.

In the field of theological polemics, he wrote a series of treatises against the Pelagians, against the Luciferans (⇒Lucifer of Cagliari), against his old colleague ⇒Rufinus, and against several other opinions that appeared to him to be wrong. J. made himself known as a historian, particularly in his treatise *De viris illustribus* (On Illustrious Men). He also wrote several biographies of saints. But it was as a biblical scholar that J. was preeminent. He wrote manuals on the etymology of the Hebrew proper names in the Old Testament and also on the geography of the Holy Land. In addition, he wrote homilies and commentaries on several books of the Bible. While he attempted to read and interpret the texts in their historical and geographical context, in these commentaries he always sought ulterior meanings, some of them allegorical. Thus, like Origen and a good part of the Alexandrian school, J. showed himself willing to find several messages in the same passage, as the interpreter penetrates more deeply into the mysteries of God.

J.'s theology was quite traditional. Perhaps his chief innovation, with respect to what was then generally held, was his inclination not to accept the authority of the deuterocanonical books—that is, those that, although they formed part of the traditional Septuagint and as such had been accepted by the church, were not part of the Hebrew canon.

———
JLG

Jerome of Prague (ca. 1371–1416).
Czech prereformer, a member of the Bohemian Brothers. Nephew of Archbishop Rokycana, who distributed both elements of the Communion and who appointed J. the head of a community of faith. He left the Utraquist community in order to establish a new community in Kunvald, in eastern Bohemia. He was a collaborator of the Englishman ⇒Wycliffe and translated several works written by him. It was J. who exposed his friend John ⇒Huss to the ideas of Wycliffe. He not only translated but also reproduced several of Wycliffe's works, for which he was excommunicated in 1409; a year later Sigismund of Hungary forbade him to share his ideas in the court. Like Huss, J. died at the stake as a heretic, after having been declared such by the Council of ⇒Constance. His death moved the University of Prague to declare him a martyr and to use him as a standard to rid itself of German domination in the university. In addition, the Hussite movement in Bohemia was revived by his testimony and death.

———
GC

Jerotheus (or Hierotheus).
Personage, perhaps fictitious, to whom ⇒Dionysius the Areopagite attributes his mystical knowledge.

———
JLG

Jewel, John (1522–71).
Bishop of Salisbury who was educated in Merton and Corpus Christi colleges at Oxford. He became one of the intellectual leaders of the reforming party. During the reign of Mary Tudor, J. agreed to sign a series of articles against Protestantism, but in spite of this action he was persecuted and forced to flee to Frankfurt, where he wrote against John ⇒Knox and opposed the Calvinists. When Elizabeth I was crowned, J. returned

to England and in 1560 was consecrated bishop of Salisbury. From then on he defended the middle way of Anglicanism, between Roman Catholicism on one side and the Puritans on the other.

Jiménez de Cisneros, Francisco (1436–1517).

Franciscan cardinal, confessor of Queen Isabella the Catholic beginning in 1492, and a shrewd politician and diplomat.

From his see in the Archbishopric of Toledo he led the Spanish church from 1495 to 1517, completing an important reform of the religious orders and preventing the disappearance of the Mozarabic rite, a liturgy used for centuries by Christians who lived under Muslim rule. For these reasons he is considered a reformer of the Spanish church previous to the reforms of the Council of ⇒Trent. He founded the University of Alacalá de Henares and directed the production of one of the great critical works of the period, *Biblia Políglota Complutense* (Polyglot Bible of Alcalá de Henares), published in 1522. This work included the first printed edition of the New Testament in Greek. In the political arena, J. combated all attempts to make Joanna the Mad the heiress of Isabella. He led the Inquisition in Spain and supported the expulsion of the Jews authorized by Queen Isabella in 1492. Through a request in the will of King Philip, he was made regent of Castille until the arrival of the young successor Charles I (Charles V, emperor of the Holy Roman Empire), who on the way to Spain removed him from office, sending him to a monastery, where he died.

Joachim of Fiore (or Flora) (ca. 1132–1202).

Abbot of the Cistercian monastery of Fiore or Flora who devoted himself to mystical contemplation and careful study of the Apocalypse. On the basis of that study he developed a vision of history known as Joachimism. His two chief works were the *Concordance between Both Testaments* and a commentary on the Apocalypse or Revelation of John under the suggestive title of *Apocalypsis nova*, which could be understood as "new revelation." With perhaps the teachings of ⇒Gilbert de La Porrée as a starting point, J. developed an outline of history based on a strange understanding of the Trinitarian doctrine.

According to this schema, history is composed essentially of three stages, each of them corresponding to one of the three persons of the Trinity. The first stage goes from Adam to Jesus Christ, and is the age of the Father. The second stage is that of the Son. Since from Adam to Jesus there are forty-two generations, and it is to be expected that the second stage, that of the Son, will be more perfect than the previous one, having generations of equal length, the forty-two generations of the second age, at the rate of thirty years per generation, point to the year 1260 as the end of that second age. Then the third age will come, that of the Spirit, about whose duration J. offers no indication.

In each of these ages, and especially as the transition to the next stage comes near, forerunners or heralds of the age to come appear. Thus, for example, the prophets in general, and John the Baptist in particular, are heralds of the second age. In the same way the monastic movement in general, and its great founders in particular, such as ⇒Benedict, are heralds of the age of the Spirit.

The theories of J. are another one of many cases in which Christians, pained by the apparent lack of faithfulness and consecration of their coreligionists and even of themselves, long for a new age of greater holiness and purity. In any case, on the death of J. many considered him a saint, above all because of his mysticism and his constant call to holiness of life.

But as his teachings became known, church authorities rejected them. This first occurred in the Fourth ⇒Lateran Council, which rejected his understanding of the Trinity, although in that case Gilbert de La Porrée was the one whom the council was really rejecting.

Later, when the "spiritual" Franciscans began to criticize the rest of the Franciscans and the church (⇒John of Parma), Joachimism emerged in all its strength. Soon it was said that ⇒Francis of Assisi had been the precursor of the age of the Spirit, just as John the Baptist had been the precursor of the age of the Son. Thereafter the institutional church came to be spoken of as a new Sanhedrin, willing now to smother the work of the Spirit.

Rejected and frequently persecuted by ecclesiastical authorities, Joachimism continued to gain followers well into the fourteenth century, when the failure of its predictions about the end led to its decline. Still, elements of its teaching survived, some of them within the framework of Freemasonry.

John XXIII (1881–1963). Angelo Giuseppe Roncalli, John XXIII, occupied the papacy from 1958 until his death in 1963. From a poor family in the rural area of Bergamo, he was assigned to serve as secretary of the bishop of Bergamo after his ordination. After the First World War, Father Roncalli was named national director of the Congregation for the Propagation of the Faith, the missionary arm of the Vatican. Later he was chosen for a diplomatic career, first in Bulgaria and then in Turkey and Greece. During the Second World War and under the German occupation, he led rescue task forces and stopped the deportation of many Jews to Nazi concentration camps. In France Roncalli became acquainted with the worker priest movement, thus gaining experience of great importance for his theological and social formation. In 1953 he was named patriarch of Venice, his last post before being elected pope.

Because of his age at the time when he was elected, it was expected that his papacy would focus chiefly on housekeeping within the church. Nevertheless he began an age of reforms as had never been before. J. XXIII called the Roman Catholic Church to an *aggiornamento*, a "bringing up to date." First, he created the largest and most international body of cardinals in history. Second, he convened the Second Vatican Council (⇒Vatican II) with the purpose of bringing up to date the teaching, discipline, and organization of the church. In addition, he began the revision of canon law. Unfortunately, he died before the second session of the council.

Among his encyclicals, he wrote *Pacem in Terris* (1963), in which he proposes the importance of peace as a theological criterion for coexistence. This encyclical continues to be a plan of action for the Christian religion in the entire world. J. XXIII is remembered as a visionary pope, full of passion and compassion for the world, and possessing a uniquely sensitive pastoral conscience.

———

CCO

John Cassian (ca. 360–ca. 435). Born in the Roman province of Scythia Minor, from a very early age he was a monk in Bethlehem, but he left for Egypt in 385 to make a careful study of monasticism in that country. In Egypt he was under the guidance of ⇒Evagrius Ponticus, who had a strong influence on J.'s later thought. In 404 he became a deacon of the church of Constantinople, from which he traveled to Rome as part of a delegation sent by Patriarch ⇒John Chrysostom to Pope Innocent I. From that time on he remained in the West. He is recognized as having introduced monasticism into western Europe. Around the year 415 he founded two monasteries near Marseilles, in what is now France. There he wrote two great works: the *Institutes* and the *Conferences*. The first furnishes a simple rule for the use of monks and the organization of monasteries (it inspired ⇒Benedict of Nursia to write his famous *Rule*). The second work is a series of conversations (perhaps some of them fictitious) between the author and the great leaders of Eastern monasticism of his time. J.C. objected to the teaching of ⇒Augustine on grace, and he strongly attacked it in his *Conferences*. Consequently he was branded as Semi-Pelagian, although incorrectly. He also wrote *De Incarnatione Domini*, at the request of Pope ⇒Leo I, in order to familiarize westerners with the heresies of ⇒Nestorius, which were condemned by the Eastern church.

———

OOE

John Chrysostom (ca. 347–407). Patriarch of Constantinople and ⇒doctor of the church. A native of Antioch in Syria, he studied law there with Libanius, and theology with ⇒Diodore of Tarsus. He felt the call to monastic life, but the austerities of the monastic rule severely injured his health, leading him to the ministry of preaching, in which he earned the epithet of "Chrysostom" (golden mouth). He was ordained a deacon in 381, and a presbyter in 386 by Flavian, bishop of Antioch, who commended him to preaching and teaching as his chief ministries, in which he soon excelled.

His first great series of sermons, in 387, was motivated by street demonstrations in Antioch against the erection of statues in that city. But his great homiletic production was directed to the instruction and correction of the Antiochian society of his time, which was barely Christianized. His homilies on the books of the Bible (especially Genesis, Psalms, Isaiah, Matthew, John, Acts, and the Pauline epistles) earned him fame as one of the great biblical expositors of all time, since he was able to explain and apply what he understood to be the significance of the biblical texts to the social and ecclesial reality of his epoch. Some of his sermons still ring with force in our contemporary situation. His homiletical method contrasted the text with the social reality, calling listeners insistently (and sometimes ferociously) to conversion. Although he was opposed to a chiefly allegorical interpretation of the Bible, common in his time, he knew how to take advantage of the best of the allegorical method (without limiting himself to it) to apply the Bible to the real conditions of society and church.

Against his wishes, in 398 he was elected patriarch of Constantinople, where he encountered a difficult situation of corruption and abuse that permeated the imperial court as well as the local church. Nectarius, his predecessor as bishop of Constantinople, had been neither vigilant nor admirable in the episcopal function. J. devoted himself immediately to the reform of society, the court, and the church. His zeal, which was sometimes extreme, earned him numerous enemies. His lack of tact in his dealings with the imperial court was famous, especially with the powerful empress Eudoxia, who came to believe (not without reason) that the preaching of J. against corruption and immorality was in reality directed personally against her. J.'s chronic lack of tact (assisted by the hatred that the empress came to feel for him) resulted in the undermining of the pastoral work of the patriarch as well as of his own permanence in the see of Constantinople.

When he welcomed to his bishopric several refugees from Alexandria who had been accused there of heresy, he suddenly found himself involved in a struggle without respite with Theophilus, patriarch of that Egyptian city. In the so-called Synod of the Oak, convened on the outskirts of Chalcedon by imperial order in July of 403, the patriarch of Alexandria achieved the condemnation of J. and his separation from the bishopric of Constantinople. The accusation and deposition through heresy, invented and manipulated by Theophilus and his group of bishops, were ratified by Emperor Arcadius, who ordered his exile. When they heard the news, the Christian population of Constantinople went out into the streets to demand the return of their bishop. Out of fear of a major revolt, and the fear produced by an unexpected earthquake, the emperor rescinded his order, and J. returned to his patriarchal see. Nevertheless, his continual lack of tact again gained for him the hatred of the empress and of a major part of the court. By the following year (404) he was exiled again, this time accused of having returned to his episcopal functions in Constantinople after having been canonically deprived of them. Although the entire Western church, and especially Pope Innocent I, interceded in favor of the deposed patriarch, and although the people again demanded that the imperial order be rescinded,

nothing could prevent his exile to Antioch in Syria and later to the Hellespont. He died in 407 after a series of forced removals to ever more secluded areas ordered by imperial edict ruined his already wretched health.

J. is remembered for his personal holiness, which even his enemies did not doubt; for his reforming zeal; and for his magnificent sermons (above all, his expositions of the Bible). One of his most influential works is a treatise on the priesthood, in which he emphasizes and explains the personal and pastoral responsibilities of the Christian ministry. Many of his letters also survive. But the jewel of his literary production is still his sermons, which are models of eloquent preaching.

———

OOE

John Climacus ⇒Climacus, John

John Italos (12th century). Teacher of the Patriarchal School of Constantinople, where he succeeded Michael ⇒Psellus. His erudition was so great that he was given the title of second Plato. In spite of his philosophical interests, he was convinced that only theology is capable of leading to ineffable truths, and all the objections and dead ends of philosophy are to yield to it.

———

JLG

John of Antioch (7th century).
Author of a *Universal History*, of which only some fragments remain. Little is known about his life.

———

JLG

John of Ávila (1500–69). An older contemporary of ⇒Teresa of Ávila, with whom he sustained an interesting correspondence. He is known as the apostle of Andalusia. His writings, published in six volumes by the Biblioteca de autores cristianos, include sermons, biblical commentaries, letters, and a series of treatises on the reformation of the church and the spiritual life. Outstanding among the reformist treatises are *Reformation of the Ecclesiastical State*, two *Memorials to the Council of* ⇒*Trent* (one in 1551 and another ten years later), *What Should Be Informed to the Bishops*, *Causes and Remedies for the Heresies*, and *Necessary Warnings to Kings*. Outstanding among his works on spirituality are his *Treatises on the Love of God*, *Rules of the Spirit*, and

Prayers. He was beatified by ⇒Leo XIII in 1894.

———

John of Cournailles (12th century).

Author of a treatise, *On the Humanity of Christ*, in which he refuted the theories of ⇒Abelard and of ⇒Gilbert de La Porrée, who seemed to understand that the humanity of the Savior is nothing more than a vestment in which the Word presents itself. J. insisted on the complete humanity of Jesus Christ and called his opponents nihilists, since, according to his understanding, for them the humanity of Christ has no reality, is nothing.

———

John of Damascus (ca. 670–749).

Generally considered to be the last of the great fathers of the Eastern church. A native of Damascus, he was a high official of the caliphate. Although some say he was the grand vizier of the caliphate, it is most likely that he represented Christians before the government and collected the taxes that the caliphate levied on Christians. In any case, around the year 726 he was ordained a priest in Jerusalem, and from then on served in Palestine under John IV, the patriarch of Jerusalem. It is very likely that this transition was the result of the policies of the new caliph, Omar II, who forbade Christians to have public offices. Perhaps it is because of this that the records of the Seventh Ecumenical Council (⇒Nicaea, 787) praise him for having preferred "the shame of Christ above the riches of Arabia."

Besides sermons, poems, and some brief treatises on the vices, the virtues, and the ascetic life, J. wrote *Commentary on the Epistles of St. Paul*, which in reality is a compendium of what was stated previously by authors such as ⇒John Chrysostom and ⇒Cyril of Alexandria. He also wrote *Brief Introduction to Doctrine* and two treatises *Against the Nestorians* (⇒Nestorius).

His most famous work is the *Fount of Wisdom*, and especially its third part, which was frequently published separately from the rest and which is known as *Exposition and Declaration of the Orthodox Faith*. The first part of the *Fount* deals with philosophical themes. In it J. summarizes the teachings of some of the great philosophers of antiquity, as well as some Christian authors who had concerned themselves with philosophy. The second part is a historical compendium of 103 "heresies," among which

Islam is included, as well as opposition to images. While his discussion of the most ancient heresies is completely derived from previous authors whose statements and comments J. summarizes, his discussion of the most recent ones is original and provides interesting data on the theological debates of the eighth century, as well as on the way in which Christians under Muslim rule viewed that other religion.

Exposition and Declaration of the Orthodox Faith presents that faith in one hundred chapters. Following the order of the Nicene Creed, J. expounds the Christian doctrines systematically in the early chapters. However, in the last twenty-five chapters, before dealing with eschatological topics, he includes a series of themes that are of special interest to him. It is there that the concerns and interests of J. are best seen and his theological originality and creativity are most clearly manifested.

The core of J.'s theology is the doctrine of the incarnation. On this point, his teaching adheres to what was previously determined by the Council of ⇒Chalcedon and by those of ⇒Constantinople in 553 and 680–81. That christological doctrine is the basis of his defense of the use of images.

The iconoclastic controversy had broken out shortly before, and J. sided with the defenders of images. For that defense J. distinguished between true worship, which is due only to God, and veneration, which is due to saints and their images. Although both manifest themselves in genuflection, in reality they are very different, and therefore whoever kneels before an image does not commit idolatry.

Having made this distinction, J. declares that there is no reason for not venerating images. Human beings have the obligation to venerate one another, because we are all made in the image of God. Certainly, to wish "to give a concrete form to God would be the height of madness and impiety." Consequently, "we do not venerate what is material, but what those things signify." But it is Godself who, in mercy and love for humanity, became human, making Godself known in human form. To pretend then that it is impossible to see God through material realities is to deny the very incarnation of God in Jesus Christ, who is the center of the Christian faith. Since God has given Godself to us in a figure, it is possible that the figures of Jesus Christ and of those human beings in whom the image of God has revealed itself with greater purity can help us to see the invisible.

———

John of Jandum (?–1328). Principal defender of Latin Averroism in France in the fourteenth century, supporting the views of ⇒Siger of Brabant. He asserted that although reason and philosophy contradict much of the Christian faith, he accepted by faith the teachings of the church. He was excommunicated in 1327, with his colleague ⇒Marsilius of Padua. After being restored to the communion of the church, he was named bishop of Ferrara shortly before dying.

JLG

John of La Rochelle (1200–45). Franciscan successor of ⇒Alexander of Hales at the University of Paris. Among other works, he wrote *Essence (Summa) on the Soul* and *Essence (Summa) on the Virtues.* He differed from Alexander and the Augustinian tradition regarding the hylomorphic composition of intellectual beings. According to the majority of the Franciscans of the thirteenth century, every created being, including the spiritual or intellectual beings, consists of form and matter. Opposing this idea were ⇒Thomas Aquinas and the majority of the Aristotelians, who insisted that intellectual beings have no matter, but only form. On this point J. agreed with Thomas, and not with Alexander and the majority of Franciscans.

JLG

John of Parma (13th century). Professor in Paris and then general minister of the Franciscans from 1247 to 1257. Defender of the strict disciplinarian party within that order, he insisted on literal obedience to the will and testament of ⇒Francis of Assisi, and therefore on absolute poverty. This caused conflicts with Rome, as well as with the more moderate among the Franciscans. In the midst of these struggles, he became a follower of the apocalyptic ideas of ⇒Joachim of Fiore. After he was judged a heretic under the direction of his successor ⇒Bonaventure, the proceedings ended quietly, and J. was permitted, apparently thanks to papal intervention, to retire to the cloister, where he spent the rest of his days.

JLG

John of Salisbury (?–1180). Archbishop of Chartres, where he had previously studied. After studying in Chartres and in Paris, he went to England, where he served as secretary to Archbishop Becket, of whose death he was a witness. He was one of the first theologians to take into account the new Aristotelian perspectives that were penetrating western Europe. His chief work is *Metalogicus*, in which he defends the use of dialectical reason against the obscurantist tendencies of his age. A cautious theologian, he knew how to combine these new ideas with the old orthodoxy.

JLG

John of Spain (12th century). Also known as John of Seville. After serving as vizier of the Moorish king al-Mutamid of Seville, he served under the direction of Bishop Raymond of Toledo as one of the "translators of Toledo" through whom western Europe came to know Arab thought and a good deal of ancient Aristotelian philosophy.

JLG

John of St. Giles (?–1258). Dominican theologian of the first generation who taught in Paris, Tolosa, and Oxford. He had to face the objections of those who said that mendicants had no place in the universities.

JLG

John of the Cross (1542–91). Spanish mystical theologian. Founder, with ⇒Teresa of Ávila, of the Order of the Barefoot Carmelites. After a childhood and youth in the most abject poverty, he was ordained a priest in 1567. He soon laid aside his priestly responsibilities, hoping to devote himself entirely to the contemplative life by joining the Carthusian order. But Teresa dissuaded him from doing so and then called him to be the spiritual director and confessor of the Convent of the Incarnation in Ávila. By joining the reform movement led by Teresa, he exposed himself to persecution and was imprisoned for nine months in Toledo. He would live the rest of his life in precarious health, which he interpreted as a divine reply to his prayer "to suffer and be despised" like Jesus Christ himself. It is said that when he died his body remained uncorrupted for several years, and later portions of his body were distributed as relics among neighboring towns, where there soon began to appear visions of Christ, the Virgin, Elijah, and ⇒Francis Xavier, according to the personal devotion of each presumed witness. Among his best-known mystical poems are "The Ascent to Mount Carmel,"

"The Dark Night of the Soul," and a paraphrase of the Song of Songs, "Where Have You Hidden?" These spiritual canticles contain a mystical theology whose cornerstone is the conviction that the human soul needs to empty itself of itself and fill itself with God until, purified of all earthly dross, it can participate fully in the divine nature. This divine aspiration is at the root of the ascetic rigor of J., which led him to mortify his body and, up to a point, even to desire physical death.

He was canonized on December 27, 1726, and subsequently was declared a ⇒doctor of the church.

GCC

John Paul II (1920–2005).

Karol Wojtyla was elected to the papacy in 1978. Upon the death of his mother, he was brought up by his father, an official of the army, near Kraków, Poland. After a difficult experience under the German occupation during the Second World War, Wojtyla felt called to the priesthood. After serving as priest in a parish, he worked as professor of ethics. In 1963 he was named bishop of Kraków, a task he managed with great diplomacy and astuteness. He also traveled widely, a practice that he continued as pope, giving him an enormous international exposure.

The papacy of J.P. II was marked by extremes. On the one hand, he used his papal influence to contribute to the downfall of the Soviet bloc and to support the workers' movements in Poland against the communist regime. On the other hand, he confronted Latin American liberation theology by pointing out its dangers because of its participation in projects of a Marxist political nature. This posture was clear in his visit to Nicaragua, where he publicly reprimanded the priests in the Sandinista government.

The extremes are not limited to the political arena but are also seen in the theological and social spheres. For example, J.P. II wrote encyclicals and documents, such as *Redemptoris Missio* and "Dialogue and Proclamation," and other pastoral letters that show a continuity with the tradition of the Second Vatican Council (⇒Vatican II) relation to other religions, ecclesiology, and soteriology. Nevertheless, his position with respect to women in the ministry, abortion, and the role of the church in society indicated a strongly conservative tendency.

In 1998 J.P. visited Cuba, the only communist bastion in the West. There he demonstrated his conservative diplomacy when he invited Cuba to change, without at the same time offering a strong critique of the embargo that the United States has imposed on that Caribbean island.

CCO

John Peckham (ca. 1225–92).

Franciscan theologian, a disciple of ⇒Bonaventure in Paris, and later archbishop of Canterbury. A defender of traditional Augustinianism, he tenaciously opposed the innovations of ⇒Thomas Aquinas and other Aristotelians.

JLG

John Philoponus (6th century).

Monophysite theologian who argued that, since the hypostatic union of Jesus Christ also requires the union of nature, the fact that in the Trinity there are three hypostases (persons) requires that there also be three natures. This caused him to be accused of tritheism, although J. repeatedly rejected this accusation.

JLG

John the Deacon (8th century).

Author of an extensive *Life of ⇒Gregory,* composed between 770 and 780. Apparently it was J. who first gave Gregory the title of "the Great." His biography has little historical value and serves rather as an indication of what the eighth century thought was the life of an exemplary Christian.

JLG

John the Grammarian (6th century).

Orthodox theologian of Palestine who wrote in defense of the Council of ⇒Chalcedon against ⇒Severus of Antioch and Monophysitism. Severus responded to this with *Against the Grammarian*, in three books.

JLG

John the Teuton (ca. 1170–ca. 1245).

His real name was John Semeca, but because he spent almost all of his career in Italy he was given the name Teuton as a reminder of his Germanic origin. He was professor of canon law in Bologna, and his chief work is a *Summa Decretalis*. The most interesting point of his theology may be his vision of the relationship between penitence and forgiveness. According to him, contrition is sufficient for the remission of sins, but confession and penitence are necessary in order to reach greater purification. In this he agreed with ⇒Peter Lombard.

———

JLG

Jonas, Justus (1493–1555). German theologian and humanist. He obtained academic degrees in theology and law and became expert in classical languages (Greek and Latin). He translated several works of ⇒Luther, his friend and collaborator. He was also an admirer of the great humanist ⇒Erasmus. His major contributions as a reformer were to the theological curriculum in the academy and to the renewal of preaching in the church.

———

NRG

Jones, Rufus Matthew (1863–1948). North American mystic, a long-standing (1893–1947) professor at Haverford College in Pennsylvania, which was sponsored by the Quakers. J. served as an unofficial spokesperson for the Society of Friends for half a century. His background was that of a farmer from Maine. He converted his mystical piety and profound scholarship into a practical demonstration of compassion through feeding programs for destitute Germans and Belgians immediately after the First World War. J. also helped to found the Friends' Service Committee and was its president for many years. His many writings reveal an ardent optimism, a pacifist conviction, and radiant love for God.

———

RPT

Joye, George (ca. 1495–1553). Promoter of the Reformation in England. He was born in the county of Bedford and was educated in Peterhouse College in Cambridge, where he obtained his master of arts degree in 1517. Later he worked as associate pastor with ⇒Tyndale, for which he was accused of heresy in 1527 and had to flee to Germany. During his stay in that country, he was one of the translators and supervisors of the publication of the Tyndale Bibles printed in Antwerp. The place of his death is unknown.

———

HMT

Juana Inés de la Cruz (1651–95). First Christian feminist theologian of the American continent. She was born in S. Miguel de Nepantla (a name that comes from *Náhuatl*, meaning "in the middle"), Mexico. Her birth name was Juana Ramírez de Santillana, surnames taken from her maternal grandfather. She was an "illegitimate" daughter of Isabella, who herself was the descendant of Spaniards born in Mexico (a *criolla*), and of Captain Pedro Manuel de Asbaje. She used the paternal surname only when she entered the convent (1669) so as not to stain the good name of the Order of Saint Jerome. Thus J.I. "was Nepantla": she was neither Indian nor Spanish.

She lived in the century of the repression of witches, when more than 80 percent of the executions of the Inquisition were of women. In the convent she sustained a furious struggle with her confessor, the misogynist Antonio Nuñez de Miranda.

She was precocious, brilliant, and clever. Hiding from her mother, she learned to read at the age of three. At the age of six she discovered that there were schools for males, and she asked that her mother dress her as a boy in order to matriculate. This never happened. When she was still a small child, she went to live with her grandfather Pedro in Panoayan. There J.I. devoured her grandfather's library, learning Náhuatl with the Indians and a little of the languages of the African slaves—J.I. herself owned a slave. Her aunt and uncle from Mexico City adopted her at the age of eight. The following year she learned Latin in twenty lessons. When she turned sixteen she went to live at the palace of the marquis of Mancera, as the favorite of the vicereine. In her zeal for wisdom J.I. rejected matrimony and opted for the monastic life in order to cultivate her intellect. She studied theology, philosophy, gastronomy, herbology, astronomy, mathematics, geography, geometry, and literature, but poetry was inborn in her.

In Hispanic America J.I. inaugurated the literary genre of autobiography with her *Reply to Sor Filotea de la Cruz*. The occasion for this was her response to a sermon by Antonio Viera, the great defender of the Brazilian Indians. She was astonished to see her refutations published and criticized in the *Athenogorical Letter*, which also condemned her secular knowledge. The bishop of Puebla, under the pseudonym "Sor Filotea," was the author. Her *Reply* provides overwhelming biblical exegesis in which she defends the right of women to cultivate the mind.

———

EPA

Julian of Eclanum (?–454). Chief defender of Pelagianism after the condemnation of ⇒Pelagius, and thus one of the chief protagonists of the controversy with ⇒Augustine. He attacked Augustine's teaching on grace in four books *To Turbantius*; and when Augustine refuted J., he in turn responded with another eight books *To Florus*. These writings of J. have been lost and can be reconstructed only on the basis of the quotations from them in the works of Augustine.

———
JLG

Julian of Halicarnassus (?–ca. 528). Monophysite theologian who radicalized the principle of the *communicatio idiomatum,* or interpenetration of the properties of the humanity and divinity in Christ, by saying that the body of Jesus was incorruptible. Apparently (although some interpreters differ) J. maintained that the divinity took possession of the humanity of Jesus in such a way that his body could not suffer any harm or natural corruption. The sufferings of Jesus were then not the natural result of the harm that his executioners wished to cause him, but the result of a miracle that allowed the incorruptible body of Jesus to suffer. His critics gave this posture the name of Aphthartodocetism, that is, the Docetism of incorruptibility.

———
JLG

Julian of Norwich (1342–1420?) Very little is known of her. What is known is that for more than twenty years she reflected on the mystical experience she had when she was about thirty years old, an experience that lasted a day and a night. Her reflections, *Book of Showings*, the oldest surviving book written in English by a woman, are a source of light and hope in the midst of the pessimism, fear, and anxiety that characterized England in the fourteenth century. In the midst of a historical period full of mortal anguish caused by the bubonic plague, the One Hundred Years' War, and the possibility of eternal damnation, J. insisted that God loves and delights in human beings. This mystical theologian presents a God whose power is expressed through love, and not punishment. The God she experienced is a maternal God who lovingly creates, compassionately restores, and caringly sustains. Although J. is not the first to use the image of mother to speak of God, it must be noticed that she places God the Mother on the same level as God the Father. She uses maternal physiological functions to describe the ways in which God

relates to human beings, and resorts to the maternal image not only to speak of each person of the Trinity, but to speak of the Trinity itself. The maternal womb is to her an instructive symbol of the cycle of human life and the path toward divinity: life begins in the maternal bosom of God and will arrive at the eternity, which is life in the heavenly bosom of eternal beginnings. J. uses maternity as a means to understand and point to what is divine in a way that does not reduce women to an object of veneration, but that represents the way in which women are treated in society and church. The image of God the Mother is a bold claim that breaks down the argument of the superiority of men based on the idea that they are a more faithful image of God than women. If Jesus nurtures with his body and blood in order to sustain the life of his progeny, then women are better equipped than men to act *in persona Christi.* Although in her first writings J. accepts the feminine attitude of diminishing her own importance, years later, in her more extensive writings, we see a woman who is free from that attitude, who no longer speaks of the soul, humanity, and God as "He," but as "She." Her way of speaking about creation, redemption, and eternal life, just like her extensive use of "God the Mother," kept her precariously between the understandings of heresy and orthodoxy prevailing in her time.

———
AMID

Julian Pomarus (5th century). A native of North Africa who established himself in southern Gaul, apparently fleeing from the Vandals who invaded his native Mauritania. Although the ancients mention several of his works, today he is known only by his treatise *On the Contemplative Life*, whose purpose is to help clergy combine the contemplative life with the active life that their ministry requires. Although he deals extensively with the different virtues and vices, for him the root of all evil is in pride and in the misguided will (*cupiditas*). The principal and only antidote against them is love.

———
JLG

Julius Africanus ⇒Sextus Julius Africanus

Jung, Carl Gustav (1875–1961). Swiss psychologist and psychiatrist, the son of a Reformed pastor, and founder of the school of analytic psychology. He studied medicine in Basel, psychiatry in Zurich, and psychology in France. He was professor in the universities of Zurich and Basel and was a collaborator of ⇒Freud, who considered him his right hand. Nevertheless, J.'s interpretation of the human psyche and of the dynamics of the unconscious, and his definition of libido, marked his rupture with Freud in 1917 with the publication of *The Psychology of the Unconscious*. With his emphasis on the relationship of the unconscious with the experience of the person, J. did away with the Freudian emphasis on the libido as the primary force behind personal motivations and devoted himself to the exploration of the "internal space" of individuals.

His theoretical contribution rests on his broadening the psychoanalytic approach of Freud, interpreting mental and emotional disturbances as attempts to find personal and spiritual integrity. He expanded Freud's concept of the unconscious with his notion of a collective unconscious and deepened its content by the concept of the "archetypes" as ancient primordial images that belong to the common treasure of humanity: maternity, the hero, the virgin, the shadow, and so on. These images are found in all mythology, and J. understood them as an integral part of the deep unconscious. Other areas of interest for J. were alchemy, astrology, I Ching cards, and the Tarot. In 1921 he published an important work, *The Psychological Types*, in which he establishes the link between the conscious and the unconscious and proposes the types of personality known as extroversion and introversion. Then he made a distinction between unconscious or repressed sensations and thoughts, which are developed during the life of an individual, and what he called "collective unconscious," which represents sensations, thoughts, and memories shared by all of humanity. The Myers-Briggs system of tests to establish personality types is based on J.'s psychology of the personality.

J. divides the psyche in three parts: the ego, which identifies with the conscious mind; the personal unconscious, which includes what is not present in consciousness, but which is not exempt from being present; and the collective unconscious, which includes "the common treasure of humanity": innate knowledge that we all share through archetypes or primordial or mythological images that act as an "organizing principle" in our daily life. The therapeutic approach of J. attempts to reconcile the different states of the personality (introversion and extroversion, thought, intuition, sensation, and

perception) with the goal of helping the client or parishioner to confront the personal unconscious and to integrate it with the collective unconscious. J. maintains that such a patient can reach a state of individuation or of self-integrity.

Outstanding among his principal works are *Transformations and Symbols of the Libido*, *The Ego and the Unconscious*, *Wealth and Its Current Problems*, *The Relationship between Psychotherapy and the Cure of Souls*, *Reality of the Soul*, *Psychology and Religion*, *On the Psychology of the Unconscious*, *The Psychology of Transference*, *Symbology of the Spirit*, and *Conscious and Unconscious*.

—

JR

Justin (ca. 100–ca. 165). Known as Justin Martyr. He was the most important of the Greek Apologists of the second century. J. was a native of Samaria, the son of pagan parents, and he spent a good part of his youth in a philosophical quest for truth. After testing Stoic, Aristotelian, Pythagorean, and Platonic teachings, J. met an old man whose name he does not give us, but who engaged him in a long dialogue. In the end J. says, "The old man left . . . and I did not see him again. But I immediately felt that a fire lit up my soul and love for the prophets and those men who are friends of Christ overpowered me. And reflecting on the reasoning of the old man, I found that only this one is the safe and useful philosophy." Then there began a career in defense of Christianity, which manifested itself in his teachings in Rome, where he established a Christian school; in his written works; and, in the end, in his martyrdom.

Three works of J. survive: two *Apologies* and *Dialogue with Tripho*. Since the second *Apology* appears to be only an appendix of the first, it can be said that his works are two. One of them, the *Dialogue with Tripho*, deals chiefly with the relationship between Christianity and the faith of Israel, while the other one deals with the relationship between Christianity and classical culture.

The interlocutor of J. in the *Dialogue* may well have been the famous rabbi Tarpho, but this could also be an imaginary dialogue, used by J. as a way of presenting his teachings. What interests J. in this work is the question of how to interpret the Old Testament. At the time there were Christians who thought that the OT should be rejected by the followers of Jesus (⇒Marcion), since what is presented there is very different from the teachings of the Master. On the other hand, Jews insisted that Christians interpreted the OT incorrectly when they saw in it the preparation for the coming of Jesus.

J.'s argument in this dialogue can be summarized by saying that for him the OT points toward Jesus chiefly in two ways: through its prophetic words, and through deeds or actions that are "figures" or "types" which also point toward Jesus. Thus, J. quotes the sayings of the prophets which by that time were linked with Jesus. But it is also necessary to take into account the "types," for example, that of the Passover lamb with whose blood the doors of the children of Israel in Egypt were marked. Thus, just as those Israelites were saved through the blood of the Passover lamb, so also the followers of Jesus are saved through the blood of the Lamb. Furthermore, the fact that the lamb is roasted opened in the form of a cross is a sign and announcement of the cross of Christ.

This is what is commonly called typological interpretation, which should not be confused with the allegorical method typical of ⇒Origen and the Alexandrians. In allegorical interpretation the historical facts are left aside. What is important is the text, which then becomes an allegory that must be deciphered. In typological interpretation the historical events themselves point toward other historical events, particularly in the life of Jesus.

J. discusses the relationship between Christianity and classical culture mostly in his two *Apologies*. In order to explain that relationship, he makes use of the doctrine of the Logos. In this he had ⇒Philo of Alexandria as a precedent. For a long time Greek philosophy had affirmed that human reason is capable of understanding and capturing reality because under both human reason and reality there lies a fundamental reason or order, the Logos. Without such a Logos, it is impossible to know or understand anything. Little by little, some philosophers had given substance to that Logos, and some even spoke of it as a power that inspires all knowledge. The Gospel of John begins by affirming that Jesus Christ is the Logos or Word of God through whom all things were made. J. then blends both traditions, affirming that the one who became incarnate in Jesus Christ is the eternal Word or Logos of God through whom all things were made and through whom all knowledge is given. This means that all that the ancients knew, they knew thanks to the same Logos who became incarnate in Jesus Christ. What the ancients knew "in part," the Christians know completely, in his incarnation. Thus Christians can claim for themselves any knowledge of antiquity, because it is knowledge given by their Lord. Furthermore, we can even say that Heraclitus, Plato, and all the wise people of antiquity were wise thanks to the Logos, and thus in a certain sense were "Christians."

J. thus opens the way for Christian theology to accept and appropriate for itself whatever good and whatever truth it finds in the surrounding culture, and at the same time invites his coreligionists to see that culture in a positive way, as something that, at least in part, is a work of God.

His works are also an important source for our knowledge of early Christian worship.

———

JLG

Justinian (482–565).

Justinian (482–565). Byzantine emperor from 527 until his death. Under his regime the Byzantine Empire recovered some of its lost brilliance and for some time it conquered North Africa again. Some of that new flourishing was reflected in the compilation and reorganization of Roman law. J. is important for the history of theology because he tried to win the support of his discontented subjects in Egypt and Syria, the majority of whom were Monophysites. This led him to a series of measures and edicts that in the end only served to underscore differences.

J. first convoked an encounter between Chalcedonians and Monophysites, the result of which was so dismal that it is known as the Contradictory Conference. There the Monophysites insisted on the formula "one of the Trinity suffered," which was an expression of traditional Alexandrian Christology. But the other faction refused to affirm such a formula. J. was then convinced that it was the Chalcedonians who were not willing to seek unity, and from that time forward he was inclined toward policies that supported the "unitive" Christology of Alexandria at the expense of the Antiochene tradition and of the Chalcedonian affirmation of the "two natures" in the Savior. This culminated in the debate about the "Three Chapters," when J. condemned the teachings of three great Antiochene teachers, ⇒Ibas of Edessa, ⇒Theodore of Mopsuestia, and ⇒Theodoret of Cyrus.

The West reacted strongly against the action of J. Pope ⇒Vigilius, who was taken to Constantinople by imperial order, in the end agreed to sign a *Iudicatum* against the Three Chapters. But this exacerbated the opposition of those Westerners, who were outside J.'s reach. Vigilius himself felt strengthened and withdrew his *Iudicatum*.

Then J. convoked a council, the Second Council of ⇒Constantinople (553). It condemned the Three Chapters, although at times distinguishing the persons from their teachings, and trying not to contradict the Council of ⇒Chalcedon, where a letter of ⇒Ibas had been used as a sign of orthodoxy.

For some time Vigilius resisted imperial pressure. But he finally acceded to what was done in the council and produced a new *Iudicatum* in which, through subtleties and subterfuges similar to those of the council, he tried to safeguard his integrity at the same time that he affirmed the conciliar decisions. A whole series of disagreements and schisms in the West followed this. But little by little the disputants became calm again, and with the passing of the years everyone accepted the council of 553 and its decisions. Consequently, it is considered the Fifth Ecumenical Council.

—

JLG

Justus Jonas ⇒Jonas, Justus

Justus Menius ⇒Menius, Justus

Kähler, Martin (1835–1912). Lutheran systematic theologian, a native of Eastern Prussia. He established the difference between the historical Jesus and the redeeming Christ, arguing that all the texts of the New Testament are testimonial literature. He also insisted that the missionary task is an integral part of the gospel. He greatly influenced the thought of Rudolf ⇒Bultmann.

—

JDRR

Kant, Immanuel (1724–1804). One of the chief philosophers of the eighteenth century, he has strongly influenced modern theology. In his *Critique of Pure Reason*, he argues that it is impossible to have objective knowledge of the external world, for in the very process of knowing, the mind prints its seal on what is known. Our perceptions are filtered and organized according to the categories of our mind, which has to order them within the structures of space and time and of its own categories (such as cause, relationship, and so on) without which it is impossible for us to know or think. Therefore knowledge cannot give us things just as they are in themselves.

This has had an enormous impact on all the fields of knowledge, for it implies that knowledge itself is always a relationship between mind and reality, and that the mind always leaves its mark on all knowledge, however objective it may seem. Notions such as substance, causality, and the like are not really "out there," but are structures that the mind must imprint on things in order to know them. Just as it is impossible to prove that substance really exists, it is impossible to prove the existence or nonexistence of God, the immortality of the soul, or life after death.

Nevertheless, for K., God, the immortality of the soul, and eternal life are necessary postulates for the existence of the moral institution, as he demonstrates in *Religion within the Limits of Reason Alone*. These postulates assure us that at the end of all time our own happiness will depend on good moral conduct. If these theological postulates are not real, moral life makes no sense. On the other hand, for K. religion has no value apart from its moral content. The contribution of religion is to allow us to change our character and help us to overcome evil with the inclination to do good. The church is the means through which this transformation can be achieved, and therefore it is one of the principal communities of moral formation.

According to K., the morality of human action is not based on its result or end, but on the motivation and intention of the actor, as he indicates in *Critique of Practical Reason*. The only thing that can be called good without more qualification is goodwill. To wish what is good is to wish according to the universal laws that reason gives us. Reason allows us to formulate the "categorical imperative," the moral principle which calls us to act in such a way that the basis of our action (our maxims or rules for acting) can be made a universal rule. In such a case we act in an autonomous way. The moral act is expressed in terms of duty. Morally we are called to fulfill our duty without taking into account the consequences of our actions. We do not act morally when our motivation is to obtain some benefit, such as pleasure, or when we seek to gain God's favor or personal salvation. The purpose of all moral action is that the action itself be moral. Among the duties that correspond to universal moral laws are not to lie, to keep our promises, to affirm and maintain our existence (not to commit suicide), and to treat other human beings as ends in themselves—that is, with respect and dignity, and never as mere means for the satisfaction of our own ends.

—

IG

Käsemann, Ernst (1906–98). German Lutheran theologian, professor of New Testament at the University of Tübingen, and a disciple of Rudolf ⇒Bultmann. K. was one of the chief proponents of the "new search" for the historical Jesus. Among his chief works is his commentary on the Letter to the Romans, in which he reemphasizes the centrality of justification by faith as the key to understanding the book.

———
NRG

Katoppo, Henriette M. (1943–). A native of Indonesia, K. is a writer, novelist, journalist, and theologian. Among her theological works are *Compassionate and Free: An Asian Woman's Theology.* A graduate of the Theological Seminary of Jakarta, K. has served in several ecumenical capacities around the world. Her theological work is rooted in the daily experience of Indonesian and Asian women and in the search for a new feminine identity that is liberated from patriarchy and other oppressive aspects of Asian cultures.

———
CCO

Kaufmann, David (1852–99). Jewish literary critic. Born in Kojetein (Moravia). He studied in the rabbinic seminary and the university of Breslau. He received his doctorate from the University of Leipzig in 1874. In 1877 he was named professor of the rabbinic provincial school of Budapest, where he taught courses in Jewish history, religious philosophy, and homiletics until the end of his life. The scholarship of K. was broad and deep. He published thirty books and more than five hundred essays, including book reviews.

———
JDR

Keble, John (1792–1866). Anglican theologian, poet, and leader of the Oxford movement, also known as a hymnologist and as a translator of ⇒Irenaeus. In 1816 he was ordained a priest, resigned his post at Oxford University, and devoted the rest of his life to parish work, especially among the most poor and humble. His sermon on the relationship between church and state, "National Apostasy," preached in 1833, mobilized the Anglo-Catholic group in what is known as the Oxford movement or tractarianism. Together with K., the organizers of this movement were Froude

and ⇒Newman; Pusey joined two years later. K. formulated the principles of the movement. He wrote seven of the ninety *Tracts for the Times.* He also wrote *On Eucharistical Adoration* (1857). Although other leaders of the movement joined the Roman Catholic Church, K. remained an Anglican priest.

———
CS/JDR

Kempis, Thomas à (ca. 1380–1471). German monk and writer who was born in the small city of Kempem in Prussia, and who died on July 25 at the approximate age of ninety-one years. His original name was Thomas Hammerken, and his surname was changed to reflect his place of origin. At the age of twelve he was sent to the well-known school of Deventer in Holland, which was founded by the Dutch mystic Geert de ⇒Groote. There he received his spiritual formation. In 1399 he entered the Augustinian order in the monastery of the Mount of St. Agnes, near Zwolle, where his brother was the superior. He deepened his mystical and simple devotion to the person of Christ. In 1413 he was ordained a priest. He had to earn his living by copying manuscripts in the poor monastery of Zwolle. Aside from the time he devoted to fulfilling his obligations after he became superior of the monastery, he lived in isolation, meditation, and the writing of his books. Of his numerous works the most important are *De tribus tabernaculis, De recognitione propiae fragilitatis, Meditatio de incarnatione Christi, Orationes de passiones Domini et beata Virgine et aliis sanctis, Orationes et meditationes de vita Christi,* and *Soliloquium animae.*

His masterwork is *The Imitation of Christ,* which has been attributed by some scholars to Groote and to others such as ⇒Gerson and ⇒Bernard of Clairvaux. After the Bible, this book has been the one most translated into other languages, because it is the most famous and the most influential of all the medieval ascetic and monastic writings.

———
RPT

Khomiakoff, Alexis (1804–60). Russian Orthodox lay theologian who sought to clarify the roots of Orthodox piety and its importance vis-à-vis other Christian traditions. He influenced important figures within the Russian Orthodox tradition and within Orthodoxy in general, such as J. ⇒Meyendorff,

G. ⇒Florovsky, and A. ⇒Schmemann. He provided the foundations for the formulation of Orthodox ecclesiology that served as the basis for the participation of Eastern Orthodoxy in the ecumenical dialogue and for the formation of a solid Orthodox theology in the twentieth century.

Of special interest is his insistence that the Orthodox tradition should be distinguished from Western Christianity, both in its Catholic and in its Protestant expressions, and that it should rediscover its own ecclesiastical identity that distinguishes it from those other traditions. For K. the Orthodox tradition had been excessively influenced by those Western currents, and it was necessary to insist on the rich tradition of Eastern Christianity, especially the Russian.

———

CEA

Kierkegaard, Søren Aabye (1813–55).

Danish Lutheran pastor. He considered himself primarily a religious writer and a critic of religion as commonly practiced in his native land. His thought has significantly influenced the fields of theology, philosophy, depth psychology, and communication, among others. In a solitary environment, he began a crusade against rationalistic moralism, philosophical idealism, and nineteenth-century theological and scientific triumphalism.

In spite of the importance of his life and work, K. has not yet been evaluated in his full dimension. This is due to at least three reasons: First, Walter Lowrie, his biographer, translator, and propagator in the English-speaking world, has painted the portrait of the shy, chronically melancholic, and bourgeois Dane. Second, if the Nordic Socrates has been an interlocutor of small importance, this is because of the partial reading of his writings, which has been limited to the philosophical ones. Finally, regarding the evolution of his ideas, we have failed to distinguish at least three Kierkegaards: from 1840 to 1846, the young conservative characterized by direct and indirect communication; from 1846 to 1852, the K. influenced by the Danish transition from an absolute to a democratic monarchy that occurred in 1848, and in whom direct communication is dominant; from 1852 to 1855, the mature and radical intellectual who assaulted a hardened Christianity and whose social, economic, and religious criticism is on the way to being rescued.

K. belonged to a first generation of city dwellers. He inherited from the rural areas the profound religiosity of the Moravians. He faithfully attended the Sunday morning services in the Cathedral of Our Lady, and in the evenings he met with a Moravian community, at a time when religious services lasted three hours. His progenitors were humble folk. But his father, the businessman Michael Peter, amassed a considerable fortune, which gave the family entrance to the select circle of leaders in Copenhagen during the golden age of Denmark (1800–1860). That era and social class destined male children for the university, commerce, and banking, in that order. Søren, the seventh in number but the first in the favor of his father, was able to follow in the footsteps of his older brother Peter Crispin. He obtained a doctorate in theology, but in contrast to Peter, who became bishop of Aalborg, Søren remained tied to his idea of becoming a small-town parish pastor. After rebelling against his prescribed work of managing the family business, his brother Neils Andrew (1809–83) emigrated to New Jersey. After having been there a short time he died in poverty, leaving unfulfilled his desire to make a fortune on his own.

The romantic life of K. has been the object of many psychological explanations. Having been engaged to Regina Olsen in 1840, he broke off the engagement in 1841 because at times he felt that she was pitying him. Shortly afterward Regina was married and later emigrated to the West Indies (today the Virgin Islands), where her husband was governor general.

K. was a prolific writer. In fourteen years he produced a corpus that would include twenty-six books in their English translation. In addition there are twenty-two bulky volumes of his diaries and papers in the Danish edition, which have been translated into English only in fragmentary form.

His production comprises three major groups: the pseudonymous or "interim" works, the *Edifying Discourses*, and his *Journals*.

The pseudonymous works may be subdivided into the aesthetic, the philosophical, and the psychological. Through them he wanted to address people by means of "indirect communication." He uses the Socratic method of "midwifery" to help the pregnant mind give birth to its own ideas. Through polynomy, using various pseudonyms, K. seeks to free people from the influence of the author and to confront them with the challenge to a personal appropriation of the truth. As a religious writer he uses aesthetic and philosophical categories to "approach from behind persons who are under the illusion" of being Christian and, as soon as they have swallowed the hook, bring them back to authentic Christianity.

From the beginning his pseudonymous production was continuously accompanied by his explicitly religious production. Thus, in *Diary of a Seducer* (1843), *Philosophical Fragments* (1844), or his most philosophical book, *Concluding Unscientific Postscript to the Philosophical Fragments* (1846), we become aware of the tension introduced by their author. In his own words: "I offered the world *Either/Or* (1843) with the left hand and the *Edifying Discourses* with the right hand; but all or almost all grasped with their right hand what I held in my left hand."

On the other hand, the *Journals* seek to join knowledge with being, thought with life. For this reason his intellectual work includes an illuminating autobiography written during twenty of the forty-two years of his life: "Life is only understood facing backward, but is lived facing forward." Here in his *Journals* one sees the K. who is an outrageous peripatetic, friend of children and of the working class, the Dane who is a talker, jocose, merry, and highly sensitive to the needs of the poor in the country and in the city.

It is common to associate K. with his teaching about the aesthetic, ethical, and religious stages. According to him these stages are closed worlds that are connected only through a qualitative leap. Nevertheless, these spheres are intertwined in the life of an individual, since no one can be the pure prototype of one of these stages. In fact, the three can be confused. This confusion occurs because, among other things, the passage from one stage to another does not negate the previous stage, but saves it.

By "aesthetics" K. means a passive attitude toward life, the absence of passion and decision, or choosing not to choose. The person is overwhelmed by a multitude of distractions. One's center is located at the periphery of the self. Both the irresponsible Don Juan and the Hegelian philosopher (⇒Hegel) who finds fulfillment in pure ideas and never comes down to earth for action are aesthetic prototypes. Vis-à-vis all of this, K. proposes a desperate leap into the ethical.

In the "ethical" sphere, or that of "Judge William," husband and father, the lost ego comes back to itself. One makes a decision for the ethic of the universal imperative. Through that decision this sphere leads to repentance, but not to forgiveness, because forgiveness is antiethical. For that reason, it is necessary to make the mortal leap, with *Fear and Trembling* (1843), to the religious stage.

When Abraham attempts to sacrifice his son he stands on this highest stage, but this attempt does not spare him the anguish of having to suspend ethical demands. The ethical sphere is always experienced side by side with the religious, although in a subordinate way, as is observed in *Works of Love* (1847), K.'s best work on Christian ethics.

K. influenced his society with his book *Either/Or*. Later he developed his three *Stages on Life's Way* (1845), and in his last years he fell back on the radical stance of being or not being a Christian. In one of his best books, *Sickness unto Death* (1849), he shows that the aesthetic sphere is like being well educated but ignorant of one's own being, or like the bourgeois who is desensitized by the illusions of Christendom and by the abstract universal Hegelian state.

The adult K. broke with institutionalized Christianity. He refused to go to Communion on Fridays. He invited the public to boycott the Sunday service. At the hour of the morning service he made his appearance in the reading room of the public library. In the newspapers *The Nation* and *The Moment* he called all of society to abandon outward Christendom, which has betrayed the Christianity of the New Testament.

His *Attack upon Christianity* (1854–55) shows him as the radical Christian who denounces the connections that exist between material poverty and the social system based on competition, and the connections between the privileged condition of the clergy and the divine sanction they give to an unjust society. K. saw no sense in continuing to cure sick individuals when the entire hospital building is contaminated. He also did not see how it is possible to put out a huge fire with buckets and dishes when it has to be done by the firefighters in the front line. K. thought in political categories when, in his campaign to save his age, he placed the inner revolution in tension with the outer.

———
EPA

Kilwardby, Robert (13th century).

Professor at Oxford and then archbishop of Canterbury (1273–78). His theological position was a traditionalist Augustinianism, opposed to the innovations inspired by the new Aristotelian philosophy. In 1277, a few days after a similar action in Paris by the archbishop of that city, Stephen ⇒Tempier, K. condemned thirty propositions apparently drawn from the writings of ⇒Thomas Aquinas and other Aristotelians.

—

JLG

King, Martin Luther, Jr. (1929–68).
African American Baptist pastor, and the most prominent figure in the struggle to eradicate racial discrimination and prejudices in the United States. He was born in Atlanta, Georgia. At the age of fifteen he entered Morehouse College, where he met Benjamin E. ⇒Mays, who inspired him to enter the ministry and who served as his mentor and counselor for life. He graduated from Crozer seminary in Pennsylvania, and finished his doctorate in theology at Boston University. In Boston he met and married Coretta Scott (1927–2006), with whom he shared the struggle for civil rights and with whom he had four children. He was assassinated in 1968 in Memphis, Tennessee, by James Earl Ray while, in an act of solidarity, he was visiting with the trade union of garbage collectors. At this time K. was organizing the Poor People's Campaign, which represented a radicalization of the civil rights movement, emphasizing the importance of guaranteeing to every citizen the right to work and to a minimum wage.

K. was a public speaker and preacher of the first order, with the result that he won the support of many in the struggle against racism. Some see him as one of the forerunners of liberation theology in the United States. For K. all authentic theology implies a transforming social practice. Theology is based on a practical testimony not only at the personal level, but also in the political arena, where human beings confront most of their existential problems. He believed that Christians who refuse to become involved in the social and political sphere contribute, intentionally or not, to injustice. All human practice is political, and the worst, or the most irresponsible, politics is that which does not know its own consequences. Just as for liberation theologians, theology for K. is authentic when it identifies with the victims of injustice.

In his "Letter from Birmingham City Jail," he replies to a group of white pastors who criticized the civil rights movement for violating the law and provoking violence. K. denounces and criticizes the social myopia of those pastors. They do not recognize that it is precisely the structures and laws of racial segregation that are unjust and violent. He points out that the civil rights movement is not the cause of the tension and conflict. Peaceful protest only makes more evident the violence of the racial structures already there. Regarding the violation of civil laws, K. alleges along with ⇒Augustine and ⇒Thomas Aquinas that it is indispensable to distinguish between just and unjust laws. Unjust laws are not laws in the full sense of the word and therefore are not valid. The main mistake of white pastors is that they do not recognize or do not wish to admit that their interpretation of the Christian faith makes them accomplices of the social injustice that is committed against the black population. Intentionally or not, they make of Christianity a tool that supports racism and social injustice.

For K., the struggle against injustice creates conditions for the birth of what he called "the Beloved Community." This is an inclusive community in its racial, class, and ethnic composition. It is a community of reconciliation, of solidarity among the different social groups, based on the principle of mutual support, where everyone will have a real opportunity to participate actively in the organization and direction of the local and national community. For this reason K. insists on nonviolence as an integral and essential part of the process of social change. Peaceful resistance, which K. appropriated from Gandhi, has the virtue of allowing us to attack sin without harming the sinner. It is a method of social change that mitigates the desire for vengeance and the memory of cruelty among combatants, and therefore accelerates the process of reconciliation among the factions in conflict. It is a humanizing way of fighting against the enemy, and it corresponds to the principle of love that rules creation.

—

IG

Kingsley, Charles (1819–75).
Clergyman of the Church of England, social reformer, and novelist. Under the pseudonym "Parson Lot," he promoted the Christian Socialist movement. Like other socialists of his time, his political stance was more reforming than revolutionary. His political goal was to promote the education of workers, the formation of cooperatives, and sanitation reforms. He hoped that the Christian middle class would take the lead in the promotion of these social reforms.

—

IG

Kirk, Kenneth (1886–1954).
Anglican priest, professor at Oxford (1932–37), and bishop of the same city beginning in 1937. He

combined the Thomist (⇒Thomas Aquinas) tradition and modern freedom. This synthesis stimulated a rebirth of interest in moral matters. Among his most important works are *Some Problems of Moral Theology* (1920) and *The Vision of God* (1931).

—

IG

Kitamori, Kazoh (1916–). One of the most creative Protestant thinkers in Japan, he was professor of systematic theology at Union Seminary of Tokyo. His book *Theology of the Pain of God* (1965) is a testimony to the difficult task of understanding the Christian theological tradition in an Asian context, especially the Japanese. K. was one of the first modern theologians to write Christian systematic theology from his Asian context.

—

CCO

Knitter, Paul F. (1939–). Roman Catholic and North American member of the Missionary Society of the Divine Word (SVD) in Asia, and one of the forerunners of the project of religious pluralism, as he shows in his book *No Other Name?* (1985). His most recent works, *One Earth Many Religions* and *One Jesus Many Religions*, explore new models of interreligious dialogue with a liberating and ecological perspective and an ecclesiological proposal for living in the religious pluralism of our times.

—

CCO

Knox, John (ca. 1514–72). Leader of the Protestant reformation in Scotland. He had a turbulent life, living in exile for several years and suffering persecution when in his own country. Bold and dogmatic, he helped Presbyterianism become the chief Protestant body in Scotland.

Ordained in 1536, K. also worked as a lawyer and tutor. In 1543 he became a Protestant under the spiritual direction of George Wishart, a Lutheran reformer. Wishart was accused of heresy by Cardinal Beaton, who had him condemned to the stake. This provoked a crowd to occupy the castle of St. Andrew and to imprison and assassinate the cardinal. K. joined the revolutionaries, becoming their chief teacher and preacher.

When the castle fell in 1547, K. was taken to France and sentenced to the galleys. After gaining his freedom in 1549, he returned to England, where he soon expressed his discontent with the second Book of Common Prayer of the Church of England. The ascent of Mary Tudor to the English throne precipitated his flight to the Continent. In 1554 he was named pastor of the English congregation in Frankfurt. Another dispute about liturgical manuals led to his dismissal and return to Geneva, where he led an English congregation from 1556 to 1559. During those years K. collaborated with ⇒Calvin. It was at this time that he wrote *The First Blast of the Trumpet against the Monstrous Regiment of Women* (1558), in which he attacked Mary Tudor, Catherine of Guise, and Mary Stuart, all Catholic queens. Later, when Mary Tudor was succeeded by the Protestant Queen Elizabeth, this writing would come back to haunt him.

K. returned to Scotland in 1559, where he promoted Calvinist theology and developed the presbyterian form of government. His return as well as his preaching provoked disturbances and confrontation. In 1560 he drew up the Scottish Confession of Faith, a document through which Parliament established Presbyterianism as the national faith. From that moment, K. devoted himself to strengthening the new church. In this task he clashed with Mary Stuart. After the queen was deposed in 1567, the new Scottish church felt secure.

K. was married at the age of forty-eight and had two children during his marriage. He died in Edinburgh, Scotland, on November 24, 1572.

—

PAJ

Knudson, Albert Cornelius (1873–1953). North American theologian, philosopher, and Methodist pastor. The greater part of his academic career was spent at Boston University, where he was professor of Bible and of theology, in addition to being dean. Among his works on the Scriptures are *The Old Testament Problem* and *The Religious Teaching of the Old Testament*. Under the influence of B. P. ⇒Bowne he became interested in personalist philosophy and wrote *The Philosophy of Personalism*, *The Validity of Religious Experience*, and *Present Tendencies in Religious Thought*. He also wrote *The Doctrine of God*, *The Doctrine of Redemption*, *The Principles of Christian Ethics*, and *The Philosophy of Peace and War*.

—

CS/JDR

Kohlbruegge, Hermann Friedrich (1803–75). Dutch, born and reared in a pietist Lutheran family in Amsterdam. He was the pastor of an independent Reformed church in Elberfeld, Germany. Although he was considered a dissident and an "irregular" theologian, and was not accepted by many of his colleagues in the academic circles of his age, his theology influenced a good part of the European church during the nineteenth century. In the twentieth century he influenced Reformed theology, particularly such notable theological figures as ⇒Barth and ⇒Bonhoeffer. The spirit of resistance promoted by K. was a significant element in the formulation many years later of the ⇒Barmen Declaration, the fundamental document of the Christian resistance to the government of Hitler.

The theology of K., influenced to a great extent by that of ⇒Calvin, shows an intense interest in the word of God. According to K., the word of God has three chief expressions, in Christ, the Bible, and preaching—a paradigm that Barth would also use. For K., theology arises from the church, which is not only a community of faith, but also a new social reality.

————

LGP

Kohut, Heinz (1913–81). Born in Vienna, Austria. He left Freudian theory behind and founded the "psychology of the self," a theory of great importance in the psychology, theology, and pastoral psychology of the United States. One of his most important contributions was to redefine empathy as a clinical tool and vicarious means of introspection. In addition, he developed a theory of the self that does not depend on Freudian libidinous energy (⇒Freud), but on empathetic relations that give cohesion to the psychic world of the infant. He introduced a theory of narcissism based on the "object relation" as necessary for development and psychic cohesion. He postulated two lines of independent development: narcissism and the instinctive-objectival. He analyzed narcissistic transferences, described narcissistic personality disorders, and offered empathetic immersion and introspection as a treatment that compensates for the narcissistic needs not satisfied by the primary objectival relations of the individual. His most important works are *The Analysis of Self* (1971), *The Restoration of the Self* (1977), and *How Does Analysis Cure?* (1984).

————

JR

Köllin, Conrad (1476–1536). German theologian, Dominican, and apologist of Thomist theology (⇒Thomas Aquinas). He was an important theologian in Germany during the Protestant Reformation. He defended Catholic teaching against what he saw as the deviations of the new Lutheran teaching.

————

CEA

Kosma, Presbyter (10th century). Priest and preacher at the royal court of Bulgaria during the second half of the tenth century. His most important work was his *Discourse against the New Heresy of the Bogomils*. The book, written in popular and accessible style, includes a description of the morality that Christianity and the Christian state should promote.

————

CCO

Koyama, Kosuke (1929–). Japanese theologian and missionary. His experience in Hiroshima and Nagasaki during the nuclear bombarding mark his theology and missiology. He studied in Tokyo and at Princeton Theological Seminary. His book *Water Buffalo Theology* (1974) shows his concern for the themes of inculturation, indigenization, and acculturation. In addition, K. shows the theological dangers in these processes in a study about idols and idolatry in Japanese and Christian spirituality, *Mount Fuji, Mount Sinai* (1984). He was professor of world Christianity at Union Theological Seminary in New York.

————

CCO

Kraemer, Hendrik (1888–1965). Dutchman who, as a result of his work in Indonesia under the Dutch Biblical Society, acquired enormous experience of Islam. Ever since that time he showed great interest in the religions of the East and in the work of missionaries. He also expressed his frustration over the state of the "young churches" and the failure of missionaries whose continued domination hindered the development of the leadership and structures of those churches.

In 1936 the International Missionary Conference asked him to write a book in preparation for the second world conference on mission to be celebrated in Tambaram, Madras, India, in 1938, and in response to the work of W. E. ⇒Hocking, *Laymen's Report: Rethinking Missions*. His book *The Christian Message in a Non-Christian World* (1938) confronted a growing liberal tendency in the missionary movement and generated a controversy, the effects of which are still being felt in mission-ary circles. In this book K. promotes "biblical realism" in contrast to other religions. Deriving the inspiration for his work from the theology of Karl ⇒Barth, K. proposes a discontinuity between the revelation of God in Jesus Christ and other religions. But he goes beyond Barth in the recognition that in other religions there exists a "religious conscience" that points toward the revelation in Jesus Christ.

After this confrontation, K. returned to Holland, where he taught phenomenology of religion in Leiden. During the Second World War he was a prisoner in a German concentration camp. Afterward he participated in the formulation of the constitution of the Dutch Reformed Church, which for the first time recognized mission as an integral part of the life of this church. In 1947 he was invited to be the first director of the Ecumenical Institute of Bossey in Switzerland, where he promoted a mission-oriented ecumenical conscience.

—
CCO

Krauth, Charles Porterfield (1823–83).
Born in Martinsburg, in what is now West Virginia, K. studied in the College of Pennsylvania and at Gettysburg Lutheran Seminary. He was licensed by the Lutheran Synod of Maryland in 1841. He then served a mission in Canton, a suburb of Baltimore, Maryland, and was ordained in 1842. He served as a pastor in Baltimore (1842–47), Martinsburg, Shepherdstown (1847–48), Winchester (1848–55), Pittsburgh (1855–59), and Philadelphia (1859–67). He was a professor at the Theological Seminary in Philadelphia (1863–83) and the University of Pennsylvania (1868–83). He was instrumental in the organization of the General Council of the Evangelical Lutheran Church, serving as its president from 1870 to 1880. K. is remembered as one of the most eminent leaders of the English-speaking Lutheran church in the United States, having been a person of great knowledge, staunchly committed to pure Lutheran doctrine. *The Conservative Reformation and Its Theology* stands out among his works. He was also editor of the *Lutheran Church Review*.

—
JDR

Küng, Hans (1928–).
Swiss Catholic theologian, prolific author, noted academic, and international lecturer. He studied in Switzerland, Rome, and France, and was ordained a priest in 1957. His doctoral thesis, *Justification*, proposed the compatibility between the Catholic tradition and the theologian K. ⇒Barth on this particular theme. He was a theological adviser at ⇒Vatican II.

K. has stood out as a reformist and ecumenical theologian within Catholicism. His focus and positions have been the reason for great controversies with the Vatican and the German bishops. K. has favored the revision of several dogmas and canonical practices, among them the mandatory celibacy of the clergy, papal infallibility, the teaching on birth control, the power of the Roman curia, and the inequality of women in the church. The Congregation for the Doctrine of the Faith unilaterally revoked his status as a Catholic theologian in 1979. However, the University of Tübingen in Germany permitted him to continue as professor and director of the Institute for Ecumenical Investigation.

K. has developed a theological agenda with the following emphases: the theological and ecclesial reformation of Catholicism; a contemporary and ecumenical theology of the Christian faith in critical dialogue with the most important currents of modern Western thought; ecumenical and interreligious dialogue as a contribution to processes of justice and peace in the world.

In the 1960s and 1970s his major contributions were to ecclesiology (*The Church*), Christology (*On Being a Christian*), and theology (*Does God Exist?*). Since the 1980s he developed what he considers a new paradigm in the history of Christian theology, which he calls the "ecumenical paradigm" (*Theology for the Third Millennium*).

This project reinterprets the gospel of Jesus Christ for a postmodern, postcolonial, and polycentric world where there are four principal challenges: the relationship of humanity with nature, the struggles for the equality of women, distributive justice, and, especially, relations among religions in favor of peace. This last aspect has been the central focus of K.'s latest publications, in which he attempts to formulate an ecumenical Christian theology in dialogue with the world religions and a global ethic (*Christianity and World Religions: Paths of Dialogue with Islam, Hinduism, and Buddhism*; *Judaism*; *Global Responsibility: In Search of a New World Ethic*).

—
LRR

Kuyper, Abraham (1837–1920).
Calvinist theologian of the Reformed Church

of the Netherlands. He served his faith, his church, and his nation as pastor, journalist, professor of theology, and politician. He studied in Leiden, where he was influenced by modernist rationalism, but in his pastorates from 1863 until 1874 he came to accept a more orthodox Calvinism, with faith in biblical authority and in divine activity in all areas of life. These convictions, in addition to a preoccupation with the liberalism that had made its way into the Reformed Church of Holland as a state church, led K. to enter politics as a member of the Lower Parliament, where he was active from 1874 until 1878, representing the Antirevolutionary Party, which was Protestant and conservative. When the state became involved in the selection of professors of theology in the university, K. established the Free University of Amsterdam (1880), where he taught until 1901. In 1886, over against the growing liberalism of his own church, K. helped to form a new group, the Reformed Churches. In all of this, his conviction was that the Calvinist theological system (⇒Calvin), including predestination and the sovereign grace of God, affirms not only the certainty of faith for the individual, but also the individual's responsibility before the church, culture, and the order created by God. Therefore the believer should become involved in every sphere of life (home, school, and state) for the good of all and so that the entire nation might honor God. In addition, K. affirmed common grace and the presence of God in nonbelievers such that we should respect the divine providence in all creation. K. shared his ideas in the United States in his famous lectures at Princeton Seminary, *On Calvinism* (1898). He wrote more than two hundred works on theology, culture, and politics, including *Pro Rege*, where in three volumes he developed his theme of establishing the authority of Christ over society, art, culture, education, and politics. From 1901 to 1905 he was the prime minister of the Netherlands, and in 1907 the nation celebrated his seventieth birthday, recognizing its debt to him.

—

EA

La Ramée, Pierre de ⇒Ramus, Petrus

Labadie, Jean de (1610–74). French theologian, originally Jesuit, who founded the sect of the Labadists. He insisted on the necessity of receiving the Holy Spirit, affirming that the Spirit's inspiration was necessary for the correct understanding of the Scriptures. His theology influenced the development of pietism.

—

PAJ

Lactantius (ca. 250–ca. 318). His real name was Lucius Cecilius Firmianus. A native of Africa, he studied with ⇒Arnobius and then moved to Asia Minor, where he lectured on rhetoric in Nicomedia. The persecution of Diocletian forced him to flee, and he experienced times of great need. After the Edict of Tolerance he was a member of the court of Constantine and tutor of one of his children.

His two chief works are the *Divine Institutions* and his treatise *On the Death of Persecutors*. Although the latter work deals with persecutions since the beginning of Christianity, in reality its historical value is much greater with respect to the years in which L. himself lived. In fact, in the first six of his seventy-two chapters L. comes as far as the persecution of Aurelianus in the third century, and all the rest deals with the more recent persecutions. The thesis of L. is that God punishes those who persecute the church, particularly by allowing them to die in pain and anguish. Sometimes L. seems to take pleasure in telling of the last sufferings of some of the emperors, as in the case of Galerius, whom he describes as dying consumed by worms.

Divine Institutions also has an apologetic purpose. In it L. offers a presentation in an elegant style, and directed to well-educated readers, of the teachings of Christianity. L. himself called it an *Epitome*.

—

JLG

Ladd, George Eldon (1911–82). Evangelical New Testament theologian who taught in Fuller Seminary for three decades, beginning in 1950. A graduate of Gordon Divinity School and Harvard University, L. promoted the acceptance of critical methods in the study of the New Testament among evangelicals. His most recognized work, *The Presence of the Future* (1974), describes the kingdom of God as a reality inaugurated in the person and ministry of Jesus Christ that still awaits its final consummation.

—

JLG

Laínez, Diego (1512–65). Spanish Jesuit who studied theology in Paris. With

Ignatius of ⇒Loyola he promoted the Catholic reformation by creating the Company of Jesus as a modern pillar of the reformation within Catholicism. As a fervent defender of the Catholic faith and a provincial of the order, L. gave momentum to the company in Italy. He was a papal theologian in the Council of ⇒Trent, above all in the discussions on justification, the sacraments, and purgatory.

———

CEA

Lamennais, Hughes-Félicité-Robert de (1782–1854).

French Catholic writer, originally anti-Gallican, who affirmed the independence of the church over against the state. A self-taught theologian, in 1809 he wrote *Reflections on Church and State*, a document censored by Napoleon that pointed to his new Gallican sympathies. He became a monk in 1811, joining the seminary of Saint-Malo, an institution founded by his brother John. In 1814 he returned to Paris, where he became involved in the public life of the country. On September 1, 1830, he founded the newspaper *L'Avenir*, with the aim of defending Gallican ideas. This became a forum where several young writers defended the elimination of the Concordat, administrative decentralization, the extension of electoral rights, and the freedom of conscience, the press, and association. L. is considered one of the founders of liberal Catholicism.

———

PAJ

Lampe, Armando (1958–).

Catholic priest who is a native of Aruba. One of the most important theologians and historians in the Caribbean. He studied natural sciences at the Free University of Amsterdam. Among his theological and historical works are *Discovering God in the Caribbean* and *Christianity in the Caribbean: Essays on Church History*. The latter has been published in English and Portuguese. In 2000 L. was named president of the Commission of Studies on the History of the Church in Latin America (CEHILA).

———

CCO

Land, Steven Jack (1947–).

Educator, author, and professor of Pentecostal theology and dean of the Theological Seminary of the Church of God in Cleveland, Tennessee. As an ordained minister of the Church of God, he has served as pastor, urban missionary, and organizer of communities for the defense of civil rights. He is an active participant in many academic organizations and associations. He is coeditor of the *Journal of Pentecostal Theology*. Among his publications is the valuable work *Pentecostal Spirituality: A Passion for the Kingdom* (1993). In his theology he underscores the central role of the affections (orthopathy) in the integration of pastoral tasks and practices and therefore in the contribution of Pentecostal theology.

———

EV

Lanfranc (1005–89).

Italian, a professor of law and literature in France, he finally devoted himself to the monastic life, becoming abbot of the monastery of Bec, in Normandy. There he was a teacher of ⇒Anselm of Canterbury, while he wrote against ⇒Berengar and produced commentaries on the Pauline epistles. He was finally called to England by William the Conqueror and was made archbishop of Canterbury. His theology, which was rather traditional, nonetheless showed a certain openness toward studies, and the impulse that led Anselm to his speculative efforts can be seen in it.

———

JLG

Langton, Stephen (?–1228).

Englishman who was a professor in Paris and then returned to England, where he became archbishop of Canterbury. From that time on his life was in turmoil, since he became involved in the conflicts that led to the Magna Carta, which in turn created difficulties for him with the pope. He attended the Fourth ⇒Lateran Council, where he became reconciled with Rome. When the conflicts in England died down, he returned to his native land. His most important contributions in theology took place in the field of biblical studies, where he composed a number of longer commentaries. He also made an effort to establish a system for the division of chapters based on the Vulgate.

———

JLG

Las Casas, Bartolomé de (1484–1566).

Chief protagonist of the theological debates on the conquest and Christianization of America in the sixteenth century. He was a secular priest, then a Dominican friar, and later bishop of Chiapas. He arrived in America in 1502 with the new governor of the Indies, Nicolás de Ovando. He exercised priestly functions and obtained land concessions and grants. On August 15, 1514, "the day of the Assumption of Our Lady," having been moved by the suffering of the Antillian natives, he proclaimed from the pulpit that the military conquest and enslavement of the native people constituted a grave violation of divine and natural laws. He freed his indigenous people and devoted the rest of his life to defending the rights of the American aboriginal communities.

He wrote an enormous number of works of a diverse character: doctrinal treatises, stories, chronicles, memorials, epistles, juridical accusations, sermons, guides for confessors, and, finally, his will. He participated in multiple juridical, ecclesiastical, and state debates, among which stands out his sharp controversy with the humanist Juan Ginés de Sepúlveda in the presence of the Council of Valladolid, which was made up of several of the most important theologians in Spain. In those writings and debates he defended the following theses:

1. Evangelization is the purpose of the discovery of America. In his opinion, the objective of Pope Alexander VI, when in 1493 he conferred upon the Catholic sovereigns the authority over the native nations of America, was evangelization. The fulfillment of the universal missionary mandate of the church is the only fundamental justification for European authority. Any other political or economic intention must be subordinate to that missionary purpose.

2. The only legitimate missionary strategy is peaceful persuasion. L.C. rejected every attempt to justify wars against the indigenous nations on missionary or theological grounds. He wrote a book, *Del único modo de atraer a todos los pueblos a la verdadera religión* (On the Only Way to Attract All Peoples to the True Religion), defending this thesis. Against many theologians, jurists, functionaries, and conquistadors, he denounced the theological validations of war as an instrument of Christianization.

3. The indigenous peoples have the full right to their freedom. Although L.C. did not deny the possibility of justifying the enslavement of some peoples, he refuted it with respect to the Americans. In his opinion, they had not committed any wrong that merited enslavement. Neither did he accept the *encomienda*, a system of servile labor that is legally distinguished from slavery. He denounced it as a veiled slavery that caused the accelerated death of the indigenous peoples. Although on several occasions he suggested that African slaves be imported, at the end of his life he was convinced that the servitude imposed on them was also unjust, and he denounced it in his *Historia de las Indias* (History of the Indies).

4. The indigenous peoples are fully human. Against the efforts to picture the natives of America as inferior, L.C. defended their complete humanity. In order to demonstrate this thesis he wrote an extensive work, *Apologética historia sumaria* (Concise Apologetic History). His objective was to make evident through the description of their cultural and cultic traditions that the American indigenous peoples have nothing to envy the Europeans with respect to rationality, creativity, and free will. He rejected every attempt to diminish the humanity of the indigenous peoples.

5. The military conquest of the American peoples is a grave sin against God and a serious offense against those communities. His chief historical works, *Historia de las Indias* (History of the Indies) and *Brevísima relación de la destrucción de las Indias* (Very Brief Account of the Destruction of the Indies), are written from a perspective of indignant prophetic denunciation. As with all the chronicles of the period, they have a purpose that goes beyond description: they seek to denounce, call to repentance, and demand respect for the life and liberty of the native peoples. In his last writings he made the Spanish political authority over America conditional on the consent of the native nations and Spanish respect for their own authorities and sovereignty.

6. The Spaniards are obliged to render restitution. From his sermon of 1514 until his last writings five decades later, L.C. insisted on the obligation to restore the misappropriated property as the indispensable condition for obtaining sacramental absolution. Restitution included material, moral, and political goods; properties, freedom, and sovereignty. As bishop of Chiapas he drew up a guide for confessors, with the directive to the priests not to absolve anyone who was in any way involved in wars against the indigenous peoples or in their servitude, unless they restored to the aboriginal communities what had been taken by those means.

We see arising from his tortuous polemics the utopia of a church in solidarity with the poor, the marginalized, and the humiliated peoples of the earth. The aged L.C., his soul weighed down by fatigue and bitterness, but with the same tenacity as always, described it in his last letter to Pope Pius V (1566). In it he demands, going against the grain of contemporary imperialisms, the birth of a poor church that restores the goods obtained by the blood and sweat of the oppressed, a church that knows and respects the languages of the peoples, that identifies with their cultures, that humbles itself along with those who are despised, and that in the last instance, if necessary, is ready to offer its life as a sacrifice for those who are persecuted.

Since then, L.C. has been a controverted figure. Bitterly criticized by the apologists of the empire, he became a symbol of resistance and liberation for those who, like Simón Bolívar and José Martí, sought to break the colonial bonds of Latin America with Spain. Even today he figures very prominently in the different interpretations of the conquest and Christianization of the Americas.

———
LRP

Lateran Councils (4th to 16th centuries).

A series of fourteen councils, five of which were considered ecumenical, were celebrated in the complex of buildings known as Lateran, on Mount Celius, in Rome. The basilica of St. John in the Lateran palace served as the assembly hall for these councils, which were sometimes known as Lateran. During the Middle Ages the Lateran palace was the papal residence.

1. (413) Convoked by Miltiades. Its principal concern was the African schism provoked by the conflict between the Donatists (⇒Donatus) and their staunch enemy ⇒Augustine. Beginning with the time of this council, the locale emerged as the administrative center of medieval Catholicism.

2. (649) Censured the Monothelite christological heresy (⇒Sergius of Constantinople).

3. (769) Legislated in matters of papal election and confirmed the use of images.

4. (1059) Restricted the election of the pope to the recently created college of cardinals.

5. (1060) Denied ordination to simoniacs, that is, to those who purchased church offices with money (Acts 8:18–24).

6. (1079) Made a pronouncement on eucharistic doctrine.

7. (1102) Legitimated the papacy of Paschal II and repudiated Emperor Henry IV. Continued the investiture dispute.

8. (1112) Condemned the treatise of Ponte Mammolo derived from Paschal II.

9. (1116) Ratified the previous council.

10. (1123) The First Ecumenical Lateran Council (⇒Councils). Convened by Pope Calixtus II while Henry V was emperor. It was composed of three hundred bishops and archbishops and approximately six hundred abbots. It legislated on the administration of the sacraments and the investiture of the clergy, indulgences during the Crusades, the protection of pilgrims and merchants, and the eradication of abuse.

11. (1139) The Second Ecumenical Lateran Council. Called by Innocent II while Conrad II was emperor. Condemned anti-Pope Anacletus II. Approximately one thousand representatives attended, including some from the East. Regulated monastic garb and activity; denied Christian burial to usurers; forbade the marriage of the clergy; turned to the secular power in order to combat heresy; sanctioned those who opposed the baptism of infants; forbade charging fees for the administration of confirmation, funeral rites, and extreme unction; and denied the study of medicine and civil law to members of religious orders.

12. (1179) The Third Ecumenical Lateran Council. Convened by ⇒Alexander III while Frederick I Barbarossa was emperor. Numerous abbots and about three hundred bishops attended. It annulled the legitimacy of a succession of antipopes. In order to prevent new divisions, it mandated a two-thirds majority of votes for papal elections. It established cathedral schools, the germ of the future universities. It regulated ecclesiastical benefices. It forbade simony and pluralism. It set thirty as the minimum age for bishops and twenty-four for the priesthood. It repudiated clerical concubinage. It forbade the charging of fees for funeral rites.

13. (1215) The Fourth Ecumenical Lateran Council. Ratified the declaration of Innocent III proclaiming Frederick II emperor of the Holy Roman German Empire. This "Great Lateran Council," whose importance is almost equal to that of the Council of ⇒Trent, was the first ecumenical council to be convened in the name of the pope. Four hundred bishops and archbishops and some eight hundred priors and abbots attended. It prohibited the creation of new ecclesiastical orders, although the Franciscan order was ratified. It promulgated the dogma of transubstantiation, a term already in use, to explain the presence of Christ in the Eucharist. It laid on Christians of the age of reason the duty of confession, penance, and Communion at Easter, or at least once a year. It suspended priests who lived in concubinage. It canceled any fees charged for the administration of the sacraments. It demanded the authentication of relics. It imposed on Jews and Muslims a different attire in order to avoid interreligious

marriage with Christians. It forbade Jews to appear in public during Holy Week in order to avoid tensions with Christians. It anathematized the Waldensian (Peter ⇒Waldo), Cathar, and ⇒Albigensian movements. It ordered preaching to be done in the vernacular language. It decided to launch a new crusade. It denied clergy any participation in secular justice.

14. (1512–17) The Fifth Ecumenical Lateran Council. Convened by Julius II and continued by Leo X while Maximilian I was emperor. It was composed of sixty-nine bishops and fifteen cardinals, mostly Italians. It repudiated the Council of ⇒Pisa, which was sponsored by the French king Louis XII. It approved a crusade against the Turks. Instead of listening to the cry for the reformation of the church, Pope Leo X followed the steps of his father and of his Renaissance court: "Let us enjoy the papacy, since God has given it to us."

—

EPA

Latin American Theological Fraternity ⇒Fraternidad Teológica Latinoamericana

Latimer, Hugh (ca. 1485–1555).
English reformer born in the region of Leicestershire. He studied for the Roman Catholic priesthood at Cambridge University, but after his ordination he devoted himself to preaching the Reformation. His sermons emphasized human sin and total dependence on the atonement of Christ. He supported the divorce of Henry VIII and his marriage with Anne Boleyn, whose chaplain L. was. He was bishop of Worcester from 1535 until 1539, when he resigned his post because of his support of the Reformation. Queen Mary Tudor denounced him as "Lutheran," and he was condemned as such. He died at the stake in October of 1555.

—

EA

Latomus, James (1475–1544).
Roman Catholic theologian born in Cambron, Belgium. He studied in Paris and then went to Louvain, where he received his doctorate, in order to teach theology. He became rector of the University of Louvain (1537). A great scholar and skillful scholastic, he debated ⇒Erasmus and the humanists. Beginning in 1520 he wrote against the Reformers, becoming a vigorous critic of the theological proposals of ⇒Luther.

His writings were gathered and published by his nephew in Louvain (1550). Among them are *De trium linguarum et studii theologici ratione* (1519) and *Articulorum doctrinae fratris Martini Lutheri per theologos, Lovanienses damnatorum ratio* (1521). L.'s polemical works, considering the limitations of the times, are examples of a movement away from decadent scholasticism and toward the development of a literary polemical genre eventually perfected by ⇒Bellarmine.

—

JDR

Latourette, Kenneth Scott (1884–1968).
North American Baptist, possibly the most important historian of missions in the twentieth century. He studied at Yale University and worked in the Yale-in-China program in Changsha, China, where he taught for two years after completing his doctoral studies. His academic works began by focusing on the region of East Asia, especially in his work *The Chinese: Their History and Culture* (1934), and culminated with his great work in seven volumes, *The History of the Expansion of Christianity* (1937–45). According to his interpretation, the history of the church displays a pattern that repeats itself, because each movement of reform leads to successes which ultimately produce new corruption and require a new reform. In addition to his academic work, L. distinguished himself by his participation in a number of missionary and ecumenical organizations and agencies.

—

COO

Lausanne, Movement of (1974–).
The Lausanne Movement was created partly as a result of the work of evangelist Billy ⇒Graham and under the auspices of the Lausanne Committee for World Evangelization. This international movement is devoted to motivating and supporting Christians and churches to pray, study, plan, and work for the evangelization of the entire world. The movement has a voluntary character and is united under the Lausanne Covenant. It is evangelical in its tone and grounds the evangelizing task on the Scriptures. It holds to the following:

1. In the evangelizing task, cooperation and the exchange of resources are better than competition.
2. The fullness of the gospel includes both the proclamation of the Word and work for justice.

3. Biblical theology and missionary strategies should be coherent.
4. The purpose of the movement is to unite all evangelical groups, no matter what their tradition or denominational affiliation.

The prophetic character of the movement is born of the participation of evangelicals from the third world, such as Samuel ⇒Escobar, Carlos René ⇒Padilla, and Orlando ⇒Costas.

—
CCO

Lee, Ann (1736–84). Leader of the "Shaking Quakers" movement, which is a variant of the Quakers. Commonly called Mother Ann or Mother Ann Lee. She was born on February 29, 1736, in Manchester, England and began to work at a very early age in the textile mills. At the age of twenty-two and without any formal education she joined the movement of the Shakers, and months later she convinced her husband, her brother, and another six followers to emigrate to New York, where they founded a colony in Watervliet. Under the leadership of Mother Ann, the Shaker movement grew to such a degree that soon there were thousands of followers. Based on visions she received, L. believed that she was the feminine incarnation of Christ and that purity, equality, and community life were essential elements of the Christian life. These beliefs and her personality inspired others to form similar colonies that followed the disciplines she dictated. She died on September 8, 1784. The Shakers developed celibate communities of men and women, and these became model farms as well as centers of production. Their worship included, and eventually became known for, ecstatic circle dancing.

—
HMT

Lefèvre d'Étaples, Jacques (ca. 1450–ca. 1537). Also known as Jacobus Faber; Fabri; surname Stapulensis. French priest, professor, translator, and exegete. Recognized as the most prominent religious figure at the beginning of the Reformation in France, he prepared the way for ⇒Calvin and ⇒Farel. His career began in Paris and Florence, and he was noted for his translation of the works of ⇒Aristotle into Latin. His theological production could be divided into two genres: his editions of patristic works and of mystical writers and, of much greater importance, his translations of and commentaries on the Scriptures. In

1507 he was appointed as librarian by his disciple Guillaume Briçonnet, director of the Benedictine monastery of St. Germain-des-Près. His first exegetical work was *Psalterium quintuplex* (1509). He published his commentaries on Galatians and Romans in 1512. His *Preface to the Epistles of Paul* is extraordinary in that it promulgated fundamental principles for the Reformation five years before ⇒Luther published his Ninety-five Theses (1517) in Wittenberg. He affirmed the authority of the Holy Scriptures in doctrinal matters and the importance of the unmerited grace of God for receiving redemption, while he opposed the idea of merit earned before God though works and the requirement of clerical celibacy. He insisted on the need to reform the church. In 1520 he fell under the suspicion of being a Lutheran, based chiefly on his critical essays on Mary Magdalene (1518). Protected and encouraged by Briçonnet in 1520, he went to live in Meaux, where his disciple was bishop. Briçonnet elected him vicar general and encouraged him to embark on a translation of the Vulgate into French. It was published in Antwerp in 1523. During this period he published his *Commentary on the Four Gospels* (1522) and *Commentary on the Universal Epistles* (1525). In his exposition of these texts he pointed out the errors of the Vulgate and prepared the way for a more adequate exegesis. Later in Blois he prepared another translation of the Bible that was more modern and accessible to the people. This translation became very popular in France and was used by R. ⇒Olivetan in his translation of 1535, which became the official version of the Reformed Church. In spite of the fact that L. completely affirmed the principles of the Reformation, he did not withdraw from the Roman Catholic Church, since he had the hope of renewing it through the power of the gospel.

—
ALG

Lehmann, Paul (1906–96). In the spirit of H. R. ⇒Niebuhr, L. develops an antilegalist ethics based on his interpretation of human nature. Against Niebuhr, L. defines the human being, as ⇒Barth does, by looking at Jesus the Christ, who reveals the essential elements of the moral life that is proper for Christians. Christ reveals that God's historical purpose is to promote our humanization. Our moral duty, therefore, is to contribute to that humanizing purpose of God. When we give ourselves over to God and live in God's community of faith, we can see what we should do. The mature conscience is theonomous: it is not ruled by moral laws or by institutions created by human beings. It is ruled and allows itself to be governed by the spontaneous and humanizing activity of God. The result is an ethics without rules, which is totally open to the changes that God brings about in the world.

—

IG

Leibniz, Gottfried Wilhelm (1646–1716).

Philosopher and mathematician who was born in Leipzig, Germany. At the age of fifteen he entered the University of Leipzig and then transferred to the University of Jena, where he studied jurisprudence, mathematics, and philosophy. In the field of mathematics he distinguished himself through his work on integral calculus. Regarding the philosophical question of the communication of substances, which was posed by the entire Cartesian (⇒Descartes) tradition, L. declared that there is no such communication, but all of reality consists of a number of "monads" that do not communicate among themselves. (Hence his famous phrase, "Monads do not have windows.") There is a "preestablished harmony" among the monads, so that it appears that they do communicate and affect one another. In his work as well as in his writings, L. defended the traditional belief in the existence of God. His rational understanding of Christianity led him to maintain that it was the sum of all the religions and that the evil in the world was a simple necessary consequence and an essential part of the created universe. In the political sphere, L. always sought peace among the nations.

—

HMT

Lenski, Richard Charles Henry (1864–1936).

Lutheran pastor and theologian born in Greifenberg, Prussia. He emigrated to North America, where he was ordained into the ministry of the Ohio Synod. At Capital University he served in different capacities, sometimes concurrently: professor of languages and theology (1919–35); professor of dogmatics, exegesis of the New Testament, and homiletics (1919–35), professor of systematic theology (1928–36); and dean (1919–35). For twenty years he was editor of the journal *Lutherische Kirchenzeitung*. His principal work was a monumental commentary on the entire New Testament, in eleven volumes.

—

CS/JDR

Leo I, "the Great" (ca. 400–61).

Bishop of Rome, or pope, from 440 until his death. He lived in an age when the imperial order was crumbling before the invasions of the Germanic peoples and others. The church began to fill the void left by the order that was disappearing, and this made the actions of L. stand out prominently. Of those actions, the most famous was his crossing of the Tiber River to speak to Attila when the latter was preparing to attack the practically defenseless city of Rome. It is not known what L. told him, but Attila decided to withdraw his armies without attacking and sacking the city. As bishop of Rome, L. intervened in the ecclesiastical matters of distant places, such as southern France and North Africa. Some of those interventions had to do with matters of canon law or with the date on which Easter was to be celebrated. Others were attempts to end movements that L. considered heretical, such as the Manicheans (⇒Mani), the Pelagians (⇒Pelagius), and the Priscillianists (⇒Priscillian).

The chief theological contribution of L. was related to Christology. For L. the doctrine of the incarnation of the Word of God in a human being was of fundamental importance. This may be seen in his sermons, in which he constantly relates the incarnation and other christological matters with the theme of the day. When he saw the doctrine of the incarnation threatened by the excessively disjunctive tendencies of ⇒Nestorius and his followers, he opposed them. And when the opposite tendencies of the Monophysites appeared to endanger the true humanity of the Savior, he also opposed them. He did this in a famous *Tome* or *Dogmatic Epistle to* ⇒Flavian, who at that time was patriarch of Constantinople.

In that epistle L. expounded his christocentric faith and his understanding of the incarnation. According to him, in the same way that God does not cease to be divine by having compassion for us, the humanity of Jesus does not cease being human because it is united to the divinity. Therefore, "Without a diminishing of the properties of either of the two natures and substances united in one person, majesty clothed itself in humility, strength in weakness, eternity in mortality. . . . And just as the Word does not cease possessing a glory equal to the glory of the Father, in the same way the flesh does not lose that which is proper to our race."

When the council that had been convened to deal with that matter met in Ephesus, the Alexandrian party, with the support of the emperor, made sure that no opportunity was given to their opponents. The epistle of L. was not read and Flavian was physically mistreated, with the result that he died shortly afterward. L. protested against such an outrage by giving that synod the name by which it is generally known: "the robbery of Ephesus." When political circumstances changed, the Council of ⇒Chalcedon undid what had been done in the "robber synod" by incorporating the *Tome* of L. into its minutes and affirming what had long been the Western doctrine, namely, that in Jesus Christ there are two natures, one human and one divine, which are united in a single person.

—

JLG

Leo XIII (1810–1903). Pope of the Roman Catholic Church (1878–1903) and author of the encyclical *Rerum Novarum* (1891), promulgated at the time of the greatest social, political, and economic changes of the nineteenth century. The encyclical seeks a just solution for the benefit of the working class and for the alleviation of the misery of the poor. It rejects the socialist solution because it is atheistic, because it rejects private property, and because it foments envy and antagonism among social classes.

The right to private property is fundamental for individual and social well-being. Private property fosters discipline in individuals and the incentive to produce and use their talents in such a way that they contribute to their own well-being and to that of their fellow citizens. Only if we increase social productivity can we improve the condition of the poor.

For Christians, the contribution to social well-being is not based only on the acquisitive instinct and on the institution of private property, but also on the theological condition that all that exists must serve God and contribute to the well-being of its neighbor. The conviction that God is Lord over all that exists moves us to redistribute social wealth for the common good.

The Christian social vision is based on the principle of love. The love of God and of Christ for human beings does not allow us to be indifferent in the presence of the suffering that poverty and social injustice cause. Among the policies that should rule the social order, it is indispensable that the salaries of workers allow them to live with dignity, that children should not be forced to work, and that the workers have the right to organize and defend their interests.

The state has the responsibility of promoting the well-being of individuals and of creating opportunities for them to form independent associations in order to promote their interests.

The state should not intervene in these spheres of voluntary associations. The state also has the responsibility to promote and protect the common good.

In particular, the state must organize all individuals and their associations in such a way that they can contribute to the common good. But when one sector of society falls into poverty and need, the state has the responsibility and the obligation to help them.

This encyclical led to the creation of Catholic political and workers' organizations and fostered social and political activism in several European and Latin American countries.

L. directed that a new edition of the writings of ⇒Thomas Aquinas be prepared and published, the resulting edition therefore being called the Leonine Edition. He also wrote on the value and desirability of Catholic countries, where Catholic teachings dominate civil life. Thus, he may be seen both as the source for reforming elements within the Catholic Church and as a very conservative force.

—

IG

Leo of Ochrid (11th century). Archbishop of that city in Bulgaria who wrote a letter to a bishop in Apulia delineating his disagreements with Western doctrines and practices. This letter was one of the factors that precipitated the schism of ⇒Cerularius.

—

JLG

Leontius of Antioch (4th century). Arian bishop of that city, a disciple of ⇒Lucian of Antioch, and therefore one of the "fellow Lucianists" to whom Arius appealed. Although some attacked him because of his anti-Trinitarian position, what provoked a greater scandal was that when L. was criticized for living with a young woman and was ordered to separate from her, he decided to emasculate himself rather than leave her. This gave rise to a series of canons against voluntary emasculation.

—

JLG

Leontius of Byzantium (ca. 500–ca. 543). Monk and Orthodox theologian, one of the chief defenders of the christological teaching of the Council of ⇒Chalcedon. A native of Constantinople, he entered the monastic life in Palestine, where he came into contact with the teachings of ⇒Origen. His early contact with Origenism has led some historians to try to detect this influence in the development of his Christology. The analysis of his writings has convinced the majority that the Christology of L. is fundamentally in agreement with that of ⇒Cyril of Alexandria, the most influential Orthodox theologian in this subject.

Three of the works of L. have survived. One is a collection of three treatises grouped under the title of the first, *Against Nestorians and Eutycheans*. This includes his major defense of the faith of Chalcedon; it was an attack on Monophysite ideas, that is, the teaching of those who proclaimed the unity of the divine and human nature in Jesus Christ in a single divine nature.

His two other works are also polemical: *Dialogue against the Aphthartodocetists* and *Criticism and Triumph over the Nestorians*. Two other works that once were attributed to L. are now ascribed to at least one of his homonyms.

L. basically defended a diophysism, that is, the view that in Jesus Christ two natures coexist, the human and the divine, in one person. These two natures must be properly distinguished but not separated. On the one hand, there is an emphasis on the element of unity, in the hypostasis of the Logos. On the other hand, the full humanity of Jesus as well as his divinity are simultaneously emphasized.

For L. the key for understanding the formula of Chalcedon is that the two natures of Jesus Christ cannot be mixed or confused, nor can the one be subordinated to the other. L. declared himself against all who divided, separated, or confused the two natures, instead of simply distinguishing the one from the other.

Although his Chalcedonism has been placed into doubt by some scholars in favor of a supposed Origenism, the fact is that L. himself spoke against Origen and explained that it was only in his youth that he felt attracted to him. Besides, shortly before the death of L. Origenism was condemned as heretical, and this did not touch his reputation.

In spite of his participation in the theological and ecclesiastical debates of his time, L. does not appear to have decisively influenced subsequent generations. His work remained almost forgotten until the beginning of the seventeenth century, when translations into Latin appeared.

———

NRG

Lessius, Leonhard (1554–1623).
Jesuit Belgian theologian. He studied art and philosophy in Louvain in preparation for his ordination in 1580. After teaching in the faculty of Douai, he continued his theological studies in Rome under ⇒Bellarmine and ⇒Suárez. He then became a professor at Louvain, where he was accused of Semi-Pelagianism by the followers of ⇒Baius, who initiated a vigorous controversy with the Jesuits. The dispute was resolved in 1590 with the exoneration of L.

L. defended papal authority in a manuscript that had limited circulation for fear of the interference of the king. In *De gratia efficaci*, he defended the theology of ⇒Molina on the relationship between efficacious grace and human free will. His most notable work is *De justitia et jure*, in which he deals with themes of justice and morality, especially those concerning fair contracts, prices, and wages, and the exploitation of the recently discovered lands of America.

———

LGP

Leuthard of Chalons (ca. 1000). A
little-known heretic of imprecise teachings. Some historians believe that he represents the first presence of the ⇒Albigensians in western Europe.

———

JLG

Lewis, C. S. (1898–1963). English novelist and religious writer. Clive Staples Lewis was born in Belfast, Ireland, and was educated at Oxford University, where he taught until 1954. There he was a member of a group of illustrious young scholars called Inklings. Several of them would become famous, such as J. R. R. Tolkien, Charles Williams, and Dorothy Sayers. Later he was distinguished professor of literature at Cambridge. Between 1929 and 1931, L. returned to Christianity. He then began to write for the general public on religious and ethical problems. Among these writings was his science-fiction trilogy, *Perelandra* (1938–45). Some of his radio readings during the Second World War were compiled in three books: *Beyond Personality*, *Miracles*, and *Mere Christianity*. But better known was his book *The Screwtape Letters* (1942), in which a devil writes to his nephew about human temptation. In *Surprised by Joy* (1955) he describes his conversion. He also wrote a series of seven popular books for children, but also for adults, since they are a profound allegory: The Chronicles of Narnia (1950–56).

———

EZ

Liberius (?–366). Bishop of Rome from 352 to 366. At the time Emperor Constantius, the only survivor of the children of Constantine, favored the Arian cause (⇒Arius) against the Nicenes (Council of ⇒Nicaea, 325). For some time L. was the focus of resistance against imperial politics. But imperial pressure was strong. L. had to go into exile, and everything appears to indicate that somehow the emperor succeeded in getting the elderly pope to consent to his Arian politics and to reject the Nicene teaching. This sad story of Liberius was one of the problems to be faced by those who, in preparation for the First Vatican Council (⇒Vatican I), advocated the proclamation of papal infallibility.

———
JLG

Licinianus of Cartagena (6th century). Late participant in the controversies surrounding the teaching of ⇒Augustine on the incorporeal nature of the soul. He wrote an *Epistle to Epiphanius* in which he refutes the arguments of ⇒Gennadius of Marseilles, who had criticized Augustine by adducing that only God is incorporeal.

———
JLG

Liguori, Alphonsus María de' (1696–1787). Catholic moral theologian of Neapolitan origin. After practicing for some years as a lawyer, he was ordained to the priesthood in 1726. In 1731 he founded the Congregation of the Redemptorists for women and in 1732 the Congregation of the Most Holy Redeemer for men. Both communities were devoted mainly to mission among the poor in rural areas.

His theology reacted against Jansenism (⇒Jansen) and probabilism (⇒Medina). His balanced teaching, as found in his *Moral Theology*, eventually obtained the approval of the Roman Catholic Church. For this reason L. is considered the father of moral theology. He was beatified in 1816, canonized in 1839, and declared a ⇒doctor of the church in 1871. In 1959 he was proclaimed heavenly patron of confessors and moralists.

———
PAJ

Lindbeck, George Arthur (1923–). North American Lutheran theologian and one of the names associated with the postliberal school of thought developed at Yale University. Born in China, L. studied at Gustavus Adolphus College in Minnesota and at Yale, where he would return as professor. L. was selected by Lutherans to serve as a Protestant observer invited to the Second Vatican Council (⇒Vatican II).

Having been influenced by the narrative theology of Hans Frei, L. devoted himself to examining theological doctrines by employing linguistic and cultural concepts, thus determining the significance of religion within the cultural, social, and linguistic system of those who practice it. His best-known book, *The Nature of Doctrine: Religion and Theology in a Postliberal Age* (1984), attempts to maintain religious belief systems in the face of philosophical attacks concerning the verification of the particular beliefs of each doctrinal system.

———
LGP

Livingstone, David (1813–73). Son of poor Scots, L. was reared in the atmosphere of evangelical piety and decided to be a missionary. He was named missionary to Africa under the London Missionary Society. His missionary work resulted in great discoveries, providing for the West valuable geographical, ethnographic, and exploratory information. L. conceived his missionary vocation as one of opening the way for the arrival of Christianity in the unknown heart of Africa. His missionary and exploratory work established the foundations for the mission in Africa.

L. believed that the slave traffic, besides being immoral, was a great obstacle for the propagation of the Christian faith. As an antidote to this traffic, he proposed opening the heart of Africa to legitimate commerce—hence his interest in geographical exploration. He died in Africa, where, as he had directed, his heart was buried, while his body received honors in Westminster Abbey in England.

———
CCO

Locke, John (1632–1704). Philosopher whom many consider the father of empiricism and of English political liberalism. Among his chief works are *Essays concerning Human Understanding* (1690), *Treatises on Civil Government* (1690), and *Letters concerning Toleration* (1690). His work is focused on the theory of knowledge. For L., ideas are derived from sensory experience and from intellectual reflection. His ideas on human rights, society as a product of a social contract, the need to limit the power of government, and the division of political power took on concrete form in the Constitution of the United States.

In *The Reasonableness of Christianity* (1693), L. tries to present a "reasonable" biblical Christianity, independent of the dogmas of the church and purified of all false teaching.

—

IG

Loehe, Johann Konrad Wilhelm (1808–72).

Educator and pastor from Neuendettelsau, Bavaria, who helped to found a Lutheran seminary in Fort Wayne, Indiana. He differed from C. F. W. ⇒Walther in that he did not believe that the authority to ordain to the ministry of the church rested on the local congregation. His greatest contribution was founding, in 1854, the Association of Deaconesses and the Deaconess Home in Neuendettelsau. This marks the first historical step of the Evangelical Lutheran churches in the United States in recognizing the ministry of women in the church.

—

ALG

Loisy, Alfred Firmin (1857–1940).

Catholic modernist, a native of Ambrières, France. After his studies at the seminary of Châlons-sur-Marne and at the Institute Catholique de Paris, he was ordained to the priesthood in 1879. He worked for several years as a parish priest before returning to the Institute Catholique as professor of Bible. He was one of the first Roman Catholics to apply the historical-critical method to the study of the Bible. He rejected the historicity of the book of Genesis and did not believe Moses to be the author of the Pentateuch. Because of his teachings, considered heterodox, L. lost his post at the Institute, and he became chaplain of a convent. Later he returned to teach at the Sorbonne, but he was also dismissed from there in 1903.

Because of his critical work, L. is considered one of the pioneers of the Catholic modernist movement. His book *The Gospel and the Church* (1902) is a critical response to ⇒Harnack's *The Essence of Christianity*. In it L. argues that the church did not develop according to the plan of Jesus and that the essence of the teachings of Jesus, which according to Harnack still existed in the Christian faith, has been lost. According to L. only the teachings of the church remain, which are what constitutes the true Christian faith. Although L. presented his book as a defense of the true faith, its publication, together with his critical studies of the Gospels, caused alarm in Rome, resulting in his excommunication in 1908.

Although he was able to continue teaching the history of religion in a secular college until he retired in 1930, all of his subsequent works were considered heretical. In his studies he arrived at the conclusion that in all the religions there exists a common moral base in the thirst for justice. The culmination of his thought is found in the book *The Birth of Christianity* (1933).

—

LGP

Lonergan, Bernard Joseph Francis (1904–84).

Canadian Jesuit philosopher and theologian who was particularly interested in methodological matters. The son of a surveyor, he was born near Ottawa. His family was of Anglo-Irish origin, and he was the eldest of three sons. At the age of fifteen he was near death, and his mother stayed by his bedside. At eighteen he entered the Company of Jesus, and his program of formation led him first to Guelph, Ontario, for his novitiate, and then to Heythrop College in England to study philosophy. After teaching for three years in Loyola College in Montreal, he was sent to study theology in the Gregorian University of Rome. He was ordained as a priest in 1936. He completed his licentiate the following year and his doctorate in 1940. He taught theology for twenty-five years, thirteen of them in Jesuit seminaries in Montreal and twelve in the Gregorian University. In 1965 an operation for lung cancer forced him into partial retirement, although he continued writing and giving lectures. During this period he served as professor and researcher at Regis College in Toronto, as Stillman Professor at Harvard, and as distinguished visiting professor at Boston College. Upon his final retirement in 1983 he returned to Canada, where he died the following year, at the age of nearly eighty years.

He worked chiefly in three fields: theology, philosophy, and economics, although his last work on economics remained unfinished. A number of scholars believe that someday his studies in economics will be as much appreciated as are his theological and philosophical works today. Among the thinkers who most influenced his thought are ⇒Plato, ⇒Aristotle, Euclid, ⇒Augustine, ⇒Suárez, Maréchal, and ⇒Newman, whose *Grammar of Assent* he read repeatedly.

His first works were studies of ⇒Thomas Aquinas and his Aristotelian background: *Grace and Freedom* (which was his doctoral thesis) and *Verbum: Word and Idea in Aquinas.* But soon he showed himself capable of going beyond the sphere of Thomism. *Verbum* was an original work in which a new way of viewing Thomist epistemology emerged and which served as a starting point for his classic work of 1957: *Insight: A Study of Human Undertanding.* This work transcends Thomism and involves the science, psychology, and political and social theory of the twentieth century. The lifetime dream of L. was to discover a theological method that would incorporate modern advances in science and at the same time be capable of replying to the criticisms posed by modern philosophy. The purpose of *Insight* was to establish the foundations for a theological methodology through the process of outlining methods for other disciplines, such as mathematics, physics, and biology. In the same way he also dealt with the methodology of psychotherapy, political theory, metaphysics, and ethics.

His second most famous work is *Method in Theology*, published in 1972. Some believe that this is his masterwork, because in it he recognized the great changes that modern culture has brought with it and how theologians have to adjust to those changes if their work is to be adequate. He proposes a transcultural method discovered by paying attention to our own mental operations, which are essentially a matter of experience, understanding, judgment, and decision. It is necessary to consider all of these operations when dealing with the content of the Christian faith and tradition (just as with any other religion), in the light of the present and the future.

His contributions to modern theological method are fundamental. Both L. and Karl ⇒Rahner are credited with having promoted a methodological change that concerns itself not only with Scripture and tradition, but also with the life and mind, the context and interests of those who concern themselves with theology. Frequently described as a historical conscience, this concept underscores the existence of what is concrete and passing and thus challenges classicism, which pretends that reality (the truth) is essentially static, fixed, and independent of history and culture. The world of L. is mediated by meaning. Like Rahner and ⇒Gutiérrez, he insists that theology is not the task of experts, the result of which is then filtered to the common people in order to be applied. If one takes culture and cultural change seriously, it is necessary to pay attention to the agents of change, including persons.

In the area of ecumenism and interreligious dialogue, L. approaches religious experience with great openness, firmly declaring that a contemporary Catholic theology must be directed not only to all Christians, but also to non-Christians and atheists. Following this norm, for example, Frederick E. Crowe, SJ, has linked the Trinitarian theology of L. to other religions in his book *Son of God, Holy Spirit, and World Religions: Bernard Lonergan's Contribution to the Wider Ecumenism* (1984). The works of L. are also linked with the psychology that stems from ⇒Jung, with mystical theology, and with popular religions. All of these materials, as well as his unpublished works, are available in the Lonergan Research Institute of Toronto. One of the greatest achievements of this Canadian Jesuit is his proposal of a concrete method, a paradigm for the theological task.

—

EF

Lorenzo de Brindisi ⇒Brindisi, Lawrence of

Lores Zucarino, Rubén (1923–92).
Born in Cuba, where he received his first biblical formation. He continued his studies in the United States, to which he had moved while still young, before going to Spain as a missionary. After having been expelled from Spain, he lived in Tangier, where he labored in the pastorate and in evangelical radio programming in Spanish. Upon returning to the United States he worked in New York with the American Bible Society and as pastor of an independent church. Later he joined the Latin American Mission and lived in Costa Rica. There he was a pastor, associate director of the mission, and rector of the Latin American Biblical Seminary, where he promoted the creation of a system of distance education (PRODIADIS). Having received his licentiate in philosophy from the University of Costa Rica with a thesis on ⇒Kierkegaard, he later obtained his master's degree in theology from Princeton Theological Seminary. He was also an evangelist and mission strategist. He wrote many articles on mission, evangelization, and theological education.

—

PAB

Lowrie, Walter (1868–1959). North
American Episcopal priest. In his twenty-three-year pastorate in Rome, he made contact with

the thought of Søren ⇒Kierkegaard, who was unknown in the English-speaking world. After learning Danish at the age of sixty-five, he wrote two hagiographic biographies and translated totally or partially fifteen volumes containing more than half the work of Kierkegaard.

———

EPA

Loy, Matthias (1828–1915). Lutheran theologian and translator of hymns from German into English. Born in Cumberland County, Pennsylvania. He was president of the Lutheran Synod of Ohio (1860–78 and 1880–94); editor of the *Lutheran Standard* (1864–91), professor of theology at Capital University (Columbus, Ohio) between 1865 and 1902; and president of the same university from 1881 to 1890.

———

HMT

Loyola, Ignatius of (1491–1556). Mystic and founder of the Company of Jesus, better known as the Jesuits. Íñigo López de Loyola was the son of a noble Basque family. As a young man he enjoyed a life full of duels, love affairs, and escapades, until during the French siege of Pamplona (1521) a cannonball injured one of his legs and fractured the other. He suffered several painful operations to straighten and save his leg. His long recovery gave him time to read voraciously. First he read chivalric literature, which he soon discarded, and then spiritual works of the age, which inspired in him the desire to undertake great works for God. When his injuries were healed, he decided to leave on a pilgrimage to the Holy Land, and on the way he stopped at the Benedictine monastery of Monserrat, where he spent a night in vigil, abandoned his possessions, and swore to become a knight in the service of God. While he prayed he hung up his sword and garb as knight and exchanged them for a pilgrim's habit.

Passing through Manresa, where he lived for eleven months, he experienced a mystical transformation that led him to write the first parts of the *Spiritual Exercises*, one of the classic works of Christian spirituality. In this work we see the importance of military life for the inner development of L. and for the development of the institutional vision of the future order. He divided his work into four stages or weeks in which the devout should remove themselves from their secular activities in order to occupy themselves with various spiritual exercises whose purpose is to submit the mind, imagination, understanding, and will to the will of God, under the guidance of a spiritual director.

From Manresa the pilgrim continued toward Jerusalem, where he arrived in September of 1523. When he was denied permission to live in the Holy Land, he decided to return to Spain. During the next eleven years he became engrossed in studies, in the hope of eventually serving God adequately. He began his studies in Barcelona, where he studied Latin for two years (1524–26); he then studied philosophy in Alcalá and Salamanca. His talks and his pastoral care of several followers and women of the area aroused the curiosity of the Holy Inquisition, which under an accusation of being an *alumbrado* (a follower of a mystical movement of that time that was persecuted by the institutional church) imprisoned him for forty-two days in Alcalá, and later twenty-two more days in Salamanca. In both cases he was exonerated. After this ecclesiastical pressure, L. decided to leave for the University of Paris, from which he graduated in 1534 with the degree of a master of arts in philosophy. On August 15, 1534, while in Paris, he and six companions (among them ⇒Francis Xavier and Diego ⇒Laínez) dedicated their lives to the service of others and took the vows of chastity and strict poverty. They also decided to leave for the Holy Land, or if not, to place themselves at the disposition of the pope. One year later three new associates increased the number of members of the incipient order to ten persons. On the way to Jerusalem the group met in Venice in January 1537, where, on seeing the impossibility of their trip to Jerusalem, they decided to create a permanent structure with the name of Company of Jesus.

The aim of the order was "to militate for God under the banner of the cross and to serve only the Lord and the Pope, his vicar on earth." The new order was confirmed by Pope Paul III in September 1540. Since then its followers have taken four vows: the usual three of poverty, chastity, and obedience, and a fourth vow of faithfulness to the pope. In 1541, in Rome, the other nine cofounders elected Ignatius as superior general of the order for life. During the next fifteen years, until his death, the order grew rapidly, attaining a membership of one thousand Jesuits. By 1556 Jesuits were serving in Europe, Africa, Asia, and the new colonies of Spain in America. This activity greatly advanced the development of Christianity in those territories, while it created suspicions among the civil authorities, who eventually expelled the Jesuits from several colonies and countries. Their work emphasized pastoral and missionary service and education. The Jesuits stood out for their missionary work in Asia, where men like Matteo ⇒Ricci, Francis Xavier, and others risked their lives preaching Christianity. Their militancy and courage led them to be leaders in the Catholic reformation, always under the direction of L., who when he died left a collection of about seven thousand letters. L. also wrote the Constitutions of the order and other documents.

In Rome he founded the Roman College (now the Gregorian University) and the German College for the preparation of German priests who were interested in serving in the Protestant territories of their country. A year after its foundation (1551), the Roman College had more than three hundred students.

Ignatius was the founder and leading figure of one of the most important religious orders of the contemporary world, which currently has about thirty-five thousand priests around the world. Of these, about eight thousand serve in the missionary field. Contemplative, a man of vision and action, L. demonstrated in his life the highest ideals for the promotion of the greater glory of God. Ever since then the phrase *ad majorem Dei gloriam* has served to distinguish the followers of the Jesuit spirit. L. was beatified by the Roman Catholic Church in 1609 and canonized in 1622.

———
LMcA

Lubac, Henri de (1896–1991). French
Jesuit who distinguished himself as a theologian and historian of the church. He was one of the chief members of the movement known as the *nouvelle théologie* (lit., new theology). He also advocated a return to the study of patristics and scholastic theology.

He was born in Cambrai, France, and became a Jesuit in 1913. He fought in the First World War, receiving a head injury that affected him for the rest of his life. He was ordained a priest in 1927. From 1935 to 1950 he taught in the Faculty of Theology of Fourvière, near Lyon. He was involved in the French Resistance movement during the Second World War. During the 1950s he was marginalized because of some of his theological positions on supernatural phenomena. He was publicly restored in 1960 and went on to play a leadership role in the preparatory commission of the Second Vatican Council (⇒Vatican II). He was named cardinal in 1983. Among his publications are *The*

Religious Thought of Father ⇒*Teilhard de Chardin* (1967) and *Atheism and Meaning of Man* (1969).

———
PAJ

Lucaris, Cyril (1572–1638). Patriarch
of Constantinople and theologian, L. studied in Venice, Padua, and Geneva, where he was influenced by Calvinism and came to include Reformed perspectives in his Orthodox theological thought. For this reason he was strongly criticized by his colleagues. Based on his Calvinist perspectives, L. strongly opposed union with the Church of Rome. His most debated theological work was his Confession of Faith, which had strong Protestant overtones and led many within Orthodoxy to view him as a heretic. For this reason, there are significant ecumenical values in his theological legacy. Also, it was he who made known the *Codex Alexandrinus*, which he delivered to the British ambassador to Constantinople.

During his stormy patriarchy (he was deposed and restored on six different occasions between 1620 and 1638), L. managed politically difficult moments in the empire and violent conflicts with the Muslim caliphs. He was murdered by the troops of Sultan Murad.

———
CCO

Lucian of Antioch (3rd–4th centuries). Celebrated teacher of that city, said
to be a disciple of ⇒Paul of Samosata and teacher of the chief Arian leaders, such as ⇒Arius, ⇒Eusebius of Nicomedia, and ⇒Asterius the Sophist. Some scholars have suggested that in Antioch there were two teachers with the same name, so that the disciple of Paul of Samosata was not the teacher of Arius and Eusebius. In any case, the teacher of Arius was certainly a convinced Origenist, although he differed from his Alexandrian model in that he insisted on literal and historical exegesis in the Antiochene style and rejected the allegorical method of ⇒Origen. His understanding of God was similar to Origen's. For him the Word or Logos was an intermediate being that allowed the immutable and impassible God of the Platonic tradition to be related to this mutable and passible world. It was precisely this way of understanding God and God's relationship with the Word and with creatures that led to Arianism.

———
JLG

Lucifer of Cagliari (?–ca. 370). One of the protagonists of the resistance against Emperor Constantius, when the latter sought to impose Arianism (⇒Arius). His writings against the emperor and his edicts are strong and at times even insulting. Among them are *Defense of Saint Athanasius* and *To Die for the Son of God*. When, after the death of Constantius, the controversy died down, L. appeared annoyed by the ease with which those who earlier had submitted to the emperor were forgiven. This gave rise to the sect of the Luciferians, which did not last long. His most famous follower was ⇒Gregory of Elvira.

———

JLG

Luis de León (1527–91). Spanish theologian, philosopher, poet, and teacher. He was born in Belmonte, Cuenca, in the region of La Mancha, in a prosperous family. Educated in Salamanca, he entered the Order of St. Augustine at the age of fourteen. He studied philosophy in the monastery, and later theology in the university. He taught theology among Augustinians in Salamanca, Soria, Alcalá, Valladolid, and possibly Toledo. In Toledo he graduated with a bachelor's degree, and then moved to the University of Salamanca in 1558. He received the licentiate and master's degrees in 1560, and the following year obtained his first chair, on ⇒Thomas Aquinas, in the same university.

The environment at the University of Salamanca was then characterized by internal struggles provoked by competition among persons and religious institutions, and also by the frequent intervention of the Inquisition. The University of Salamanca was divided into two schools of thought, with different points of view on biblical methods of interpretation: the scripturalists and the scholastics.

L. and two other professors, Martínez Cantalapiedra and Gaspar de Grajal, maintained the traditional position regarding the Vulgate and the rabbinical interpretations of the Scriptures. L. had made a Spanish translation, with comments, of the Song of Songs. The Inquisition had forbidden the reading of the Scriptures in a vernacular language, and the enemies of L. accused him of having broken that rule in his commentary. He had also written a dissertation on the Vulgate, and this resulted in additional accusations of undermining the authority of that version.

Charges against him alleged that (1) he said only Requiem masses, even on a feast day; (2) what he said was not understood; (3) he finished too quickly; (4) he spoke badly of the Septuagint; (5) he ridiculed the Holy Fathers; and (6) he translated the Scriptures into Spanish.

After a complicated trial, L. was found guilty of the imprudence of treating matters like the authenticity of the Vulgate in public, and of translating biblical books into the vernacular. These activities were considered dangerous, for they were points of possible contact with Lutheranism. He and the other two professors were condemned to prison.

In spite of the bitter ecclesiastical and academic conflicts that surrounded him, L. was characterized by a singular moderation. Although he was imprisoned for five years, he never questioned the legitimacy of the court that judged his faith. He complained about the false religious zeal of his accusers, about lies and envy, but not about the Inquisition itself. In the midst of the illnesses and hardships that he suffered during his imprisonment, he retained inner peace, as reflected in the poetry he composed while in prison.

Also while in prison he worked on a commentary on Psalm 26 and composed what many consider the masterpiece of Spanish prose of the sixteenth century: *De los nombres de Cristo* (On the Names of Christ). In an imaginary conversation, three friends expound on ten biblical names of Jesus (Shepherd, Way, Mount, among others).

In 1576 L. was exonerated and returned to the lectureship in Salamanca. Six years later he was again denounced to the Inquisition, but the charges were dropped. In the last years of his life he avoided university struggles, finding comfort in the friendship of the disciples of ⇒Teresa of Ávila. He died in Madrigal at the age of 64, while he served as Augustinian provincial of Castile.

It would be difficult to exaggerate the influence of L. on Spanish literature and theology. He is perhaps the greatest lyrical poet of Spain. Poems such as "Noche serena" (Serene Night) made him a model for subsequent generations of Spanish classicists, who struggled to preserve in their literature a flavor that was native rather than Latin. His treatise on the duties of the Christian wife, *La perfecta casada* (The Perfect Married Woman), published in 1583, is also considered a literary classic. His translations from Greek, Latin, Hebrew, and Italian of books from the Old Testament on which he commented established him as a classical translator. He is one of the great Spanish mystics, together with ⇒John of the Cross and Teresa of Ávila.

———

RAR

Luis of Granada (1504–88).

Spanish mystic, preacher, and writer of the Dominican order. He was born in Galicia, in a very poor family. He lost his father at the age of five. His mother had to wash clothes for a living. The experience of poverty in his childhood marked his life. Subsequently the governor of the city took him into his service as a page. Thus he had contact with the world of the nobility and became familiar with the contradictions of the age.

In 1529 he was sent to the College of St. Gregory in Valladolid, an intellectual center seething with the spirit of religious reform and rivaling the more conservative Salamanca. There he assumed the name of Luis of Granada and was introduced to Christian humanism and to mysticism. He was conscious of the preoccupations of his contemporaries and insisted that the renewal that they sought could only come from the inner life, through a total surrender to the life of prayer.

His spirituality was centered on meditation on the life and passion of Christ; inner piety, free from every intellectual consideration and centered on Christ; and the remembrance that makes possible an intimate union with God. He regarded external ceremonies as relatively unimportant in comparison with the inner religious life, which was the life of grace.

Around 1548 he became a prior in Badajoz. In 1553 he was elected provincial of his order for Portugal, where he spent the last three decades of his life. He was a spiritual guide among the laity at large as well as to religious prelates and members of the nobility. His works enjoyed ample circulation. Outstanding among them are *Libro de oración y meditación* (1554; Book of Prayer and Meditation) and *Guía de pecadores* (1567; Guide of Sinners). At the time Spain was threatened by heresies, and the inquisitors suspected all books that promoted inner piety. His were condemned, but this did not intimidate him or keep him from writing.

He was a man of his time. He opened a new chapter in religious history, balancing the spirituality of remembrance of the Franciscans and the apostolic zeal of the Jesuits. He emphasized the practice of Christian virtues that give a sense of confidence, liberation from sin, illumination, and transformation by the Holy Spirit.

RAR

Lull, Ramón (1232–1316).

Spanish missionary and philosopher, born in Majorca. At the age of thirty he had a vision in which Christ sent him to be a missionary among Arab Muslims. Interpreting the vision as a call from God, he studied Arabic, Islam, and Christian thought.

Traveling to North Africa and to the Mediterranean, L. made contact with Arab Muslims and developed a new missionary strategy for dealing with Islam, the Christian apology. By this time Christianity had long been involved in the Crusades to recover the Holy Land, and violence had become the normal mode of encounter among Christians, Muslims, and Jews. Therefore L. opened a new way for the encounter between Christians and Arab Muslims and established the antecedents for interreligious dialogue, although his purpose was the conversion of Muslims to Christianity.

CCO

Luther, Martin (1483–1546).

Recognized as the founder of the sixteenth-century Reformation and of Protestantism. He not only precipitated the birth of a third Christian theological branch, together with Roman Catholicism and Eastern Orthodoxy, but also influenced the theological, social, economic, and political thought of future generations in all those branches of the church. For more than a century the critical edition of Luther's works has been published in Weimar. These include sixty volumes of theological and devotional treatises in Latin and German, fourteen volumes of correspondence, twelve of his translations of the Bible into German with his prefaces, and six of his "Table Talks," compiled by his students. He wrote almost all of his works under pressure and as a response to criticism, and he did so while breaking through the patterns of theology of his age.

L. was born at a time when Europe was discovering new civilizations in new continents, the Renaissance reigned with its admiration of Greek and Latin classical culture, and scholars were returning to the sources of antiquity. It was the age when the movement that the eighteenth century would call humanism was born. Mainly in Italy and Germany, rhetoric, grammar, and dialectics confronted the logic of the scholasticism of ⇒Thomas Aquinas and Duns ⇒Scotus. The *via antiqua* of those giants, with its metaphysical realism, began to be criticized by the *via moderna* of the nominalist metaphysics of William of ⇒Ockham and ⇒Gregory of Rimini.

But L. was also born in a society that was full of superstitions and witches. He was born at a time when kings questioned the authority of the pope, when common folk began to resent the autocracy of the nobility, and when the printing press with movable type—an indispensable instrument for the dissemination of ideas—had already existed for some years.

L. was born in a middle-class family in Eisleben, Saxony. His father, Hans, and his mother, Margarethe, were pious persons who reared their son with fear and rectitude. Hans longed for his son to become a lawyer, and to this end L. completed his bachelor of arts (1501) and master of arts (1505) degrees in the University of Erfurt, subsequently entering the Faculty of Law. It is known that he was a good student. It is possible that by that time he was influenced by the *via moderna*.

L. tells in his "Table Talks" that on July 2, 1505, returning from Eisenach to Erfurt, on the occasion of a visit with his parents, he was surprised by an electrical storm, and, terrified of dying, he cried: "Help me, St. Anne, and I will become a monk." Much has been written about this experience. Some suggest that L. was already worried about his spiritual situation or by his sinful condition as a mortal man, and for this reason he entered the Augustinian cloister in Erfurt that same month. It is known that he entered the monastery without much enthusiasm. There he professed as a monk in 1506, and the following year he was ordained a priest. He was selected to pursue theological studies in Wittenberg, where in a few months he was declared a bachelor in biblical studies. He returned then to Erfurt to begin his theological career as reader and commentator on the *Sentences* by ⇒Peter Lombard. His disdain for the intrusion of the philosophy of ⇒Aristotle in the theological field can already be seen here. But that could simply be a prejudice that was learned from his nominalist professors. The spirit of those times was to ignore, not to study, the scholastics.

During his studies in Wittenberg he met his confessor John Staupitz, vicar general of the Augustinians and occupant of the chair of Bible. Staupitz preferred the mystical and spiritual theology of the *devotio moderna* and the christocentric emphasis of ⇒Bernard of Clairvaux to both classical scholasticism and nominalism. Staupitz was the mentor and friend of Luther, whom he sent to Wittenberg to earn the doctorate. Luther obtained this degree in 1512, and he then assumed the chair of Staupitz in biblical theology. Because of his rigid administration of the Augustinians, Staupitz caused a conflict in which the dissident group went to

Rome to appeal. It is ironic that Luther was the companion of the brother who represented the dissidents.

He spent one month in Rome and observed the disorder, the low level of morality of Pope Julius II and his attendants, and the decadent piety among them. In his heart he began to have the desire, which was already present in other Roman Catholic leaders, to reform the church. But Luther would not accomplish this before he made a deeper study of the Holy Scriptures—especially, as he indicated later, because he did not understand the meaning of the righteousness of God.

There are different opinions on the date when Luther discovered the meaning of the righteousness of God in the Pauline epistles. Early dates are suggested, beginning with his first lectures on the Psalms, *Dictata super Psalterium* (1512–13), or his lectures on Romans (1515), and as late as his second course of lectures on the Psalms, *Operationes in Psalmos* (1518). Probably it was a gradual development. L. was well acquainted with the ethics of Aristotle and had taught it in Wittenberg in the Faculty of Arts. There he understood the concept of righteousness (justice: *justitia*) as punishment or retribution. The works of several nominalists also defined the righteousness of God as an active and harsh punishment of sinners by God. This was how the "righteousness of God" in Romans 1:17 was generally understood. My opinion is that beginning in 1515 Luther began to struggle with that concept in a specific way, because we can see him struggling with key concepts, above all in his lectures on Romans 3:10 and 4:7. Here Luther exhibits an anthropology according to which the human being is not made such by being constituted of body and soul in their ontological reality. We are human beings in our totality and in our relation to God.

Thus Luther tells us: "In my temerity I do not distinguish body, soul, and spirit, but I present the complete human being in its relation to God." Because of original sin, the concern of the human being revolves around itself, and it lives unconcerned about God and about its brothers and sisters. The nominalist theology of Gabriel ⇒Biel, which Luther had studied, contradicted the Pauline vision of a being that is totally a sinner who could not obtain a proper relationship with God and be truly absolved and forgiven. Because of his theological training, Luther understood the righteousness of God to be like judicial justice, and for this reason he resented it.

He describes his breakthrough in his Preface to his Latin writings, published in 1545:

Finally, God had mercy on me while I meditated day and night about the connection of the words: "The righteousness (justice) of God is revealed in this," as the Scriptures say: "The just (righteous) shall live by faith." I began to understand that "the righteousness (justice) of God" is that by which the righteous one lives as a gift of God properly by means of faith, and this phrase "the righteousness (justice) of God is revealed" refers to a passive righteousness (justice) by which our merciful God justifies us by faith.

L. found that with faith given as a gift by God, forgiveness is received and a new relationship with God is established. It was for him a "passive righteousness (justice)," because what was accepted was the work of Christ on the cross. There the righteousness (justice) of God is found. In his treatise *Christian Liberty*, written in 1520, it is clear that for Luther this righteousness (justice) of God is an incarnational, christological reality. The reality of the life of faith is such that faith in Christ is a "happy exchange" in which the righteousness (justice) of Christ is interchanged for our unrighteousness (injustice). Christ in his incarnational reality lives in us with supreme freedom over sin and in a new relationship of community in service to the neighbor. He sums it up: "The Christian is a free lord over all things and is not subject to anyone. The Christian is servant of all things and is subject to all."

In his study on Romans, Luther begins to use a phrase that is the key to his anthropology and his vision of the justification of believers: *simul justus et peccator* ([a believer is] simultaneously righteous and sinful). It means that as human beings we continue to be sinners centered on ourselves (*incurvatus in se*), but in our relationship of faith in Christ we are righteous. Thus L. sees that this reality of being righteous is lived in Christ. Christ lives in us through the gospel and through his sacramental reality in baptism and Communion.

L. gives a very special place to his baptism and to the image Paul uses in Romans 6 as a key to his life and pastoral ministry. In his Large Catechism, written in 1530 as a text of instruction for the ignorant clergy of his region, he declares that baptismal reality. All Christians should remember their baptism daily as the death of their sinful being and their resurrection to a new life in Christ. For L. this new life in Christ is not a return to a past state of integrity, but an eschatological situation of new life in communion with Christ and with our neighbor.

From this perspective L. develops an ecclesiology in which the church is such by demonstrating the true marks of the gospel and is nurtured by the sacraments of baptism and the Lord's Supper in order to live in true community. This is clearly expressed in his *Schmalkald Articles*, in the section on "The Gospel." From this starting point, although L. does not annul but rather affirms pastoral ministry, he also emphasizes the important ministry of all believers in preserving and communicating this reality of the gospel. His treatise *To the Nobility of the German Nation* (1520) affirms that right, which is given to all believers, and not only to the clergy.

But the most important result of his realistic anthropology and his doctrine of justification by faith is that they led L. to formulate his theology of the cross as the central and key point of his method of doing theology. This can be seen particularly in the theses that he prepared for the Heidelberg Disputation.

The Heidelberg Theses do not always receive the attention that they deserve, since they have been eclipsed by the famous Ninety-five Theses that were the immediate cause of his rupture with Rome. Already in 1518 L. was having great difficulties with Pope Leo X because of the Ninety-five Theses that he had placed, in Latin, on the door of the Church of All Saints in Wittenberg on October 31, 1517. He had written them only to have a dialogue with theologians about the sale of indulgences and the need to reform the church through the free offer of grace in the Bible. Leo X had given orders to Gabriel de la Volta, governor of the Augustinian Order in Rome, to silence L. But those theses deal chiefly with the matter of indulgences, and not with the function and method of theology, a subject with which L. deals in the Heidelberg Theses.

For this reason the Heidelberg Theses are very important. Theses 19, 20, and 21 are the most significant. In thesis 19 he says: "That person does not deserve to be called a theologian who looks upon the invisible things of God as though they were clearly perceptible in those things which have actually happened." Here, as in other writings, L. despises the use of reason as an instrument to lead us to a righteous relationship with God and to be received by God. L. never denies reason and the presence of the order of God under the tutelage of reason in creation, society, and government.

This can be clearly seen in his explanation of the first article of the Apostles' Creed in his Catechisms (the "Large" and the "Small"). In his realistic anthropology he sees the human being completely separated from God, with the result that neither reason nor any type of *analogia entis* (ontological analogy) can lead us to a saving relationship with God. Only an analogy of faith reveals God to us in Christ, the crucified God. He says in thesis 20: "That person deserves to be called a theologian who understands the visible and rearward things of God (*visibilia et posteriora Dei*), considering them in the light of the passion and the cross."

Here L. maintains a concrete christological perspective wherein God is revealed in Christ by assuming a posture of suffering for our sins and by affirming God's own solidarity with our human situation. Thus L. does not reject the Council of ⇒Chalcedon, but he does transcend in several ways the substantial problem of the relationship of the two natures of Christ, divine and human. His attitude is neither modalist nor deipassionist, since he distinguishes the person of Christ in relation to the Father and thus emphasizes the role of the person of Christ as divine and human. God the Father abandons God the Son. God struggles with God so that in the light of the Spirit there might be true community in the Trinity through its solidarity with humanity. This is a relationship of love and not of vengeance. Thus L. understands the sacrifice of Christ in a very different way from ⇒Anselm. This sacrifice is not merely a propitiation, but a relational action through which God the Father lives once and for all in a relationship of solidarity and love with humanity, on remembrance of the sacrifice and cross of God's Son. L. highlights this in his *Operationes in Psalmos.*

With this vision L. directs the work of the theologian in thesis 21: "The theologian of glory calls evil good and good evil; the theologian of the cross calls things what they really are." The human experience of power does not compare with the true power of the solidarity of the love of the crucified God. Our faith in Christ is an active faith in that love. In his *Operationes*, L. affirms this dynamic faith of the Christian in the face of the world. There he writes: "Living, or rather dying and being damned make a theologian, not understanding, reading or speculating."

L. dedicates his Preface to the edition of his writings in German (1539) to the "study of theology." Gabriel Biel had written that one becomes a theologian through *oratio, medita-*

tio, lectio (prayer, meditation, and reading). L. replaced *lectio* with *tentatio*. In this formulation one becomes a theologian through prayer, meditation, and living in temptation (tribulation, *Anfechtung*)—the way of the cross in the world. This is a position in which pain is taken not to elevate it, but to liberate it from the consequences of sin.

In his affirmation of creation and the incarnation, L. shows greater appreciation for music and art than his contemporaries ⇒Carlstadt and ⇒Zwingli, who were almost Platonic in this aspect of their theology. The heritage in Protestantism that elevates music and art as magnificent expressions of the divine originates with L.

On the other hand, L. was a child of his times. He frequently expressed himself with rough language, and he almost even asks for the death of "heretics." But he did not instigate or participate in the executions of heretics, as Zwingli and ⇒Calvin would do. Even so, two of the darkest chapters of his life are his attitude at the time of the peasants' revolt in 1525 and his posture toward the Jews. Although he complained of the oppression to which the peasants were subjected, he wrote severely against them when they revolted. We must understand that he owed his life to Frederick the Wise, who obtained a safe-conduct enabling him to be present at the Diet of Worms in 1521 and protected him when Charles V asked for his death. Many rulers supported his position against the pope, but they feared that the mob would take matters to an extreme. And in a certain way the rebellion of the peasants appeared to confirm that fear.

The attitude of L. against the Jews arose from his frustration when he did not see them accepting the gospel. This feeling became more urgent in his old age, when he believed that he was living in the last of days and seems to have forgotten that Jesus never called his followers to act in such a way.

Finally, it must be said of L. that one of his major contributions was the translation of the Bible into a German that was understood by the people. He began this task in his exile in Wartburg Castle (1521), and then in Wittenberg he had the cooperation of ⇒Melanchthon. The impact of this work can be seen in the translation of the Bible into other vernacular languages.

———

ALG

Lyon, Second Council of (1274).

Considered the Fourteenth Ecumenical Council by the Roman Catholic Church. It was convoked by Gregory X with three principal purposes: to promote support for the cause of the Crusades, to unite the Western church with the Eastern, and to reform the church, above all in the matter of papal elections, which had become a cause of scandal. The first goal was attained by the pope through a series of private negotiations with the members of the council and the representatives of different governments. The second was achieved on July 6, when the Byzantine prelates and the emperor's chancellor signed a document in which they accepted the primacy of the bishop of Rome, the teaching of purgatory, and the seven sacraments. This accord was celebrated with a solemn mass. But all was in vain, since what the delegates accepted in Lyon was flatly rejected by the bishops and by the Byzantine population.

The council had a more lasting impact on papal elections, since its decree on this matter, *Ubi periculum*, outlines the system of elections which, with some adjustments, has been in effect until this time. According to this decree, ten days after the death of a pope the cardinals were to meet behind closed doors (in conclave). While the conclave was meeting, the cardinals would lose their income, by which measure the council hoped to avoid useless delays. If the election lasted for more than three days, the diet of the electors would begin to be restricted, and after the fifth day they would have only bread and water.

———

JLG

Macarius the Great (ca. 300–90).
Monk of the Egyptian desert, famous for his holiness and wisdom. Several treatises and above all homilies are attributed to him. But it is very probable that almost all those writings are not his and that they have been attributed to him simply because of his fame and holiness. At any rate, the corpus of writings attributed to M. is a treasure for the history of Christian spirituality.

———

JLG

Macedonius of Constantinople (?–362).
Semi-Arian theologian who was patriarch of Constantinople for two periods when political circumstances were favorable to him. Several contemporaries affirm that, although M. was willing to accept the divinity of the Son, he was not willing to do the same with respect to the Holy Spirit. Those who

adopted such a position were at times known as Macedonians and sometimes as Pneumatomachians (i.e., enemies of the Spirit).

———

JLG

Machen, John Gresham (1881–1937).
Calvinist New Testament scholar and founder of two Christian denominations. Born in Baltimore, Maryland, of a wealthy family. Graduated from Princeton Theological Seminary in 1905. In 1905–6 he did postgraduate study in Göttingen and Marburg. From 1906 to 1929 he taught at Princeton. He was ordained to the pastorate in 1914 and stood out for his zeal for the ⇒Westminster Confession of Faith.

In 1923 he published *New Testament Greek for Beginners*, in addition to *Christianity and Liberalism*, in which he attacked liberalism. Although he was a lecturer and preacher in fundamentalist circles, M. disagreed with that movement on the use of tobacco and alcoholic beverages. He likewise distanced himself from fundamentalism by attacking the Dispensationalist views of Cyrus ⇒Scofield.

In 1929 M. founded Westminster Seminary in Philadelphia, Pennsylvania, as a reaction to the liberal positions of Princeton. In 1936 he organized the Presbyterian Church of America, which later split into the Orthodox Presbyterian Church and the ultrafundamentalist Presbyterian Biblical Church.

He died suddenly of pneumonia in January 1937.

———

EPA

Machiavelli, Nicholas (1469–1527).
Writer of the Renaissance and an early exponent of political science. He was born in Florence under Medici rule. He occupied political posts of little importance that were granted to him by Cardinal Julius Medici (who later became Pope Clement VII). He developed his theory of political science in *The Prince*, published in 1513. In this work he explains how the principle that "the end justifies the means" should dominate in politics. He also affirms that in order to be realistic it is necessary to divorce politics from morality. Based on these declarations, he developed an entire science of hypocrisy and deceit in order to gain political advantage.

For M., religion ought to be thought of as an instrument or means of domination. For this reason he detested Christianity, because it stands in the way of the fulfillment of political objectives. The principles that were expounded by M. became the handbook of many politicians and sovereigns of that time, among them Catherine de Médicis in France and Thomas Cromwell in England.

———

Macintosh, Douglas Clyde (1877–1948).

Protestant theologian who was born in Canada and who taught systematic theology at Yale Divinity School from 1901 until 1948, when he retired for health reasons. He wrote *The Reaction against Metaphysics in Theology* (1911), *The Problem of Knowledge* (1915), *God in a World at War* (1918), *Theology as an Empirical Science* (1919), and *Social Religion* (1939). He was also special editor for Protestant terms in *Webster's New International Dictionary*, second edition.

———

Mackay, John Alexander (1889–1983).

This Scottish Presbyterian was one of the most important personalities of the Committee on Cooperation in Latin America (CCLA), a missionary body organized in 1916 that left a mark on Protestantism in Latin America and on the development of the ecumenical movement. His best-known works are *The Other Spanish Christ*, *That Other America*, and *Ecumenics: The Science of the Church Universal*. His book *Preface to Christian Theology* was very popular among beginning students of theology. M. articulated an ecumenical missiology for Latin America in the Latin American Missionary Congresses held in 1916, 1925, and 1929, and participated in the International Missionary Council and the World Missionary Conferences.

———

Mackintosh, Hugh Ross (1870–1936).

One of the greatest early-twentieth-century teachers of Scottish Reformed theology. He was the eldest of three sons of the Rev. Alexander Mackintosh and his wife, Jannet Ross. He was born in Pailey, Glasgow, where his father was pastor of the Welsh Free Church. He studied philosophy and the classics at the University of Edinburgh, then went on to study for the ministry in New College, a seminary of the Free Church of Scotland. After his graduation from New College in 1897, he became a preacher in Queen Street Free Church in Tayport. He died suddenly while giving a lecture to missionaries in June 1936.

M.'s contribution can be appreciated from two perspectives: as preacher and church leader and as theologian and teacher. As preacher and church leader, M. was a spirited preacher ever since his early days in Tayport and a prolific writer, having produced several volumes of sermons. Among them the most influential was *The Highway to God* (1932). As church leader he received the high distinction of being the fourth moderator of the General Assembly of the reunified Church of Scotland from 1932 to 1933. Although he did not participate directly in the 1910 World Missionary Conference in Edinburgh, where the foundations for the ecumenical movement were laid, he was a promoter of the ecumenical effort of Scottish Presbyterianism. Subsequently, he was active in the Faith and Order movement. Because of his friendship with theologians and church leaders in Germany and because of his participation in the Student Christian Movement, he had the opportunity to visit, preach, and lecture for missionaries and students on several occasions in Hungary, Denmark, Czechoslovakia, Romania, and Germany. During the period of the Third Reich in Germany he had connections with the clandestine Confessing Church and was a critic of the posture assumed by the Evangelical German Church.

As theologian and teacher, in 1904, at the age of thirty-four, M. was appointed to the chair of systematic theology at New College, where he functioned as a theologian for preachers. His contribution to the theological task was vast. What stands out in it is the use of historical-critical studies of the New Testament for the formulation of his Christology, his treatises on dogmatics, and his works on eschatology. His contribution was greatly influenced by the research of Wilhelm ⇒Wrede, Johannes ⇒Weiss, and Albert ⇒Schweitzer.

In the last stage of his life, 1928–36, M. was under the influence of the dialectical theology of Karl ⇒Barth. This led him to revise many of his theological positions and his previous writings, which had been strongly influenced by the liberal theology of ⇒Schleiermacher, ⇒Ritschl, and ⇒Troeltsch. In his posthumous work, *Types of Modern Theology* (1937), M. reformulated Reformed theology and dogmatics and reevaluated the patristic tradition in the light of his critical reading of Barth and ⇒Kierkegaard.

M.'s theological production was immense. Some of his other outstanding works are *The

Doctrine and the Person of Jesus Christ (1912); *The Person of Jesus Christ* (1913); *Studies on Christian Truth* (1913); *Immortality and the Future* (1915); *The Originality of the Christian Message* (1920); *The Divine Initiative* (1921); *The Christian Experience of Forgiveness* (1927); and *The Christian Apprehension of God* (1928).

————

FMA

Macquarrie, John (1919–). Scottish theologian formed at the University of Glasgow, where he taught after serving as a pastor for several years. He then taught at Union Theological Seminary in New York, and later at Oxford. The theology of M. developed initially under the influence of the existentialism of ⇒Heidegger, as can be seen in his book on systematic theology, *Principles of Christian Theology* (1966), and in his translation into English of Heidegger's *Being and Time*. His more recent works include books on Christology.

————

LGP

Macrina. This is the name of two saints, one being the grandmother of the second one, who belonged to the family of the ⇒Cappadocians ⇒Basil and ⇒Gregory of Nyssa. The grandmother was born in Neocaesarea, probably before 270, when ⇒Gregory of Neocaesarea was still bishop of that city. She had a profound influence on the religious education and the intellectual life of her grandchildren, particularly Basil, Gregory, and the younger M. She sowed in them the seeds of piety and the desire to seek Christian perfection. The date of her death is unknown.

M. the granddaughter (ca. 330–79) was the eldest child in her family. We are acquainted with her life principally through her brother Gregory, who wrote about her and the theological conversations he had with her about the resurrection, *Dialogue on the Soul and the Resurrection*. There we see how brilliant Macrina was. She had received an education based mainly on the Scriptures and not on the classical literature of the time, to which she refers as "profane literature." Her father had made arrangements for her marriage at the age of twelve with a young man from an excellent family. But the youth died, and M. decided to devote her life to Christian perfection and to perpetual virginity. She had a great deal to do with the education of her younger brothers, especially Peter, who became Bishop Sebaste.

After the death of her father she went with her mother to Pontus, where they devoted themselves to a life consecrated to God, which consisted of a strict asceticism, meditation on Christian truths, and prayer. Other women formed part of this community. Upon the death of her mother, M. became the head of the community. ⇒Gregory of Nazianzus and ⇒Eustace of Sebaste were associated with this pious community. Upon returning from the synod in Antioch at the end of 379, Gregory of Nyssa visited his sister, who was very ill. It was during this last visit that M. consoled her brother by conversing with him about life after death and the restoration of all things. In writing the dialogue, Gregory portrayed M. as the master of the dialogue. The day of Saint M. is July 19.

————

ECF

Maduro, Otto (1945–). Venezuelan philosopher and sociologist of religion with significant ties to both Latin American and U.S. Hispanic theologies. After years of research, teaching, and writing in Latin America and Europe, he has made the United States his home since 1987. He is known especially for his work on how socioeconomic interests and their conflicts influence human knowledge and religious dynamics. Among his main publications are *Religion and Social Conflicts* (1982) and *Mapas para la Fiesta* (1999).

————

PAJ

Maistre, Joseph-Marie de (1753–1821). French nobleman who, in reaction to the French Revolution, maintained a radically conservative posture. According to him, a society without order cannot function, and that order has been established by God once and for all. Thus, rebellion is never justified. If the king makes a mistake or commits some crime, only the pope can judge him, since spiritual authority is always above that of the secular. But the pope is not subject to any human judgment.

————

JLG

Major, Georg (1502–74). German Lutheran theologian, native of Nurenberg, and professor at the University of Wittenberg. He was also preacher of the castle church in the same city. Under the influence of the humanistic thought of Philipp ⇒Melanchthon, he wrote textbooks on the catechism, grammar, and rhetoric. His chief work focuses on the doctrine of biblical inspiration and the catholic consensus of the ancient church. His ideas about the necessity of good works for salvation caused many misunderstandings and were the focus of the so-called Majorist Controversy among the Lutherans of the sixteenth century.

———

NRG

Malchion (3rd century). Philosopher and Origenist theologian (⇒Origen), about whose life little is known. Some ancient authors aver that he was a Christian priest and also a teacher of philosophy at a secular school. At any rate, it was M. who persuaded a synod gathered in Antioch in the year 268 to reject the teachings of ⇒Paul of Samosata as false. The debates of that synod indicate that M. resorted to philosophical arguments, some of which were similar to those of Origen, in order to demonstrate that the teaching of Paul of Samosata implied a negation of the complete divinity of Jesus Christ.

———

JLG

Mamertus, Claudianus
⇒Claudianus Mamertus

Manegold of Lautenbach (?–ca. 1110). Person about whose life very little is known, since during the same period there was also a Manegold of Raitenbuch who some believe is the same person. In any case, M. wrote in defense of ⇒Gregory VII in his conflicts with Henry IV. According to M., the authority of monarchs is not by divine right, but has a contractual origin, through which the nation has delegated its authority to the sovereign. If the king does not govern as he should, the pope can declare that he has broken the contract, and the people do not have to obey the king.

———

JLG

Mani (216–ca. 276). Founder of Manicheism. M. was born in the Persian Empire, in the region of Babylonia, of an aristocratic family related to the royal family. Apparently his father and his brother were members of a religious sect that had ⇒gnostic tendencies. From the time of his youth, M. had visions. Then he journeyed to India and on his return gained a degree of favor with the new sovereign, Sapor, who permitted him to preach his new religion with a measure of freedom. Persecuted by the

Zoroastrian priests, in the end he was incarcerated and died in prison. Some authors say that he was flayed alive, but this appears to be a legend.

The central note of Manicheism is a radical dualism. There are two principles, one of good and one of evil. The first is spiritual and the second material. The first is light and the second darkness. In this world, and especially in human beings, these two principles are intertwined and therefore are in continual conflict. The good and spiritual element is imprisoned in the body and needs to recognize its divine origin and destiny in order to be liberated.

The good principle has been revealed through a whole succession of prophets that includes Buddha, Zoroaster, Jesus, and M. himself. He is the last of the prophets and completes the imperfect revelation given through his predecessors. This revelation includes mythical explanations about the origin and functioning of the world. Everything is explained in terms of a constant struggle between good and evil, or between light and darkness. In the end, these two elements will be separated (because evil, just like good, is eternal and indestructible). The spirits of light will return to the kingdom of light, and the darkness will be submerged in its own black night.

All this led to an ethic of extreme renunciation. The "perfect" were permitted to have only some foods that, according to M., contained elements of the good. By consuming them, the believers helped to liberate those good elements. But the number of such foods was extremely limited; therefore the majority of the Manicheans, instead of aspiring to reach the status of the "perfect" ones, were "hearers." The hope of hearers was not to go to the kingdom of light when they died, but to be reincarnated in a "perfect" individual, in order to reach final liberation.

The movement that M. founded continued to exist for a long time. It even reached a level of organization similar to that of the Christian church. The Manicheans soon spread to India and China and were numerous in the Roman Empire during the fourth and fifth centuries. It was there, for instance, that ⇒Augustine became acquainted with their teachings and for some time followed them, although he never went beyond the status of hearer.

———

JLG

Manning, Henry Edward (1808–92). Prominent pastoral and theological leader of the

Church of England (1833–51) and then of the Roman Catholic Church (1851–92). He defended the Catholic wing of the Anglican communion, and his frustration with religious, doctrinal, and administrative aspects of that church eventually led him to join the Roman Catholic Church. He was received and supported by Cardinal Wiseman and by Pope ⇒Pius IX. He set in motion an impressive course of reforms in the Roman Catholic Church of England, contributing to Catholic educational reform and to the establishment of the Order of the Oblates of St. Charles, an agency of social service. He was named archbishop of Westminster and cardinal and participated prominently in the First Vatican Council (⇒Vatican I), where he defended papal primacy and infallibility.

———

LRR

Mansi, Giovanni Domenico (1692–1769). Archbishop of Lucca who is known particularly for his publication of a collection of the minutes and documents of the councils, *Sacrorum conciliorum nova et amplissima collectio.* This collection consists of thirty-one volumes, although only the first fourteen were edited by M. himself. Like every work of this magnitude, it has errors and imperfections. In spite of this, it continues to be one of the principal sources for the study of the councils.

———

JLG

Map, Walter (1135–1210). English theologian who was distinguished for his satirical style. His principal work was *De nugis curialum* (On Courtiers' Trifles). History remembers him above all because it was he who, by means of a theological subterfuge, ridiculed Peter ⇒Waldo. The result was that the movement directed by Waldo was not authorized, and the Waldensians broke with Rome.

———

JLG

Marathon of Nicomedia (4th century). Obscure person about whose life little is known. He was one of the principal promoters of the position that the Son is divine but the same cannot be said fully of the Holy Spirit. His followers received the name of Pneumatomachians, enemies of the Spirit, and were also called Macedonians (⇒Macedonius of Constantinople).

———

JLG

Marca, Pierre de (1594–1662). Archbishop of Toulouse at the time of Richelieu. He defended Gallicanism in a treatise, *On Peace between the Priesthood and the Empire.* M. rejected the old conciliar ideas and affirmed papal supremacy within the church, but at the same time he affirmed the sovereignty of the king and his obligation to defend "the ancient canons of the Gallican Church," which the pope cannot abolish. Some critics have seen in M. a docile instrument in the hands of the policies of Richelieu.

———

JLG

Marcellus of Ancyra (?–ca. 375). Bishop of that city, which today is called Ankara. He participated in the Council of ⇒Nicaea (325) and in the condemnation of the teachings of ⇒Arius. Later, the Arians as well as ⇒Athanasius and several others of the chief defenders of the Nicene faith rejected his teachings. In 336 an Arian council held in Constantinople removed him from office. He was perhaps later restored to his seat, but it is not possible to know this with certainty.

According to M., God is one and reveals Godself as Father, Son, and Holy Spirit, not as three successive phases of revelation, but as three modalities of divine action. Although the Word was with God from eternity, the Word is the Son only through the incarnation. What is not clear and caused difficulties to Athanasius and others is whether that Word, which always existed in God, really subsisted together with the Father from eternity, or whether the Word was only a potential Word, pronounced in order to create and redeem. Since the writings of M. have been lost, it is difficult to know whether his critics interpreted him correctly.

———

JLG

Marcion (ca. 100–ca. 160). Theologian and philosopher of gnostic tendencies and founder of a Christian sect that bore his name (Marcionites). He was born in Sinope, Pontus (a region in what is now Turkey), and was probably the son of the bishop of that city.

Among the works attributed to M. are his *Antithesis* and a letter he wrote to the church in Rome in which he gave a systematic presentation of his beliefs. However, these writings are not available to us. What we know today about M. comes through some of the most prominent representatives of the established church of the second century, who were bitter opponents of M.: ⇒Irenaeus, ⇒Justin, and, ⇒Tertullian.

According to the testimony of these "heresiologists," M. believed in the eternity of matter, but he also taught a duality of gods. Based on the teachings of ⇒Cerdo (gnostic leader in Rome), M. made a clear distinction between the god of the Old and the God of the New Testament. The first was the creator of the material world and the judge of those who disobey him. M. characterized this god as "vain," "angry," "cruel," "ignorant," and "inferior" (a version of the demiurge of classical culture). The second was the "eternal," "transcendent," and "absolutely good" God revealed in Jesus Christ. Because he came directly from the Father, Jesus was very superior to the god of the old covenant. His principal mission was to save humanity from its slavery in the material world. Nevertheless, Jesus was not the messiah promised to Israel and was not born of a virgin, but appeared in the world as an adult. On this ideological foundation, M. rejected all the books of the OT, almost all the NT, and every reference to the incarnation and resurrection of Jesus (who did not really come in the flesh, but only in the appearance of such). He accepted as authoritative documents only an altered version of the Gospel of Luke and ten letters of Paul. According to M., his purpose was not to introduce new teachings, but to restore what had become corrupted.

M. traveled to Rome in the year 140. For four years he attended the meetings of the churches and shared his ideas with them. This activity gave rise to a great controversy. This forced the church to demand from M. a formal explanation of his beliefs. His defense was futile, and M. was declared a heretic and was excommunicated in 144.

Soon after the church in Rome rejected him, M. founded and organized his own church, differing in this from various gnostic leaders who only created schools of thought. From that time onward Marcionism grew and took root in many parts of the world: Italy, Egypt, Palestine, Arabia, Syria, Cyprus, and even Persia. For more than two hundred years it was the most serious threat to the Western church. We can trace vestiges of its influence in the Eastern church, even up to the Middle Ages. The followers of M. had faith in Christ, were well organized, and practiced asceticism and celibacy. They accepted women into the priesthood. They also celebrated the sacraments of baptism and the Lord's Supper (although without using wine).

M. was much more than someone who assimilated the dominant culture of paganism and whose teachings consequently were branded as heretical. From a wider point of view, the case of M. is a small sample of the many social tensions and differences of thought which the church had to face in its process of formation. Not everyone thought the same way, and there were internal struggles in the church. The Christian faith during the New Testament period and afterward was much more varied and complex than what we at times think. Dialogue and tolerance do not appear to have been central values.

M. is also the reflection of a church that continued to struggle to define its identity and to reaffirm the theological foundation left by the apostles, although in order to do so it had to use force to rid itself of members whose beliefs attacked the essence of faith in Christ. Nevertheless, in the end the teachings and the mutilated canon of M. proved to be beneficial for the church, because they accelerated the process of canonization of the New Testament as a reaction to the abbreviated canon of M.

———

AEM

Maritain, Jacques (1882–1973).
French philosopher, disciple of ⇒Bergson, and one of the most prominent lay theologians of the twentieth century. This Catholic thinker, who, with his wife, was converted from Protestantism in 1906, was one of the principal proponents of neo-Thomism. As an exponent of natural law, he alleges that the human being has the ability to intuit moral rules of conduct and the ability to apply these laws and rules to the moral problems of daily life. Among his most significant political postulates is his affirmation of the autonomy of the secular world and of the state. His political philosophy emphasizes democracy, economic liberalism, and the rights of the individual. Two of his most significant works are *Integral Humanism* and *Man and the State*.

—

IG

Marius Mercator (4th century).
Friend and colleague of ⇒Augustine and, like him, of African origin. He traveled to Constantinople, where he spent some time, and for this reason served as a bridge by which the West was informed about ⇒Nestorius and the controversies revolving around Christology, and the East learned about ⇒Pelagius and the controversies surrounding his teachings. He wrote in Greek

about the Pelagian controversy. He then translated into Greek a summary of the actions of Celestius against Pelagius and dedicated it to Emperor Theodosius II for the purpose of keeping him informed. With regard to the Nestorian controversy, he translated into Latin a number of the sermons, letters, and other writings of Nestorius, ⇒Cyril of Alexandria, and ⇒Theodore of Mopsuestia, in whom M. saw the root of both Nestorianism and Pelagianism.

———

JLG

Marius Victorinus (ca. 300–ca. 363). Neoplatonic philosopher who was converted to Christianity around the year 355. The story of his conversion strongly influenced ⇒Augustine, who refers to it in his *Confessions*. In addition, M. pointed to the way in which Augustine made use of Neoplatonic philosophy in the development of his theology. The greater part of his literary work has been lost, but ⇒Jerome refers to his commentaries on Galatians, Ephesians, and Philippians, and also to several treatises against Arianism (⇒Arius), which, according to Jerome, are difficult to read because of their use of philosophical language and concepts.

———

JLG

Marrero, Domingo (1909–60). Puerto Rican theologian, philosopher, and Protestant pastor. Professor at the Evangelical Seminary of Puerto Rico and the University of Puerto Rico. Author of an important work on the religiosity and the theological thought of the Spanish philosopher José Ortega y Gasset. He also wrote many essays and articles on the philosophy of religion, in addition to a volume of sermons on the passion of Jesus Christ.

Central themes in his writings are the paradoxical relation between reason and faith; human existence as an enigma leading to philosophical and theological reflection; the contingency of existence and its relationship to grace (the classical theme of free will and providence from the viewpoint of existential theology); the similarities and differences between classical, modern existential, and Christian tragedy; the convergences and correlations between philosophy and theology; and the overcoming of essentialist categories in theology.

He belonged to a generation of Latin American theologians that sought to link the evangelical understanding of the Christian faith with Hispanic literature and thought, in an effort to answer the criticism of cultural foreignness that was brandished against his church. His literary style was distinguished by its elegance and his preaching stood out because of his eloquence.

———

LRP

Marsden, George M. (1939–). Author, educator, and scholar considered to be one of the outstanding researchers on the history of North American Protestantism. He has written extensively on the history of North American fundamentalism and on the place of religion in the academy and the culture of the United States. He has been professor of history at Calvin College and Duke University. Since 1992 he has occupied the Francis A. MacAnaney chair of history at Notre Dame University. He has received numerous honors for his historical research. He is a member of the Christian Reformed Church. In 1992 he served as president of the American Society of Church History. Some of the outstanding works of this prolific author are *Fundamentalism and American Culture: The Shaping of Twentieth-Century Evangelicalism* (1980), *Reforming Fundamentalism: Fuller Seminary and the New Evangelicalism* (1987), *The Soul of the American University* (1994), *The Outrageous Idea of Christian Scholarship* (1997), and *Jonathan Edwards: A Life* (2003).

———

EV

Marsh, Adam (?–ca. 1258). Known as *Doctor illustris*, he studied at Oxford under ⇒Grosseteste. Later he was the first Franciscan teacher in that university (1247–50). His theology is a traditional Augustinianism.

———

JLG

Marsilius of Padua (ca. 1275–1342). Eminent philosopher and politician. He was born in Padua, Italy, where he began his academic career in medicine, but then he studied jurisprudence, philosophy, and theology in the University of Paris, where he was named rector in 1312. In 1324 he published *Defensor Pacis s. de re imperatoria et pontificia* (Defender of the Peace or concerning the Sphere of the Empire and the Pope), in which he criticizes the papacy by affirming that the pope is the greatest enemy of universal peace and prosperity. In order to confirm his declarations he cites as examples the whims of

⇒Boniface VIII, which caused disputes with King Philip of France. He also cites the arrogance of Clement V in his dealings with Emperor Henry VII and the unjust treatment of King Louis of Bavaria by John XXII.

M. affirms that the nature, origin, and aim of the state ought to be centered on the concept of peace, which should be considered the highest value in social life. Therefore he defines the relation between church and state by establishing the following rules:

1. The obligations and the authority of priests are limited to the study and preaching of the Scriptures and to the celebration of the sacraments. Every priest, even a bishop or pope, is subject to civil authority.
2. Every priest, independently of his authority and position, should have the same spiritual rank and authority.
3. The church has only one divinely appointed head, which is Christ, and no one is exempt from Christ's reign.
4. The maximum authority of the church is not found in one person, but in a general council made up of lay and ordained persons.
5. Only the Holy Scriptures should regulate the life and conduct of the church.

In all these points M. was the forerunner of democratic reforms that later would take place in both church and state.

His work was condemned in 1327. It is not clear how his life ended, for he lived the rest of his days under constant persecution. Nevertheless, his thought and work were critically important during the Reformation.

————

HMT

Martin of Braga (ca. 515–80). Bishop of Braga, in the northwest of the Iberian peninsula. He was born in Panonia, in what today is Hungary. M. traveled extensively in the Near East before arriving in Braga at an undetermined date. There he played an important role in the conversion of the Suevi, who abandoned Arianism and embraced the Nicene faith. The majority of his writings are moral in character or deal with the organization of the church. His brief treatise *On Triune Immersion* is interesting. In it he replies to a bishop who had asked him whether the practice of triple baptismal immersion did not emphasize excessively the difference between the three divine persons,

and therefore was Arian. M. answered that everything depends on the name or names in which the immersion is performed. If one baptizes by immersing the person three times in "the name" of the Father, the Son, and the Holy Spirit (only one name), such a baptism is a sign of orthodoxy. But if the baptism is performed in three "names" (the name of the Father, the name of the Son, and the name of the Holy Spirit), then this is a sign of an Arian stance.

————

JLG

Martineau, James (1805–1900). A member of the Unitarian Church known for his analysis of various types of ethical theory. His work *Types of Ethical Theory* (1885) is considered a classic in the field of ethics. He rejected ethical naturalism and therefore opposed the utilitarianism, the positivism, and the evolutionism that were dominant in his time. He rejected the idea that there is a supreme moral principle. On the contrary, morality is made up of a plurality of moral principles and goals.

————

IG

Marty, Martin E. (1928–). Religious educator, editor, Lutheran minister, and emeritus professor of the University of Chicago. He was born in Nebraska. The author of about fifty books, M. has published on the history of Christianity, the religious history of the United States, and particularly on the place of religion in civil and public life. His specialty is the period between the end of the eighteenth and the twentieth century. His principal work, in three volumes, is *Modern American Religion*, in which he explores the role of public Protestantism in the social history of the United States during the first half of the twentieth century. His major contributions include the many doctoral students whom he has helped shape and his personal dedication to both the Christian church and to society in general. M. has been a defender of the need for a public theology and ministry.

————

NRG

Marx, Karl (1818–83). Around 1844 he and Friedrich Engels (1820–95) founded an atheist version of socialist theories that later was called Marxism. M. was superficially Christian—the son of Jews who were forced to embrace Christianity—and Engels was profoundly such before both were converted to atheism when they were about twenty years old. This was before they accepted socialism, an originally and predominantly Christian movement until then. Both of them, but especially Engels, retained throughout their lives a certain interest in the study of religions. Thus Engels is considered a pioneer in the sociology and social history of religions. The theories of both have had a gradual and important impact on theology, beginning with the Christian-Marxist dialogue in postwar Europe (⇒Barth, ⇒Tillich, ⇒Reinhold Niebuhr), continuing in the political theology of ⇒Metz, the theology of hope (⇒Moltmann), and the theology of liberation (⇒Gutiérrez, ⇒Boff, ⇒Schüssler Fiorenza), up to the materialist and feminist critiques of the Bible (Belo, Gottwald, Fewell), among many other fields and movements related to theology.

For M. and Engels, economic life (i.e., the production, distribution, and control of the material goods necessary to maintain human life) constitutes the chief basis of human life in society. It is the economic life that provides the conditions of possibility, the limits, and the orientation for any other human activity, including religious activities (liturgy, theology, ministries). Economic life changes historically, from epoch to epoch, from society to society, and as it changes, it provokes changes in all the other spheres of human life (religious, political, military, and so on). When economic life becomes organized (through scarcity, wars, or other reasons) not in an egalitarian way, but rather around private appropriation of the chief means of production by an elite within society, then that society tends to divide itself internally into social classes with unequal economic, social, political, and cultural (class domination) power relations and with conflicting interests among them (class struggle). For M. and Engels these divisions, domination, and class struggles profoundly influence all the other dimensions of collective life, including the religious dimension. Thus there appear intra- and interreligious divisions, domination of some religions or religious tendencies over others, and conflicts among theological, clerical, and other factions. In this sense, M. and Engels seem to uphold the theory that religions are only secondary products of the economic-social dynamic, that their differential traits are barely specific effects of the sudden attacks which religions are subject to under the class struggles that characterize the greater part of human societies, and that religions are definitely destined to disappear under the economic

dynamic of capitalism. Theories such as these have been particularly scandalous for the churches, but they also motivate self-criticism that is transformative. This is even more so when correlative Marxist notions are added, namely that "religion is the opium of the masses" (a narcotic produced and consumed by the oppressed in order to be able to survive spiritually under oppression) and that the dominant ideas in any epoch are the ideas of the dominant classes, that is, the particular interests of the dominant classes, which are ideologically expressed as universal principles (including the religious, theological, and moral ideas that predominate in any society). For M. and Engels, the most important social processes (including religious dynamics) are much more the result of unconscious mechanisms than of deliberate decisions—which, of course, suggests an invitation to critical self-examination of the origin and the consequences of religious traditions.

According to M. and Engels, the exploitation of some human beings by others is not an eternal nor inevitable phenomenon. It is an ancient and profound phenomenon, but definitely historical and transient. Capitalism, for them, represents the exacerbation and the final point of that history of exploitation. The classes that are dispossessed and exploited by the capitalists (the proletariat) will gradually grow in number, organization, and class consciousness and will contribute to the creation of a peaceful, fraternal, and egalitarian society. In the meantime, the very dynamic of capitalism, when it lays bare the economic root of all religious dynamics, will undermine the bases of religion and will lead it, first, to become privatized and, finally, to lose all significance or importance. The political, intellectual, and organizational efforts of M. and Engels were directed, in fact, toward accelerating the inevitable arrival of that new society. In this and many other points, M. and Engels did not differ much from the communists and the Christian and Jewish socialists who preceded them (Cabet, Weitling, Hess, among others), neither did their horizon differ much from the Hebrew *shalom* or from the *basiléia tou theou* of Judeo-Christian teleology. In a certain sense, Marxism is a secular, atheist version of Judeo-Christian teleology. Where M. and Engels depart radically from earlier socialism (religious or not) is in their double conviction that socialism is really possible only where there are already material means capable of satisfying the basic material necessities of all human beings, and in the place where the working classes have already reached the level of knowledge of reality, of class consciousness, and of self-organization capable of taking advantage of those material conditions in order to create an egalitarian, fraternal, and peaceful society. In fact, the polemics of M. and Engels with the Christian socialists (Weiling and others) have much less to do with the religious question and much more with what they saw as the scorn of the latter toward the need for the effort to know and analyze reality, and as their naive confidence in the transforming power of example, will, or the preaching of the "truth" by themselves. M. and Engels systematically opposed those who understood atheism as a revolutionary article of faith (for example, Bakunin), as a requirement for enrollment in the socialist workers' movement, or as the constitutional principle of a new society. For them, atheism was barely an ideological reaction to religion—just as limited, divisive of the oppressed, and historically transient as religion itself.

In the theological field, Marxism has frequently been scorned as irrelevant or attacked as an enemy of the faith and of the church (and, of course, the antireligious politics of many self-designated Marxist governments have contributed to the latter). But increasingly, after the trauma of the Holocaust and the Second World War, and even more so since the decolonization of Africa, Asia, and Latin America, more and more theologians have taken seriously many Marxist challenges. Among others, it is worth pointing out the challenge of analyzing to what extent and in which aspects of history and religious life one can discern (and perhaps criticize and transform) the influence of the interests and conflicts in which the dominant classes have become involved. To what extent have the predominant theologies been much more of a sacralization (by commission or by omission) of the dominant interests than humble service to the "smallest ones"? Or in what sense have our churches contributed—among other things, by insisting on absolute authority, uniformity, and blind obedience—more to hiding and perpetuating all kinds of oppression than to the prophetic mission of freeing the oppressed in which Jesus enrolled and for which he was arrested, tortured, and executed by the Roman authorities?

Thus, in fact, M. and Engels have contributed indirectly to this theological revolution which today affects the entire field of biblical studies, church history, missiology, and ecclesiology, not to speak of Christology or pneumatology, among other fields, and which relocates the option for the oppressed in the center of Christian reflection, in order to deconstruct and reconstruct the entire life of the churches from the perspective of the oppressed.

Marxism, not any less than Christianity itself, is a reality that is multiple, variable, and contradictory. What for some Marxists is an article of faith is for others anathema. And in matters of religion, the variety and the intra-Marxist discussions are increasingly greater. For those who are interested in religion and theology, among the most interesting Marxist thinkers is the Italian Antonio Gramsci (1891–1937). Gramsci formulated a much more open and fresh version of Marxism, also in religious matters, than that which was developed beginning with Lenin or Trotsky. Gramsci valued the role of culture in general, and in particular that of religion, in the sociopolitical processes that concern the consolidation of old hegemonies and in the construction of new "historical blocks" that are conducive to important social changes. Likewise he emphasized the variable function that intellectuals (including religious leaders) can carry out, whether as traditional intellectuals, in the service of the conservation of a social hegemony in crisis, or as organic intellectuals, contributing to the emergence and consolidation of new class alliances and projects of society. And in the same way he paused to analyze sociologically the concrete changes of Christianity in Italian history, economy, and politics.

It is customary to declare Marxism irrelevant. Notwithstanding, the most recent efforts of social and cultural criticism (postcolonialism, feminism, poststructuralism) as well as the new tendencies in religious, theological, and biblical studies carry, implicitly or explicitly, the mark of the concern of M. and Engels for the socioeconomic conditions of the production of "knowledge," that is, for the weight of the interests of the powerful in the orientation of the material and symbolic life of societies, for the conscious or unconscious effectiveness of the resistance of oppressed communities and nations, and for the possibilities of transformation in the midst of situations that appear to be unreformable.

———

OM

Mascall, Eric Lionel (1905–93).

Anglo-Catholic theologian; that is, a representative of that branch of Anglicanism that seeks to maintain strong contacts with the tradition that predates the Reformation. He was a mathematician and then an Anglican clergyman. After serving as pastor, he was professor at Oxford and at the

University of London. In his theology he made use of the Thomist tradition (⇒Thomas Aquinas). Several of his books consist of summaries of the positions of other theologians, followed by the position of M., which is often a synthesis of elements taken from several of the theologians under discussion. Among his works are *He Who Is* (1943), *Christian Theology and Natural Science* (1956), *Theology and History* (1962), *The Secularization of Christianity* (1965), and *The Triune God* (1986).

———

JLG

Mather, Cotton (1663–1728). Son of

Increase ⇒Mather. He studied at Harvard and then at the University of Glasgow. For a time he collaborated with his father in the pastorate. He was, like his father, a Calvinist of strong Puritanical conviction. His formal theology is based on the ⇒Westminster Confession, and his personal piety carries the seal of a strong emphasis on spiritual discipline. On the other hand, he was very interested in all kinds of natural and supernatural phenomena. His medical studies, for example, were admired by many in New England as well as in old England, where he was a member of the prestigious Royal Society. At the same time, he was also interested in visions, angelology, private revelations, and even magical practice. His sermons and theological writings made a strong impact on the theology of New England for several generations, especially in matters such as missiology, eschatology, and the concept of covenant as a fundamental theological notion.

———

JLG

Mather, Increase (1639–1723). Puri-

tan pastor of the Second Church of Boston (Old North Church), where his father, Richard, and his son Cotton ⇒Mather were also pastors. Increase was born in Boston and studied at Harvard, which he entered at the age of twelve. Later he obtained his master's degree from Trinity College in Dublin, Ireland. He preached for three years in England, but his Puritanism in an Anglican environment led him to return to Massachusetts, where he accompanied his father in the pastorate, beginning in 1661. He devoted himself to defending traditional Puritanism in the midst of social changes in New England. Initially he resisted those who proposed the idea of a "halfway covenant" that allowed the church to baptize children in those cases in which at least the father or the mother

was a converted Christian who gave proof of the grace of God. In 1662, a group of ministers, including Richard Mather, wished to mitigate this rule in such a way that it would include also the grandchildren. M. and other conservatives resisted until a synod resolved the matter in favor of moderation. M. was also president of Harvard (1685–1701), but theological conflicts provoked his resignation. He devoted the rest of his life to serving as pastor of Second Church and, in his many writings, to defending traditional Puritanism—attempting, for example, to deny the right to vote to members of the colony who were not members of the Congregational Church. This effort also failed. By contrast, M. was instrumental in the cessation of the trials and executions of the so-called Salem witches.

———

EA

Matthew of Aquasparta (ca. 1240–

1302). Franciscan theologian, and after 1289 a cardinal, generally held to be a continuer of the work of ⇒Alexander of Hales and of ⇒Bonaventure. Like them, he defended a theology that, without completely rejecting ⇒Aristotle, insisted on the moderate Platonism of the Augustinian tradition, and he opposed the new synthesis proposed by the Dominicans ⇒Albertus Magnus and ⇒Thomas Aquinas.

———

JLG

Maurice, Frederick Denison (1805–

72). Anglican theologian who sought to relate the Christian faith to the problems of poverty and poor working conditions. He was fully confident that, in spite of sin, Christians can significantly improve the human condition in history. H. R. ⇒Niebuhr identified him as one of the prototypes of "Christ transforming culture." For M. the church can resolve many of the social problems that affect us. The kingdom of God became present in history, and it can be partially realized in the intimate spiritual dimension as well as in the economic, political, artistic, and social spheres. Not to recognize this makes the community of faith morally irresponsible. His political position was not revolutionary, but reformist. M. was an independent thinker whose originality and honesty brought him into conflict with the church. He lost his teaching position at King's College in London for opposing the doctrine of eternal punishment.

———

IG

Maximus the Confessor (ca. 613–62).

Monk and mystic who distinguished himself by his opposition to the Monothelitism proposed by ⇒Sergius of Constantinople, even though this won him the enmity of the Byzantine authorities, and in the end exile and perhaps death. After serving for a time in the imperial court, shortly after turning thirty years of age he devoted himself to the monastic life. It was there that it fell to him to face Monothelitism, which came with the seal of approval of the imperial authorities. M. argued that if there are two natures in Christ, there must also be two principles of operation (two *energeias*), for nature requires such a principle in order to be complete. In addition, if that principle of operation should reside in the person and not in the nature, it would be necessary to state that there are three such principles in God, one for each of the three persons, which is false. With regard to the wills, also the will belongs to the nature, and therefore in Christ there are two wills, one human and one divine. This does not mean, however, that Christ desires two things, since the human will is subject to the divine will.

The mysticism of M. is derived chiefly from the works attributed to ⇒Dionysius the Areopagite. M. also derives much of his philosophy, especially his Neoplatonic inclinations, from that source.

JLG

Mays, Benjamin Elijah (1894–1984).

African American Baptist who stood out as an educator and won the prestigious Spingarn medal. He obtained his doctorate at the University of Chicago. He served as dean of the School of Religion of Howard University, and during the years 1940–67 he served as president of Morehouse College in Atlanta, Georgia. Martin Luther ⇒King Jr. was one of his disciples. Two of his best-known works are *The Negro's God as Reflected in His Literature* (1938) and *The Negroes' Church* (1933).

M. was an active participant in the ecumenical movement. In the Oxford conference on church, community, and state (1937) and also in the first assembly of the ⇒World Council of Churches, in Amsterdam (1948), he contributed to the documents that denounced racial discrimination and segregation both inside and outside the church. His autobiography, *Born to Rebel*, was published in 1971. A program of theological scholarships for African Americans offered by the Theological Education Fund bears his name.

IG

Mbiti, John S. (1931–).

An Anglican and a native of Kenya, M. is one of the most distinguished theologians of Africa. He is known for the hundreds of articles and reviews he has written. Two of his most ambitious theological works are *African Religion and Philosophy* and *Introduction to African Religion*.

M. is a forerunner of the theological proposal of the contextualization of African Christianity on African soil. He not only discusses the social and cultural implications of that contextualization, but also studies and reflects on the impact of the African worldview and its traditional religions on the Christian faith and the theological task.

In addition to his theological work, M. has been a leader in the ecumenical movement, particularly in the ⇒World Council of Churches and as director of the Ecumenical Institute at Bossey.

CCO

McClendon, James W. (1924–2000).

North American Baptist theologian, exponent of Anabaptist theology and ethics, but of a clear ecumenical persuasion. He placed his ethical or practical concerns in the very center of his theological work. He was critical of the tendency in philosophy and theology to establish epistemological foundations, as well as of postmodern relativism. His best-known work is *Biography as Theology*, followed by *Convictions: Defusing Religious Relativism*, of which he is coauthor. However, his main work, which he finished shortly before his death, is his *Systematic Theology* in three volumes, under the titles *Ethics, Doctrine*, and *Witness*

NRG

McFague, Sallie (1933–).

North American feminist theologian. Professor of theology at Vanderbilt University. She has developed a theology of liberation challenging oppression on the basis of gender, race, and class. She has also written about the nuclear and environmental crises. In her work she develops a metaphorical understanding of religious language and a religious epistemology based on the metaphorical imagination. She explores social and ecological models (mother, lover, friend, body) to understand the relationship between God and the world. Her chief works are *Metaphorical Theology*, *Models of God*, and *The Body of God: An Ecological Theology*.

——
LRR

McGavran, Donald Anderson (1897–1990).

Born in India of North American missionary parents, M. was educated in the United States and then served as a missionary under the auspices of the United Christian Missionary Society. He was an ordained minister of the Christian Church (Disciples of Christ). His missionary work was concentrated in the areas of hospital administration, education, and rural evangelism. He translated the Gospels into several Indian languages. He obtained his doctorate from Columbia University in 1936.

M. experienced great frustration in missionary work, especially with regard to the growth of congregations. Observing the conduct of the great masses in India, he developed new theories about congregational growth and missiology. His books *God, Man and Church Growth* and *Understanding Church Growth* explain his proposals, which continue to be controversial. Above all, his use of the social category "homogeneous unity" as a means for church growth is frequently contested. M. was also the founder of the Church Growth movement based in Fuller Theological Seminary, which was very popular in the 1970s and 1980s.

——
CCO

McGee, Gary B. (1945–).

Church historian and ordained pastor of the Assemblies of God. He was born in Canton, Ohio. He has promoted dialogue between Pentecostalism and Roman Catholicism. An expert in studies on Pentecostalism, he is an author, lecturer, professor, and preacher.

——
EPA

McGiffert, Arthur C. (1861–1933).

Professor of the history of Christian thought at Union Theological Seminary in New York (1893–1927). He also served as president of that institution (1917–26). As a theologian he was a student of ⇒Harnack and a follower of Protestant modernism. He wrote several volumes on different periods of church history, including *History of Christianity in the Apos-*

tolic Era (1897). Some of his positions in that book led to his resignation as an ordained minister of the Presbyterian church and his transfer to the Congregationalists. As president of Union, he established a sound financial foundation for the school and introduced several innovations, one of which was a program of practice in ministry as part of the curriculum of theological education.

——
EA

McGrath, Alister Edgar (1953–).

Irish Anglican theologian, historian, and scientist, popularizer of theology. He became convinced of the truth of Christianity in his studies at the Methodist University of Belfast, his native city. He studied theology in Oxford and Cambridge. During his pastorate (1980–1983) in Nottingham, England, he became disenchanted with liberalism. In 1983 he began teaching at Wycliffe Hall in Oxford.

His book *Luther and the Theology of the Cross* (1985) is often required reading in courses on that subject. At present he is working on his three volumes of systematic theology, in which the main interpretive key is also the cross.

——
EPA

McPherson, Aimee Semple (1890–1944).

Born in Ontario, Canada, she converted to Pentecostalism in 1907. In 1908 she married and went with her husband as a missionary to China, where she served until her husband's death. After returning to the United States she devoted herself to preaching. She was the first woman in her tradition to preach by radio. In 1927 she founded the Pentecostal denomination International Church of the Foursquare Gospel. The four bases of the denomination are the work of Christ as Savior, as Baptizer in the Holy Spirit, as Healer of the sick, and as the One who one day will return as king.

——
LGP

Medellín Conference (1968).

The Second Conference of the Latin American Episcopal Council (⇒CELAM II), celebrated from August 26 to September 6, 1968. This conference became one of the most significant events in the history of the Roman Catholic Church in Latin America, given its ecclesial and doctrinal authority and its impact.

After the Second Vatican Council (⇒Vatican II) and the subsequent launching of Paul VI's encyclical *Populorum Progressio* (on the need to promote the development of peoples, 1967), which was considered by many the most daring political document in the history of the Roman Catholic Church, and after the growing world political radicalization that characterized the 1960s and included vast sectors of Roman Catholics, especially in the third world, M. attempted to apply the Second Vatican Council and its implications to Latin America. M. is definitely a sequel to Vatican II. Argentine Methodist theologian José ⇒Míguez Bonino has called it "the Vatican II of Latin America."

Gathered in M. were 146 cardinals, archbishops, and bishops, 14 male religious, 6 nuns, 15 laypeople and consultants at various levels, plus non–Roman Catholic observers. The central theme of the conference was "The Church in the present transformation of Latin America in the light of the Council."

The documents of M. were published in Spanish in two volumes. The first contains the inaugural addresses, the initial papers devoted to the analysis of the Latin American reality, and the consequent ecclesial reflection. The second volume incorporates the documents produced by the sixteen commissions and subcommissions of the conference.

These papers attempt to respond to three questions that express the areas of greatest pastoral concern at M.: (1) how to serve Latin American men and women authentically, starting from the basic requirements of justice (documents 1–5); (2) how to develop an evangelization and maturation in the faith, starting from renewed catechesis and liturgy (documents 6–9); and (3) how to transform the structures of the church in order to make it a visible reality and sign of liberation among the exploited masses of Latin America (documents 10–16).

M. also involved significant methodological shifts. The deductive theological method, traditionally adopted by the Roman Catholic Church and also privileged by Vatican II, begins from an understanding of the essence or nature of the matter obtained from revelation, which is then applied to the reality or problem. Without making it explicit in any of its documents, M. assumes an inductive theological method. The conclusions of M. do not start out from the essence of justice or peace, although these are important biblical themes. M. begins instead with the historical and present-day Latin American reality, analyzing it with the assistance of the social sciences. The methodological

sequence was facts, theological reflection, and then pastoral orientations or conclusions. M. thus inaugurated a new relationship of the categories and theological and pastoral language with the social sciences, which seek to interpret concrete reality. It is here where the agenda, ideas, and vocabulary of Latin American liberation theology, which at that time was in its initial stage, would ground their legitimacy. Themes such as peace, justice, marginalization, and poverty are key elements in the theological-pastoral discourse of M. Without abandoning ideas such as the binomial "underdevelopment and integral development," which are central to the language of Vatican II and *Populorum Progressio*, the documents begin to speak also about "domination and dependence," "liberation from every oppressive situation," "social situation of sin," "institutionalized violence," "rapid, vigorous, urgent, and profoundly renewing change," "conscientization," "liberating education," "the people, agents of their own progress." That is, M. inserts into the discourse of the church the category of "liberation," which quickly became the central axis of an ecumenical theological project that was soon baptized as "liberation theology," not only in Latin America, but also in other contexts. The documents of CELAM II thus constituted the Magna Carta of liberation theology. It was not in vain that the Peruvian Catholic theologian Gustavo ⇒Gutiérrez, called "the father of liberation theology," and a significant number of theologians and pastoralists who would later become inspiring leaders of that theology, were influential theological consultants at M.

Whether in the papers or in the conclusions, some emphases are reiterated in the course of all the documents. These are the vocation (calling) of the human being to his or her integral development; the idea of integral salvation that includes the human totality (soul and body, individual and society, history and eternity); and the church as a sacrament of unity between God and human beings and of these among themselves, through Word and sacrament.

The multiplicity of subjects considered in M. does not dilute certain central directions and concerns of the Roman Catholic Church in Latin America. Among these matters or theological-pastoral concerns, the painful reality of the growing masses of the poor in the subcontinent was given first place. Because of their importance in the documents, the poor have a central and privileged place in CELAM II. An attempt was made to respond to pastoral questions such as these: How can the church speak to the poor about the justice and peace of Jesus? What sense does evangelical poverty make to the millions of marginalized people in our countries? What does the church say and do for the poor?

Although the documents of M. show a number of ambiguities and vacillations, such as are typical of a time of transition in the church, their agenda, methodology, and especially their pastoral conclusions are a decisive milestone in the Christian world.

———

OLM

Medina, Bartolomé de (1528–80).
Dominican teacher at the University of Salamanca, and therefore successor to and continuator of the work of ⇒Vitoria, ⇒Soto, and ⇒Cano. The facet of his theology that has been most discussed is his so-called probabalism. M. considers whether, in doctrinal or moral matters in which opinions differ, it is permissible to follow a probable opinion even when another more probable one exists, or whether one is always obliged to follow the one of greatest probability. The answer of many was that in such cases one must follow the most probable opinion, as when a doctor who is not sure which treatment would be better chooses the one that has the greatest chance for success. M. disagreed, declaring that in moral matters as well as in doctrinal ones, it is permissible to follow any probable opinion, even though there may be another more probable one. Later, using some of the arguments of M., a casuistic ethic arose which held that in moral matters it is permissible to follow any path that is likely to have a good result. But that does not seem to have been what M. thought. For him, "probable" did not mean "possible" (as it does for many today), but rather "capable of being proven"— that is, reasonably sustained. A teaching is probable if there are solid arguments that seem to prove it, even if there are more solid arguments to the contrary. A moral action is probably good when there are sound reasons to believe that it is effectively so, and not a mere possibility that it could be.

This does not mean that there is complete freedom to follow the path that strikes our fancy. What M. means is that in cases of contradictory probabilities one must not necessarily choose the most probable alternative, for in such a case it would no longer be probable but sure. Shortly afterward, Domingo Ibañez defended the probabalism of M. But with the passage of time, and especially in the hands of

some Jesuit interpreters, probabilism became broader, to the extent that it appeared to endorse a great moral latitude. Some even said that if there are doubts about whether an action is sinful, it is permissible to act as if it were not. As a result, the Dominicans turned against M. and abandoned the theory of their old teacher.

———

JLG

Mehl, Roger (1912–97).
French Protestant ethicist and sociologist who taught in the Protestant Faculty of Theology in Strassbourg. Outstanding among his publications are *Catholic Ethics and Protestant Ethics* (1973) and *Who Is My Neighbor? Reflections on Communication between People* (1966).

———

PAJ

Melanchthon, Philipp (1497–1560).
German humanist and reformer, educator, philologist, and theologian, also known as the Teacher of Germany because of his many contributions to the education and culture of the nation. He was born in Bretten and studied in Pforzheim, Heidelberg, and Tübingen. In 1518 he was appointed professor of classical Greek in the University of Wittenberg in Saxony. There he was influenced by the thought of Martin ⇒Luther, with whom he closely collaborated, in spite of their differences. In Wittenberg he began his studies in theology, and he received a degree in that discipline the following year. As part of the requirements for the theology degree, M. wrote what is considered his most important work, *Loci theologici* (Theological Topics), which is thought to be the first book of Protestant dogmatics.

As a humanist, M. was influenced by ⇒Erasmus, the most important humanist of his time. M. learned from him the method of the *topoi* or *loci*, identifying the basic concepts in the exposition of a text. However, M. broadened the use and significance of this method by developing a methodology that extracted from the text itself—for example, the biblical text— its fundamental themes and structure.

Throughout his career, M. continued to revise and expand his *Loci theologici*. He did the same with a number of his works on logic and rhetoric and with his commentaries on books of the Bible.

As an educator he carried out a number of curricular and administrative reforms, beginning in Wittenberg but also in several other universities, as well as in parochial schools. As a man of the church he was a proponent of evangelical reforms, ranging from matters pertaining to the liturgy and worship, doctrine and preaching, to canonical or constitutional issues. He was an active participant in a considerable number of ecumenical dialogues, both with Roman Catholics and with other Protestants.

M. consistently strove to establish clearly fundamental doctrinal principles, that is, affirmations with which different groups could be in agreement. Nevertheless, he defended a number of theological principles that served him as a guide in defending his own convictions. For example, his emphasis on the clear distinction between law and gospel served to maintain a unity between his interest in the humanities and the sciences and his theological convictions without mixing or confusing them. In this way he avoided the anti-intellectualism of other reformers, while also refraining from imposing philosophies and other idealisms on Christian faith and theology.

M. is the author of the most important confessional document of the Lutheran churches, the ⇒Augsburg Confession (1530). This document represented the evangelical self-definition over against the religious and political-civil system of Roman Catholicism. The themes of justification by faith and Christian liturgy are repeatedly addressed in its articles.

M. championed simultaneously faith, freedom of conscience, and the ethical responsibility of the Christian. He also supported granting the greatest possible autonomy to local churches. As a good ecumenist, he was often ready to concede points in certain aspects of ecclesiastical teaching and practice that are not indispensable for the truth of the gospel, but are necessary to maintain the unity of the faith and of the Christian church, the *adiaphora*. He was ready to accept the ecclesiastical authority of the pope and of bishops, but only by human, not divine, right. Nevertheless, he also held that the way in which the Roman papacy had acted historically reflected the kingdom of the antichrist more than the gospel of Jesus Christ.

———

NRG

Meletius of Antioch (?–381).

Bishop of Antioch from 361 to 381. Although his theological position is not entirely clear, it appears that little by little he developed and drew near to the Nicene teaching, particularly in response to a schism in his flock that was apparently led by those who rejected the decisions of ⇒Nicaea. In 363 a synod under his leadership

affirmed the Nicene *homoousios*, although they interpreted it in terms that some Niceans looked on with suspicion, because the teaching of the three hypostases was also accepted.

Sadly, for some reason this development did not produce a rapprochement between M. and ⇒Athanasius, who at the time was maneuvering in the same direction and therefore should have been a natural ally of M. Consequently, Athanasius insisted in the presence of ⇒Damasus that M. was a heretic, and as a result Rome joined Alexandria by taking the side of the enemies of M. This provoked the intervention of ⇒Basil of Caesarea, who for many years had insisted on the need to unite all those who in one way or another affirmed the Nicene faith. But Rome was inflexible, always taking the side of the enemies of M. When M. died in 381, he was succeeded by ⇒Flavian, who finally achieved reconciliation with Rome and the end of the schism.

———

JLG

Meletius of Athens (?–1714).

Historian of the Greek church who, with ⇒Dositheus of Jerusalem, participated in an awakening of historical studies as a means of reaffirming the identity of that church in the modern world.

———

JLG

Meletius of Lycopolis (4th century).

Bishop of that city in Egypt. When the persecution of Diocletian diminished, he protested against the liberality with which the rest of the church forgave those who had apostatized. This gave rise to a rupture known at times as the schism of Meletius, and therefore often confused with the schism of ⇒Meletius of Antioch. Although the Council of ⇒Nicaea (325) intervened in the matter, the schism continued until the time of the Arab invasions.

———

JLG

Meletius Pegas (ca. 1537–1601).

Greek patriarch of Alexandria who wrote a treatise against Roman Catholicism, *On the True Catholic Church and Its True Head.*

———

JLG

Melito of Sardis (2nd century).

Prolific author whose works have been almost totally lost. He wrote an apology directed to Marcus Aurelius of which only a few fragments remain, as well as several treatises mentioned or quoted by ancient authors, all of which are lost: *On the Apocalypse of John*, *On God Incarnate*, *On Baptism*, and others. At a relatively recent date a *Paschal Homily*, which the majority of scholars believe was written by M., was discovered. In it all the history of Israel is summarized, with particular emphasis on the exodus and the institution of the Hebrew Passover. Everything is then related to Jesus Christ by means of typological interpretations. Thus, for example, M. says that Jesus Christ "is the one who in Abel was killed; in Isaac, was bound; in Jacob, was a stranger; in Joseph, was sold; in Moses, exiled; in the lamb, sacrificed; in David, persecuted; in the prophets, dishonored."

JLG

Menander (1st century). Gnostic teacher and, according to ⇒Justin Martyr, a follower of ⇒Simon Magus. According to ancient Christian authors, M. taught that the world has been created by angels and that the only way that humans can free themselves from the power of these angels and ascend to eternity is by learning the secrets and receiving the baptism which only M. can give.

JLG

Menius, Justus (1499–1558). Lutheran reformer of Thuringia. He was born in Fulda, Germany. He studied in the universities of Erfurt and Wittenberg. He was one of the first followers of Martin ⇒Luther. He was superintendent of the church in Eisenach (1529), took part in the visitations of the congregations in that area, and participated in the Marburg Colloquy, in the meeting of the Schmalkald League (1537), and in the Colloquy of Hagenau. Together with other leaders of the Lutheran Reformation he signed the Wittenberg Concord (1536) and the Schmalkald Articles. He wrote extensively against the Anabaptist movement. His treatment of this matter became the traditional Lutheran perspective. In his theological debates he maintained that the beginning of a new life in the believers is necessary for salvation.

JDR

Menno Simons ⇒**Simons, Menno**

Mercator, Marius ⇒**Marius Mercator**

Mercier, Jean (?–1570). French linguist who was born at the beginning of the sixteenth century in Uzès. He studied law and then, attracted by his inclination toward Semitic languages, he entered the College of France. Persecuted because of his religious ideas, he left his country in 1567 and returned to France after the peace of St. Germain. He was the first to discover the quantity and measure of Hebrew verbs. He left interesting commentaries, *On the Old Testament* and *On the Gospel of St. Matthew*. Among his other works are *Tabulae in grammaticam linguae chaldae* and *Alphabetum hebraicum*.

JDR/AL

Mergal Llera, Angel M. (1909–71). Puerto Rican writer, theologian, and humanist. Born in Cayey, he studied at the University of Puerto Rico, the Evangelical Seminary of Puerto Rico, Union Theological Seminary in New York, and Columbia University, where he graduated with a PhD with high honors in 1943. He taught at the University of Puerto Rico, the Universidad Interamericana, and the Evangelical Seminary of Puerto Rico, a position from which he contributed to the religious and social formation of a generation of Puerto Rican and Latin American ministers. He collaborated with several publications inside and outside Puerto Rico, such as *El Mundo* of Puerto Rico and *Cuadernos Teológicos* of Argentina. He was also a Baptist minister, lecturer, and vice president of the Institute of Puerto Rican Literature. Among others, he wrote these works: *El agraz* (1945; Sour Grapes), *Reformismo cristiano y alma española* (1949; Christian Reform and Spanish Soul), *El arte cristiano de la predicación* (1952; The Christian Art of Preaching), *Puerto Rico: enigma y promesa* (1960; Puerto Rico: Enigma and Promise), and *El reino permanente* (1965; The Permanent Kingdom).

LMcA

Merton, Thomas (1915–68). Trappist monk, mystic, and writer. He was born in Prades, France, and studied at Ockham and Clare colleges in Cambridge, England. When he became an orphan he went to live with his maternal grandparents in New York City, where he completed his studies at Columbia University. In 1938 he left Protestantism and became a member of the Roman Catholic Church. In 1941 he joined the Trappist order in a ceremony in Kentucky. After that event he devoted himself to reflection and writing about the Christian faith. His work and writings reflect a desire for Christian unity, opposition to war and nuclear weapons, and a marked opposition to segregation and racial discrimination. With a unique literary style he describes his pilgrimage through the Christian life, emphasizing the importance of Roman Catholic customs as a source of spiritual aid and strength, thus inviting other Christian and non-Christian traditions to a dialogue about unity. He was accidentally electrocuted in a shower in his room in Thailand, where he was participating in an encounter of religious leaders.

———
HTM

Mesters, Carlos (1931–). Brazilian Carmelite exegete, author of *Flor sem defesa* (Defenseless Flower) and *Deus, onde estabas?* (God, Where Were You?), as well as many other popular biblical commentaries. He was one of the precursors and pacesetters of the hermeneutic of liberation in the Latin American continent.

———
CCO

Methodius of Olympus (?–310). Very little is known of his life, although it is said that he was bishop of Olympus and a martyr. He represents the theological voice that opposes the theology of ⇒Origen concerning the eternity of the world, the preexistence of souls, spiritualist eschatology, and allegorical hermeneutics. While he criticized Origen for his use of philosophy, he himself was profoundly influenced by Platonic thought, to the extent that he composed several dialogues in the style of ⇒Plato. The only one of them that has survived complete is *Symposium*, an encomium to virginity.

———
CCO

Metz, Johann Baptist (1928–). Disciple of the prominent Roman Catholic theologian Karl ⇒Rahner. He attempted to free himself from the individualist categories that dominate theological thought and to construct a theology that underscores the historical and political dimension of the Christian tradition. His political theology, his vision of the human being, his historical emphasis, and his criticism of bourgeois society are closely related to the thought of Jürgen ⇒Moltmann.

He holds that in the contemporary world, biblical texts and the Christian tradition have to be reinterpreted in the light of the historical, political, and social reality. This political dimension of Christianity is based on the symbol of the kingdom of God that is at the center of the teaching of Jesus. Christians cannot reduce the politics that are proper to the practice of faith to the partisan politics of their country or to a particular alternative program.

The Christian position should question all political absolutism and must resist the ideological use of faith to justify limited partisan positions. The church must be a critical and prophetic community that denounces the limitations of all political positions.

M. criticizes the consumer culture dominant in wealthy countries that live under the illusion of freedom, when in reality they are under the tyranny of technological rationality. This means that our conduct is dominated by a consumer utilitarianism that measures everything we do in terms of the monetary benefit that is produced. Our being is defined by our capacity to consume; that is, the purpose of having is not to benefit our being, but rather we are in order to have more things.

Authentic Christianity represents a criticism of this conformity. It calls us to live values that produce life for the poor, the marginalized, and all those who do not count socially. The memory of Christ's suffering, which is embodied in those who are exploited and oppressed in our time, calls us to serve the less privileged.

—
IG

Meyendorff, John (1926–92). Born in France of Russian parents, M. devoted his ministry to the mission and renovation of the global church. Theologian and historian of the Orthodox church, M. represents the spirit of the Neopatristic movement in that church. Consequently, he was instrumental in the promotion of unity, the importance of the universal church over and above the nationalist spirit, and the quest for unity in the concrete life and structure of the church.

He was a moderator of the Commission of Faith and Order of the ⇒World Council of Churches (1967–75) and one of the leaders who supported and promoted the work for the document *Baptism, Eucharist, and Ministry* of the World Council of Churches. In addition to being professor and academic dean of St. Vladimir Orthodox Theological Seminary in New York, he wrote a great number of academic works and, in a popular tone, books such as *The Orthodox Church: Its Past and Its Role in the World Today* and *Christ in Eastern Christian Thought*.

———

CCO

Michael of Antioch (12th century).

Jacobite patriarch of that city, who was one of the chief protagonists of a controversy with the Copts on whether it was necessary to confess sins before taking Communion.

———

JLG

Michael Italicus (12th century).

Teacher of the Patriarchal School of Constantinople, where he succeeded Michael ⇒Psellus. His learning was such that he was given the sobriquet of Second Plato. In spite of his philosophical interests, he was convinced that only theology is capable of leading to ineffable truths and that all the objections and dead–end alleys of philosophy should yield to theology.

———

JLG

Migetius (8th century). Obscure person, apparently Spanish, who, according to ⇒Elipandus of Toledo, said that David was the Father, Jesus the Son, and Paul the Holy Spirit.

———

JLG

Míguez Bonino, José (1924–).

Methodist theologian and ethicist born in Argentina. He worked as a Methodist pastor in Bolivia and Argentina for more than a decade. He obtained his licentiate in theology from the Evangelical Faculty of Theology in Buenos Aires, which is now the Higher Evangelical Institute of Theological Studies (ISEDET), in 1948; his master's degree in theology from Emory University in 1952; and his doctorate in theology from Union Theological Seminary in New York in 1960. He was professor of theology and ethics in the Evangelical Faculty of Theology in Argentina (1954–69) and then in ISEDET (1970–85), where he also served as dean. He is a recognized Latin American ecumenist who was one of the Protestant observers at the Second Vatican Council (⇒Vatican II) and a president of the ⇒World Council of Churches. He was one of the founding leaders of ISAL (⇒Iglesia y Sociedad en América Latina [Church and Society in Latin America]) and a human rights activist. He is an interpreter of and contributor to Latin American liberation theology from a Protestant perspective.

Outstanding among his publications are *Espacio para ser hombres* (Room to Be Human), *La fe en situación revolucionaria* (Doing Theology in a Revolutionary Situation), *Christians and Marxists: The Mutual Challenge to Revolution*, *Los rostros de Jesús en América Latina* (The Faces of Jesus in Latin America), and *Towards a Christian Political Ethics*. One of the central concerns in the work of M. is the discernment of a Christian praxis and ethic that critically guide Christians to become involved in social and political processes of transformation with actions and criteria that are suitable to the context of political struggle for the freedom and humanization of life in the world and that are faithful to the gospel, proclaiming a righteous and liberating God.

———

LRR

Mill, John Stuart (1806–73). Nineteenth-century English philosopher and economist who was educated by his father, James Mill, also a philosopher. He was prolific as an author of philosophical essays. M. served as administrator of the East India Company in London for many years. His major work, *System of Logic* (1843), presents the inductive method (from the particular to the universal) as the most effective in argumentation. His writings on logical reasoning influenced many fields in his time, including economics, political theory, sociology, and ethics. In *The Subjection of Women* (1861) he defended women's rights, and suffrage in particular. After his death a collection of his *Three Essays on Religion* (1874) was published. In the essay "On Nature," M. argues that the old declaration of "following nature" presumes that what is natural is always the best, but this is not so. M. holds that there is a God and that God is good, but not omnipotent. God depends on God's creation, humanity, in order to intervene with nature and produce what is good. In this sense, M. is also considered a utilitarian philosopher: the knowledge produced by logical reason ought to be useful for the good of society. In "On Theism" M. supports the attempt to prove the existence of God through the order of the universe: when one looks at creation, it is logical to believe in an intelligent being as Creator. In "On the Usefulness of Religion" he also supports the idea of a "religion of humanity" that promotes the human character which is necessary to do good in the world. On the other hand, a "supernatural religion" creates polemical attitudes without resolving social problems.

—

EA

Miller, William (1782–1849). Founder of the Adventist Church. He was born in Pittsfield, Massachusetts, and years later moved to Low Hampton, New York, where he worked in the construction business and studied several academic disciplines that led him to become a deist and to doubt the truthfulness of evangelical Christianity. In 1816, at the age of thirty-four, he experienced a dramatic conversion and joined a Baptist church, where he became a preacher and evangelist. Based on his studies of the book of Daniel and of the second coming of Christ, M. arrived at the conclusion that Christ would return between March of 1843 and March of 1844. His predictions caused great admiration, and thousands believed him and followed him. They were called Adventists because of the marked emphasis on the second advent of Christ. When the dates given by M. passed and Christ had not returned, there was great disillusionment and frustration among his followers, to which the leaders of the Adventist movement responded with a new date for the coming of Christ, which was set for October 22, 1844, after correcting the calculations of M. Nevertheless, on that date as on the previous ones there was no such coming, and thus the movement almost disappeared completely, leaving room for other groups and interpretations, of which the Seventh-day Adventists are the largest.

—

HMT

Milton, John (1608–74). After Shakespeare, the most important English poet. He is chiefly known for his epic poem *Paradise Lost*, which is about the fall of humanity. This poem and several others are a strong expression of the Puritan vison of the world and of history. He was a defender of religious and civil rights. He studied at Cambridge University (1625–32). Although for some time he considered entering the ordained ministry, at the university he began to write poems in Latin, Italian, and English, and from then on devoted himself mainly to literature.

His literary work is divided into three periods. The first covers the years 1632 to 1640. During that time he lived in his father's house, studied the Greek and Latin classics, and traveled throughout Europe.

The second period (1640–1660) is characterized by his political activity and by writings that were chiefly opinionative in character, in addition to some sonnets. His pamphlets dealt with matters such as his opposition to the episcopacy (1642), his opinion on divorce (1643; M. married three times, and none of those marriages resulted in a happy family life), and his defense of the deposition of a tyrannical king (1649). In all of this we see the application of his Puritan ideas to civil and political life.

In 1651 he became blind. With the Restoration of Charles II, he was fined and briefly imprisoned. From 1660 until his death in 1674, he withdrew to Burnhill, where the third stage of his literary production transpired. At that time he wrote three epic poems, all of which had a great impact on the Puritanism of that period and of later centuries: *Paradise Lost* (1667), *Paradise Regained* (1671), and *Samson Agonistes* (1671).

—

EZ

Minucius Felix (2nd century). Author of an apology in the form of a dialogue known by the name of its protagonist, *Octavius*. Scholars debate whether the first Christian author in the Latin language was M. or ⇒Tertullian. In the dialogue of M., which is probably fictitious, the Christian lawyer Octavius argues with the pagan Cecilius. Both are walking from Rome to Ostia when Cecilius makes a sign of worship in front of a statue of Serapis. Octavius admonishes him, and thus a dialogue ensues, which in the beginning is a strong defense of paganism by Cecilius. Among other things, Cecilius accuses Christians of being lowly and ignorant people belonging to the masses. Octavius responds in a moderate tone, declaring that all human beings, regardless of their low social station, are gifted with reason and must use it. From there he goes on to demonstrate that there must be a creator God, and that this God must not be more than one. Paganism, as opposed to Christianity, is nothing but a series of fables which the ancients have bequeathed to us and which people accept without giving it much thought. Then the dialogue goes on to the topic of the calumnies that are spread against the Christians, and Octavius replies to them. In the end Cecilius accepts the faith, and both continue happily along the way.

—

JLG

Miranda, José Porfirio (1924–2001). Born in Monterrey, Mexico. Prolific writer, philosopher, theologian, and scientist, M. is known worldwide for his books *Marx y la Biblia* (Marx and the Bible) and *El Cristianismo* *de Marx* (Marx's Christianity). His philosophical as well as his theological work is founded on a critique of capitalist oppressive ideology and the promotion and support of the revolution of the poor. M., who was educated by the Jesuits, left the order with the conviction that it participated in the capitalist structures of oppression.

——

CCO

Moffat, Robert (1795–1883). Pioneer of missionary work in South Africa, and a Scotsman of the Anglican tradition, M. was considered one of the most important British missionaries in the mid-nineteenth century. His work focused on the translation of the Scriptures into Tswana, a language used in the entire southern region of South Africa. He also wrote *Missionary Labours*, in which he describes the missionary work that had been carried out until then in South Africa by the London Missionary Society.

——

CCO

Moffatt, James (1870–1944). Biblical scholar and church historian born in Glasgow, Scotland, who was especially known for his translation of the Bible into a modern and familiar English (the New Testament in 1913, the Old Testament in 1924, and a revision of both in 1935). This work was the basis of a number of biblical commentaries on the New Testament, which were edited in seventeen volumes between 1928 and 1949.

——

ODV

Mogila, Peter (1596–1646). As a Russian theologian from the school of Kiev, M. adopted the Latin theological methodology within the frame of Russian Orthodox theology, during an era of profound anti–Roman Catholicism in Russia. His *Orthodox Confession of the Catholic and Apostolic Church of the East* shows this methodological adaptation at the same time that it maintains two basic principles of Orthodoxy: the procession of the Holy Spirit only from the Father and the nonacceptance of papal authority.

——

CCO

Molina, Luis de (1536–1600). Jesuit theologian who attempted to refute Protestant teachings on grace and predestination through his book *La concordia entre el libre albedrío y*

los dones de la gracia (Concord between Free Will and the Gifts of Grace). M. proposes a distinction between two kinds of freedom: "freedom from all coercion" and "freedom from necessity." In the strict sense, only the second is true freedom. A stone that falls does not suffer coercion, but it is not truly free, for it falls by necessity. This implies that the Protestant argument that predestination does not destroy the will, for the will does not suffer coercion, is false.

In his own theological construction, M. begins by distinguishing three modes of knowledge in God. The "natural" knowledge of God includes everything that exists or could exist. The "free" knowledge of God includes only those things that God through the divine will has decided should exist. But there is also a third or "intermediate" knowledge (a *scientia media*) through which God knows the "future contingents," that is, those things that are to happen through the work of other wills which God has created and gifted with freedom. The fact that such future things are not the product of the free knowledge of God is what makes them contingent, what makes them a product of the free will of creatures.

When Adam was created he had, in addition to natural human freedom, supernatural gifts that allowed him not to sin, as ⇒Augustine had previously affirmed. With the fall, his nature and his natural freedom were not corrupted, but Adam simply lost the supernatural gifts. Consequently, in our present state, we have full freedom to decide our actions, but not to not sin. God supplies that freedom with a "general aid" or prevenient grace that is given to all human beings, allowing them to believe. From then on, God grants to whoever decides to believe the assistance that is needed to continue believing and acting correctly in full freedom.

Consequently, neither the knowledge of God nor the priority of grace require a teaching of predestination such as ⇒Luther, ⇒Calvin, and other Protestants promulgated.

Even before its publication, M.'s book *On Divine Knowledge and Predestination* provoked debates among Roman Catholics. The Dominicans thought that his theology came too close to Pelagianism (⇒Pelagius), and they halted the sale of the book until an appendix written by Domingo ⇒Báñez, with the objections of the Dominicans, and a second appendix in which M. replied to these objections, were added. From then on there were strong debates among the Dominicans and Jesuits concerning the opinions of M.

——

JLG

Molinos, Miguel de (ca. 1640–97).

Spaniard who spent a good part of his career in Italy, where he became famous for his devotion, especially after his publication of a book under the title *Guía espiritual* (Spiritual Guide). Almost immediately he was attacked by several theologians, Dominicans as well as Jesuits, who saw in his teaching and devotional practice an unacceptable passivity. According to M., the soul does not have to do anything but hope in God. Everything that might be an effort to approach God should be rejected—including devotional practices. Such teachings were given the name of quietism or Molinism. Soon a number of nuns who followed his teachings refused to participate in the devotional life of their communities. In 1685 M. was imprisoned for his teachings. Although he retracted them, he was then accused of being immoral, and he spent the rest of his days in prison. It is impossible to know whether such an accusation was true. Madame de ⇒Guyon was one of his most distinguished followers and defenders.

———

JLG

Moltmann, Jürgen (1926–).

One of the outstanding theologians of the last five decades. His creativity and original theological thought opened up new paths whose purpose was to raise again the political themes of our time. Such creativity can be confirmed in the manner in which he has integrated the best of the biblical, theological, philosophical, and sociological knowledge of his time in an eloquent and pertinent discourse vis-à-vis those crucial challenges that human life must unavoidably face. His originality can also be seen in his effort to transcend abstract and descriptive thought in the theological task, in order to offer an understanding of the faith that effectively reaches the very center of one's human experience and thus transforms it in a radical way. The end of theology is not to soar in mere concepts and ideas, but to illumine reality from the perspective of a faith that is thoughtful, that preserves its fundamental identity, and that is relevant to its particular context.

In *Experiences of God*, M. tells his dramatic personal history from the time he finished high school until he finally decided to follow a theological career. Those were years of a search for meaning in a Germany that swelled with pride as it projected itself on the world stage. At first it appeared that mathematics and physics would win him over in the professional field. That was due mainly to the admiration he had for Max Planck and Albert Einstein. The poetry of Goethe and the philosophy of ⇒Nietzsche moved him to believe in the greatness of Germany, with the result that he joined the military forces of his country in the Second World War. For three years and two months he was a prisoner of war in Scotland, Belgium, and England. Those years were dominated by humiliation and bewilderment; but, far from drowning him in the existential abyss, they allowed him to find himself with God in deafening silence and loving solidarity. Having the powerful mystery of such an experience behind him, he was finally liberated and returned to a Germany that was different from the one that he left, since he found it in spiritual and national ruin.

In the face of the collapse of the dreams of German greatness, the horrifying stories of the war, and the national and personal shame for what had happened, M. identified with those persons of his generation who proposed to reconstruct what remained of the old Germany on new existential and social assumptions. To this end he would have to criticize the ideological assumptions that led Germany to its own destruction, and from the perspective of that criticism seek a new orientation that would hopefully lead Germany toward national fulfillment. In addition, he would have to vindicate Germany in the face of history, offering the best of his soul to construct collectively a world that is more wholesome and just.

M. sought in theology that new orientation that would allow him to contribute to that decisive effort of national and world reconstruction. He studied theology in Göttingen under the direction of Otto ⇒Weber, who had been a disciple of Karl ⇒Barth. He wrote his dissertation under Weber. At the beginning of his theological career he wrote about doctrinal themes that had been studied by theologians such as ⇒Amyraut, Christoph Pezel, ⇒Ramus, and ⇒Cocceius. M. sought in the theologies of the Reformation and in reflection about them the clarity that is necessary to understand important doctrinal issues. All of it strengthened his fundamentally Barthian formation. It is clear that the theologies of Barth and of the Reformation offered him an ideal theoretical framework for distancing himself from the dominant culture that was determined by the crisis, in order to then become anchored in the Word of God as the only way that leads to human fulfillment.

In 1964 M. published *Theology of Hope*, which provoked discussion. It was immediately translated into a number of languages. Soon it became a classic in what later was called

European political theology, which had strong repercussions on other theological currents that also seek to meditate on faith within the political domain. In this work M. raises again the place of eschatology in promissory hope, which should become the center and vitality of the community of believers as they look forward to the transformation of the world. The criticism of M. that demolishes other eschatological interpretations is most valuable.

In order to present the importance of transforming hope, he borrows from von Rad, who had stressed the God of promise in the theology of the Old Testament. In addition, M. dialogues with the monumental work of the German philosopher Ernst Bloch titled *The Principle of Hope*, which proposes that human nature irreversibly tends toward its future fulfillment. One can detect in this work the interest of a Marxist atheist, who is also marginalized by the orthodoxy of the communist parties, in an in-depth reading of the Bible as a source of hope. Faith that wishes to speak of what is political must deal with Marxism and be capable of offering the kind of hope that opens up the space that is necessary for planning the future of humanity on the basis of solidarity and full justice. Other works of M., such as *Faith and Politics, Hope and Planning for the Future*, and *The Experiment Hope*, have broadened the theme of Christian eschatology, placing it on the solid terrain of social and historical experience.

In 1972 M. published *The Crucified God*, in which he shows the importance of a theology of the cross in a community of believers who wish to communicate the Christian message to the present-day world. With this work, M. did not leave behind the eschatological theme conceived as a promissory hope for humanity. Instead, he presented the Crucified One as the authentic way of hope that it is necessary to understand and assume in the totality of human life. M. has insisted that from the perspective of the Crucified One, God has clearly revealed Godself to us, and that from the same perspective all of the antivalues that are predominant in the religious, cultural, and political domains are stripped away.

The church and religion could remain trapped in ideology as a distortion of reality if they do not allow themselves to be molded by the Crucified One, since only he can move them to break decisively with the comfortable position that they enjoy in the social structure and with their scandalous complicity with a society that oppresses and dehumanizes. Taking this path undoubtedly would lead one to experience suffering, incomprehension, taunts, repressions, frustrations, and even martyrdom. But precisely in all of that, the message of the Crucified One would truly reign, since all of this would be irrefutable and conclusive proof of the solidarity of the church with suffering humanity. In spite of the fact that M. distances himself from natural theology as a way to know God, his understanding of God from the perspective of faith in the Crucified One is in total opposition to the arguments that ⇒Freud, ⇒Marx, ⇒Feuerbach, and Nietzsche used to deny the existence of God. The Crucified One speaks in an eloquent way about a God who not only surprises through his incarnation, but who is also capable of total self-humiliation in order to offer a new historical way to humanity. Faith in the Crucified One thus approaches reality in order to understand it better and encourages the believer to continue working to transform it with a view to its supreme fulfillment.

In addition, the Crucified One invites the believer to maintain a critical distance from those political projects that pretend to be absolute or totalitarian in their understanding of the truth and in its concrete application, because in every one of them seeds of evil and destruction may be detected. M. would therefore not go along with the defeatist pessimism of the myth of Sisyphus, according to which one struggles, knowing that in the end nothing makes sense. The hope that comes from the Crucified One always issues the call to struggle for the transformation of history and for a fuller humanization, knowing that in the end the victory will be fully realized not by our own efforts, but conclusively through the divine work. This hope also distances itself from Promethean optimism. Against such optimism, with humanizing projects that see God as the enemy of humanity, M. argues that the hopeful struggle for the humanization of history nurtures and sustains itself in a God who has given his own life in the Crucified One in order to give life in abundance to all of humanity.

The work *Trinity and the Kingdom of God* deals with the doctrine of God from the perspective of the communitarian relations between the Father, the Son, and the Holy Spirit. This way of understanding things differs radically from others who have approached Trinitarian discourse on the basis of assumptions of homogeneous substance or identical subject, which have ended by speaking of a monarchical and authoritarian God. The problem that M. sees in this discourse centered on the unity of God is that it ignores the intra-Trinitarian relations, which, far from closing in on themselves, overflow into human history. For M. the unity of the triune God can be seen clearly in the relations between the Father, the Son, and the Holy Spirit and how these relations can model a better understanding for social life and the church. The way in which M. assesses the understanding of God in Judaism and in the Christian tradition is very valuable because in the end it allows him to construct his communal and social Trinitarian way of understanding things while thinking in ecological terms that include the world, humanity, and God in a coherent whole.

Following this line of thought, M. wrote *God in Creation: An Ecological Doctrine of Creation*, which is a magisterial response to one of the grave problems that humanity faces, the ecological problem. He investigates in depth the present situation and its ill-fated consequences as well as the theoretical way in which secular and religious thought has looked at it. He proposes a different way, based on the Trinitarian relation. He maintains that starting from that dynamic and creative communion, a theory and a practice that assume complete responsibility for protecting the divine creation can be constructed. The understanding of God that has frequently predominated in theology, based on domination or authoritarianism, is thus challenged. M. detects that this way of understanding God in relation to humanity is very much like the way in which humanity has been relating to nature.

M. has dug into anthropological themes concerning humanism in industrial society in his work *The Human*. He has seen human misery vis-à-vis the bewilderment of the historical moment that we live. Over against this situation, he has proposed God as a critic and source of hope for contemporary anthropology. He has also suggested a messianic christological road in his work *The Way of Jesus Christ: Christology in Messianic Dimensions*. Vis-à-vis the so-called Christologies from above and from below, M. has suggested a Christology that serves as a lodestar for humanity, providing guidance for living the way Jesus Christ has laid out toward the promised future. In the field of pneumatology M. has written *The Church in the Power of the Spirit: A Contribution to Messianic Ecclesiology* and *The Spirit of Life: A Universal Affirmation*. This last work emphasizes the place the Holy Spirit is occupying in the Protestantism of our time and the theological necessity of understanding this in its proper perspective.

————

JNR

Moody, Dwight L. (1837–99). Evangelist born in Northfield, Massachusetts. At the age of thirteen he left school, and at seventeen he went to Boston to work in a shoe store. In Boston he attended the Congregational Church of Mount Vernon, and under the influence of his Sunday school teacher, Edward Kimball, he fervently converted to Christianity. In 1856 he moved to Chicago, where he worked as a commercial agent and traveling salesman. He joined the Plymouth Church and in 1858 organized the Sunday school of North Market, appointing John V. Farwell, a prominent businessman, as the person in charge. Two years later he left his secular work to devote himself to Sunday school and the Young Men's Christian Association (YMCA). During the Civil War he established the nondenominational church of Illinois Street. In 1873, on his third trip to England, he organized several evangelistic campaigns with great success. On his return to the United States he continued with evangelistic campaigns that led him to Brooklyn, Philadelphia, Boston, Baltimore, St. Louis, Cleveland, and San Francisco. In addition to gathering crowds to hear his preaching of the gospel, in 1879 he organized Northfield Seminary, a school for women. Two years later he founded Mount Vernon, a school for men. In 1886 he organized the Evangelistic Society of Chicago, which later became the Moody Bible Institute. He died in December of 1899, a few days after having ended his last campaign in Kansas City.

————

HMT

Moore, George F. (1851–1931). Born in West Chester, Pennsylvania, on October 15, 1851. He was educated at Yale University and at Union Theological Seminary in New York. Between 1877 and 1878 he served as pastor of the Presbyterian Church of Bloomingburg and from 1878 to 1883 as pastor of Putnam Presbyterian Church in Zanesville, both in Ohio. Then he was appointed professor of Hebrew and literature at Andover Theological Seminary, where he worked from 1883 until 1902. Finally, from 1902 until his retirement he served as professor of the history of religion at Harvard University.

————

HMT

More, Thomas (1477–1535). A man of a great humanist culture who was ambassador, chancellor, and an author in his native England.

He chiefly had a religious vocation, although he decided to serve his Roman Catholic Church principally as a layperson. In that role he promoted the cultural and religious program of ⇒Erasmus, especially the intensive study of Greek as key in the study of theology, in order to understand in depth the Scriptures and the fathers of the church. His most impressive work was his *Confutation of Tyndale's Answer* (1532), in which he comments on the doctrine of the church. He defended King Henry VIII in a dispute with ⇒Luther on the sacraments in his scholarly work *Responsio ad Lutherum* (1523). He is recognized chiefly for *Utopia* (1516), in which he describes a city-state of communist character governed only by reason. In that work he analyzes religious pluralism, women's rights, divorce, euthanasia, abortion, and state education. His chief place in history is the result of his posture over against Henry VIII for not supporting his divorce from Catherine of Aragon, and especially for not attending the coronation of the new queen, Anne Boleyn. For this reason he was accused of sedition and beheaded, thus earning the title of martyr and later that of saint (1935).

———

ALG

Morse, Jedidiah (1761–1826).

Congregationalist clergyman who was recognized in the secular world chiefly as the father of North American geography. As a clergyman he occupied an important place in the foundation of Andover Theological Seminary (1808) and of the American Bible Society (1816). In addition, having been one of the first to use tracts for evangelism, he also founded the New England Tract Society (1814). Of an orthodox Calvinist persuasion, he fought against the dominant religious position, especially in Harvard University, which was a combination of the teachings of ⇒Arminius with those of the Unitarians.

———

ALG

Mott, John R. (1865–1955).

North American Methodist, and one of the great leaders of the Protestant missionary and ecumenical movements. He was one of the young people who, under the inspiration of D. L. ⇒Moody, signed the declaration for missionary work at the end of the nineteenth century. His leadership in the YMCA and in the Student Christian Movement led him to found the World Student Christian Federation in 1895,

taking missionary enthusiasm and ecumenical inspiration to world levels.

In 1910 he presided over the World Missionary Conference in Edinburgh, which is a milestone in the development of the missionary and ecumenical movements. With his evangelizing spirit and his gift for speaking, M. continued to give direction and shape to missionary and ecumenical conferences until 1948.

The missiological contribution of M. is more motivating and structural than reflective and critical. It is possible that his most important missiological legacy was his constant demand for cooperation in the missionary task among denominations and missionary agencies. The great world missionary and ecumenical conferences and the national and regional ecumenical councils, united for the task of Christian witness, are the fruit of the administrative genius and of the tenacious spirit of this visionary evangelist in the transition from the nineteenth to the twentieth century.

———

CCO

Mott, Lucretia (1793–1880).

Leader of the abolitionist movement and of the struggle for women's rights. She was born in Nantucket, Massachusetts, into a family of Quakers, a tradition in which she became a preacher in 1821. Like the majority of Quakers, M. devoted herself fervently to the abolition of slavery and to the promotion of the legal and religious rights of women. After it seemed that these causes had been won, or at least advanced, M. devoted herself to promoting the right of African American citizens to vote.

———

HMT

Muller, Max (1823–1900).

German historian of religions and scholar in the fields of philosophy and comparative religions. His work began through the meticulous study of Sanskrit, which led him to translate many of the religious documents of Hinduism and Buddhism. In addition to his scholarship in this field, subsequently, as professor of comparative philology, he developed a scheme for the comparative study of religion. After his retirement, he devoted himself to history and the scientific analysis of religion.

M. did not see his work only as a contribution to the science of the religious phenomenon, but rather hoped and proposed that through this study relations among religions and cultures could be improved. In this sense, his work contributed to the knowledge of the cultures and religions of India in the West. Moreover, from a theological perspective, M. sought to develop a "theological theory" for the study of religion, which became an antecedent of the contemporary theology of religion.

His most important works in this last field are "Comparative Mythology" in *Oxford Essays* (1856), *Introduction to the Science of Religion* (1873), and *Contributions to the Science of Mythology* (1897).

—

CCO

Mullins, Edgar Young (1860–1928).
Pastor, theologian, and president of Southern Baptist Theological Seminary, of the Southern Baptist Convention, and of the World Baptist Alliance (1928). Some of his works are *The Axioms of Religion*, *The Christian Religion in Its Doctrinal Expression*, and *Why Is Christianity True?*

—

JDRR

Münzer, Thomas (1490–1525).
Prominent figure of the Radical Reformation. He was a Roman Catholic priest, and during his stay in Wittenberg (1519–20) became a follower of ⇒Luther. Later he denounced the Lutheran Reformation for not being sufficiently radical and for not responding to the religious and moral anxieties of the epoch. He especially rejected the position that Luther took against the rebellion of the peasants. He believed that Luther and other Reformers depended excessively on the Scriptures and that their notion of justification by faith had conservative implications. For M. it was the Bible that depended on spiritual and religious experience. The true reformation gives rise to the church of the truly elect. This community of the chosen would in turn lead to the creation of a new social order ruled by justice and love. He actively participated with the peasantry of Germany in several armed conflicts and also supported the peasants in France and Switzerland. In the twentieth century some socialist movements claimed him as a forerunner.

In the ecclesial sphere he opposed any kind of embellishment of the church with images, statues, or any other type of ornament. For him all decoration is an expression of a materialism that opposes the true spiritual development of the believer. He also opposed the baptism of children.

His radical ideas led him to join the Peasants' Revolt. After the defeat of the movement,

he was imprisoned, tortured, and decapitated as a rebel. Some claimed that before his death he returned to the Catholic faith.

—

IG

Murray, John (1741–1815).
At first a participant in the Methodist revival led by John ⇒Wesley and George ⇒Whitefield, M. became convinced that God's love required universal salvation. He then abandoned both his native England and the Methodist movement and settled in New England, where he met others with similar ideas. Mostly under M.'s leadership, a Winchester Confession was issued in 1803, and this became the common link among people and congregations from diverse theological backgrounds, but all agreeing on the principle of universal salvation. This was the origin of the Universalist Church, which long after M.'s death, in 1961, joined with the Unitarians in the Unitarian-Universalist Association.

—

IG

Murray, John Courtney, SJ (1904–67).
Theologian who had a great influence on the formation of North American Roman Catholicism. His special contribution was the redefinition of the relationship between state and church. For him, given the social and political context of North America, the church should not attempt to dominate the state, nor should the state dominate the church. He was a promoter of ecumenism. He made important contributions at the Second Vatican Council (⇒Vatican II), particularly to the "Declaration on Religious Freedom."

—

IG

Müsaeus, Johannes (1613–81).
German Lutheran theologian who had studied philosophy and humanities in the universities of Erfurt and Jena before deciding on theology. In 1643 he taught history in the University of Jena. In 1646 he was appointed professor of theology in the same university. During his thirty-eight years as professor of that university, he was also rector on seven occasions. M. had an exceptional philosophical acumen and was an avid student of the methodology of the medieval scholastics. He resisted the mere repetition of formulas he had received and devoted himself to distinguishing between the theological task and the confession of faith. He opposed

elevating any theological system to the level of norm and insisted that even the deeply orthodox theologians inevitably would have to differ in their efforts to teach, expound, and defend the teachings of the faith.

M. was a victim of the synergist controversy, which took place between the faculties of the universities of Wittenberg and Helmsted. In his *Quaestiones theologicae inter nostrates hactenus agitatae de Syncretismo et Scriptura sacra* (written in 1671, but published in 1679), he rejected, even with scorn, the accusation of syncretism that was characteristic of the faculty of Helmsted.

Among his other works are *Dissertatio theologica de quaestione: An sive principiorum rationis homo ad aeternam salutem pertingere possit?* (1667), *De usu principiorum rationis et philosophiae in controversiis theologicis* (1644), *Der Jenischen Theologen aussfuehrliche Erklaerung uber drei und neunzig vermeinete Religions-Fragen* (1676–77; Detailed Clarification of the Jena Theologians on Ninety-Three Alleged Religious Questions), and *Introductio in theologiam* (1677–78).

——

JDR

Musculus, Andreas (1514–81).

German Lutheran theologian, pastor, and professor of theology in the region of Brandenburg. He was one of the editors of the Formula of ⇒Concord (1577), one of the principal confessional documents of the Lutheran churches. He was accused of antinomianism because of his opposition to the use of the law as a guarantee of good works in the believer and because of his support of Johann ⇒Agricola. He defended the independence of the clergy and the church against the civil authorities.

——

NRG

Narses (?–507).

Nestorian theologian of the fifth century, known in the Nestorian tradition as the Harp of the Holy Spirit because of his hymns and homilies, in which he expresses his Nestorian Christology. The Monophysite Jacobite tradition called him Narses the Leper.

N. had the responsibility of directing the doctrinal school of ⇒Barsumas in Nisibis, Persia. The Christology of N. can be summarized in his words in a homily: "We believe in one Lord Jesus Christ, the Son of God: one person, in two natures, each one with its hypostasis." This points towards a Christology that affirms the integrity of each of the two natures of Christ, although this is achieved at the expense of their unity.

——

CCO

Nasedka, Ivan (16th century).

Russian Orthodox priest who wrote a letter in the name of the patriarch to the Danish and Protestant prince Waldemar, giving him the reasons for which Russian Orthodoxy is the unique and true expression of the Christian faith. In this letter N. proposes that the church fathers have the same authority as the Scriptures.

——

CCO

Nash, Roland (1936–).

Evangelical philosopher and director of the Institute of Advanced Christian Studies, which organized conferences in various venues. Among his most important works are *The Philosophy of Gordon H. Clark* (1968), *Ideas of History* (1969), and *The Light of the Mind: St. Augustine's Theory of Knowledge* (1969).

——

AEM

Neale, Robert (1929–).

Minister of the United Church of Christ, chaplain, professor of psychiatry and religion at Union Theological Seminary of New York, and an amateur juggler. After a successful career of twenty-four years at Union (to 1985), he devoted himself to exploring the psychology of magic and juggling, an area in which he has a great number of publications.

Among his many theological books are *In Praise of Play: Toward a Psychology of Religion* (1969), *The Art of Dying* (1973), *Loneliness, Solitude, and Companionship* (1984), *Tricks for the Imagination* (1991), and *Life, Death, and Other Card Tricks* (2000).

——

JDRR

Neill, Stephen C. (1900–84).

Englishman of the Anglican and evangelical tradition, N. was a missionary, bishop, and missiologist. Following the tradition of his family, he was a missionary for twenty years under the auspices of the Church Missionary Society, an expression of the evangelical wing of the British Anglican tradition. In 1939 he was named bishop of Tinnevelli in India, where he devoted a great part of his ministry to community development projects. He occupied this position until 1944. He also taught missiology in different parts of the world, among them the universities of Hamburg and Nairobi.

N. is known as a historian of the Christian missionary movement, particularly in Asia, and of the ecumenical movement. Together with Ruth Rouse he is editor of *History of the Ecumenical Movement, 1517–1948*. His books include *A History of Christian Missions, The Interpretation of the New Testament, 1861–1961*, and his best-known work, *A History of Christianity in India*. Along with these works are more than one hundred articles in the field of history and missiology.

————

CCO

Neri, Philip (1515–95). A mystic who favored the poor, N. was affable and even comic. He was influenced by ⇒Savonarola. He renounced the position of notary, his father's occupation, and the world of business in his native Florence. He sold his library and devoted himself to serving the poor. He was the cofounder of the Confraternity of the Most Holy Trinity (1548). He ministered in the Hospital of the Holy Spirit of Vassia and created the Order of the Oratorians (1564). Ordained a priest in 1551, he was beatified in 1615 and canonized in 1622.

————

EPA

Nestorius (?–ca. 452). Patriarch of Alexandria who was condemned and deposed by the Council of ⇒Ephesus in 431 for having declared that Mary was not the "mother of God" (*Theotokos*), but the "mother of Christ" (*Christotokos*). The controversy surrounding N. is an episode in the long conflict between the Alexandrian and the Antiochian Christologies. The first, which was profoundly influenced by ⇒Origen and in the time of N. was represented by ⇒Cyril of Alexandria, was a "unitive" Christology. This means that the theologians of the Alexandrian school insisted on the necessity of safeguarding the unity of the person of Jesus Christ, even when this might imply that his humanity was to be subordinated to or eclipsed by the divinity. Over against them, the Antiochenes maintained a Christology that historians call "disjunctive." They insisted on the complete humanity of Jesus Christ and, in order to safeguard it, they tended to distinguish more clearly the divinity from the humanity, and sometimes even to separate the two.

What was debated in the controversy surrounding N. was not so much the Mariological theme of the titles owed to Mary, but rather the christological question of whether the unity between the humanity and the divinity in Jesus Christ is such that what is said of the one should also be affirmed of the other. This is the principle of the *communicatio idiomatum*, the communication of the properties or predicates. Thus, for example, according to this principle it must be said that when Jesus walked about in Galilee, it was God who walked in him. Before N., another great Antiochene teacher, ⇒Theodore of Mopsuestia, had expressed doubts about such a principle, and particularly about whether this meant that Mary had given birth to God. Theodore himself retracted in the end, saying that the *communicatio idiomatum* was indeed necessary if in reality God became incarnate in Jesus Christ.

The conflict broke out when the chaplain of N. declared his rejection of the title of *Theotokos*, as applied to Mary, and N. defended him. Shortly afterward, N. himself preached a series of sermons on the same topic. Criticism was not long in coming. From Alexandria, Patriarch Cyril protested and wrote a series of letters seeking the support of other colleagues. John, his counterpart in Antioch, came out in defense of N. Rome took the side of Alexandria. Finally it was decided to convene a council, which met in Ephesus in the year 431. It rejected the teaching of N. and deposed him. The Antiochenes, for their part, met in a separate council and condemned the other party. Cyril promulgated twelve anathemas against N., who did the same against Cyril. In the long run, after a complicated series of negotiations, in the year 433 a Formula of Union was reached. N. was deposed as patriarch of Constantinople and spent the rest of his life in exile. In his last days he believed that the Council of ⇒Chalcedon had vindicated his position.

In his *Book of Heraclides*, composed shortly before his death and rediscovered at the end of the nineteenth century, N. explains and defends his teachings. There N. appears to use the term "hypostasis" in the sense of what he calls a "complete nature." There are incomplete and complete natures. An incomplete nature is, for example, that of the body, since when it joins with the soul it forms the complete nature of a human being. But both human and divine natures are complete, and therefore cannot join one another as the body and soul are joined. For this reason N. says that in Jesus Christ there are "two natures and two persons or hypostases." This, along with his affirmation of a "voluntary union" between both, as if they were two persons who agree in their wishes, was what created confusion and caused his teaching to be rejected.

Eventually the followers of N. took refuge in Persia, where for a period of time a church commonly known as Assyrian Christians, and which other Christians call the Nestorian church, flourished. Today only a few thousand remain, dispersed throughout the Levant, and some are in Europe and the Americas.

———

JLG

Newbigin, J. E. Lesslie (1909–98).

English missiologist, bishop, and ecumenical leader. N. received his education at Cambridge University, where through the British Christian Student movement he came to know and accept the Christian faith. In 1936 he was ordained in the Church of Scotland to serve as a missionary in India. His work as a missionary included being an interpreter of the work and development of the Church of South India, of which he was bishop from 1947 to 1959.

After his term as bishop, he served in the International Missionary Council and was one of the missiological architects who made from that council the Unit of Mission and Evangelism of the ⇒World Council of Churches in 1961. His passion for India made him return and remain in that country until 1974.

From 1974 until 1979 he was professor of mission and ecumenism in Selly Oakes College in Birmingham and moderator of the United Reformed Church. During those years and upon his return to his place of birth, N. observed the deterioration of the Christian church in the West. His works *Foolishness to the Greeks* (1986) and *The Gospel in a Pluralistic Society* (1998) demonstrate a critical missiological reflection that is directed to the churches of the West. Moreover, as a good missiologist, he also organized the group The Gospel and Our Culture, the purpose of which is to continue that reflection and develop missionary strategies for the West.

His contribution and ecumenical style are evident in many articles and studies published around the world and especially in his books *The Household of God* (1953) and *The Open Secret: Sketches of a Missionary Theology* (1978).

———

CCO

Newman, John Henry (1801–90).

Theologian, philosopher of education, apologetic writer, and cardinal of the Roman Catholic Church. Born in England, he graduated from Oxford University, where he was a tutor and preacher until his conversion to Roman Catholicism in 1845.

As intellectual leader of the Oxford movement, N. influenced the Anglican Church in its eventual restoration of patristic teachings and liturgical practices. One of his best-known works is *The Idea of a University Defined and Illustrated*, in which he emphasizes general education as the center of university education, with a strong devotion to the liberal arts. Following this was *Apologia pro vita sua*, in which he speaks about the development of his own religious ideas and his Catholic conversion. The work that possibly had the strongest impact, especially on subsequent generations, was his *Essay on the Development of Christian Doctrine*, in which he introduces the concept as well as the terminology of "doctrinal development" to the modern theological vocabulary.

N. was a controversial public figure who caused a commotion because of his ecumenical ideas. His life was divided between his Anglicanism and his subsequent Catholicism. In both contexts he made use of Protestant ideas, such as justification by faith and the importance attributed to biblical exposition and preaching. For this and other reasons, he has been considered by some (for example, Jaroslav Pelikan) as the most important theological thinker of modernity.

———

NRG

Nicaea, Council of (325).

Generally recognized as the first of the great ecumenical ⇒councils. It was convened by the Emperor Constantine, and its principal action was to condemn the teachings of ⇒Arius and to formulate a creed that, with some additions and changes, is still recited in Western as well as in Eastern churches as the Nicene Creed.

The teachings of ⇒Arius had created a deep division in the Eastern church, since while ⇒Alexander of Alexandria had condemned and deposed him, several of the disciples of ⇒Lucian of Antioch, to whom Arius had appealed as "fellow Lucianists," defended him. The emperor asked ⇒Hosius of Cordoba to intervene in the matter and seek reconciliation between the parties. But after meeting with several bishops in the East, Hosius informed him that the topic which was disputed was very serious and that there was no hope of reaching a reconciliation. It was then that Constantine convened a great universal council that was to meet in Nicaea, near

Constantinople, in 325, to discuss the Arian question as well as a host of administrative matters it was necessary to resolve now that the persecutions were over. For those who had undergone persecutions, the meeting of such an assembly, sponsored by the emperor, was nothing short of a miracle. More than three hundred bishops from all the regions of the empire, and even from beyond its borders, met in Nicaea. For the majority of these bishops, the Arian controversy was not a matter of great concern. Aside from the Lucianists who were willing to defend Arius, and the small group formed by Alexander and his followers on the opposing side, the rest of the bishops were more preoccupied with the practical matters of the life of the church. If something about the Trinitarian doctrine concerned them, it was the fear of Sabellianism (⇒Sabellius), for they knew very little about the teachings of Arius. But when the Lucianists, led by ⇒Eusebius of Nicomedia, expounded their teaching with great clarity, the majority of bishops rejected it. It seemed to them, with good reason, that Arius made of the Word or Son of God a being who was inferior to the Father, and in some sense less than God. This in turn implied that the church worshiped a creature.

After some attempts to show its rejection of Arianism by means of biblical quotations, the council decided to promulgate a creed, apparently based on the ancient baptismal formula of the church of Caesarea, and originally proposed by ⇒Eusebius of Caesarea. But to that creed were added several phrases and clarifications that clearly demonstrated that Arianism was not acceptable. Those phrases are still recited in the Nicene Creed (which is not exactly the same one that was adopted in Nicaea, but rather that creed with some changes). There it is stated, for example, that Jesus Christ is "begotten . . . of the substance of the Father; God of God; light of light; true God of true God; begotten, not made; consubstantial [*homoousios*] with the Father."

In addition, in order to make things very clear, the council added a series of anathemas that were clearly directed against Arius and the Lucianists: "To those who say, then, that there was [a time] when the Son of God did not exist, and that he did not exist before he was begotten, and that he was made of the things that are not, or that he was formed from another substance [hypostasis] or essence [*ousia*], or that he is a creature, or that he is mutable and variable, the Catholic church anathematizes these."

When the council ended, its decisions were not accepted without resistance. When many of the bishops returned to their sees, they again faced a situation in which Sabellianism seemed to be a more serious threat than Arianism. Some of the formulas adopted in Nicaea, and above all the *homoousios*, lent themselves to Sabellian interpretations. It is interesting to read the way in which Eusebius of Caesarea tries to explain to his congregation what the council decided, since in his explanations it is clear that he was not entirely convinced. Criticism soon surfaced against what was done in Nicaea. At the same time, Eusebius of Nicomedia and others intervened before the emperor, asking him to undo what was done. The day arrived when Constantine vindicated Arius and his followers, and on his deathbed Constantine himself was baptized by the Arian Eusebius of Nicomedia. A long period in which the Nicene cause suffered setbacks followed this. Several of those in Nicaea who had condemned Arius were deposed, among them ⇒Marcellus of Ancyra and ⇒Eustathius of Antioch. During those years, the great defender of Nicaea was ⇒Athanasius, who because of his defense had to endure several periods of exile. When Constantius became the only emperor, as ⇒Jerome said, "The world awoke from a deep slumber and discovered that it had become Arian." But in the end the Nicene cause began to prosper, convincing more and more bishops and theologians and clarifying its positions in order to answer the objections of those who were afraid of falling into Sabellianism. Finally, in the Council of ⇒Constantinople in 381, the decision of the Council of Nicaea was reaffirmed.

JLG

Nicaea, Second Council of (754).

Generally recognized as the seventh of the great ecumenical ⇒councils, it officially put an end to the iconoclastic controversy. In the year 725 the Byzantine emperor Leo III had promulgated the first of a series of edicts against the use of images in Christian worship. An extended controversy, in which ⇒Germanus of Constantinople, ⇒Theodore the Studite, and ⇒John of Damascus distinguished themselves, followed this event. In 754 an iconoclastic council had forbidden the use of images on the basis of the prohibitions of the Decalogue and on the basis of the nature of the divine, which is indescribable. Facing such a position, the "iconodules" insisted that they were worshiping not the images, but the divine reality behind them. In addition, they argued that since in Jesus Christ God has come to us in human form, this provides a basis for representing the divine in a physical form. The council declared: "It is permissible to represent Christ, the Mother of God [*Theotokos*], the angels and the saints, because whoever contemplates such representations is led to think about their prototypes and is encouraged to imitate them. The worship [*proskynesis*, genuflection] that is rendered to the images is directed to their prototypes and is different from the worship [*latria*] that is due only to God."

Although after these decisions there was resistance to the use of images in various sectors of the church, especially in the Carolingian kingdom, it can be said that with this decision the controversy ended, and it would not arise again in all its power until the time of the Protestant Reformation.

—

JLG

Nicephorus (ca. 758–829).

Patriarch of Constantinople from 806 to 815. At first he clashed with ⇒Theodore the Studite because of imperial policy, but then he became the great ally of Theodore in his struggle in defense of images. He was deposed from the patriarchy because of his opposition to the iconoclastic imperial edicts. In spite of this, he continued writing in defense of images. His chief work is *Antirrheticus*, in three volumes, in which he attacks the positions and policy of Emperor Constantine "Copronymus" (thus dubbed for having soiled the waters of his baptism).

—

JLG

Nicetas Stethatos (11th Century).

Byzantine monk who wrote against Western practices such as priestly celibacy and the use of unleavened bread in Communion. His brief treatise, as well as the response of Cardinal ⇒Humbert, show that behind the theological debate there were deep prejudices on both sides.

—

JLG

Nicholas of Cusa ⇒Cusa, Nicholas of

Nida, Eugene A. (1914–).

North American missiologist, linguist, and biblical translator who is known for his work in the translation of the Bible. He was founder of the journal *The Bible Translator*, in which he was able to communicate in a clear manner and with aca-

demic rigor an analysis of the problems in the linguistic processes in Bible translation, the challenge and complexity of cross-cultural communication, basic and practical concepts in Bible translation, and the structure and form of communicating meaning from one language to another.

The most important contribution of N. to linguistics and to the translation of the Bible is the "theory of dynamic equivalence," proposed in his work *Toward a Science of Translating* (1964). Other important works are *Morphology: The Descriptive Analysis of Words* (1949) and *Message and Mission* (1960).

—

CCO

Niebuhr, H. Richard (1894–1962).

It is significant that two members of the same family had so much influence on the development of theological and ethical thought in the United States. N. was born in Missouri and, like his brother ⇒Reinhold, was educated at Elmhurst College, where he later served as president, and at Eden Theological Seminary. He also studied at Washington University and at Yale University, where he served as professor of theology and ethics. A great number of the ethics professors who now teach in theological seminaries and universities are disciples, directly or indirectly, of N.

For N., theology must always be practiced in a practical context focused on the activity of God in history. His theoretical works represent a synthesis between theology, sociology, and ethics. In *The Responsible Self* (1963) he gives his most mature thought. Three theories of the human being lead to three different ways of interpreting our ethical responsibility. When human beings see themselves as political beings or as citizens, ethical responsibility is defined in terms of obedience to laws or rules. Christian life is then legalistic and obedient to the commandments of God. When people interpret themselves as creators of institutions and artifacts, ethics emphasizes the fulfillment of ends or goals. In such a case Christian life consists in conforming to the ends that God dictates, whether it is the search for the kingdom or the creation of a society ruled by peace and justice. Finally, humans may see themselves as beings in dialogue who respond to the multiple challenges that appear in their life and historical moment. The human being, more than anything else, is a being who is responsible before God, before other human beings, and before all of creation. According to N., our action should be interpreted as a response to God, the Being who acts through all that takes place in creation. Therefore, in all that we do we should act in a way that fits with the creative, ordering, and redeeming activity of God. The result of this vision is that it increases the space in which we are called to act responsibly.

N. rejected the idealism that dominated the ethical thought of his period. Human beings are not to seek to fulfill personal or social ideals. They constitute themselves through the multiple material relations that they establish with other human beings and with nature. Their sin is not their disobedience to commandments and moral rules, nor their lack of vision or determination in fulfilling ideals or moral goals. Their sin is their infidelity, their lack of faith, and their irresponsibility toward God and others in their historical existence. Their responsibility is to contain evil and promote the good for all people and communities to which they belong.

Among the chief works of N. are *The Social Sources of Denominationalism* (1929), *The Kingdom of God in America* (1937), *The Meaning of Revelation* (1941), *Christ and Culture* (1951), and *Radical Monotheism and Western Culture* (1960).

—

IG

Niebuhr, Reinhold (1892–1971).

Along with Paul ⇒Ramsey, the theologian who has had the greatest influence on the political life of the United States. He was a pastor in the United Church of Christ, and studied in Elmhurst College and in Eden Theological Seminary. He served as pastor of Bethel Evangelical Church in Detroit (1915–28) and as professor of theological ethics at Union Theological Seminary, New York. From the beginning of his ministry, N. became involved in the social and political spheres. He was a counselor to several presidents and political executives. In his youth he belonged to the Fellowship of Socialist Christians and to the pacifist movement. Later he abandoned the socialist ideals and the pacifist movement and joined the progressive liberal wing of the Democratic Party. Faced with the Nazi threat, he encouraged Christians to take part in the struggles for peace and justice, even though this might imply the need to use violence. His political realism was thus born.

His chief contribution to theological thought and the basis of his historical and political realism was his teaching on human nature and sin. Following ⇒Augustine, ⇒Kierkegaard, ⇒Calvin, and ⇒Luther, and basing himself on the Bible, N. rejected the notion that we human beings can significantly alter our moral attitudes. Neither religious piety nor education and social reforms make us morally better. N. also insisted that collective life is more prone to sin than personal life.

For N., human nature is transcendent and free, and at the same time it is also finite and tied to the limits of nature. As transcendent beings, we recognize that it is God alone who provides us with the norms that lead to the fulfillment of our being. As finite beings, we know that death threatens and makes us feel that our life has no meaning. This tension in our being leads us to sin. Sin is a manifestation of our wish to resolve the anxiety that is born of our dual being. Sin is pride and idolatry. Sin makes us arrogant, makes us pretend that we can live in terms of ideal possibilities that, in moments of honest introspection, we know we cannot achieve within the limits and finitude of our historical existence. When we are honest with ourselves, we also recognize that every historical action carries with it imperfections that are inevitable.

According to N., love is the norm of history and the fundamental law of all human reality. Love that voluntarily sacrifices itself for others constitutes "the possible impossibility of history." This love cannot be realized in history, but its historical relevance is very significant, for it shows that the most we can achieve in history are approximations of love. At the same time it points to the possibility of making any situation more just.

Although we cannot realize social and personal projects of a utopian character, two elements of our faith free us from falling into social pessimism: our security in the love and mercy of God, who gives God's Son so that we may have life; and the resurrection of Christ. These two theological convictions give us confidence and certainty in the final victory of the kingdom of God. This liberates us and motivates us to struggle to improve the human condition in the light of our real possibilities, in the full consciousness of our sin and finitude. We have the freedom to commit ourselves to the fulfillment of penultimate moral goals, knowing that what assures us of the final victory is the forgiveness and love of God.

Among his chief works are *Moral Man and Immoral Society* (1932), *The Nature and Destiny of Man*, 2 vols. (1941–43), *Faith and History* (1949), and *Christian Realism and Political Problems* (1953).

—

IG

Niemöller, Martin (1892–1984). German pastor and leader of the Confessing Church in Germany. A fervent nationalist, at first he supported Hitler, but it did not take him long to recognize his error. His congregation became famous for its resistance to the Nazi movement. N. also publicly opposed the movement of the German Christians, who not only supported the politics of Hitler but also wanted to eliminate the Old Testament and all that is "Judaizing" from the New and to reinterpret Jesus in a way that would justify the Nazi philosophy.

IG

Nietzsche, Friedrich (1844–1900). German philosopher and writer who has influenced theologians, philosophers, and other intellectuals in modern and postmodern times. He was born into a devout Lutheran family in which his grandfathers and his father were pastors, although his father, who was demented, died during N.'s infancy. In his youth, N. studied theology, and then in Leipzig he was the favorite disciple of the classicist F. W. Ritschl, who considered him his most brilliant student. Ritschl recommended him for a position in Basel, which he obtained before receiving his doctorate. In Leipzig he was influenced by A. Schopenhauer and R. Wagner, although he later abandoned them (especially Wagner) because of their chauvinism and anti-Semitism. During that time he explored aesthetics as a starting point of knowledge.

His intellectual legacy is located in his exploration of the relationship between suffering and culture(s). He maintains that the Enlightenment leads us to declare the "death of God" culturally. He does not propose atheism, but simply affirms that ideologically societies exist without God and that their ideological powers must be unmasked. His call is to a "Wille zur Macht," badly translated as a "will to power," but which in reality is a "will to be," to assert the creativity and vitality of the "Übermensch," the "superhuman." This superhuman is not a dictator, but rather a person whose creativity stands out and who does not succumb to the ideological criterion of the masses. Because of this it seemed to him that Christianity, with its invitation to turn the other cheek and its ascetic tendencies, was a religion for the weak.

Among his most important works are his *Thus Spoke Zarathustra* (1883–85) and *Beyond Good and Evil* (1886).

ALG

Niles, Daniel Thambyrajah (1908–70). A native of Sri Lanka, N. came from a family with Methodist roots dating back to 1821. He studied theology at the Seminary of Bangalore in India, and then obtained his doctorate at the University of London.

N. was an ecumenical leader and theologian of evangelism. The motto "evangelism is a beggar telling another beggar where to find food" sums up his theology of evangelism, which is filled with an ecumenical spirit that joins the riches of the Orthodox tradition, his Protestant background, and the spirituality of the religious traditions in Asia, especially Hinduism. Even with this diverse theological integration, N. proposes a discontinuity between the non-Christian traditions and the Christian faith.

N. was executive secretary of the Division of Evangelism of the ⇒World Council of Churches and strongly promoted the ecumenical spirit in the local congregation. In 1957 N. founded a council of churches in East Asia. This council became the precursor of other ecumenical movements and councils in the region. Such works of his as *That They May Have Life* (1952), *Upon the Earth* (1962), *Who is Jesus* (1968), and *A Testament of Faith* (1972) reflect the enormous work and breadth of his evangelizing and ecumenical ministry. As few have done in the twentieth century, N. united a passion for evangelizing with openness and ecumenical conviction.

CCO

Nobili, Roberto de (1577–1656). Jesuit priest who was born in Italy and died in Madras, India. Together with ⇒Francis Xavier and ⇒Ricci, N. can be considered one of the most creative missionaries in his context. The Jesuits sent him to Madura, India, in 1606, where he noticed the great resistance to the Christian faith on the part of the Hindus. To belong to Christianity meant to be Portuguese and therefore was not culturally acceptable.

As he faced this situation, he began to study Tamil and Sanskrit as well as Indian philosophy and religious literature. He decided to become a *sannyasis* or "holy man" of India, adopting such a man's clothing, diet, and many other customs. In addition, he decided to find points of contact between the Christian faith and Hinduism, distancing himself from the traditional missionary form of confrontation.

It was evident that N. appropriated and accepted Hindu customs without much critical reflection, obscuring the boundaries between the Christian faith and religious Hindu practices. His missionary strategy created enormous controversies with other missionary groups, especially because of his acceptance of the caste system of India. N. focused his efforts on the higher castes of India, although he never forgot the need to evangelize the lower castes. His missionary method, which is known today as adaptation of Christianity to a non-Christian culture, provoked strong opposition. Nevertheless, it was approved by Pope Gregory XV in 1623 in the apostolic constitution *Romanae Sedis antistes.*

CCO

Noetus of Smyrna (2nd century). Obscure person who apparently began to teach a doctrine in Smyrna according to which the Father, the Son, and the Holy Spirit are only three ways in which God is revealed. ⇒Hippolytus wrote a treatise *Against Noetus,* which is our chief source of information about him. He is considered a precursor of the teachings of ⇒Sabellius.

JLG

Noll, Mark A. (1946–). North American historian and professor. He teaches at Wheaton College, where he received his bachelor's degree with a specialization in English. After graduating from Wheaton, N. pursued at Vanderbilt University his doctoral studies in the history of Christianity, completing them in 1975. A member of the faculty of Wheaton since 1979, N. has taught in the most prestigious universities of the country. In his lectures and publications he defends the traditional evangelical point of view in the areas of theology and politics, the history of Protestantism, and the cultural and literary history of the Bible. He is recognized worldwide as one of the most distinguished historians of Christianity.

HMT

Novatian (3rd century). It is believed that he was a native of Rome, where he also practiced his ministry. Together with a group of followers, he broke away from the Roman episcopacy, becoming an "antipope" and leader of a separatist faction. The controversy that led him to this had to do with the restitution of those who had not remained faithful in times of persecution. With harsh rigorism, N. and his party denied the possibility of restoring the apostates.

N. also wrote a treatise *On the Trinity.* The theological contributions of N. on this theme were the most important since the days of ⇒Tertullian. In that work he defended the full divinity of Jesus, although the purpose of his writing was to refute Sabellianism (⇒Sabellius) by demonstrating that the Father and the Son are different persons. The emphasis on this last point and the kenotic tension led him to subordinate the Son to the Father, and for that reason many take him as a forerunner of Arianism (⇒Arius). But such a conclusion is incorrect, since the disciples of N. were among those who strongly attacked Arianism in the Council of ⇒Nicaea. Thus the theological legacy of N. was of great importance in the development of the Trinitarian doctrine.

GC

Nuñez, Emilio Antonio (1923–). Latin American theologian, a native of Guatemala, N. is known as one of the evangelical theologians associated with the ⇒Fraternidad Teológica Latinoamericana and as one of the critics of liberation theology in Latin America. Among his works are *Teología de la Liberación* (1984; Liberation Theology) and *Crisis in Latin America: An Evangelical Perspective* (1989), written with William David Taylor.

CCO

Nygren, Anders (1890–1971). One of the most influential representatives of the Lundensian school of theology, thus named for its origin in the Swedish University of Lund. He was ordained to the ministry in the Lutheran Church of Sweden in 1921, at the same time that he accepted the post of instructor in the faculty of theology in the University of Lund. In 1924 he was promoted to professor of systematic theology and ethics. In 1948 he was elected bishop of the diocese of Lund, a post he held until his retirement in 1959. Since the time of his participation in the Conference on Faith and Order in Lausanne (1927), he took a very active part in the ecumenical movement. He exercised a very important leadership role in the Edinburgh Conference on Faith and Order (1937) and presided over the commission on Christ and the Church of that organization for more than a decade. He was one of the leaders who shaped the Lutheran World Federation, serving as its first president (1947–1952).

Although his first writings were in the area of philosophy of religion, his interests were very broad and included historical theology, ethics, and biblical exegesis. Part of his method was what the Lundensians called the "investigation of motifs," which consisted in following certain motifs or themes throughout history in order to determine and clarify theological options. A classic work in this sense is his *Agape and Eros*, in which he discusses different types of love, contrasting Christian agape and the eros of Platonic philosophy. Among his most important works, which are accessible in English translations, are *Religious Apriori: Its Philosophical Presuppositions and Theological Implications* (1921), *The Scientific Foundation of Dogmatics* (1922), *Basic Questions in Ethics* (1926), *Agape and Eros* (1932), *Primitive Christianity and the Reformation* (1932), *Commentary on the Epistle to the Romans* (1949), *The Gospel of God* (1951), and *Christ and His Church* (1956).

——
JDR

Obadiah of Babilonia. Fictitious name that the author of *Histories of the Apostles* gave himself. These *Histories*, apparently composed by a Frankish author in the sixth century, contain legends about each of the apostles. The author seems to have taken the name Obadiah from the legend of ⇒Abgar, which cites a person by that name who, according to other traditions, became bishop of Babylon.

——
JLG

Ochino, Bernardino (1487–1564). Reformer born in Siena, Italy. While he was still young he joined the Franciscans under the impact of ⇒Savonarola. In 1534 he joined the Capuchins, and on two occasions was elected general of the order. Because of his exemplary life and his inspired oratory he was recognized as a holy and pious man. In 1541, through the teaching and influence of Juan de ⇒Valdés, he accepted and allied himself with the positions of the Protestant Reformation. When representatives of the Roman Catholic Church were about to put him on trial before the recently reorganized Inquisition, he fled from Italy and found refuge in Geneva, Basel, Augsburg, Strassburg, and finally London, where he was a preacher to the Italian Protestant community. Upon returning to Switzerland in 1553, he settled in Zurich, where his positions on matters of doctrine and morality, and especially his opposition to the doctrine of the Trinity and his defense of polygamy, earned him the opposition of the Calvinists. Because of this he was exiled in 1563. From then on he wandered about until he became a victim of the plague.

Among his works are *Thirty Dialogues on the Trinity*, in two books, several *Sermons*, *Six Hundred Apologies against the Abuses and Errors of the Papal Synagogue*, *Defense of the Doctrine of the Supper,* and *Dialogues on the Mass*.

——
CS/JDR

Ockham (or Occam), William of (ca. 1280–ca. 1349). English Franciscan philosopher of the "Spiritual" branch who, like several other coreligionists, found refuge in the court of Emperor Louis of Bavaria. From there he wrote several treatises on the authority of the pope. Their fundamental argument was that civil authority has been instituted by God independently of religious authority. His dispute with John XXII was based on the fact that this pope had declared his opposition to "evangelical poverty" as understood by O. and the Spiritual Franciscans. For these reasons he was excommunicated in 1328 and expelled from the Order of Friars Minor in 1331, although his branch of the Franciscans came to recognize him as its general.

With regard to universals, it has often been stated that O. was a nominalist. The fact is that, in contrast to the true nominalism of ⇒Roscelin and others of earlier times, O. and the majority of his colleagues defended a realist conceptualism, maintaining that universals really existed, although only as concepts and only in the mind.

O. did not believe that reason could get very far in theological matters. This belief was based on the distinction, which was typical of the nominalism of the end of the Middle Ages, between the *potentia Dei absoluta* (absolute power of God) and the *potentia Dei ordinata* (ordered power of God). By God's *potentia absoluta*, God could and can do anything, because even reason itself is beneath such absolute power. But through God's own decision the divine power is limited, establishing and following a certain order. The power of God that functions under this order is the *potentia ordinata*. In all of this we see the extreme expression of "voluntarism," which had characterized the Franciscan tradition for a long time. According to this tradition, will has primacy over reason in God. That which establishes the principles of reason is the absolutely free will of God. As some would say, "It is not as exact to say that God does what is good as it is to say that what God does is good"—in other words, the sovereign will of God is what determines what is good and what is not.

All of this led O. and his school to assert that, while they believed the doctrines of the church to be truths revealed and established by God, they did not believe that they could be proven by reason. The process of distancing faith from reason, which had been undermining traditional scholasticism for some time, was thus completed.

———
JLG

Odo also ⇒Eudes

Odo of Beauvais (9th century).
Bishop of that city who opposed some monks who claimed that there is one single soul, in which all individual souls participate. At the request of O., ⇒Ratramnus intervened in the debate, chiefly through *Treatise on the Soul to Odo of Beauvais*.

———
JLG

Odo of Tournai [or of Cambrai] (?–1113).
Philosopher and theologian who was a native of Orleans. He adopted an extreme realism on the question of universals and used it to explain the doctrine of original sin. According to O., neither traducianism nor creationism correctly explain original sin, because the truth is that humanity is one in such a way that it was fully present in Adam. Thus literally "in Adam all sinned," in that all individual humans exist in the universal humanity, which was present in its totality in Adam.

———
JLG

Odo Rigaud (13th century).
Franciscan, successor of ⇒Alexander of Hales as a teacher in Paris and as a teacher of ⇒Bonaventure.

———
JLG

Oduyoye, Merci Amba (1934–).
Methodist, a native of Ghana and one of the best-known African feminists. She has been a member of the Executive Committee of the ⇒World Council of Churches, a president of the Ecumenical Association of Third World Theologians, and a leader in the African Conference of Churches. Currently she is the coeditor of a third volume on the history of the ecumenical movement. O. is an author of several theological works, such as *Hearing and Knowing: Reflections on Christianity in Africa* (1986), *The Will to Arise: Women, Tradition, and the Church in Africa* (1992), and *Daughters of Anowa* (1995).

———
CCO

Oecolampadius, John (1482–1531).
His original name was Hussgen. He was a Protestant reformer who was born in Weinsberg and died in Basel. After studying in the humanities in his native country, he went to Bologna to pursue a career in law. In 1499 his theological interests led him once more to Bologna and Heidelberg, where he devoted himself to studies in scholastic theology and mysticism.

He established friendships with ⇒Melanchthon, ⇒Brenz, ⇒Capito, and ⇒Erasmus, and these contacts led him to reconsider his Roman Catholic roots. In 1515 he was parish priest in Basel, and in 1520 he surprised those who thought he was imbued with Protestant ideas, embracing the monastic life in Altmünster. About that time he was a strong partisan of ecclesiastical celibacy, although later on (1528) he married the widow Rosenblatt. Erasmus gave him a tongue-lashing with his satire because of this weakness. Shortly afterward he had to leave Altmünster because of his Lutheran proclivities. When he left the cloister he was without resources. He went on to Basel where, with his eloquence, he did more than anyone else to consolidate the Reformation, making Erasmus say that in his writings there was something capable of seducing and deceiving, if it were possible, even the elect. Lutheran in regard to justification by faith and Zwinglian in his interpretation of the Lord's Supper, he participated on the side of ⇒Zwingli against ⇒Luther in the colloquy of Marburg, where he had to endure the anathemas of the latter.

———
JDR

Oikonomos, Constantine (1780–1857).
Conservative Greek theologian, opponent of Theocletus ⇒Pharmaquides. He held fast to everything that was traditional, even to the extent of writing a work in four volumes, *On the Seventy Translators of the Old Testament*, in which he argued that the ancient legends about the inspiration of the Septuagint were true and that to deny them was to reject the inspiration of the Scriptures. For the same reason he opposed the translation of the Bible

into modern Greek and was against the autonomy of the Greek Orthodox Church, which according to him should continue to be subject to the patriarch of Constantinople, even though Greece was now independent from Turkey.

———

JLG

Oldham, Joseph H. (1874–1969).
Englishman who was born of Scottish missionary parents in India. O. is one of the pioneers of the ecumenical movement of the twentieth century. In 1908 he was named secretary in charge of organizing the World Missionary Conference of Edinburgh in 1910. Subsequently he was named secretary of the Committee on Continuity of the conference and in 1912 founded the *International Review of Missions*, one of the most important journals in the field of missiology.

His work in the missionary and ecumenical world led him to see the problems of colonialism, and in 1924 his book *Christianity and the Race Problem* became a touchstone for the theological discussion of racism and the encounter between cultures. Moreover, O. promoted a conciliatory spirit after the First World War and warned about the danger that was developing in Germany under Nazi power.

O. suffered from a hearing problem that prevented him from making himself known as well as other colleagues of his time.

———

CCO

Olevianus, Caspar (1536–87).
German reformer who was born and died in Trier. He studied law in Paris, Orleans, and Bourges (where he deepened his knowledge of Calvinist doctrine). Later he moved to Geneva, where he studied theology. In 1559 he obtained a teaching post in Trier. There he wished to establish the Reformation according to the Calvinist perspective, but his attempt estranged him from the leaders and inhabitants of the region. He had to flee to Heidelberg, where he was professor, church counselor, and preacher of the Palatinate. In that post he collaborated in the drafting of the ⇒Heidelberg Catechism (1562).

———

JDR/ALN

Olivetan, Pierre Robert (1506–38).
A relative of John ⇒Calvin, with whom he was associated in the University of Paris. Together they worked on the French version of the Bible. It is possible that he was the predecessor of Guillaume ⇒Farel in the dissemination of the teachings of the Reformation in Geneva. In Neuchâtel he worked with the Waldensians of the Piedmont. He prepared a French translation of the Bible for them, which appeared in June of 1535.

———

JDRR

Optatus of Milevis (4th century).
Bishop of that city in the region of Numidia. He wrote chiefly against the Donatists (⇒Donatus) and against their second-generation head, ⇒Parmenianus. His principal work is *On the Schism of the Donatists, Against Parmenianus*, in seven books (six were published initially, and the seventh was added later). He rejected the argument of the Donatists that the church is a community of the righteous, and insisted on the distinction between the visible and the invisible church. In addition he argued, also against the Donatists, that the validity of the sacrament does not depend on the virtue or the faith of the one who administers it. In all of this, O. was a forerunner of the theology of ⇒Augustine, who built on the foundations that O. had laid.

———

JLG

Orange, Synod of (529).
The second of two synods which met in that city. (The first, in 441, was presided over by ⇒Hilary of Arles and dealt mainly with legislative matters.) The teaching of ⇒Augustine was reasserted there and the Semi-Pelagianism of ⇒Faustus of Riez and others was rejected. The synod reasserted the Augustinian doctrine of original sin and its consequences, which corrupt the human being in its totality, in such a way that it can no longer choose the good. Therefore it also reasserted the Augustinian doctrine of the necessity and primacy of grace for salvation. In short, the synod rejected any position that would locate the *initium fidei* (the beginning of faith) in human decision and not in the action of God. However, it conjoined prevenient grace with the act of baptism, thus undermining Augustine's insistence on grace given only to the elect. The synod also rejected double predestination, condemning those who said that God predestined some for evil and perdition. It was through the decrees of this synod, and later through the writings of ⇒Gregory the Great, that the Middle Ages read and interpreted the works of Augustine.

———

JLG

Origen (ca. 185–ca. 254). One of the most prolific and original Christian authors of antiquity. He was born in Alexandria of a Christian family. His father, Leonidas, suffered martyrdom in 202 during the persecution of Septimius Severus. It is said that on that occasion the only way his mother could keep O. from offering himself as a martyr was by hiding his clothes. All of this led O. to write an *Exhortation to Martyrdom*. Shortly after that date O. began to teach literature and philosophy as a means of earning a living. Bishop Demetrius entrusted him with the instruction of catechumens, even though O. was still an adolescent. His fame spread rapidly, and soon the school where O. taught began to receive visitors who came to listen to his lectures. Among such visitors were future bishops and theologians such as ⇒Gregory of Neocaesarea as well as distinguished persons such as the governor of Arabia and the emperor's mother.

O. had strong mystical and ascetic tendencies. In order to practice what he considered the "philosophical life," he sold his books in exchange for a very small pension that would allow him to live in extreme austerity. When his sexual impulses seemed to him to interfere with his studies and devotion, he emasculated himself. This was one of the reasons for a series of conflicts with the new bishop of Alexandria, ⇒Heraclas, who had previously been his disciple. Finally O. left the city and established himself in Caesarea. There he was imprisoned and tortured during the persecution of Decius. When he was set free, he found refuge in Tyre, where he died shortly afterward, when he was almost seventy years old.

The literary production of O. was enormous. His surviving writings are more voluminous than the sum of those of all the other Christian authors of the first three centuries. His *Hexapla* was a monumental work of biblical scholarship that unfortunately did not survive in its entirety. It was a presentation in six parallel columns of the Hebrew text of the Old Testament, a transliteration in Greek characters, and the four most common versions which at that time circulated in Greek. When, as in the case of the Psalms, there were more versions, they were also included, with the result that some sections of *Hexapla* had up to nine columns. O. added to all of this a system of symbols to indicate the differences (alterations, omissions, and additions) between the Hebrew and the Greek text. Thus O. produced a work that would not be surpassed until the modern period.

In addition to homilies and brief explanations of difficult passages (the *scholia*), in the field of biblical studies O. produced commentaries on several books of the Bible. Ample portions of those he wrote on Matthew, John, Romans, and the Song of Songs are extant.

In defense of Christianity, O. wrote *Against Celsus*. Celsus was a philosopher of the Platonic tradition who some time before had written a detailed and very well-informed attack against Christian teachings and practices. At the request of a friend, O. wrote a refutation in which he quoted Celsus extensively, with the result that O.'s work is the only way we have of knowing what Celsus wrote.

The chief theological work of O. is *On First Principles*, in four books. Most of it survives only in a Latin translation by ⇒Rufinus, an admirer of O., who for that reason made an effort to eliminate or mitigate in the work of the great Alexandrian teacher anything that might appear to be heterodox. Thus although this work is useful for following the general order of O.'s thought, it must always be compared and corrected through other writings of his that have not been altered by well-intentioned attempts to make him appear more orthodox.

O. bases his theology on the Scriptures and on his own philosophical convictions, which generally fell within the Platonic tradition. For him the Bible is certainly divine revelation and the source of all Christian doctrine, but that Bible should be interpreted in such a way that it does not contradict reason (that is, reason as the Platonic tradition understood it), and this is why O. tended to favor allegorical interpretation. According to O., the biblical texts have a literal meaning, another which is moral, and another which is intellectual. This is parallel to the presence in humans of body, soul, and spirit, and is based on what ⇒Philo had previously said and done. But O. did not always follow this triple scheme; instead he frequently included only the allegorical sense, and at times found a multitude of different senses in the same text. As a guide in his biblical interpretation, in addition to this allegorical inclination, O. maintained that nothing should be said of God that is unworthy of God's majesty, and that every text should be interpreted in the light of the rest of the Scriptures and the rule of faith.

All of this led O. to a series of interpretations that appear arbitrary and at times even preposterous. Thus, for example, wherever the word "horse" appears, it means "voice"; "thigh" means "beginning," and so on. Consequently, in the twentieth century it was said that O.'s exegesis is like a spiritual crossword puzzle whose solution is hidden in the mind of O. himself.

The God of O. is triune: Father, Son, and Holy Spirit. O. is not entirely clear about the relationship among the three, since at times he appears to affirm the complete divinity of the three persons, while at other times he appears to make distinctions among them on the basis of subordinationism. For this reason, among the followers of O., historians distinguish between an "Origenism of the right" and another "of the left." While the first emphasizes the divinity of the Son (and, when in question, that of the Holy Spirit), the second emphasizes his subordination, making of him almost a secondary god or an intermediate being between God and creatures. Arianism (⇒Arius) emerged from within this second branch of Origenism.

According to O., this God is the creator of all that exists. But considering that in the first chapters of Genesis there are two parallel stories of creation, and uniting this fact with his Platonic perspective, O. came to the conclusion that creation is double. First, God produced a purely spiritual creation. It is of humanity in that state that Genesis says that it was "male and female," that is, there were no gender distinctions, for they were not corporeal. Then these spiritual beings fell into sin when they no longer contemplated the ineffable One, and God produced the present second creation, which is physical, and where the spirits reside temporarily until they are saved and return to their state of pure spirituality. This in turn led O. to theories about the preexistence and transmigration of souls, and to an entire hierarchy in which demons are nothing but spirits who have fallen lower than humans, and angels are essentially spirits themselves, although in a higher state. Such theories were never accepted by Christians in general, and they were soon officially rejected by the church.

God's purpose for this creation is a total restoration. This implies a return to the original creation, which was purely spiritual. Physical creation will disappear, and everything will be purely spiritual. This total restoration is such that even the devil will be saved, for otherwise God's plans would be frustrated. Moreover, since that restoration includes the return to the original freedom, which allowed the spirits to fall in the first place, O. was not sure whether other parallel processes are to follow this process. The restored spirits would have the free-dom that would allow them to fall again. On the other hand, although there could be an infinite series of future worlds, O. was sure that Jesus Christ would not suffer again, since his work of redemption is sufficient for eternity. Once more, it need not be said that such speculations were not generally accepted.

Jesus Christ is the Word of God made flesh. The Word has united itself with a spirit that had not fallen and with it has taken a human body. Thus, in Jesus Christ there is the equivalent of a human soul, although a soul that has not sinned. In his incarnation, Jesus Christ penetrated this world where the devil dominated and thus began his victorious work. In his crucifixion and death, he entered the deepest dens of the devil. With his resurrection and ascension he broke the power of the devil in the abyss of death, and therefore the faithful can now follow him on his path of return to the spiritual heaven.

In this way of viewing the saving work of Jesus Christ, the teaching of O. is very much like that of ⇒Irenaeus and other ancient Christian authors. But to this O. added a broad interpretation of the work of Jesus Christ as a messenger who comes from beyond to remind us that we are fallen spirits and to teach us the way of virtue and truth.

The impact of O. was enormous. His library in Caesarea was the chief source to which ⇒Eusebius of Caesarea turned for his historical studies. His teachings on the nature of God and God's relation to the Word and the Holy Spirit were the background of the Trinitarian controversies of the fourth century. His allegorical interpretation became a general practice, although seldom with the speculative flights of O. himself. His biblical studies were never equaled in Alexandria, and could well have inspired Antiochian theologians such as ⇒Theodore of Mopsuestia. For several centuries in the entire Eastern church, what was not Origenism was anti-Origenism. Rufinus translated some of his writings into Latin, through which the influence of O. extended to the West, although not with the power that it had in the East. In the end, several of his theories were rejected and even condemned as heretical. But in spite of this, O. continued to be respected and admired as the great wise man of antiquity, and his use of Platonic philosophy became an example that most theologians of the early Middle Ages followed.

———
JLG

Orosius, Paulus (ca. 380–420?).

Spanish priest who, having read some of the writings of ⇒Augustine, traveled to Africa to meet him. He took along a work of his, *Contra Priscilliano* (Against Priscillian), the reading of which inspired Augustine to write about the same subject. Augustine then sent him to Palestine with letters for ⇒Jerome. There O. collaborated with Jerome in the refutation of Pelagianism (⇒Pelagius). On his return to Africa, the reading of *The City of God* by Augustine inspired him to write seven books of *History against the Pagans*. In that history, just as Augustine had done in *The City of God*, he refuted the argument that the recent calamities had befallen Rome because the Romans were abandoning their gods in favor of Christianity. O. tells both the history of Rome and that of the rest of humanity with which he was acquainted, trying to demonstrate that calamities prior to the advent of Christianity were worse than the present ones and that history is in the hands of divine Providence, which punishes the ungodly and makes the nations fall because of their wickedness. *History* was widely read throughout the Middle Ages.

—

JLG

Orr, James (1844–1915).

Protestant theologian. He was a professor of apologetics and theology in Glasgow, under the auspices of the United Free Church of Scotland. His theology offers little originality. He devoted himself above all to propagating German thought, chiefly that of ⇒Ritschl. Among his works are *The Christian View of God* (1893), *The Ritschlian Theology and the Evangelical Faith* (1897), and *Essays on Ritschlianism* (1903).

—

ALN

Ortega, Miriam Ofelia (1936–).

Cuban Presbyterian pastor, feminist, and ecumenical theologian, part of the staff of and then adviser to the ⇒World Council of Churches, and rector of the Evangelical Theological Seminary in Matanzas, Cuba, until 2004. Elected as president of the World Council of Churches in 2006.

—

SHR

Osiander, Andreas (1498–1552).

Contemporary of ⇒Luther, whom he followed at first. O. succeeded in obtaining the conversion to Lutheranism of the grand master of the Teutonic Order, Albert of Brandenburg. Subsequently in the Colloquy of Marburg of 1529 he began to oppose the doctrines of Luther, which he continued to do from then on, publicly preaching with great acrimony against the one whom he now called a heresiarch. This angered Luther to such a point that it was said that O. had to arm himself while preaching in order to be able to defend himself against those who defended his old teacher. The essence of O.'s teaching is that God not only covers sins in virtue of the merits of Christ, as Luther said, but also sanctifies the heart and mind of the human being, and that this is so because Christ dwells in the human being in such a way that what God sees is not the wickedness of the sinner, but the essential righteousness of Christ. In other words, when God justifies the human being, God does so not simply by a nonimputation of sins, but because God dwells in the human being. What most disturbed the theologians of that time regarding the theories of O. was that this seemed to turn justification into a sort of deification. For this reason Luther and others attacked him repeatedly, particularly ⇒Calvin in the last editions of the *Institutes of the Christian Religion*. Among his works, which are numerous but which have been almost completely forgotten, those that deserve to be mentioned are *Coniecturas de ultimis temporibus* (Conjectures about the Last Times), *Harmoniae Evangelicae* (Gospel Harmonies), and *Biblia sacra*.

—

ALN

Otto, Rudolf (1869–1937).

German Lutheran theologian born near Hanover. A graduate of the University of Göttingen, he spent the greater part of his teaching career in Marburg. Although during his first years his theology reflected the influence of ⇒Ritschl, he was later influenced by colleagues such as the philosopher Edmund Husserl and the historian and theologian Ernst ⇒Troeltsch. Another important influence on the thought of O. was ⇒Schleiermacher, whose ideas served as a starting point for his reflections on religious experience. His most influential and important book was *The Idea of the Holy*, published in 1917. In it he deals with the theme of religious experience, presenting God as the *mysterium tremendum*, which is "completely other." In addition, he stood out through his writings on Hinduism, a subject in which he became interested after traveling in the East.

—

PAJ

Padilla, Carlos René (1932–). Ecuadorian Baptist missiologist who is a resident of Argentina. P., Samuel ⇒Escobar, and Orlando ⇒Costas were founding leaders of ⇒Fraternidad Teológica Latinoamericana (FTL), of which P. was secretary general for many years. In addition, P. stood out in the first meeting of the ⇒Lausanne Movement in 1974, when he stressed the dimension of social justice in the very nature of the gospel, before an audience that was not always sympathetic.

P. has been a writer and editor of many works in several languages. He is associate editor of the journal *International Bulletin of Missionary Research* and general editor of the journal *Mission*. P. has helped to develop in Latin America a theology of evangelical mission that is founded on the Scriptures, with a biblical hermeneutics that recognizes social conflict, and that is in dialogue with others on subjects such as ecclesiology, eschatology, and social justice. These aspects of his theology of mission are evident in his work *Mission between the Times* and in many of his articles in the journal of the FTL. P. represents a generation of Latin American evangelicals who are developing a contextual missional theology.

CCO

Paine, Thomas (1737–1809). Son of an English Quaker, he was born in Norfolk, England. He is famous for his revolutionary activities and pamphlets against the monarchy and in favor of the revolutions in the United States and France. Like many of his revolutionary colleagues, P. held to a deist philosophy, which was based on a high concept of natural law in both morality and human reason. Although he was not original in his ideas, P. was able to express complex ideas clearly and simply for the common people. His book *The Age of Reason* (1794) criticizes the institutional church as an instrument of aristocracy for subjugating the people. It expresses a simple belief in the existence of God and in the human moral duty of practicing justice and mercy.

LGP

Palamas, Gregory (1296–1359). Born in Constantinople, P. became the most important Orthodox theologian of the fourteenth century. He was educated in the Byzantine imperial court until he took monastic vows. He was ordained to the ministry in Thessalonica, where he remained until he became archbishop. Besides being a theologian, P. was a mystic and a defender of Hesychasm against the criticisms of ⇒Barlaam and others. Although in its origins Hesychasm was a method of meditation without great theological depth, practiced by some monks on Mount Athos, P. defined it and shaped it theologically, so that Hesychasm came to be known as Palamism. In that context he wrote *In Defense of the Hesychast Saints* and the *Hagionetic Tome*, in which he expresses the need to obey those saints who have had profound mystical experiences with the Holy Spirit.

P. also clashed with Barlaam and others regarding the procession of the Spirit, writing against those who accepted the Western doctrine of the *filioque*. In that polemic his most important work is *Apodictic Treatises on the Procession of the Holy Spirit* (1335). Finally, he wrote a compendium of his moral theory, *Exposition of the Decalogue*.

The theological legacy of P. is highly appreciated within the Orthodox tradition, for which reason after his death he was declared a saint of the church.

GC

Paley, William (1743–1805). English theologian and philosopher. He was educated in Cambridge, where he was also professor of mathematics, ethics, and Greek. He worked as pastor from 1767 to 1795, becoming rector, vicar, and prebendary. His teleological arguments attempt to demonstrate the existence of God by means of the order in creation and serve as a basis for his natural theology. P. is the author of the famous argument that someone who finds a watch in the desert takes for granted the existence of another who made it, and that finding the complex machinery of the universe, we must believe that someone made it. His vision of the world was mechanistic, as can be seen in his books *Evidences of Christianity* (1794) and *Natural Theology* (1802).

LGP

Pamphilus of Caesarea (?–309). As an enthusiastic follower of the teachings of ⇒Origen, P. saved and enlarged the library Origen had left in Caesarea, which ⇒Eusebius of Caesarea then used as one of the chief sources of his *Ecclesiastical History*. His principal work was *Defense of Origen*, in five books, to which his disciple and admirer Eusebius added another. Only the first of these books survives, and only in a Latin translation by ⇒Rufinus.

—

Panikkar, Raimundo (1918–). Indian Catholic priest and theologian. He has doctorates in philosophy, chemistry, and theology. He has contributed to the dialogue between religion and modernity and among Christianity, Hinduism, and Buddhism. His reflection is interdisciplinary, interreligious, and international. At the center of P.'s theology and spirituality is the vision of the cosmotheandric principle which declares that the divine, the human, and the earthly are the three irreducible dimensions of the real. Any instance of the real (God, humanity, world) has this irreducible trinitarian structure: matter-energy, conscience, and infinite inexhaustibility or transcendence. This vision represents the third great kairological moment in the development of the human conscience and is the foundation for a cosmotheandric spirituality in a pluralist and postcolonial world. All of this is best expressed in his work *The Cosmotheandric Experience.*

—

Pannenberg, Wolfhart (1928–). German Lutheran theologian who studied philosophy in Berlin and Göttingen before devoting himself to theology, which he studied in Basel with ⇒Barth. He then continued his studies in Heidelberg, where he became a professor. In 1958 he accepted a teaching position in systematic theology at Wuppertal, where he was a colleague of ⇒Moltmann. He then taught in Mainz before accepting a post in the faculty of Munich in 1968.

In contrast to ⇒Bultmann, the theology of P. is defined by a universal historical emphasis. History, according to P., can only be understood in its totality and interpreted by means of its end or goal. This end is manifested in the life, death, and resurrection of Christ, which should be interpreted through an apocalyptic lens, which is key for understanding the New Testament. For P., divine revelation is manifested by means of historical and public events that are interpreted as acts of God in history.

Theological work requires an objective analysis of those historical events. Consequently, for P. the resurrection of Christ is a historical event that announces the end of history and anticipates the final revelation of God at the end of history. In his defense of the historicity of the resurrection in *Jesus—God and Man* (1968), he proposed that those who deny the historicity of the resurrection take a human and prejudiced point of view, assuming from the beginning that the resurrection could not occur. P. proposes an objective investigation of the historical evidence for the resurrection and concludes that it is a historical reality which affirms for the disciples the presence of God in Christ. His other books include a systematic theology in three volumes (1993).

—

Pantaenus (3rd century). Christian scholar who, after traveling extensively, settled in Alexandria. There he met ⇒Clement of Alexandria, who saw in the teachings of P. the end of his long intellectual pilgrimage. Apparently P. did not leave a single piece of writing. Therefore, although the central vision of the Alexandrian school, a confluence between classical philosophy and the Christian faith, can well be attributed to him, there is no way of confirming how much of this comes from P. and how much from Clement.

—

Panteugenos, Soterichos (12th century). Antiochian deacon who touched off a controversy when he declared that the eucharistic formula "You are the one who offers; you are the one that is offered" smacks of Nestorianism (⇒Nestorius), because it implies an excessive distinction between the two natures of Christ. He also affirmed that the Eucharist is a sacrifice that is offered only to the Son and not to the Trinity. His positions were rejected by a synod that met in Constantinople in 1156.

—

Papias (ca. 60–140). Bishop of Hierapolis (in what today is Turkey) of whom we know mostly through the writings of ⇒Eusebius of Caesarea and ⇒Irenaeus. In his work *Against Heresies* the latter speaks of P. as a man of yesteryear, a disciple of "John," who was associated with ⇒Polycarp and was the author of a work in five volumes titled *Expositions of the Words of the Lord.*

Among the most interesting contributions of P. to the contemporary study of the Bible are his statements on the authorship of the Gospels of Mark and Matthew, which were preserved by Eusebius in his *Ecclesiastical History.* According to P., Mark had been the interpreter of Peter, writing down faithfully, but not in order, what he remembered of the preaching of the apostle. He tells us that Matthew put in order the oracles of the Lord in the Hebrew dialect (he possibly meant Aramaic) and that everyone interpreted them as they could.

Currently biblical scholars attribute little value to the testimony of P., mainly because biblical criticism has demonstrated that the Gospels were written on the basis of oral traditions that were of a communal origin, and not the product of the memory of a single person.

———
ODV

Paredes, Tito (1949–). Peruvian missiologist and anthropologist, a member of ⇒Fraternidad Teológica Latinoamericana (FTL). He is a pioneer in the evangelical context and is developing a theology of contextual mission jointly with indigenous evangelical groups. Many of his works have been published in the journal of the FTL.

———
CCO

Paris, Council of (1210). Assembly that condemned the teachings of ⇒Amalric of Bena and of ⇒David de Dinant. This condemnation was confirmed five years later by the Fourth ⇒Lateran Council. The C. of Paris also prohibited the use of the "natural philosophy" of ⇒Aristotle. This included all of the Aristotelian corpus except his logic and his ethics, which had been used for a long time previously. This was part of the reaction in Paris against the studies that took place in the Faculty of Arts and that would finally lead to the Latin Averroism of ⇒Siger of Brabant. In 1215 the chancellor of the University of Paris, Robert of Courçon, ratified this prohibition.

———
JLG

Parmenianus (355–91). Successor of ⇒Donatus as director of his movement. He wrote several treatises against ⇒Augustine and ⇒Optatus of Milevis.

———
JLG

Pascal, Blaise (1623–62). French scientist, mathematician, and religious thinker. He began his academic and scientific work as a freethinker and atheist. Because of his interest in the exact sciences he wrote on sounds and mathematical equations and a treatise on the equilibrium of liquids.

In addition to his scientific interests, P. had deep religious concerns. As the possessor of a keen mind and a restless spirit, he devoted his short life to the attempt to reconcile faith and reason. The relationship between faith and reason concerned him as a matter of vital importance for his life, so that his conversion in 1654 was followed by a ceaseless search for truth based on a faith that comes from the heart and not from the mind. At bottom P. aspired to establish his faith on a personal experience with Jesus Christ, as a reaction to the cold and calculating rationalism that discards an experience of the heart. P. chose a personal gospel that leads the believer to accept his or her sinful situation. His adherence to Jansenism (⇒Jansen) offered him a framework for strengthening his faith theologically and at the same time for maintaining a critical spirit over against the orthodoxy of his time. Thus P. chose a path of witness to Jesus Christ and discipleship to which he gave beautiful shape in his *Pensées*, a classic of Christian literature and piety.

The theology of P. revolves, on the one hand, around an experience of authentic faith that does not exclude human reason and, on the other hand, around a rationality that validates the gospel as reasoned truth. P. emphasizes the human condition of misery that finds in Jesus Christ a new meaning and a path which leads to God.

God is known by faith through proofs found in miracles, prophesies, the testimony of history, and Scripture. These are eloquent testimonies of the loving revelation of God. The paradox of human existence is located in insecurity, inconstancy, and anxiety, and in a certainty of faith that progressively overcomes pessimism and uncertainty until it encounters Christ. The peace that leads to God is a path beginning with a personal encounter with Jesus Christ. When the human being is capable of thinking correctly, it is ready to seek its full liberty.

The great value of the thought of P. lies in having achieved a balance between the anthropological pessimism of the Protestant Reformation and the moral and rational optimism so strongly emphasized by rationalism and the Enlightenment. The radicalization and polarization of one extreme or the other have led to many theological and doctrinal confusions and occasionally to sterile debates. In both Roman Catholic and Protestant theologies of the modern and contemporary period, the subject of the relationship between faith and reason continues to be debated. The genius of P. can help lay Christians, pastors, and theologians to ground their theology on a sound equilibrium between mind and heart, so that they can believe with passion and at the same time think through the faith.

——

CEA

Paschasius Radbertus (9th century).
A monk of Corbie, author of the treatise *On the Body and Blood of the Lord.* According to P., in the Eucharist bread ceases to be bread and wine ceases to be wine, for they are changed into the body and blood of the Lord. This is the same body that was born of the virgin Mary, lived in Galilee, was crucified, died, and was buried, and then rose from the dead. Bread and wine, now changed into body and blood, retain their physical appearance, although the vision of their true nature is given to a fortunate few (and P. devotes an entire chapter of his treatise to the narration of such incidents). In addition, the Eucharist is a repetition of the sacrifice of Christ.

When King Charles the Bald read this treatise, he asked another monk of Corbie, ⇒Ratramnus, for his opinion about the work of P. Ratramnus replied with a work that presented a very different version of the presence of Christ in the Eucharist, and this was the beginning of a controversy in which, in addition to P. and Ratramnus, ⇒Rabanus Maurus, John Scotus ⇒Erigena, and others participated.

——

JLG

Patton, John (1930–).
Pastoral theologian of the United States and supervisor of clinical pastoral training. Following the model of Seward ⇒Hiltner, he has proposed "relational humanism" as the basis of pastoral care. He changes the psychological paradigm and tackles with clinical-theological rigor the experience of guilt and forgiveness. His works include *Is Human Forgiveness Possible?* (1985), *Pastoral Counseling: A Ministry of the Church* (1983), and *Pastoral Care in Context: An Introduction to Pastoral Care* (1993).

——

JR

Paul of Samosata (3rd century).
Bishop of Antioch, beginning approximately in the year 260, and civil servant of Queen Zenobia of Palmyra. It is said that he surrounded himself with pomp and that he was tyrannical, but such statements are found only in the writings of his adversaries. In the area of theology he opposed Origenism (⇒Origen) and considered himself to be a tenacious defender of Christian monotheism. For this reason he resisted referring to the Word as something more than the immanent reason of God, that is, as a "person" or "hypostasis" different from the Father. This Word or Wisdom of God is called "Son" because of its presence in Jesus Christ, who is the Son of God, begotten in the bosom of Mary by the Holy Spirit. But it is the same power of God that inhabited Moses and the prophets, and therefore Jesus Christ is distinguished from them only by the degree in which the Word inhabited and manifested itself in him. Jesus is not divine, but rather "from here below," and in him the Word or Power of God inhabited "as in a temple." (This phrase would soon become characteristic of Antiochene Christology; ⇒Theodore of Mopsuestia.)

Since P. referred to the Word as the Power (*dynamis*) of God, historians call his monarchian doctrine "dynamic," to distinguish it from the "modalist" monarchianism of ⇒Sabellius, ⇒Noetus, and others.

P. was summoned to several synods and discussions, but his teaching was not declared to be erroneous until the Origenist ⇒Malchion, in a debate before a synod in Antioch, succeeded in clarifying what was at stake. The synod declared P. a heretic and decreed his deposition. In spite of these decrees, P. was not deposed, since he had the support of the authorities.

——

JLG

Paulinus of Aquileia (ca. 725–802).
Bishop of that city, and an important participant in the rebirth of studies at the time of Charlemagne, a task in which he collaborated with ⇒Alcuin. His main theological work was motivated by the adoptionist controversy. He wrote treatises against both ⇒Elipandus of Toledo and ⇒Felix of Urgel, and he was a leader in the councils that condemned adoptionism, particularly in Regensburg in 792, and two years later in Frankfurt.

——

JLG

Paulinus of Nola (351–431).
Civil servant who, with his wife, Therasia, devoted himself to a life of asceticism and service to the poor. In 399 he became bishop of Nola. Most of his writings have been lost, and only some letters and poems remain, as well as a story, *The Passion of Genesius of Arles.* Although he corresponded with theologians of the caliber of ⇒Ambrose, ⇒Augustine, and ⇒Jerome, his

works are not mainly theological. What is seen in them is a devoted spirit, but a piety grounded on the admiration and imitation of the saints who preceded him, especially Felix of Nola.

—
JLG

Paulus Orosius ⇒Orosius, Paulus

Peale, Norman Vincent (1898–1993).
Ordained minister of the Dutch Reformed Church in New York. He was pastor of the Marble Collegiate Church in Manhattan for fifty-two years, increasing the membership of this church to more than five thousand. He published more than forty-two books. Foremost among these is *The Power of Positive Thinking*, of which almost 20 million copies were sold. P. took clinical psychology as a hermeneutical norm, especially the schools of ⇒Jung and ⇒Freud. He used their psychology as therapeutic means from a Christian perspective, in order to arrive at emotional health, which P. called the foundation of Christian life. In this congregation he founded a center of psychology and therapy called The American Foundation for Psychiatry and Religion. For fifty-four years he directed a radio program, *The Art of Living*, which was broadcast by one of the main radio networks in the United States. His sermons were sent regularly to 750,000 persons. P. is also known for his dialogue with other religions, to which he gave recognition as authentic means of divine revelation. This dialogue included the great monotheistic religions (Judaism, Christianity, and Islam) as well as Asian religions.

—
ELR

Pelagius (4th–5th century).
A native of the British Isles (probably England, but perhaps Ireland), who is said to have been a monk. He arrived in Rome at the end of the fourth century, and there he gained respect because of the holiness of his life and his commentaries on the epistles of Paul. Apparently it was around the year 405 that P. was scandalized on hearing that ⇒Augustine in his *Confessions* asked God: "Give what you command, and command what you will." This appeared to P. to imply that in order to obey the commandments of God, divine grace was necessary. It also appeared that this in turn undermined every call to obey the commandments of God. Soon afterward, when the Goths approached Rome, P. and his disciple ⇒Celestine fled to Africa, where Celestine remained, while P. continued his journey to the

Middle East. Thus the Pelagianism with which Augustine became closely acquainted, and against which he wrote several works, was the teaching of Celestine rather than of P. In Palestine P. gained a certain amount of support. But then ⇒Jerome learned about his teachings and attacked him. ⇒Orosius, the disciple of Augustine, aided Jerome in his attacks. Soon several synods in the East condemned P. In Rome, Bishop Innocent I confirmed the decisions of those synods. His successor ⇒Zosimus, who at first hesitated, at the end confirmed that condemnation. Finally, the Council of ⇒Ephesus confirmed the rejection of Pelagianism.

P. apparently feared the consequences of the determinism of the Manicheans (⇒Mani). But his concerns were above all of a practical nature: to prevent people from saying that they sin owing to their own sinful nature, and from using this as an excuse to sin against God's commandments. According to P., God has given us freedom, and by virtue of this freedom we are able to do both good and evil. Ever since the creation and even after the fall, we have the freedom both to sin and not to sin, because the sin of Adam does not corrupt the freedom of the rest of humanity. God gives to all humans an "original grace," which sin cannot remove. To this is added the "grace of revelation," through which God tells us what we are to do. And then, if we repent by our own free will and do good, God gives us the "grace of forgiveness," through which God frees us from the guilt of the sins committed. Since the sin of Adam does not affect the rest of humanity, newborn children are innocent and totally free of sin. Finally, although Paul speaks of a divine "predestination," he does not want to say that God truly decides who are the ones to be saved, but that God in God's foreknowledge knows who will make the right decisions and therefore "predestines" these to salvation.

For his part, Augustine offers a list of the errors of P., among which he mentions that the sin of Adam harmed only him, and not the rest of humanity; that newborn infants are in the same state of innocence as Adam before the fall; that it is possible to get into the kingdom through both the law and the gospel; that among the ancients there were some who lived without sin; that if humans so desire, they can live without sin.

Although the Pelagian controversy came to an end with the Council of Ephesus, the teachings of Augustine also provoked opposition on the part of those whom some called Semi-Pelagians (⇒Faustus of Riez). Much later, ⇒Luther accused almost all the scholastic theologians of Pelagianism. ⇒Calvin argued that Roman Catholicism had fallen again into Pelagianism. At the Synod of ⇒Dort, the strict Calvinists accused ⇒Arminius and his followers of falling into the error of P. Thus the debate between Augustine and P. has left a profound mark on the entire trajectory of Christian theology.

—

JLG

Pellicanus, Konrad (1478–1556). Also known as Kürsner Pellikan. Franciscan priest converted to the Protestant cause after visiting Rome and under the influence of ⇒Zwingli. He was professor of Hebrew in Basel and Zurich for more than thirty years. In this capacity he published a Bible in Hebrew (1527). He promoted the publication in Basel of the works of ⇒Luther, with whom he was somewhat friendly, although he supported Zwingli in the latter's position on the Lord's Supper.

—

ALG

Pérez de (la) Pineda, Juan (ca. 1500–67). Spanish educator and translator of unknown origin. His life and accomplishments are known from the time of his work as director of the Colegio de la Doctrina in Seville and his consequent advocacy of the ideas of the Protestant Reformation. Together with other followers of the Reformation in Andalusia, he found refuge in Geneva, where he became preacher of the Spanish-speaking congregation. In Geneva he translated the New Testament and the Psalms. According to literary historian Marcelino Menéndez y Pelayo, his is the best translation of the Psalms into Spanish prose. In addition to these translations, he wrote many letters and treatises of a pastoral nature to console and strengthen the spirits of the Spaniards who were persecuted by the Inquisition. In the last years of his life he took up residence in Montargis Castle, where he served as chaplain to Princess Renata de Ferrara, an ardent Calvinist and protector of persecuted Protestants.

—

JRI

Perkins, William (1558–1602). Anglican theologian famous in England and elsewhere for being one of the pioneers of "Protestant casuistry," combining elements of Reformed theology with the piety of the Puritans, and acquainting the public in general with basic aspects of Christian theology. He took the Protestant Reformation to the practical level by concentrating on the personal relationship of the Christian with God and by speaking of the need to preach the gospel. He also sparked a dialogue between scholarship and spirituality, submitting the two to the authority of the Scriptures and highlighting the role of the Christian conscience in making correct decisions.

—

AEM

Peter Chrysologus (ca. 400–50). Bishop of Ravenna and doctor of the church (⇒Doctors). It is not known with certainty where he was born nor where he was educated. It is known that his episcopate coincided with the years in which Empress Gala Placidia lived in Ravenna. With her P. shared an enthusiasm for architecture, but he preached more than one sermon against her. A large collection of his sermons survives, and for these sermons he won the nickname of "Chrysologus" ("word of gold," possibly so that the Western church could have its great preacher, just as the Eastern Christians had their John ⇒Chrysostom). In spite of being externally a subject of the Byzantine emperor, P. always insisted that the Roman see had the last word in matters of orthodoxy, and he made this known to ⇒Eutyches (the famous Monophysite).

—

OOE

Peter Damian (1007–72). Medieval reformer. He was born in Italy and entered the Benedictine order, in which he founded new monasteries and reformed the existing ones. He was named cardinal bishop, but he was not so much interested in being a hierarch as in reforming the church. He attacked the moral decadence in the church, in particular among the clergy. In his writings his criticism of the church is evident, but they also reveal his deep contemplative life and his Catholic folk piety. He was named a ⇒doctor of the church by Benedict XIII in 1728. His work still has an impact on a great deal of missionary work, and his influence has made itself felt in the monastic life.

—

CEA

Peter Lombard (ca. 1100–60). Theologian of Italian origin, as his name indicates. He arrived in Paris around 1130 and studied with ⇒Hugh of St. Victor and possibly with

Peter ⇒Abelard. His works include commentaries on the Psalms and on the epistles of Paul, but his most important work is his four books of *Sentences*. Uniting the piety and the devotional and practical spirit of the school of St. Victor with the rational thought of Abelard, in this work P. produced a systematic summary of Christian doctrine. Although without great originality, the *Sentences* are characterized by their logical order, their didactic clarity, and their reference to authors who wrote on the subjects under discussion.

The first book of the *Sentences* deals with God, and in it P. discusses the doctrine of the Trinity and the divine attributes. His presentation is highly traditional. The chief exception to this is his suggestion that the Holy Spirit is the bond of love that unites human beings. This suggestion gave rise to repeated criticisms and accusations against P.

The second book treats of creation, the angels and other creatures, and the human being. It proceeds from that point to grace and sin (these last two subjects are treated in that order, the reverse of the order many other authors follow).

The third book deals with Christology, redemption, the gifts of the Holy Spirit, and the commandments. It is here, in the christological section, that P., as if in passing, poses what has been called his "christological nihilism," when he declares that Jesus Christ, insofar as he is a human being, is not "something." Some of his enemies interpreted this as a form of Docetism, or at least Monophysitism. But in reality P. simply proposes what ⇒Cyril of Alexandria had previously understood as the "anhypostatic" union.

The fourth and last book of the *Sentences* deals with the sacraments and the last things. A list of seven sacraments is offered, and reasons are given for limiting the number of the sacraments to seven. This appears to have reflected the common opinions and practices of the twelfth century and to have helped to fix the number of the sacraments at seven.

The *Sentences* were not accepted without opposition. Their use of reason did not please mystics who had fideistic tendencies, like ⇒Gautier of St. Victor. Others accused P. of heresy because of his christological stance. There were repeated attempts to condemn him, and the use of the *Sentences* was prohibited in some universities. But little by little the book gained acceptance because of its usefulness and clarity, and finally the Fourth ⇒Lateran Council endorsed it. From then on the *Sentences*

were the principal textbook of theology in the universities, where it was expected that one of the first tasks of every aspirant to a professorship was to comment on the *Sentences*.

——

JLG

Peter Mongo (5th century).

Theologian of Monophysite tendencies who collaborated with Emperor Zeno in the drafting of the ⇒Henoticon. He can be considered a verbal Monophysite or a Severian.

——

JLG

Peter of Auriole (?–1322).

Archbishop of Aix who had been a disciple of John Duns ⇒Scotus. The theory of universals that dominated the late medieval period is attributed to him. This theory, although at times it receives the name of nominalism, is in reality a conceptual realism, because it understands that universals are real, but only as concepts in the mind. To a certain extent he is the link between Scotus and ⇒Ockham.

——

JLG

Peter of Auvergne (?–1304).

Canon of Paris, and then possibly bishop of Clairmont. He was particularly known and admired for his commentaries on the works of Aristotle.

——

JLG

Peter of Bruys (?–ca. 1131).

French preacher, great critic of the church of his time, for which he died at the stake. He confronted the abbot of Cluny, ⇒Peter the Venerable, who vigorously opposed him. His fervent passion led him to reject fundamental teachings of Catholicism such as infant baptism, the real presence of Christ in the Lord's Supper, and good works applied to the dead. His main focus was his insistence on personal faith as the only means of salvation.

——

CEA

Peter of John Olivi (1248–98).

Franciscan of the "Spiritual" party, follower and defender of the theories of ⇒Joachim of Fiore, which he expounded in his own commentary on the book of Revelation.

——

JLG

Peter of Poitiers (12th century).

Defender of ⇒Peter Lombard and his *Sentences*.

He probably was the first to establish the practice of giving lectures commenting on the *Sentences*.

JLG

Peter of Sebaste (4th century).

Brother of ⇒Basil of Caesarea, ⇒Macrina, and ⇒Gregory of Nyssa. His inclination for the ascetic life was evident from an early age, and he appears to have influenced Basil in the same direction. He supported the Nicene cause, although he never achieved the prominence of Basil, Macrina, and Gregory.

JLG

Peter of Tarantaise (1225–76).

Dominican master at the University of Paris who participated in the Council of ⇒Lyon, was archbishop of Lyon, and became pope during the last six months of his life, with the title of Innocent V. In theology he followed the traditional Augustinian line, although he appeared willing to accept elements of the new Aristotelian philosophy. He was known as Doctor Famosissimus. His principal work was a treatise against the theory of the eternity of the world.

JLG

Peter of Trabibus (13th century).

Obscure person, apparently a defender of Joachimism (⇒Joachim of Fiore) and of the "spiritual" Franciscans. Some scholars have suggested that he is the same person as ⇒Peter of John Olivi.

JLG

Peter the Devourer (or *Comestor*) (?–ca. 1198).

An eminent scholar given the name of "devourer" because he apparently devoured books. He was a defender and promoter of the *Sentences* of ⇒Peter Lombard. He wrote a large compilation of historical data which in its time was very famous and which, as modern languages developed, was translated into several European tongues.

JLG

Peter the Fuller (?–488).

Monophysite bishop of Antioch in three successive periods whose career is an indication of the way in which the political vicissitudes of the time affected the course of theological discussion. P.

belonged to the group that historians call verbal Monophysites or Severians (⇒Severus of Antioch). At any rate, P. stirred up a controversy when he added to the *Trisagion* (the hymn that proclaims God as thrice holy) the phrase "who was crucified for us." Because of this he was accused of theopaschism, that is, of declaring that God suffered on the cross. P. based his position on the *communicatio idiomatum*, a christological principle according to which the properties of one of the natures of the Savior can be predicated of the other nature, by virtue of the hypostatic union.

JLG

Peter the Venerable (–1156).

Abbot of Cluny of whom several apologetic works and also epistles are preserved. His principal theological work consisted of a number of defenses of the Benedictine ideal (⇒Benedict of Nursia) as it was practiced in Cluny, and against the reformist criticisms of ⇒Bernard of Clairvaux.

JLG

Peter Waldo ⇒Waldo, Peter

Pfefferkorn, Johannes (ca. 1469–1524).

Jewish writer converted to Christianity in 1505. He is known chiefly for his campaign of persecution against the Jewish people in Germany. He urged the authorities to force the Jews to hand over for burning all their books appearing to be anti-Christian. He also insisted that Jews should be required to attend church so that they could listen to Christian sermons. He was supported by the Dominicans of Cologne and by Emperor Maximillian in 1509. In the face of protest against this action, the emperor sought the advice of theologians, humanists, and scholars, in particular ⇒Reuchlin, the most prominent Hebraist of his time, who opposed these radical positions and defended the Jews. This controversy stands out among many that broke out between the conservative professors in the universities and the humanists, who defended their new methodology.

ALG

Pharmaquides, Theocletus (1784–1860).

Greek theologian, educated in Göttingen, who opposed the radical traditionalism of Constantine ⇒Oikonomus. P. distinguished between the true tradition and the practices, beliefs, and customs added with the passing of years. In order to distinguish between the former and the latter, the historical-critical method that was in vogue then was to be applied. Although the Septuagint was of value to the ancient church, it was not inspired by God, and therefore the modern Greek church had the freedom and the need to translate the Bible again from the original languages into modern Greek. In addition, the Greek church had to take into account the new political realities; thus, now that Greece was independent of Turkey, the Greek church should also become independent of the patriarchate of Constantinople, which was located in Turkey. P. encountered great opposition among the more conservative elements of the church, and therefore he was transferred from theological teaching to the field of philosophy.

————

JLG

Philip Neri ⇒Neri, Philip

Philips, Obbe (ca. 1500–60). Anabaptist pastor born in Holland. In 1534 he organized the first Anabaptist congregation in Frisia. In this congregation he baptized Menno ⇒Simons in 1536, and in 1537 ordained him as pastor. In 1540 Simons took over the leadership of the congregation, which gradually began to call itself Mennonite. Years later P. distanced himself from the Mennonites, and it is believed that he returned to the Roman church, which he had left when he joined the Anabaptists.

————

HMT

Philo of Alexandria (ca. 20 BCE–42 CE). Hellenistic Jewish philosopher, son of a prominent family in Alexandria. He is the outstanding interpreter of Alexandrian Jewish philosophy and the most influential exponent of the allegorical method of biblical interpretation, commonly found later in patristic literature. He influenced the Greek patristic writers ⇒Barnabas, ⇒Justin, ⇒Theophilus of Antioch, ⇒Eusebius of Caesarea, ⇒Clement of Alexandria, and ⇒Origen, and, among the Latin authors, ⇒Jerome, ⇒Ambrose, and ⇒Augustine of Hippo. In his *Ecclesiastical History*, Eusebius offers a long, though incomplete, list of Philo's works, which are of three types: exegetical, philosophical, and political.

His exegetical works are the clearest and the most accessible. They can be subdivided into three topics: cosmogonic, historical, and legislative. In his cosmogonic writings he uses allegory to explain the creative work of God as it is described in Genesis. His historical studies interpret allegorically, chapter by chapter, the meaning of the Genesis narratives. In his legislative writings he presents a universal ethic beginning with the Decalogue and the Hebrew rituals in the light of Exodus, Leviticus, and Deuteronomy, which are also interpreted allegorically.

P. uses the allegorical method in his exegesis of the Bible in order to establish a close relationship between the Jewish faith and Greek philosophy. He thus interpreted numerous anthropomorphic narratives in the Pentateuch which, like Greek mythology, were problematical for Greek thought. For this purpose P. uses philosophical language and numerous concepts taken from Plato and Stoicism. He applied the allegorical method when it seemed to him that the literal interpretation presented God in an unworthy manner, there existed apparent contradictions, or the text itself used figurative language. As a fundamental principle of his interpretation he affirmed a strict Jewish monotheism and consequently God as the only source of creation.

For example, in his exegesis of the creation story in Genesis he took into account Plato's *Timaeus*. In the two narratives God exists before creation. In *Timaeus* the eternal ideas also exist before creation. P. did not think that the existence of such eternal ideas was incompatible with the biblical tradition, but he did believe that the eternity of such ideas cannot be the same as that of God. Then he reconciled the biblical tradition with Plato by granting to the world of ideas a gradual process of double existence. First they exist in eternity as ideas in God, and then they also exist before the creation of the world as real entities created by God.

Another way of reconciling the two traditions consists in posing intermediary beings between the infinite God and the finite world. The Logos is the principle of the image of God and the eloquent mediator of the act of creation. In that way P. reconciled Greek ontology with the Jewish tradition of creation. Although in that ontology the human being has the image of God, it is created as imperfect because it is created by the Logos and other intermediate powers.

According to P., Moses is presented in the Scriptures as the earthly mediator, just as the

Logos is the heavenly mediator. The law of Moses is in reality a written expression of the natural law of God. Thus P. gives a universal openness to Hebrew thought, although for him the people of Israel occupied a special place as the messenger of God. In the same way, P. also employs the order of moral virtues of Plato and of the Stoics in his reading of Moses' ethics, although his Jewish faith leads him to emphasize piety and faith as superior virtues.

That faith is rooted in a contemplative mysticism, in which the human being does not lose its identity in the Absolute. It affirms a monotheistic Mosaic ethic that allows the conscience to open itself and see clearly in order to perceive the nature of things.

It is important to point out that the teachings of P. differ from the fundamental doctrines of Christianity concerning the person and work of the Word or Logos. His use of the Logos is similar to the Logos of John only as a matter of terminology. The Logos of P. is a cosmic power with no personal identity, while the Logos of the New Testament is the One who in his incarnation becomes the Messiah.

———

ALG

Photius (ca. 820–ca. 890). Scholar and patriarch of Constantinople, whom history remembers above all as one of the protagonists in the schism of Photius. P. was a widely respected layman when a series of political intrigues and controversies within the church led to his election to the patriarchate. In that election both parties of the conflict agreed, and in the course of one week P. received all the degrees of ordination and was consecrated patriarch. When one of the factions in the dispute changed its mind, declaring the election of P. to be null and void and sending protests to Pope Nicholas, the conflict grew worse. To this was added a dispute between Rome and Constantinople on whether the Latin or the Greek church would have jurisdiction over Bulgaria. When Emperor Basil rose to the throne because of the murder of Michael III, a political change in Constantinople caused P. to be deposed. The Fourth Council of Constantinople (869–70) (⇒Councils) declared P. deposed but was not able to obtain the support of the majority of the clergy or the faithful. The result is that this council, which until the present day is considered ecumenical by the West, is not considered so by the Greek church. All of this led to a long dispute between Rome and Constantinople. Having been restored to the patriarchate, P.

made efforts toward reconciliation with Rome. Currently, scholars agree that it was all an unfortunate episode of misunderstandings and faulty information, complicated by the ill will of some.

None of this should overshadow the importance of P. as a scholar and theologian. At a time when in western Europe, even in the midst of the brief Carolingian renaissance, the knowledge of the most erudite was limited to the contents of a few books, P. was an encyclopedist of broad knowledge. His works comprise four thick volumes in the *Patrology* of Migne. Among them is the *Library* or *Myriobiblon*, a list and summary of the books read by P., which gives witness to the breadth of his scholarship, including, in addition to theological and philosophical works, broad knowledge of classic philosophy and literature.

In the field of theology, in addition to a very ample correspondence, sermons, and biblical commentaries, P. wrote a long treatise *On the Holy Spirit*, in which he refuted the position of the West that the Spirit proceeds from the Father and the Son (*filioque*), and did so on the basis of biblical exegesis as well as of dialectics. Scholars debate the authorship of a long treatise, *Against the Manicheans,* which traditionally is attributed to him. Naturally, in the midst of the controversy with Rome, P. also wrote polemical works in which he denies the argument that the visit and death of St. Peter in Rome gives the bishop of that city primacy over the rest. In other works he makes use of his ample scholarship to point out cases in which popes erred in their relations with Constantinople and other sees.

———

JLG

Pieris, Aloysius (1934–). Jesuit theologian and priest from Sri Lanka, and the first non-Buddhist to receive a doctorate in Buddhist studies from the University of Sri Lanka. Author of a vast number of articles and chapters in collections in several languages, P. is particularly known for his work *An Asian Theology of Liberation* (1988). In addition, he was founder and director of the Tulana Research Center in Sri Lanka, where his theological contributions focused on the theology of religion, folk religiosity, and liberation, all from an Asian perspective. P. is also a member of the Ecumenical Association of Third World Theologians (EATWOT) and has taught in well-known universities around the world.

———

CCO

Pierius (3rd century). Alexandrian teacher whom some called the Second ⇒Origen. Except for a few brief fragments, his works are lost. It is said that he suffered martyrdom and that his teachings included speculations similar to those of Origen, particularly regarding the preexistence of souls. It also appears that he declared that the Holy Spirit is inferior in glory to the Father and the Son.

———

JLG

Pierson, Arthur Tappan (1837–1911). North American Presbyterian promoter and theoretician of mission and author of the book *The Crisis of Mission* (1886). Author of more than fifty books and editor of the journal *Missionary Review of the World.* P. was one of the most important promoters of mission at the end of the nineteenth century. Both his written works and his ministry reflect the theoretical/practical duality of mission in the North American context.

———

CCO

Pigge, Albert (1490–1542). Dutch humanist and theologian who was born in the city of Kampen, in the province of Overijssel. He died in the city of Utrecht. He studied in Louvain, where he received the master of arts degree. The date of his ordination to the priesthood is unknown. After several years in Paris, he went to Rome in 1522. Through his writings, as adviser to papal nuncios, and through his participation in religious debates, he made great contributions to the Roman Catholic position in the sixteenth century. In the ecclesiastical context, he was known for his close relation with and defense of the papal system. His interpretation of papal infallibility went beyond the opinion of his contemporaries, questioning even the possibility that a pope could fall into heresy. His opinions were accepted by many theologians, especially by ⇒Bellarmine. He was one of the most quoted authors in the Council of ⇒Trent. His critical examination of sources earned him recognition in the area of church history. His theory that the minutes of the Councils of ⇒Nicaea and ⇒Constantinople were falsified in the parts relating to the condemnation of Pope Honorius I was accepted until the nineteenth century.

———

JDR

Pineda, Ana María, RSM (1945–). Catholic theologian of Salvadoran origin who has contributed to the articulation of Hispanic/Latin theology in the United States. In her theological work she emphasizes the importance of the Mesoamerican roots of Hispanics. She asserts that oral tradition, which has been part of Hispanic culture for centuries, is a fundamental source of Hispanic/Latin theology. P. is coeditor of the book *Dialogue Rejoined: Theology and Ministry in the United States Hispanic Reality.*

———

NLD

Pisa, Council of (1409). Convened by the cardinals in order to end the Great Schism of the West, in which two rival popes claimed to be the legitimate bishop of Rome. When the council began in Pisa, both contenders for the Roman see convened their own councils in other cities, but the cardinals, bishops, and other representatives who were in Pisa declared themselves to be legitimately and canonically a council of the church and proceeded to depose both popes. The council then elected Alexander V as the only bishop of Rome, but unfortunately this election only complicated the schism, because as a result there were three popes, each one insisting that he was the only legitimate one. The schism came to an end only by action of the Council of ⇒Constance in 1417, although the majority of historians consider Pisa as the necessary preamble to Constance.

———

OOE

Pithou, Pierre (1539–96). Outstanding French lawyer and theologian who gave impulse to the Gallican movement. He embraced Catholicism at the same time as Henry IV, who named him attorney general. He wrote *The Liberties of the Gallican Church* (1594), in which he affirmed that the pope has no temporal authority in the territories governed by Christian kings and that his spiritual authority is limited by the canons of the ancient councils.

———

PAJ

Pittenger, William Norman (1905–97). Anglican theologian born in Bogota, New Jersey. He studied at Princeton University and at the General Theological Seminary (GTS) in New York. He was invited to join the faculty of GTS in 1935. He worked for more than thirty years in that institution as professor of apologetics. After his retirement from

GTS, he lectured at Kings College. He made use of process philosophy (⇒Whitehead), especially in his writings on Christology and the Eucharist.

——
HMT

Pius IX (1792–1878). His name was Giovanni Maria Mastai-Ferretti, and he occupied the Roman see from 1846 until his death. His pontificate was the culminating point of the conflict between Roman Catholicism and modernity, in both the political and the theological spheres. In the political sphere P. had to face the growing nationalist, republican, and revolutionary sentiments. A short time before his ascent to the papal throne, it fell to him to respond to the challenges of the revolutions of 1848. Toward the end of his pontificate, the growing force of the Republic of Italy finally snatched from the papacy the temporal authority over Rome and its surroundings. As a consequence P. felt a deep antipathy toward every kind of republicanism or laicism, and a good deal of the impetus of modernity appeared to him to be an attack against the very nature of the church. In the theological sphere three great milestones mark the pontificate of P.

The first was the proclamation in 1854, in the bull titled *Ineffabilis*, of the dogma of the immaculate conception of Mary. This was the first time in the history of the church that a pope promulgated a doctrine based on his own authority, without the intervention of a council.

The second theological milestone in the pontificate of P. was the proclamation in 1864 of the *Syllabus of Errors*. This was a list of "errors" which the Roman see condemned, and included matters such as the secular state, schools under the control of such a state, the separation of church and state, the autonomy of the sciences, freedom of worship.

Third, it was during his pontificate that the First Vatican Council (⇒Vatican I) proclaimed papal infallibility.

In all of this we see that the tendency of Roman Catholicism during the nineteenth and the first decades of the twentieth century was to reject a major part of the presuppositions and practices of modernity. This explains why the *aggiornamento* proposed by ⇒John XXIII was so necessary.

——
JLG

Pixley, Jorge (1937–). Among contemporary biblical scholars in Latin America, P. has developed in the most detailed and systematic fashion the theme of the interpretation of the exodus. In his exposition, the biblical interpretation of the exodus is developed in four stages. In the first, the exodus is interpreted as a heterogeneous movement of peasants in Egypt who, together with a group of immigrants from the East, escaped from Egypt under the leadership of Moses the Levite. The second stage understands the exodus as a popular movement of Levites who joined a group of Canaanite rebels, constituted the people of Israel, and organized in order to struggle against exploitation. The third interpretation is produced when Israel is a monarchy, and the exodus is seen as a national (not a class) rebellion against Egypt. Finally, at the fall of the monarchy, the exodus is interpreted as a strictly religious event in which God liberates the people without their participation. For P. this change in the interpretation of the exodus reveals how the dominant classes can destroy the good news or the gospel of God. The heart of the exodus is seen in its character as a political-religious movement and not as an apolitical religious movement. The good news is denied when religion separates itself from popular struggles.

——
IG

Plantinga, Alvin (1932–). U.S. philosopher and theologian in the Reformed tradition. A native of Michigan, he studied at Calvin College and at the University of Michigan. He taught at the universities of Yale, Wayne State, Calvin College, and Notre Dame. In his philosophy, the use of logic dominates his arguments, in which he considers complexes of possible alternatives to the present world in which we live. Using logic, he confronts the problem that the existence of evil posits for the concept of God. He develops a theodicy based on the freedom of the human being. His works include a study of the ontological proof of the existence of God of ⇒Anselm, in which he uses the new arguments of ⇒Hartshorne. His most important books are *The Ontological Argument from St. Anselm to Contemporary Philosophers* (1965), *God, Freedom, and Evil* (1974), and *Does God Have a Nature?* (1980).

——
LGP

Plato (428–348 BCE). His real name was Aristocles, and the name "Plato" was given to him because of his broad shoulders. He was a member of an aristocratic family of Athens and a disciple of Socrates, in defense of whose memory he wrote a number of dialogues. In 388 BCE he founded a school that received the name "Academy" because it was close to the temple of Academus. The Academy continued operating until it was closed by ⇒Justinian in 529 CE. Aside from a few letters, all that is preserved of his writings is his *Dialogues*.

The philosophy of P. is an entire system, which it is not necessary to review here. What is important for the purposes of this dictionary is the impact P. has had on Christian theology. This impact is due in the first place to the fact that when Christians were accused of ignorance or of teaching irrational doctrines, they appealed to P. and his teachings to show that their preaching was not as irrational as it was said to be.

When Christians were accused of being atheists or of preaching the strange notion of one invisible God, they frequently replied by showing the similarities between their teachings and what Plato had said about the Supreme Idea of the Good. Thus Platonism soon began to influence the way in which theologians spoke about God, so that many came to think that the Platonic language was better or more exact than that of the Scriptures, and that therefore the latter ought to be interpreted allegorically. The goal was that the Scriptures should be reconciled with what Plato and other philosophers had said about the nature of the Supreme Good.

When Christians were accused of being foolish because of their belief that they would live after death, they replied by appealing to the Platonic doctrine of the immortality of the soul. The result was that soon the doctrine of the resurrection of the dead was supplanted or at least eclipsed by the doctrine of the immortality of the soul.

When it was said that Christians were mistaken in promising a kingdom of heaven, their reply was that Plato had taught the existence of a "world of ideas," and that this purely spiritual world was what they meant to say when they spoke about the kingdom.

All of this, which undoubtedly had great apologetic value, in the end shaped a major part of Christian theology and piety. The result was that God, the soul, and the eschatological hope were interpreted in terms that owed at least as much to Plato as to the Bible.

The impact of P. increased thanks to the work of several Christian authors who were convinced that the Platonic tradition (that is, not only Plato but other philosophers who followed and developed his positions, such as ⇒Philo and ⇒Plotinus) was an instrument God had been preparing for the preaching of the gospel to the gentiles (⇒Clement of Alexandria, ⇒Origen, ⇒Augustine, ⇒Dionysius the Areopagite).

Possibly the greatest impact that P. had on Christian theology had to do with the theory of knowledge. P. did not believe that the senses are a reliable source for the knowledge of truth, and therefore he explained true knowledge in terms of reminiscences which the soul has of a previous existence. When Christian theologians discarded the theory of the preexistence of souls, they were obliged to explain knowledge in another way. ⇒Justin, Clement of Alexandria, Augustine, and others did this in terms of the theory of illumination, according to which the Word of God deposits truths in the human mind.

These theories of knowledge dominated medieval theology until the rediscovery in the thirteenth century of the philosophy of ⇒Aristotle offered other alternatives.

———
JLG

Plessis, David Johannes du (1905–87).

South African Pentecostal, international leader in Pentecostalism and in the ecumenical movement. His ecumenical and theological leadership led him to become secretary of the Pentecostal World Conference of 1947. He participated in several assemblies of the ⇒World Council of Churches and in the last sessions of the Second Vatican Council (⇒Vatican II). He also established the formal dialogue between Roman Catholics and Pentecostals, of which he was president from 1972 until 1982.

He lived in the United States, from where he was able to communicate the contribution and perspective of Pentecostalism to important theological circles in the nation. With his deep Pentecostal conviction and ecumenical perspective, he challenged churches and charismatic movements to recognize that the work of the Holy Spirit leads to ministries that cross denominational and confessional borders. This brought him conflicts with the most conservative sectors of world Pentecostalism.

———
CCO

Plotinus (205–70).

Neoplatonist philosopher, a native of Egypt, but fundamentally Greek in his education and culture. He studied philosophy in Alexandria and taught this discipline in Rome. He was surrounded by a number of disciples, among them Porphyry, who edited the writings of the master in six *Enneads* (six groups of nine treatises), and who in the introduction to this collection recounts the life of the philosopher.

His vision was essentially Platonic, except in his teaching of the final "mystical union." P. believed that all reality emanated from the One and consisted in a series of concentric spheres, much like circles emanating from the impact of a stone on water. He thus affirmed the existence of several hypostases in a hierarchy of values, distinguishing among the One, the mind, and the soul. The greater the distance of a reality from the One (for example, the material body), the less is the divine element in it. P. attempted to understand the divinity of his own soul in relation to the One or the Good, which was his conception of God. His philosophy was also a means of ascent from the Many to the One.

This was not merely a philosophy but a religion that included mystical experience. It was a method by which the mind could ascend to God by means of intelligence and virtue. P. was venerated by his own disciples and influenced generations of Christian thinkers, among them ⇒Augustine.

———

NRG

Pneumatomachians (4th century).
A group of theologians of indefinite profile who in the midst of the Arian controversy (⇒Arius) showed a readiness to accept the absolute divinity of the Son (the *homoousios*), but not that of the Holy Spirit. The term "Pneumatomachians" means "enemies of the Spirit." Their principal leader appears to have been ⇒Macedonius of Constantinople, and for that reason at times they are called Macedonians. They never established themselves firmly, and apparently they disappeared after the Council of ⇒Constantinople (381).

———

JLG

Pobee, John S. (1937–). Protestant theologian, native of Ghana, P. was director of the Program on Theological Education of the ⇒World Council of Churches from the late 1980s until the end of the twentieth century. His theological contribution is extensive. He has promoted African contextual theology without losing sight of the ecumenical and global character of the theological task. Many of his writings have been published worldwide in journals

of theology and mission. His books include *Toward an African Theology* (1979) and *Persecution and Martyrdom in the Theology of St. Paul* (1985).

———

CCO

Polanus von Polansdorf, Amandus (1561–1610).
He was born in Troppau, Silesia, and died in Basel. Educated in the universities of Tübingen, Basel, and Geneva, he received the doctoral degree from the University of Basel in 1590. He was named professor of Hebrew Scriptures at the University of Basel (1596) and served as dean of the faculty of theology of that university from 1598 until 1609. He translated the New Testament into German. Among his most important works are *Partitiones theologicae* (Part 1, 1590; Part 2, 1596) and *Syntagma theologiae christianae* (1609).

———

JDR

Polanyi, Michael (1891–1976). Hungarian-British philosopher and scientist with an interest in epistemology. P. developed a philosophy that questions the objective character of scientific knowledge. His most important book is *Personal Knowledge* (1958), which has played a vital part in the development of postmodern theology and science.

———

CCO

Politi, Lancelot ⇒Catharinus, Ambrosius

Polycarp (ca. 69–ca. 155). Bishop of Smyrna and martyr during the reign of Marcus Aurelius. According to Irenaeus, P. was a disciple of the apostle John, but in the *Epistle of Polycarp to the Philippians* no reference to John is found. Two works related particularly to Polycarp exist in the Christian literature of the second century. *The Martyrdom of Polycarp*, which is perhaps the better known of the two, is a marvelous and inspiring story about the clash of Christianity with emperor worship. The words of Polycarp when he replied to the proconsul who interrogated him, "For eighty-six years I have served him, and he has done me no harm. How can I curse my King who has saved me?" articulate Christian defiance in the face of persecution in the Roman province of Asia. The *Martyrdom* purports to be written by an eyewitness and is directed to the church of Philomelium and the surrounding area.

Although the authenticity of the *Epistle of Polycarp to the Philippians* has been questioned by some scholars, it is a very important witness to the text of the New Testament, because it uses New Testament language freely, for instance, quoting 1 John 4:3. The epistle supposedly was written after the visit of ⇒Ignatius of Antioch, who was not able to write to the Philippians from Troas.

According to ⇒Eusebius, P. was consecrated as bishop by the apostles and therefore is an important link between the apostolic and the subapostolic eras. Ignatius of Antioch wrote a letter to P. when he was traveling from Syria to Rome, where martyrdom awaited him. Apparently P. knew the illustrious persons of his day, such as Ignatius, ⇒Marcion, ⇒Anicetus of Rome, and ⇒Irenaeus, and was a person of great influence. He consulted with Anicetus during the Quartodeciman controversy concerning the date for the celebration of the resurrection of the Lord. They concluded that each church could continue with its own practice.

—

AP

Ponce de la Fuente, Constantino (1502–60).

Leader of the Protestant reformation in Seville. Professor of theology and very famous preacher in Seville, until he was accused of being a "Lutheran" by the Holy Office in 1558. He died as a result of torture, and his remains were exhumed and burned on December 22, 1560. His works include *Summary of Christian Doctrine* (1543), *Christian Catechism* (1547), and *Christian Doctrine* (1548).

—

JFM

Pontianus (?–235).

Bishop of Rome who was criticized by ⇒Hippolytus for being too willing to forgive sinners and welcome them again into the church. He died as an exile in the mines of Sardinia, where it is said that he was reconciled with Hippolytus.

—

JLG

Potter, Philip (1921–).

Methodist theologian and leader of the ecumenical movement in his native Caribbean and throughout the world. P. was the third executive secretary of the ⇒World Council of Churches (1972–84) and the first person from the third world to be named to this post. His period as secretary was very controversial because of his stance in favor of the theologies of liberation and his

decided option for justice in the midst of the tensions of the Cold War and its effects on the third world. His theological and ecumenical legacy can be summed up in a profound conviction of the correlation between faith and action and in a spirituality that moves Christian people to obey the gospel.

His personal, theological, and ecclesial trajectory is depicted in two biographies, one written by William Gentz, *The World of Philip Potter* (1974), and the other by Ans J. van der Bent, *The Whole Oikoumene* (1980). Many of his articles have been published in the journals of the World Council of Churches.

—

CCO

Praxeas (3rd century).

Obscure person, apparently of Eastern origin, who settled in Rome in the third century and taught a modalism according to which the Father, the Son, and the Holy Spirit are only three modes of God's revelation. One scholar thinks that this "Praxeas" to whom ⇒Tertullian refers is none other than the Roman bishop ⇒Calixtus, whom Tertullian did not wish to attack by name because he had already died, but whose teachings he thought it necessary to refute.

—

JLG

Preger, Johann Wilhelm (1827–96).

Lutheran theologian born in Schweinfurt in Bavaria, Germany. He studied at the universities of Erlangen and Berlin. He published an edition of ⇒Luther's *Table Talk* of 1531–32. His works also include a life of Matthias ⇒Flacius (1859–61) and the history of German mysticism in the Middle Ages.

—

JDR

Priscillian (ca. 340–85).

Bishop of Ávila, Spain, whose teachings were rejected by several Spanish councils. When P. appealed to the emperor, the latter condemned him to death because of heresy, immorality, and magical practices. This condemnation caused a great commotion in the church, because it was the first time in the history of Christianity that someone was condemned to death because of supposedly heretical teachings.

With regard to what P. himself taught, there are many doubts. He was accused of being a Sabellian (⇒Sabellius), of teaching a docetic Christology, and of undermining the moral teachings of the church, apparently because he demanded of the mass of believers an ascetic morality. What is known of his teachings is derived chiefly from the work of Paulus ⇒Orosius, *Warning against the Errors of the Priscillianists and the Origenists*. At the end of the nineteenth century, several writings attributed to P. were discovered in which his teaching does not appear as extreme as Orosius depicts it.

———
JLG

Procopius of Gaza (465–529).

The main teacher of the famous school of Gaza. He wrote on several theological subjects, with special attention given to inspiration and the doctrine of creation.

Regarding the first of these subjects, he strove to demonstrate that a vision like that of Isaiah does not consist in a suspension of rationality by the work of the Holy Spirit but, on the contrary, it is the maximum exaltation of reason by the work of the Spirit. In this argument his purpose is to refute the fideism of his opponents, for whom faith demanded the suspension of rationality.

As to creation, P. wrote *Refutation of the Theological Arguments of Proclus* and *Commentary on Genesis*. The first of these works is lost. In the second, he argues against the eternity, not only of the world, but also of matter. At the same time he has a dynamic vision of the creative work of God, a work that God continues in God's providence and guidance of history.

———
JLG

Procopovic, Theophanes (1681–1736).

Russian prelate born in Kiev. He won fame as an orator and preacher, for which he is known as the Chrysostom of the Russian church (⇒John Chrysostom). After studying in Rome, he was appointed professor of rhetoric in the Academy of Kiev. When he sojourned in Kiev, Czar Peter I was attracted by the oratory of P. and named him abbot of the monastery of Kiev. In his desire to establish good relations between the church and the Russian government, P. wrote a tract in which the church is presented as a civil institution and the clergy are seen as employees of the government. This proposal set the tone for much of the life of the Russian church. P. had the honor of crowning Peter II. He died in Saint Petersburg.

———
HMT

Prosper of Aquitaine (390–463).

Possibly a lay monk. He supported the theology of ⇒Augustine, but then he distanced himself from it, rejecting predestination to eternal damnation.

P. wrote *A Call to All Nations,* in which he distances himself from the "privatizing" of Augustine with respect to predestination and affirms the responsibility of the church: "Let us pray, then . . . because God, who desires that everyone come to the knowledge of the truth, cannot reject anyone without any cause at all." In addition to this work, P. compiled a *Book of Declarations of the Works of Saint Augustine* which was used as a theological resource in the Synod of ⇒Orange in 529.

Finally, P. also wrote about the relationship between the life of the church, particularly its liturgy, and its doctrine. His famous words are *ut legem credendi lex statuat supplicandi* (the rule of prayer establishes the rule of faith, or: what is said in worship establishes what is believed).

———
CCO

Prudentius, Aurelius (348–410?).

Native of Spain, and possibly the most distinguished poet of his time. He published his verses at the age of fifty-seven, declaring that both they and all his literary work were written as a way to atone for the sins of his youth. When he was about fifty years of age, after serving as a public servant, he decided to devote himself entirely to Christianity, which had been his religion since birth. His literary work began on that date. He wrote in poetic form two books *Against Symmachus*, in which he defended Christianity against paganism. His *Apotheosis*, also in verse, was a defense of the deity of Jesus Christ. The teachings of Priscillian possibly motivated this work. Other long poems treat of spiritual struggle (*Psychomachia*) and the origin of sin (*Hamartigenia*), in addition to liturgical and biblical themes.

———
JLG

Prudentius of Troyes (9th century).

Theologian whom ⇒Hincmar asked for help in his controversy with ⇒Gottschalk. Contrary to what Hincmar expected, P. declared himself in favor of double predestination, limiting the saving will of God and the scope of the atoning work of Jesus Christ to the elect. When John Scotus ⇒Erigena intervened in the controversy, P. wrote a treatise *On Predestination against John Scotus*, in which he rejected the methodology of Erigena and insisted that matters like the one that was being debated be resolved not on the basis of philosophical reason, but of Scripture.

———

JLG

Psellus, Michael (1018–96).

Celebrated master of the University of Constantinople, philosopher, and theologian. He established in Constantinople a curriculum that began with rhetoric and dialectics, continued on to mathematics, music, and geometry, and culminated in philosophy. Nevertheless, theology is above all other human knowledge in the same way that gold is more valuable than bronze. He was convinced that the Greek philosophical tradition, in particular the Platonic (⇒Plato) tradition, had been provided by God as a preparation for the gospel. But his vision of Greek philosophy is in reality Neoplatonic, and therefore tends to hide the contrasts between the different philosophers and to understand Greek philosophy as a homogeneous whole. As in the entire tradition to which he belongs, P. solves the apparent contradictions between the Bible and philosophy by means of the allegorical interpretation of the Scriptures. P. was a person of mystical tendencies who nevertheless criticized occultism and refused to accept the arguments of those who claimed to have knowledge of things that were received by mystical revelation or a similar phenomenon.

———

JLG

Pseudo-Dionysius ⇒Dionysius the Areopagite

Ptolemy (2nd century).

A gnostic, disciple of ⇒Valentinus. In his *Letter to Flora* he provides firsthand information about the gnostic system taught by Valentinus. He maintained that the Law was not bad, but inadequate, because it had not been ordained by God the Father but by an imperfect lower being who needed to be perfected by another. This intermediate being is a lower image of the Father, but ignores the existence of the Father and is responsible for the creation of the imperfect universe in which humanity lives. His commandments are not in accord with the nature of God. Both ⇒Irenaeus and ⇒Tertullian pay special attention to the gnostic teachings of P. as a threat to primitive Christianity.

———

DCF

Puebla, Conference of (1979).

The Third Conference of the Latin American Bishops Conference (CELAM III) was originally convened by Pope Paul VI to be celebrated on October 12–18, 1978. The death of the pope on August 6, 1978, followed by the death of his successor, John Paul I, on September 27 of the same year, caused the new pope, ⇒John Paul II, to postpone the event. It was finally held in the Mexican city of Puebla de los Ángeles from January 28 to February 13, 1979. John Paul II inaugurated the conference, which had as its theme "Evangelization in the Present and the Future of Latin America." The conference was highly significant for the life and mission of the Roman Catholic Church in Latin America, owing to the ecclesiastical, social, and political developments that took place between the ⇒Medellín Conference (CELAM II, 1968) and P. As the Brazilian Catholic theologian Clodovis ⇒Boff says, P. can only be understood by reference to its past, its present, and its future. The period previous to P., which has been called post-Medellín, was a decade of great theological, pastoral, and popular vitality in the Roman Catholic Church in Latin America. Some analysts rightly affirm that in certain contexts the church continued as if Medellín had not happened. On the other hand, Latin American liberation theology, following the inspiration of CELAM II, reached a high degree of development, maturity, and worldwide influence. The base communities that arose throughout the continent represented a new, contextual, and popular way of being the church in the liberating line of Medellín. In Santiago, Chile, which at that time had a leftist government led by the Socialist Salvador Allende, the First Latin American Encounter of Christians for Socialism was held on April 23–30, 1972. Those were days of revolutionary euphoria. The Christians for Socialism movement spread rapidly throughout Latin America and the rest of the world. On September 11, 1973, a coup d'état overthrew this Chilean government, and a stage of repression of the popular forces began at the continental level.

As a consequence of this development, certain hierarchical circles of Catholicism, especially in CELAM itself, questioned whether P. should continue with the liberating focus of

Medellín. In 1972 the conservative bishop Alfonso López Trujillo succeeded the progressive Eduardo Pironio as secretary general of CELAM. This deepened the polarization already present between traditionalist groups and popular movements of Catholicism.

The three years previous to the celebration of P. generated a broad dialogue that prepared for the event. In spite of the tensions and dissensions that can be expected in a polarized church, this dialogue was greatly enriching. The conference did not produce dogmatic declarations or institutional or disciplinary measures; rather, it was characterized by its eminently pastoral nature. The inductive theological method that prevailed in CELAM II was repeated in P. The latter finally confirmed without ambiguity the pastoral focus originally assumed by Medellín.

The conference was structured in twenty-one commissions and plenary sessions. The final report, published in Spanish, Portuguese, and English and later translated into other languages, is a document of 220 pages and a good number of appendices. It deals with the general theme of P. in five broad areas: (1) pastoral vision of Latin American reality; (2) the designs of God for Latin American reality; (3) evangelization in the church of Latin America: communion and participation; (4) the missionary church at the service of evangelization in Latin America; and (5) evangelization under the dynamism of the Holy Spirit: pastoral options.

The greatest achievements of P. were the confirmation of the preferential option for the poor and its emphasis on a liberating evangelization, without the ballast of antiecumenical sectarianism.

OLM

Quadratus (ca. 130). The first of the Christian apologists. His work has been lost. Some scholars think that at least part of it is found in the discourse To ⇒Diognetus.

JLG

Quenstedt, Johann Andreas (1617–88). German Lutheran theologian who studied in Helmstadt. He attained the doctorate in theology and soon thereafter obtained a teaching post in geography in the same university. He moved to Wittenberg in 1644 and there taught several courses on morality and metaphysics. He was appointed a tenured professor of theology in 1660 after having been assistant professor for eleven years. In 1684 he was appointed superintendent and consistorial counselor. Because of his rigid Lutheran orthodoxy he can be considered one of the most faithful representatives of Protestant theology in the seventeenth century (the so-called Protestant orthodoxy or Protestant scholasticism). Among his works are *Disputationes exegeticae in Epistolam ad Colossenses* (1664; Exegetical Debates on the Epistle to the Colossians), *Ethica pastoralis* (1678; Pastoral Ethics), and *Theologia didactico-polemica, sive systema theologicum* (1685–96; Didactic and Polemical Theology, or Theological System). He also pursued historical studies and published some monographs, such as *De sepultura veterum* (1648; On the Burial of the Ancients) and *Antiquitates biblicae et ecclesiasticae* (1699; Biblical and Ecclesiastical Antiquities), which includes other previously published works.

ALG

Rabanus Maurus (776–856). One of the main scholars of the Carolingian renaissance. He studied with ⇒Alcuin, and then took his methods of study and teaching to Germany, where he became archbishop of Mainz from 847 until his death. His works are very numerous, including commentaries on the majority of the books of the Bible, in addition to an extensive treatise *On the Universe*, which has an eclectic and encyclopedic character, and a brief essay *On the Immortality of the Soul*.

Against the teachings of ⇒Gottschalk on predestination, R. wrote a treatise *On Foreknowledge and Predestination, and on Free Will*, in which he attacked the monk of Orbais, and which was one of the chief causes for which Gottschalk was punished and imprisoned by order of ⇒Hincmar.

According to R., predestination is nothing but the foreknowledge of God, according to which God predestines to salvation those who will accept it and condemns those who will reject it. R. presents this as if it were the teaching of ⇒Augustine. This is an indication of the way in which the Middle Ages read and interpreted Augustine. On the other hand, his rival ⇒Ratramnus of Corbie appears to have had a clearer understanding of the teachings of Augustine.

JLG

Rahner, Hugo (1890–1968). The contribution of the Rahner brothers to Roman Catholic thought is similar to the contribution of the Niebuhr brothers to Protestant thought. Hugo, the elder brother of Karl ⇒Rahner, was born in Pluffenberg-Baden, Germany. He was ordained as a Jesuit priest in 1919. Like his brother, he was educated at the University of Innsbruck, Austria. In 1934 he finished his doctoral studies in Bonn in the area of church history. In 1937, fleeing from the Nazis, he was exiled in Switzerland. In 1945 he resumed his professorship in Innsbruck, where he also served as dean and professor of history and patristics. His historical studies on the relationship between church and state in the first eight centuries enjoy international recognition.

—

IG

Rahner, Karl (1904–84).

German Jesuit theologian and philosopher. He pursued advanced studies in Austria, Germany, and Holland, specializing in the philosophy of ⇒Kant, ⇒Hegel, and ⇒Heidegger. His theology expresses his commitment to the Roman Catholic tradition and to the thought of ⇒Thomas Aquinas. His doctoral thesis, *Spirit in the World*, establishes a synthesis between the thought of Heidegger and that of Thomas Aquinas which is known as Thomist transcendentalism. His doctoral adviser, Martin Honecker, who was an opponent of that theological current, rejected the thesis. Convinced that his viewpoint was correct, R. moved to Innsbruck. In 1936 his thesis was approved, and three years later he was able to publish it. In Innsbruck he began his career as professor of theology, a career that was abruptly interrupted by the advent of the Nazi regime. The Nazis closed the university and R. went into exile. From 1939 to 1944 he lived in Vienna, where he engaged in pastoral work. This pastoral experience helped him to understand that all authentic theology necessarily includes a practical dimension and a commitment to people.

The transcendental theology of R. is based on his interpretation of human nature. As a natural being, the human depends on and responds to the universal laws that govern nature. But what distinguishes the human being from the rest of creation is its spiritual dynamism, which defines it as a creative being. As a spiritual entity the human being is radically free, a being which gives itself the laws by which it governs its options and goals. Since it is free, the human being has the ability to manipulate and transform its natural and social world. Since it is free, it appears impossible to determine the limits of its creative capacity. Nevertheless, R.

asserts that the goal of the human being is found in its turning to God. Humanly authentic action must correspond to our human nature as free beings. Our deeds, our social arrangements, our intervention in nature and cultural development, all have as their purpose and goal the growth of our freedom. These are the good deeds. The deeds that negate or destroy our freedom are forbidden and are evil. The realization and preservation of our freedom constitute, according to R., the fundamental theological and moral norm. The goal of religious, moral, and social activity is the realization of our nature as free beings.

Freedom is the necessary condition for the human to realize its particular and unique personality, that is, for the realization of human dignity. And the realization of human dignity is the goal of creation, attained through the grace of God. The order of creation and the purpose of divine activity is the sustenance of our freedom. According to R., every human being has the consciousness, implicit or explicit, that God is the unique and authentic horizon of its spiritual dynamism. By affirming positively its being and by realizing its freedom, the human being acts in accordance with the purposes of God. When it acts in a way that violates its freedom, it denies and rejects God.

R. asserts that the human being is a social entity, created to enjoy its freedom in the company of other beings who are equally free. In the realization of our creative freedom and in our historic activity, we become interdependent. The human being is creator of community. To be a person and to live in community are correlative realities and experiences. By the grace of God we are inclined to live in community. R. questions the individualism that defines our present cultural life. Our perfection is correlative with our ability to serve and love others. As social beings we also should recognize that we must accept sacrifice in the present in order to improve conditions in the future. According to R., the priority of grace means that God is a God for humans, and that God's grace extends to every human being. Since this is the case, even non-Christians, whom he calls "anonymous Christians," can respond to the grace of God.

R. is probably the theologian who has written most on God as mystery. Our experience of God is a transcendental experience, that is, a primary experience, and therefore is not a product of human reflection. Because of our finitude, our theological concepts, no matter how refined, cannot capture the totality of God. To pretend otherwise is to say that God is merely one object among the many other objects of creation. The best way to describe God is through the silence and reverence that are experienced in the moment and context of worship.

Therefore theology must be humble in terms of the certainty it alleges. At the same time, theology is necessary and indispensable for a being which knows that its destiny is directed toward God and which inevitably asks about the meaning and purpose of its life. It is in our nature to attempt to understand our transcendental orientation toward that mystery which is God. Although, according to R., God is the foundation of all that exists, God is fundamentally distinct from every creature and created thing. Nonetheless, although God is different, God does not exist as a dual reality or as distinct from creation. The immanent and transcendent reality of God is what, in the final analysis, permits us to know and relate to all that exists in creation. For this reason our relations with others and with the objects of our world provide us with analogies by means of which we can understand something of the mystery of God. Theology grows in the measure that our creative ability grows. It is developed on the basis of new scientific understandings, historical experiences, human interdependence, and concerns about future generations.

R. was one of the most prolific theologians of the twentieth century. He preferred to publish short essays and theological monographs. His work covers the whole gamut of theological doctrines: the Trinity, Christology, grace, ecclesiology, anthropology, and eschatology. His analysis of the church as an institution that experiences the tension of being both hierarchical and charismatic, his defense of freedom of thought in the church, and his commitment to a pastoral practice that motivates the laity to be agents of critical decisions rather than persons who adapt to the established order all had great influence on the reforms of the Second Vatican Council (⇒Vatican II). His pastoral concern led him to discuss a variety of theological themes having to do with the life of the church: the authority of the Scriptures, the practice of the church in the diaspora, the relationship between faith and works, and the authority of the church. He supported ecumenical work and maintained a close dialogue with the theology of hope and European political theology. His writings on moral theology have had great influence in Europe and the United States. His moral concerns are evident in several essays on nuclear

weapons and on the technological manipulation of the human being and of nature.

According to R., authentic theology should guide and illumine the moral and spiritual problems of the moment. The theologian should be a spiritual guide and pastor who edifies believers and helps them to develop their thought in a rigorous way by means of reflection on experience, ecclesial tradition, and the Scriptures.

The theologian faces the future with hope but without false illusions. He or she lives and acts in the present with an optimistic attitude, but maintains a realistic stance. The theologian does not expect utopian transformations, and understands that suffering and evil are a part of the world, but such realism does not make the theologian passive or defensive. On the contrary, faith helps to maintain an adventurous spirit that is open to the new. God is involved as the theologian is also involved in the temporal and historical process of the human community, leading it toward a more loving and inclusive community. God is our future; God is active presence who calls us to respond to what God is doing in the world. The theologian is a participant in this future creativity of God. The theologian should incarnate the spirit of love, seeking new forms of community among human beings.

—

IG

Raiser, Konrad (1938–). German theologian and fifth executive secretary of the ⇒World Council of Churches. R. has an impeccable ecumenical trajectory accompanied by an openness to the historical changes that affect the ecumenical movement. His book *Ecumenism in Transition* (1991) is a critical reflection and a proposal for the ecumenical movement in the twenty-first century.

—

CCO

Ramée, Pierre de La ⇒**Ramus, Petrus**

Ramm, Bernard L. (1916–92). Evangelical theologian who was professor of philosophy and theology at several Baptist institutions, such as Baylor University, Eastern Baptist Seminary, and American Baptist Seminary of the West. R. devoted his teachings and written works to the intellectual defense of the conservative Protestant position. His book *Protestant Biblical Interpretation* (1950) argues that faith in the inspiration of the Bible does not eliminate the need for a rigorous scientific hermeneutic which studies the historical and linguistic context of the various literary genres of the Bible. In works on Christianity and science, R. rejected the literal interpretation of scientific references in the Bible. According to him, the Bible makes us "wise unto salvation," not in terms of science. Therefore R. tried to disconnect evangelical theology from fundamentalism and sought methodologies that would be in dialogue with modern criticism. His book *After Fundamentalism: The Future of Evangelical Theology* encourages evangelicals to look as ⇒Barth did for a theology faithful to the Reformation and to the Word of God, but in dialogue with the intellectual currents of the modern world.

—

EA

Ramsey, Ian (1915–72).

English philosopher who studied sciences and religion at Cambridge. He was professor of philosophy at Oxford before becoming bishop of Durham. His book *Religious Language* (1957) expounds his philosophy, which can be classified as a Christian empiricism rejecting the empirical-linguistic narrowness of positivism and the antiempiricism of the dialectical theologians.

—

LGP

Ramsey, Paul (1913–88).

R. stands out among North American Protestant ethicists for his influence on the political environment of the country. He supported the war in Vietnam, was active in the debates on abortion and on nuclear weapons, and contributed to the national policies on medical ethics.

His ethics emphasizes explicitly theological norms and the formulation of laws and principles that provide criteria by which we can choose ethical means to achieve good ends. His principal opponents, then, are the situational ethics of ⇒Fletcher and the contextualism of ⇒Lehmann, who emphasize moral ends and relativize means.

Christian ethics has a specific content: *agapē* love. *Agapē* provides firm criteria for determining whether the end and the means are moral.

Three types of rules express and implement Christian love:

1. Summary rules serve as advice about love. These rules are not categorical in nature.
2. General rules reveal those deeds that are always and unconditionally loving. They

are revealed in the covenants that God establishes with God's people.
3. Rules governing social customs and institutions that regulate our mutual relations, which R. calls "practical" rules, limit our inclination to act in the light of the immediate situation and remind us that the moral life has to do with relations and institutions that are continuous with the past and also relevant for the present and the future.

—

IG

Ramus, Petrus (1515–72).

Also known as Pierre de La Ramée. French philosopher and theologian who was prominent chiefly for his *Dialectics* (1555) and *Logic* (1556) because he related the study of logic to the art of discourse and because he put what he called dialectics in the place that the quantified logic of medieval scholasticism had previously occupied. His work inspired William ⇒Ames in his method of doing theology and influenced the rhetoric of ⇒Melanchthon. He also indirectly influenced ⇒Descartes with his emphasis on method. Nevertheless, his works on ⇒Zwingli, to whom he gave great attention, were not well received in his time.

—

ALG

Ratramnus of Corbie (?–868).

Scholarly monk who intervened in several of the theological controversies of the Carolingian period. He participated in the debate on predestination provoked by the teachings of ⇒Gottschalk and the reaction of ⇒Rabanus Maurus, ⇒Hincmar, and others. His treatise *On Predestination*, which some expected would support Hincmar over against Gottschalk, was exactly the opposite. R. knew the works of Augustine, and he therefore declared in his treatise that all humanity, as a consequence of the fall, is a "mass of perdition," and that God in love has predestined some individuals from that mass for salvation, while the rest are predestined for the condemnation that all deserve.

R. also intervened in the eucharistic controversy when Charles the Bald asked for his opinion about the treatise of ⇒Paschasius Radbertus on that subject, in which the latter affirmed that the body of Christ that is present in the Eucharist is the very body of the incarnate Lord. R. replied to this with a treatise *On the Body and Blood of the Lord*, in which he declared that the body of Christ in the Eucharist is present only "figuratively," and not "in reality." What this means is that although the body of Christ is indeed present, this presence cannot be proved in any way by the senses, in contrast to Paschasius Radbertus's assertion that many had seen the host bleed, and so forth. Finally, the eucharistic body is not the historical body of Jesus, which at present is at the right hand of the Father, but is an invisible spiritual body.

Other controversies of that time dealt with the nature of the soul. Against those who maintained that the soul is in a certain sense corporeal, R. wrote a treatise *On the Nature of the Soul*, in which he repeated the arguments of Augustine to deny that the soul is in any sense corporeal. The controversy on the existence of a universal soul was more prolonged. This controversy dealt with an obscure passage of Augustine which seemed to assert that the soul of all of humanity is one. In this controversy R. wrote a treatise titled *On the Soul, to* ⇒Odo of Beauvais. This is the main extant writing from that debate, but fortunately in this work R. summarizes the different phases of the controversy. The position of R. himself is that a multitude of souls exists, one for each person. In order to support this stance, R. makes use of his understanding of universals, which are real only as concepts. Thus, although the concept of "soul" is one, a multitude of individual and real souls are included in it.

Finally, while R. maintained the perpetual virginity of Mary, he criticized those who, in order to defend that virginity, said that the birth of·Jesus did not take place in the natural way, but that the Savior emerged from the womb in some miraculous fashion. According to R., Jesus came into the world "by the natural door," but this occurrence did not affect the physical virginity of his mother.

———

JLG

Ratzinger, Joseph (1927–). Pope Benedict XVI since 2005. Cardinal and theologian, native of Bavaria, who was known above all as the prefect of the Congregation of the Doctrine of the Faith, a position to which ⇒John Paul II appointed him in 1981. He was also president of the Pontifical Biblical Commission and of the International Theological Commission of the Vatican. He served as the principal theological expert for Cardinal Joseph Frings of Cologne during the Second Vatican Council (⇒Vatican II). He was cofounder of the international journal *Communio* in 1972, together with Hans Urs von ⇒Balthasar and Henri de ⇒Lubac. In 1977 Paul VI named him archbishop of Munich and

Freising, and the following year he was made a cardinal.

The theology of R., profoundly influenced by patristic sources, revolves chiefly around the theme of the church. His thesis, *Volk und Haus Gottes in Augustins Lehre von der Kirche* (People and House of God in Augustine's Doctrine of the Church), examines the ecclesiology of ⇒Augustine. The latter, with ⇒Bonaventure, von Balthasar, and Romano ⇒Guardini are the theologians who have had the most influence on R. In addition, the themes of truth and freedom prevail in his thought, and he has written on liturgical, catechetical, and sacramental theology.

After the death of John Paul II on April 2, 2005, R. was elected his successor and took the name Benedict XVI.

———

MAG

Rauschenbusch, Walter (1861–1918). North American Baptist pastor and theologian who inspired the social gospel movement at the end of the nineteenth century and the beginning of the twentieth. This movement sought to relate personal faith to the challenges of justice and social transformation, beginning from the biblical, theological, and ethical nucleus of the kingdom of God. R. has been called the father of this movement because of the exceptional influence he exercised over it.

Theologians such as Reinhold ⇒Niebuhr and pastors like Martin Luther ⇒King Jr. recognized the decisive influence of R. on their thought.

August Rauschenbusch, father of Walter, was the sixth in an uninterrupted family line of German Lutheran pastors. In 1846 he emigrated from the land of his birth as a Lutheran missionary to the United States. In the United States he adopted Baptist beliefs and was rebaptized. During his forty-four years in the United States, he traveled to Germany frequently, and thus maintained an active ministry in both contexts. His intense Westphalian pietism totally filled his life, thought, and ministry.

Walter R. is best understood against the cultural and religious background from which he came. In the words of Paul ⇒Tillich, August and Walter were "theologians on the frontier" between Germany and the United States.

R. was born in Rochester, N.Y., but received his basic education and began his ministerial work in Westphalia. There, at the age of sixteen, he had a personal experience of Jesus Christ. As he himself affirmed, "It determined my path forever, and I thank God for it."

Although this experience and his baptism did not have for Walter the same sense of rupture as in the case of his father, they helped him experience the presence of God as the source of all power to undertake the daily imitation of Jesus Christ. He finished his university (1884) and theological (1886) studies in the university and the seminary of Rochester, where he was able to observe and analyze the different theological currents of his time. He wanted to be a missionary, but his application was rejected because of his sympathy for the historical-critical method.

In 1886 he succeeded his father as pastor of the Second German Baptist Church of New York, where he served until 1907. His pastoral influence went beyond the life of the congregation, and he became a community leader. He inspired and founded the Brotherhood of the Kingdom, a group of Christians committed to social change. His ministry in Hell's Kitchen, as that wretched neighborhood came to be known where the poor and the immigrants lived, produced in R. the conviction that an intense private devotional life is not enough for a life of faithful discipleship to Jesus Christ nor as an answer to the challenges of the mission of the church. In 1891 his theology began to take shape, starting from the kingdom of God as the central concept that includes personal faith and social transformation. His chief work, *The Righteousness of the Kingdom* (1968), probably written during those decisive years of his pastorate, was not published until long after his death.

In 1907, when he published his *Christianity and the Social Crisis*, which rapidly made him famous, he began his teaching career in Rochester Seminary. There he taught New Testament (1897–1902) and church history (1902–17).

Four elements characterize the life and thought of R.: an intense quest for communion with God through Scripture and prayer; a certain influence of liberal theology, which is expressed in his concepts of Jesus Christ and the kingdom of God; a profound knowledge of the history of the church, which is manifest in his writings; and an understanding, unusual in his time, of socioeconomic realities, which he acquired by linking with Marxist notions. His life and ministry are a combination of evangelical piety, liberal theology, and reformist activism. His greatest theological contribution was his acute articulation of "social sin," a category that only recently has reappeared in theological parlance.

He died shortly before the end of the First World War. At the time, his German origin and his opposition to the involvement of the United States in the war had dimmed his popularity.

OLM

Rayan, Samuel (1920–). Charismatic Roman Catholic priest and one of the most important theologians of India. He studied at the Gregorian University in 1960 and has served as professor of theology and dean of the Vidya Jyoti Institute in Delhi, India. His theology of the Holy Spirit, developed in his book *The Holy Spirit: Heart of the Gospel and Christian Hope* (1978), proposes a divine activity as agent of transformation in society. This activity leads the church to participate in society in favor of justice. It also leads to openness in the encounter with other religions.

CCO

Raymond of Peñafort (ca. 1175–1275). Spanish canonist. Born in Barcelona, he taught rhetoric and logic and specialized in law at Bologna. He joined the Dominican order and returned to Spain. He assisted Peter Nolasco in founding the Mercedarians, a religious order dedicated to the rescue of Christian captives. He became so interested in the conversion of Jews and Muslims that he resigned his ecclesiastic offices in order to establish schools of Hebrew and Arabic. Apparently it was he who asked ⇒Thomas Aquinas to write the *Summa contra gentiles*. He was canonized by Clement VIII in 1601.

CEA

Raymond of Toledo (12th century). Bishop of that city. He showed great interest in the sciences and the philosophy of the ancients, and also of the Arabs. He gathered around himself the famous "translators of Toledo" (Domingo ⇒González; ⇒John of Spain), whose work had an enormous impact on Western theology from the thirteenth century onward (⇒Thomas Aquinas).

JLG

Reimarus, Herman Samuel (1694–1768). Professor in Hamburg, Germany, who wrote, but did not publish, *A Defense of Rational Worshipers of God*. After his death, Gotthold Lessing published extracts of this work which questioned, on the basis of reason, a number of fundamental Christian teachings, among them the historical character of the Gospels. For this reason R. became one of the fathers of the "quest of the historical Jesus." The publication of his work influenced not only his contemporaries but also, a hundred years later, first David F. ⇒ Strauss and then Albert ⇒Schweitzer.

—

EA

Reina, Casiodoro de (1520–94).

Spanish friar of the monastery of San Isidoro del Campo in Santiponce, near Seville. He accepted the ideas of the Reformation and had to flee the Inquisition, settling at first in Geneva. However, he soon came to the conclusion that Geneva had become "a new Rome" because of the rigidity and intolerance imposed by the leaders of the Reformation in that city. He moved to Frankfurt, where he was received by the French-speaking church. He then went to England, where he became pastor of a congregation made up of Spanish exiles. In England he began the first translation of the Bible into Spanish on the basis of the original languages, and when he returned to Frankfurt he devoted himself full time to this labor. As an aid he had the work of predecessors who had translated portions of the Bible into Spanish, such as the New Testament of Juan ⇒Pérez de (la) Pineda (which in the end he was not able to use, because it had been confiscated by the authorities) and of Francisco de ⇒Encinas, the Psalms of Juan de ⇒Valdés, and the Old Testament of the Jews of Ferrara.

It was not until 1569 that, while living in Basel and with the financial support of a Calvinist banker, he was finally able to publish the translation of the entire Bible into Spanish, with a printing of 2,600 copies. This edition is known as the Bible of the Bear (*Biblia del Oso*) because of its frontispiece, which depicts a bear.

—

JRI

Reitzenstein, Richard (1861–1931).

German classical philologist who studied mystery religions, Gnosticism, and Mandaeanism. He also studied the influence of these currents on the development of the faith and practices of primitive Christianity.

—

AEM

Rembao, Alberto (1895?–1962).

Mexican Protestant theologian. He belonged to the first generation of Latin American Protes-

tant theologians who came to maturity in the missionary conferences of Panama (1916), Montevideo (1925), and Havana (1929). His theological work has at least three dimensions: First, R. was executive secretary of the Committee on Cooperation in Latin America and worked with John ⇒Mackay, Samuel ⇒Inman, Stanley ⇒Rycroft, Sancte Uberto ⇒Barbieri, Gonzalo ⇒Báez Camargo, and others. He was an ardent promoter of missionary cooperation in the Latin American continent and the Caribbean.

Second, R. was one of the first Protestant theologians who reflected on the relationship of Protestantism with Latin American culture and politics. His book *Discourse to the Evangelical Nation* is a theological proposal for the legitimate place of Protestantism in the continent. Other books that reflect this concern are his novels, among which the best known is *Lupita*, and his many articles in the magazine of the Committee on Cooperation in Latin America, *La nueva democracia*.

Third, R. was an itinerant teacher in many seminaries in Latin America. His presentations and lectures affirmed Latin American identity and the Protestant faith as an agent of modernization in the continent.

In the last decade of the twentieth century, members of ⇒Fraternidad Teológica Latinoamericana (FTL) went to R.'s writings to explore once again the relationships among culture, gospel, and Protestant faith in Latin America. R. was undoubtedly one of the most prolific theologians in Latin America until the middle of the twentieth century.

—

CCO

Remigius of Auxerre (9th century).

Disciple of ⇒Heiric of Auxerre in the monastery of St. Germain, in that city. In 893, at the request of the archbishop of Reims, he went to Reims to teach in its cathedral schools, and then went to Paris for the same purpose. He wrote commentaries on Genesis and the Psalms, as well as on some of the writings of ⇒Augustine and John Scotus ⇒Erigena. Following Erigena, he was a realist on the matter of universals. His biblical interpretation is allegorical. The image of God in humanity consists in rationality, while the likeness of God consists in holiness. Sin has deprived us of the likeness, but not of the image.

—

JLG

Renan, Ernest (1823–92). French historian and philosopher. From infancy on he showed a vocation for the priesthood, but while he was studying at the Major Seminary of St. Sulpicius he had a crisis of faith. He then abandoned religion and devoted himself to the study of science. When he was twenty-five years old, he wrote *The Future of Science*, in which he insists that science is a religion that is capable of solving by itself every problem and will one day replace religion. He became an authority on Eastern languages and on the history of religions. His writings reveal a profoundly critical and rationalistic attitude, especially in the explanation of the miracles of Christ. Particularly through his famous *Life of Jesus*, he was one of the main exponents of the skeptical position vis-à-vis Christianity that was adopted by the French intellectuals of the second half of the nineteenth century.

———

RAR

Renato, Camilo (ca. 1500–75). Sicilian Anabaptist whose original name was Paul Ricci. In his youth he was a Franciscan monk and had contact with reformers such as Juan de ⇒Valdés, developing an eclectic Protestant-style theology. When he was accused of heresy in 1540, he wrote a courageous defense titled *Apology*. In 1541 he adopted the name Renato (i.e., born again). Due to his heterodox views on the Trinity, he was persecuted by Catholics and Protestants alike. He had a strong influence on the theology of Laelius Socinus.

———

PAJ

Reuchlin, Johannes (1455–1522). German humanist and pioneer in the scientific study of classical Greek. He published a Latin lexicon in 1475–76. He then became interested in the study of Hebrew, and in 1506 his scholarly work *De rudimentaris hebraicis* appeared. He was the most important professor of Greek and Hebrew in his country, so that the humanists thought only ⇒Erasmus surpassed him. He was judged by the Inquisition at the initiative of the Dominicans (⇒Pfefferkorn), but was exonerated by Pope Leo X.

———

ALG

Rhegius, Urbanus (1489–1541). Also known as Regius or Rieger. Educator, author, priest, and Lutheran pastor. He was influenced by humanism. ⇒Eck, a major opponent of ⇒Luther, was his mentor at the beginning of his career. In 1520 he was assigned as preacher in Augsburg cathedral. After the Diet of Augsburg (1530) he was dismissed as preacher by the emperor. His efforts to reconcile the positions of Luther and ⇒Zwingli were in vain. He achieved his greatest reforming work as superintendent in Lüneburg by providing faithful and effective preachers for the congregations. Among his best-known works are *De dignitate sacerdotum* (1521; On the Dignity of Priests), *Novae doctrinae ad veterem collatio* (1526; Comparison of the New Doctrine with the Old), *Formula caute loquendi* (1535; *Preaching the Reformation*, 2003), and *Doctrina certissima* (1545; Most Certain Doctrine).

———

ALG

Ricci, Matteo (1552–1610). An Italian Jesuit, R. is considered the founder of modern missions in China. He arrived in Macao, China, in 1580. There he learned the Chinese language and three years later received permission to settle in Chao-ch'ing, to the west of Canton. One of the great accomplishments of R. was the translation into Latin of the "Four Books," which were the academic sources for the knowledge required of every Chinese scholar of that time. By this exploit he merits the title of founder of Sinology, the Western study of Chinese culture.

In 1601 R. asked for permission to preach and teach the Christian faith. With his knowledge of the language and the culture of the country, and with the purpose of starting a contextual mission, which was approved by his superior Alessandro Valignano, R. began to adopt the cultural styles of Confucian scholars. Even more, he proposed that the honors given to ancestors, in particular the honors rendered to Confucius, were not a superstition or a religious rite, but part of the academic formation of Chinese scholars. Those elements of his missiology led to what is known as the controversy about Chinese rites, which was not resolved until 1742.

Finally, through his many translations of scholarly works, both from Latin into Chinese and from Chinese into Latin, R. became an important figure in the Confucian scholarly world. His last work was a history of the introduction of Christianity into China. By special permission of the emperor, whom he never met, R. was buried in Ch'a-la, in a cemetery that bears his name, where there are more than sixty graves of other Jesuits who served as missionaries in China.

———

CCO

Richard of Middleton (?–ca. 1308).

Franciscan, disciple of ⇒Bonaventure, who was probably the most respected Franciscan theologian in the time between Bonaventure and ⇒Scotus. While he followed the Franciscan line in matters such as the priority of the will over reason and the absurdity of an eternal creation, in epistemology he adopted an intermediate position between traditional Franciscanism and Thomism, granting to the senses an important place in the development of knowledge. He also asserted that philosophy—which ought always to be subject to the teachings of revelation—is an independent science with its own method and is capable of arriving at its own conclusions even aside from theology or from the guidance given by faith.

—

JLG

Richard of St. Victor (?–ca. 1173).

Famous teacher of that school, born in Scotland, and successor of ⇒Hugh of St. Victor. Like Hugh, R. sought to relate rational theology or dialectic with contemplative or mystical theology. According to him, there are three stages of knowledge: *Cogitatio* is based on the imagination and drags itself on the ground in spite of all its efforts. *Meditatio* is based on reason and walks through a combination of effort and results. *Contemplatio* has to do with the intellectual spirit, and by the grace of God it flies without any effort and with the highest results. This last level of knowledge leads to the contemplation of God, although not in such a way that the mind grasps God, but through an intuitive knowledge which permits the soul to know that which is greater than the soul itself, what medieval thinkers called "knowledge of excess." R. discusses all of this in his mystical works, which include *Benjamin the Lesser*, or *Book of Preparation of the Soul for Contemplation*, and *Benjamin the Greater*, or *Book of the Grace of Contemplation*. He also wrote allegorical commentaries on the Bible, particularly on the Song of Songs and on Revelation.

In his six books *On the Trinity*, he argues that Trinitarian doctrine is an expression of the love that is the very nature of God, because love requires a plurality of persons.

—

JLG

Richard, Pablo (1939–).

Chilean Roman Catholic priest, biblical scholar, and sociologist of religion. R., who is one of the best-known liberation theologians in the world, has been professor at the National University of Costa Rica, researcher of the Ecumenical Department of Investigations (DEI), and visiting professor in universities and seminaries all over the world. His contribution to liberation theology has been the rediscovery of a popular hermeneutic for the reading of the Bible in ecclesial base communities and a sociology for understanding the history and development of the church and theological thought in Latin America.

Many of his writings have been published by DEI and in the journal *RIBLA*, which is also a publication of DEI. Some of these writings have been translated into different languages, among them, into English, *Death of Christendom, Birth of the Church* (1987) and *The Struggle of the Gods* (1983). Among his most recent works is an exegetical commentary on the book of Revelation, published by DEI.

—

CCO

Richer, Edmond (1559–1631).

French theologian who was instrumental in the development of Gallicanism. In 1611 he published *On Ecclesiastical and Political Power*. This brief book asserted that Christ, as the head of the church, delegates his authority to every believer. He thus rejected the idea that the church necessarily has a hierarchical structure.

—

PAJ

Ricoeur, Paul (1913–2005).

French philosopher. Born in Valence, R. lost his parents at an early age and was brought up by his grandparents in French Brittany. He studied in Rennes, and at the Sorbonne in Paris he studied under the guidance of Gabriel Marcel. Until the Second World War he was a schoolteacher. During the war he participated as a combatant (receiving the Croix de Guerre for heroism) and was prisoner in a concentration camp. After the end of the armed conflict he was appointed professor in the universities of Strasbourg and Nanterre, and later in Paris and Chicago. His first philosophical interest was the phenomenology of Husserl (whose works he translated into French). His reflection about the problem of evil led him to hermeneutics and to the study of the symbol. His first great work was *Philosophy of Will*, in three volumes. His essays on *Biblical Interpretation* explore the way in which religious texts speak of God. R. has shown great interest in the comparative study of texts and perspectives. In addition, he has published many books on diverse hermeneutical subjects, almost always from a philosophical perspective that is respectful of faith and in dialogue with it. Among his books the following ones stand out: *The Symbolism of Evil*, which is part of the work *Finitude and Culpability*; *Freedom and Nature: The Voluntary and the Involuntary*; *Interpretation and Ideology*; and *The Rule of Metaphor*.

———

OOE

Ridley, Nicholas (ca. 1500–55).
English martyr, reformer, chaplain, and bishop. He was influenced not only by the Reformers but also by the medieval theology of ⇒Ratramnus. He was burned at the stake in Oxford because he rejected transubstantiation in the Eucharist. He used his religious influence to create hospitals and schools.

———

EPA

Ritschl, Albrecht (1822–89).
German Lutheran theologian; important exponent of liberal German Protestantism. Together with ⇒Schleiermacher he was one of the two top figures of Continental Protestant theology of the nineteenth century. His influence extended to England and the United States. Son of a Lutheran bishop who was a member of the Prussian elite in Bonn, R. developed a vocation for theology and obtained his education in important theological centers: Bonn, Halle, Heidelberg, and Tübingen. He initiated his teaching career in Bonn (1846–64) and brought it to culmination in Göttingen (1864–89). His areas of research, publications, and teaching were theology and ethics, historical studies of the church and its theology, and New Testament.

Among the formative influences in his work are the Scriptures; the theology of the Reformers, in particular ⇒Luther; the thought of ⇒Kant, ⇒Schleiermacher, F. C. ⇒Baur, and Richard Rothe; and his debates with and opposition to two currents in German Lutheranism: confessionalism and pietism. His work reflects an understanding of theology as the reconceptualization of Christian faith in dialogue with the epistemological and ethical challenges of the modern world, including the natural sciences, the historical method, and the comparative approach to religions and philosophy.

The contribution of R. as a historian of the church and of theology, and as a systematic theologian, first appears in his book *The Rise of the Old Catholic Church* (1850, 1857), written against his famed teacher Ferdinand Christian Baur. There, anticipating the work of his disciple A. ⇒Harnack, he argues that Catholicism is not a synthesis between Jewish Christianity and gentile-Hellenic Christianity, but a totally gentile phenomenon which is a deviation and an alienation from the Judaic heritage of early Christianity. His work in three volumes, *Justification and Reconciliation* (1870–74), is his greatest contribution to theology. In this work R. proposes, in a form novel for his time, that the Christian faith is centered in the revelation of God in Jesus, whose life and message are centered in the will of God to establish God's kingdom. God makes it possible in Jesus Christ to receive the gift of the kingdom (justification) and to realize this kingdom by means of the ethical life in the context of society with its vocations and institutions (reconciliation). This in turn leads R. to defend the subjective or moral theory of the atonement of ⇒Abelard over against the objective or juridical theory of ⇒Anselm. His *History of Pietism*, also in three volumes (1880–86), is a massive critical study of the primary sources of Dutch, German, and Swiss pietism. Its purpose was to combat pietism as a theological option for the reformation of the church.

In his time R. had great influence and popularity in the theological academy and the church, where his work was both accepted and debated. His theology was disseminated in the academic world by several of his famous disciples whom he sponsored, and by other followers: Harnack, ⇒Troeltsch, and ⇒Rauschenbusch, among others. The first generation of neo-orthodox theologians (⇒Brunner, ⇒Barth) severely criticized R., thus contributing to the eclipse and neglect of his work.

Contemporary interpreters of R. consider him a pioneer and a contributor to modern historical studies of the Reformation and of Luther. He is also credited with an understanding of theology as a critical and constructive task based on the revelation that is available in the Scriptures, but which is interpreted as centering in Jesus Christ and in the ecclesial context. R. has also contributed to the development of the method of correlation in theology and to the emphasis on the centrality of the kingdom of God for Christian theology, including its religious and ethical dimensions.

———

LRR

Rivera Pagán, Luis (1942–).
Puerto Rican theologian and researcher. Professor of humanities in the University of Puerto Rico, adjunct professor in the Evangelical Seminary

of Puerto Rico. Later he went on to occupy the John A. ⇒ Mackay Chair of World Christianity at Princeton Theological Seminary. His books include *Entre el oro y la fe: El dilema de América* (Between Gold and Faith: The Dilemma of America); *Mito, exilio y demonios: Literatura y teología en América Latina* (Myth, Exile, and Demons: Literature and Theology in Latin America); *Los sueños del ciervo: Perspectivas teológicas desde el Caribe* (The Dreams of the Stag: Theological Perspectives from the Caribbean); and *Evangelización y violencia: La conquista de América* (A Violent Evangelism: The Political and Religious Conquest of the Americas).

—

LMcA

Robert of Courçon (?–1218). Englishman, professor in Paris, and later cardinal. In 1215, as chancellor of the University of Paris, he participated in and endorsed the condemnation of the reading of the works of ⇒Aristotle on natural philosophy.

—

JLG

Robert of Melun (?–1167). Englishman, professor in Paris and later in Melun, where he founded his own school. His theology combines the perspectives of ⇒Abelard and ⇒Hugh of St. Victor. He participated in the synod of Reims in 1148, which condemned the teachings of ⇒Gilbert de La Porrée. He wrote *Sentences* in the style of those of ⇒Peter Lombard, although he strongly criticized the "christological nihilism" of the latter.

—

JLG

Robert of Retines (12th century). Philosopher and theologian who went to Spain because he was attracted by the work of the translators of Toledo (Domingo ⇒González). He then contributed to the introduction of Aristotelian and Arabian philosophy into France and England.

—

JLG

Robinson, James M. (1924–). North American theologian, professor of New Testament and early Christian history, and internationally known specialist in the gnostic literature of Nag Hammadi. He studied in Basel (Switzerland) under the tutelage of Karl ⇒Barth, but he was mainly influenced by the demythologizing ideas of Rudolf ⇒Bultmann.

R. contributed to the new search for the historical Jesus and also to the reconstruction of the hypothetical source (or Gospel of) Q.

—

NRG

Robinson, John Arthur Thomas (1919–83). Bishop, theologian, and biblical scholar. Born in Canterbury, he was educated at Cambridge under C. H. ⇒Dodd. He taught in that university until he was elected Anglican bishop of Woolwich, although soon afterward he returned to teaching in Cambridge, where he remained until his death. He appears to have been a rebel in New Testament studies, especially because of his two books *Redating the New Testament* (1975) and *The Priority of John* (1984). In the first book he insists that all the New Testament was written after the destruction of Jerusalem in the year 70; in the second, he proposes that the Gospel of John is earlier than the Synoptics. R. is known internationally for another work, *Honest to God* (1963), which received both applause and fierce criticism. This book is a theological reflection on radical German (and European) thought of the time and its implications for the Christian believer.

—

OOE

Rogers, Carl R. (1902–87). North American humanist and existentialist psychologist. He began studies for the ministry in Union Theological Seminary in New York, but he left them to enter the program of clinical psychology at Columbia University, where he received his doctorate in 1931. He put aside psychoanalysis and created a therapy centered in the person (or client). The central hypothesis of R. is that individuals have vast resources for understanding themselves and for altering their behaviors and reorienting the attitudes and conduct that affect them. Hence his emphasis on the thesis that the types of a person's behavior are better understood when they are examined from the internal frame of reference of the individual in an environment in which the therapeutic climate is created or the necessary conditions are provided to bring about change: authenticity, positive unconditional respect, and empathetic understanding.

His theories transformed the fields of secular and pastoral psychology. His principal works are *Client-Centered Therapy* (1951), *On Becoming a Person* (1961), and *A Way of Being* (1980).

—

JR

Rogers, William (1818–96). Anglican, reformer of education in England. As a pastor from 1845 to 1863 he devoted himself to elementary education, establishing a network of schools in his poor parish in St. Thomas, Charterhouse. In 1863 he continued with this work in middle-class schools. He was severely criticized because he tried to exclude religious teaching from school, asserting that this was the work of parents and the clergy.

————

JFM

Roland of Cremona (?–1271). Teacher in the Dominican center of studies in Paris. When the University of Paris disbanded in 1229 owing to a number of conflicts, the Dominicans began to admit students who were not Dominicans to the classes of R. When the university was reorganized, R. remained in it as a professor, and thus the Dominicans gained their first chair in the University of Paris.

————

JLG

Rolle, Richard (ca. 1300–49). His full name was Richard Rolle de Hampole. He was an English mystic, author of ascetic and mystical treatises. He lived a hermit's life and served as spiritual mentor of the nuns of Hampole. R. is known chiefly for his devotional prose, which was written in a vernacular language and directed particularly to female readers.

————

ALG

Romero, Oscar Arnulfo (1917–80). Archbishop of San Salvador, El Salvador. R. assumed the leadership of the diocese of San Salvador in the midst of a warlike conflict in the entire country. A churchman whose pastoral style was traditional and whose theological formation was conservative, R. was soon forced to assume spiritual and moral leadership vis-à-vis the situation in which his people were living. He then took the difficult stance of pastor and prophet over against the suffering caused by extreme poverty and by the marginalization and persecution of the people, taken to the ultimate consequence of torture and martyrdom.

As the Salvadoran civil war became more violent, R. continued to attune his ear and to raise his voice. The famous phrase "I am the voice of those who have no voice" resounded all the way from the pulpit to episcopal conferences. His own sermons and biblical studies progressively challenged him to assume his role as a prophetic voice and finally led to his martyrdom. Because he opted for a pastoral practice of accompaniment and solidarity, R. knew that his life was in danger. He succeeded in articulating a theology of discipleship with a clear christological profile.

Monsignor R. was murdered in the chapel of Providence Hospital in San Salvador on March 24, 1980, just at the moment of preparation for the eucharistic consecration. His death moved the whole world, and in particular Central America. His memory remains precisely as he desired: "If they kill me, I will arise in the Salvadoran people." His body rests in the cathedral of San Salvador.

————

CEA

Roscelin (1050–1120). Philosopher and theologian who was condemned in Soissons (1092) but was able to continue teaching in other places. He was particularly interested in dialectics, or the use of reason in theological matters. What caused him the greatest difficulties was his nominalist stance regarding the question of universals, while his contemporaries were inclined toward realism. According to R., universals do not exist and in reality are no more than "the wind of the voice." Thus, for example, "humanity" does not exist. What exists are individual human beings, whom we join through the word "humanity." This in turn led him to prefer, in the matter of the Trinity, the vocabulary of the Eastern church to the Latin vocabulary. The Eastern church says that there are three hypostases in God, while the Western church asserts that there are three persons and one substance. Because "hypostasis" can be translated as "substance," this stance caused the accusation of tritheism to be made against him. Among those who criticized him was ⇒Abelard, to whom R., in his own defense, directed an *Epistle to Abelard*. Also ⇒Anselm attacked him in an *Epistle on the Incarnation of the Word*. Although his Trinitarian teaching is not entirely clear, and it is probably distorted by his adversaries, there is no doubt that his nominalist stance made it difficult for R. to accept a large part of the philosophy and theology of his time.

————

JLG

Roscio, Juan Germán (1763–1821). Lawyer who became the most important theologian of the Hispanic American Revolution.

He was born in Venezuela and earned his doctorate in canon and civil law. As a jurist he was characterized by his anticlerical liberalism and by his defense of freedom of worship. Together with Francisco de Miranda he made possible the publication of the articles of William Burke, an Irishman who promoted religious tolerance. All his works are a coherent theological apology for democracy, for the legal status of the citizen, and of religious liberty. He translated Thomas ⇒Paine's works into Spanish. His most important work was published in Philadelphia (1817) under the title *The Triumph of Liberty Over Despotism*. He also published a treatise in which he demonstrated the ambiguities of the Catholic curia, giving as an example Bishop Chiaramonti, who as bishop supported the French Revolution and later as pope repressed the Hispanic American Revolution.

The Political Catechism is also attributed to R. Later his works helped shape the political-religious thought of Benito Juárez.

———

GC

Roswitha (10th century). Also known as Hrosvitha. German poet, theologian, and abbess. Coming from a noble family, she was abbess of Gandersheim in Saxony. Famous in her day, but forgotten soon after her death, the manuscripts of her works were discovered in Regensburg by the humanist Conrad Celtis and were published for the first time in 1501. Today R. has again aroused great interest. Her works are poems and theatrical pieces through which she comments on biblical texts, on the lives of several saints, and on some theological subjects. Her writings show that she had an excellent knowledge of the church fathers and of the Greco-Roman classics. According to her, Terence was her literary model, although she did not hesitate to criticize his image of women fiercely.

———

OOE

Rouse, Ruth (1872–1956). A native of England, ecumenical leader, and promoter of the missionary and ecumenical movement in the entire world. She was one of the first women to participate actively in the Student Christian Movement and in the YWCA (Young Women's Christian Association). R. is considered the feminine counterpart of John R. ⇒Mott. Toward the end of her career she contributed significantly as a writer on the history

of the missionary and ecumenical movement, as is shown by her work *History of the Ecumenical Movement, 1517–1948*, edited with Stephen ⇒Neill.

———

CCO

Reuther, Rosemary Radford (1936–). Activist in favor of civil rights, an ecumenist, and forerunner of feminist criticism in Christian theology. Her vast theological production covers several thematic areas and disciplines, among which are patristics, feminism, Catholicism and its relation with ecumenism, anti-Semitism, international politics, globalization, and ecology. The methodological principles of her criticism are sketched in her book *Sexism and God-Talk*. In this classic of feminist theology, she establishes the bases for a reinterpretation of the Judeo-Christian tradition starting from the experience of women. This reinterpretation attempts to humanize and dignify women by rediscovering the prophetic and liberating tradition of sacred texts. This "usable tradition," as R. prefers to call it, is opposed to texts and traditions that legitimate patriarchal relations in society and the church. R. upholds a broad understanding of patriarchalism as a system maintaining hierarchies of domination and a dualistic conception of reality. Beginning with feminist criticism, she establishes the bases for the reflection that will identify the greater part of her written work on other patriarchal systems, such as colonialism, the exploitation of the environment, economic oppression, racism, and heterosexism.

———

JRI

Rufinus (345–411). Monk, translator, and historian. He studied in his native city, Aquileia, and then in Rome, where he became a friend of ⇒Jerome. After traveling through Egypt for some time, he settled in Palestine, where he founded a monastery and continued his friendship with Jerome. Upon his return to Italy, R. was a protagonist in a bitter controversy concerning the theology of ⇒Origen, whose works he was translating into Latin. When some people complained about the strange ideas that appeared in those works, R. suggested that Jerome had approved them. This caused a misunderstanding between the friends, who were reconciled for a time, but then criticized each other again in a dispute that R. appears to have tried to resolve, but which Jerome, with his vehement temperament, would not put to rest.

The result has been that later centuries have viewed R. with mistrust, through the eyes and the interpretation of Jerome.

An important feature of the work of R. is his translations, not only of Origen, but also of ⇒Gregory of Nazianzus, ⇒Pamphilus of Caesarea, ⇒Eusebius of Caesarea, and others. In some cases, as occurs with the major part of Origen's treatise *On First Principles*, the original Greek text is lost, and only the translation of R. survives. Unfortunately, since R. himself affirms that, at least in the case of Origen, he has tried to clarify some of the doubtful teachings that appeared in the original text, the translations of R. should be read with a degree of mistrust. The *Commentary on the Creed* of R. is one of the principal sources we have for the study of the Old Roman creed, known among scholars as R, that gave shape to the Apostles' Creed.

Finally, besides giving publicity in the West to the *Ecclesiastical History* of Eusebius of Caesarea, R. added to it an appendix bringing that history up to the death of Theodosius in 395, and this is a most important source for the study of the history of the church in the fourth century.

———
JLG

Russell, Letty Mandeville (1929–).
Born in Westfield, New Jersey, where she was a member of the Presbyterian church. She graduated from Wellesley College in Massachusetts in 1951. She participated in the Student Christian Movement of New England, an experience on which she grounded much of her ministry. On graduating from the university, she taught third grade while also directing the program of Christian education in a small Methodist church in Connecticut. Then, in 1952, she went to the East Harlem Protestant Parish in New York as director of religious education. Her conviction that the gospel is a source of transformation was her guide during this ministry.

She continued her studies at Harvard Divinity School, graduating in 1958. She was one of the first women to be ordained to the ministry in the Presbyterian Church in the United States. She returned to the ministry in East Harlem as pastor for ten more years, during the civil rights movement. Her experiences there shaped her educational theory and her feminist theology. In 1967 she obtained the master's degree in theology (STM) from Union Theological Seminary, specializing in Christian education and

theology. The following year she left the ministry in East Harlem to continue her theological studies. In 1969 she received the doctorate in theology (ThD), with a specialization in the theology of mission and ecumenism. She taught at Manhattan College until 1974, when she joined the faculty of Yale Divinity School.

For R. the biblical foundations have been central. The concept of *oikodome*, edification (Eph. 4:11–16; 1 Cor. 3:10–11), gave initial shape to her educational work. In the 1970s, when liberation theologies began to be heard and evaluated, she began to view Christian education through those lenses. She continued to define education as the process through which one comes to understand liberation in Christ. Starting from that concept, R. has developed the theme of partnership in her works on feminist hermeneutics, theology, and education. She defines this idea as "a relation of mutuality and trust based on the gift of the partnership of God with us." Her chief works on this subject are *The Future of Partnership* (1979) and *Growth in Partnership* (1982). She is the wife of Johannes Christian ⇒Hoekendijk.

———
ECF

Ruysbroeck (or Ruusbroec), Jan van (1293–1381).
Mystic. Born near Brussels, R. was educated in the Belgian capital, where he also was ordained as presbyter in 1317. Twenty-eight years later he retired to the valley of Groenendaal, where, with several companions, he founded a community of contemplative regular canons. R. served as superior of the community until his death. The popularity of this Flemish mystic and of his group spread throughout Europe, and the community in the valley of Groenendaal became a prominent center of the later movements known as the *devotio moderna* and the Brothers of the Common Life. Thomas à ⇒Kempis is perhaps the most famous disciple of R. The best-known literary work of R. is *Spiritual Marriage*, in which he teaches the surrender to God in love. His prose was of the highest importance in the development of the Flemish language.

———
OOE

Rycroft, W. Stanley (1899–1993).
Englishman and minister of the Free Church of Scotland. He was a missionary in Peru, where he worked in the University of San Marcos and followed in the steps of John A. ⇒Mackay. In

1940 he was named executive secretary for the Committee on Cooperation in Latin America, a missionary organization and ecumenical promoter in the Latin American continent. Chief among his writings is *Religion and Faith in Latin America* (1958), an analysis of the condition and future of religion and the evangelical faith in Latin America much influenced by ⇒Barth's theology.

CCO

Sabellius (2nd–3rd centuries). A

rather obscure person of Libyan origin who moved to Rome and there continued to elaborate on the teachings of ⇒Noetus and ⇒Praxeas. It is difficult to know with certainty what were his teachings, because everything he wrote has been lost, and only the testimony of his opponents remains. The teaching that is attributed to him, Sabellianism, is also called Patripassionism, modalism, and Monarchianism. Apparently, according to S., God is triune, not in Godself, but only in God's revelation. The names Father, Son, and Holy Spirit are only three modes in which God reveals Godself or relates to the creation. It is possible, although it cannot be proved, that S. said that God appears as Father in the creation and in the Law, then as Son in the incarnation, and lastly as Holy Spirit after the ascension of Jesus. At any rate, the orthodox theologians of the fourth century feared the consequences of Sabellianism. Many of those who at the beginning opposed the decisions of the Council of ⇒Nicaea did so because it seemed to them that the affirmation of the *homoousios*, or the consubstantiality of the Father with the Son, could easily be understood in Sabellian terms.

JLG

Saint-Cyran, Abbot of (Jean Du Vergier de Hauranne, 1581–1643).

French theologian who strongly promoted Gallicanism and Jansenism. His interest in the Gallican movement arose from his suspicion of the monastic orders, especially of the Jesuits. In a treatise published under the pseudonym Petrus Aurelius he defended the authority of the bishops over against the pope and the religious orders. S.-C. asserted that God gives authority directly to the bishops. In addition, he asserted that parish priests reflect, and therefore share, episcopal authority. Thus his central thesis was that the basis of authority in the church lies in the bishops and their clergy, not in the pope and the monastic orders.

His interest in Jansenism arose from his close and lasting professional relationship with ⇒Jansen, who was his companion when he studied at the University of Louvain. S.-C. played a very important role in his time, both because of his theological writings and because of his influence on important people.

PAJ

Salvianus (5th century). Orator, priest,

and moralist who spent the greater part of his life in Gaul. His two most important works are *Against Avarice* and *On the Government of God*. In the first of these he invites the rich to leave their fortunes to the church, so that they can be used to help the poor. In the second he deals with the calamities that had recently occurred, in particular the Germanic invasions. According to S., it is not right to think that the reason for these invasions is that the Romans have abandoned their old gods, nor is it right to think that God punishes wickedness only in the last judgment. These misfortunes that have befallen the Roman Empire have as their cause the vices of the empire itself and those of its subjects, including some Christians. According to S., in certain respects the "barbarians" are more virtuous than the Romans. Here we note an echo of the *City of God* of ⇒Augustine and one more expression of a theme that would soon become part of the Christian apologetic tradition: the Roman Empire fell because of its own vices and as a punishment from God.

JLG

Samartha, Stanley (1920–2001).

Protestant theologian of the Church of South India. Together with ⇒Panikkar and ⇒Pieris, he is one of the pioneers in the theology of religion and the interreligious dialogue in Asia. His theological contribution is focused on the encounter of Christianity with the Hindu faith as seen from a perspective of religious pluralism. S. maintains continuity with predecessors such as ⇒Chenchiah and ⇒Devanandan, but he takes the theology of religion and the interreligious dialogue to a new level.

S. was the first director of the Subunit on Dialogue with Peoples of Other Religions and Ideologies of the ⇒World Council of Churches (1970–81). Among his books are *The Hindu Response to the Unbound Christ* (1974), *Living Faiths and Ultimate Goals* (1974), *Faith in the*

Midst of Faiths (1977), and *Courage for Dialogue* (1980).

———

Samuel the Moroccan (11th century).

A Jew converted to Christianity who wrote in Arabic a *Book on the Past Coming of the Messiah*. In it he tries to prove that Jesus is the promised messiah and asserts that because they have not accepted him the Jews have been condemned to wander as vagabonds throughout the world—a theory that was not original with him, but which has had unfortunate consequences throughout the centuries. An interesting aspect of the work of S. is that he cites not only the traditional passages of the Old Testament but also passages from the Koran in defense of his thesis that Jesus is the Messiah.

———

Sandoval, Alonso de (1576–1652).

Spanish Jesuit born in Seville. As a very young man he went to Peru when his father served in the colonial government. In 1605 he entered the Company of Jesus and was sent to Cartagena, in what is now in Colombia. In his missionary work he gave himself totally to the evangelization of the thousands of African slaves who arrived in Cartagena every year. His work was focused on giving them the catechism, baptizing them, and taking care of their physical needs.

S. wrote an important treatise on the evangelization of black slaves, *De instauranda Aethiopum salute* (How to Promote the Salvation of Africans). In this work he gives details on the culture and customs of the African slaves and also on the methods of evangelism that were used.

Pedro Claver, another Jesuit who would be famous for his sacrificial ministry to the slaves, was introduced by S. to this evangelizing task. S. was also supervisor of the Company of Jesus in Colombia and for a short time was rector of the University of Cartagena.

———

Santa Ana, Julio de (1934–).

Uruguayan, theologian, ethicist, and ecumenical leader. S.A. has been a shaper of liberation theology from a Protestant perspective. Two of his works, in addition to his many articles published in the journal ⇒*Iglesia y Sociedad en América Latina*, are *The Challenge of the Poor to the Church* (1977) and *Toward a Church of the Poor* (1979). S.A. also served as coordinator of the Department of Development of the ⇒World Council of Churches and executive secretary of ISAL. Some of his most recent works deal with the theological and ethical problems of neoliberalism and with the protection of the environment in Latin America and the Caribbean.

———

Saravia, Hadrianus (1532–1613).

One of the few leaders of the Protestant movement of the sixteenth century who promoted the missionary task. S., of the Reformed tradition, was one of the translators of the King James Version of the Bible. Born in Belgium and educated in France, he served for a long time in England, where he accepted the Anglican tradition. His work *De diversis ministrorum evangelii gradibus* (On the Different Ranks of the Ministry) reflects the controversy concerning the function of bishops and the Reformed/Presbyterian government. One of his arguments in favor of episcopal government is that without a bishop the church is divided. In addition, S. argues that the church has a missionary mandate based on its apostolic succession. Therefore bishops are needed to send missionaries to the Middle East and to the "wicked" people in the world. His work is a forerunner of missiology and ecumenism because it considers the relationship between mission and the unity of the church.

———

Savonarola, Girolamo (1452–98).

Italian Dominican friar who was a reformer and a preacher of social justice. He was born in Ferrara of a middle-class family who planned for him a career in medicine. However, in 1475 he suddenly entered the novitiate of the Dominican order in Bologna. In 1482 he was sent to preach in Florence and in other Italian cities. In 1491 he returned to Florence as prior of the monastery of St. Mark. As a monastic leader he promoted the study of languages other than the biblical ones, such as Chaldean, Latin, and Arabic, with a view to establishing missionary work. As a prior he also had access to the pulpit of the cathedral in Florence and was also able to order the sale of some of the properties of the monastery and to distribute the proceeds among the poor.

His wide biblical knowledge was put to use in his incendiary sermons, in which he thundered against the corruption of both the church and the governing family of Lorenzo and Piero de' Medici. In 1494 the Medici family fell from power because of the French invasion. S. interpreted the presence of the French king Charles VIII as providential for social and ecclesiastical reform. The friar dissuaded the foreign king from plundering the city. With this action his influence grew on the new Florentine republican government.

S. worked incessantly so that the poor could have employment. He encouraged the distribution of the riches of the church among needy people. The main plaza of Florence was a witness on repeated occasions to the "bonfire of vanities," when the citizens mobilized to throw into the flames their beauty accessories, silks, worthless books, games of chance, and jewels. This friar, the sworn enemy of Renaissance luxury and ostentation, was behind it all.

His prophetic mission of denouncing social injustice and eroding the Petrine authority caused him serious problems with Pope Alexander VI. The latter unsuccessfully tried to suborn S. by offering to make him a cardinal, to which it is said that S. replied: "The only hat I want is red: a hat of blood." Finally the pope excommunicated him on May 13, 1497. S. claimed to pay more attention to the call from on high, disregarded the excommunication, and in its place asked for the celebration of a universal council to depose the pope. In these struggles, S. pioneered in the use of the printing press to spread his reforming religious ideas. The "meddlesome monk" ended his days by being tortured in prison, and on May 23, 1498, he was hanged and his body was burned. His ashes were spread on the Arno River as symbol of a second and definitive excommunication: the denial of Christian burial.

—

EPA

Scannone, Juan Carlos (1931–).
Argentine philosopher and theologian of liberation, S. is particularly known for his work in the philosophy of liberation, theology, and science, and the theological study of popular piety. Among his many works are *Theology of Liberation and Popular Praxis* (1976), *The New Evangelization of the World of Science in Latin America* (1995), and *The Political Factor in Latin America* (1999).

—

CCO

Schaeffer, Francis A. (1912–84).
North American conservative theologian and apologist. He studied at Faith Theological Seminary and in 1938 was the first minister ordained by the Bible Presbyterian Church. After several pastorates in Pennsylvania and Missouri, S. and his wife, Edith, went to Switzerland in 1948 as missionaries. In 1955 they founded L'Abri, a center of theological studies and spiritual formation for young university students and others in search of a relation between faith and the secular world. S. promoted the return to a conservative Christian faith over against a growing humanism in society, both in Europe and in the United States. His most popular books are *The God Who Is There* (1968), *Escape from Reason* (1968), *How Then Shall We Live* (1976), and *True Spirituality* (1979).

—

EA

Schaff, Philip (1819–93).
Church historian born in Switzerland and educated in Germany. After beginning his career in the University of Berlin, he was invited to teach in Mercersburg Seminary of the German Reformed Church in Pennsylvania (1844). Together with the theologian John W. Nevin he developed the Mercersburg theology, which proposed the theory of a true development in the history of the church, so that each era produces advances in the church, and it is therefore not a question of returning to a perfect era of the primitive church. S. in particular argued that the Protestant Reformation resulted from the development, and not from the complete rejection, of the best aspects of medieval Catholicism. In fact, throughout his career S. expressed himself in favor of the future reunification of Protestantism and Catholicism in an "Evangelical Catholicism." Because of his positive ideas on Catholicism and historical development, he had to leave Mercersburg in 1863, and in 1870 he began thirty years as professor at Union Theological Seminary in New York. During that time he founded the American Society of Church History (1888) and devoted himself to various ecumenical endeavors. Among his more than eighty works, the following stand out: *What Is Church History* (1846), *Creeds of Christendom* (3 vols., 1877), and *History of the Christian Church* (6 vols., 1882–92). He also edited the *Schaff-Herzog Encyclopedia of Religious Knowledge* (3 vols., 1882–84) and the first volumes of the series *Nicene and Post-Nicene Fathers* (28 vols., 1886–1905). His theory of ecclesial historical development is summarized in his first book, *The Principle of Protestantism* (1845).

—

EA

Schell, Herman (1850–1906). German Roman Catholic theologian who was born in Freiburg and died in Würzburg. From 1884 on he was a professor of apologetics and comparative religions (history of religions) in the University of Würzburg. Educated in the school of Brentano, he inherited from it his broad vision of philosophical problems. His interest in the renewal of the church led him to write "Theologie und Universität" (university lecture, 1899) and, in 1898, the pamphlets *Der Katholizismus als Prinzip des Fortschritts* (Catholicism as Principle of Progress) and *Die neue Zeit und der alte Glaube* (The New Times and the Old Faith). The Sacred Congregation of the Index condemned not only these pamphlets, but also his dogmatic works, among which were *Katholische Dogmatik* (1889–93) and *Die göttliche Wahrheit des Christentums: Gott und Geist* (1895–96; The Divine Truth of Christianity: God and Spirit). S. submitted, but there are doubts about the sincerity of his retraction.

In the work that motivated his condemnation, *Catholicism as Principle of Progress*, he combats the organization of Catholic society of that time as completely opposed to Protestantism: unilateral, authoritarian, centralist, enforcing uniformity, conservative, deprived of all Roman or medieval character that would permit each nation to be Christian according to its own individual essence. He attempted to renew the tendency of several nineteenth-century German theologians who accepted from modern philosophy (principally German) religious or metaphysical views that were incompatible with Roman Catholic dogmas. His desire to reconcile religion and philosophy led him to a conception of the divinity subject to the same contradiction that theologians have repeatedly pointed out in modern philosophy.

———

JDR

Schelling, Friedrich Wilhelm Joseph (1775–1854). German philosopher, companion and friend of ⇒Hegel during his studies in Tübingen. He taught in the universities of Jena, Würzburg, Erlangen, Munich, and Berlin. His philosophy is characterized by his emphasis on nature in opposition to the scientific materialism of the era and to the simplistic mechanism of physics. S. proposed that all nature is imbued with mind or spirit, although it is not always conscious of it. The philosophy of S. also moves toward aesthetics, by means of which the Absolute (God) expresses itself through creation and the development of his-

tory, which moves toward the final revelation of the Absolute.

———

LGP

Scherer, James (1926–). U.S. missiologist and Lutheran ecumenical leader. S. has contributed to missiological reflection from a Lutheran and global perspective. Among his works are *Missionary Go Home!* (1964) and *Gospel, Church, and Kingdom* (1987). Together with Stephen ⇒Bevans, he is editor of the series published by Orbis Books titled New Directions in Mission and Evangelization.

———

CCO

Schillebeeckx, Edward Cornelius (1914–). Born in Antwerp, Belgium. Studied with the Jesuits in Turnhout and then with the Dominicans in Ghent. After serving in the army of his country, he studied theology in Louvain and taught there for a time. After finishing his doctorate, he continued studying theology in Paris, where he made the acquaintance of the principal Dominican theologians of the time. In 1958 he began his long teaching career at the University of Nijmegen, Holland, where he continued teaching even after his official retirement. He was an expert at the Second Vatican Council (⇒Vatican II), where he distinguished himself for his knowledge and theological depth. However, this did not prevent him from being investigated at least twice by the Roman authorities.

S. guided the doctoral formation of numerous theologians who today have growing influence on Catholic theology around the world, and through their efforts his work has considerable impact. Among his principal books are *The Language of Faith: Essays on Jesus, Theology, and the Church*; *Mary: Yesterday, Today, Tomorrow*; *Church: The Human Story of God*; *The Church with a Human Face: A New and Expanded Theology of Ministry*; *God among Us: The Gospel Proclaimed*; *Ministry: Leadership in the Community of Jesus Christ*; *Jesus, Sacrament of God and Humanity* (which gained him international fame during the council); *The Eucharist*; *Ministry: A Case for Change*; *Interpretation of the Faith* (a work that is now classic, from the postconciliar period); and the trilogy *Jesus*, *Christ*, and *Church* (works of maturity that together are a true interdisciplinary tour de force). He has also written dozens of articles that have been published in specialized journals all over the world.

S. always placed his theology in dialogue with the best and most recent biblical research and made maximum use of patristics and church history. His knowledge of the social sciences and especially of non-Christian religions is impressive. He increasingly attempted to dialogue with those religions through his writings. He promoted ecumenism among the Christian churches and made public his increasing dissatisfaction with what he considers the insufficiency of the reforms of the Second Vatican Council—and, above all, his dissatisfaction with the restorationist attempts (and interferences) of the Roman see. In his last works S. appears to be very interested in intercultural theological methodology and well acquainted with Latin American theology and the Latin theology of the United States.

———

OOE

Schleiermacher, Friedrich (1768–1834).

Born in Breslau, Silesia (now Poland), son of a Calvinist clergyman. He is one of the most important German theologians of the nineteenth century. S. was formed in the Reformed tradition but was educated in Moravian and Lutheran schools. He appreciated the Moravians' piety and study of Latin, Greek, and Hebrew, but he bemoaned their resistance to considering the philosophical tendencies of their time. He studied Kantian philosophy and was a student of F. von Schlegel, one of the leaders of Romanticism in the literary circles of Berlin. Ordained to the ministry in 1794, he was a clergyman in Berlin, where he began his association with the circles of Romantic philosophy. S. was the first Calvinist to be invited to teach in the Lutheran university of Halle, in 1804. In 1810 he was the first theologian to teach in the University of Berlin. S. was a convinced ecumenist. He advocated the union of the Calvinist and Lutheran churches in Prussia.

Vis-à-vis the exhaustion of Kantian rationalism and the traditional dogmatism of the church, S. presented a theological alternative in which he related Romanticism to theology. In dialogue with ⇒Kant, S. denied the possibility of knowing God by means of reason. But against Kant, who maintained that the locus for knowing God is ethics and morality, S. questioned ethics as the locus for knowing the deity. For S. the way to the knowledge of the deity is the feeling of total dependence on the deity, and intuition. In his works *Addresses on Religion to Its Cultured Despisers* (1799) and *The Christian Faith* (1822), S. defined religion as "the feeling and intuition of the universe." He understood all religion as "the feeling of dependence on God." For S. religion could not be studied properly either through the rationalist philosophy of the Enlightenment or through ecclesiastical dogmas. Feeling and intuition are the best ways to enter into relationship with the deity. In his *Soliloquies* he wrote, "As many times as I look inside my most intimate being, I am in the sphere of eternity." The pious and mystical experience of believers is the locus of theological reflection. Theology therefore has a new locus: human feeling and intuition. S. asserted that the feeling of absolute dependence on the deity is "the essence of piety itself." The Christian religion deals more specifically with the dialectical experiences of sin and grace in the believer.

This understanding of religion as absolute dependence had implications for theology and dogmatics in the thought of S. Doctrine is important as a means for the church to judge which experiences maintain continuity with those in the past who experienced God in Christ. S. questioned the dogma of the Trinity and the resurrection because these are beyond the realm of our experience.

In agreement with his view of religion as absolute dependence on the divinity, he understood sin as the weakening of the sense of dependence on God, thus increasing concern for one's own pleasure. Those who experience dependence on God are sent into the world to alter it in the direction of the kingdom of God. Sin is seeking one's pleasure rather than the kingdom and is transmitted and strengthened through the influence of a sinful society.

Christ is the Savior because in him the consciousness of absolute dependence on God shone forth to others, giving them the experience of sin and grace, with grace always overcoming sin. This mystical union with Christ which unites the human being with God is the justification by faith of the human being as sinner and the beginning of the work of sanctification.

S. was later criticized for making of theology an essentially subjective enterprise at the expense of the revelation of God. Jesus was the Savior of human beings because he was the stimulator par excellence of this absolute dependence on the divinity in the particular form of the Christian religion. The church is the place where this experience is reproduced in the midst of the community. The church is a place of true human community, and it has been given the mission of spreading the gospel and working toward the kingdom, even at the expense of its own pleasure or convenience.

In his approach to the New Testament, from 1819 to 1832 S. focused his reflection on Jesus. S. asserted the undeniable difference between the Gospel of John and the Synoptic Gospels (Matthew, Mark, and Luke). But contrary to the tendency of his time to identify the Synoptics as the primary texts that are closer to Jesus of Nazareth, S. argued in favor of the preeminence of the Johannine Jesus. For S. the Gospel of John came from an eyewitness, while the Synoptics were the work of the disciples of the apostles and therefore were secondary works. S. was of the opinion that John shows us Jesus as the human being who depended totally on the divinity and who teaches us to strengthen this dependence. Human salvation consists in recognizing this dependence on the divinity.

S. was of the opinion that the Gospel of Matthew mentioned by ⇒Papias in the *Ecclesiastical History* of ⇒Eusebius of Caesarea is not the same as the canonical Matthew. The Matthew mentioned by Papias was used by the canonical Matthew as a source for constructing his narrative. He held similar opinions concerning what Papias says about Mark being written by a disciple and interpreter of Peter. Thus, while his views on the matter are not held by scholars today, S. was one of the first scholars to question the traditional views about the authors of the Gospels. S. also tackled other matters related to the New Testament.

He questioned the Pauline authorship of the Pastoral Epistles. S. was a scholar in the field of ancient Greek—he translated the writings of Plato into German—and he perceived linguistic differences between the authentic Pauline letters and the Pastorals.

Another great contribution of S. to theology was his articulation of a hermeneutical theory. For S. the task of hermeneutics is "to understand the discourse as well as the author did, and then better than he." S. attempted to present a coherent theory about the process of interpretation of texts. This made him the father of modern hermeneutics. S. presented the theory of communication between a sender and a receiver based on a common social and linguistic context. This common context is what makes communication possible between two people. S. proposes a circular system similar to what we now know as the hermeneutical circle. An interpreter needs to penetrate the social and individual dimension of the author in order to understand a text. This understanding on the part of the reader is what S. calls comparative comprehension. But S. asserts a second level of comprehension, the intuitive. This level is subjective and "divinatory." In this interpretation the reader understands the individuality of the author of a text.

ELR/CGG

Schmemann, Alexander (1921–83).
Orthodox theologian, expert in liturgy, and church historian. He attempted to give to the Orthodox faith an ecumenical emphasis that would make it more visible in the ecumenical movement. His *Introduction to Liturgical Theology* (1966) is a definitive work in its field.

CEA

Schmidlin, Joseph (1876–1944).
Catholic theologian and missiologist born in France, although greatly shaped by German culture. S. was one of the most distinguished Catholic missiologists of the twentieth century. In an era in which it appeared that missiology was in Protestant hands, S. wrote prolifically on the history and science of mission, particularly on the relation of mission to ecclesiology. Thus he stimulated interest in missiology in Catholic university centers. Almost all his works were written in German. The best known is *Einführung in die Missionswissenschaft* (1917; Introduction to the Science of Mission).

CCO

Schmidt, Karl Ludwig (1891–1956).
German scholar whose research made significant contributions to biblical exegesis in the areas of lexicography, form criticism, and theology of the New Testament.

AEM

Scholarios, Georgios (ca. 1400–68).
His monastic name was Gennadius. He was a Byzantine theologian who participated in the Council of Florence (⇒Councils, 17), where he declared himself in favor of union with Rome. But on his return he changed his mind and became a most resolute opponent of that union. When Constantinople was conquered by the Turks, the sultan made S. patriarch (with the name Gennadius II) and came to an agreement with him that regulated the relations between the Turkish government and the Orthodox church until the twentieth century. In the field of theology he continued his dialogue with the West, and he even translated portions of the *Summa theologica* of ⇒Thomas Aquinas.

JLG

Schreiter, Robert (1947–). Catholic theologian and missiologist in the United States, one of the best-known Christian thinkers on the connection between theology and missiology. In *Constructing Local Theologies* (1985) he affirms the contextual and local character of theology. On the other hand, without discarding this theological and ecclesial reality, S. proposes several directions for the unity of the people of God in *The New Catholicity* (1997). His work also includes a critical reflection on the meaning of the Christian ministry in a world filled with conflicts, in his book *Reconciliation* (1992).

———

CCO

Schüssler Fiorenza, Elisabeth (1938–). Feminist theologian who, from the store of her profound knowledge, proposes a liberating feminist hermeneutic. Among her contributions are the rediscovery of the leadership role of women in the daily life of early ecclesial communities and a rereading of biblical passages that often have been decontextualized and manipulated with oppressive and subjugating intentions.

Her pioneering work has offered important norms for dialogue among the different feminist theologies in the world. Her book *In Memory of Her* (1983), translated into Dutch, French, Italian, Japanese, Portuguese, Spanish, and Swedish, is her biblical/theological work that is best known in Bible study circles at the international level, particularly in the ecumenical movement. S.F. occupies a chair at Harvard University, is the mentor of young biblical scholars from all over the world, and actively participates in the Society of Biblical Literature, of which she became the first female president in 1987. She is also cofounder and coeditor of *Journal of Feminist Studies in Religion*.

———

CEA

Schweitzer, Albert (1875–1965). German theologian, physician, and musician who made significant contributions in the field of biblical theology, especially in eschatology. In his chief work, *The Quest of the Historical Jesus* (1906), he proposed that the key for interpreting Jesus is his deeply eschatological view of history. All the preaching of Jesus should be understood as a call to an ethic that is radicalized by the imminent coming of the end. Since this did not occur, Jesus chose the road of self-sacrifice as a way to force the arrival of the end.

For S. the historical Jesus is less important than the Christ of faith, who still is present with us through the faith we confess. It was that Christ who called him to serve as a medical missionary in Africa, where he founded a hospital in Lambarene, in what is now Gabon. In 1952 he was awarded the Nobel Peace Prize. Some of his most important works include, aside from the one already mentioned, *The Mystery of the Kingdom of God* (1901), *Paul and His Interpreters* (1911), and *Philosophy and Civilization* (1923), in which he summarizes his humanitarian principles in the phrase "reverence for life"—which for him meant all forms of biological life, including plants and insects.

Before beginning his renowned ministry of service to the poor and sick people of French Equatorial Africa, he served as pastor in Strassburg and was a lecturer at the university of that city.

———

ODV

Schwenkfeld, Caspar (1489–1561). German radical reformer. Initially converted to Lutheranism, he slowly changed his perspective because of his critical attitude toward the Lutheran doctrines of justification by faith, predestination, and the "real presence" of Christ in Holy Communion. He maintained that Christ could not be really present in the material elements of the Lord's Supper. This emphasis, linked to the conviction that the majority of believers were not well informed about the Christian faith, led him to support, along with other local reformers, the suspension of the Lord's Supper in Legnica. Because of religious persecution, S. took refuge in Strassburg with numerous dissidents of his time. But also there he caused controversy, even among the Anabaptists. He spent his last days in Ulm, where he wrote a considerable number of books and letters, chiefly of a polemical nature.

———

NRG

Scofield, Cyrus (1843–1921). Bible teacher who popularized the Dispensationalist interpretation of the Bible by means of his biblical notes (*Annotated Scofield Bible*). He was one of the key leaders of the Dispensationalist movement, together with Dwight ⇒Moody and J. N. ⇒Darby. S. had been a soldier in the Southern army during the American Civil War (1861–65). When the war ended, he studied law and began to practice as an attorney in 1869. In

1879 he had a conversion experience and was educated in the Christian faith by James Brookes, a Presbyterian pastor who was a sympathizer of Darby. He was ordained in 1883 and was pastor of the First Congregational Church in Dallas, Texas, for many years.

As part of his ministry S. began to give lectures on the Bible and prophecy, using the Dispensationalist interpretation, which became very popular through biblical conferences held throughout the United States. The result of these efforts was the *Annotated Scofield Bible*, published in 1907. The Scofield Bible has been translated into several languages and has been one of the chief means for the propagation of the Dispensationalist interpretation of the Bible, particularly in Latin America.

The Dispensationalist interpretation understands that God works with the human race in different ways during different periods of history. These periods or dispensations reflect different aspects of God's plan. At present we are in the dispensation of the church, and the secret rapture of the church is awaited soon. After the rapture there will be seven years of tribulation and suffering in which the antichrist will be revealed. After the tribulation Christ will come to the earth to establish his millennial reign. During this reign the promises to Israel will be fulfilled on earth. When the millennium ends, the last judgment will take place and the eternal kingdom of God will be revealed.

The influence of S. was felt in Latin America not only through the Bible. He also played a key role in the formation, in 1890, of the Central American Mission, an organization that began missionary work in several Central American countries. The Central American Church and the Central American Theological Seminary (SETECA, in Guatemala) are a direct result of this effort.

———
JFM

Scotus, John Duns (ca. 1265–1308).

Theologian and philosopher. Little is known of his life, although it is believed that he was born in Duns, near Roxburgh in Scotland. Around the year 1280 he became a Franciscan and in 1291 was ordained a priest in England. He studied theology in Oxford and in Cambridge, commenting especially on the *Sentences* of ⇒Peter Lombard, and in 1301 completed his doctorate in Paris, where he also taught for some years. In 1307 he established himself as a teacher in Cologne, where he died the following year. S. was a profound and meticulous thinker, and his untimely death left many of his works unfinished. Not until the twentieth century were his authentic works distinguished from the pseudonymous ones, so that his genius could be better appreciated and his great influence on medieval philosophy and theology could be explained.

His chief authentic work was a commentary on the *Sentences* by Lombard. Three complete versions remain, and one was left unfinished at the time of his death. He also wrote commentaries on the logic of Aristotle and on Porphyry, another commentary on the metaphysics of Aristotle, a treatise on the "first principle," and a collection of disputed issues (the *Quodlibeta*) on theological and philosophical subjects.

S. wrote after the condemnation of Aristotle and of several scholastics (among them ⇒Thomas Aquinas) by the archbishop of Paris in 1277. In that anti-Aristotelian climate he attempted to mediate between the Aristotelianism of some and the Augustinianism of others (especially that of ⇒Henry of Ghent). He rejected much of the former, explicitly opposing Thomas Aquinas and his effort to reconcile Aristotelianism with the Christian faith. S. was convinced that faith cannot simply be established or proved through purely rational means. With this, and perhaps without anticipating it, he contributed to the definitive separation of medieval theology from philosophy.

His chief contribution to philosophy can be summarized in his emphasis on the reasonableness of the "particularity in itself" of what is individual (which he called *haecceitas*). And although he would reject Aristotelian enthusiasm for the capabilities of human reason, he equally objected to the Augustinian position (above all of Henry of Ghent), which supposed that all certainty of truth is possible only through the illumination of God.

His theology emphasized the primacy of Christ as the supreme manifestation of the love of God. S. said that the incarnation was not "provoked" by human sin or by any created human need. Even if there had not been sin, there would have been an incarnation, since it occurred only because of the love of God (and therefore as a result of the faithfulness of God). S. thought that this in turn implied the reasonable possibility of the immaculate conception of Mary, and he was one of the first theologians in history to defend this doctrine.

S.'s impact and influence were great during the latter Middle Ages and remained in the Franciscan theological tradition until well into the eighteenth century. His theological contribution has begun to be recovered today, thanks especially to his emphasis on the affective dimensions of the human being and also to his theory of the reasonableness of the particular.

———

OOE

Segundo, Juan Luis (1925–96).

Uruguayan Jesuit and theologian. He studied theology in Argentina, Louvain, and Paris and was ordained a priest in 1955. In Montevideo he created and directed the Pedro Faber Center for the study and investigation of the sociology of religion. As one of the most original liberation theologians, he emphasized the grace of God and the human initiative, both operating in a particular social context.

He wrote *A Theology for Artisans of the New Humanity* (5 vols.); *Spirituality of Hope*; *An Evolutionary Approach to Jesus of Nazareth*; *The Historical Jesus of the Synoptics*; *The Liberation of Dogma: Faith, Revelation, and Dogmatic Teaching Authority*; and *Faith and Ideologies*, among others. In *The Liberation of Theology* he proposes that the function of theology is to unite the disciplines that open up the past with those that explain the present. He attempts to achieve this by means of a contextualized methodology that he calls the "hermeneutical circle," in which he emphasizes the eternal dialogue between the revelation of God and the historical realities of the present.

The hermeneutical circle includes four steps: (1) the study of the reality which surrounds us, starting from an ideological suspicion that the social context which we perceive in our surroundings is not as it initially appears to be; (2) an approach to the Scriptures to discover in them norms for action; (3) the application of these conclusions to the context for the purpose of transforming it, in order finally (4) to initiate again the process in the new context and social reality which emerged from the previous circle.

A book that became particularly significant after the election of ⇒Ratzinger as Pope Benedict XVI is S.'s *Theology and the Church: A Response to Cardinal Ratzinger and a Warning to the Whole Church.*

———

LMcA

Sergius of Constantinople (?–638).

Patriarch of that city beginning in 610. Of Syrian origin, S. knew the objections that were raised in that region and in Egypt against the Definition of Faith of ⇒Chalcedon. Conscious

of the interest of the Byzantine government in gaining the good will of the Monophysites (or at least of the verbal Monophysites, ⇒Severus of Antioch), S. first proposed "monergism," the theory of "one energy" in Christ, and then put forward what was called Monothelitism, that is, the theory that there is only "one will" in the Savior. Although it is true that there are "two natures" in Christ, as Chalcedon affirmed, according to the monergist theory there is in him only one "energy," one principle of activity, which is divine. Thus one should speak not only of one "hypostasis," but also of one "energy." The criticisms of this theory, particularly those coming from ⇒Sophronius of Jerusalem, were such that S. withdrew it and in its place proposed Monothelitism. It is impossible to know exactly what S. meant by this term, and for that reason some have said that Monothelitism is "the chameleon-like heresy." At any rate, the theory of S. gained imperial support and also, for some time, the approval of Pope ⇒Honorius. But this theory also had opponents, especially ⇒Maximus the Confessor, who insisted that a human nature without its own will is not truly human. In the end, some time after the death of S., the Council of ⇒Constantinople of 681 rejected Monothelitism. By that date the Muslim conquests had nullified the interest of the Byzantine government in gaining the sympathy of the Syrian and Egyptian Monophysites.

———

JLG

Servatus Lupus (ca. 805–62).

Distinguished scholar and one of the chief promoters of the Carolingian renaissance. His most important theological work is the book *On Three Questions*, in which he proposed and defended the Augustinian position. According to it, after the fall human free will only has the power to sin, and from among the resulting mass of perdition God has predestined the elect to salvation. The rest have been predestined to condemnation. Although his teaching was similar to ⇒Gottschalk's, his posture was less rigid and legalistic.

———

JLG

Servetus, Michael (1511–53).

Physician and anti-Trinitarian theologian, born in Spain. He conscientiously studied the biblical languages, mathematics, philosophy, theology, and law. As a man saturated with radical theological ideas, and sought after by the Inquisition, he moved to Basel and Strassburg, where he met the Protestant reformer Martin ⇒Bucer. His radical ideas led him to the stake in Geneva, because he challenged the belief in the eternal existence of the Son and, ultimately, the unity, difference, and equality of the persons of the Trinity. He rejected infant baptism and challenged the great reformer John ⇒Calvin, responding to the latter's *Institutes of the Christian Religion* with his *Christianismi restitutio* (1553).

His death at the stake has provoked very different reactions, from extreme condemnation as a heretic to the attempt to restore him as a creative and original thinker. Many theologians acknowledge both his creativity and the possible heresies of S., and rue his death by burning.

CEA

Severus of Antioch (ca. 465–538).

After studying in Alexandria and Beirut, he became a monk and was made patriarch of Antioch in 512. The emperor Justin deposed him, and S. took refuge in Alexandria. From there he continued writing in defense of what has been called a verbal or moderate Monophysitism. Thus those who adopted this position were called Severians. His principal christological work is *The Lover of Truth*, in which he denounces the falseness of those who quote ⇒Cyril of Alexandria in defense of the Chalcedonian formula (Council of ⇒Chalcedon) of the "two natures" in the Savior. S. argues correctly that Cyril always upheld the formula of "one nature incarnate of God the Word."

This does not mean, however, that S. was really a Monophysite in the strict sense. On the contrary, he affirmed that Jesus Christ is at the same time "consubstantial with the Father" and "consubstantial with us." What worried S. and his followers was the possible Nestorian (⇒Nestorius) interpretation of Chalcedonian doctrine, since for them "nature" was the same as "hypostasis," and therefore the assertion of two natures appeared to them to endanger the unity of the person of the Savior.

In the end, the majority of the so-called Monophysites adopted the position of S., with the result that the debates between Monophysites and Orthodox regarding the one or the two natures of the Savior became largely a matter of semantics, in which each side viewed the other according to its own prejudices.

JLG

Sextus Julius Africanus (?–ca. 245).

Apparently of Palestinian origin rather than African, he was converted to Christianity after a long period of military service and extensive travel. He corresponded with ⇒Origen about the authority of the deuterocanonical writings of the Old Testament, in particular about the passages in Daniel not found in the Hebrew text. While S.J. cast doubt on their authority, Origen affirmed it. He also wrote a huge encyclopedia titled *Tapestries*. His most influential work was his *Chronicle*, which does not survive in its totality. In it S.J. established a chronology of all human history until the year 221, based on the biblical narratives. Its purpose was to show that the biblical doctrines are older than pagan teachings.

According to him, the world will last seven thousand years. Jesus was born in the year 5500 after creation and will return in the year 6000. Although this work has been lost, ⇒Eusebius of Caesarea and other later authors used it, and thus his vision of history left a deep impression on Christian tradition.

JLG

Sharpe, Eric (1933–).

Australian scholar in the field of religious studies and the history of religions. He has contributed significantly to the integration of religious studies with theology, missiology, and ecumenical studies. He has translated and written numerous work on the philosophy and history of religions, Indology, Hinduism, and the impact of the Christian missionary movement in India.

Among his many works, three are of great importance: *Comparative Religion* (1975), *Understanding Religion* (1983), and *Faith Meets Faith* (1977).

CCO

Shaull, Richard (1919–2002).

U.S. missionary, theologian, and ecumenist who worked in Colombia and Brazil for many years. On the basis of his article "The Church in the Diaspora" he is considered one of the forerunners of Latin American liberation theology. Later much of his work was focused on the development of Latin American theology and its relationship with historic Protestantism, as is shown by his book *The Reformation and Liberation Theology* (1991). During the last decade of his life S. devoted himself to the study of the Pentecostal phenomenon in Latin America. With the Brazilian sociologist Waldo

Cesar, he wrote *Pentecostalism and the Future of the Christian Churches: Promises, Limitations, and Challenges* (2000). His last book, *Surprised by Grace: My Struggle against Cancer*, narrates his ecumenical and missional journey and his continuous concern for the social witness of the church.

CCO

Shedd, William Greenough T. (1820–94).
Presbyterian systematic theologian who also taught the history of doctrine. In Andover Seminary (1854–62) and Union Seminary in New York (1862–93), he defended traditional Calvinist thought and the ⇒Westminster Confession of Faith.

EZ

Shenk, Wibert (1935–).
North American Mennonite, S. is an exponent of evangelical missiology in the United States dealing with both the history and the theology of mission.

CCO

Sibylline Oracles (2nd and 3rd centuries).
A collection of fifteen books, written in verse, which pretend to be predictions of an ancient pagan sibyl. It is possible that these books included some texts that were originally pagan, as well as Jewish interpolations. But the books that remain today (three of them have been lost) are undoubtedly of Christian origin and are probably the product of the imagination of some believer who in this way tried to shore up the Christian faith through predictions about it on the lips of a pagan prophetess of antiquity. Scholars generally agree that the Jewish interpolations, which include references from the time of the Maccabees up to the second century, are earlier than those which are Christian, which could well be from the third century. Thus it is possible that the original work was of Jewish origin and that later on Christians appropriated it, adding new interpolations to it, and apparently entire books. In any case, already in the second century there were Christian authors who used these books, such as ⇒Theophilus of Antioch and ⇒Clement of Alexandria. According to the testimony of ⇒Origen, the pagan Celsus criticized the Christians for using them and believing that they were really predictions. During the Middle Ages these oracles were highly thought of, for they were held to be authentic, and they appeared to show that even in the midst of the pagan culture and

religion God had been announcing the coming of Jesus Christ. During the Spanish "Golden Century" they were still read frequently, since several passages from them seem to have inspired Calderón de la Barca.

JLG

Sider, Ronald J. (1939–).
Evangelical theologian and professor at Eastern Baptist Theological Seminary who stimulated a generation of students and seminarians with his book *Rich Christians in an Age of Hunger* (1977). In this book S. presented a gospel of social activism based on a biblical vision in favor of the poor and questioned the lack of economic analysis in the evangelical church, with its automatic acceptance of capitalism. S. organized Evangelicals for Social Action and also Just Life, a political action committee that advocated a consistent ethic in favor of life, which ultimately was opposed to abortion, but also to the death penalty, nuclear weapons, poverty, and everything that is "antilife." His most recent works have moderated his criticism of capitalism, declaring that the causes of poverty are complex and that a mixed economy with decentralized decisions in the market can offer more opportunity and power to the poor.

EA

Siger of Brabant (ca. 1234–ca. 1282).
Master of the Faculty of Arts of the University of Paris from 1266 until 1277. He was a defender of the extreme Aristotelianism (⇒Aristotle) known as Latin Averroism (⇒Averroës). Apparently the repeated condemnations of different Aristotelian positions on the part of the authorities in Paris were directed mainly against S. and his followers, although they also were directed, at least in part, against the more moderate Aristotelianism of ⇒Thomas Aquinas.

S. maintained that philosophy should continue its studies on the basis of reason and not let itself be led or dominated by theology or the dogmas of the church. Thus, for example, he maintained that philosophy leads to conclusions such as the eternity of the world, the "unity of the active intellect" (which implies that all souls are only one), and determinism. He perhaps also maintained the theory of "double truth," according to which philosophy comes to some conclusions and theology to others, and in such cases it is necessary to yield to the theological authority, but with the insistence that reason leads to different conclusions. In 1277 he was accused before the Inquisition and fled from Paris. A few years later he was murdered by his secretary.

————

JLG

Sihler, Wilhelm (1801–85).

One of the founding pastors of the Lutheran Church—Missouri Synod, elected as its first vice president in 1847. He served as president of Concordia Seminary in Fort Wayne, Indiana. In his youth he was influenced by ⇒Kant and ⇒Schleiermacher, but later he was converted to a confessional Lutheranism. He was one of the first Lutherans to discover the power of the printed word in North America. His writings had to do chiefly with practical problems of theology. One of his most influential works was *A Conversation between Two Lutherans about Methodism* (1878), in which he highlighted the evangelizing work of the Wesleyans who gained for their movement religious immigrants with little education, among them many Germans.

————

ALG

Silva Gotay, Samuel (1935–).

Puerto Rican sociologist and researcher. He is the author of *Revolutionary Christian Thought in Latin America and the Caribbean* and *Protestantism and Politics in Puerto Rico (1898–1930): Toward a History of Evangelical Protestantism in Puerto Rico*. He is director of the Project on History and Sociology of Religion of the University of Puerto Rico.

————

LMcA

Silvester II ⇒Gerbert of Aurillac

Simeon of Polock (17th century).

A monk of Kiev who directed a theological school in Moscow and devoted himself chiefly to refuting Protestant teachings. He had been strongly influenced by Roman Catholicism, and for this reason many Russians reacted violently against him. It was even said that he was a secret agent of the pope. The greater part of his refutation of Protestantism is nothing but a translation of Latin Catholic works, with slight adaptations for the Russian context. When the reforms of Patriarch Nikon resulted in the protest of the "Old Believers," and a synod that met in Moscow condemned them, the task of refuting them was entrusted to S. This refutation did not have the desired result. The Old

Believers rebelled, were suppressed by force, and became an ever more radical sect with pronounced eschatological expectations.

————

JLG

Simeon the New Theologian (949–1022).

A mystic to whom the Byzantines gave the title of New Theologian to indicate that he was the greatest theologian since ⇒Gregory of Nazianzus, whom they called the Theologian. For S., as for Gregory, theology is not a question of intellectual exercise or of philosophizing about God, but is, rather, based on the vision of the divine. Humans have lost their freedom because of sin, and the only thing that remains is the desire to be free. But humans cannot achieve freedom by their own efforts; they can only attain it through an action of the grace of God that leads to an encounter with the divine light. In this respect S. differs largely from the Neoplatonic mystical tradition (⇒Dionysius the Areopagite), for which the contemplative life is a process of ascending to God through purification, contemplation, and so on. After their encounter with the divinity, people are not the same, because what takes place is a "deification." On the other hand, that encounter does not consist in the loss of the identity or the consciousness of the I, as many mystics maintained; it is, rather, the case that those who participate in the encounter know themselves to be other than God. The mysticism of S. gained many followers, and later it had an effect on ⇒Palamas and Hesychasm.

————

JLG

Simon Magus (1st century).

According to Acts 8:9–24, S. was a magician of Samaria who claimed that he was "something great" and whom some Samaritans identified with "the great power of God." Although, according to Acts, there is no reason to doubt the conversion of S. and his repentance, many ancient Christian authors considered him the founder of ⇒Gnosticism. According to Christian authors attacking him, S. claimed to be the supreme God, who had remained hidden in antiquity but had descended to earth to be reunited with his companion, Helen—who according to S. was the Holy Spirit. The traditions about S. and his relation to Gnosticism are found in the writings of ⇒Justin Martyr, ⇒Irenaeus (who considered S. to be the father of all heresies), ⇒Hippolytus, the Pseudo-Clementine literature (⇒Clement of

Rome), and the apocryphal book *Acts of Peter*. In later times, the practice of buying ecclesiastical offices came to be called simony, in reference to the desire of S. to buy the gift of the Spirit.

———

AEM

Simon of Tournai (?–ca. 1219). A professor in Paris who was known for his innovations in the methodology of academic debates. He was a strong defender of the authority of the spiritual power over the temporal—so much so that, according to him, the pope has authority to depose kings and emperors.

———

JLG

Simons, Menno (1496–1561). A leader among the Dutch Anabaptists in the sixteenth century. He was not the founder of Anabaptism, nor even of his group of followers, but because of his leadership in a key moment, the Anabaptists of that region came to be known as Mennonites. M. was born in Witmarsum in 1496. At the age of twenty-eight he was ordained a priest. After a few years in the ministry he was exposed to the preaching of the Sacramentarians, who denied transubstantiation, and of the Anabaptists, who practiced the baptism of adults. These issues provoked a crisis in him. When he did not find a biblical basis for transubstantiation or infant baptism, he came to the conclusion that they were unacceptable. However, M. did not join the Anabaptists at that time.

In 1535 many Anapabtists in Münster died at the hand of the civil authorities. Among the dead was a brother of M. These events caused M. to reflect more seriously on his own commitment. In January 1536 he made a clear commitment and left the priesthood. He had to flee persecution and found refuge among secret Anabaptist communities. Soon he became the leader in the communities, and he was asked to lead some of the dispersed Anabaptist congregations. He spent the rest of his life fleeing from the authorities, until he died in 1561.

His influence on the Anabaptist movement was crucial. He was one of the few Anabaptist leaders who did not suffer martyrdom. For that reason he was able to influence the Anabaptist communities that were dispersed throughout northern Europe. Above all he guided them to adopt a pacifist stance. He wrote many pamphlets and treatises, which are published in *M. Simons, Complete Works*.

———

JFM

Smart, Ninian (1927–2001). Philosopher, theologian, and Anglican professor at the University of Birmingham for many years. He devoted a good portion of his life to the study of natural theology, the concept of "the death of God," and the most important religions of the West and the East, especially Hinduism and Buddhism.

———

AEM

Smith, Joseph (1805–44). Prophet, visionary, and spiritual leader, S. established The Church of Jesus Christ of Latter-day Saints (known as the Mormon church). He did not think of it as a new religion, but as a new beginning. Born of a farming family in New England, he had several visions that convinced him of the need to restore the good news in preparation for the return of Jesus Christ. His next vision, in 1820, convinced him that no church was true. In 1823 he said that an angel had appeared to him and given him a sacred document of an ancient people, written on golden tablets. In 1827 he published a translation of these writings, which are known as the Book of Mormon. Because of these and other revelations, S. organized his church in 1830. Frequently persecuted and misunderstood, S. was killed, along with his brother, by a mob in 1844.

———

EZ

Sobrino, Jon (1938–). Spanish Jesuit theologian, working in El Salvador since 1957. University professor of theology and prolific author. His contribution has been mostly in Christology, ecclesiology, and the spirituality of liberation. Among his works are *Rethinking Martyrdom*; *The Principle of Mercy: Taking the Sacrificed People from the Cross*; *Jesus the Liberator: A Historical-Theological Reading of Jesus of Nazareth*; *Spirituality of Liberation: Toward Political Holiness*; *Jesus in Latin America*; *The True Church and the Poor*; and *Christology at the Crossroads*.

———

LRR

Socinus, Faustus (1539–1604). Born in the city of Siena, S. died in the city of Luclavia, close to Kraków. Having studied theology, he was instrumental in the unification of the anti-Trinitarian Anabaptist movements of the sixteenth century, which came to be known as Socinianism. His intelligence, elegant manners, and eloquence gained him many followers. He was persecuted as a heretic by both Roman Catholics and Protestants.

The Socinians, also called Unitarians or Anti-Trinitarians, have their roots in the teachings of ⇒Servetus, well known both in medicine and in theology. Not finding the dogma of the Trinity in the Bible and prodded on by the impossibility of penetrating the dogma by reason alone, they ended up denying it. S. believed that although there was no sin in Christ, his nature was not divine, and that his significance in the divine providence was to show the way of salvation by serving as a model and by inviting us to endure sufferings and attain moral perfection through a life of penitence and service in harmony with the divine will.

S. expounded his teaching, at least in its general lines, in his work *Del Salvatore Gesu Cristo*, which enjoyed great popularity in Transylvania, Poland, and Hungary. Andrew Wissowatius, a nephew of S., published his works in the first two volumes of *Bibliotheca Fratrum Polonorum* (1656; Library of the Polish Brothers).

———
JDR

Socrates (ca. 390–450).

Historian who updated the *Ecclesiastical History* of ⇒Eusebius of Caesarea. His work covers the period from 309 until 439. His interest lay more in political and personal conflicts than in theology, so that some think that he said little about the theological debates because he himself was not totally in agreement with the orthodoxy that had issued from them. His *Ecclesiastical History* is one of the main sources we have for the study of the history of the church in the fourth century, and in many points it proves to be more objective than other documents of the same period.

———
JLG

Solle, Dorothy (1929–2004).

German feminist theologian who taught in Germany and in the United States at Union Theological Seminary, New York. Her theology is informed by decades of political praxis in different movements of social protest. Her writings articulate the theology and spirituality of a radical Christianity which rejects traditional theism and asserts that faith and politics are inseparable. This radical theism affirms the Christian vocation to fight for justice, peace, and the liberation of human beings and of creation.

———
LRR

Song, Choan-Sang (1929–).

Taiwanese Reformed theologian. His work is focused on the contextualization of Christian theology on Asian soil. S. also uses non-Christian symbols to communicate the centrality of the gospel. His most important works are *Third-Eye Theology* (1980), *The Compassionate God* (1982), and *Theology from the Womb of Asia* (1988).

———
CCO

Sophronius of Jerusalem (ca. 561–638).

Patriarch of that city, beginning in 634. He was one of the principal opponents of Monothelitism (⇒Sergius of Constantinople). Apparently of Egyptian origin, he attacked chiefly the form that Monothelitism assumed in Egypt. He was patriarch of Jerusalem when that city fell into the hands of the Arabs.

———
JLG

Sorbon, Robert (?–1274).

Chaplain of the king St. Louis who was known by the title Devout Doctor. He wrote chiefly on moral theology and also some annotations on biblical texts. He founded a college in Paris for students of theology who could not pay their expenses. The present-day Sorbonne derives its name from him and from that college.

———
JLG

Soto, Domingo de (1494–1560).

A scholar who studied first in Alcalá and later in Paris. In 1532 he occupied a chair of theology in the University of Salamanca, where he was a colleague of ⇒Vitoria and ⇒Cano. He interrupted his teaching to attend the Council of ⇒Trent, where he defended the position of ⇒Thomas Aquinas concerning grace over against the attacks of a group led by Ambrosius ⇒Catharinus. He remained in Germany as the confessor of Charles V, and in 1532, when Cano was made a bishop, he returned to Salamanca as his successor. There he continued the work of Vitoria, attempting to lay the foundation for international law as it should be applied in the Spanish colonies.

———
JLG

Sozomenos (5th century).

Author of an *Ecclesiastical History* in nine books that continues and updates the work under the same title of ⇒Eusebius of Caesarea, and which covers the period from 323 to 423. He apparently takes much of his material from ⇒Socrates. Like the latter, he was not greatly interested in theological debates. Although his style is more refined than that of Socrates, his analysis of events is frequently less profound. His work is of special interest for anything having to do with the expansion of Christianity toward the East, and also among the Goths.

——
JLG

Speer, Robert E. (1867–1947). Presbyterian layman and leader in the missionary movement at the beginning of the twentieth century. S. was one of the voices justifying and legitimizing missionary presence and activity in Latin America and the Caribbean. A man whose impact was comparable to that of John R. ⇒Mott, S. was an administrator and visionary of the missionary movement, participating significantly in the world missionary conferences until 1938.

S. was one of the architects of the missionary movement in Latin America. He was the first president of the Committee on Cooperation for Latin America, an organ of missional cooperation for the continent. His missionary vision for the region is given concrete form in the books *The Case for Missions in Latin America* (1912) and *South American Problems* (1915), which precede the first missionary conference on Latin America, held in Panama in 1916.

——
CCO

Spener, Phillip Jacob (1635–1705). Father of pietism and one of the outstanding personalities of the church in the seventeenth century. He was born in Rappoltsweiler, Alsace, and grew up in a family dedicated to Puritanism and mysticism. He studied theology in Strassburg, where he learned Lutheran theology. Then he went to the University of Basel, where he studied Hebrew. In 1663 he was named preacher of Strassburg and in 1664 received a doctorate from the university of the same city. From 1664 to 1685 he served as pastor and dean of the ministerium in Frankfurt am Mein. It was in the discharge of his duties as pastor and dean that he emerged as leader of the pietist movement. In Frankfurt, he restored the practice of confirmation, set dates for prayer and fasting, and preached on the need for a conversion experience and a holy life. In addition, in 1670 he organized a group of pastors and laypeople who met periodically to study the Bible and pray together for mutual edification. His outstanding written work, in which he explains his theological and pastoral view-

point, is *Pia Desideria* (Pious Desires), published in 1675 as the prologue to Johann ⇒Arndt's *True Christology*. S. offers six pious desires: (1) that small groups will help believers develop a deeper and clearer understanding of their faith; (2) that the universal priesthood of all believers will be rediscovered; (3) that Christianity will be seen more as an experience of faith than as a series of doctrines; (4) that controversies might take place in a spirit of charity; (5) that ministerial education will include devotional readings and practices; and (6) that there be a renewal of preaching for the spiritual feeding of the flock.

His publications and his ministry created controversy, with the result that he had to leave Frankfurt and go to Dresden (1686–91) and then to Brandenburg, where he was pastor of the church of St. Nicholas in Berlin, where he died.

——
HMT

Speroni, Hugo (?–1174). Jurist and consul of Piacenza who originated a current of antihierarchical notions that some authors have considered a remote precedent of the teachings of John ⇒Calvin. For other scholars, the movement that was directed by S. was one of the antecedents of the Quakers. As a consul in Piacenza, S. participated with families and other groups of the community in lawsuits against the monastery of St. Julia, lawsuits related primarily to matters of customs duties on bridges and coasts. Eventually, these endeavors led him to more radical views.

S. rejected the validity of the priesthood, which he understood to be indelibly stained by sin, and the sacraments, especially baptism, the Eucharist, confession, and penance, which he replaced with the spiritual communion of the Word of God. For S. justification did not depend on the sacraments, but on internal purity. Neither was it possible to gain salvation by means of good works, because the internal holiness that made justification possible did not depend on them but on the grace of God, granted to those who were predestined to receive it. His perspective on these matters is known thanks to the refutation written by his former friend ⇒Vacarius (who died in 1198). In spite of his theological radicalism, the position of S. rejected violent attitudes or protests. His individualistic position, opposed even to any kind of missionary plan, diminished the possibility of establishing this minority movement, which was known as the Humiliati or Speronians among the educated laity of the time. Thus he was condemned to play a purely testimonial role. In fact, it is thought that this movement never had great influence outside the region of Piacenza.

Aside from generic appeals to evangelical poverty and protestations against the priesthood, his teaching appears to have been characterized by a strong predestinationist individualism. Its diffusion was so minimal that it was not until the pontificate of Innocent IV (who died in 1254) that the church condemned some whom it declared to be Speronians.

—

JDR

Spittler, Russell (1931–). Professor of New Testament and Pentecostal theologian. Ordained pastor of the Assemblies of God. He was part of a group that founded the Society for Pentecostal Studies in 1974. He has been professor at Fuller Theological Seminary in California since 1976.

—

JFM

Spurgeon, Charles Haddon (1834– 92). Notable Baptist preacher, born in London. He was converted to the Baptist faith and began to preach at the age of sixteen. At twenty-two he was already the most popular preacher of his time, preaching to congregations of more than ten thousand persons. He then built the Metropolitan Tabernacle, where he would preach until his death. He was a fervent conservative evangelical his entire life. He published more than two thousand sermons and several books, of which the best known is *The Saint and His Saviour*.

—

LGP

Stam, Juan (1928–). A native of the United States, but naturalized in Costa Rica, S., Baptist and biblical theologian, has been professor of biblical studies and theology at the Latin American Biblical University (and formerly in its predecessor institution, the Latin American Biblical Seminary) for most of his life. Some of his writings are *Las buenas nuevas de la creación* (1995; The Good News of Creation), *Apocalipsis y profecía* (1998; Apocalypse and Prophecy), and his most recent book, *Profecía bíblica y la misión de la iglesia* (2001; Biblical Prophecy and the Mission of the Church).

—

CCO

Stancaro, Francesco (ca. 1501–74). Theologian who, in opposition to ⇒Osiander, declared that Christ is our mediator only by reason of his humanity, and not of his divinity (as Osiander affirmed). This teaching provoked a strong rejection on the part of ⇒Calvin, who declared that Jesus Christ saves us in his hypostatic union, and that therefore everything which has to do with our redemption should be referred to the person of the Savior, and not to only one of his two natures.

—

JLG

Stendahl, Krister (1921–). Bishop of the Church of Sweden (Lutheran) from 1984 to 1988. He participated in the ⇒World Council of Churches as moderator of the consultation on the church and the Jewish people. His works include *The School of St. Matthew* (1954, 1968), *The Bible and the Role of Women* (1966), *Paul among Jews and Gentiles* (1976), *Meanings* (1984), and *Energy for Life* (1990).

—

ODV

Stephen of Niobe (6th century). Alexandrian sophist, founder of the sect of the Niobites, who upheld an extreme Monophysitism. According to S., the union of the incarnation is such that a human nature of Jesus Christ can no longer be spoken of in any way, so that one should not speak of "a divinity and a humanity" in the Savior. Thus Niobism is a real Monophysitism, in contrast to the moderate or verbal Monophysitism of ⇒Severus of Antioch.

—

JLG

Stephen of Tournai (1128–1203). Canonist, known above all for his commentary on ⇒Gratian, *Summa decreti*. Because of his emphasis on natural law and its relation to "positive law," he is considered a forerunner of ⇒Thomas Aquinas.

—

JLG

Steuernagel, Valdir R. (1931–). Brazilian Lutheran, and a leader in ⇒Fraternidad Teológica Latinoamericana, S. is a theologian of mission. Director of the Center for Mission and Pastoral Studies in Curitiba, Brazil, his best-known work, in addition to many articles, is *Missionary Obedience and Historical Practice*. S. has been an interpreter of the ⇒Lausanne Movement in Latin America and has contributed to the development of a social justice perspective among evangelical missionary movements.

———
CCO

Stoddard, Solomon (1643–1729).

Congregationalist pastor and theologian in the English colony of Massachusetts. He was born in Boston and was educated at Harvard University. In 1670 he became pastor of the Congregational church of Northampton, in the valley of the Connecticut River, where he became a famous preacher. During his time as pastor, the congregation had five revival periods, which were called "harvests." In his sermons S. emphasized the need for every person to experience individually the "new birth." During the disputes about what was called the Half-way Covenant, S. permitted the participation in the Lord's Supper of baptized persons who did not have a conversion experience. He viewed the Lord's Supper as "an ordinance that converts." Although he was in constant debate with Increase and Cotton ⇒Mather on salvation and conversion, S. had a strong influence on the entire Connecticut valley. His grandson, Jonathan ⇒Edwards, joined him as associate pastor in Northampton in 1726 and was his successor after his death.

———
EDA

Stott, John R. W. (1921–).

Evangelical Anglican pastor and preacher who for more than fifty years has carried out a worldwide evangelizing and ecumenical ministry. He was pastor of All Souls Church in the center of London from 1950 until 1975, when he was made rector emeritus so that he could devote himself to his worldwide ministries. The heart of his ministry has been the expository preaching of the Bible. S. affirms the authority of the Bible and the centrality of Christ, the cross, and conversion. But he also emphasizes, as an evangelical who is more progressive than many of his contemporaries, the necessity of a contextualization of the Word in the culture, both ancient and modern, and the need for a biblical vision that includes the social responsibility of Christians in the world. Perhaps the primordial expression of this stance is found in the ⇒Lausanne Covenant, one of whose principal authors was S. In this covenant it is asserted that the Bible is the Word of God "without error in all that it affirms." It also declares the dual responsibility of evangelization and social action on the part of each believer. Among the many works of S., the best known is *Basic Christianity*, translated into fifty languages, and six biblical commentaries in the series The Bible Speaks Today.

———
EA

Strachan, R. Kenneth (1910–65).

Born in Argentina and brought up in Costa Rica, of North American parents, S. was one of the evangelical leaders behind the work of the Latin American Mission (LAM). He continued in the steps of his parents, serving as director of LAM from 1945 until his death in 1965. His leadership and his evangelizing passion led him to carry out missionary campaigns and to articulate a theology of mission and evangelization for all of Latin America that later bore the name of "evangelization in depth." His theological and practical contributions to the theology of evangelism in depth are found in *Revolution in Evangelism: The Story of Evangelism in Depth in Latin America* (1967). One of his two biographies is *Who Shall Ascend: The Life of Kenneth Strachan of Costa Rica* (1968), written by Elizabeth Elliot.

———
CCO

Strauss, David Friedrich (1808–74).

German theologian. His academic education was influenced by great figures of liberal German theology: F. C. ⇒Baur, ⇒Schleiermacher, and ⇒Hegel. He began to teach in Tübingen (1832–35), but the publication of *The Life of Jesus* (2 vols., 1835) generated so great an opposition that he was ousted from his teaching position and eventually suffered academic ostracism. His incursion into politics, as defender of the Prussian monarchy, was brief and disastrous. He made a living as an author until his death.

Of all the writings of S., *The Life of Jesus* is the most important because of its proposal and its reception. It is a deconstructive work criticizing the historicity of the Gospels. It interprets this material using a theory of myth; criticizes the constructive efforts of orthodox and rationalist theologies, which assume the historicity of the Gospels; and proposes a christological interpretation that is rooted in Hegel: humanity as a species in its unity with the Spirit is the true God/man of orthodox faith. Jesus is the representation of the religious imagination of that religious idea and truth. This work has left its mark both on biblical studies and on theology by contributing to the modern debate on the "quest of the historical Jesus." It has contributed to the development of critical studies of the Gospels, to the mythological interpretation of the Scriptures, to the discussion on the historical Jesus and the Christ of faith, to the relationship between historical method and constructive theology, and to the criticism of classical theism, among other things.

——

LRR

Strigel, Victorin (1524–69). Professor in Jena, later in Leipzig, and finally in Heidelberg. A follower of the more moderate stances of ⇒Melanchthon. He was opposed to the strict Lutheranism of ⇒Flacius, especially with regard to the participation of the believer in conversion.

——

JLG

Strong, Augustus Hopkins (1836–1921). U.S. Baptist theologian and pastor. He is famous for his voluminous *Systematic Theology*. This has been very widely used by Baptists and others. S. was born in Rochester, New York. He graduated from Yale University and from Rochester Theological Seminary, and pursued complementary studies in Berlin. He was a pastor (1861–72) in Massachusetts and Ohio. He was professor and president of Rochester Theological Seminary for forty years. He added Walter ⇒Rauschenbusch to the faculty, showing thereby that Rauschenbusch was not as radical—or that S. was not as conservative—as was generally thought.

In spite of being a friend and a relative by marriage of John D. Rockefeller, S. disapproved of the founding of the University of Chicago by the former. Instead of this, he fought for the creation of a Baptist university in New York City.

He received honorary doctorates from Brown, Yale, Princeton, Bucknell, Alfred, and Rochester universities. He was president of the American Baptist Foreign Missionary Society (1892–95), the Northern Baptist General Convention (USA) (1905–10), the Historical Society of Rochester (1890), and the board of directors of Vassar College (1906–11).

——

EPA

Strong, Josiah (1847–1916). Evangelical theologian and expert in missiology who focused on the study of the major modern religions and on Christian ecumenical work.

——

AEM

Stuart, Moses (1780–1852). Congregational minister, theologian, and professor of Bible, born in Wilton, Connecticut. He studied under Timothy ⇒Dwight at Yale University and served as pastor of the First Church in New Haven, where the spirit of the Second Great Awakening was still felt. Later he was professor of sacred literature in the new Andover Theological Seminary, near Boston. S. exercised a profound influence on the development of biblical studies in the United States. He wrote a Hebrew grammar that became the standard textbook in that subject. As a defender of Trinitarian theology, S. opposed Transcendentalism and Unitarianism. He retired in 1848 and died in Andover in 1852.

——

EDA

Suárez, Francisco (1548–1617). Spanish philosopher, theologian, and jurist. He was born in Granada, and his father was a rich lawyer. At the age of sixteen he joined the Company of Jesus, which had then existed for less than three decades. Although at the beginning he had difficulties with his studies, he later did exemplary work in philosophy. He returned to Salamanca, where he had previously studied canon law, to study theology from 1566 to 1570. In that time there was an awakening of Thomism in the university. In 1571, one year before his ordination as priest, he was sent to teach philosophy in the Jesuit college of Segovia, and for the next ten years he taught philosophy and theology in several Jesuit colleges of Castile, among them the college of Valladolid, where he gave an acclaimed series of lectures on the first part of the *Summa theologica* of ⇒Thomas Aquinas. Having been called to the College of Rome in 1580, he continued there his lectures on the second part of the *Summa*. In 1585 his health forced him to return to Spain, this time to Ávila, where he concluded his work on the third part of the *Summa*. In 1592 he was sent to Salamanca, and in 1597, at the request of Philip II, to Coimbra, where he taught until 1616. He died in Lisbon one year later, at the age of sixty-nine.

S. was part of the late scholasticism of the sixteenth century, centered in Salamanca, Alcalá, and Coimbra. Many of the thinkers of this movement had been educated in Paris or

Rome. Returning to Thomism and the great medieval systematic works, they affirmed the scholastic tradition over against the criticism of the Renaissance scholars. They did not do this by simple repetition, but rather by elaborating on what had been said before. This included addressing new social and political issues that had arisen beginning with the Renaissance, as, for instance, in matters of international law.

The vast literary labor of S., a total of twenty-six volumes, can be classified in two principal categories: theology and philosophy. His theological writings are much more than commentaries on Thomas. In several ways they are autonomous treatises that deal systematically with the different areas of theology. His first published work, *De Deo Incarnato*, which arose from his lectures on the third part of the *Summa*, appeared in 1590. Later other works appeared. *De divina substantia* deals with natural theology, while *De angelis* studies the problem of intellectual knowledge. *De gratia* explores the relationship between divine and created liberty. *De ultimo fine* and *De voluntario* present fundamental principles and norms for a natural ethic.

Although S. was a convinced Thomist, he frequently departed from classical Thomism. As a product of his time, his christological thought had less to do with the soteriological orientation of the New Testament and more with the way in which the union of the divinity and the humanity in Christ takes place.

For S., philosophy was the foundation for theological research. His works of a more philosophical character are found in a large work in two volumes, *Disputationes metaphysicae*. It is said that ⇒Descartes carried a copy of this work on his travels. Published in 1597, it was reprinted eighteen times in the seventeenth century. His metaphysics, while fundamentally Aristotelian and Thomist, is highly original, according to the consensus of scholars. The modern Spanish philosopher Zubiri praises him, saying that "Suárez represents the first attempt since ⇒Aristotle to make of metaphysics a corpus of independent philosophical teaching. With Suárez metaphysics is raised to the rank of an autonomous and systematic discipline."

S. exhibits a deep comprehension of the medieval thinkers, as well as a great ability to address the problems of his own time. For example, in his last publication, *De defensione fidei* (1613), he confronted the theory of the divine right of kings that was upheld by James I of England. In other places he maintained that, while ecclesiastical authority comes directly from God, temporal power proceeds directly from the people. The people are above the ruler, whose power comes from them. What is more, the people can legitimately overthrow a ruler who does not favor the interests of the people, as is the case when a tyrant governs. In the same way, he believed firmly in the application of the principle of subsidiarity in civil society. This principle of Catholic social teaching maintains that nothing should be done by a higher agency that can be done equally well, or better, by another one that is lower. In both cases S. shows his modernity by rejecting the medieval ideal of imperial power. His teaching on the *ius gentium*, which is rooted in the principle that the precept of love goes beyond national or racial divisions, contributed to the evolution of international law.

S. is frequently spoken of in the context of the debate in the seventeenth century between Dominicans and Jesuits concerning the relationship between grace and free will. Although he himself did not participate directly in the debate, he did work behind the scenes to promote the Jesuit stance. In the field of ethics he worked in favor of the probabilist school, which maintains that one can follow a theological or moral position that is proposed by a person who has sufficient authority to maintain it (⇒Medina). Later this position was associated with the confessional practice of the Jesuits.

Some maintain that S. is the greatest of all the Jesuit theologians. There is no doubt that he made a very valuable contribution to Catholic intellectual life and to society in general. For example, during the seventeenth and eighteenth centuries his *Disputationes* served as an important text in Catholic European universities, and even in some Protestant schools. Philosophers of the importance of Spinoza, Berkeley, and Vico declared themselves in debt to him. He played an important role in the transition between the medieval concept of natural law and the modern concept, particularly through his influence on ⇒Grotius. His influence can be seen also in the Spanish mystics ⇒Teresa of Ávila and ⇒John of the Cross, who in turn affected French spirituality.

—

EF

Suchoki, Marjorie Hewett (1933–).

U.S. theologian, known for her work in process theology, particularly in her books *God, Christ, and Church: A Practical Guide to Process Theology* and *The End of Evil: Process Eschatology in Historical Context*. S. has also contributed to the theology of religion from perspectives that include feminism and process theology.

———

CCO

Suidas, Nicetas (11th century).
Byzantine theologian who upheld the doctrine of Pentarchy, according to which there are five patriarchs: those of Jerusalem, Antioch, Alexandria, Rome, and Constantinople. S. asserted that one of the five senses corresponded to each of these five patriarchs: the sense of sight to Jerusalem, the sense of smell to Antioch, and so on. The most important of the senses is touch, which feels things directly and which corresponds to Constantinople, whose patriarch is above the other four.

———

JLG

Sulpitius Severus (ca. 360–ca. 422).
Refined author who after a brief political career withdrew to the life of retirement. His most famous work during the Middle Ages was *Life of St. Martin*, a hagiographic work whose purpose is to inspire the reader rather than to tell the life of the famous bishop of Tours. His two books of *Chronicles* are a history of Israel according to the Old Testament, and then of the church, until the year 400. A great deal of it depends on the *Ecclesiastical History* of ⇒Eusebius of Caesarea and yields little new information. The sections of greatest interest are those that deal with ⇒Priscillian and Priscillianism.

———

JLG

Suso, Heinrich (ca. 1295–1366).
Dominican, disciple and defender of Meister ⇒Eckhart. S. compiled his own writings, possibly out of fear of false interpretations and accusations like those his teacher had suffered. His two chief writings are the *Book of Eternal Wisdom* and the *Book of Truth*. They consist of two dialogues, the first between S. and Wisdom, and the second between S. and the Truth. The first deals principally with the way in which one should live and die, always praising God. The second is an attempt to refute some of the teachings of that time which S. considered erroneous. Here he went to the defense of Eckhart, mainly taking some of the phrases and propositions of Eckhart which had been condemned by the church authorities and showing that although what those authorities had condemned was certainly a theological error, it is possible to interpret what was said by Eckhart

in another way. Just like Eckhart, S. at times let himself be carried away by the mystical Neo-platonism of (pseudo) ⇒Dionysius the Areopagite, so that he could refer to God as "the eternal nothing." Because he wrote in the German vernacular, S. can be considered one of the principal figures in early German literature.

———

JLG

Swedenborg, Emanuel (1688–1772).
Founder of the Church of the New Jerusalem, sometimes known as Swedenborgian. He studied science, philosophy, and theology. Through a combination of these three disciplines he developed a speculative, mystical, and theological pattern of thought that he claimed was due to a special revelation. His mysticism led him to seek communication with the world of spirits. This process produced in him a profound crisis, which was resolved by a vision of Jesus Christ, leading him to a new understanding of Christianity.

His conception of the church made him emphasize the need to return to the sources of primitive Christianity. Some of his speculations and his powerful mysticism, united with his intellectual formulations, have won for him the admiration of philosophers like Coleridge, novelists like Balzac, and short-story writers like Borges. His church still exists, with a small nucleus of followers. The work of S. is considered in literary circles as romantic literature, with esoteric-psychic tendencies.

———

CEA

Tamez, Elsa (1950–). Theologian and biblical scholar whose main contribution is in the integration of her feminist criticism and practice with her critical commitment to the poor. She was born in Mexico and lives and works in Costa Rica, where she was rector and is professor of Bible in the Latin American Biblical University in San José, and a researcher in the Ecumenical Department of Investigation. As a Methodist theologian, she is a theological adviser to the Latin American Council of Churches and is active in the World Methodist Council. As a liberation theologian, she is a member of the Ecumenical Association of Third World Theologians, and in that forum she is an important spokesperson for the Latin American perspective and reality. She is author and editor of many publications, which have been translated into several languages. Among her best-known books are *When the Horizons*

Close: Rereading Ecclesiastes (1998); *The Amnesty of Grace: Justification by Faith from a Latin American Perspective* (1991); *Through Her Eyes: Women's Theology from Latin America* (ed.; 1989); *Liberation Theologians Talk about Women* (ed.; 1986); *The Scandalous Message of James: Faith without Works Is Dead* (1985); *The Feminine Face of Theology* (ed.; 1985); *The Bible of the Oppressed* (1979); and *The Time of Life* (1978).

———

SHR

Tanquelm (12th century). Popular leader in the diocese of Antwerp who was condemned as a heretic, accused of pretending to be the Son of God. Scholars wonder whether this accusation was intended to silence his radical social ideas.

———

JLG

Tatian (ca. 120–?). Apologist, native of Syria or Assyria, who apparently was converted to Christianity in Rome, perhaps as the result of the teachings of ⇒Justin. After the martyrdom of his teacher, T. directed a school in Rome for some time, but later departed for his native land, where he died. In the meantime he had embraced the extreme asceticism of the Encratites, who considered matrimony impure. It was then that he wrote the treatise *Perfection according to the Savior,* which has been lost and which ⇒Clement of Alexandria refuted. Other ancient authors, particularly ⇒Irenaeus, say that he also began to teach gnostic doctrines such as Docetism and the existence of several "eons."

Among the works of T., the one of greatest influence has been his *Diatessaron,* a compilation of the four canonical Gospels, which for some time was the version of the Gospels that was most used in the church of Syria.

His principal theological work is his *Discourse to the Greeks,* in which T. defends the "barbarian religion" against the criticisms of those who maintained that the Hellenistic culture and religion were superior, while Christianity was a religion for stupid or uncultured people. More than a defense of Christianity, it is an attack on Hellenism. Thus, for example, it says the Greeks in reality did not invent or create anything, but simply borrowed and learned everything from their neighbors. Their philosophers never were in agreement among themselves, and in any case what is told about them is very far from being admirable. The

Greeks themselves tell the most disgraceful stories about their gods. Those who worship the images of the gods in reality worship the women of ill repute who were the models for those images. And, as if all this were not enough, the small portion of good that is in the philosophy and culture of Hellenism was learned by the Greeks from the "barbarian" Jews, because Moses lived long before Homer, and all the philosophers said that was good and true they copied from the Hebrews. In all this the attitude of T. over against classical culture contrasts with that of his teacher Justin, who valued that culture.

T. agrees with Justin regarding the centrality of the doctrine of the Word or Logos, which emerges from God in the same way that a light is kindled by another light, and yet this does not imply any loss for the first light. This Word was in God from the beginning and is the creator of all that exists, first unformed matter and then the ordered cosmos.

A part of that creation of God is the human being, who is mortal by nature, in both body and soul, but to whom God can give life after death, because the soul that knows the truth does not die with the body.

———

JLG

Tauler, Johannes (ca. 1300–51). One of the outstanding German mystics of the Rhine Valley. At a very young age he entered the Dominican order in Strassburg and probably studied with Meister ⇒Eckhart. His sermons, although mystical and inspired by Eckhart and Neoplatonism, had the goal of awakening a faith active in the love of God. He emphasized the necessity of the grace of God in his mysticism and influenced the young ⇒Luther.

———

ALG

Taylor, Jeremy (1613–67). Puritan Anglican pastor, known for his preaching and talent as a spiritual director. His moral and practical theology (*The Rule and Exercise of Holy Living,* 1665, and *Of Holy Dying,* 1655) were very influential. He provided practical guidance for daily living and for critical moments. He sought to discern the nature and authority of the moral conscience and also that of civil, revealed, natural, and ecclesiastical laws. As an integral part of their commitment to God, it is supremely important for believers to make public their moral commitment. John

⇒Wesley was one of the theologians influenced by T.

—

IG

Taylor, Nathaniel W. (1786–1858).

Congregationalist theologian, minister, and intellectual, he was born in New Milford, Connecticut. He studied theology with Timothy ⇒Dwight at Yale University and then served as professor of didactic theology at Yale (1822–58). He believed that human beings are able to choose and to do good. His theological adversaries in 1833 established a Theological Institute in East Windsor that became Hartford Theological Seminary. T. died in New Haven, Connecticut.

——

EDA

Teilhard de Chardin, Marie-Joseph-Pierre (1881–1955).

He was born in Sarcenat, France. In 1899 he entered the Jesuit novitiate in Aix-en-Provence. He was ordained a priest in 1911. His theological education was augmented by his scientific interest—in particular, his interest in geology and paleontology. In the First World War he served as a stretcher-bearer. Between the two world wars he lived as an exile in China, where he engaged in paleontological studies. His sympathies with the theory of evolution placed him in conflict with his church, and his order forbade him to disseminate his ideas. His participation in the discovery of Pithecanthropus, Java man, and Sinanthropus, Peking man, brought him international recognition in the scientific community (*The Apparition of Man*). When he returned to France, his order did not permit him to publish what later was his famous work, *The Phenomenon of Man*. He spent his last years in the United States, involved in anthropological research with the Wenner Green Foundation. He died in 1955 on Easter Sunday.

T. was an existentialist theologian who asked: given our finitude and death, what is the meaning and purpose of our creative activity? For him the answer is in the theory of evolution. Evolution makes us conscious that we humans have a special history and an extraordinary future. Evolution is not only a scientific postulate, but it is also a part of the Pauline vision of Christ. For Paul, according to T., Christ is the origin, the present center, and the end of the cosmos. Everything that is evolves toward the end that is revealed in Christ. Therefore evolution is not anti-Christian, but on the contrary, it is the clearest expression of the universal cosmic law.

Following ⇒Bergson, T. asserts that there is continuity between the animal/material world and human beings. Nature, like humanity, has a historical character. Both manifest the tendency toward the integration of different forms of life (the "tangential tendency of energy"), and both manifest the development of more complex forms of life (the "radial tendency of energy"). T. calls these two tendencies the Law of Complexity of Consciousness. With this term he points to the evolutionary process by which more complex forms of matter are accompanied by more sophisticated forms of consciousness. Matter and consciousness are present at every level. The history of evolution, with all its contradictions and positive moments of progress and negative moments of regress, points to the development and the future of human personality and to the creation of the universal community of various cultures. With the development of the human being (hominization), the evolutionary process enters a new stage, the conscious stage, where the continuity and future of evolution, in all its spiritual and social dimension, are the responsibility of human beings. What is now at stake is the conversion of humanity into a harmonious and creative family.

T. alleges that if humanity is to accomplish its historic mission, its evolutionary responsibility to live in unity and under conditions that promote human personality, it must live under the power of love ("amorization"). For him, the center of the cosmos incarnates the absolute power and presence of love. This cosmic presence ultimately motivates and sustains loving attitudes among human beings and gives us the assurance of the final success of the evolutionary process. It is here that T. postulates a synthesis between his scientific and religious convictions and confesses that the risen Christ is the center of the cosmos and the culmination of the evolutionary process.

According to T., Christian doctrines and beliefs must make sense in the scientific context, and science gives us hope only in the christocentric context. This combination implies that both science and theological postulates must be creatively reformulated. For example: (a) creation no longer is understood as a final and complete reality in itself, but is rather a reality that continues to evolve ("cosmogenesis"); (b) Christ is not only the incarnation of God, but also the evolution of the new community (the mystical body) and the goal of human personality ("Christogenesis"); (c) sin is interpreted as an obstacle to the evolutionary process, but not as a permanent reality; (d) the redemption that Christ offers us is his contribution to the development of the evolutionary process; (e) eschatology is the history and process of the coalescence between the natural and the supernatural worlds, and the culmination of the evolutionary process in the "Omega point"; (f) prayer, spiritual development, and piety motivate and aid us on the road of the evolutionary process; finally, (g) God is interpreted as the creative agent *par excellence*, the creator of diversity and the creator and power of unity among all the dimensions of creation. God is not the Omega, but is the one who determines that all reality points to the Omega.

The evolutionary vision of T. is attractive for those who underline the necessity 'and the positive character of social change. Many who are committed to social justice, human progress, and international and interreligious relations find affirmation and hope in his works *The Future of Man* and *The Divine Milieu*. Juan Luis ⇒Segundo is one of the Latin American theological figures who are much influenced by his thought.

—
IG

Tempier, Stephen (13th century).
Bishop of Paris who opposed the new philosophical currents and who in 1210 condemned thirteen teachings of extreme Aristotelianism such as predeterminism, the eternity of the world, and the unity of all souls in one single "intellectual agent." In 1277 he published a much longer list of 219 propositions that he proscribed as bishop of Paris. Most of these propositions were taken from the writings of ⇒Siger of Brabant, and others from his colleagues in the Faculty of Arts, but some of them were from ⇒Thomas Aquinas.

—
JLG

Temple, William (1881–1944).
Archbishop of Canterbury (1942–44) and leader of the international ecumenical movement in the first half of the twentieth century. He was born in Exeter, England, and was educated at Oxford University, where he was also an instructor. T. was a man of great intellectual ability and energy, recognized for his oratorical ability and for his passionate support for the church and its ministry. As a priest he formed part of a group promoting reforms in the polity of the Anglican church. He was a prolific writer who published several works of a philosophical and theological nature that also touched on social ethics. In them he showed his mastery of a form of critical idealism (in the style of ⇒Hegel). T. openly supported the cause of the workers' movement both in his own country and at the international level. Politics was one of his passions. He firmly believed in the responsibility of the church to speak out on political matters and on social and economic problems.

—
NRG

Tenaka, Masao (1925–).
A member of the Kyodan Church in Japan, T. is one of the most important contextual theologians in Japan and Southeast Asia. His theological contribution lies in the relationship of the Christian faith with Asiatic cultures and the imperative of ethnic reconciliation. His best-known and most controversial work is *God Is Rice: Asian Culture and Christian Faith* (1986).

—
CCO

Tepedino, Ana Maria (1941–).
Brazilian theologian who obtained her doctorate in systematic and pastoral theology at the Pontifical Catholic University of Rio de Janeiro, where she remains as a professor. She has been coordinator of the Latin American area of the Ecumenical Association of Theologians of the Third World. She has distinguished herself through her contributions to feminist theology and her inclusion of the voices of marginalized men and women in theological discourse. Her two most important publications are *The Women Disciples of Jesus* (1990) and, with María Pilar ⇒Aquino, *Between Indignation and Hope: Latin American Feminist Theology* (1998).

—
OOE

Teresa of Ávila (1515–82).
Teresa de Cepeda y Ahumada lived in the Spain of the Counter-Reformation, which was marked by a very intense mysticism and longing for holiness. She came from a family of converted Jews or "new Christians," who were more inclined toward a private and affective spirituality that was open to mystical experiences. This tendency put them in conflict with the Inquisition, which supported an outward piety and traditional rituals. Growing up in a well-to-do family, at the age of twenty T. entered the Convent of the Incarnation of the Carmelite nuns of Ávila. During her first year in the

cloister she became gravely ill and suffered paralysis. Her father insisted on taking her away from the convent so that she could be cared for. But when she recovered from her illness, she returned to the convent, noting that her spiritual life had become lukewarm and superficial. However, the condition of the convent was not helpful to her. The rigorous Carmelite rule had been relaxed, and the convent appeared to be a boardinghouse for wealthy young women, since the nuns spent a good deal of their time in the visitors' salon. At the age of thirty-nine T. had a conversion experience while she was contemplating Christ nailed to the cross. This was the beginning of her raptures, ecstasies, and mystical visions.

For years she worked arduously for permission to establish a convent that would return to the original spirit of the Carmelite rule. At last, in 1562 she founded the convent of St. Joseph of the Discalced Carmelite nuns in Ávila. In this community strict poverty was maintained; the nuns earned their living by begging and working. A strict enclosure and a rigorous schedule of prayer were observed. T. founded thirty-two reformed convents, in spite of the opposition of her own order, the suspicion of the hierarchy, and a formal investigation by the Spanish Inquisition. Only the protection given by confessors and theologians like ⇒John of the Cross, her friend and disciple, and by King Philip II made it possible for her to elude the judgment of the Inquisition. Her character, which was both strong and charismatic, and her sense of humor were of help to her in all her work. Her public success did not stand in the way of a fervent life of prayer and profound mystical experiences.

Obeying her confessors and superiors, T. collected her mystical experiences in several books. The one which she considered her best work was *Castillo interior o las moradas* (1577; The Interior Castle or the Dwelling Places). This title refers to the stages of a person's inner journey toward union with God. On this journey one should not be in a hurry, and one should only be concerned to follow God freely, since it is God who guides each one in an appropriate way. The journey is not the same for all; rather, there are many possible variations that can be perceived as one comes to understand better the different manifestations of the love of God. Other books of T. are *Constitutions, Book of the Foundations, The Book of Life,* and *The Road to Perfection.*

For T. holiness is manifested in an active love for the neighbor and not through mystical experiences. In everything that she did, she showed a basic confidence in God and in the goodness of people, and her actions demonstrated that she was convinced that God loved her gratuitously. It was not possible for her to consider the body as separate from the soul. In her writings three requisites for the Christian life can be perceived: love for God and neighbor, true humility, and detachment from material things and from persons. This last quality, however, did not lead T. to deny the value of friends. On the contrary, she was sure that heaven consists in enjoying the presence of God and in continuing the relation with friends. The personality of T. was healthy, affable, and open. She was not afraid of novelty or anything different; she did not fear the challenges that life presents. Mixing gentleness with firmness, she guided her nuns in such a way that each one would be led by God without comparing herself to others.

T. died on October 4, 1582. She was canonized in 1622, and in 1970 she was the first woman to be declared a ⇒doctor of the church.

———

AMID

Tertullian (ca. 155–ca. 220). Possibly the first Christian theologian to write in Latin, an honor that some attribute to ⇒Minucius Felix. Certainly he was the creator of a great deal of the Latin theological vocabulary that is used to this day. Having coined and determined the theological sense of words such as "person," "substance," and "satisfaction," T. seems to have been a lawyer, and some scholars identify him with a jurist of the same name who is quoted in the *Corpus iuris civilis.* He was a native of northern Africa, although he lived in Rome during his youth and even after his conversion, when he was around forty years old. He then returned to Carthage, where he wrote extensively in defense of his new faith against the pagans and against the different heresies circulating at that time. In spite of being the great champion of orthodoxy, his rigorist tendencies led him to become a Montanist (⇒Montanus) around the year 207. Some ancient writers say that later Montanism itself did not seem to him to be sufficiently rigorous, and he abandoned it, founding the sect of the Tertullianists.

The rigorism of T. is not only moral but also theological. For him, all theological errors and all heresies have their origin in the incursion of pagan philosophy and its reasoning into doctrine and theology. He asked: "What does Athens have to do with Jerusalem? What does the Academy have to do with the Church? What do heretics have to do with Christians?" Occasionally, he would even affirm that the death of the Son of God "must be believed because it is absurd," and that the resurrection "is true because it is impossible." But this does not mean that what proves Jesus' death is the fact that it is absurd, but rather that because it is absurd, the only way one can affirm it is through faith.

On the other hand, while T. repudiated any incursion of philosophy within theology, he himself is largely a Stoic, and his vision of the reality and order of the cosmos derives largely from his Stoic perspectives. This is not surprising, since Stoicism dominated the intellectual circles of the Latin-speaking world to such an extent that it was often taken for granted and therefore went unnoticed.

The chief work of T. in defense of Christianity over against the pagans is *Apologeticus adversus gentes pro christianis*, generally known simply as *Apology*. In it T. defends his new faith with all the rhetorical and legal weapons at his disposal. While he shows respect for the authorities and their laws, sharp and even sarcastic criticism against their injustice and wrongdoing is not lacking. In another of his apologetic works, *The Testimony of the Soul*, T. examines the human soul as if it were a witness before a tribunal, and finally he forces it to confess that "the soul is by nature Christian." In his attack on heresies, T. produced *Prescription against Heretics*. In the legal language of that time, a "prescription" was something similar to what we today call a "previous question," that is, an argument which, rather than entering into the discussion of the debated subject, affirms that the debate itself cannot take place, because the opponent does not have the right to debate. In a few words, T. argues that the Scriptures are the property of the church, which has long used them as its own, and no one has questioned its right to do this. Therefore heretics do not have the right to use the Scriptures, and the debate about their correct interpretation has no place at all. But this argument did not keep T. from writing tracts against different heresies, especially when, because he had become a Montanist, he himself appeared to contradict his own "prescription." Thus he wrote a long work in five books, *Against ⇒Marcion,* and also tracts *Against ⇒Hermogenes* and *Against ⇒Praxeas.*

His own ethical rigorism led T. to write several tracts on practical and moral matters, such as *On Monogamy, On Fasting, On Modesty, On Chastity, On Patience, On Penance,* and *To His Wife.*

Possibly the most important theological contributions of T. are his discussions about the Trinity and the incarnation. Both are found chiefly in *Against Praxeas*. In it T. refutes the theory that Father, Son, and Holy Spirit are only manifestations of God, and he does it based on two terms that were in common use in the jurisprudence of that time: "person" and "substance." Apparently T. does not give the term "substance" its metaphysical sense, but he refers to its legal meaning, according to which the substance is what determines one's legal status. Thus, for example, the substance of the emperor is the empire. In the same way, divinity is the substance of God, and the three persons participate in it in complete and indivisible fashion, just as occasionally there were emperors who shared the empire with their sons. Therefore in God there is "one substance in three persons." Although this formula is quite ambiguous in T., after a long struggle (⇒Arius, Council of ⇒Nicaea) it came to be the mark of Trinitarian orthodoxy.

Apparently, Praxeas connected his Modalistic Monarchianism—that is, the teaching that the three "persons" are only modes of action and revelation of God—with a confused Christology, asserting that in the Savior the divinity, which is called Christ, is the Father, and the term "Son" refers to the flesh or the humanity, which is called Jesus. T. begins by clarifying that "Christ" is not really a name, but an adjective that means "anointed." When we speak of Jesus as the Christ, what we are saying is not that Christ is one and Jesus another, but that Jesus is the anointed or the Messiah of God. Then he goes on to discuss how it is that the Word becomes flesh. This does not take place through a mixture of the divinity with the humanity so that Jesus is neither totally divine nor completely human, but something in between, a *tertium quid*. The truth is that, just as in God there are three persons who share one substance, in Jesus Christ there are two substances—the divinity and the humanity—shared by one person. Since T. occasionally uses the term "nature" as a synonym of "substance," it can be said that he was the first to use the formula "two natures in one person," which after long debates also became the sign of christological orthodoxy (Council of ⇒Chalcedon).

Another point in which T. influenced the theology of later centuries was his way of understanding original sin. Already in the New

Testament we find the idea that in some way "in Adam all sinned." But this is not explained any further. Because of his Stoic background, T. understood that the soul is a bodily substance—although it is an extremely subtle body—that is inherited by one person from another. Thus the soul of Adam, once it is corrupted by sin, transmits that inheritance to all of his descendants. This interpretation of original sin as an inheritance from the first parents was not the only one that existed in the ancient church, nor is it the oldest. However, owing in part to the influence of T., until the present time the most common interpretation of original sin in Western Christianity, both Catholic and Protestant, is in terms of inheritance.

Toward the end of his life the rigorism of T. led him to withdraw from the rest of the church and finally to join a group considered to be schismatic. But in spite of this action his works continued to be read by the great theologians of North Africa, so that ⇒Cyprian referred to him as the Teacher. Through them, and especially through ⇒Augustine, the lawyer T. has left his imprint on all of Western Christianity, in which the tendency is to view the human condition in terms of a legal debt owed to God, and the work of Jesus Christ in terms of the payment of that debt.

———
JLG

Theodore bar Koni (8th century).
Nestorian theologian about whose life little is known. His only surviving work is a number of *Scholia* or notes on miscellaneous subjects, in eleven books. Of these the most interesting is the tenth, "Dialogue between a Christian and a Pagan" (although in reality the "pagan" is a Muslim).

———
JLG

Theodore of Mopsuestia (350–428).
Bishop of that city, in the province of Cilicia, from 392 until his death. He was a native of Antioch, where, like ⇒John Chrysostom, he studied under the distinguished teacher of rhetoric Libanius. Famous during his life for his exegetical work, after his death he was rejected because of some of his teachings, both in reference to the Bible itself and in the christological field. In both fields, exegesis and Christology, T. was a faithful exponent of the Antiochene tradition. His exegesis rejected allegorical interpretations, against which T. wrote two works: *On Allegory and the Histor-*

ical Meaning and *On the Perfection of Works*. He therefore preferred a historical and typological interpretation. For that reason he declared that the Song of Songs is a love poem composed on the occasion of the marriage of Solomon with an Egyptian princess, and that the book of Job is a drama composed by a Jew in imitation of Greek dramas. He also came to distinguish between two levels of authority in the Bible, relegating to a second level books such as Ezra, Job, Song of Songs, James, 2 Peter, 2 and 3 John, and Revelation. He also rejected many of the messianic interpretations of Old Testament passages that had become common among Christians, limiting such predictions to a few passages. These opinions did not earn him sympathy among the most traditional sectors, particularly among the Alexandrians, whose allegorical interpretations T. flatly rejected. Among his exegetical works are commentaries on much of the Bible, of which some are extant—on the Psalms, the Minor Prophets, the Pauline Epistles, and John.

As a theologian, what was most discussed and is still discussed of the teaching of T. is his Christology. T. wrote a treatise against the teachings of ⇒Apollinaris of Laodicea, another one with a similar purpose titled *He Who Assumes and He Who is Assumed*, and a large work in fifteen books, *On the Incarnation*. The title *He Who Assumes and He Who is Assumed* suffices to show that the Christology of T., which is typically Antiochene, tends to distinguish clearly between the humanity and the divinity of the Savior, in order to safeguard the integrity of the former. For the same reason T. resisted the *communicatio idiomatum* (sharing of predicates), and therefore denied to Mary the title of *Theotokos* (mother or bearer of God).

Because T. died shortly before the Nestorian controversy broke out (⇒Nestorius, Council of ⇒Ephesus), during his life his christological positions only gave rise to minor controversies. But after the condemnation of Nestorius there were repeated efforts to condemn the deceased T., whom many saw as the teacher and forerunner of Nestorius. This ultimately led to the condemnation of T. by the Council of ⇒Constantinople of 553, as one of the "Three Chapters."

In recent times there has been an awakening of interest in T. on the part of scholars, who see in his biblical works a level of scholarship and careful research that was unusual in his time.

———
JLG

Theodore of Raithu (6th century).
Monk who wrote in defense of the Definition of Faith of ⇒Chalcedon, although he understood it from an Alexandrian perspective. Thus, for example, he considered ⇒Theodore of Mopsuestia to be a heretic.

——

JLG

Theodore the Studite (759–826). Also called Theodore of Studius, Theodore Studites. Champion of the autonomy of the church over against the empire. Promoter of the Byzantine monastic revival, and honored as a saint on November 11. He was born in Constantinople of a well-to-do family and entered the abbey of Mount Olympus, in Bithynia, Asia Minor (780). He was ordained a priest (787) by the patriarch Tarasios. He succeeded his uncle as director of that monastery (794). Banished, persecuted, and incarcerated by the emperors Constantine VI (796), Nicephoros I (809), Leo V (815), and Michael II (820), he never capitulated before the power of the empire. He rebuilt a monastery that was founded in 463 in Constantinople (799). He organized monastic life and drew up rules for it, including the prohibition of visits by women and even by female animals. He wrote hymns, poems, letters, catechisms, liturgies, penitential prayers, and apologetic treatises.

——

EPA

Theodoret of Cyrus (ca. 393–485).
Historian, exegete, and theologian of Antiochian origin, who beginning in 423 served as bishop of Cyrus, near the Euphrates River. His principal historical works are *History of Monasticism*, which is largely a series of anecdotes about the first monks in the East and which concludes with a treatise on the ascetic life, and his *Ecclesiastical History*, which is a continuation of the work with the same title by ⇒Eusebius of Caesarea. This continuation or appendix covers the period from 323 until 428, and much of it is taken from similar works by ⇒Sozomenos and ⇒Socrates. What is most original and useful for the study of the fourth century is the material that deals with the church in Antioch and its surroundings.

The exegetical production of T. was enormous. Besides brief notes on individual texts and a vast number of sermons, he wrote commentaries on most of the Bible. These commentaries are scholarly, careful, and quite traditional. They conform to the exegetical method of Antioch, which he had learned from the writings of ⇒Theodore of Mopsuestia.

As an apologist, T. wrote *Cure for the Illnesses of the Greeks*. In it he expounds the traditional opinions about a number of philosophical and theological matters and compares them with Christian teaching.

However, what drew most attention to his theology were his christological positions. T. studied in Antioch with ⇒Nestorius and ⇒John of Antioch, and therefore his Christology is typically Antiochene, although it does not go to the extremes of Nestorius. For him it was essential to uphold the complete humanity of Christ, and therefore he was inclined to make a sharp distinction between that humanity and the divinity of the Savior. An interesting corollary which T. derives from his Christology is that in the Eucharist there is also a duality of natures in a single reality, because the eucharistic bread, at the same time that it is the body of Christ, continues to be bread—as is also true of the wine.

When the Nestorian controversy broke out, T. defended his old fellow student. In the Council of ⇒Ephesus he was aligned with John of Antioch and his council. When ⇒Cyril of Alexandria promulgated his *Twelve Anathemas*, T. published *Reprimand of the Twelve Anathemas of Cyril*. Later, although he appears to have taken part in drawing up the Formula of Union of 433, he did not sign it until two years later. The "robber synod" of Ephesus in 439 deposed him and ordered him to be incarcerated in a monastery. In 447, in his *Eranistes* or *The Beggar*, he was the first to call attention to the dangers of the Monophysitism, which was appearing among the most extreme Alexandrians. The Council of ⇒Chalcedon vindicated him and restored him to his see. However, even after his death, his enemies of Alexandrian tendencies continued to attack him. When in the year 553 the Council of ⇒Constantinople rejected the "Three Chapters," the latter included the writings of T. against Cyril, even though the council refused to condemn T. himself.

——

JLG

Theodulf of Orleans (ca. 750–821).
Bishop of that city, distinguished figure of the Carolingian renaissance, who toward the end of his life was exiled because he was accused of conspiring against Louis the Pious. Among his works is a treatise *On the Holy Spirit*, in which he defends the position of the Latin West regarding the *filioque*—that is, that the Holy

Spirit proceeds from the Father *and from the Son*. He was also the author of many hymns, among them the classic hymn for Palm Sunday, *All Glory, Laud and Honor*.

———
JLG

Theognis of Nicea (4th century). Former student of ⇒Lucian of Antioch, and therefore defender of ⇒Arius in the Council of ⇒Nicaea, where T. was bishop. He was one of five bishops who refused to sign the creed that was adopted there. When he at last agreed to sign it, he refused to sign the anathemas against Arius. For this refusal, Constantine ordered him to be deposed and sent into exile.

———
JLG

Theognostus (?–ca. 282). One of the successors of ⇒Origen as director of the school of Alexandria. His writings have been lost, although some of them are found in quotations by ⇒Photius and other authors. He was a theologian respected in his time, and ⇒Athanasius appealed to his authority against the stance of the Origenists who refused to accept the decisions of the Council of ⇒Nicaea.

———
JLG

Theophilus of Antioch (2nd century). Bishop of Antioch and one of the early Christian apologists. ⇒Eusebius of Caesarea places him sixth in the line of descent from the apostles as bishop of Antioch. Of his writings we have only his *Apology*, divided into three volumes and directed to his pagan friend Autolycus, therefore also known as *To Autolycus*. It is believed that he wrote it around the year 180, at the end of the reign of Marcus Aurelius, or shortly thereafter, at the beginning of the reign of Commodus. The objective of the books is to convince his learned friend and the pagan world at large of the truth of Christianity. Among the subjects he discusses in his *Apology* are the Christian concept of God, the interpretation of the Old Testament, and the superiority of the Christian teaching on creation to the immoral myths of the Olympian religion. Among the writings of T. that do not exist today, Eusebius mentions *Against the Heresy of Hermogenes*, *Against Marcion*, and several catechetical manuals. ⇒Jerome adds some commentaries on Proverbs and on the Gospels to the list of books attributed to T., but he doubts their authorship.

In the field of theology, T. introduced several concepts and terminology to refer to the Christian doctrines of God and the Word. For instance, he was the first theologian to use the word *Trinity* (*trias*) to refer to God. According to him, and in agreement with ⇒Justin Martyr, ⇒Tatian, and, ⇒Athenagoras, the second person of the Trinity is the Logos, whom they at times also call Sophia. T. brought to Christian theology the distinction made earlier by ⇒Philo between the immanent Logos or Word (*Logos endiathetos*) that has always existed in God, and the expressed Word (*Logos prophorikos*), pronounced before all creation—"the only begotten of all creation." This new distinction would come to be adopted by several eminent theologians and would play an important role in the controversies of the following centuries.

In contrast with later Nicene theology, the theology of T. tends to reflect some previous tenets or characteristics of Jewish Christianity. For example, Jesus is differentiated from the rest of humanity by his obedience to God and not, as later Christian theology postulates, by his incarnation. It is this obedience that wins for him the name that is above every name. However, following the line of gentile and then Nicene Christianity, T. affirms that the title "Son of God" refers to the generation of the Logos before the creation of the world.

His writings show a superficial knowledge of Greek literature and philosophy. Nonetheless, they were used later by ⇒Irenaeus, ⇒Novatian, and ⇒John of Damascus.

———
ZMP

Thielicke, Helmut (1908–86). German Lutheran preacher who served as professor of theology at the University of Heidelberg until he was ousted by the Nazi regime in 1940. After the war, he was professor of theology and then rector of the University of Tübingen until 1954, when he became rector of the University of Hamburg. Both in Germany and in the United States he was acknowledged as a great preacher because he was able to respond to the spiritual hunger among educated people, for whom the typical sermons of the 1950s left much to be desired. He published a great number of works, among which are close to thirty-five books of sermons, in addition to *Man in God's World*, *Theological Ethics*, and *The Evangelical Faith*, in three volumes, one of the major systematic syntheses of the twentieth century.

———
JDRR

Thierry of Chartres (?–ca. 1128). One of the great masters of the school of Chartres, who was characterized by his realism regarding the matter of universals. That realism was based on a philosophical position with Platonic overtones. In the case of T. that regard for ⇒Plato was manifested in an attempt to show the compatibility between the creation stories and the worldview of Genesis, on the one hand, and the *Timaeus* of Plato, on the other.

———

JLG

Thomas, Gospel of. Accidentally discovered near the village of Nag Hammadi, Egypt, (ca. 1945–46) by a Bedouin who was looking for fertilizer for his plants. The *Gospel of Thomas,* written in the ancient Egyptian dialect called Coptic, is one of several documents found on that occasion that evidently formed part of a gnostic library of the middle of the fourth century.

This Gospel consists of 114 sayings of Jesus in the form of aphorisms or proverbs. The total absence of historical narrative and of any mention of the death and resurrection of Christ is conspicuous. The purpose of the sayings is to bring eternal life to those who understand them. The first saying of the Gospel makes this explicit: "These are the secret words which the living Jesus spoke, which Didymus Judas Thomas wrote. And he said, 'The one who finds the meaning of these words will not taste death.'"

Although there are several sayings that are very similar to the Synoptic material, others do not have any parallel, for example: "In the day that they were one they became two. But when they become two, what will they do?" This and other sayings in the Gospel appear to reflect a certain gnostic tendency known as Encratism, which asserted that originally humankind was androgynous—that is, of both sexes—and that in the fall the sexes had separated. However, there still exists in the human being a divine spark which, if it is ignited through the words of Jesus, is capable of providing the knowledge necessary to escape from the prison of sexuality and the material world and to return to the undifferentiated primordial state where the soul will obtain eternal rest and dominion over everything.

This Gospel reflects the notions of a group of Christians who understood the ministry of Jesus in a different way. They believed salvation was obtained not through the sacrifice of Christ, but through a correct understanding of his words.

———

ODV

Thomas, Madathilparampil M. (1916–97). Native of Kerala, India, lay member of the Church of South India, T. was one of the most important ecumenical leaders in Southeast Asia. His ecumenical activities included serving as president of the Executive Committee of the ⇒World Council of Churches (1968–75) and as moderator of the Department of Church and Society of the World Council.

His theological work focused on social matters and the Christian faith, particularly the relationship of Christianity to other religions and to Marxism in Asia. Among his many works are *The Christian Response to the Asian Revolution* (1966), *The Acknowledged Christ of the Indian Renaissance* (1970), *Salvation and Humanization* (1971), and *Risking Christ for Christ's Sake* (1987).

———

CCO

Thomas à Kempis ⇒Kempis, Thomas à

Thomas Aquinas (ca. 1225–74). Dominican theologian of Italian origin, ⇒doctor of the church, and patron saint of Catholic schools. Without a doubt, he is one of the most important and influential scholastic theologians, not only because of his works and thought, but also because of his impact on the life and thought of the church throughout the ages. Among other honorary titles, he has been called *Doctor Communis* (in the twelfth century) and *Doctor Angelicus* (fifteenth century).

He was the son of Landolfo d'Aquino, an Italian nobleman in the service of the emperor, and of his second wife, Theodora de Chieti. He had five sisters, three older brothers, and at least three half brothers. The ancestral castle of Rocca Secca, where T. was born, was halfway between Rome and Naples. It was part of the kingdom of Sicily, governed by Emperor Frederick II, of the house of Hohenstaufen (1194–1250), who was constantly at war with the papal armies of Honorius III and his successors. Thus the position of the Aquinas family, located between two loyalties, was precarious.

After spending the first five years of his life at home, T. was sent to the Benedictine abbey of Monte Cassino, in the hope that he would join that order and become the abbot. There he was trained in the spiritual life, particularly through the Latin Psalter. In addition, he learned the basic skills of reading, writing, and mathematics. As a result of the conflicts between the emperor and the pope, the imperial troops occupied the monastery, and consequently the youths who studied there were sent to the imperial university in Naples, founded in 1244. There T. encountered the philosophy of ⇒Aristotle for the first time.

After attending mass regularly in the priory of Santo Domingo in Naples, T. became interested in the lifestyle of the Dominicans, and eventually joined that order, receiving the religious habit at the age of nineteen. The Order of Preachers—the formal name of the Dominicans—had been founded a few decades earlier, in 1216, by ⇒Dominic of Guzmán, an itinerant Spanish preacher. From the beginning Dominic had devoted himself to preaching, study, and community life. His apostolic zeal, his poverty, and his simple life impressed the young T. Because his family did not support him in his decision to enter the order, and because his superiors thought that Benedictine monasticism was better suited to a youth of the nobility than a mendicant order, the Dominicans felt that it was better to send him far away, first to Rome and then to Paris, for his novitiate studies and the rest of his education. In Paris his mentor was ⇒Albertus Magnus, another Dominican who soon became a provincial and bishop.

At the beginning, T. did not appear to be exceptional at all, neither in appearance nor in intellect. Because of his timidity and corpulence, they called him "the silent ox." One of his companions decided to help him in his studies, fearing that otherwise he would not pass. When T. helped his friend to understand a passage that he did not understand, this student was surprised. Another companion showed the notes of T. to his teacher, Albert the Great, who was impressed and examined him in public. An eighteenth-century chronicler of the lives of the saints, Alban Butler, recorded a quotation attributed to Albert: "Until now we have called brother Thomas 'the silent ox'; but I assure you that his mooing will be heard in the whole world."

T. followed his teacher to Cologne, where he went to establish a new *studium generale*, according to a mandate of the General Chapter of the Dominicans in 1248. While Albert lectured on ⇒Dionysius and discussed the *Ethics* of ⇒Aristotle, T., his bachelor of arts assistant, lectured on Isaiah, Jeremiah, and Lamentations.

Later T. returned to Paris, where he studied in order to occupy the teaching post for non-Parisian students. He began there to study under Elias Brunet de Bergerac in the autumn of 1252, while he lectured on the *Sentences* of ⇒Peter Lombard. There he achieved an excellent reputation as a teacher and author. Even though in those years there were several strong attacks on the Dominicans, T. graduated and continued to teach and write. Between 1256 and 1259 he lectured on the Bible, directed scholastic disputations (*Quaestiones disputatae de veritate*), preached, and began to write his *Summa contra Gentiles*, which he completed in 1264. This work, apparently written for Dominican missionaries in Spain and North Africa, is a systematic summary in which T. proposed strong arguments "against the gentiles," that is, nonbelievers and heretics. In this context it is necessary to remember the diversity of religions that characterize those centuries of the Middle Ages, when Christianity, Judaism, and Islam encountered one another repeatedly.

T. then returned to his native Italy to continue teaching, writing, and preaching. At the request of Pope Urban IV he composed the liturgy for the new feast of Corpus Christi. (His hymns *O Salutaris* and *Tantum Ergo* are still sung at eucharistic celebrations.) He also wrote *Against the Errors of the Greeks*, concerning the doctrinal differences between Greek and Latin Christians. In the process of writing this work he discovered the doctrinal riches of Greek patristic writings. The result was the *Catena Aurea*, a continuous gloss or commentary on the Gospels, made up of quotations from the Latin and Greek fathers of the church. This work was an immediate success and was one of the books of T. that were most read and published, at the time in manuscript form and later in printed editions. Although the book is only a compilation and does not have one word of T. himself, the *Catena* appears to have been a milestone in his thought, because of the influence of the ancient Greek authors.

In July 1265, the Dominicans asked T. to open a school in Santa Sabina in Rome. He quickly realized that the *Sentences* of Peter Lombard, the basic text in common use, was not adequate for students who were beginning their theological studies. He then began to think about an exposition of Catholic theology, in three parts, that would be simpler, better organized, and more inclusive than the existing textbooks. By 1268 the first part of what would become his famous *Summa theologica* was already in circulation. During the rest of his life, aside from other writings (some of them in response to frequent requests for him to express his opinions on controversial matters) and preaching and teaching, he devoted himself to the completion of this monumental work, which has never been surpassed in the history of Christian theology. When death overtook him, the third part was still unfinished, and his secretary completed it by compiling fragments of what T. had previously written when he commented on the *Sentences*.

Other teaching assignments took him back to Paris, where he wrote the second part of the *Summa* between 1269 and 1272. He again returned to his beloved Naples, where he was sent to establish another *studium*. After five years of intense work there, he had a traumatic experience while celebrating mass in the chapel of St. Nicholas on December 6, 1273, a few months before his death. His medieval biographers do not agree about what happened. Some think that it was a mystical experience, while others suggest that it was a psychological breakdown. According to Bartholomew of Capua, something extraordinary occurred: "After the mass he never wrote or dictated anything more. Moreover, he hung up his writing instruments." Here there is an allusion to the Jews in exile hanging up their musical instruments. This refusal to write was strange for a man who, after mass and the thanksgiving, was accustomed to devoting the entire day to writing, lecturing, and teaching. His companion Friar Reginald asked him why he was not writing. T. answered: "It is no longer time to write. Everything that I have written appears to me to have been only straw, in comparison with what has been revealed to me." Once more, what happened is not clear; but what is certainly clear is that his career as scholar and author had come to an end.

Pope Gregory X invited him to attend the Second Council of ⇒Lyon, where the union between the Greeks and the Latins was to be discussed. After leaving Naples with Friar Reginald and others early in February, T. suffered a serious accident near Maenza, hitting his head on a branch and falling to the ground. Since he already had bad health and was rapidly growing weaker, he received the last rites and died in the nearby monastery of Fossanova on March 7, 1274. He was less than fifty years old. The news of his death spread quickly, as did the news of the miracles that took place in connection with his death. The result was that people began to venerate him as a saint in the monastery and its surroundings. He was buried in the abbey, and the peasants began to bring the sick to his tomb, where it was said that miracles of healing occurred. Reginald returned to Naples after preaching at his funeral in Fossanova, and he appears to have invited William of Tocco and Batholomew of Capua to write the biography of T. Soon the convent of Santo Domingo in Naples became a center of devotion.

T. was canonized by John XXII in a great public ceremony at Avignon on July 18, 1325, in the presence of the king of Sicily. His mortal remains were moved by Urban V to Toulouse, where they still rest. As happens in connection with any great figure, legends sprang up concerning his person. For example, it is frequently said that when he was on his deathbed he dictated to the monks of Fossanova a commentary on the Song of Songs. The nonexistence of any manuscript of this commentary casts doubt on this report.

Butler relates an incredible incident about a theological controversy of that time over the manner of the presence of Christ in the Eucharist, or, as is commonly said, the Real Presence.

> But nothing can give us a more precise idea of the fame of the saint than the decision of the university [of Paris] to abide by his opinion on a matter that was much debated until that time: whether in the most holy Sacrament the accidents remain in reality or only in appearance. After a fervent prayer, St. Thomas wrote his reply in the form of a tract and placed it on the altar before giving it out to the public. The university accepted his decision, which the church later adopted, and the tract is still preserved. As far as we know, this was the first time that the Lord showed St. Thomas, in a perceptible way, his approval of what he had written, saying to him in an apparition: "You have spoken well of the sacrament of my body." When he heard this, the saint went into such a lengthy ecstasy that the friars had time to meet and see him elevated above the floor. Then there was heard a voice coming from the crucifix and repeating: "You have spoken well of me, Thomas. What do you want as a reward?" The saint replied: "I want no other reward than You, Lord."

T. Aquinas was above all a theologian whose teachings have been officially approved by the Roman Catholic Church. When he was declared a doctor of the church in 1567, he was added to a distinguished list that included such teachers as ⇒Augustine, ⇒Jerome, ⇒Ambrose, and ⇒Gregory the Great. He is the only theologian who is mentioned in the *Codex of Canon Law* of 1918, with the instruction that priests of the Roman Catholic Church are to receive their philosophical and theological instruction "according to the method, doctrine, and principles of the Angelic Doctor." Chesterton has described him as belonging to a physical type that is "not very common in Italy. . . . Because of his corpulence he was humorously compared to those ambulatory pot-bellies which are common in the comedies of other nations. He himself joked about it. . . . But, above all, his head was powerful enough to govern that body. He had a type of head that is easily recognizable, to judge from the traditional portraits and the personal descriptions."

His companions and biographers describe him vividly: "One of his main physical recreations was to walk alone through the cloister with his head raised." "His dreams were daytime dreams. . . . Like those of a greyhound, they were dreams of hunting, dreams of going after error as well as going after truth, dreams of following all the twistings and turnings of falsehood." But in many ways, T. was always a mystery. ⇒Dante says of him: "Thomas was very courteous, well-mannered in his conversation, and soft in speech. He never seemed to be disturbed by anything, always looking at higher things. He never talked about himself. We know anecdotes about his life, but the secret remained with him. His contemplative and mystical experience has not been transmitted to us. We know the arguments of the professor, but we do not know his mystical experience." Also in this respect he was, as he was for his companions, "the mute ox."

Before describing the historical content of his writings, it is important to add something about the *Summa*—his best-known and most influential work—as well as about his philosophical and theological method. While he gave primacy to the revelation of God to the people of Israel and through Jesus Christ, T. also recognized the importance of human reason. In contrast to many of his contemporaries who confused reason with faith, T. underlined the particularity and importance of Aristotelian philosophy and of the sciences, even for theology. Thomistic theology is different from pure philosophy and depends on the divine gift of faith, which comes to humans through revelation, worship, the spiritual life, and human speculation about these three activities. The field of faith is in the strict sense supernatural, because its truths, values, and efficacy transcend what is natural. Faith is the free gift of God, given for salvation, and is beyond the reach of human nature (Rom. 11:5–6). Thus reason is not opposed to faith, but is at its service.

The theology of T. belongs to scholasticism, a theological and philosophical movement of the Middle Ages, which was practiced in the schools (thence the name) and which concerned itself with the systematic interpretation of texts, particularly the texts of other theologians and philosophers, rather than biblical or patristic texts. Yet at the same time it is important to point out that T. did not write his *Summa* as a substitute for the Bible, but as an aid for beginners who needed a summary of "sacred doctrine." At that time every teacher of sacred theology had to lecture on the Bible, preside over scholastic debates on specific disputed questions, and preach regularly before the university community. The sources of the theology of T. are, therefore, the Bible (in the translation known as the Vulgate), the life and practice of the church, and the writings of the ancient Greek and Latin writers, although the former were available to him only in Latin translations. On the other hand, its terminology is traditional, largely philosophical, and frequently Aristotelian. Therefore, in order to read and understand T., it is necessary to know the meaning of Aristotelian technical terms such as matter and form, substance and accidents, essence and existence, nature and operations, the soul and its faculties.

The first part of the *Summa* considers God and the origin of all things in God. The other two parts are concerned with the final goal of human life and the return of all things to God. The two subdivisions of the second part deal with the intrinsic means, such as the virtues, law, and grace; and the third part considers Christ and his sacraments as extrinsic means, which are indispensable for salvation. This last was the part that was completed by his companion after the death of T.

T. did not propose to "prove" the sacred mysteries, because these truths, revealed by God, are beyond total human comprehension. What he attempts to do is clarify the terms that are used, determine what can and what cannot be said, and defend the truth of the revealed mysteries against the attacks of nonbelievers. T. considers that two of the revealed mysteries are absolutely fundamental for the Christian religion: the Trinity of persons in one God, and the incarnation of the Son of God as true man born of Mary.

The volume of the works which T. produced is enormous. During his twenty years of teaching and writing (1252–73), this theological genius, who knew by heart the Bible and the *Sentences* of Peter Lombard, wrote 895 lectures on the books of Aristotle, 803 on the Scriptures, 850 chapters on the Gospels, and 2,652 "articles" (that is, tracts on specific questions) in the *Summa*. The edition of his complete works consists of twenty-five volumes in folio. This enormous production shows the intellectual ability of T., as well as his commitment to the search for truth. His manuscripts that survive are full of revisions; some paragraphs were written and corrected four times. His thought was so prolific that he kept four secretaries constantly occupied. They busied themselves drafting what he outlined, for which he gave them copious notes. His biographers say that he worked sixteen to eighteen hours a day.

His principal contribution was to create the most complete and systematic presentation of the Christian faith that has been written until the present. His teachings about God, the human being, the soul, human knowledge, the social order, the church, and the supernatural life occupy a central place in Christian theology.

T. was without doubt an innovator. A historian of philosophy in the twentieth century, the Jesuit Frederick Copleston, says that T. was an innovator whose adoption of Aristotelian philosophy was daring and at the same time modern:

St. Thomas confronted a system which was growing in influence and importance, and which in many ways appeared to be incompatible with the Christian tradition, but which naturally captivated the minds of many students and professors—particularly in the faculty of arts of Paris—precisely because of its majesty, its apparent cohesion, and its breadth. Aquinas took the bull by the horns decisively and utilized Aristotelianism to construct his own system. His was not a retrograde action, but rather an extremely "modern" one, and was of enormous importance for the future of scholastic philosophy and of all philosophy.

—
EF

Thurneysen, Eduard (1888–1974).
Swiss theologian and pastor, a native of Wallenstadt. He was the friend and faithful collaborator of K. ⇒Barth. He was pastor in Leutwil and in the cathedral of Basel before becoming a professor in Zurich. T. was distinguished for his work in pastoral theology, in which he was much influenced by Barth. His book *Theology of Pastoral Care* argues that pastoral care is an individual communication of the Word of God, on a par with the communication to the community in preaching and the sacraments.

—
LGP

Tillich, Paul Johannes (1886–1965).
Protestant theologian and philosopher, son of a Lutheran pastor. T. studied in Berlin, Tübingen, Halle, and Breslau in his native Germany. During the First World War he served in the German army as a Lutheran chaplain. After the war he taught theology in Dresden and Marburg and was professor of philosophy in Leipzig and Frankfurt. In this last city he became a member of the Christian Socialist Movement. Because of this membership, he was persecuted once the Nazis came to power. In 1933 he was forced to flee from Germany, and he emigrated to the United States, becoming a U.S. citizen in 1940. There he taught first at Union Theological Seminary, New York, and from 1955 at Harvard Divinity School. From 1962 until his death he was professor of theology in the Divinity School of the University of Chicago. The influence of T. on a large part of Protestant and Catholic theology in the 1960s and 1970s, especially in the United States, cannot be exaggerated.

The central interest and principal goal of the theology of T. is to establish a reasonable and authentic bridge between Christian faith and revelation, on the one hand, and modern culture, on the other. To that end he developed what he called the "method of correlation," in which the content of Christian revelation is presented as the response to crucial questions arising from modern existence. The correlation between Christianity and modernity cannot, according to T., falsify either revelation or the deepest concerns of modern humanity. For his comprehension and analysis of both revelation and modern culture, T. used the contributions of existentialism, of ontology, and of the psychology of Carl ⇒Jung, so that his theology in large measure depends on the latter. He applied his method to the correlation of themes such as reason and revelation, being and God, human existence and the Christ, existential ambiguities and life in the Spirit, the meaning of history and the kingdom of God. T. spoke of God as "the ground of being" whom we find by means of ultimate questions, and he spoke of Jesus Christ as the "New Being." The contribution of T., thanks to his method of correlation, permitted the establishment of fruitful dialogues between theologians and specialists in other branches of human knowledge, and opened spaces to think about the content of revelation in modern terms. It is not an exaggeration to say that the theology of T. made possible the understanding of the faith and its acceptance among sectors that had previously been marginalized by theology and the churches. However, T. never thought of the correlation between Christianity and non-Western cultures, nor did he think of what these cultures could offer. Likewise, T. did not think outside of European and androcentric epistemological frameworks. Nevertheless, his theological contribution opened up these spaces so that two decades later he was able to contribute (indirectly) to the establishment of correlations between Christianity and non-Western cultures, as well as to the legitimacy of postandrocentric theological thought.

His many books had great acceptance in the theological world, especially the three-volume *Systematic Theology* (1951–64). Among his other publications the following are worthy of mention: *Church and Culture* (1924), *The Interpretation of History* (1936), *The Protestant Era* (1948), *The Shaking of the Foundations* (1948), *The Courage to Be* (1952), *The New Being* (1955), and *The Eternal Now* (1963). Several of these books are collections of his lectures and sermons.

OOE

Timothy Aelurus (5th century). The first anti-Chalcedonian patriarch of Alexandria after the deposition of ⇒Dioscorus by the Council of ⇒Chalcedon. Although he has been called a Monophysite, in reality his Monophysitism was verbal, like that of ⇒Severus of Antioch. In spite of this, he was considered a champion of heterodoxy, so that in the time of Justinian, after his death, T. was accused of Docetism.

JLG

Tindal, Matthew (1655–1733). English deist who was educated in Lincoln and Exeter colleges in Oxford. In spite of his Protestant education and faith, for a short period during the reign of James II he was converted to Roman Catholicism. He returned to the Church of England in 1688. The writings of T. assert that there is a common law which is present and evident in every thinking being, and that this is the law of reason or natural law, which is at the same time eternal, absolute, and immutable.

HMT

Toland, John (1670–1722). British deist born in Ireland. A Roman Catholic by birth, he became Protestant at the age of sixteen. After a careful education in Scotland, Holland, and England, he published his first work in 1696 with the title *Christianity Not Mysterious*. There he tried to show the compatibility of the gospel with the most modern philosophy of his time, represented, according to him, by John ⇒Locke. The book was badly received, especially by the more traditional people of his native Ireland, where it was burned in public. Equally controversial were his later works on religious, political, and philosophical subjects. Critics considered them the fruit of an intellectual who was more inclined to criticize and negate than to construct and propose coherent ways in which to understand the world. His principal legacy is contained in his *Letters to Serena* (1704), in which he asserts that movement is intrinsic to matter (challenging ⇒Descartes). His magnum opus is *Pantheisticon* (1720), in which he develops his pantheistic ideas by combining a strict materialism with an almost religious veneration of the universe. Recently the intellectual activity of T. has been reevaluated positively. He is recognized as a forerunner of modern scientific materialism and of contemporary sensitivity concerning the integrity and dignity of nature.

GCC

Tolstoy, Leo (1828–1910). Russian novelist and man of letters, a writer on ethics and religion. Descendant of an ancient Russian family of the nobility, his individualism compelled him to question the validity of formal education. For this reason he did not complete university studies. However, he focused on the education of peasant children, for whom he founded a school and developed original pedagogical methods that anticipated the modern movement of progressive education. He participated in the Crimean War (1851) and obtained a commission as an artillery officer because of his brave conduct. At the age of thirty-four he married Sophia Bers, with whom he had thirteen children. For fifteen years he abandoned the educational experiments and devoted himself to family life on his farm, Yasnaya Polyana, in the province of Tula. During that time he produced his two masterpieces, *War and Peace* (1863–69) and *Anna*

Karenina (1873–76). Subsequently he entered a period of deep doubt and moral questioning about the purposes of his life, a crisis that led him to the edge of suicide. The aid that he did not find in theologians and philosophers was given to him by peasants when he asked them to explain their way of life. Their answer was that one must serve God and not live for oneself. Then he turned to the Bible, especially the New Testament, where he found answers. He decided to found a new "religion of Christ," purified of the dogmas and mysteries of traditional Christianity. He ended up producing a type of Christian anarchy in which he rejected personal immortality, the authority of the church, private property, and the state (because of its sanctioning of violence). He became a vegetarian, renounced vices, and lived simply, emphasizing physical work and philanthropical activities. His new teachings attracted followers who formed communes to preach his lifestyle, but they caused him serious family problems. At the age of eighty-two, seeking a solitary place to live and be closer to God, he fled to a small railroad station far from the paternal farm where he had lived. Shortly thereafter he died of pneumonia.

T.'s influence was one of the most powerful factors in the complex development of the period that encompassed Russian realism. He stands out not only as a literary author but also as a man and a thinker on the subject of the social and moral life that was the background on which the literature of the second half of the twentieth century developed.

———

RAR

Torrance, Thomas Forsyth (1913–).

Scottish theologian, founding editor of the *Scottish Journal of Theology*. He was born in China, where his father was a missionary. He studied in Edinburgh, Basel, and Oxford before assuming posts in theology and then in history at Auburn Seminary in New York. From 1952 he was professor at New College, Edinburgh. Influenced by ⇒Barth, the theology of T. is christocentric, as can be seen in the way he holds that the Word of God incarnate in Christ is the objective norm for dogmatics. His theological work makes connections between science and religion, including drawing parallels between the methods of theology and of science in his book *Theological Science* (1968). Other books include *Space, Time, and Resurrection* (1976) and *Space, Time, and Incarnation* (1997).

———

LGP

Tracy, David (1939–).

Catholic theologian born in Yonkers, New York. He studied at the Gregorian University in Rome during the time of the Second Vatican Council (⇒Vatican II) and taught at the Catholic University of America and at the University of Chicago. His studies are focused on the theology of the Jesuit theologian ⇒Lonergan, whose influence can be noted in the methodological interests of T. As a part of his theological methodology, T. has devoted himself to the development of theological models and to the exploration of the relationship between Christian texts, human experience, and language. His interests embrace equally the disciplines of systematic, fundamental, and practical theology.

His theological work notes the importance of cultural and social pluralism as a resource for the development of theology. He examines how forms of cultural expressions such as literature and art open new dimensions of understanding that can enrich our theological perspectives. His best-known and most influential book is *The Analogical Imagination: Christian Theology and the Culture of Pluralism* (1980).

———

LGP

Travers, Walter (ca. 1548–1635).

English Puritan who was educated at Christ College, Cambridge University. Because of his friendship with Theodore ⇒Beza and his own convictions, T. rejected the thirty-nine articles of the Church of England. However, in 1594 he was named dean of Trinity College in Dublin. In his writings he defends the presbyterian form of church government and emphasizes purity as the essential element in the life of the Christian.

———

HMT

Trent, Council of (1545–63).

A council in which the Roman Catholic Church proposed to respond to the Protestant challenge through the reform of the church's customs and organization and through the reaffirmation of the traditional dogmas over against the Protestant positions. It is the nineteenth ecumenical council according to the reckoning of the Roman Catholic Church. Since in Latin "Trent" is *Tridentum*, the reforms and directives of that council are called Tridentine, and historians refer to the Catholic Church from that point forward to the Second Vatican Council (⇒Vatican II) as the Tridentine or Postridentine church.

The long duration of the council (almost two decades, during which Popes Paul III, Julius III,

Marcellus II, Paul IV, and Pius IV succeeded one another) was not so much due to the many topics of discussion as to the interruptions caused by political and military tensions. When Paul III first convened the council, he did it in agreement with Charles V. The very choice of Trent as the place of meeting was an indication of the tensions between the pope and the emperor, because Trent was a city under imperial rule on the border of Italy. It was also the time of the Schmalkald League, which was organized by the Protestants as a defense against a possible invasion by Charles V. The plan was to find a military solution to that situation, and then proceed to the sessions of the council. But the Schmalkald War lasted longer than had been expected, and therefore the first sessions of the council were affected and at times even interrupted by the military vicissitudes and the tensions between the pope and the emperor. For a time a typhus epidemic forced the council to move to Bologna, although some refused to leave Trent. Although at the beginning the intention was to invite the Protestants, this was not accomplished until Charles V defeated them. At the Diet of Augsburg, while he imposed on them the Interim of Augsburg, he made them promise to attend the council. The Protestants agreed to this, on the condition that the council would be free from the authority of the pope and that the decisions made up to that point would be reconsidered. When this did not happen, the few Protestants who had attended the council withdrew. In the meantime, the king of France, who previously had prevented the French prelates from participating in the council, now ordered the French bishops to participate in view of new political circumstances, and above all because of the rapid growth of Protestantism in his country. While these measures increased the attendance at the council (which never surpassed 150 bishops), they also complicated the political tensions in the assembly itself. It could be said that, although the leading political and secular power during the first years of the council was the emperor, toward the end of the council the impact of France was greater.

From the first time that it was convened, the council had the double purpose of reforming the church and defining Catholic dogma over against Protestantism. The first of these goals did not turn out to be easy. Thus, for instance, when the Spanish bishops proposed strong rules against absenteeism and pluralism and declared that the residence of bishops in their dioceses is a divine command, the curia and others were tenaciously opposed. It was not

until the sessions were about to conclude and when a new leader of the council, Cardinal Morone, put forth an entire program of reforms with fifty-two articles that the council adopted definitive measures to reform the life and customs of the church. These measures included the establishment of seminaries in which future priests should be trained and where they should follow a certain curriculum; the manner in which diocesan and provincial synods should be organized and implemented; and the responsibilities of bishops. These Tridentene reforms were the foundation on which the modern Catholic Church was reorganized.

With respect to dogmatic issues, the Council of T., in contrast to other councils, had to deal with an enormous variety of subjects. This was the case because Protestantism challenged Catholic dogma, not only in one or two points, but almost in its totality, excluding the traditional points that had been defined by the first councils, such as the Trinity and christological doctrine. Thus, one of the first actions of the council was to discuss the relative authority of the Scriptures and tradition. Without in fact making them equal, the council decreed that apostolic traditions should be seen with the same pious affection, that is, the same devotion, with which the Scriptures are viewed. This includes "the traditions, whether they have to do with faith or with morals, which have been orally dictated by Christ or by the Holy Spirit and preserved in the Catholic Church in uninterrupted succession." In addition, the council decreed that the Vulgate was sufficient to prove dogmatic truths. Although this did not prohibit the study of the original biblical languages, it in fact lessened their importance.

Concerning original sin, the council insisted on its reality and on baptism as the washing that cleanses it, and it condemned the opinions of those Protestants who maintained that the corruption of sin remains in human beings even after baptism.

Likewise, the sacraments are declared to be seven—against most Protestants, who limited them to two—and their efficacy does not depend on the faith of believers nor on the promises of God, but takes place through the ritual action itself, *ex opere operato*.

Naturally, the major portion of the theological work of the council had to do with the doctrine of justification and its corollaries. For that reason, the decree on justification consists of sixteen chapters, which are followed by thirty-three canons and a series of anathemas. Their point of departure—with which Protestants agreed—is that as a consequence of the fall, humans are unable to obtain justification. The work of Christ takes place in response to this reality. The work of Christ enables those who believe in him to receive Christ's merits and thus obtain salvation. This process in the believer begins with prevenient grace, which is given without any human merit, but which then enables the human will to accept or reject salvation. The justification which results from this process is not only that God declares the believer righteous, as ⇒Luther would say, but is also a process by which God makes the believer truly righteous, that is, sanctifies the believer. This justification is not an imputation of the grace of God, but an objective reality in the believer, so that to say that the believer is "righteous and sinner at the same time" (Luther) is a grave error. Moreover, the righteousness of the believer, which is justification, can increase by means of good works. And, since justified believers, without being sinners in their nature, can still commit venial sins, the sacrament of penance is offered as a remedy for such sins. Through the use of penance and, above all, by the practice of good works, believers can fully satisfy the divine law and come to merit eternal life.

The anathemas that follow simply clarify the theological positions against which the council makes its declarations. Thus, for example: "If anyone says that the sinner is justified by faith alone, meaning that no other thing at all is required to cooperate in order to obtain the grace of justification, and that it is not possible in any way to be prepared or disposed through the action of the will, let him be anathema."

Soon after the council had ended, Pius IV confirmed its decrees, and a half year later he created a commission of cardinals whose task was to ensure the correct interpretation of and obedience to the Tridentine decrees.

—

JLG

Troeltsch, Ernst (1865–1923). German historian of religion, theologian, and philosopher. He served as professor in the universities of Göttingen, Bonn, Heidelberg, and Berlin. His principal interest was the history of religion, using the historical methodology of Wilhelm Dilthey. He maintained that religion can be analyzed only in the light and in the context of the spiritual and cultural development of humanity.

Christianity is the most advanced religion of Western culture, but it is not an absolute religion. Other religions can be as valid as Christianity. The theological problem that defines a great part of the work of T. is to establish the relationship between revelation and the historical character of the Christian faith. His historicism led him to allege that the Christian revelation is relative and made him question the truthfulness of the biblical miracles and of postulates that are not based on human experience. For this reason, ⇒Barth and other theologians rejected much of the thought of T.

T. contributed in a significant way to the historical understanding of the development of the Christian church. Following Max ⇒Weber, he alleged that religion is not merely a social product. It is, rather, an autonomous reality that has great influence on all the dimensions of culture. At the same time, the different elements of culture exercise their influence on religion.

His typological classification of the church as a sectarian community that rejects the wisdom of the world, as an ecclesiological community that incorporates and adapts to its culture, or as a mystical community, continues to influence contemporary theological understanding. H. R. ⇒Niebuhr polished and developed this typology and used it to analyze the different ways in which the Christian community responds to cultural forces.

—

IG

Turretin, Benedict (1588–1631). Italian Calvinist theologian whose original name was Turretini. He took refuge in Geneva, where he founded a theological dynasty that lasted for three generations. As a conservative and scholastic Calvinist, he interpreted the doctrine of predestination in the style of his compatriot ⇒Zanchi. He tenaciously opposed Arminianism (⇒Arminius) and intervened in the negotiations that led to the Synod of ⇒Dort. However, once the synod had come to an end, he criticized those who treated the Arminians with violence and intolerance.

—

JLG

Turretin, François (1623–87). Son of Benedict ⇒Turretin. One of the most important theologians of Calvinist scholasticism of the seventeenth century. He opposed the more open Calvinism that came from the school of Saumur in France (⇒Amyraut). His principal work is *Institutiones theologicae elenchticae*, in three volumes, which attempts to systematize all of Christian doctrine. Its point of departure is the authority of the Scriptures, which is above all tradition. That authority is of such a nature that

it is necessary to affirm that the transmission of the text through a number of copies has not corrupted it in any way, because any error or change that could have been inserted by the copyists would be a failure of divine Providence, which has determined to reveal itself completely and definitively through the Bible. This stance of T. is reflected also in the Helvetic Consensus of 1675, a document that is typical of Calvinist scholasticism and in part a product of T. himself. This Consensus asserts that even the vowel points of the Hebrew text, even though they were subsequent to the original text, are inspired by God.

His doctrine of predestination is typical of later Calvinism, because instead of interpreting predestination as an expression of the experience of grace, as in ⇒Calvin, T. presents it as a corollary of the very nature of God. Consequently, T. devoted much attention to the question of the order of the divine decrees and concluded that God first resolved to create humanity; then, to permit the fall; third, to elect those who were to be saved from among the resulting mass of perdition; fourth, to send Jesus Christ for the salvation of the elect (because Christ died only for them); and last, to call those elect to faith. This is the classical expression of infralapsarianism, which maintains, not that the fall of the human being took place before the decree of election, but that before any creative or redemptive action, the decree concerning the fall preceded the decree concerning election.

In all this, T. typified the scholastic Calvinist orthodoxy of the seventeenth century.

JLG

Turretin, Jean-Alphonse (1671–1740).
Reformed theologian, son of ⇒François and grandson of ⇒Benedict. His theological stance was very different from that of his grandfather and even more from that of his father. He sympathized with the more open Calvinism of ⇒Amyraut than with the orthodoxy of his ancestors, and he therefore led a reaction against that strict orthodoxy. The result was that in 1725 the government of Geneva repudiated both the decrees of ⇒Dort and the Second Helvetic Confession.

JLG

Tutu, Desmond (1931–).
Anglican archbishop of South Africa, T. is one of the most important theologians and prophets of that continent. A great part of his ministry has been devoted to dismantling apartheid and, after the fall of that unjust racial system, he has been engaged in the process of national reconciliation. His book *No Future without Forgiveness* is a testimony to the arduous task of reconciliation which T. had as the president of the Commission on National Reconciliation in South Africa. Eloquent orator and the recipient of the Nobel Peace Prize, T. has shown the world the demands of the black African people and of all oppressed groups. His ministry has been broad and ecumenical, going beyond Anglican circles and serving as general secretary of the South African Council of Churches (1978–85) and in 1987 as president of the African Council of Churches. He also served as the program assistant of the Theological Education Fund of the ⇒World Council of Churches.

Among his many articles and publications, two books stand out: *Crying in the Wilderness* (1982) and *Hope and Suffering* (1984).

CCO

Twesten, August Detlev Christian (1789–1876).
German Lutheran theologian. He was born near Hamburg and died in Berlin. He was educated at the universities of Kiel and Berlin. T. was much influenced by the thought of ⇒Schleiermacher. He was professor of philosophy and theology in the University of Kiel, beginning in 1814. He also occupied chairs of dogmatics and New Testament exegesis in the University of Berlin. He worked arduously for the union between Lutherans and Reformed and maintained that the confessions of the Reformation period should be fundamental in the formation of the church in Prussia.

T.'s works include *Die Drey Ökumenischen Symbola, die Augsburgische Confessio, und die Repetitio Confessionis Augustanae* (1816; The Three Ecumenical Creeds, the Augsburg Confession, and its Repetition); *Vorlesungen über die Dogmatik der Evangelisch-Lutherischen Kirche* (1826; Lectures on the Dogmatic of the Evangelical Lutheran Church); and *Zur Erinnerung an Friedrich Daniel Ernst Schleiermacher* (1868; In Memory of Friedrich Daniel Schleiermacher).

JDR

Tyndale, William (1494–1536).
Reformer of the church in England. He studied Greek and the New Testament in the universities of Oxford and Cambridge. He was ordained to the

ministry in 1521. Convinced of the need to make the Bible accessible to the common people, he studied Hebrew in Germany and translated the New Testament and then the Pentateuch into English. His biblical translations, published in Germany; his book *The Obedience of the Christian*; and several tracts in which he defended biblical authority against the church were smuggled into England and made significant impact among the English people. Persecuted as a heretic and traitor, he was captured in Belgium and sentenced to death.

———

LGP

Tyrrel, George Henry (1861–1909).

Roman Catholic theologian. He was born in Dublin, where he studied at Trinity College. Leaving the Anglican Church, he entered the Society of Jesus in 1880, studying philosophy in Stonyhurst and theology at St. Bruno's in Wales. His modernist tendencies created conflicts for him with the church, particularly because he denied the infallibility and perfection of Catholic theology and because of his criticism of Pope Pius X, against whose condemnations he defended modernism. He was ultimately expelled from the Jesuit order. For T. the church is an organism subject to change, development, and modification. In his last book, *Christianity at the Cross-Roads*, published posthumously, T. proposed the possibility of a religion beyond Christianity.

———

LGP

Ulfilas (311–83).

An Arian bishop who may have been consecrated in 341 by ⇒Eusebius of Nicomedia, U. was a missionary to the Goths and other Germanic groups. His missionary work is distinguished for having developed an alphabet for the Goths, based on Greek and Latin. With it he was able to translate parts of the Bible. U. excluded parts of the Old Testament from his translations in order to discourage the warring spirit of the Goths and other Germanic groups. Since U. was an Arian (⇒Arius), his converts were also Arian. When the Goths and others later invaded western Europe, they brought that faith with them, resulting in the presence of Arianism in areas that had not been affected earlier by that theology.

———

CCO

Ulrich of Strassburg (?–1277).

Disciple of ⇒Albertus Magnus, he died earlier than his master. He wrote *Summa on the Good,* in which he combined Christian theology with Neoplatonism and, to a lesser degree, with Aristotelianism. A large part of this writing is a commentary addressing the work *On the Names of God* by so-called ⇒Dionysius the Areopagite.

———

JLG

Unamuno, Miguel de (1864–1936).

Spanish writer and philosopher who was impassioned in the defense of his ideas. Always possessing a personal vision of things and events, he was often in the center of the polemics of his time. He was concerned that everyone should live with restless longing, and he fiercely rebuked everything he considered conformism, indifference, or falsehood. He came from a fairly affluent middle-class Basque family. He was an avid reader and thus familiarized himself with the ideas of many saints of the church, above all Saint Louis of Gonzaga, as well as with the works of ⇒Kant, ⇒Hegel, and ⇒Descartes. In 1884 he earned his doctorate of literature in Madrid and returned to his native Bilbao, where he devoted himself to teaching. In 1891 he was appointed professor of Greek at the University of Salamanca. That year he married Concha Lizárraga, the great companion of his life, whose memory would continually surface in his extensive literary production. In 1901 he became rector of the university.

His first novel, *Peace in War* (1897), was inspired by childhood memories of the first Carlist war, especially of the bombardment of Bilbao in 1874. *The Life of Don Quixote and Sancho* (1905), a commentary on the classic novel of Cervantes, is one of his most important works. According to U., the two heroes created by Cervantes developed their own personalities and snatched the work away from its author. In an apparent personal identification with Don Quixote, U. admired his consecration to a life of misfortune out of faithfulness to his ideals, mad as they might seem.

Fog (1914) is centered on the idea that just as a person of flesh and bone, once created, has some measure of free will, so an author can create a character but cannot control it completely. The character follows its own internal logic and therefore possesses the autonomy to make its own decisions. In fact, U. once thought of calling his novels "nivolas," because according to him they are stripped of everything that is not essential and focus on a few protagonists—or "agonists," as he would call them—and their passions and inner conflict. These agonists become real persons to the extent that they can stand up to the author.

The poetry of U. has been compared to a torrent that drags branches and rocks along with it and puts the reader at the risk of being emotionally brought down by its blows. It is the culmination of an irrational tendency. In it expression is stripped bare and becomes allusive. It avoids direct reference to things in order to point at their meaning. Such poetry does not speak of an experience, but allusively provokes it by an effective spiritual contagion.

The poem *The Christ of Velázquez* is considered to be the greatest poetic monument of Spanish literature after the Golden Age. It consists of four parts, each one divided into numerous paragraphs, which can be enjoyed independently. It is like a bundle of meditations on Jesus Christ, which ground faith for life even after death on the death of the Redeemer.

The essay was possibly the genre best fitted to his temperament. In that literary medium U. creates the most definitive expressions of his thought. The dominating themes are the problem of the concrete human being, U.'s longing for immortality, and the pain he felt for Spain.

His main philosophical work, *The Tragic Sense of Life* (1913), reveals a strong influence from Protestant theologians and a broad familiarity with the works of Kant, Hegel, Schopenhauer, and ⇒Kierkegaard. But the philosophy of U. is highly personal. It grows out of the clash between his intense desire to believe in immortality and his inability to find logical justification for it: "I need the immortality of my soul; the indefinite continuity of my individual conscience. Without that . . . I cannot live, and I am tormented by my doubt and inability to believe that I can obtain it."

U. builds his philosophy of struggle on this eternal torment. He considered himself most alive when the conflict was strongest. An ethical imperative is essential to his philosophy. He subscribed not only to the Christian concept of love for the neighbor, but also to the necessity of moral integrity. This philosophy of struggle and fidelity to his moral convictions nuanced his political ideas and caused him severe setbacks in his personal life. During the First World War he sided with the Allies. His violent campaign for the Allies and his severe criticism of the monarchy of Alfonso XIII cost him the office of rector of the University of Salamanca in 1914.

In 1924 he was exiled to Fuerteventura in the Canary Islands because of his hostility to General Primo de Rivera, who had come to power through a coup d'etat. A few months later he escaped to Paris and remained in exile in spite of official offers of amnesty. He established himself in the Basque area of France, from which he continued his verbal attack against the Spanish government.

When the dictator Rivera fell in 1930, U. returned to Spain in the midst of a tremendous reception and honors. Alfonso abdicated in 1931, and the new republican government again named U. as rector of Salamanca, as perpetual mayor of the city, and as honorary citizen of the republic. He was a member of the Spanish parliament from 1931 to 1933. At the beginning of the civil war he allied himself with the nationalist movement of General Francisco Franco. The government of the Popular Front of Manuel Azaña dismissed him from the rectorship, but in August 1936 the nationalists reinstated him. Soon he had a fight with them too, and he remained intensely critical of both factions until his death.

————

RAR

Ursacius (4th century). Bishop of Singidunum, in the region of Illyria. Together with ⇒Valens and ⇒Germinius of Sirmium, they are known as "the Illyrian trio." They were Arians (⇒Arius), although of the Homoean party, since they preferred not to speak of the *homoousios* or of the *homoiousios*—of the same and of similar substance, respectively—while rejecting the affirmation of the extreme Arians or Anomoeans, that the Son is "different" from the Father. Instead, they said that the Son is "similar" (*homoios*) to the Father. Occasionally they are called political Arians because of the ambiguity of that position.

————

JLG

Ursinus, Zacharias (1534–83). German theologian and one of the authors of the ⇒Heidelberg Catechism. He was born in Breslau and was a disciple of ⇒Melanchthon in Wittenberg. He studied theology in Geneva under ⇒Calvin and Hebrew in Paris under Jean ⇒Mercier. Beginning in 1561 he was a professor in Heidelberg, where in 1563, at the request of Frederick III, elector of the Palatinate, he drafted the Heidelberg Catechism in collaboration with Caspar ⇒Olevianus. The death of the elector in 1576 resulted in the dismissal of U., who from 1578 until his death in 1583 occupied a teaching post in Neustadt. His works were published in 1587 through 1589, and a more complete edition in 1612 by his son and two of his disciples, Pareus and Reuterus.

—

ALN

Uyttenbogaert, John (1557–1644).

Dutch theologian born in Utrecht, who died in The Hague. He was educated in the universities of Utrecht and Geneva. He occupied the pastorate in Utrecht (1584–90) and The Hague (1591–1618). After the condemnation of the Arminians in Holland he lived in Rouen, France (1621–26).

His ecclesiastical history, *Kerckelicke Historie*, stands out among his works. He contributed to the drafting of the *Remonstrantie* (1610), which some attribute to him in its entirety, since he was one of the chief defenders of the teachings of ⇒Arminius in the debates that led to the Synod of ⇒Dort.

—

JDR

Vacarius (ca. 1115–98).

Italian scholar educated in Bologna, a specialist in Roman and canon law. He is recognized as the first professor of canon law in England, where he distinguished himself in the nascent University of Oxford. He served as counselor to Theobald, archbishop of Canterbury, in his successful bid to transfer the papal representation in England from the bishopric of Winchester to Canterbury. He wrote *Liber pauperum* (Book of the Poor), a book based on the civil code of Justinian. It was written chiefly to educate those who were not able to study at the university. Even so, this work of nine volumes became one of the main textbooks in the legal training given at Oxford. For this reason students in the law school took the name of *Pauperistae* in honor of V.

—

ALG

Vahanian, Gabriel (1927–).

A native of France, he studied at the Sorbonne and then at Princeton. He finally settled in the United States, where he taught at Syracuse University. His theology deals with the death of the sense of God in our usage and daily life, which he considers to be a contemporary cultural phenomenon. For this reason V., ⇒Altizer, and ⇒Van Buren are the leaders of the "theology of the death of God," which was much discussed in the 1960s. This theology, which is commonly misunderstood, speaks about the death of God, not in a literal sense, but of the death of the concept traditionally associated with God, which, they assert, has lost its value and meaning for our society. His books include *The Death of God: The Culture of Our Post-Christian Era* (1961) and *No Other God* (1966).

—

LGP

Valdés, Juan de (ca. 1509–41).

His family was related to the Spanish nobility. Some suggest that his ancestors were Jews who converted to Christianity to avoid the rigors of the Inquisition. At an early age Juan was a student and follower of the lay preacher Pedro Ruiz de Alcaraz. In biblical studies and in religious meetings, Alcaraz propagated reformist ideas and criticized the church. The Inquisition accused Alcaraz of being a heretic and sentenced him to death. V. developed and systematized many of the ideas of Alcaraz. In 1526 he entered the University of Alcalá, whose founder, Cardinal ⇒Jiménez de Cisneros, wanted it to be a center of religious reform in Spain. Although V. did not study theology at the university, everything seems to indicate that he had a good knowledge of the biblical languages, of Latin, and of the thought of ⇒Erasmus and ⇒Scotus.

In 1529 he published his first work, *Dialogue on Christian Doctrine*. This catechism, an instrument for popular religious education, although it was faithful to his reforming ideas, was self-censored by V., who softened his positions to avoid persecution by the Inquisition. This book has been compared with the catechisms of ⇒Luther, which were unknown to V. The dissemination of the book was considerable and led the Inquisition to condemn it.

Fearing persecution and incarceration by the Inquisition, in 1531 V. moved to Italy. His brother lived there but died of the plague before Juan's arrival. In 1535 V. established himself in Naples and, like Alcaraz, founded a group for religious reflection in which he propagated his theological vision and continued his biblical studies, mainly among the aristocracy. But the preacher Bernardino ⇒Ochino, a follower of V., took his thought to the common people. This activity gave to the movement an anti-Catholic character. V. died in Naples, but even after his death the Inquisition accused him of heresy and identified him with the Lutheran and Calvinist movement. A number of his Italian disciples were persecuted and sentenced to death.

Some of the central teachings of V. are justification by faith and salvation by the grace of God; the limited authority of the pope; and the inefficacy of the sacraments and of good works for salvation. For him, the only truly Catholic church is the one that preaches and affirms the doctrine of justification by faith. This is the community in which the kingdom of God is incarnate. God is known through God's revelation, not by our reason, which is infected with sin. The Scriptures, in particular the divine laws and the Gospels, make us conscious of the radical nature of our sin and our inability to do good. They also show us that the good news consists in our total reliance on God, who justifies and saves us. We are able to know God through reason, but this knowledge is distorted. We also know God through the Scriptures. But only the Holy Spirit allows us to hear the words of forgiveness and the intention to save us which constitute the will of God. The only knowledge of God is that which God gives us through Christ, who reveals God's free redemption. This is the grace that frees us from fear and liberates us to love.

—

IG

Valens (4th century). Bishop of Mursa, in the region of Illyria. V., ⇒Ursacius, and ⇒Germinius of Sirmium are known as "the Illyrian trio." They were Arians (⇒Arius), although they belonged to the Homoean party, because they preferred not to speak of the *homoousios* nor of the *homoiousios*—of the same and similar substance, respectively—but would rather say that the Son is "similar" (*homoios*) to the Father. At times they are called political Arians because of the ambiguity of this position.

—

JLG

Valentinus (ca. 115–65). One of the most important gnostic figures of the second century. He was born in Egypt and was educated in Alexandria. Around the year 135 he moved to Rome, where he lived the rest of his life. He worked out a very complex theology, with a God as the beginning of all things in the universe ("Monad" or "Father"). This God generates certain "principles" or "eons," which appear in pairs: Depth and Silence, Mind and Truth, Word and Life, Human Being and Church. This first "Ogdoad" forms the "fullness" or "pleroma" of the deity and generates other principles, to make up a total of thirty. Among the latter is Sophia (Wisdom), who outside the pleroma erroneously produces a demiurge, the false God of the Old Testament, creator of the earth and of humanity, which wrongly

worships him. The pleroma, by means of Mind and a repentant Sophia, sends another "eon," Christ, who unites with Jesus of Nazareth in his conception or baptism in order to rescue humanity—that is, the divine spirit that resides in their being, for the rest cannot be saved and is not worth saving. Now there are three classes of humans: (1) the "spiritual" ones, who know these mysteries and whose spirits are finally saved; (2) the "natural" ones, who perhaps through their works and faith will be able to obtain salvation; and (3) the "carnal" ones, who will never be saved. V. apparently wrote several works, perhaps among them some of the gnostic writings that were found in Nag Hammadi, Egypt, in 1945, in particular, the *Gospel of Truth*. Aside from this, we are acquainted with his theology through the summaries of his orthodox opponents, especially ⇒Irenaeus.

—

EA

Valera, Cipriano de (ca. 1531–1602). Born in Valera la Vieja, in the region of Seville, this writer, editor, and translator entered the monastery of San Isidoro del Campo, just outside the city of Seville, where he embraced the ideas of the Protestant Reformation. In the company of other friars he fled from the threat of the Inquisition to Geneva. In exile in Geneva, Amsterdam, and London, he devoted nearly twenty years to revising the Spanish translation of the Bible made by Casiodoro de ⇒Reina. The edition made by V. improves the language of Reina and places the order of the books according to the reformist canon, as followed in the Bibles of Geneva. His most extensive work is *Two Treatises, on the Pope and on the Mass*, which in an anticlerical tone contrasts biblical theology with the Roman ecclesiastical system. Of equal importance for the dissemination of Protestant ideas among the Spanish people was his translation into Spanish of *The Institutes of the Christian Religion* by ⇒Calvin, which is still used.

—

JRI

Valla, Lorenzo (1407–57). Italian Renaissance scholar, a distinguished philologist and rhetorician. He was a teacher of Latin and Greek. His two best-known works were influential in both the ecclesiastical and the academic spheres.

His first and most famous work was *Declamation on the False Donation of Constantine* (1440), which provoked polemics in ecclesiastical circles and the admiration of literary critics in academic circles. By proving the spuriousness of a document that purported to prove that the emperor donated to the papacy a territory in central Italy, V. introduced a hermeneutical principle that was fundamental for modernity: historical proof.

The second important work by V., *The Elegance of the Latin Language* (1441), established criteria of style and literary expression. It became required reading on literary criticism. For this work, V. was admired by scholars of the stature of ⇒Erasmus.

———

CEA

Van Buren, Paul (1924–98). North American theologian who studied at Harvard, the Episcopal Theological College, and the University of Basel. After receiving his doctorate, he taught at the Episcopal Theological Seminary of the Southwest and at Temple University. He was identified with the theologians of the death of God, together with ⇒Altizer and others. This theology, commonly misunderstood, does not mean to say that God died in a literal sense, but rather points to the loss of meaning of the concept of God in contemporary life and culture. Although it was much debated in the 1960s, the interest it aroused soon waned.

———

LGP

Van Leeuwen, Arend (1918–). Dutch theologian, philosopher, and missiologist. His missiological studies analyze the phenomenon of the encounter between cultures, above all the encounter of Western cultures with Eastern cultures. He underlined the devastating impact of technology on the traditional cultures of the East. In addition, together with ⇒Kraemer and A. J. Toynbee, he pointed out the influence and role of religion in the modern processes and its connection with the impact of Western culture on the world. His works include *Prophecy in a Technocratic Era* (1968), *Christianity in World History* (1964), and *Development Through Revolution* (1970).

———

CCO

Van Til, Cornelius (1895–1987). Although he was born in Holland (of Calvinist parents), his family moved to Indiana in 1905. He was educated at Calvin College, an institution of the Christian Reformed Church. But after a year in his denominational seminary he transferred to Princeton Seminary, where he studied the Calvinist traditions of North American Presbyterianism. He completed there his master's degree in theology, and later a doctorate in philosophy at Princeton University. After one year in the pastorate he devoted himself to teaching apologetics, the philosophical defense of Christianity, first at Princeton and subsequently at Westminster Theological Seminary in Philadelphia. The latter was founded in 1930 in opposition to the theological liberalization of Princeton Seminary. In the following forty years V.T. taught and wrote, proposing a theology that he called Presuppositionism. Influenced by ⇒Kuyper, V.T. argued that all knowledge and truth have their roots in the knowledge of God, which is revealed only in the Bible. This divine knowledge, testified to in the Scriptures and in its final form by Christ, should influence every area of our lives. Because of original sin, only one who has been rescued by faith in Christ Jesus can, in the final analysis, acquire true knowledge. This particularist perspective on the role of Christian faith in society and culture left its mark on evangelical theologians such as ⇒Schaeffer, who studied with V.T. at Westminster Seminary.

———

EA

Vanderkemp, Johannes Theodorus (1747–1811). Dutch missionary and theologian. V. was the cofounder of the Missionary Society of the Netherlands (1797). In 1799 he arrived in South Africa as a missionary of that society. His work was concentrated among African slaves, and afterward among two ethnic groups in the region, the Xhosas and the Hottentots.

V. was a controversial figure for the Dutch government and for those whom he wished to evangelize. One of his missiological works is *Principles of the Word of God for the Hottentot Mission*, the first book published in South Africa. From the beginning of his missionary work and thought, V. rejected slavery and promoted racial justice, thus creating great tensions with the governments of the Netherlands and Great Britain. Ironically, although V. was in solidarity with national ethnic groups to such an extent that he adopted their lifestyles, many accused him of conspiracy and treason. Several of the missiological themes that he proposed in his life as a missionary are still to be developed in missiological reflection.

———

CCO

Vatican I (1869–70). The twentieth general council of the Roman Catholic Church (⇒Councils) was announced informally by Pope ⇒Pius IX on December 6, 1864, and was inaugurated by him on December 8, 1869. Its purpose was to deal with the problems of the day. The church was under attack from political forces that wanted to control it and from intellectual movements that wanted to discredit it before its members because it was an antiprogressive and obscurantist institution.

Vatican I concluded on October 10, 1870, without being able to deal with everything that the bishops wanted to discuss. This was due to the Franco-Prussian War and to the entrance of Garibaldi into Rome on September 20, 1870. The council fathers were only able to vote on and accept two dogmatic constitutions and a few other matters: *Dei Filius*, on the relationship between faith and reason (April 24, 1870), and *Pastor aeternus*, on the primacy and infallibility of the pope (July 18, 1870). The most important and innovative of these two constitutions was the one that dealt with the matter of papal primacy and infallibility, since the other constitution proclaimed classic Catholic teaching on God the Creator, against materialism, in favor of the inspiration of the Holy Scriptures, and the difference, but favorable relation, between faith and reason.

Pastor aeternus, or Dogmatic Constitution on the Church of Christ, consists of four chapters: the institution of the Petrine primacy, its permanence in the Roman popes, the nature and power of the primacy of the Roman pope, and the infallibility of the magisterial authority of the Roman pope. Regarding the Petrine primacy, the document proclaims a primacy that is not only honorary, but also one of universal jurisdiction in all the church. On the basis of Matthew 16:18 and Luke 22:32, among other biblical texts, the document spells out certain and determined conditions when papal pronouncements can be considered infallible or free of all error. Therefore one could say that the infallibility that is proposed by *Pastor aeternus* is much more moderate than other Ultramontane formulations that were suggested before the council took place.

The constitution affirms as dogma of faith that when the Roman pope speaks *ex cathedra*, that is, exercises his office as pastor and teacher of all Christians, by virtue of his apostolic authority, and declares that a doctrine about faith and morals must be believed by all the church, the pope possesses—by the divine assistance which God promised to Peter and his successors—the infallibility which the Savior wished his church to have when it defined doctrines of faith and morals. Such definitions are not reformable in themselves nor by the approbation of the church. *Pastor aeternus* was officially approved by a vote of 433 in favor and 2 opposed. More than two bishops had opposed the definition, but on the official day of the vote they were absent from the Basilica of St. Peter. The bishops who opposed the definition of the primacy and infallibility of the pope based their objections on historical reasons and on the untimeliness of the definition. Many were North American, Hungarian, German, and Austrian bishops who feared that the definition would complicate relations with their governments and with non-Catholic fellow citizens.

The solemn definition of the primacy and infallibility of the pope was rapidly accepted, even by those bishops who considered it untimely. In a historical moment when the Holy See had lost the Papal States to the Italian unification movement of Garibaldi and its temporal power was in decline, the definition of the primacy and infallibility of the pope was understood as a way to strengthen the spiritual and moral authority of the Roman pontiff against conciliarist and Gallican tendencies in the church. Because of the definition laid down by *Pastor aeternus*, several thousand Catholics of central Europe, under the influence of university professors, left the Roman church and formed the Old Catholic Church. The council also had the effect of reinforcing and augmenting centralist tendencies that increased the authority and juridical power of the Holy See over the bishops of the world. Because of political events beyond its control, Vatican I was not able to deal with many things, especially a more ample vision of the nature of the church, which would have to wait almost one hundred years, until ⇒Vatican II, to be discussed again in a council.

———

CMB

Vatican II (1962–65). The twenty-first ecumenical council (⇒Councils) of the Roman Catholic Church was convened by Pope John XXIII on January 25, 1959, for the spiritual renovation of the church in the light of the gospel, bringing it up to date (*aggiornamento*) so that it would be able better to carry out its mission of evangelization and to promote union with all Christians. The Second Vatican Council met in the central nave of the Basilica of St. Peter in four sessions between October 9, 1962, and December 8, 1965, when it was formally closed by Pope Paul VI.

Bishops from all parts of the world participated in the council, giving testimony, as Karl ⇒Rahner, SJ, the preeminent postconciliar Catholic theologian, wrote, that the Roman Catholic Church was for the first time a "world church." An approximate average of 2,250 bishops, out of 2,908 who had the right to attend, were present at the different sessions of the council, which produced more documents than any other council in history (a total of sixteen: four constitutions, nine decrees, and three declarations). Close to one hundred observers who were invited from other Christian churches also attended.

Without doubt, it was the most important ecclesiastical event of the twentieth century for the Roman Catholic Church. This is due to the new and surprising theological and pastoral norms that the Second Vatican Council inaugurated, incorporating the thought of great theological figures of the postwar period, such as M. D. ⇒Chenu, OP; Yves ⇒Congar, OP; Jean ⇒Daniélou, SJ; Henri de ⇒Lubac, SJ; Hans ⇒Küng; John Courtney ⇒Murray, SJ; Karl Rahner; and Joseph ⇒Ratzinger. Some of these theologians had been silenced during the pontificate of Pius XII (1939–58).

Among the new theological and pastoral norms initiated by the council, the more biblical ecclesiology of the Dogmatic Constitution, *Lumen gentium*, stands out. It emphasized that the church is not only a perfectly and hierarchically structured society, but also the temple of the Holy Spirit and the pilgrim people of God. The Pastoral Constitution, *Gaudium et spes*, proclaimed an opening to "the signs of the times," or the action of the Holy Spirit in the modern secularized world. This document is characterized by the desire to serve that secularized world and not to condemn it a priori. *Sacrosanctum concilium* formulated a new sacramental theology of the Eucharist, recognizing the presence of God not only in the consecrated elements of bread and wine, but also in the Word of God proclaimed in the assembly, in the priest, and in the community. It also authorized the Mass to be celebrated not only in Latin but in the language of the community which celebrates it.

The decree *Unitatis reintegratio* committed itself to ecumenism and the movement for the unity of all Christians that was already at work among the Protestant churches, and the declaration *Nostra aetate* promoted interreligious dialogue. Both of these last two documents of the council were based on the abandonment of the former position of scholastic Catholic theology, which asserted that error has no rights. It was also based on the new evaluation of religious liberty, founded on the dignity of human conscience, made in the image of God, which was affirmed by the declaration *Dignitatis humanae*.

Antecedents and preparation. The Second Vatican Council can be seen as the continuation of the work of ⇒Vatican I (1869–70), which could not finish its deliberations because of the Franco-Prussian War and the entrance into Rome of the forces of the Italian patriot Garibaldi on September 20, 1870. Vatican I was not able to discuss the nature of the church in depth, and it promulgated only two dogmatic constitutions, on the relationship between faith and reason (*Dei Filius*) and on the primacy and infallibility of the pope (*Pastor aeternus*). Thus Vatican II can be seen as the continuation of Vatican I, with the broader agenda of the former on the nature of the church and its relation with the world.

However, Vatican II can also be seen as a rupture with Vatican I. The style and theological substance of Vatican II testify to a Roman Catholic Church that desires to be more open to the modern secularized world; less clerical and more inclusive; and less scholastic and more biblical in its theology.

During the almost one hundred years between Vatican I and Vatican II, the church and the world experienced difficult times that were marked by two world wars and made it inopportune to celebrate an ecumenical council. In spite of this, both Pius XI and Pius XII seriously considered convening a council.

Ten years after Pius XII abandoned the idea of a council, his successor, ⇒John XXIII, announced the convening of a council on January 25, 1959. John, the octogenarian patriarch of Venice, had been elected pope in 1958, as a candidate from whom many did not expect new initiatives because of his advanced age and his reputation as a traditionalist. It was expected that he would not last long in the See of St. Peter. But this venerable old man from northern Italy, whose ancestors were farmers, began to surprise the world from the beginning of his pontificate. First, the surprises began because of his personality: He was the exact opposite of his predecessor, Pius XII, who was the personification of the infallible pope of Vatican I: ascetic, aristocratic, reserved, formal. In contrast, John XXIII was heavy, humorous, from a humble family, smiling, accessible, like a beloved grandfather. John XXIII would person-ify the new style of the church that Vatican II tried to implement with its different theological and pastoral initiatives which sought the *aggiornamento*, or the updating of the Roman Catholic Church, which many saw as ossified and reactionary against everything that has to do with modernity.

Preparations for Vatican II began when the pope invited all the bishops of the world, the leaders of male religious orders, theological faculties of Catholic universities, and members of the Roman curia or central bureaucracy of the church to suggest topics for discussion by the council. Close to 9,300 proposals were received and examined by ten preparatory com-missions appointed by the pope in June 1960.

These commissions worked between November 1960 and June 1962, formulating documents that would serve as working docu-ments or *schemata* for the consideration of the bishops who would attend the council. Before being sent to the participants, the documents were revised by the Central Preparatory Com-mission, which was controlled by cardinals of the Roman curia, and sent to the pope for his approval. In the summer of 1962, copies of some of the documents to be discussed in the first session of the council were sent to partic-ipating bishops.

Chronology. The first session of the council took place between October and December 1962. This session was the most important and dramatic of the four sessions between 1962 and 1965, because the decisions made then set the course to be followed during the rest of the ses-sions. In his opening address John XXIII described his dreams for the council, emphasiz-ing that Vatican II should be a pastoral council which would not condemn the errors of the modern world and which would discern in new human movements the imprint of the Holy Spirit. The pope also exhorted the council fathers to distinguish between the substance of the faith and the way in which it had been expressed in the past, in order to express the Christian faith to the contemporary world better.

The real battle for the heart of the council would take place over the working documents which the council fathers were to discuss in their meetings, and over the composition of the council commissions that were to amend them. The *schemata* had been written by theologians who were favored by the Roman curia and who were not interested in breaking with the Tri-dentine (⇒Trent) scholastic theological schemes.

During the first session the council fathers, headed by bishops from central and western Europe, decided to postpone the vote on the membership of the commissions. The bishops wanted to get to know one another better before deciding who would represent them in these commissions. But behind this decision there was discontent with the *schemata* that had been pre-pared by the Central Preparatory Commission.

This situation was confirmed during the debate of the council about the *schemata* on the reform of the liturgy and on the sources of divine revelation. The majority of the bishops supported the call of the pope for a renovation of the eucharistic liturgy and rejected the text on divine revelation. Although this majority did not have enough votes to remove the text from the consideration of the council, the pope inter-vened and ordered the text to be reformulated. He thus supported those bishops who were not content with the more traditional and scholas-tic theological perspectives of the Roman curia that they saw reflected in the *schemata*.

During the recess between the first and sec-ond sessions, John XXIII died, in June 1963. He was succeeded by Paul VI, archbishop of Milan, who had been a close collaborator of Pius XII before he lost the latter's favor and was exiled from Rome to the see of St. Ambrose. Nevertheless, his sympathy and interest in the new French theological currents called *nouvelle théologie*, which contributed to his appointment as archbishop of Milan, would play an important role in the biblical, patristic, and theological formulations of the documents of the council.

Paul VI did not lose time in affirming the con-tinuation of the council in the line of John XXIII. It was this cultured and refined diplomat who guided the work of the council during the major part of the three remaining sessions. Thanks to the diplomatic talents of Paul VI, the several fac-tions in the council succeeded in approving a number of constitutions, decrees, and declara-tions that began in the Roman Catholic Church a period of renewal, change, and confusion that had not been seen since the sixteenth century and the Protestant Reformation.

Documents. Vatican II produced more docu-ments than any other council, covering a great variety of topics. These documents differ from each other not only because of their themes, but also because of their weight or juridical and theological importance. The longest documents and those of greatest theological and juridical importance were the four constitutions approved by the council, which deal with the reform of the liturgy (*Sacrosanctum concilium*), the nature of the church (*Lumen gentium*), divine revelation (*Dei verbum*), and the church in the world (*Gaudium et spes*).

Nine decrees were published on the following subjects: the means of social communication, the Eastern or Orthodox churches, ecumenism, the pastoral ministry of bishops, the renewal of the religious orders and congregations, priestly formation, the apostolate or ministry of the laity, the missionary activity of the church, and the life and ministry of priests. Three declarations were also published, on Christian education, on non-Christian religions, and the highly important declaration on religious liberty.

Impact. Vatican II produced a revolution in the Roman Catholic Church. John XXIII wanted to bring the church up to date by opening the windows so that the wind of the Holy Spirit could air it out and it would look less like a moldy museum. The Holy Spirit breathed strongly by means of the reforms of the council, and their acceptance or reception by millions of Catholics in the whole world are a witness to their success. But at the same time that the reforms of the council moved the church in a direction of greater simplicity and evangelical solidarity (especially with the poor, with dechristianized people, and with other Christian churches and even non-Christian religions), the changes caused confusion and disorder for some Catholics who missed the precouncil state of affairs.

In particular, Archbishop Marcel Lefèbvre, a council father and a former superior general of the Fathers of the Holy Spirit, a missionary order, rejected the magisterium of the council, and in 1970 founded the Priestly Fraternity of St. Pius X. This society directs parishes, schools, and seminaries throughout the world for Catholics who reject the council. Lefèbvre was excommunicated by John Paul II in 1985 when he ordained three bishops of his organization without the permission and against the instructions of the pope.

However, the movement of Lefèbvre is not very numerous, and more significant has been the number of Catholics who, while they accept the teaching of the council, have followed a more conservative line of interpretation that seeks to maintain the continuity between the preconciliar and the postconciliar styles of the Roman Catholic Church.

These persons, among whom are found a number of priests, and also bishops and cardinals who attended the council—among them de Lubac, Ratzinger, and Daniélou—reject many postconciliar reforms which they consider to be an abuse of the letter of the magisterium of the council. Many of them consider themselves to be following the line of Pope John Paul II, whose pontificate (1978–2005) marked the end of the period of experimentation in the implementation of the council. Nonetheless, certain initiatives of the Polish pope (for instance, his ecumenical policy toward the Orthodox churches and interreligious dialogue, especially with Jews; his encyclicals on the social teaching of the church; and his apostolic travels throughout the world) were not entirely to the liking of traditionalist sectors of the church.

Other, more progressive Catholics have appealed to the "spirit of the council" to advocate changes in the church that were not mentioned by the magisterium of the council (for instance, the priestly ordination of women and married men; the election of bishops; a sexual morality that is more tolerant of birth control, homosexuality, divorce). Many of these progressive Catholics interpret the pontificate of John Paul II as a betrayal of the council and a restoration of the preconciliar Roman Catholic Church, even though John Paul II attended all the sessions of the council and affirmed that his pontificate, as his name suggests, continued the conciliar line of John XXIII and Paul VI.

———

CMB

Venn, Henry (1796–1873). British

Anglican of profoundly evangelical convictions, V. was an outstanding leader in missionary work in the nineteenth century, working in the areas of the administration of missionary resources, strategy, and theology of mission. His work, very similar to that of Rufus ⇒Anderson, sought the development of an autochthonous church on missionary soil.

Characterized by ecumenical thought and an adventurous spirit, V. lived in the era of British imperialism. As executive secretary of the Church Missionary Society, he proposed a vision of the autochthonous or "indigenous church," promoting its self-development, self-financing, and self-diffusion, without the necessity of missionary work coming from abroad. To achieve this vision, V. proposed the growth of the churches from the base and the creation of small interdenominational councils that would contribute to the training of a native ministerial body. This ministerial body, in time, would take the reins of work on missionary soil without the need for foreign intervention and participation.

Although V. proposed the "euthanasia" of foreign missionary work, his purpose was really to put an end to the control exercised by the missionaries over the new churches in Africa and Asia. This vision, which was advanced for its time and was accompanied by the optimism that was typical of that era, did not sufficiently recognize the tendency to dominate on the part of the missionary agencies and the missionaries.

Nevertheless, Christian leaders in Africa and Asia acknowledge the pioneering work of V. Moreover, many lay claim to the missionary strategy of V. in order to affirm the contextualization of the gospel in those continents.

———

CCO

Vermigli, Peter Martyr (1500–1562).

Reformer with a particular interest in sacramental doctrine. Son of a prosperous merchant, in 1518 V. entered the Lateran Congregation of Regular Augustinian Canons in Fiosole. After eight years of study and several assignments as preacher and vicar, he was named abbot of the urban monastery of St. Peter ad Aram in Naples in 1537. There he formed part of a group directed by Juan de ⇒Valdés. In 1541, as prior of St. Frediano, he introduced Reformation teachings to his monastery and congregation. Ordered by his congregation to appear in Genoa and to respond to the accusations against him, he fled to Zurich in August 1542. Martin ⇒Bucer called him to Strassburg, where he served as professor of theology from 1542 to 1547, and from 1553 to 1566. In 1547 he accepted an invitation from Thomas ⇒Cranmer to visit England, where he was named professor of theology in Oxford. There in 1549 he began a debate on the Eucharist in which he attacked transubstantiation, the bodily presence of Jesus Christ in the host, and the sacramental union of the body and blood of Jesus Christ with the bread and the wine. *Defensio adversum Gardinerum* (1559), in which he describes his sacramental teaching, reflects the influence of John ⇒Calvin, Martin Bucer, and Philipp ⇒Melanchthon. He was named assistant to the archbishop of Canterbury, but during the persecutions that followed Mary Tudor's accession to the throne he fled into exile with ⇒Jewel and others of his disciples. He returned to Strassburg in 1553. Finally, as a result of the controversy between Lutherans and Reformed on the ubiquity of the body of Christ, he left Strassburg and returned to Zurich as professor of Hebrew in 1556.

———

LMcA

Verona, Council of (1184).

Regional council whose chief action was to condemn the movement of Peter ⇒Waldo. As a result the Waldensians were persecuted, and they sought refuge in the valleys of the Alps, where in the sixteenth century they accepted Calvinism.

———

JLG

Victor of Rome (?–198).

Bishop of Rome from 189 until his death. Although ⇒Jerome says that he was the first Christian author to write in Latin, his writings have been lost. He took a very active part in the Quartodeciman controversy concerning the date of the celebration of Easter. He opposed tenaciously the practice of some churches in Asia of determining the date of that celebration by the Hebrew calendar, and he even broke off fellowship with those who insisted on this practice. ⇒Irenaeus, who tried to calm the debate, thought that V. was too intransigent.

———

JLG

Victorinus, Marius ⇒Marius Victorinus

Vigilius (?–555).

Bishop of Rome beginning in the year 537. History remembers V. more for his cowardly and irresolute character than for any achievement. When he came to the papacy, he made a secret pact with Empress Theodora, promising his support for the Monophysites. When he took office, he reneged on his promise. Vacillation attitude would characterize the rest of his papacy. In 548 he gave his approval to the "Three Chapters" of Emperor Justinian. This document condemned ⇒Theodore of Mopsuestia and his writings, and also the writings of ⇒Theodoret and ⇒Ibas of Edessa. Later he twice retracted his decision, finally deciding in favor of the edict. The case of V. has given cause for arguing against the Roman Catholic claim of the infallibility of the pope, and was one of the cases discussed before proclaiming that infallibility at the First Vatican Council (⇒Vatican I).

———

ZMP

Villafañe, Eldin (1940–).

Pentecostal theologian born in Puerto Rico and brought up in New York. As an ordained pastor of the Assemblies of God, he has been a leader among the Latino churches of that denomination.

V. is a professor at Gordon-Conwell Theological Seminary and founder of the Center for

Urban Ministerial Education, a multilingual and multicultural center of urban theological training in Boston. He directed this program from 1976 to 1990. He is recognized in the United States for his writings on urban theological education, urban ministry, Latin ministry, and Pentecostal studies. He has been president of the Association for Hispanic Theological Education and of the Society for Pentecostal Studies. He has published several books, of which the best known is *The Liberating Spirit: Toward an Hispanic-American Pentecostal Social Ethics.*

———

JFM

Vincent de Paul (ca. 1580–1660). A priest of French origin who studied in Toulouse and, after a period of captivity in Tunis, in Paris. He was devoted to works of charity, and for that purpose founded a monastic order for men, and another for women, dedicated to serving the needy. He was a fervent defender of Catholic orthodoxy, particularly against Jansenism (⇒Jansen). The Society of St. Vincent de Paul, whose purpose was to combat freethinkers, was not founded by him, but began in 1833, almost two hundred years after his death.

———

JLG

Vincent of Lérins (?–ca. 450). Monk of southern France who in the year 434 published a brief work, *Commonitorium*, which claimed to be a reminder of the principles that ought to guide Christians in the process of discerning the truth, because "our duty is not to take religion to where we think it ought to go, but to follow it to wherever it takes us." The name of V. does not appear in this writing, whose author gives himself the pseudonym "Pilgrim." But a short time later ⇒Gennadius, who lived in Marseilles and had good reasons for being acquainted with the origin of the book, attributed it to V. It is very possible that V. wrote under a pseudonym because it was a veiled attack against the theological innovations of ⇒Augustine. If that is the case, *Commonitorium* would be part of the controversy that arose around the teachings of Augustine, which many, particularly in southern France, considered unacceptable innovations.

V. affirmed that the norm for every doctrine is the Bible. However, since there are many different interpretations of the Scripture, it is necessary to establish other norms to determine what the church is to believe. For V. what is to be believed is that which fulfills three requirements: universality, antiquity, and consensus. He wrote:

> In the Catholic Church we are to make certain that we uphold that which has been believed everywhere, always, and by all [*quod ubique, quod semper, quod ab omnibus creditum est*]. . . . We observe this norm if we adhere to universality, antiquity, and consensus. We adhere to universality if we confess the faith which all the church in all the world confesses; to antiquity, if we do not depart from those interpretations which are clearly upheld by our holy fathers and ancestors; and to consensus if we equally follow the definitions and decisions of all, or at least almost all priests and doctors.

This norm, frequently summed up in the phrase *quod ubique, quod semper, quod ab omnibus*, is commonly called the Vincentian canon. V. himself applied it to teachings that he considered erroneous, such as Nestorianism (⇒Nestorius) and, without attacking him by name, the teachings of Augustine.

Aside from the Vincentian canon, the other chapter of great interest in *Commonitorium* is chapter 23, in which V. deals with the development of dogma. He says there that doctrines develop and that this process is permissible on the condition that it is not an alteration. The difference is that while growth or development arises from what already existed, alteration creates something new. Thus, just as the individual believer progresses in the faith, so also a development of doctrine exists in the church, and it is necessary to be sure that this development follows the rules of growth in such a way that doctrine is consolidated, enriched, refined, and polished, but at the same time that it remains uncorrupted, pure, complete, and perfect.

Thus, although it is clear that V. upholds a conservative position, it is also clear that he was one of the first to recognize the development of dogmas and to attempt to establish rules for that development.

———

JLG

Vinet, Alexandre-Rodolphe (1797–1847). French-speaking Swiss theologian, known as the ⇒Schleiermacher of French Protestantism. Ordained in 1819, he held that personal experience validates doctrine. He was a teacher of "eloquence" in the Academy of Lausanne and author of several books on homiletics. Some of his most important works are *On Freedom of Worship* (1823) and *Studies on Blaise* ⇒*Pascal* (1856).

———
PAJ

Viret, Pierre (1511–71). Outstanding leader of the French reformation and founder of the Reformed Church in Lausanne. He embraced Protestantism thanks to the influence of ⇒Farel. A friend and disciple of ⇒Calvin, in 1564 he published his *Christian Instruction on the Doctrine of the Law and the Gospel.* This work popularizes Calvinist teachings, presenting them in the form of a dialogue.

———
PAJ

Visser 't Hooft, W. A. (1900–1985). Dutchman of the Reformed tradition, a graduate in theology from the University of Leiden. Leader of the Christian Student Movement and secretary of the World Federation of Christian Students, organizations through which he was initiated into the worldwide ecumenical movement.

V.'s vision and his participation in a vast number of ecumenical and international organizations and congresses led him to be elected as the first secretary general of the ⇒World Council of Churches in 1948.

His *Memoirs* (1947) describes in an interesting way and in the form of personal testimony his journey as a leader in the ecumenical movement. His contribution to that movement and to the vision of the World Council of Churches until 1966 is summed up in the development of a profoundly Trinitarian theology, in which the unity of the church is the locus for mission and for the announcement of the reign of God to the world.

———
CCO

Vitalis (5th century). Monk of Carthage who wrote to ⇒Augustine proposing that, although it is certain that only by the grace of God are we able to do all the good that we actually do, the first step of faith, the *initium fidei,* depends on our will and not on divine intervention. This is the typical position of Semi-Pelagianism. Augustine replied with *Epistle to Vitalis,* in which he insists on the priority of grace and refutes the objections presented by the Semi-Pelagians.

———
JLG

Vitoria, Francisco de (ca. 1483–1546). Spanish theologian and jurist born in the city of Vitoria, in the Basque country. He was a friar in the Dominican order. He studied at the University of Paris, and on his return to Spain he taught in Valladolid and then in Salamanca. V. was an outstanding member of the famous Second Scholasticism in the University of Salamanca. He gained notoriety, and then celebrity, because of the contributions he made to modern international law, in the context of the conquest and colonization of the Americas by Spain.

Working out his theory of modern international law, V. insisted that the organization of the state belongs to natural law through the free determination of the civil community. The power of rulers is delegated, and not instituted directly by God. The appointment of rulers is mediated by civil society. If the authority of the state belongs to natural law, the American Indians are legitimate lords of their kingdoms, because their power has been conferred on them by a constituted civil community. The consideration of the principles of sociability and communication as the right of nations (*ius gentium*) implies that both principles belong to natural law. The indigenous rulers had no right to keep the Spaniards from communicating and socializing with one another, nor to impede the establishment of commercial relations and free transit through their territories, on the condition that the Spaniards not contravene the rights and laws that were established in the indigenous kingdoms. V. broadened these principles by proposing the exchange of ambassadors, the formulation of treaties, and even alliances in just wars as part of his conception of international law. V. insisted on the equality of the American indigenous peoples and of their systems of order with their Spanish counterparts.

V. has been admired for the development of his theory of international law, which has had notable influence in the modern world. His importance for the history of international law is comparable only to that of the Dutchman Hugo ⇒Grotius.

It is important to point out that V. assumed a moderate position between the radical solidarity of Bartolomé de ⇒Las Casas, defender of the Indians, and the opposite position of Juan Ginés de Sepúlveda, detractor of the Indians and defender of the Spanish conquest in the Americas. The three shared much of the same Thomist tradition, and they felt that they were servants of a just cause related to their native land, Spain, and its American enterprise. In all of this V. distinguished himself as a teacher, theologian, and jurist. His *Relecciones de Indias* (Lectures on the Indies) became an obligatory source for research and consultation on matters related to the rights of Spain in the Americas. In those times Salamanca was also consulted by the Spanish crown on different matters related to their intervention in the Western Hemisphere and the treatment of indigenous peoples. A variety of subjects were under discussion, ranging from the rationality of the Indians and whether they really had souls, to the questioning of their full humanity. These matters required a theological and juridical answer. Therein lies the importance of the thought of V.

Many have questioned his thought because it was not sufficiently critical of the conquest and colonization of Spain in the Americas, and ultimately accuse him of justifying the imperialist adventure of Spain in the sixteenth century.

———

CEA

Vives, Juan Luis (1492–1540). Spanish theologian and moralist who studied in France, Belgium, and finally in England, where he obtained a doctorate from Oxford University. Among his best-known works are a lengthy commentary on *The City of God* of ⇒Augustine and a work in five books, *On the Truth of the Christian Faith*. In the latter, books 3 and 4 attempt to show the superiority of Christianity over Judaism and Islam, respectively. His work *On Human Needs or On the Support of the Poor* has received little attention.

———

JLG

Voetius, Gisbert (1589–1676). Pastor and theologian of the Reformed Church in Holland. As a leader at the Synod of Dordrecht or ⇒Dort, he promoted a strict Calvinism. His theology of mission influenced important decisions of his church on the baptism of children in mission fields. He was a defender of religious liberty. He wrote polemical works against "false religion" and in defense of the "true religion."

———

NRG

Von Hügel, Friedrich (1852–1925). Roman Catholic philosopher of Austrian origin and a member of the nobility. He is known as one of the pioneers of the revival of realism and one of the chief promoters of the study of religious sentiments. He was interested in the relationship between Catholic dogmas and history, modern science, free will, and mystical experience.

———

AEM

Wagner, Peter (1930–). Missionary in Bolivia for close to sixteen years, W., of evangelical background, is one of the founders of the Committee on Evangelization of ⇒Lausanne and of the Institute for Church Growth in Pasadena, California. Among his works in English are *Church Planting for a Greater Harvest* and *Latin American Theology: Radical or Evangelical?* In Spanish his best-known work is *¡Cuidado! Ahí vienen los pentecostales* (Look Out! The Pentecostals Are Coming).

———

CCO

Waldo, Peter (?–ca. 1217). Founder of the Waldensians, also known as the Poor Ones of Lyon, and through that movement a forerunner of the Reformation. W. was a relatively wealthy man from the province of Lyon who, after the sudden death of one of his friends, began to search for the meaning and usefulness of his opulent life. He then decided to distribute his goods among the poor and to use part of his fortune for the translation of biblical books and some works of the church fathers (⇒Augustine, ⇒Ambrose, and ⇒Jerome, among others), and began advocating voluntary poverty as a means to follow Jesus. Many people joined W., but this did not prevent him from being expelled from the city by Archbishop Guichard. W. appealed to Rome, and his case was studied in the ⇒Lateran Council of 1179. He did not receive a definitive answer and asked the new archbishop of Lyon for authorization to preach. When this was categorically denied, W. did not submit to the order of the church. As a result, Pope Lucian III excommunicated him in 1183. W. might have been influenced by the ideas of Antonio de Brescia, ⇒Peter of Bruys, and Henry of Cluny. At the time of the Protestant Reformation, the Waldensians adopted Calvinism, and they are now part of the Reformed tradition.

———

GCC

Walls, Andrew (1928–). Scottish historian of the Reformed tradition, W. is considered by many the dean of the discipline known as world Christianity. Founder and former director of the Center for the Study of Non-Western Christianity in Edinburgh, W. has called attention to the demographic changes in Christianity, underlining the vitality of the faith and the new theological challenges in the non-Western world.

—

CCO

Walther, Carl Ferdinand Wilhelm (1811–87).

Pastor, theologian, leader of the Saxon Lutherans who moved in 1839 to Missouri in search of religious freedom. W. emerged as a leader among the immigrants when he declared that a congregation has the right to elect its pastor. His position, which is maintained in his work *Church and Ministry*, is the historical point that marks his separation from other Lutherans in the United States such as J. ⇒Grabau. W. is recognized as the founder of Concordia Seminary and as the first president of the Lutheran Church–Synod of Missouri and Other States (1847–50, 1864–78). His *Law and Gospel* is a classic text in that church.

—

ALG

Warfield, Benjamin Breckinridge (1851–1921).

Presbyterian who continued the tradition of Reformed theology at Princeton, previously upheld by Charles ⇒Hodge and A. A. ⇒Hodge. Defender, therefore, of the orthodox Calvinism that he called "Evangelical religion," W. helped to formulate the doctrine of biblical infallibility, which was the way the Presbyterian Church defined the authority of the Scriptures. He also advocated a diluted form of predestination, which he called "congruism," according to which the work of God coincides with the will of the individual, so that one freely decides that for which God has predestined one. His thoughts and ideas were dominant in the General Assembly of the Presbyterian Church between 1892 and 1910.

—

MAD

Warneck, Gustav (1834–1910).

German, born in Hamburg. After finishing his theological studies, he worked as pastor and professor of the "science of missions" in Halle. W. is traditionally known as the founder of Protestant missiology, the scientific study of missions. His first important contribution was the journal *Allgemeine Missionszeitschrift*,

whose purpose was to establish a scientific structure for the study of Protestant missions.

In Europe W. is known for his five-volume *Evangelische Missionslehre* (1892–1903), which systematically studies Protestant missionary work. His best-known work in the English-speaking world is *Sketch of the History of Protestant Missions from the Reformation to the Present* (1892), which has been reprinted more than five times. In this work W. establishes two fundamental principles for the study of missions. First, he emphasizes the practical and experiential character of missionary work. For W. missionary experience ratifies the Holy Scriptures, and the latter confirm the importance of missionary work and calling.

Second, W. understands missionary work as a labor of education or "civilization." For him, the great changes that occurred at the beginning of the twentieth century go hand in hand with the dissemination of the gospel of Christ. In this sense, he defines mission as the extension of the kingdom of God and as the establishment of the church in all the world. However, the function of the church is not merely the conversion of individuals but also the "Christianization" of communities by means of missions as education.

—

CCO

Warren, Max (1904–77).

General secretary of the Church Missionary Society (1942–63), an Anglican missionary society of evangelical inspiration. W. was one of the best-known missiologists of the twentieth century. A native of Ireland, his works were focused on theological reflection about decolonization, the missionary activity of God in the world from a historical perspective, and the grace of God in those religious traditions outside the covenant (Judeo-Christian) traditions. Today W. is considered one of the forerunners of the evangelical missiology and theology of religion.

In addition, W. was an interpreter of third world development for political leaders in Great Britain. An avid promoter of mission, he advocated interpersonal relations and voluntary work as bases for missionary work. His works include *Interpreting the Cross: Social History and Christian Mission* and *I Believe in the Great Commission*.

—

CCO

Weber, Max (1864–1920).

Professor of political economy in the universities of

Freiburg and Heidelberg, born in Erfurt, Prussia. In much of his work he examines the relations between the structures of religions and social and political structures. For W., who was one of the founders of the sociology of religion, this analysis should begin by investigating the conditions and the effects of communal actions and should focus on the way religious actions make for a good and long life "on the earth." W. recognized that even in the religious field one acts initially according to the rules of experience, and afterward one goes over to the field of "suprasensible powers." He insisted on the relationship between religious belief and practical rationalism, and between religious institutions (priesthood, prophetic ministry) and the here and now. For W. intellectualism is essential for religions, since it offers order and meaning for the world and life. His theories are opposed to Marxist materialism, and he rejects the theory that the means of production are the only factor conditioning human conduct. His best-known and most polemical work is *The Protestant Ethic and the Spirit of Capitalism*, in which he links the Calvinist doctrine of predestination with the interpretation of economic success as the guarantee of divine grace. However, his major contribution might be in his methodology of investigation (*Methodology of the Social Sciences*) and his studies on the relation between different social systems and on bureaucracy (*Economy and Society*, and *Studies of Sociology and Politics of Social and Economic History*). Toward the end of his life, W. participated in German politics as a member of the committee that wrote the constitution of the Weimar Republic in 1918.

AMID

Weber, Otto Heinrich (1902–66). Professor of Reformed theology, born in the city of Cologne, Germany. W. studied at the universities of Bonn and Tübingen (1921–25). In 1928 he accepted the position of director of the Theological School in Wuppertal. From 1934 until his death he held the chair of Reformed theology in the University of Göttingen.

His works include *The Plan of the Bible*, *Report on the Dogmatics of* ⇒*Barth,* and *The Foundations of Dogmatics*.

JDR

Weiss, Johannes (1863–1914). German New Testament scholar, the first to propose that the central purpose of the ministry of

Jesus Christ was to proclaim the kingdom of God as a transcendent reality and himself as the Messiah.

His work includes several books expounding and enlarging on this topic. The first was *Die Predigt Jesu vom Reiche Gottes* (1892; Jesus' Proclamation of the Kingdom of God), followed by *Kommentar zum Lukasevangelium* (1893; Commentary on the Gospel of Luke), in which he elaborates on his thesis.

In addition to his eschatological interpretation of the gospel, in an influential article that was published in 1912 W. set out for the first time the basic principles of form criticism, concepts later elaborated on by M. ⇒Dibelius and R. ⇒Bultmann.

ODV

Wells, David F. (1939–). Congregationalist minister, author of fifteen books, and a well-known conservative evangelical theologian. W. is professor of historical and systematic theology at Gordon-Conwell Seminary in Massachusetts. His writings criticize the state of the evangelical church, above all because of its close connection with secular culture, and at times its capitulation to it.

EZ

Wesley, Charles (1707–87). Born in Epworth, England, where his father, Samuel, was parish priest. Studied at Oxford, from which he graduated in 1733. He had a conversion experience on May 21, 1738, when, in his own words, he was "at peace with God."

He was a poet whose hymns became an integral part of the movement headed by his brother John: Methodism. Some of his verses can be considered among the most beautiful in the English language. He wrote 4,600 hymns, of which 3,000 were published posthumously and others have remained unpublished. It can be easily understood that in such a huge production of hymns, not all are of the same quality.

Charles W. was not a systematic theologian, but he put into verse the sublime truths of the gospel to be sung by the church. In his hymns we find allusions to and, in some cases, explanations of the meaning of the incarnation, salvation, reconciliation, the new birth, eternal life, and the whole gamut of Christian doctrine and experience.

His best-known hymns include *O for a Thousand Tongues to Sing*; *Jesus, Lover of My*

Soul; Come, Thou Long-Expected Jesus; Hark! The Herald Angels Sing; and *Christ the Lord Is Risen Today!*

———

AZ

Wesley, John (1703–91). Anglican cleric and founder of the Methodist movement, born in Epworth, England, where his father was parish priest.

W. studied at the Charterhouse school in London and in 1720 entered the University of Oxford. In 1725 he was ordained a deacon and three years later was ordained a priest of the Church of England.

His parents were Samuel Wesley, also a cleric of the Church of England, and Susanna Annesley. Both belonged to well-known clergy families, and they were lovers of study and of theological research. While she was still very young, Susanna became competent in Greek, Latin, and French and delighted in the study of the church fathers and the details of metaphysics. Susanna was number twenty-five among her father's offspring and gave Samuel, her husband, nineteen children.

One of the greatest influences in the life of W. was his home, and especially Susanna, his mother. Life in the home at Epworth was rigidly governed. The regular practice of prayer, the reading and memorization of the Scriptures, and the teachings and admonitions of Susanna formed the environment in which W. grew up and was educated.

Even though he was an ordained cleric in the established church and was knowledgeable in biblical and theological matters, W. lacked the conviction that he had attained salvation. He later saw himself as an example of how it is possible to believe, and even to believe fervently, in the doctrine of salvation by faith and at the same time lack that experience. He had in his head all the knowledge about this doctrine and believed it firmly, but he had not experienced in his heart what he believed and preached.

During a voyage to Georgia, where he wanted to be a missionary among the Indians, the boat in which he was traveling was battered by a storm. W. was filled with fear, as were most of the other travelers, but some Moravians on board were calm and fearless, including the children. This experience left a mark on W. that was deeper than the storm itself. Some days after his arrival in Georgia he had a conversation with one of the Moravians, August Gottlieb Spangenberg, who, by asking him incisive questions, brought him to the conclusion that he was not sure of his salvation. Afterward, when he returned to England, W. had a conversation with Peter Böhler and a group of Moravians in which he became convinced that Christ had saved him and was his only justification, sanctification, and redemption. Up to this point W. was convinced, but not converted. The experience of conversion was near.

This experience took place on May 24, 1738, in a chapel in Aldersgate Street in London. W. himself tells us that in the evening of that day he went, very unwillingly, to that chapel where the Preface of Luther to the Epistle to the Romans was being read. At about fifteen minutes to nine, while the words were being read that speak of the change which God effects in the heart by means of faith in Christ, he felt a strange warmth in his heart and came to trust only in Christ for his salvation. And, he adds, he was given the certainty that Christ had erased all his sins and that he was saved from the law of sin and death.

This conversion experience marks a new beginning in the life of the founder of Methodism, who became a tireless preacher and an indefatigable writer. It is estimated that during his life he traveled 250,000 miles and preached between forty thousand and fifty thousand sermons. W. was not a systematic theologian; that is, he did not develop an elaborate and logically ordered system of doctrine. But it cannot be denied that his thought was systematic and logical in relation to the faith which he professed, although he worked out only a limited number of doctrines, those that he felt the need to elaborate and organize. His theological thought, perfectly founded on the Scriptures, can be discovered by an examination of his writings.

Whoever desires to study the theology of W. should go to his sermons, because W. was concerned about the orthodoxy of his preachers and demanded that they preach the true doctrine in their meetings and services. He published his sermons not so that they would be read directly to the groups of believers, but in order that the preachers would have a source from which they could drink in order to strengthen their own experience and thus be able to use that material in their own sermons. W. did not write a treatise of theology that summed up Christian doctrine. In its place he offered to his collaborators and to Christians of all the ages his magnificent series of sermons.

———

AZ

West, Cornel (1953–). African American philosopher, theologian, and activist. He has taught in some of the great universities of the United States, such as Princeton and Harvard. Among his publications are *Race Matters* (1993), *The Future of the Race* (1996, cowritten with Henry Lewis Gates Jr.), and *Jews and Blacks: A Dialogue on Race, Religion and Culture in America* (1996, cowritten with Michael Lerner).

———

PAJ

Westminster, Confession of (1643–46).

One of the most important confessions of the Calvinist tradition. The English parliament convened the Westminster Assembly, financed it, chose its members, imposed the agenda, approved and rejected the results, named its officers, and tried to "establish the correct opinion." Its results were the Confession of Faith, the Larger and the Smaller Catechisms, and the Directory of Worship, both for Scotland and for England. England sent 121 clerics and 30 lay assessors (10 from the House of Lords and 20 from the House of Commons). Scotland, in turn, commissioned 4 clergymen and 2 laymen.

The confession consists of thirty-three chapters that deal with the chief theological doctrines and matters having to do with administration and the relation between church and state. The frame of reference of this confession is Protestant scholasticism, that is, an environment in which the following qualities predominate: a mentality that is closed to dialogue with other churches, a love of theological subtleties, epistemological dogmatism, and extreme individualism.

The confession maintains continuity with the canons of ⇒Dort or Dortrecht (1618–19): total depravity of the human being, unconditional election, limited atonement, irresistible grace, and the perseverance of the saints. Both creeds of the seventeenth century established the "sound doctrine" of the Reformed family.

On the other hand, there is also a discontinuity between the confession and the dynamic theology of ⇒Calvin. The French reformer begins his *Institutes of the Christian Religion* with a reflection on the condition of the human being in the light of the Bible; the confession begins with the Scriptures, conceived as an oracle and in a legalistic tone. Calvin struggled with predestination as a comforting doctrine in the midst of the persecution of his people; the confession eclipsed the other doctrines with the weight it gave to the "horrible" divine decree.

Likewise, Calvin never held, in contrast to the confession, to the inerrancy of the Scriptures.

From the time of its beginnings in 1647, the confession was acknowledged as "the most orthodox [confession] and the one based on the Word of God." In 1649 the Church of Scotland adopted it as the most important norm, subordinate to the Scripture. Beginning in 1690 university professors were required to subscribe to it. From 1711 onward it was necessary to affirm it in order to receive ministerial orders.

———

EPA

Westphal, Joachim (1510–74).

German theologian born in Hamburg. He studied theology in Wittenberg under the direction of ⇒Luther and ⇒Melanchthon. In 1534 he went on to teach at the universities of Heidelberg, Strassburg, and Basel. He returned to Germany and in 1541 was named preacher in his native city, where he took part in the religious polemics of the time. He enthusiastically defended the eucharistic teaching of Luther against ⇒Calvin's. This caused a break between W. and Melanchthon, and contributed to the distancing between the Lutheran and Reformed traditions. In the Adiaphorist controversy he shared the opinions of ⇒Flacius.

Among his principal writings are *Recta fides de Coena Domini* (1553; Proper Belief Concerning the Lord's Supper), *Collectanea sententiarum Aurelii Augustini de Coena Domini* (1555; A Collection of Sayings of Augustine on the Lord's Supper), and *Confutatio aliquot enormium mendiorum L. Calvini* (1558; Refutation of Some of the Enormous Lies of J. Calvin).

———

JDR

White, Ellen G. (1827–1915).

Possibly the female author whose writings have been most translated. (Some of her books have been translated into approximately 150 languages.) Born in Gorham, Maine, she was a convinced follower of the teachings of William ⇒Miller on the second coming, which was to occur in 1843 or 1844. After the failure of Miller's predictions, in October 1844 W. declared that she had received a vision concerning the way in which God would guide God's people from that moment until the return of Jesus. Her prophetic ministry continued until her death in 1915. In the course of that ministry she wrote several books. Dozens of millions of copies of some of them have been sold. Her most important titles are *Steps to Christ* (1892), *The Desire of the Ages*

(1898), *The Great Controversy* (1888, 1911), *Testimonies of the Church* (1855–1909), and *Early Writings* (1882). In addition she published more than five thousand articles, and when she died she left some sixty thousand unpublished typewritten pages. The Ellen G. White Estate, with offices in Silver Spring, Maryland, has the legal custody of this literary inheritance.

After the disappointment of Miller's followers, W. was one of the cofounders of the Seventh-day Adventist Church. The first years after 1844 made believers in the prophecies of Miller return to their Bibles in an attempt to understand their experience. Through this study of the Bible they came to the conclusion that Revelation 11:19–14:20 was a prophecy about the last times. That message not only referred to the imminence of the second coming, but also underlined the importance of the Decalogue (including the commandment concerning rest on the seventh day: 12:17 and 14:12).

W. was firmly convinced of the truth of these beliefs. Although they were the result of her study of the Bible, and not of her visions, those visions confirmed them. Also, W. believed in the conditional immortality of the soul and in its possible annihilation. She also concerned herself a great deal with the importance of health and of having a healthful lifestyle. All this took place in the context of the substitutionary atonement by Christ and of salvation by grace through faith. The central theme of her writings was the love of God.

The work of W. has made a significant contribution to the church and, more indirectly, to the world in general. Her impact on Seventh-day Adventism was multifaceted. Although she did not determine any of the central doctrines of that church, her influence was fundamental in the process of keeping it united and giving it direction. She also was a moderating voice in Adventism, even though later some of her followers used her writings to support more extreme views. One of her most visible contributions to Adventism was her advice to her followers to establish institutions. For that reason, at the beginning of the twenty-first century the denomination had 523 hospitals and clinics, 5,590 schools and universities, and 57 publishing houses, in some 205 countries. It is possible that her most visible impact on the daily life of millions of people is the existence of an enormous cereal industry, created by J. H. Kellogg as a way of following the advice of W. about healthy living.

———

EIH/GRK

Whitefield, George (1714–70).
Notable English preacher and one of the main figures of the evangelical renaissance of the eighteenth century. He was born in Gloucester and, when he was studying in Oxford, formed part of the "holy club" directed by John ⇒Wesley. Its members were mockingly called Methodists. At the age of twenty-one he was ordained in the Church of England. He preached in the open air, and his eloquence attracted enormous crowds, especially in the rural and mining areas. After some time he separated from the Wesleys because of doctrinal differences: while W. followed strict Calvinism, the Wesleys were inclined toward Arminianism (⇒Arminius). He died in North America during his seventh visit and was buried in Massachusetts.

———

AZ

Whitehead, Alfred North (1861–1947).
English philosopher and mathematician. Although in his youth he studied philosophy and theology on his own, he devoted himself to mathematics, serving as professor in the universities of Cambridge and London. After the death of a son in the First World War, he returned to the field of philosophy, publishing several works on that subject, beginning in 1917. In 1924, at the age of sixty-three, he moved to the United States and began a prolific career as philosopher at Harvard University.

W. developed an overarching system of knowledge and interpretation. His interests included classical metaphysics, science, and religion. Using an empirical methodology, he developed a metaphysic based on experience. His writings, together with those of Charles ⇒Hartshorne, initiated process philosophy and theology. For W., reality is a dynamic and creative process in which each being constantly unites in itself different possibilities and actualities to form a new being. This process functions in harmony with God, who maintains the order of the process. Everything that occurs in the world is incorporated into the totality of God and remains interconnected with the rest of the universe in an organic reality. He published his most famous book, *Process and Reality*, in 1929.

———

LGP

Wigand, Johann or Johannes (1523–87).
Lutheran theologian, born in the city of Mansfeld, Germany. W. studied at Wittenberg University and then taught at the University of Nuremberg (1541–44). He was pastor in the

Lutheran Church of Mansfeld (1546), superintendent and pastor in the city of Magdeburg (1553), and professor in the universities of Jena and Königsburg. He defended the strict Lutheran position in several controversies and was coauthor of the ⇒*Centuries of Magdeburg*.

JDR

Wilgard of Revenna (10th century).
Condemned as a heretic for maintaining that the classical Latin poets Horace, Virgil, and Juvenal had been inspired by God and were therefore as infallible as the Bible. According to some documents of the time, W. claimed that he was able to communicate directly with these poets, but it is very probable that he did not make such a claim. He was condemned to death as a heretic, but for some time after his death he had followers in Sardinia and as far as Spain.

JLG

William of Auvergne (ca. 1190–1249).
Professor in Paris and bishop of that city beginning in 1228. Like ⇒Thomas Aquinas and his other contemporaries, he faced the challenge of the new knowledge that came from the Arab world, especially from Spain. Without reaching the level of creative synthesis of Thomas, he showed himself to be open to the new philosophy, although he remained an Augustinian in his epistemology. He also refuted the ⇒Albigensians. Several of his writings were compiled, apparently by himself, but perhaps by some disciple, into a great work, *Divine Teaching*, in which the chief themes of theology and morality are discussed. He also wrote a treatise, *On the Immortality of the Soul*, which to a great extent reproduces the treatise of Domingo ⇒González on the same topic.

JLG

William of Auxerre (?–1231).
Theologian at the University of Paris who took a relatively conservative stance over against the new philosophy that was coming from the Arab world, especially over against ⇒Aristotle. Author of *Summa aurea* (Golden Compendium), which actually is a commentary on the *Sentences* by ⇒Peter Lombard and enjoyed wide circulation. Shortly before his death, Gregory IX entrusted him with the task of revising the works of Aristotle in order to be rid of what could be harmful.

JLG

William of Champeaux (1070–1122).
Professor in Paris. Regarding the question of universals, he was an extreme realist, in contrast to his former teacher ⇒Roscelin. This extreme realism asserted that individuals within a type are only accidents, or accidental modifications, of the essence of the type. His disciple ⇒Abelard criticized him strongly, and from then on they were enemies. Abelard said that because of his criticisms W. modified his teachings, but this assertion is not entirely trustworthy. W. withdrew to the monastery of St. Victor, on the outskirts of Paris, where he continued teaching until he was named bishop of Chalons.

JLG

William of Conches (ca. 1080–ca. 1154).
Member of the school of Chartres. An extreme realist regarding universals. That realism led him to affirm that the Holy Spirit is "the soul of the world." Because of this he was accused of being a pantheist, together with other teachers of the same school.

JLG

William of La Mare (13th century).
Franciscan teacher who opposed the teachings of ⇒Thomas Aquinas, against whom he wrote around 1278 a *Correction of Brother Thomas*, in which he attacked 118 propositions taken from the writings of the great Dominican. This work was repeatedly refuted by the Dominicans, several of them under the title *Correction of the Corrupter of Brother Thomas*. On the other hand, the Franciscan General Chapter of 1282 approved and recommended the treatise of G., while it forbade the Franciscans to read the *Summa* of Thomas.

JLG

William of Saint-Amour (13th century).
Professor in Paris who opposed the presence of mendicant teachers (Dominicans and Franciscans) in the university, and who for this reason published in 1255 a treatise, *On the Dangers of the Last Times*, in which he argued that the vows of voluntary poverty led to error and that those who took them had no place in the university. Although W.'s book was condemned by Alexander IV almost immediately, this did not end the controversy, in which famous teachers like ⇒Bonaventure and ⇒John Peckham participated.

JLG

Williams, Delores (1929–). African American theologian, exponent of the African American feminist theology called womanist theology. Her most important work is *Sisters in the Wilderness* (1993).

—

CCO

Williams, John Rodman (1918–). Charismatic theologian born in North Carolina. He received a doctorate in theology from Union Theological Seminary in New York. He was a navy chaplain in the Second World War. R. is a promoter of the dialogue among various churches, including the Roman Catholic Church and the Pentecostal churches.

—

EPA

Williams, Roger (1603–83). Baptist leader and founder of the colony of Providence, Rhode Island, in 1635. He was a promoter of religious liberty and of the rights of the indigenous peoples.

W. was born in England and emigrated to New England in 1630. When he arrived there he had problems with the religious authorities because he questioned their closed position and the right of the English crown to grant to English colonists lands belonging to the indigenous peoples.

In 1635 he established the colony of Providence, a place that granted religious liberty to both Christians and Jews. In 1639 he joined the Baptists and continued to advocate the separation of church and state in the English colonies of New England. In 1644 he received the official authorization from the English crown to establish the colony of Rhode Island. He was a leader in that community until his death in 1683.

W. wrote a book on indigenous languages, *Key to the Indian Languages*, in 1643. He maintained good relations with indigenous leaders and served as negotiator between English colonists and the indigenous people on several occasions.

—

JFM

Wingren, Gustaf (1910–2000). Lutheran theologian born in Tryserum, Sweden. He is known as one of the most brilliant students of Anders ⇒Nygren, whom he replaced in the chair of dogmatics at the Swedish University of Lund. He also taught in the universities of Aabo and Basel.

The theological perspective of W. combines a fresh and nontraditional interpretation of some of the most significant emphases of both ⇒Irenaeus and ⇒Luther with a critical reaction to the theological thought of his contemporaries. He also provides a number of creative interpretations of his own. In all of this, while he reflects the traditions of the Lundensian school, he is critical of it. His insistence on combining the elements of creation and law, and those of redemption and gospel, as principles for theological reflection on the Christian faith has a very persuasive foundation, which W. develops brilliantly. The importance that he attributes to the topics of creation and law does not prevent him from working constructively on christological problems. His study on baptism provides a profound contribution to the understanding of this means of grace and its significance for the Christian life. In his interpretation of Christian worship, particularly his study of the sacraments, he establishes the foundations for the practice of loving self-giving in the daily life of the believer. His most important works, originally published in Swedish, are also accessible in English. They are *Luther on Vocation* (1948), which was his doctoral thesis; *Man and the Incarnation* (1947), a study of the biblical theology of Irenaeus; *The Living Word* (1949), a study of the classical themes of Christian preaching; *Theology in Conflict* (1954), a critical examination of the anthropological and hermeneutical presuppositions of Nygren, ⇒Barth, and ⇒Bultmann; *Creation and Law* (1958); and *Gospel and Church* (1962). The last two books present the best constructive affirmation of the dogmatic viewpoint of this theologian.

—

JDR

Wise, Carroll A. (1903–85). U.S. Methodist chaplain and pastor, and clinical pastoral theologian. He was concerned over the severing of ties between the academy and pastoral practice. He proposed a theology of pastoral care as the art of communicating the deep meaning of the gospel to persons where they need it. He understood pastoral care as a creative and experimental act of incarnation in which experience prevails over any theological formulation. His most important works are *Pastoral Counseling: Its Theory and Practice* (1951); *The Meaning of Pastoral Care* (1966), and *Religion in Illness and Health* (1942).

—

JR

Wittich, Christoph (1625–87). Dutch Protestant philosopher and theologian who was born in the city of Brieg and died in Leiden. He studied, among other places, in Grongingen, began his teaching career in Duisburg, and then went to Nijmegen and Leiden. In 1659 he published in Nijmegen *Consensus veritatis in Scriptura divina et infallibili revelatae cum veritate philosophiae a Renato Descartes delecta* (Consensus of the Truth Revealed in Divine and Infallible Scripture with the Philosophical Truth Favored by René Descartes), in whose preface he combats the opinions of theologians who oppose ⇒Descartes. Among his other works are *Theologia pacificata* (1675; Pacified Theology) and *Anti Spinoza sive examen ethices B. de Spinoza* (Against Spinoza, or Examination of Spinoza's Ethics), followed by *Commentarius de Deo et eius attributis* (1690; Commentary on God and the Divine Attributes), a voluminous work of more than four hundred pages, translated into Dutch two years later.

JDR

World Council of Churches. The historical roots of the World Council of Churches (WCC) go back to the World Missionary Conference in Edinburgh in 1910, and the subsequent world conferences of Life and Work, 1925 in Stockholm, and Faith and Order, 1927 in Lausanne. These conferences provided the foundation for what eventually became the WCC.

By 1937 both movements, Life and Work and Faith and Order, had named a group of leaders to create the WCC. The process continued to the point where the possibility of a constitutive assembly was proposed for 1941. However, the impact of the Second World War would stop the process for almost a decade. It was not until August 1948, and with much more urgency owing to the effects of the war, that the first assembly of the WCC was held in Amsterdam with a broad representation of the main confessional families in the Christian world at that time, with the exception of Roman Catholicism.

Founded as a "fraternity of churches that profess the Lord Jesus Christ as God and Savior," the WCC went through a complex process in which it defined its purpose and nature. In response to the needs of the world and to the urgency for the unity of the church of Jesus Christ in the world, the WCC holds its assemblies every six or seven years and discusses issues related to the life of the church in the world, the mission of the church, and its unity.

The theological contribution of the WCC is ample and varied. Nevertheless, several themes can be identified by which the theological work of the WCC defined the theological task of the twentieth century. First, in the context of Faith and Order, the WCC contributed to theological and ecumenical reflection on baptism, the Eucharist, and the ministry. As a voice promoting the theological and ecclesial unity of the church, the WCC's Commission on Faith and Order created the Lima Document and the Lima liturgy, whereby Protestants and Catholics can participate in the Eucharist.

The document of Lima, known as Baptism, Eucharist and Ministry (BEM), is a theological reflection on the elements of convergence and divergence among the traditions represented in the WCC. BEM has achieved the mutual recognition of ministries among denominations, the mutual participation of several traditions in the Eucharist, and the renewal of baptism as the primordial sacrament in the life of Christians.

Another important theme has been the renovation of the church through its participation in the world. Under this theme, theological challenges emerge for the church in the world and in the context where it serves, such as justice for women and the poor, the effort against racism, the protection and preservation of creation, and resolution of ethnic and religious conflicts.

Finally, a central theme for the WCC is mission. Although the Commission on Mission and Evangelization was created later in the WCC, when the former International Missionary Council joined the WCC (1961), the latter contributed to mission with people of other religions, to the understanding of mission as the activity of God and of the church as participant in that activity, and to the highlighting of the vitality of the Christian faith in the non-Western world.

CCO

Wrede, Wilhelm (1859–1906). German Lutheran biblical scholar known for his contribution to the critical study of the Gospels. W. did not interpret them beginning from the historical Jesus, but starting from the social demands and the religious needs of the primitive church.

In his famous commentary on Mark, for example, W. introduced the concept of the "Messianic Secret" as the key to the interpretation of that Gospel. In an attempt to reconstruct the history of tradition behind Mark, W. argued that Jesus never openly admitted that he was the Messiah. His closest followers created this notion and used it to reinterpret the person and mission of Jesus. Therefore the christological images of Jesus that we encounter in Mark represent an attempt to reconcile the nonmessianic life of Jesus with the church's faith in him as the Christ after his death.

Together with Albert ⇒Schweitzer, W. also emphasized the eschatological orientation of the message of Jesus and maintained that the Gospel of John could be interpreted only in the context of Gnosticism and in the light of the later expulsion of Christians from the synagogue.

—

AEM

Wycliffe, John (ca. 1330–84). Reformer, philosopher, theologian, educator, and diplomat, who was said to have been "the morning star of the Reformation." He was born in Yorkshire, England. After receiving a doctorate in theology from the University of Oxford in 1372, he remained in that university as professor.

At Oxford W. was able to develop his vast theoretical production. In addition, his presence at the university gave him the opportunity to influence young priests who later would form the pre-Reformation movement called the Lollards. These were poor priests who preached biblical teachings in the language of the people.

In the political realm, W. was present in several diplomatic missions at the service of the duke of Lancaster, John of Ghent. The latter was the son of Edward III, and at the death of Edward in 1377 John governed as regent until Richard II would be old enough to rule. This circumstance permitted W. to climb the ladder of diplomatic positions and to write several works on politics, such as *On Civil Government* (1376), *On the Power of the Pope* (1379), *On Christian Order* (1379), and *Trialogue* (1382). In all these works W. provides an incisive criticism of the decadent power of Rome. In them the pope is depicted as the captain of the armies of Satan, whom it was urgently necessary to stop. The peasant revolt in England, which broke out in 1381, was attributed in part to the teachings of the prereformer. In addition to some other works in the area of logic and metaphysics, W. was able to develop his controversial theological discourse in his *Summa theologica*. In it he articulates much of the agenda that would be fully explained by his Bohemian followers and later by the different Protestant bodies. Some of the matters included are predestination, justification by faith, the state of grace, papal authority, and the church as the community of saints. One of the most controverted matters in the thought of W. was his denial of the doctrine of transubstantiation, which had become dogma in 1215. In addition to not accepting the transformation of the elements, W. insisted on giving the laity not only the host, but also the chalice.

Two other projects in which W. was involved made him famous among the lower sectors of European society. The first was the short tract *Thirty-Three Theses on the Poverty of Christ*, which became a highly popular document in Europe. In it W. attacks the vitiated medieval church structure, its opulence, and its moral deviation. The other project was the translation of the Bible from the Vulgate into English.

The works of W. were prohibited by papal decree. Authorities in Rome sought by various means to imprison W. and requested his deportation, but were not successful. After his death his body was exhumed and burned at the stake because he was considered to be a heretic.

—

GC

Ximenes de Cisneros, Francisco ⇒Jiménez de Cisneros, Francisco

Yahya ben Adi (893–974). Jacobite (Monophysite) theologian whose philosophical gifts earned for him the title *Al-Mantiqui*, that is, the Dialectician. Although the major part of his work has been lost, it is said that he wrote more than forty books. Even though much of his theological production was polemical, his fame was such that several Muslim philosophers and theologians were among his disciples.

—

JLG

Zacarias of Mitilene (ca. 465–ca. 540). Scholar, a native of Gaza, noted for his historical and rhetorical knowledge. After a long intellectual pilgrimage that led him to Alexandria, Beirut, and other intellectual centers, Z. arrived in Constantinople, where he supported Emperor Zeno in his attempts to attract the Monophysites through the imperial decree Henoticon. As a result of his presence at the court, he was named bishop of Mitilene, on the island of Lesbos. Although he supported the verbal Monophysitism of ⇒Severus and others, as did Zeno, later he rejected those formulas and defended the positions of the Council of ⇒Chalcedon. Among his works are *Ecclesiastical History*, which survives only in fragmentary form, and *Life of Severus of Antioch*, in whose conversion to Christianity Z. was an important factor, and whom he finally rejected because of his Monophysite tendencies (although in reality the Monophysitism of Severus was more verbal than real).

JLG

Zanchi, Jerome (1516–90). Reformed theologian, converted to Calvinism by Peter Martyr ⇒Vermigli. After spending some months in Geneva listening to the sermons and lectures of ⇒Calvin, he became professor in, among other places, Strassburg, Heidelberg, and Neustadt. Although for some time he subscribed to the ⇒Augsburg Confession, he was a convinced Calvinist. This can be seen in his treatise *On Spiritual Matrimony*, published posthumously, in which he argues that the finitude of the body of Jesus Christ contradicts the Lutheran teaching of the real presence. Although a Calvinist, he never left behind his scholastic training, and therefore can be considered a bridge between the Protestantism of the first generation and Protestant scholasticism, which would be predominant in the seventeenth century. This may be seen, for instance, in his teaching on predestination, which Z. derives not from the experience of grace, as in ⇒Augustine and Calvin, but from the attributes of God. Because God is omniscient and omnipotent, everything—not only human salvation or condemnation—has been predetermined by God.

JLG

Zell, Katharina (ca. 1497–1562). Her maiden name was Schütz. She and her husband, ⇒Zell, Matthäus gave refuge to persons who were persecuted for their religious convictions, including the Protestant mystic Caspar ⇒Schwenkfeld. The couple were also recognized for their works of mercy. She published several works of literature and maintained a serious correspondence on theological matters with ⇒Luther, ⇒Zwingli, ⇒Bullinger, and other famous theologians of the time.

ALG

Zell, Matthäus (1477–1548). Pastor of the cathedral of Strassburg. He was converted to the evangelical cause by ⇒Luther and by Johann Geyler. His reforming task began with a series of sermons on the Epistle to the Romans, through which he gained many for the cause of the Reformation. His work *Christliche Verantwortung* (Christian Responsibility) was written to counteract the assaults that were being made against Catholic monks. This work gave a strong impulse to the cause of the Reformation in Strassburg. He and his wife Katharina ⇒Zell abstained from participating in the theological controversies of their time. They assumed a tolerant attitude and gave refuge to those who were persecuted for their religious beliefs. He was excommunicated by Rome in 1524, when he married Katharina.

ALG

Zinzendorf, Nikolaus L. von (1700–60). German theologian of noble birth, and leader of the Moravian Church. He was educated in the Lutheran faith, under the influence of the pietist movement. Although from an early age he considered the pastorate as his vocation, because he was a member of the nobility his family urged him to pursue law as a career. Subsequently, he would become the host of a commune of exiles from Moravia, members of the Unity of the Brethren (of Hussite roots) whose leader he became. Toward the middle of the eighteenth century this community became known as the Moravian Church. In 1735 Z. was ordained as a Lutheran minister and, two years later, was consecrated bishop of the Moravians. As bishop he traveled and visited Moravian communities in Europe, England, and America. His dissatisfaction with several theological systems led him to develop his own ideas on the Bible, on ecclesiastical practices, and on the Christian life. He avoided both enlightened rationalism and the dogmatism of Lutheran orthodoxy. His emphasis fell on the religion of the heart. The experience or sense of Christ in the believer informed his basic conception of the Christian faith. Because of his lack of confidence in institutional religion, Z. exhibited for his time a broad ecumenical spirit, establishing relations with diverse church leaders.

NRG

Zosimus (?–418). Bishop of Rome for a little more than a year and a half (417–18). In this brief period a serious conflict occurred between Z. and the bishops of North Africa.

The latter had condemned the teachings of ⇒Pelagius and ⇒Celestine, who appealed to Rome. For a time Z. appeared to support Pelagius and Celestine. This apparent support produced serious tensions with the African bishops. But the latter insisted on their position and appealed to the imperial court in Ravenna. In the end Z. accepted the condemnation of Pelagianism, but the net result of his vacillation was growing conflict between Rome and Africa, the weakening of the Roman bishop against imperial intervention, and division in the church in Rome.

———

JLG

Zwingli, Huldrych (1484–1531).

The most important first-generation leader of the Protestant reformation in Switzerland and founder of the Reformed tradition in Protestantism. He was born of a middle-class family in Wildaus, Toggenburg, where his father and grandfather were magistrates of the people. His theological and political views were partly the result of his identification with the Swiss people, characterized by their independent spirit and their love for their country and its customs.

In his work *Der Hirt* (On the Pastor), he defines the work of the pastor as the daily care of the sheep. His temperament was more like ⇒Melanchthon than like ⇒Luther. He was a man of moderate behavior, like Melanchthon, and was fully influenced by humanism and the serious study of Greek and of the church fathers throughout his life. He was a friend of ⇒Erasmus, who inspired him in his study of the New Testament and of humanist hermeneutics. He preferred Christian ethics to the study of doctrine and was more inclined to point out the ways in which Christians should influence society than was Luther. That same temperament is seen in the Reformed theology of John ⇒Calvin. On the other hand, Z. identified with Luther and the other Reformers on the use of the Scriptures as the principal and fundamental source of theology and the Christian life.

He was educated in the universities of Basel and Vienna. He studied under the influence of the scholastic *via antiqua*, but the humanism he encountered in Basel had a stronger impact on him. In the university of that city he received his bachelor's (1504) and master's (1506) degrees. He was ordained a priest in 1516 and served as pastor in Glarus. From the beginning of his ministry, under the influence of Erasmus, he gave more importance to the Word of God in the practice and worship of the church.

Although from the first he criticized the abuses of the church, he did not attack the most traditional positions. For this reason he gained distinction and was named chaplain of the Benedictine monastery of Einsiedeln.

His work as leader of the Swiss reformation began when, in 1519, he was named priest in Grossmünster. There he broke with church tradition by not preaching on the texts that were designated in the lectionary of the church and by preferring to preach on entire books and topics of the Bible. From that moment on, Zurich was his home, and his love for the Swiss Confederation occupied an important place in his task as a reformer. As he carried out his ministerial work in 1519 and 1520, he suffered from the plague and recovered. This experience was crucial for his theological transformation. In his *Hymn to the Plague* (1519), his understanding of the omnipotence of God as totally absolute may be discerned. God is absolutely active in the world through God's works in human events. Z.'s *The True and the False Theology* bears the mark of the anthropology of ⇒Augustine. It identifies the human being as totally sinful and filled with self-love directed against God and the neighbor. In 1522 we see in his writings themes that are similar to those of Luther: attacks against indulgences, the penitential system, pilgrimages, the cult of the saints, the veneration of Mary, enforced celibacy, and monastic asceticism. The year 1523 marked his most important work for the Swiss reformation. In preparation for a debate with the vicar general of Constance, he wrote his famous *Sixty-Seven Articles*. These main points stand out: Jesus Christ is the Savior; the true Catholic church is composed of all believers in Christ; the Scriptures are the sole authority in matters of faith; good works are only those done by Christ. Then, he condemned a number of practices such as clerical celibacy, fasting, priestly vestments. In addition, he affirmed that God is the only one who absolves us of all sin. Thus he laid private confession aside. However, in those articles Z. was not very clear about the work of Christ. In his subsequent writings on the Mass he defined his Christology. He then affirmed the perfect sacrifice of Christ on the cross and rejected the Roman sacrificial Mass. In 1525, on the basis of this rejection, he emphasized in the Lord's Supper the remembrance of what Christ did for us, and not the transubstantial (Roman) or consubstantial (Lutheran) presence. He preferred to celebrate the spiritual presence of Christ in the community during the memorial act of the

Lord's Supper. His critics see in this teaching a Neoplatonic stance that undervalues the bodily resurrection of Christ.

Based also on the complete sacrifice of Christ on the cross, Z. criticized those who believe that nonbaptized children are condemned. On this point, his vision of the universal validity of the death of Christ admits an almost universalist interpretation. He considered as possible the salvation of non-Christians, such as Socrates in the pre-Christian era. Z. saw in baptism a sign or a rite that marks the entrance of the Christian into the community of faith, and not the actual entrance into that community. These theological positions of Z. brought about a controversy with Luther on the real presence in the Lord's Supper, and with the Anabaptists because of the insistence of the latter on rebaptizing believers.

Although Luther once thought that the theology of Z. resembled the radicalism of ⇒Carlstadt, during the Marburg Colloquy there was a certain rapprochement between them, in spite of their differences.

In view of his time and the situation in Switzerland, Z. was very harsh with the Anabaptists in Zurich. He did not promote the executions of Anabaptists in Switzerland, but neither did he condemn the action of that Reformed inquisition against the Anabaptists. On the contrary, he approved it.

————

ALG